PRELIMINARY REFERENCES TO THE EUROPEAN COURT OF JUSTICE

PRELIMINARY REFERENCES TO THE EUROPEAN COURT OF JUSTICE

Morten Broberg and Niels Fenger

OXFORD
UNIVERSITY PRESS

OXFORD

UNIVERSITY PRESS

Great Clarendon Street, Oxford OX2 6DP

Oxford University Press is a department of the University of Oxford.
It furthers the University's objective of excellence in research, scholarship,
and education by publishing worldwide in

Oxford New York

Auckland Cape Town Dar es Salaam Hong Kong Karachi
Kuala Lumpur Madrid Melbourne Mexico City Nairobi
New Delhi Shanghai Taipei Toronto

With offices in

Argentina Austria Brazil Chile Czech Republic France Greece
Guatemala Hungary Italy Japan Poland Portugal Singapore
South Korea Switzerland Thailand Turkey Ukraine Vietnam

Oxford is a registered trade mark of Oxford University Press
in the UK and in certain other countries

Published in the United States
by Oxford University Press Inc., New York

First published 2010

British Library Cataloguing in Publication Data
Data available

Library of Congress Cataloging-in-Publication Data
Data available

Typeset by Glyph International, Bangalore, India
Printed in Great Britain
on acid-free paper
by CPI Antony Rowe, Chippenham and Eastbourne

ISBN 978–0–19–956507–8

3 5 7 9 10 8 6 4

PREFACE

References by national courts to the Court of Justice for preliminary rulings have played—and continue to play—an essential role in the development of Community law. While it is true that every general textbook or standard work on EU law will discuss preliminary rulings, surprisingly few authors have written more in-depth analyses of the subject. This is why we decided to write a book on preliminary references.

The first such book we wrote in Danish and published in 2008 under the title 'Præjudicielle forelæggelser for EF-domstolen'. We then set out to prepare a similar work in English and to this end we were very happy to receive considerable financial assistance from *Margot og Thorvald Dreyers Fond* which enabled us to have the Danish manuscript translated into English. This translation was diligently prepared by Mr Steven Harris. We are very grateful to both the Foundation and Steven Harris for this.

Having received the English translation we merely intended to make a few amendments, but nonetheless soon found ourselves drawn into what seemed a quagmire of rewriting, rearranging, and rethinking most—if not all—of the original manuscript. The present work therefore has surprisingly little in common with our Danish book on the same topic. Another consequence is that Steven Harris cannot be held responsible for whatever linguistic peculiarities may have slipped into the text during this extensive overhaul.

Even though we are two authors who jointly share responsibility for the final work, we would not have been able to write this book without asking the advice of several people and drawing on the goodwill of many more. Four people should be mentioned in particular. Senior adviser in the Danish Ministry of Foreign Affairs Rass Holdgaard, PhD, has given outstanding help in relation to the mixed agreements discussed in Chapter 4. Professor Ulrik Rammeskov Bang-Pedersen, dr. jur., has done the same in relation to the treatment of the Brussels Convention in Chapter 6. Jean-Paul Keppenne, member of the Legal Service of the European Commission, has kindly commented on the parts of the book regarding Articles 35 of the EU Treaty and 68 of the EC Treaty. And Peter Dyrberg, partner with the Schjødt law firm, has commented upon several mostly cross-cutting aspects of the book. We are deeply grateful to them all. It goes without saying that we alone should be held responsible for any remaining inaccuracies and mistakes.

The manuscript was completed on 1 September 2009 and the copy-editing was finalised at the beginning of October 2009. Although at this time it appeared very likely that the Lisbon Treaty would enter into force, it was far from a foregone conclusion. This necessarily must be reflected in the book.

In a Danish, Nordic, and international Community law perspective, Ole Due, the eighth President of the Court of Justice of the European Communities, has played an extraordinarily important role. Ole, as he insisted on being called, was an exceptionally talented lawyer and had a glittering career. He began his career in the Danish Ministry of Justice and, after a period at the High Court of Eastern Denmark, he became in 1979 only the second Danish judge at the Court of Justice of the European Communities. In 1988 he was elected by his colleagues to become the President of the Court of Justice. In 1994 he retired from the Court but continued to work with undiminished energy. Not least, he accepted a post as honorary professor in the Faculty of Law at Copenhagen University. From 1994 to 2004 both his students and his colleagues benefited from Ole's infectious enthusiasm and wide knowledge. Ole passed away in 2005 at the age of 73. It is easy to see that Ole had a brilliant career. However, it is not Ole's career that those who had the benefit of knowing him talk about when they speak of him, but rather his personal qualities. Three words in particular characterise the man he was: honest, modest, and honourable—in the truest sense of the word. We have both had the privilege of working together with Ole. We have benefited from his incomparable abilities, and we have learnt much from him as a man. This book is dedicated to him.

Morten Broberg and Niels Fenger
Copenhagen, October 2009

CONTENTS

TABLE OF CASES

ALPHABETICAL

NUMERICAL

xlix

EFTA COURT

TABLE OF LEGISLATION

TREATIES AND CONVENTIONS

OTHER JURISDICTIONS

1

REFERENCES FOR
PRELIMINARY RULINGS

1. Introduction

1.1. Preliminary rulings in the Community judicial system

A reference for a preliminary ruling is a request from a national court of a Member State to the Court of Justice of the European Community to give an authoritative interpretation on a Community act or a decision on the validity of such an act. In this situation the Court of Justice does not function as a court of appeal which rules on the outcome of the main proceedings before the referring court: it makes judgment neither on the facts in the main proceedings nor on the interpretation and application of national law. Moreover, in principle, it does not pronounce itself on the concrete application of Community law in the main proceedings before the referring court. Finally, while a preliminary ruling is normally given in the form of a judgment, the ruling is addressed only to the referring court, but not to the parties to the main proceedings. Only the referring court's subsequent decision can be enforced against those parties. As a matter of principle, the preliminary reference procedure is therefore an expression of an interplay and allocation of tasks between national courts and the Court of Justice.[1] It is this interplay which is the subject of this book.

Already the Treaty establishing the European Coal and Steel Community (ECSC)—the first stone laid in founding the European Union—made provision from 1951 for the preliminary reference procedure.[2] However, it has been Article 234 (originally Article 177) in the Treaty of Rome of 1957 that has ensured the prominent position of the preliminary reference procedure on the legal map of Europe. By this provision the six original Member States of the European Economic Community gave their national courts the possibility, and in some cases the obligation, to make preliminary references. This Article states as follows:

> The Court of Justice shall have jurisdiction to give preliminary rulings concerning:
> (a) the interpretation of this Treaty;
> (b) the validity and interpretation of acts of the institutions of the Community and of the ECB;
> (c) the interpretation of the statutes of bodies established by an act of the Council, where those statutes so provide.

> Where such a question is raised before any court or tribunal of a Member State, that court or tribunal may, if it considers that a decision on the question is necessary to enable it to give judgment, request the Court of Justice to give a ruling thereon.

> Where any such question is raised in a case pending before a court or tribunal of a Member State against whose decisions there is no judicial remedy under national law, that court or tribunal shall bring the matter before the Court of Justice.

The preliminary ruling procedure has several important functions:

- It gives national courts access to help in resolving interpretative issues concerning Community law.
- It helps to ensure the uniform interpretation of Community law throughout the Community.

---

[1] For a discussion as to whether the relationship between national courts and the Court of Justice is in reality hierarchical or rather has the character of cooperation between equals see T de la Mare, 'Article 177 in Social and Political Context' in P Craig and G de Búrca (eds), *The Evolution of EU Law* (1998) 215, 227–8, and A Dashwood and A C Johnston, 'Synthesis of the Debate' in A Dashwood and A C Johnston (eds), *The Future of the Judicial System of the European Union* (2001) 55, 58–9.

[2] Art 41. The ECSC Treaty expired on 23 July 2002.

- It helps to ensure the effective application of Community law, just as it contributes to domesticating Community law and moving Community law away from assuring compliance only through a system of international surveillance so that it also contains a supplementary system of private enforcement that is not influenced by political discretion.
- It plays an important role in the political integration of the Community.[3]

Preliminary rulings have played a crucial role in the development of Community law, and some of the most fundamental principles of Community law have been laid down in connection with preliminary rulings. This includes, for example, such central principles as direct effect and supremacy of Community law. One consequence of the preliminary ruling procedure has been to bind the national courts more closely to the Court of Justice. This has meant that these courts, functionally speaking, also act as Community courts.[4]

As Article 234 has direct effect, many Member States have made no supplementary national legislation regulating when and how a preliminary reference should be made or how a preliminary ruling should be applied by the national courts. Instead, such questions are often regulated by a combination of case law of the Court of Justice and general procedural codes of the different Member States.

1.2. The structure of this book

This book examines the different aspects of the preliminary reference procedure. It is divided into 13 chapters which broadly mirror the order in which the various issues connected with a reference under Article 234 arise for a national court.

In this introductory chapter we first give an account on the development of the preliminary procedure (Section 2). Thereafter we give a brief outline of the different types of preliminary references in the Community system (Section 3). We then (Section 4) give a short account of the broadly similar reference procedure laid down in the EEA Agreement followed by an account of other ways of

---

[3] This fourth aspect will not be dealt with in this book. The question is dealt with by, among others, H Rasmussen, *On Law and Policy in the European Court of Justice* (1986) chs 8 and 14; J Weiler, 'Journey to an Unknown Destination: A Retrospective and Prospective of the European Court of Justice in the Arena of Political Integration' (1993) Journal of Common Market Studies Vol 37, No 4 December 1999 417, 421ff; M Maduro, *We, the Court—The European Court of Justice & the European Economic Constitution* (1998) 9 and 26ff; A Burley and W Mattli, 'Europe Before the Court: A Political Theory of Legal Integration' (1993) International Organization Vol 47, No 1 ss 41–76 1993; W Mattli and A Slaughter, 'Revisiting the European Court of Justice' (1998) International Organization Vol 52, No 1 January 1998 ss 177–209; and J Pitarakis and G Tridimas, 'Joint Dynamics of Legal and Economic Integration in the European Union' (2003) European Journal of Law and Economics Vol 16, No 3 November 2003 ss 357–68.

[4] R Lane, 'Article 234: A Few Rough Edges Still' in M Hoskins and W Robinson (eds), *A True European—Essays for Judge David Edward* (2003) 327, 327; M Dougan, *National Remedies Before the Court of Justice—Issues of Harmonisation and Differentiation* (2004) 3; and C Barnard and E Sharpston, 'The Changing Face of Article 177 References' (1997) 34 CML Rev 1113, 1113ff.

obtaining guidance on interpretation of Community law, namely questions to the Commission and the European Ombudsman (Section 5). The chapter ends with a discussion of what future changes one might envisage for the preliminary reference procedure in the coming years (Section 6).

Next, Chapter 2 analyses the use of the procedure and discusses the variations in frequency of references between the different Member States. Chapter 3 discusses which bodies may make preliminary references while Chapter 4 examines which questions can be referred for a preliminary ruling. Chapter 5 discusses the requirement that an answer to the preliminary question is relevant for the resolution of the main proceedings. Chapter 6 defines when a national court must make a preliminary reference. Chapter 7 discusses when a national court that is not obliged to make a preliminary reference should make such a reference. The form and content of a preliminary reference is the subject of Chapter 8. Chapter 9 provides an account of the steps that a national court may take after having made its reference while Chapter 10 contains an analysis of the procedure before the Court of Justice and discusses how written and oral observations may be presented. Chapter 11 examines the preliminary ruling as such, including the extent to which the Court of Justice reformulates the preliminary question. Chapter 12 considers the binding effect of a preliminary ruling. Finally, Chapter 13 describes the rules on costs and legal aid.[5]

2. History and Development of the Preliminary Reference Procedure

The preliminary ruling procedure laid down in Article 234 of the EC Treaty was inspired by various reference systems in the founding Member States. Of particular significance were the procedures in Italian and German law where certain matters are referred to the Constitutional Court for a preliminary ruling. The French system, in which general courts can refer different matters to administrative courts for a preliminary ruling, and vice versa, also served as a model. In comparison, at

---

[5] A brief note on terminology: in this book the Court of Justice of the European Communities is referred to as the 'Court of Justice' and only where there is no risk of misunderstanding the term 'Court' will be used. The Court of First Instance of the European Communities is referred to as the 'Court of First Instance'. A national body which fulfils the definition in Art 234 of the EC Treaty of a 'court or tribunal of a Member State' and therefore is entitled to make a preliminary reference is referred to as a 'national court' or a 'referring court'. The term 'body' is used in respect of both entities that are covered by Art 234's definition of a court and those that are not. The terms 'EC' and 'Community' refer only to the EC Treaty and circumstances covered by it. The terms 'EU' and 'Union' refer to the EU Treaty (an exception to this is the use of the term 'union citizen'). Where we refer to the Council, Commission etc, we use the term Community institution even though these institutions also cover matters under the Treaty on European Union.

the inception of the European Community there was no other system of cooperation between an international court and national courts which could serve as inspiration. The preliminary ruling procedure was thus one of the very first forms of advanced cooperation between national courts and an international court. The procedure has since been a model for the establishment of various national procedures, whereas it has not spread much internationally outside Community law.[6]

The Court of Justice received its first preliminary reference in 1961.[7] In the early years the number of preliminary references was very limited. In the 10 years from 1960 to 1969 there were only 75 references, in other words an average of fewer than eight per year. Against this background it is hardly surprising that the Court of Justice developed a practice that was characterised by a desire not to discourage references. Among other things, the Court of Justice laid down a broad definition of what was to be considered 'a court or tribunal of a Member State', and it expressly refrained from assessing the relevance of a question referred. Likewise, it applied some rather relaxed requirements regarding the referring court's description of the facts and national law as well as regarding the precision of the preliminary question as such. It was also characteristic that the Court described the relationship between itself and the national courts as that of a non-hierarchical cooperative procedure between equal partners, where each was responsible for clearly defined tasks.

Following its somewhat hesitant beginning the preliminary reference procedure has grown rapidly and today is in danger of becoming a victim of its own success.

In the period between 1961 and 1998, the number of annual references grew by 16 per cent on average, with an overall increase of nearly 100 per cent in the period from 1990 to 1998.[8] Then came a period where the volume of cases was more or less constant. However, in the last couple of years a new upward trend is recognisable, and in 2008 the Court of Justice received 288 references.[9] At the end of 2008

---

[6] See in more detail H Kanninen, Association of the Councils of State and Supreme Administrative Jurisdiction of the European Union, 18th Colloquium 2002, General Report on the Colloquium subject 'The Preliminary Reference to the Court of Justice of the European Communities', point 3. The most important example is probably the Benelux Court of Justice of 1965. Similarly, the Community Patent Convention of 1989 envisages the establishment of a system in which a supranational court may issue preliminary rulings.

[7] Case 13/61 *Bosch* [1962] ECR 45 (original reference Rec 1962 89).

[8] This significant increase of references cannot be attributed to the enlargement of the European Community. Admittedly, Austria, Finland, and Sweden joined the Community during the period, but only in 1996 so that courts in these three Member States only had a marginal influence on the total increase.

[9] The leading topics were taxation (35 cases), environment and consumers (34 cases), freedom, security, and justice (26 cases), social policy (26 cases), and freedom to provide services (20 cases).

767 cases were pending before the Court of Justice, of which 395 were preliminary references.[10]

An important consequence of the large number of references is that the average time taken to deal with each reference is now substantial. Another consequence is that it has become increasingly difficult for the Court of Justice to ensure full coherence within its case law, as it has grown to such magnitude that it has become virtually impossible even for the members of the Court to know all the cases. While in 1975 the time spent dealing with a preliminary reference case was six months, by 2008 the average time had increased to 16.8 months. Indeed, the figure of 16.8 months was a drop from a peak of 25.5 months in 2003. These figures cover wide variations between individual cases, and on several occasions a preliminary ruling has not been rendered until over four years after the national court made the reference.[11]

Presumably, the considerable time it takes to obtain a preliminary ruling deters a number of national courts from using this procedure even though otherwise the nature of the main proceedings justifies doing so.[12] In a resolution of 9 July 2008 on the role of the national judge in the European judicial system, the European Parliament observes that the duration of the preliminary ruling procedure remains excessively long and considerably reduces the attractiveness of the procedure for national judges.[13]

Presumably, the increase in the volume of cases was a contributory factor to the Court of Justice changing its practice in the mid 1990s on a number of important points regarding preliminary references. During this period the Court tightened the conditions under which a national court may make a reference and it established more stringent requirements regarding the formulation of a preliminary reference.[14] The 1990s also witnessed a change in the Court of Justice's practice

---

[10] The Court of Justice 2008 Annual Report, point 13 in the chapter on statistics.

[11] Case C-142/05 *Mickelsson* (ECJ 4 June 2009), where the reference was received at the Court on 24 March 2005. Warnings of the problems flowing from the increased number of preliminary references were given at an early stage, see J Weiler's contribution to a conference in 1985 published in 'The European Court, National Courts and References for Preliminary Rulings—The Paradox of Success: A Revisionist View of Article 177 EEC' in H Schermers, C Timmermans, A Kellermann, and J Watson (eds), *Article 177 EEC: Experiences and Problems* (1987) 366; T Koopmans, 'The Future of the Court of Justice of the European Communities' in A Bàròv and DA Wyatt (eds), *Yearbook of European Law* (1991) 1; and H Rasmussen, 'Docket Control Mechanisms, the EC Court and the Preliminary References Procedure' in M Andenas (ed), *Article 177 References to the European Court—Policy and Practice* (1994) 83, 100.

[12] See below Ch 7, s 2.2.

[13] EP Resolution of 9 July 2008 on the role of the national judge in the European judicial system (A6-0224/2008), points F and 25 available at <http://www.europarl.europa.eu/sides/getDoc.do?type=TA&language=EN&reference=P6-TA-2008-0352>.

[14] See below Ch 8. The tightening of the Court's practice regarding access to make preliminary references has not been unequivocal, however. Thus, since the 1990s it has increasingly accepted

whereby still more emphasis was put on the procedural rights of those entitled to present observations in the preliminary procedure before the Court.[15]

While the case law has become more detailed, at the same time the exposition of the principles underpinning the preliminary ruling procedure and the allocation of jurisdiction between the Court of Justice and the national courts have become more blurred. In legal literature it has even been argued that the spirit behind the preliminary ruling procedure has come under attack.[16] Moreover, Community law is primarily based on decentralised enforcement, and the most powerful—and for the Court of Justice the most dangerous—means whereby the national courts can show their dissatisfaction is by refusing to recognise the rulings of the Court of Justice. From a strategic point of view, therefore, good relations with the national courts continue to be of considerable importance to the Court of Justice.[17]

While such concerns may seem somewhat exaggerated, the continued increase in cases before the Court of Justice entails a risk that, in the long run, the system will end up in a gridlock which may put the preliminary reference system into jeopardy. For that reason, several measures have been taken in order to make the Court better suited to dealing with the pressure of cases—measures that have already shown their positive effect. Indeed, the average 16.8 months that it now takes to process a preliminary reference is the shortest for many years. Many of the measures taken concern the internal organisation of the Court's working methods and therefore fall outside the ambit of this book.[18] However, the Court has also engaged upon a number of measures that directly affect the preliminary procedure as such; for instance that it increasingly dispenses with the oral hearing.[19] Moreover, the ability to decide cases via a simplified procedure in the form of a reasoned order

---

references where, strictly speaking, Community law does not apply in the main proceedings. See Ch 4, s 5.3. Moreover, as explained in Ch 6, s 3.4.9, it has refrained from following repeated invitations to relax the national courts of last instance's obligation to make preliminary references.

[15] See Ch 8, ss 3.1 and 3.2.5.

[16] D O'Keeffe, 'Is the Spirit of Article 177 under Attack? Preliminary References and Admissibility' (1998) 23 EL Rev 509.

[17] T Tridimas, 'Knocking on Heaven's Door: Fragmentation, Efficiency and Defiance in the Preliminary Reference Procedure' (2003) 40 CML Rev 9, 37.

[18] For example, more cases may be decided by small chambers, the length of the judgments may be kept down (making translation faster), reports for the hearing are made shorter and are normally only translated into a limited number of languages, Opinions by the Advocates General are not given in less important cases and where they are given, as a main rule, the Advocates General are expected to draft their Opinions in one of only a few 'pivot' languages rather than in their own language. See in more detail V Skouris, 'Self-conception, Challenges and Perspective of the EU Courts' in I Pernice et al (eds), *The Future of The European Judicial System in a Comparative Perspective* (2005) 19.

[19] See below Ch 10, s 4.4.1.

has enabled the Court to decide simpler cases more speedily.[20] Similarly, the Nice Treaty has introduced the possibility of delivering judgments without the Advocate General giving an Opinion, which has contributed significantly to reducing the length of the proceedings; indeed in 2008, the Court of Justice made use of this possibility in around 41 per cent of all judgments handed down that year.[21] Finally, the special urgent procedure for handling preliminary references concerning the area of freedom, security, and justice has made it possible to deal more swiftly with these types of cases.[22]

3. Outline of the Different Possibilities of Making References to the Court of Justice

3.1. Overview

As observed above in Section 1, Member State courts were first granted the possibility of making preliminary references by Article 41 of the Treaty establishing the European Coal and Steel Community (ECSC).[23] In practice Article 234 (originally Article 177) of the EC Treaty, however, accounts for the vast majority of preliminary references, and today this provision has become almost synonymous with the preliminary reference procedure.

However, there are several bases for making preliminary references to the Court of Justice other than the now defunct Article 41 of the ECSC Treaty and Article 234 of the EC Treaty, some of which are gaining increasing importance. In most respects these other bases correspond to Article 234, but in certain regards there are differences, sometimes differences of considerable importance. Where such differences exist, they are identified and examined in the relevant chapters of this book. In addition, immediately below we provide an outline of these other bases. The most important other bases concern matters within the field of justice and home affairs—often referred to as the European Union's 'third pillar'. Originally the provisions on justice and home affairs were placed in Title VI, Article K, of the Treaty on European Union. Today however, the matters on 'visas, asylum, immigration and other policies related to the free movement of persons' have been transferred to Title IV of the EC Treaty whereas the regulation of police and judicial cooperation in criminal law matters continue to be part of Title VI of the EU Treaty.

---

[20] See below at Ch 10, s 5.1 and Ch 11, s 1.
[21] Art 20 of the Statute of the Court of Justice and below at Ch 11, s 1.
[22] See below at Ch 10, s 5.3.
[23] The ECSC Treaty entered into force on 23 July 1952 and expired on 23 July 2002.

Access to making preliminary references regarding Title IV of the EC Treaty, as well as those acts which are based on that Title, is regulated in Article 68 of the EC Treaty. Likewise, preliminary references regarding Title VI of the EU Treaty are regulated through Article 35 of that Treaty. We examine these two provisions below in Sections 3.2 and 3.3 respectively. Thereupon, in Section 3.4 we briefly consider references under the Euratom Treaty followed, in Section 3.5, by an examination of the possibility of making references on the basis of certain conventions. In Section 3.6 we consider the possibility of making preliminary references regarding the Community's Common Foreign and Security Policy (CFSP)—often referred to as the 'second pillar'. Finally, in Section 3.7, we explain how the Treaty of Lisbon, if it enters into force, will affect the preliminary reference procedure and the interplay between Articles 234 and 68 of the EC Treaty and Article 35 of the EU Treaty.[24]

3.2. Article 68 of the EC Treaty

With the adoption of the EU Treaty, asylum and immigration as well as most of visa policy came into the Union framework as part of the intergovernmental cooperation under the third pillar. With the Treaty of Amsterdam this competence was transferred from the EU Treaty to Title IV of the EC Treaty. As part of the EC Treaty, in principle, these matters now come within Article 234, but this is modified by Article 68(1) which provides that preliminary questions on the interpretation of Title IV or on the validity or interpretation of Community acts based on that Title can only be referred to the Court of Justice by national courts 'against whose decisions there is no judicial remedy under national law'. In other words, if a court is not one of last instance it is precluded from referring such questions to the Court of Justice.

Moreover, Article 68 also provides that not only national courts, but also the Council, the Commission, or a Member State may request the Court of Justice to give a ruling on a question of interpretation of Title IV of the EC Treaty or of acts of the institutions of the Community based on that Title (such requests from Member States, the Council, or the Commission are not preliminary references). In paragraph 3 the provision goes on to establish that such ruling shall not apply to judgments of courts or tribunals of the Member States which have become *res judicata*.

---

[24] With the exception of the Treaty of Lisbon we do not cover possible future bases for preliminary references in this book. Nevertheless, it may be observed that on 23 March 2009 the General Secretariat of the Council issued a working paper on a Draft Agreement on the European and Community Patents Court and Draft Statute (Revised Presidency text). This document also includes a proposal for a preliminary ruling procedure. See document 7928/09.

The Commission has proposed that the preliminary ruling scheme under Article 68 is brought into line with the scheme provided in Article 234.[25] So far the Council has not followed the proposal and no other measure has been taken. This arguably is in contravention of Article 67 of the EC Treaty.

3.3. Article 35 of the EU Treaty

Title VI of the EU Treaty lays down provisions on police and judicial cooperation in criminal matters. Article 35(1), which was introduced by the Treaty of Amsterdam, gives the Court of Justice jurisdiction to render preliminary rulings on the validity and interpretation of framework decisions and decisions, on the interpretation of conventions established under the EU Treaty's Title VI, and on the validity and interpretation of the measures implementing them.

However, it follows from Article 35(2) that a national court will only be competent to make a preliminary reference under the provision if its Member State has made a declaration accepting the Court of Justice's jurisdiction. In this respect the Member States may either confer the right to make a preliminary reference upon any of its courts in accordance with Article 35(3)(b) or it may confine this right to its courts of last instance in accordance with Article 35(3)(a).[26] In other words, Article 35 allows for one of three different scenarios in any Member State:

1. No access to make preliminary references regarding Title VI of the EU Treaty.
2. Any court may make a preliminary reference regarding Title VI of the EU Treaty.
3. Only courts of last instance may make a preliminary reference regarding Title VI of the EU Treaty.

At the time of writing (Summer 2009) 17 Member States have made a declaration conferring the right to make preliminary references upon their courts. Sixteen of these declarations allow any court or tribunal of the respective Member State to make such references whereas one Member State (Spain) has limited this right to courts or tribunals of last instance.[27]

---

[25] Communication from the Commission to the European Parliament, the Council, the European Economic and Social Committee, the Committee of the Regions and the Court of Justice of the European Communities—Adaptation of the provisions of Title IV of the Treaty establishing the European Community relating to the jurisdiction of the Court of Justice with a view to ensuring more effective judicial protection of 28 June 2006 (COM(2006) 346 (final)).

[26] See further Ch 3, ss 5.3.2 and 5.3.3.

[27] The Court of Justice provides a list of the declarations made pursuant to Art 35 of the EU Treaty. This list may be found at <http://curia.europa.eu/jcms/upload/docs/application/pdf/2008-09/art35_2008-09-25_17-37-4_434.pdf>.

3.4. The Euratom Treaty

The Euratom Treaty in Article 150 provides for preliminary references regarding that Treaty. Essentially this provision is identical to Article 234. The only differences are that Article 150 of the Euratom Treaty does not mention the European Central Bank and that Article 150(1)(c) provides that the Court of Justice may make a preliminary ruling on 'the interpretation of the statutes of bodies established by an act of the Council, save where those statutes provide otherwise'. The latter formulation may be contrasted with Article 234(1)(c) of the EC Treaty which provides 'the interpretation of the statutes of bodies established by an act of the Council, where those statutes so provide'.

The number of references under Article 150 of the Euratom Treaty has been extremely limited.

3.5. Conventions

Over the years, the Member States have adopted a number of 'Community conventions' outside the Treaty framework. Many of these conventions include provisions on preliminary rulings. Under these conventions the competence to refer is often restricted either to the appellate courts and the highest courts or only to the highest courts.[28]

Of particular significance when it comes to preliminary references based on conventions has been the Brussels Convention on Jurisdiction and Enforcement of Judgments in Civil and Commercial Matters. As of 2002 the Brussels Convention has been replaced by the so-called Brussels I Regulation.[29] This regulation is based on Title IV of the EC Treaty which means that preliminary references regarding this regulation are governed by Article 68. Due to the Danish opt-out on justice and home affairs, the Brussels I Regulation does not apply in Denmark. Thus, strictly speaking, the Brussels Convention continues to apply with regard to Denmark. Denmark has, however, entered into an agreement with the Community whereby vis-à-vis Denmark the rules of the Brussels I Regulation replace those of the Brussels Convention within the former's field of application.[30] This means that Danish courts have the same rights and duties to make preliminary references in this regard as have the courts of the other Member States.[31]

---

[28] See below Ch 3, s 5.4.

[29] Regulation 44/2001 of 22 December 2000 on jurisdiction and the recognition and enforcement of judgments in civil and commercial matters [2001] OJ L12/1.

[30] Agreement between the European Community and the Kingdom of Denmark on jurisdiction and the recognition and enforcement of judgments in civil and commercial matters [2005] OJ L299/62.

[31] Cf Art 6 of Agreement between the European Community and the Kingdom of Denmark on jurisdiction and the recognition and enforcement of judgments in civil and commercial matters

Moreover, it has been pointed out that the Brussels Convention also continues to apply where the Brussels I Regulation does not apply *ratione loci,* ie to overseas territories such as Mayotte (France) and Aruba (the Netherlands).[32]

Like the Brussels Convention, the Convention on the law applicable to contractual obligations,[33] the so-called Rome Convention, has been replaced by a regulation, the Rome I Regulation.[34] As with the Brussels Convention, the Danish opt-out on justice and home affairs means that the Rome I Regulation will not apply to Denmark. The Rome Convention, therefore, will continue to apply vis-á-vis Denmark.

In addition to the above, there are a number of conventions adopted on the basis of Title VI of the EU Treaty prior to the introduction of Article 35 of that Treaty. These are: the Convention on the establishment of a European Police Office,[35] the Convention on the protection of the European Communities' financial interests and the Protocol to that Convention drawn up on 27 September 1996,[36] the Convention on the use of information technology for customs purposes,[37] the Convention drawn up on the basis of Article K.3(2)(c) of the Treaty on European Union on the fight against corruption involving officials of the European Communities or officials of Member States of the European Union,[38] the Convention on the service in the Member States of the European Union of judicial and extrajudicial documents in civil or commercial matters,[39] the Convention drawn up on the basis of Article K.3 of the Treaty on European Union, on mutual assistance and cooperation between customs administrations,[40] the Convention

---

[2005] OJ L299/62. See also N Fenger and M Broberg, *Præjudicielle forelæggelser for EF-domstolen* (2008) 177–8.

[32] C Naomé, *Le renvoi préjudiciel en droit européen* (2007) 68.

[33] [1998] OJ C27/34 (consolidated version).

[34] Regulation 593/2008 of 17 June 2008 on the law applicable to contractual obligations (Rome I), [2008] OJ L177/6. The Regulation's date of entry into force is 17 December 2009.

[35] See protocol drawn up on the basis of Art K.3 of the Treaty on European Union, on the interpretation, by way of preliminary rulings, by the Court of Justice of the European Communities of the Convention on the establishment of a European Police Office [1996] OJ C299/2.

[36] Council Act of 29 November 1996 drawing up, on the basis of Art K.3 of the Treaty on European Union, the protocol on the interpretation, by way of preliminary rulings, by the Court of Justice of the European Communities of the Convention on the protection of the European Communities' financial interests [1997] OJ C151/1.

[37] Council Act of 29 November 1996 drawing up, on the basis of Art K.3 of the Treaty on European Union, the Protocol on the interpretation, by way of preliminary rulings, by the Court of Justice of the European Communities of the Convention on the use of information technology for customs purposes [1997] OJ C151/15.

[38] [1997] OJ C195/2. See Art 12.

[39] Protocol, drawn up on the basis of Art K.3 of the Treaty on European Union, on the interpretation, by the Court of Justice of the European Communities, of the convention on the service in the Member States of the European Union of judicial and extrajudicial documents in civil or commercial matters [1997] OJ C261/18.

[40] [1998] OJ C24/2. See Art 26.

drawn up on the basis of Article K.3 of the Treaty on European Union on driving disqualifications,[41] and the Convention on jurisdiction and the recognition and enforcement of judgments in matrimonial matters.[42]

3.6. Preliminary references and the Common Foreign and Security Policy

It follows from Article 46 of the EU Treaty that the Court of Justice has virtually no competence over the Common and Foreign Security policy. A preliminary reference on one of the provisions on the CFSP is therefore very likely to be declared inadmissible.[43]

Nevertheless, it cannot be completely excluded that situations may arise where the Court of Justice will admit a preliminary reference relating to the CFSP. This might occur where the reference concerns the interaction between the EC Treaty and the CFSP.[44] Thus, if a national court considers that a CFSP act encroaches upon the EC Treaty, it is likely that in accordance with the EU Treaty's Article 47 read in conjunction with Article 46(f), the Court of Justice will consider itself to be competent to rule on the matter.[45] For example, this situation could arise in connection with a claim for damages allegedly flowing from the adoption of CFSP acts, and where in this regard there is a question whether the Council has encroached on the competence of the Community.[46] Likewise, it seems arguable that the Court of Justice may admit a preliminary reference on access to documents under Article 255 of the EC Treaty, even if some or all the documents concern the CFSP.[47]

3.7. The Treaty of Lisbon

In 2005 the Treaty establishing a Constitution for Europe was rejected by the French and the Dutch voters. It was therefore abandoned and in its place the Member States subsequently adopted a reform treaty, normally referred to as the Treaty of

---

[41] [1998] OJ C216/2. See Art 14.

[42] Protocol drawn up on the basis of Art K.3 of the Treaty on European Union, on the interpretation by the Court of Justice of the European Communities of the Convention on Jurisdiction and the Recognition and Enforcement of Judgments in Matrimonial Matters [1998] OJ C221/20.

[43] See in support of this Case C-167/94 *Grau Gomis* [1995] ECR I-1023, para 6; and Case T-299/04 *Selmani* [2005] ECR II-20, paras 52–6.

[44] K Lenaerts and P Van Nuffel, *Constitutional Law of the European Union* (2005) 903, 905.

[45] Ibid, 808 *quaere* whether the Court also has jurisdiction to inquire whether a CFSP act of an institution respects a fundamental right.

[46] See in support of this Case C-354/04 P *Gestoras pro Amnistía* [2007] ECR I-1579, paras 53–4 and Case C-355/04/02 P *Segi* [2007] ECR I-1657, paras 53–4.

[47] See in support of this reasoning of the Court of First Instance in Case T-174/95 *Svenska Journalistförbundet* [1998] ECR II-2289, para 85 and (implicitly) Case C-353/99 P *Hautala* [2001] ECR I-9565. See also generally M-G Garbagnati Ketvel, 'The Jurisdiction of the European Court of Justice in Respect of the Common Foreign and Security Policy' (2006) 55 International and Comparative Law Quarterly 77–120.

Lisbon. At the time of writing (Summer 2009) it remains uncertain whether all Member States will ratify the Treaty of Lisbon. If it is ratified it will bring about some—limited—changes to the preliminary reference system. There follows an examination of these changes.

Under the present Treaty scheme, the European Union is based upon three pillars, namely (1) the Community pillar, (2) the pillar on the common foreign and security policy (CFSP), and (3) the pillar on justice and home affairs (of which important parts have earlier been transferred to the Community pillar). The Treaty of Lisbon will abandon this pillar structure, in particular by placing the regulation of justice and home affairs on a par with the regulation of Community matters. Therefore, if the Treaty of Lisbon enters into force, subsequent acts within the field of justice and home affairs will come within the ordinary preliminary reference procedure which today is found in Article 234.[48] The procedures which today are provided for in Articles 35 of the EU Treaty and 68 of the EC Treaty will be abandoned. Some limited exceptions will continue to apply in the field of justice and home affairs, however. Thus, Article 276 of the new Treaty on the Functioning of the European Union will provide that the Court of Justice of the European Union shall have no jurisdiction to review the validity or proportionality of operations carried out by the police or other law-enforcement services of a Member State or the exercise of the responsibilities incumbent upon Member States with regard to the maintenance of law and order and the safeguarding of internal security.[49]

The two principal changes to the current preliminary reference arrangement brought about by the Treaty of Lisbon's extension of full jurisdiction to all areas of justice and home affairs (or freedom, security, and justice as it is also called) are as follows.

First, under Article 267 of the new Treaty on the Functioning of the European Union, preliminary references will become possible from all national courts and tribunals on questions relating to asylum, immigration, and civil law matters (ie existing Title IV of the EC Treaty), and not just from courts of last instance.

Secondly, references under Article 267 of the new Treaty on the Functioning of the European Union in the area of criminal law and policing can be made by any national court or tribunal with the exception of courts or tribunals of a Member State that has opted out of this area of the law.

It follows that if the Treaty of Lisbon enters into force, this will have a substantive impact on the possibility of making a preliminary reference in the field of justice

---

[48] With the Treaty of Lisbon Art 234 will be renumbered Art 267.
[49] Today the same limitation is found in Art 35(5) of the EU Treaty.

14

and home affairs. Nevertheless, this does not mean that the limitations on preliminary references which presently apply vis-à-vis legal acts in the field of justice and home affairs will cease to apply immediately. On the contrary, Article 35 of the EU Treaty will continue to apply with regard to those legal measures that have been adopted before the entry into force of the Lisbon Treaty. For a number of years this provision will therefore continue to be relevant with regard to preliminary references in the field of police and judicial cooperation in criminal matters.[50]

The Lisbon Treaty also introduces the possibility of an expedited procedure for people in custody. Thus, as a new final paragraph to Article 267 of the Treaty on the Functioning of the European Union (ie Article 234 of the EC Treaty) it will be laid down that if a preliminary question 'is raised in a case pending before a court or tribunal of a Member State with regard to a person in custody, the Court of Justice of the European Union shall act with the minimum of delay'.[51]

Whereas the Court of Justice's jurisdiction will be considerably increased in the field of justice and home affairs (the 'third pillar'), the same is not the case with regard to the Common Foreign and Security Policy (the 'second pillar'). Thus, Article 275 of the Treaty on the Functioning of the European Union will provide as follows:

> The Court of Justice of the European Union shall not have jurisdiction with respect to the provisions relating to the common foreign and security policy nor with respect to acts adopted on the basis of those provisions.
>
> However, the Court shall have jurisdiction to monitor compliance with Article 40 of the Treaty on European Union and to rule on proceedings, brought in accordance with the conditions laid down in the fourth paragraph of Article 263(4) of this Treaty, reviewing the legality of decisions providing for restrictive measures against natural or legal persons adopted by the Council on the basis of Chapter 2 of Title V of the Treaty on European Union.

In other words, the Court of Justice will not have jurisdiction to answer preliminary references regarding the Common Foreign and Security Policy—with only some very narrow exceptions regarding compliance with certain procedural rules and with the extent of the powers of the institutions.

---

[50] Protocol No 36 on Transitional Provisions in Art 10(1) lays down that the powers of the Court of Justice under Title VI of the Treaty on European Union, in the version in force before the entry into force of the Treaty of Lisbon, shall remain the same, including where they have been accepted under Art 35(2) of the Treaty on European Union. However, in Art 10(3) the Protocol goes on to establish that these transitional measures shall cease to have effect five years after the date of entry into force of the Treaty of Lisbon.

[51] See further below Ch 10, s 5.3.1.

4. References to the EFTA Court

The preliminary reference procedure is not only of relevance to the courts in the Member States of the European Community. It is also important for the national courts in Iceland, Lichtenstein, and Norway, as a result of the participation of these countries in the European Economic Area (EEA).

According to Article 107 and Protocol 24 to the EEA Agreement, an EFTA State that is party to the EEA Agreement can decide that its courts may make references for preliminary rulings to the Court of Justice. So far no such decisions have been taken. The courts in these three EFTA States cannot therefore refer preliminary questions to the Court of Justice. Instead, they must make such references to the EFTA Court.[52]

The procedure for making a preliminary reference to the EFTA Court is laid down in Article 34 of the 'Agreement between the EFTA States on the Establishment of a Surveillance Authority and a Court of Justice' (SCA). On most points the procedure under this provision is similar to that laid down in Article 234 of the EC Treaty. These similarities are emphasised by the fact that the EFTA Court follows the practice of the Court of Justice in its interpretation of Article 34 of the SCA. Thus, among other things, the EFTA Court has adopted the case law of the Court of Justice on which criteria to apply when deciding whether a given body constitutes a national court entitled to make a preliminary reference.[53] The same applies to the Court of Justice's practice whereby it declares inadmissible questions that are hypothetical and without relevance for the decision in the main proceedings, but at the same time gives the national courts quite wide discretion in assessing the matter.[54]

The EFTA Court has also followed the case law of the Court of Justice in refraining from giving preliminary rulings on issues which the parties to the main proceedings raise before the EFTA Court but which the referring court has not asked about. At the same time, as with the Court of Justice, the EFTA Court has found that this case law does not prevent it from taking into account EEA rules other than the ones mentioned by the referring court in its preliminary reference.

---

[52] On the other hand, courts in the EU Member States can, and in certain situations shall, make preliminary references to the Court of Justice in relation to the EEA Agreement under the normal rules in Art 234 of the EC Treaty; see Ch 4, ss 3.3.8 and 5.4.

[53] Case E-1/94 *Rastamark* [1994–95] EFTA Court Report 17; and Joined Cases E-8/94 and E-9/94 *Mattel* [1994–95] EFTA Court Report 113. See in more detail Ch 3, ss 2–3.

[54] Case E-1/95 *Samuelsson* [1994–95] EFTA Court Report 145; Case E-5/96 *Nille* [1997] EFTA Court Report 30; Case E-6/96 *Wilhelmsson* [1997] EFTA Court Report 53; Case E-1/00 *Islandsbanki* [2000–01] EFTA Court Report 8; and Case E-2/03 *Asgeirsson* [2003] EFTA Court Report 185. For a further discussion, see Ch 5.

Furthermore, the EFTA Court has adopted the case law of the Court of Justice on the requirement that an order for reference should describe the relevant facts and national law sufficiently clearly and comprehensively to enable the EFTA Court to give a useful preliminary ruling based on a correct understanding of the case and its general context.[55] Finally, with regard to the possibility of interpreting international agreements, the EFTA Court has adopted a view which is substantially similar to that taken by the Court of Justice in relation to the parallel issue in Community law.[56]

However, there are a number of significant differences between the procedure under Article 34 of the SCA and that which applies under Article 234 of the EC Treaty. The main differences are the following: first: under Article 34 of the SCA there is no obligation for courts of last instance to make a reference. Secondly, the EFTA Court only gives an advisory opinion which is not binding on the referring court, let alone on other national courts. And thirdly, the EFTA Court does not have jurisdiction to examine the validity of secondary EEA legislation in the same way that the Court of Justice has jurisdiction to examine the validity of secondary Community legislation.[57]

5. Other Ways of Obtaining Legal Guidance from Community Bodies

5.1. Asking the European Commission for guidance on the interpretation of Community law

5.1.1. *Questions on competition and State aid law*

Procedures whereby national courts may seek assistance from the European Commission have been laid down in the fields of competition and State aid. In some cases these procedures may serve as a substitute for a preliminary reference to the Court of Justice. In this respect, it is of particular importance that the Commission normally will be able to provide an opinion within a significantly shorter time-frame than it takes to receive a preliminary ruling from the Court of Justice. Another important difference is that whilst a preliminary ruling by the Court of Justice is binding on the referring court, such an opinion by the Commission is not binding. Obtaining an opinion from the Commission neither

---

[55] Case E-10/04 *Piazza* [2005] EFTA Court Report 76; and see in more detail Ch 8.

[56] Case E-2/03 *Asgeirsson* [2003] EFTA Court Report 185. For a further discussion, see Ch 4, s 3.3.

[57] See further on these differences N Fenger, M Sanchez-Rydelski, and T van Stiphout, *European Free Trade Association (EFTA) and the European Economic Area (EEA) in International Encyclopaedia of Laws—Intergovernmental Organisations* (2005) 150ff.

affects the national court's possibility of making, nor (where applicable) its obligation to make, a preliminary reference to the Court of Justice.

In competition matters the Commission's provision of assistance to national courts has been set out in Regulation 1/2003 on the implementation of the rules on competition laid down in Articles 81 and 82 of the Treaty[58] together with the Commission's 'Notice on the co-operation between the Commission and the courts of the EU Member States in the application of Articles 81 and 82 EC'.[59] According to this notice, the Commission's duty to assist national courts in the application of Community competition law first of all consists of an obligation to transmit factual information to these courts. For example, a national court may request certain documents from the Commission or may ask for information of a procedural nature regarding such matters as whether a certain case is pending before the Commission, whether the Commission has initiated a procedure on a certain matter, or whether it has taken a position in a given case. A national court may also obtain information about when the Commission expects that a decision will be taken. Indeed, knowledge thereof may be relevant if the national court considers staying proceedings or adopting interim measures.[60]

The notice also provides that a national court may ask the Commission for its opinion on questions concerning the application of the Community competition rules, including its assessment of economic, factual, and legal matters. In this respect, the Commission will, however, limit itself to providing the national court with the requested information or clarification, without considering the merits of the case pending before the national court. Moreover, the Commission will not hear the parties to the case before it submits its opinion to the national court. The parties must therefore deal with the Commission's opinion as part of the case and in accordance with the relevant national procedural rules.[61]

---

[58] [2003] OJ L1/1.

[59] [2004] OJ C101/4.

[60] The national court's request for assistance may be submitted in writing to: European Commission, Directorate General for Competition, B-1049 Brussels, Belgium or sent electronically to <comp-amicus@cec.eu.int>. Further description of the Commission's practice in cooperating with national courts is given in the Commission's annual reports on Competition Policy.

[61] According to Regulation 1/2003 Art 15(3), the Commission is also competent to submit observations as *amicus curiae* on issues relating to the application and effectiveness of Arts 81 or 82 of the EC Treaty to a national court which is called upon to consider those provisions, see Case C-429/07 *X BV* (ECJ 11 June 2009), and, before the entry into force of Regulation 1/2003, the English case *Hasselblad v Orbinson* [1985] All ER 173. In this respect, Regulation 1/2003 distinguishes between written observations, which the Commission may submit on its own initiative, and oral observations, which can only be submitted with the permission of the national court. As the regulation specifies that observations shall only be submitted when the coherent application of Arts 81 or 82 of the EC Treaty so requires, the Commission in practice limits its observations to an economic and legal analysis of the facts underlying the case pending before the national court. Moreover, the Commission normally only presents observations in appeal cases.

In the field of State aid the Commission has issued a 'Commission notice on the enforcement of State aid law by national courts'.[62] This notice by and large mirrors the above-described notice on cooperation in competition matters. Thus, the State aid notice also envisages two different forms of Commission support for national courts; first, the national court may ask the Commission to provide information that is in the Commission's possession, and second, the national court may ask the Commission for a non-binding opinion concerning the interpretation of the State aid rules. As in the field of competition, the parties involved in the national proceedings are not heard before the Commission renders its opinion in a State aid matter. Moreover, an opinion under the State aid notice does not consider the merits of the case pending before the national court.[63]

In a case concerning subsidies within the limits of the environmental support framework, the Dutch *College van Beroep voor het bedrijfsleven* (Administrative Court for Trade and Industry) put various questions to the European Commission that were answered in less than three months. The answers were reproduced *in extenso* in the judgment of the Dutch court.[64]

In *Airport of Eelde*, the Dutch *Raad van State* put questions concerning State aid to the Commission that were answered in less than four months. The Dutch court allowed the parties to the proceedings the possibility of commenting first on the draft questions and, subsequently, on the Commission's answers.[65]

5.1.2. Questions that do not concern competition or State aid law

It is not often that national courts ask the Commission for assistance when deciding disputes involving Community law other than that of competition or State aid law.[66] It appears that they prefer either to solve the cases themselves or to use the preliminary procedure.

In the limited number of cases where the Commission has been faced with such a request from a national court, the Commission has generally been relatively open to supplying the national court with factual information. Indeed, the Commission is under an obligation to aid the national court with regard to such information, subject to the confidentiality provision in Article 287 of the EC Treaty and applicable secondary law.[67]

---

[62] 2009/C 85/01.

[63] Requests for support in the field of State aid must be addressed to: European Commission, Secretariat-General, B-1049 Brussels, Belgium.

[64] AWB/05/59, judgment of 10 July 2007.

[65] Case 200603116/1, judgment of 11 June 2008.

[66] H Kanninen, Association of the Councils of State and Supreme Administrative Jurisdictions of the European Union, 18th colloquium 2002, General report on the colloquium subject 'The Preliminary Reference to the Court of Justice of the European Communities', points 3.8 and 3.10.

[67] Case C-2/88 *Zwartveld* [1990] ECR I-3365.

In *Canadane Cheese Trading*, the Greek Council of State asked the Commission for information concerning the issue whether Feta cheese was first and foremost sold in Greece. In the opinion of the Greek court an answer to that question was relevant for deciding whether an exclusive right to use the Feta name for cheese made in a special manner was justifiable. After having received this information the Greek court made a preliminary reference to the Court of Justice.[68]

In contrast, the Commission has generally abstained from providing a legal opinion on the interpretation of the Community provisions at issue in the national proceedings. Until now, the Court of Justice has not clarified whether this approach is compatible with the general loyalty clause in Article 10 of the EC Treaty. It is, however, submitted that the obligations of the Commission must depend on the kind of Community rule that the question relates to.

If the dispute before the national court concerns an area where the Commission can issue binding decisions, such as in the fields of State aid and competition law mentioned in Section 5.1.1 above, the Commission arguably both can and should assist the national court with an interpretation of Community law. In this situation, the competence of the Commission to issue an opinion follows logically from its more embracing power to issue binding decisions on the same matter. Moreover, it may sometimes be necessary for the Commission and the national court to coordinate their respective actions regarding these types of Community rules in order to avoid irreconcilable positions being taken.

The legal situation is less clear where the national court's question relates to a Community rule that does not grant the Commission competence to issue binding decisions so that the Commission may only enforce its legal position by initiating infringement proceedings before the Court of Justice under Article 226 of the EC Treaty.

On the one hand, Article 10 of the EC Treaty establishes a general duty on the Commission to loyally cooperate with national courts and to assist them when needed in order to ensure a correct application of Community law. Moreover, the Commission might wish to steer the development of Community law and to make sure that it is applied correctly. Besides, in many instances the Commission has published guidelines and notices on how various Community rules should be applied. It would thus not be a major step if the Commission would assist national courts in specific cases as long as it only makes general observations and refrains from providing a suggestion for the resolution of the specific case before the national court.

---

[68] Case C-317/95 *Canadane Cheese Trading* [1997] ECR I-4681; and decisions from the Greek Council of State nos CE 1873/1993, CE 3381/1995, and CE 2469/1997.

It may also be argued that, particularly where the applicable Community act has been issued by the Commission, it would be less appropriate if the Commission were to refuse to provide a national court that requested an interpretation of this act and hide behind a statement that only the Court of Justice may provide an authoritative interpretation of the relevant rule. Similarly, some might find that the Commission should be open to assisting the national court in situations where the latter is barred from making a preliminary reference to the Court of Justice, for example because the question concerns an area of Community law where only courts of last instance have been given the right to make preliminary references.

On the other hand, the obligation for the Commission to cooperate loyally with national courts must be construed in light of the overall judicial system laid down in the EC Treaty. Under that system, only the Court of Justice may authoritatively determine the content of Community law. Moreover, with Article 234 the EC Treaty has introduced a special mechanism for national courts to request such authoritative interpretations without giving the Commission any equivalent competence.

Where a national court entertains doubts of such magnitude that it contemplates asking the Commission for advice, it might be presumed that the right interpretation of the relevant Community provision is open to doubt. However, if the Commission offers the assistance requested by the national court the result might be that the national court refrains from making a preliminary reference to the Court of Justice on the matter. Thus, not only will the Court of Justice not be given the possibility of authoritatively clarifying the obscure Community law provision; if the ruling of the national court is not subject to appeal the failure to refer the question to the Court of Justice may constitute a violation of the obligation on courts of last instance to make a preliminary reference as laid down in Article 234(3).[69]

Moreover, even when the question stems from a court against whose decision a right to appeal exists, for the Commission to provide the national court with a form of assistance that the Treaty has placed in the hands of the Court of Justice could constitute a *'détournement de procedure'*. At the very least, one would have to admit that such a practice would not provide for the same legal guarantees as does the preliminary reference procedure laid down in Article 234.

First, an opinion given by the Commission cannot be considered to reflect the position that the Court of Justice would have taken in a preliminary ruling on the same matter. Indeed, this is clear from the fact that the Court of Justice does not invariably follow the observations made by the Commission as *amicus curiae* in

---

[69] See below Ch 6, s 5.

preliminary rulings. In fact, there is not even a guarantee that an opinion given by one of the Commission's directorates general (departments) will eventually correspond to the position that the Commission may take should the same question subsequently be raised in a preliminary reference.

Second, whereas both Member States and Community institutions have a right to present observations in a preliminary reference procedure before the Court of Justice,[70] neither will normally be invited to present their view on the matter before the Commission provides an opinion to the national court. Not only does this mean that the Commission's answer is likely to be given on a less informed basis than is a preliminary ruling by the Court of Justice; it may also raise issues of rights of defence in cases where the Commission's interpretation implies that national law is incompatible with Community law. Indeed, the alternative to having the national court striking down the national legislation on the basis of a Commission opinion might sometimes be that the Commission commences infringement actions against the Member State regarding this legislation. In such proceedings the Member State concerned will have a right to be heard both before the Commission reaches its own position on the matter in a reasoned opinion and if the case ends up before the Court of Justice.

5.2. Asking the European Ombudsman for guidance on the interpretation of Community law

National ombudsmen do not qualify as courts within the meaning of Article 234 and they can therefore not obtain preliminary rulings from the Court of Justice.[71] However since in some respects ombudsmen's workings resemble those of an administrative court and, generally speaking, public authorities comply with ombudsman opinions, it has been recommended that national ombudsmen should have access to obtaining authoritative advice on the correct interpretation of Community law.[72] To some extent, this need is met by the national ombudsmen's access to a 'report' of the European Ombudsman on a query concerning EU law and its interpretation.

Thus, in September 1996 the national ombudsmen and similar bodies together with the European Ombudsman agreed upon a procedure whereby the European Ombudsman will receive queries from national ombudsmen about Community law and either provide replies directly or channel the query to an appropriate

---

[70] See below at Ch 10, s 3.1.
[71] See Ch 3, s 3.2.4.
[72] M Broberg, 'Preliminary References by Public Administrative Bodies: When Are Public Administrative Bodies Competent to Make Preliminary References to the European Court of Justice?' (2009) 15 European Public Law 207, 220.

Union institution or body for response.[73] As of January 2009, 35 such queries had been received with a tendency towards an increase.[74]

The query procedure is based on a non-binding policy agreement between the members of the European network of ombudsmen and is not mentioned in the European Ombudsman's Statute or the Ombudsman's Implementing Provisions. Basic guidelines for the handling of queries are, however, provided in the European Ombudsman's *Legal Officer Handbook*.[75]

In practice the European Ombudsman will forward the query to the relevant Community institution (usually the Commission) for an opinion and, normally, the Ombudsman does not consider it necessary to carry out an independent and separate examination of the legal issues involved if the opinion obtained is satisfactory.[76]

This has been reflected in the European Ombudsman's report on a query from the Danish Ombudsman where for reasons of confidentiality the Danish Ombudsman asked the European Ombudsman not to submit the case to any other authority, including the European Commission. The European Ombudsman observed that he had no authority to engage in a procedure such as the Article 234 procedure under the EC Treaty, by providing interpretation of Community law provisions in pending cases, which concerned national authorities. Although one could argue that nothing hinders an abstract interpretation of the provisions in question by the European Ombudsman, such an interpretation would in reality find either in favour of or against the national authority concerned. Due consideration had also to be given to the fact that the Statute of the European Ombudsman explicitly provided that no authorities other than Community institutions and bodies came under his mandate. Therefore, the European Ombudsman had to limit himself to undertaking research to provide the Danish Ombudsman with all necessary elements for the case he was examining.[77] In the actual case the European Ombudsman concluded that there was no case law that directly took a view on the question, that no literature dealing with the question had been found, and that in the preparatory works on the relevant Community act there appeared to be no view on the specific questions that interested the Danish Ombudsman, although a passus

---

[73] Letter from the European Ombudsman to the Network of National Ombudsmen and similar bodies of 4 October 1996. The quotation has, inter alia, been reproduced in the European Ombudsman's Annual Report 2000 at p 197. See also Statement adopted at the Sixth Seminar of the National Ombudsmen of EU Member States and Candidate Countries, Strasbourg 14–16 October 2007 available at <http://www.ombudsman.europa.eu/liaison/en/statement.htm>.
[74] Letter of 30 January 2009 from the European Ombudsman P Nikiforos Diamandouros to the authors.
[75] The Legal Officer Handbook is a purely internal and non-binding document.
[76] eg The European Ombudsman's Annual Report 1999 at p 242.
[77] Query Q1/99/PD reported in The European Ombudsman's Annual Report 1999 at pp 243–4.

in the explanatory memorandum on that act 'could have a bearing on the question'.[78]

It thus appears that the query procedure primarily functions as a kind of transmission service whereby the European Ombudsman assists the national ombudsmen (and similar bodies) in obtaining an opinion by the relevant Community institution.

In 2008 the European Ombudsman received a query from the Danish Ombudsman on the interpretation of 2003/4 on public access to environmental information. Following an eight-page reply from the Commission the European Ombudsman welcomed the Commission's thorough and well-reasoned opinion on the query and, in the light of the content of that opinion and recalling that the Danish Ombudsman had no comments to make on it, the European Ombudsman considered that the issues raised in the query had been adequately addressed and clarified. The European Ombudsman therefore closed the query.[79]

Where for one reason or another it is not possible to obtain such an opinion the European Ombudsman will assist the national ombudsman who has made the query by providing relevant legal sources that may be of relevance in answering the query. In contrast, the European Ombudsman will normally not express his own opinion as to the interpretation or validity of the Community act in question.[80]

The assistance provided by the European Ombudsman to the national ombudsmen and similar bodies may be of substantial help to the latter. Nevertheless, we have a reservation regarding the European Ombudsman's practice of transmitting the query to the relevant Community institution to obtain its view on the interpretation or validity of the Community act in question and, in most cases, simply forwarding this opinion to the national ombudsman who has made the query with the rubric that the European Ombudsman has no remarks to make on the Community institution reply. To our mind, the Community institution cannot always be regarded as an independent arbiter in relation to these Community acts where it may have been responsible for their adoption or is responsible for enforcing Member State compliance therewith. Indeed, this presumably is one of the reasons why the national ombudsmen do not contact the Commission (or other Community institution) directly in order to obtain guidance on the interpretation

---

[78] The European Ombudsman's Annual Report 1999 at p 245.

[79] Query Q5/2008/PB from the Danish Ombudsman to the European Ombudsman on the interpretation of Directive 2003/4 of 28 January 2003 on Directive 2003/4 of 28 January 2003 on public access to environmental information and repealing Council Directive 90/313 [2003] OJ L41/26.

[80] This has also been established in the European Ombudsman's Legal Officer Handbook for the handling of queries. For an apparent exception, see the case reported in the European Ombudsman's Annual Report 2007 at p 93.

of Community law. It is therefore problematic that through the formal intervention of the European Ombudsman the opinion of the Community institution is given a rubber stamp which does not appear fully justified. It follows that it may be worth considering a revision of the present practice.

6. The Preliminary Reference System in the Future

6.1. Overview

As explained above in Section 2 of this chapter, the number of references is so high that the time it takes to receive an answer has become inconveniently long. In order to meet these problems the Court of Justice has taken a number of steps to manage its case load more effectively and has succeeded in bringing down the time it takes to process a preliminary reference. Indeed, the present average length of preliminary proceedings is the lowest in 20 years, and over the past five years there has been a continuous reduction in the average handling period.

To some extent the more recent reduction in the average handling time may be attributed to the two latest enlargements of the European Union and the consequent increase from 15 to 27 judges sitting in the Court. Until now this expansion has not been followed by a similar increase in cases from the new Member States.[81] There is normally a certain time-lag before the full weight of a new Member State is reflected in the Court's case load.[82] Thus, it may be expected that within the foreseeable future there will be a substantial growth in the number of both preliminary references and direct actions relating to the new Member States. At the same time there has been an extension of the areas of law in which it is possible to make a preliminary reference. The Court is increasingly called upon to deal with asylum, immigration, and the Schengen *acquis*, and a number of areas under the heading of judicial cooperation have come under the EC Treaty (ie the 'first pillar') and are therefore now subject to references for preliminary rulings.[83]

The future challenge for the preliminary procedure is thus to achieve a balance where the Court is not asked to treat more cases than it can handle while still ensuring that Community law is being developed primarily by the Court of Justice itself. Indeed, if no measures are taken it is not unlikely that both the unity and the

---

[81] See Tables 2.2 and 2.3 in Ch 2, s 1. M Bobek, 'Learning to talk; Preliminary Rulings, The courts of the new Member States and the Court of Justice' (2008) CML Rev Vol 45 1611, 1642, notes that the increase in the number of judges has not been matched by a proportionate reduction in the length of proceedings. However, a proportionate reduction was not to be expected considering that much of the time spent on a preliminary reference is connected with work such as translation which is not dependent on the capacity of the Court's judges.

[82] See below Ch 2, s 1.2.

[83] See below at Ch 4, s 2.3.

impact of the Court's decisions will diminish as their number increases and as they deal more frequently with questions of secondary importance or of interest only in the context of the case concerned.

In the following sections we will discuss various measures that may be taken in order to cater for the problems that will flow from the expected increase in the number of references. We first consider the possibility of transferring (some) preliminary reference cases to the Court of First Instance (Section 6.2). Thereafter we examine the so-called green light procedure, ie a procedure where the referring court explains how it believes that the preliminary question should be answered following which the Court of Justice may either give a green light to the proposed solution or admit the case for normal consideration, thus itself giving a preliminary ruling (Section 6.3). Following this, we look at what is normally referred to as docket control, meaning that the Court of Justice is given the power to choose which of the preliminary references it will admit for a normal examination and which it will decline to consider (Section 6.4). Another way that has been suggested for coping with the expected problems is to limit the right of national courts to make preliminary references so that only references by courts of last instance will be admitted. This suggestion will be discussed in Section 6.5. We then consider the possibility of introducing decentralised Community courts to relieve the pressure on the Court in Luxembourg (Section 6.6). Finally, in Section 6.7 we sum up what, in our opinion, is the best way forward.

6.2. Transfer of preliminary cases to the Court of First Instance

With the Nice Treaty, Article 225 of the EC Treaty was amended so as to allow the Council to decide that the Court of First Instance shall be given jurisdiction to give preliminary rulings in 'specific areas' which are to be laid down by the Court's Statute. The relevant parts of Article 225 read as follows:

> 3. The Court of First Instance shall have jurisdiction to hear and determine questions referred for a preliminary ruling under Article 234, in specific areas laid down by the Statute.
>
> Where the Court of First Instance considers that the case requires a decision of principle likely to affect the unity or consistency of Community law, it may refer the case to the Court of Justice for a ruling.
>
> Decisions given by the Court of First Instance on questions referred for a preliminary ruling may exceptionally be subject to review by the Court of Justice, under the conditions and within the limits laid down by the Statute, where there is a serious risk of the unity or consistency of Community law being affected.

To date the Court of First Instance has not been attributed any such preliminary cases. Nor is a future transfer on the immediate agenda. To some extent this may be explained by the fact that presently the case load of the Court of Justice is smaller than that of the Court of First Instance meaning that on average the Court of Justice spends less time on processing its cases than does the Court of First Instance.[84] A prerequisite for transferring cases therefore seems to be an increase of judges in the Court of First Instance from the present 27.

Several provisions in the Statute of the Court of Justice and its Rules of Procedure have already been introduced to cater for such a transfer.[85] These provisions shall ensure that where there is a serious risk of the unity or consistency of Community law being affected, the Court of Justice shall be given the powers to review a preliminary ruling of the Court of First Instance. In the first place this review will be performed by the First Advocate General of the Court of Justice who may propose, within one month of delivery of a preliminary ruling of the Court of First Instance, that the Court of Justice reviews that ruling. Within one month of receiving this proposal, the Court of Justice shall decide whether or not the preliminary ruling should be reviewed. If it decides in the affirmative it will deal with the case by means of an urgent procedure. If at that point the Court of Justice finds that the preliminary ruling of the Court of First Instance affects the unity or consistency of Community law, the answer it gives to the preliminary question will replace the one initially given by the Court of First Instance.

In addition, instead of processing a preliminary reference at the very outset of the procedure the Court of First Instance may itself refer a case to the Court of Justice if the case requires a decision of principle likely to affect the unity or consistency of Community law. While arguably these safety valves are necessary to ensure the coherence of Community law, they simultaneously make the preliminary reference procedure more complicated and in those situations where these special procedures are actually put into use, they are likely to mean that the procedure will take even longer than is the case today.

One problem in relation to a transfer of 'specific areas' of preliminary cases to the Court of First Instance is the difficulty in identifying areas of Community law that constitute separate bodies of law whose interpretation is unlikely to affect other areas of law. It has been argued that transferring certain groups of cases to the Court of First Instance may risk compromising the need for uniform interpretation.[86] Indeed, considering that any subject matter of Community law may involve aspects of Community constitutional law, it would not be easy to separate so-called 'constitutional issues', to be reserved to the Court of Justice, from other types of issues, susceptible to be transferred to the Court of First Instance.[87]

---

[84] C Naomé, *Le renvoi préjudiciel en droit européen* (2007) 34.

[85] Arts 62–62b of the Statute as well as Arts 123a–123e of the Court's Rules of Procedure.

[86] R Colomer, 'La réforme de la Cour de justice opérée par la traité de Nice et sa mise en oeuvre future' (2001) Revue trimestrielle de droit européen Vol 37, No 4 2001, ss 705–725.

[87] K Lenaerts, 'The unity of European law and the overload of the ECJ—the system of preliminary rulings revisited' in I Pernice et al (eds), *The Future of The European Judicial System in a Comparative Perspective* (2005) 212, 233.

That being said, it seems likely that this problem will only materialise infrequently.[88] Most preliminary questions are of a rather technical nature. They thus relate to questions that would in many national legal systems never arrive at a supreme court and it is therefore not obvious why in a two-instance system Community law should not be able to live with a similar treatment to that in national legal systems. Moreover, it is not easy to see why every single constitutional issue or problem of unity and coherence must necessarily be dealt with by the Court of Justice; in our opinion only novel, complex, and important issues need to be decided by the Court of Justice itself as the 'supreme court' on European Community law.

The above outlined reservations regarding a transfer of competence to the Court of First Instance seems to be based on a belief that the safeguards provided by the Treaty of Nice and the Statute of the Court of Justice would not suffice to avoid such risks. It is, however, not clear why that should be the case.[89] Not even the present system guarantees full coherence and unity as most of the cases in the Court of Justice are decided by smaller chambers. Hence, incoherence may already arise under the present scheme where there is no system of rectification like the one envisaged if a transfer of jurisdiction is made to the Court of First Instance.

Others fear that national courts of last instance, in particular, might be less inclined to refer preliminary questions to a court which is not the ultimate court within its own legal system. The logic seems to be that a change of partner in a long-standing relationship might endanger the mutual confidence that the present system is believed to represent.[90] The validity of these arguments is very difficult to assess. However, they should probably not be overemphasised. Indeed, it does not seem very likely that courts of last instance of the Member States would disregard the obligation to refer laid down in Article 234(3) of the EC Treaty merely because jurisdiction is transferred from the Court of Justice to the Court of First Instance.

In our opinion it might not be ideal to divide competence in the field of preliminary references between the Court of Justice and the Court of First Instance. Nevertheless, if the number of cases before the Court of Justice develops as it is feared they might, radical steps will be necessary. In such a scenario, transferring competence to the Court of First Instance in certain limited fields of the law

---

[88] T Tridimas, 'Knocking on Heaven's Door: Fragmentation, Efficiency and Defiance in the Preliminary Reference Procedure' (2004) 40 CML Rev 9, 20–1.

[89] B Vesterdorf, 'A Constitutional Court for the EU?' in I Pernice et al (eds), *The Future of the European Judicial System in a Comparative Perspective* (2005) 83, 88, but contrast with Advocate General Colomer in paras 71–4 of his Opinion in Case C-17/00 *De Coster* [2001] ECR I-9445.

[90] See A Dashwood and A C Johnston, 'Synthesis of the Debate' in A Dashwood and A C Johnston (eds), *The Future of the Judicial System of the European Union* (2001) 55, 63.

appears to represent the best long-term solution compared to other solutions that have been tabled until now.

Possible areas to be transferred to the Court of First Instance are customs matters and trade mark cases[91] as well as questions relating to the Brussels I Regulation on jurisdiction and the recognition and enforcement of judgments in civil and commercial matters.[92] Moreover, it has been argued that a substantial proportion of preliminary questions involve indirect challenges to the validity of Community legislation and that the substance of such cases is very similar to direct actions under Article 230 of the EC Treaty which at present are already heard by the Court of First Instance. It has therefore been suggested that the Court of First Instance should also be able to deal with such issues of law when they emerge indirectly via national courts as requests for preliminary rulings.[93]

It is true that a transfer of this type of case might create a certain synergy effect. Moreover, at first sight it may seem odd that different courts hear the case depending on whether it has gone directly to Luxembourg or originates from national proceedings. Nevertheless, as pointed out by Judge Lenaerts, such reasoning overlooks the fact that a judgment of the Court of First Instance in a direct case is subject to full appeal to the Court of Justice on points of law thereby giving the latter an effective vehicle to steer the interpretation and development of Community law. In contrast, a preliminary ruling by the Court of First Instance will not be subject to a right of appeal, but will in principle be definitive, subject only to exceptional review on the proposal of the First Advocate General of the Court of Justice. It could therefore just as well be argued that the parallelism between direct actions and preliminary rulings would be more likely to be broken than achieved by such a transfer, as the Court of First Instance would effectively be delivering quasi-final preliminary rulings in areas of law in which it acts as a true first instance court on points of law when it hears similar issues in direct actions. It will only be possible to achieve full parallelism in those special areas where the Court of First Instance in direct cases functions as an appellate court.[94]

---

[91] P Dyrberg, 'What Should the Court of Justice Be Doing' (2001) 26 EL Rev 291, 296–7 and J Azizi, 'Opportunities and Limits for the Transfer of Preliminary Reference Proceedings to the Court of First Instance' in I Pernice et al (eds), *The Future of The European Judicial System in a Comparative Perspective* (2005) 241, 251–3.

[92] Regulation 44/2001 of 22 December 2000 on jurisdiction and the recognition and enforcement of judgments in civil and commercial matters [2001] OJ L12/1. See further O Due, 'The Working Party Report' in A Dashwood and A C Johnston (eds), *The Future of the Judicial System of the European Union* (2001) 87, 89.

[93] P Graig and G de Búrca, *EU Law, Text, Cases and Materials* (2007) 499.

[94] K Lenaerts, 'The Unity of European law and the Overload of the ECJ—the system of preliminary rulings revisited' in I Pernice et al (eds), *The Future of The European Judicial System in a Comparative Perspective* (2005) 212, 234–6 and 256.

Hitherto the Court of First Instance has only had this function in areas that do not give rise to preliminary references, namely staff cases.

6.3. Green light procedures

Another way of dealing with the expected increase in the number of preliminary references is via a so-called 'green light procedure'. Under this procedure, when making a preliminary reference national courts would be encouraged, and perhaps even obliged, to include a proposal suggesting the answers to be given. The Court of Justice may then dispose of the case by giving a 'green light' to this proposal, with or without modifications. Where the Court of Justice does not immediately agree with the referring court's proposal, or where for other reasons the Court is of the view that the case should be dealt with in a more elaborate manner, the case will be submitted for the ordinary preliminary reference procedure.[95]

The green light procedure may take many different forms. In particular, it may be of importance whether the Member States and Community institutions are given the possibility of presenting their view on the substance of the question, whether they are only given the right to comment on the feasibility of giving the green light, or whether they are not given any possibility at all of presenting their view before the Court of Justice has decided whether or not to give the green light.

A variant of this idea consists of a 'red light procedure' whereby the referring court delivers a 'judgment *nisi*', ie a 'draft judgment' that is sent to the Court of Justice together with a preliminary reference; if the Court of Justice then fails to respond to the reference within a given time limit, the national court's 'draft judgment' becomes final.[96]

Depending on the way in which the referring court presents its proposal, both a green light system and a red light system could provide an efficient means for the Court of Justice to dispose of a considerable number of preliminary references. At best, the procedure could enable the Court to find the right balance between, on the one hand, its limited resources and, on the other hand, the need for unity and consistency in the interpretation and development of Community law. In the long run the role of the Court could evolve from its present role of de facto semi-adjudication into a role of partial monitoring of the administration of Community law at the national level.

---

[95] On such a model see further the Court of Justice's 1999 'Report on the Future of the Judicial System of the European Union'; and the 2000 Report of the Working Party on the Future of the European Communities' Court System (the so-called 'Due Report'). In a resolution of 9 July 2008 on the role of the national judge in the European judicial system, the European Parliament has called for the consideration of a 'green light' system, see point 13 of the resolution.

[96] A Dashwood and A C Johnston, 'Synthesis of the Debate' in A Dashwood and A C Johnston (eds), *The Future of the Judicial System of the European Union* (2001) 45, 68–9.

A green light procedure is not without its problems however. For such a procedure to work well, the referring court must have a good knowledge of the relevant field of Community law.[97] While it might already be tricky to identify the relevant Community law question, it is an altogether more difficult matter to come up with a qualified proposal for its resolution. For that reason, a green light procedure would probably work best if it is merely an option for the referring court which may continue to pose questions under the classical preliminary reference procedure.

In addition, a green light procedure would raise a host of questions concerning the precedent value of the referring court's opinion when it is accepted by the Court of Justice. It should, for example, be clear whether the Court of Justice agrees only with the proposed conclusions or also with the national court's legal reasoning. Presumably, it should be provided that under such a system only a 'normal' preliminary ruling of the Court of Justice with reasons would constitute a binding precedent on national courts other than the referring court.

6.4. Docket control

The US Supreme Court applies a so-called *certiorari* system—sometimes referred to as docket control—whereby it carries out a preliminary examination in order to decide whether to hear a case or let the decision of the lower court stand without having been tried by the Supreme Court. It has been discussed whether the Court of Justice should apply a similar system.[98]

Introducing a docket control system would provide a structural response to the expected growth in the number of preliminary references. By allowing the Court of Justice to weed out, at a preliminary stage, cases of lesser importance from the point of view of the uniformity and development of Community law, such a system would enable the Court to concentrate on the most notable issues of Community law. Thereby, the Court might be able to influence the development of the law in a more effective manner than under the present system where much of its time is spent on trifling cases.

A docket control system however involves a risk of distorting judicial cooperation between the national courts and the Court of Justice, which has hitherto been heralded as the heart and soul of the preliminary procedure.[99] A way of diminishing this risk could possibly be by combining a docket control system with the green light system discussed above, so that in its preliminary reference the national

---

[97] X Groussot et al, *Empowering National Courts in EU Law* (2005) 26.

[98] H Rasmussen, 'Remedying the Crumbling EC Judicial System' (2000) CML Rev Vol 37, 2000, ss 1071–1112.

[99] A Arnull, 'Judicial Architecture or Judicial Folly? The Challenge Facing the EU' in A Dashwood and A C Johnston, *The Future of the Judicial System of the European Union* (2001) 41, 45, as well as A Dashwood and A C Johnston, 'Synthesis of the Debate', ibid, 55, 64.

court would include a proposed reply to the question referred. Such a combination also has the advantage that the proposed reply could provide a basis for the Court's decision as to whether to admit the preliminary question or whether to leave it to the national court to interpret the relevant Community rule itself.

Another advantage of a docket control system is that it is likely to prompt national courts to exercise increased selectivity regarding which questions to refer and thus encourage them to exercise more fully their own functions as Community courts. The other side of the coin however is that if the national courts become too restrained this could jeopardise the preliminary ruling system's objective of ensuring a uniform interpretation of Community law. Moreover, this would place the Court of Justice in a position to 'pick and choose' enabling it to circumvent sensitive issues;[100] arguably it might be possible to eliminate this risk by leaving the decision of which cases to admit to an independent review body.

Finally, one should be hesitant in drawing parallels with the US system. While the US system functions as part of an appeal procedure, the preliminary reference system does not. The US Supreme Court exercises its discretion upon a reading of a decision of a lower federal court, and if the Supreme Court refuses to hear a case, the decision of the lower federal court will stand. In comparison, if a docket control system were to be introduced as part of the preliminary reference system, the Court of Justice would be required to decide on whether to admit the case before the referring court has pronounced its own view on the matter. Moreover, if the Court of Justice refuses to hear the case because it is not sufficiently important or novel, no Community court will have pronounced itself on the issue in doubt.[101] Whereas the US Supreme Court occupies a superior hierarchical position vis-à-vis the court whose decision is subject to the docket control decision, the Court of Justice and national courts do not form part of one and the same judicial system and are thus not in a hierarchical relationship with one another. Rather, the preliminary reference system is based on cooperation and dialogue between different types of court each having their respective function.[102] These important differences may make it difficult to introduce a docket control system in a satisfactory manner.

---

[100] T Koopmans, 'The Future of the Court of Justice of the European Communities' in A Bàròv and DA Wyatt (eds), *Yearbook of European Law* (1991) 1, 30.

[101] P Graig and G de Búrca, *EU Law, Text, Cases and Materials* (2007) 496; and T Koopmans, 'The Future of the Court of Justice of the European Communities' in *Yearbook of European Law* (1991) 1, 29.

[102] The Due Report, p 21, and above at s 1 of this chapter.

6.5. Limiting the right to refer to courts of last instance

Another option could be to limit the right to make a preliminary reference to national courts of last instance.[103] Indeed, this system is already applied today with regard to references under Article 68[104] of the EC Treaty as well as to references made under Article 35[105] of the EU Treaty provided a Member State has made a declaration under Article 35(3)(a) to this effect.[106]

Today a large number of references are made by courts other than those of last instance.[107] Therefore allowing only courts of last instance to refer is likely to lead to a considerable reduction in the number of references and thus to a reduction of the time it takes to deliver a preliminary ruling in those few remaining cases.

However, limiting the right to make preliminary references to courts of last instance could have the perverse effect of encouraging litigants to pursue their cases to the highest court simply to gain access to the Court of Justice.[108] This will not only create unnecessary work at the national level, it will also mean that some national cases will take even longer time to solve than is the case today. Moreover, if such a practice were to become widespread, the desired reduction in the workload of the Court of Justice could be more limited than is otherwise expected. In this connection it should not be forgotten, as a main rule, that national courts of last instance are under a duty to refer questions of Community law which arise in the main proceedings.

Second, preliminary references from lower courts have played a crucial role in the development of Community law, and there is no reason to assume that this will not continue to be the case in the future as well. Therefore, restricting lower courts' access to make preliminary references may adversely affect the future development of Community law.

Thirdly, a system with restricted access to make preliminary references may negatively affect the uniform interpretation and application of Community law amongst the national courts. Not only may this adversely affect the legal protection that

---

[103] For an advocate of such a system, see H Rasmussen, 'Remedying the Crumbling EC Judicial System' (2000) CML Rev Vol 37, ss 1071–1112.

[104] Concerning visas, asylum, immigration, and other policies related to free movement of persons.

[105] Concerning police and judicial cooperation in criminal matters.

[106] The Treaty of Lisbon abandons this limitation on the right to refer. See further s 3.7 above and Ch 3, s 5.3.3.

[107] See below at Ch 2, s 1.3.

[108] O Due, 'The Working Party Report' in A Dashwood and A C Johnston (eds), *The Future of the Judicial System of the European Union* (2001) 87, 88, and Schermers, 'Problems and Prospects', in the same book at 31 (33–4).

Community law offers, it could also be argued that it might alienate lower courts from Community law.[109]

Moreover, a limitation like the one set out here will mean that questions which primarily arise in cases that rarely reach the highest national courts are unlikely to be referred to the Court of Justice. In practice it means that important questions of Community law may never reach the Court of Justice if such questions arise in those cases where normally the parties do not have the necessary resources to bring the question all the way to the highest national courts.

Fourthly, the Court of Justice has sole jurisdiction to declare a Community act invalid. Therefore, if a question of the validity of a Community act arises before a national court this court is obliged to make a preliminary reference to the Court of Justice before it may declare the Community act invalid. However, where a national court is not competent to make a preliminary reference it will be placed in an unacceptable position where it will either have to declare the Community act invalid in contravention of the practice of the Court of Justice, or will have to pass judgment based on a Community act that the national court considers to be invalid.[110]

In conclusion, limiting the access to make preliminary references to courts of last instance would not be a recommendable solution to the problems connected to the Court's case load.

6.6. Decentralised Community courts

Finally, a radical way of relieving the preliminary reference pressure on the Court of Justice is by setting up a number of regional courts that may undertake parts of the work that weighs on the Court today.[111] This could be done either by setting up a number of new Community courts or by appointing a number of existing national courts to act as specialised Community law courts. Either way, the regional courts would be subject to some kind of control by the Court of Justice.

Creating such regional courts to answer preliminary questions would do much to put the Court of Justice in a position where it could focus upon the most important Community law issues. Another advantage of a system whereby regional courts answer preliminary references would be its proximity to the referring national courts and the parties to the main proceedings. This would particularly be the case if one were to establish decentralised Community courts in all Member

---

109 See further the discussion by F Jacobs, 'Introducing the Court's Paper' in A Dashwood and A C Johnston, *The Future of the Judicial System of the European Union* (2001) 9, 11.

110 See below at Ch 6, s 4.2.2.

111 J Jacqué and J Weiler, 'On the Road to European Union—A new Judicial Architecture: An Agenda for the Intergovernmental Conference' (1990) 27 CML Rev 185, 192.

States, as these courts would then be able to operate in the language of the referring court, thereby also removing the need for expensive and time consuming translation.

At the same time a decentralisation of the system will make it more difficult to ensure the requisite unity and coherence of Community law. Indeed, it has been argued that the location of the Court of Justice in one place has a significant integrative effect and contributes to ensuring the unity and coherence of the law. In comparison, decentralising the system entails a risk that 'national' or 'regional' Community law may develop.[112] Therefore some kind of appeal procedure to the Court of Justice would have to be established.[113] Such a structure would, however, bear a clear resemblance to a federal structure. Moreover, whenever a ruling by one of the regional courts was examined by the Court of Justice this could lead to unduly long delays.[114]

In conclusion, in our opinion, regional courts should not be the first choice for solving the problems stemming from the expected increase in the number of preliminary references.

6.7. The best way forward?

To sum up, today the time it takes for the Court of Justice to answer a preliminary reference has become inconveniently long. To meet this problem the Court has taken a number of steps and this has indeed brought the average length of preliminary proceedings to its lowest in 20 years. Nevertheless, the time it takes to receive a preliminary ruling continues to be inappropriately long and in addition it is likely that the number of references will increase significantly in the future. Firstly, it may be expected that courts in the new Member States will use the preliminary reference procedure increasingly in the years to come. Secondly, references concerning matters relating to Title IV of the EC Treaty and Title VI of the EU Treaty

---

[112] S Prechal, 'The Preliminary Procedure: a role for legal scholarship?' in *The Uncertain Future of the Preliminary Rulings Procedure*, Symposium Council of State, the Netherlands, 30 January 2004; A Arnull, 'Judicial Architecture or Judicial Folly? The Challenge Facing the EU' in A Dashwood and A C Johnston, *The Future of the Judicial System of the European Union* (2001) 41, 45; and O Due, 'The Working Party Report', ibid, 87, 88.

[113] According to the proposal made by J Jacque and J Weiler, preliminary rulings made by the regional courts would be open to appeal by the parties in the main proceedings, the Commission, the Council, the European Parliament, and/or the Member States, but it would still be within the discretion of the Court of Justice whether to hear the appeal. An appeal would be granted if the case raised an important issue of Community law, if the regional court decision created inconsistency between the jurisprudence amongst the regional courts, or if the Court of Justice believed that a clear error of law had been committed, see J Jacqué and J Weiler, 'On the Road to European Union—A new Judicial Architecture: An Agenda for the Intergovernmental Conference' (1990) CML Rev Vol 27 185, 193.

[114] T Koopmans, 'The Future of the Court of Justice of the European Communities' in A Bàròv and DA Wyatt (eds), *Yearbook of European Law* (1991) Vol 11, 28.

are likely to continue to increase. Thirdly, if the Treaty of Lisbon enters into force it will mean that more Member State courts will be able to make preliminary references regarding those matters which today are covered by Title IV of the EC Treaty and Title VI of the EU Treaty.

In other words, if no preventive measures are taken there is a risk that the efficiency of the preliminary ruling system will be seriously threatened. To meet this threat, should it materialise, a number of different solutions have been put forward. The most important of the proposed solutions have been considered above. All of these proposed solutions display strengths as well as weaknesses. One solution, however, stands out as superior, namely the transferring of (certain) preliminary references to the Court of First Instance.

2

VARIATIONS IN MEMBER STATE USE OF PRELIMINARY REFERENCES

1. The Distribution of Preliminary References among the Member States

1.1. Overview

This chapter examines various questions concerning the reference patterns of Member State courts. First, Section 1 looks at the number of preliminary references from each Member State (Section 1.2) and analyses whether these references primarily originate from lower courts or from higher courts (Section 1.3). Then, in Section 2, we examine why some national courts refer more preliminary questions than other courts.

1.2. The number of references from the different Member States

Tables 2.1–2.3 below show the average annual number of preliminary references for the 27 Member States. As already mentioned in Chapter 1 above, there is normally a certain time-lag before the full weight of a new Member State is reflected in the Court's caseload. Or to put it differently, the number of preliminary references from the courts of a given Member State is usually significantly lower in the first years of membership. Therefore, the figures for the newer Member States are given separately in Tables 2.2 and 2.3. Table 2.1 shows the average number of preliminary references from the EU15 measured over an 11-year period from 1 January 1998 to 31 December 2008 while Table 2.2 shows the average number of references from the 10 Member States which acceded on 1 May 2004 (the EU10) measured over a four-year period from 1 January 2005 to 31 December 2008. Finally, Table 2.3 relates to the two newest Member States, Bulgaria and Romania, and lists the average number of references from courts of those States in the two-year period 1 January 2007 to 31 December 2008.[1]

Whereas the left hand column of the three Tables shows the average figures in absolute terms, the right hand column shows the number of references relative to each Member State's population size thereby adjusting for the considerable differences of Member States' population size.[2]

As the left hand columns in Tables 2.1–2.3 below show, there is a wide variation in the number of preliminary references from courts of the different Member States. The average number of references from the EU15 courts is considerably higher than the average figure from the EU10 and EU2 courts. Moreover, the number of references also varies appreciably within the three groups of Member States set out in the three tables. Lastly, the right hand columns of the three Tables show that when one takes account of the difference in population figures of the Member States, the variations diminish significantly, although they do not completely disappear.

1.3. Distribution of references between higher and lower courts

Precise figures on the distribution of preliminary references between courts of last instance and other courts do not appear to exist. Indeed, in order to calculate these figures it would be necessary to have knowledge of both the various national procedural rules and the actual cases before the national courts. According to

---

[1] The figures in Tables 2.1–2.6 in this chapter on the number of cases are all derived from the 2008 Annual Report of the Court of Justice while the population figures are the 2009 figures from Eurostat at <http://epp.eurostat.ec.europa.eu/tgm/table.do?tab=table&language=en&pcode=tps0 0001&tableSelection=1&footnotes=yes&labeling=labels&plugin=1>.

[2] See in this respect in more detail at s 2.2 below.

Table 2.1 References per year 1998–2008 in absolute terms and relative to number of inhabitants—EU15

	Average no of references per year 1.1.1998–31.12.2008	Average no of references per year 1.1.1998–31.12.2008 per 10 million inhabitants
Austria	26.4	31.6
Belgium	17.6	16.4
Denmark	4.6	8.4
Finland	4.3	8.0
France	16.1	2.5
Germany	55.3	6.7
Greece	7.8	6.9
Ireland	1.5	3.5
Italy	39.6	6.6
Luxembourg	2.2	44.0
Netherlands	22.5	13.7
Portugal	3.6	3.4
Spain	13.2	2.9
Sweden	5.5	6.0
UK	18.5	3.0
EU15—total	15.9	6.0

Table 2.2 References per year 2005–2008 in absolute terms and relative to number of inhabitants—EU10

	Average no of references per year 1.1.2005–31.12.2008	Average no of references per year 1.1.2005–31.12.2008 per 10 million inhabitants
Cyprus	0.3	3.2
Czech Rep.	1.8	1.7
Estonia	1.0	7.5
Hungary	4.3	4.2
Latvia	0.8	3.3
Lithuania	1.3	3.7
Malta	0.0	0.0
Poland	3.5	0.9
Slovakia	0.5	0.9
Slovenia	0.0	0.0
EU10—total	1.3	1.8

Table 2.3 References per year 2007–2008 in absolute terms and relative to number of inhabitants—Bulgaria and Romania

	Average no of references per year 1.1.2007–31.12.2008	Average no of references per year 1.1.2007–31.12.2008 per 10 million inhabitants
Bulgaria	0.5	0.7
Romania	0.5	0.2
Bulgaria + Romania, total	0.5	0.3

some studies, lower courts have in total produced a minority of all preliminary references, with most references originating from intermediate courts and relatively few from the highest courts.[3] According to others, around three-quarters of the preliminary questions have come from courts other than those of final instance.[4] It has also been stated that courts of last instance account for the majority of preliminary references in about a third of the Member States.[5]

Presumably, the lack of credible data can to some extent be explained by a lack of definition of what constitutes a 'lower' and a 'higher' court. Should, for instance, a city court of first instance be categorised as a lower court if its decisions are not subject to appeal? And how should one classify a court if some, but not all, its decisions are subject to appeal; for instance because only cases where the value of the subject matter exceeds a certain minimum level may be appealed? Some scholars seem to focus exclusively on the formal rank of the court in the national judicial system, thereby disregarding the point that limitations on the right of appeal frequently mean that lower or intermediate courts may qualify as courts of last instance within the meaning of Article 234(3).[6]

It is clear, however, that the reference patterns of the different Member States diverge so that in some Member States such as Portugal and the Netherlands a high percentage of preliminary references originate from the highest courts whereas lower or intermediate courts account for the lion's share of references in the majority of the Member States.[7]

---

[3] A Stone Sweet and T Brunell, 'The European Court and the National Courts: A statistical analysis of preliminary references 1961–1995', Jean Monnet Working Paper No 14/1997, and similarly with special regard to UK courts D Chalmers, 'The Much Ado about Judicial Politics in the United Kingdom: A Statistical Analysis of Reported Decisions of United Kingdom Courts invoking EU Law 1973–1988', Harvard Jean Monnet Working Paper 1/00, point VII.

[4] See the so-called Due Report (Report by the Working Party on the Future of the European Communities' Court System) p 13 with regard to the situation up until the 31 December 1998. Similarly, according to Advocate General Tizzano in Case C-99/00 *Lyckeskog* [2002] ECR I-4839, para 68, in the period 1960 to 2000, out of a total 4,381 preliminary rulings 1,173 references originated from courts of last instance.

[5] E H Schepel and E Blankenburg, 'Mobilizing the European Court of Justice' in G de Búrca and J Weiler (eds), *The European Court of Justice* (2001) 9, 33–4 and E Fahey, *Practice and Procedure in Preliminary References to Europe* (2007) 36.

[6] See eg H P Graver, 'The Effects of EFTA Court Jurisprudence on the Legal Orders of the EFTA States' in C Baudenbacher, P Tresselt, and T Örlygsson (eds), *The EFTA Court—ten years on* (2005) 79, 85; and H Haukeland Fredriksen, 'Om mangelen på tolkningsspørgsmål fra norske domstoler til EFTA-domstolen' (2006) Jussens Venner Vol 6, 386.

[7] Court of Justice 2008 Annual Report, point 20 in the chapter on statistics.

2. Why do Courts in Some Member States Refer more than Others?

2.1. Overview

Essentially, the applicable Community legislation in Luxembourg—a small country—is the same as in the much larger Germany. At first sight, the basis for making a reference should therefore be the same. However, in order for a reference to be made at least two requirements must be met: first, a party must initiate court proceedings in which Community law may arguably be relevant and, second, the competent national court must be ready to make a preliminary reference. Therefore, it may come as no surprise that in practice the number of preliminary references differ considerably between the Member States, as shown in Tables 2.1–2.3 above.

The question remains, however, as to what factors actually affect the number of preliminary references. Below there is an examination of different factors that might explain the variations in frequency of reference between courts in different Member States. The examination commences by looking at four factors which all have in common the fact that they relate to the amount of cases concerning Community law before the national courts and thus concern the condition *sine qua non* for making a preliminary reference, namely that a dispute is pending before a national court in the sense of Article 234. The first of those factors is difference in country size (Section 2.2). Next, we consider to what extent a Member State's level of cross-border activities can explain the number of references (Section 2.3). The third factor to be considered is whether the extent to which the different Member States comply with Community law affects the number of references (Section 2.4). Fourthly, we examine to what extent national differences in willingness to litigate may have an impact on the frequency of references (Section 2.5).

We then turn to six other possible factors that all focus on the behaviour of the national court when it is faced with a dispute where a preliminary reference can be made; in other words, theories that set out to explain why different Member States' courts react differently when deciding whether to refer under Article 234 or decide the case without the involvement of the Court of Justice. The analysis of these six factors begins with a discussion of the relevance of the different constitutional traditions amongst the Member States (Section 2.6). Next, there is an examination of the suggestion that lower courts use the preliminary reference procedure in order to circumvent higher courts (Section 2.7), and we consider whether the national court's policy preferences may affect the willingness to make a reference (Section 2.8). It has been argued that differences in reference frequency may be explained by the degree to which a Member State's judiciary has been organised in specialised courts and this argument is explored in Section 2.9. Special factors in the different national judicial systems that may influence the reference patterns will then be discussed (Section 2.10). Finally, we examine to what extent there is a link between the number of references and the national courts' overall attitude towards Community law (Section 2.11). An overall conclusion is given in Section 2.12.

In several respects the following examinations are reminiscent of statistical analyses. In this regard a word of caution must be sounded, due to the limited size and quality of the 'samples', meaning that considerable restraint must be exercised when drawing inferences from the data.

2.2. Differences in population figures

In smaller countries there are fewer people and undertakings to initiate legal proceedings and thereby create the basis for a preliminary reference than in larger countries. Therefore, all things being equal, it seems reasonable to expect that the number of cases in which there is a basis for making a preliminary reference is somehow correlated to the size of the Member State populations.[8]

Moreover, the larger a Member State's population is the more attractive it will normally be as a market for exporters in other Member States. Therefore, the incentive to challenge impediments to trade is greater with regard to larger Member States' legislation than with regard to smaller Member States' legislation. The more such legal challenges, the more cases there are which may lead to a preliminary reference. Indeed, it has been calculated that out of the 832 references concerning free movement of goods which had been made up until 1998, 303 concerned challenges to German legislation. Whereas this could indicate that German legislation has been particularly protectionist, another natural explanation could be that the German market's considerable size has led to a greater interest for those trading the goods in securing access to that particular market, inter alia by challenging those parts of the German legislation that impede trade.[9]

Tables 2.1–2.3 above seem to confirm the existence of a certain link between population size and the number of preliminary references made from each Member State. However, the correlation is not linear. Whilst in absolute terms larger Member States usually generate more references than do smaller Member States, in relative terms smaller Member States are generally the source of

---

[8] H P Graver, 'The Effects of EFTA Court Jurisprudence on the Legal Orders of the EFTA States' in C Baudenbacher, P Tresselt, and T Örlygsson (eds), *The EFTA Court—ten years on* (2005) 79, 84.

[9] A Stone Sweet and T Brunell, 'The European Court, National Judges and Legal Integration: A Researcher's Guide to the Data Set on Preliminary References in EC Law 1958–98' (2001) European Law Journal Vol 6, No 2 June 2000, 117.

more references. This is hardly surprising. As observed above, the amount of national legislation that might potentially be in conflict with Community law is likely to be more or less the same in all Member States. The inclusion of population size as a relevant factor is only intended to cater for differences in the probability of the emergence of litigation with regard to such legislation. It is thus only natural that the Tables generally display higher figures per capita for smaller countries and lower figures for larger countries.

Nevertheless, the figures vary widely, even for countries which have more or less the same population size. For example German and Italian courts make more than twice as many preliminary references per inhabitant as do French and UK courts. Likewise, in relative terms Austrian, Belgian, and Dutch courts make approximately four times more references than do Irish and Portuguese courts. Thus, whilst arguably Member State size is a factor that partly explains the differences in number of preliminary references, other factors must also be taken into account.

2.3. The amount of cross-border activity

Some scholars have argued that there is a close correlation between the amount of a Member State's cross-border activities and the number of references from courts of that State. According to this theory, the greater the cross-border trade, the more likely it is that questions of Community law may be raised in litigation and thereby prompt preliminary references.[10]

This theory certainly points to one amongst several factors that are likely to influence the amount of litigation involving Community law. However, the importance of this factor appears somewhat limited. It disregards for example the fact that more and more Community legislation applies regardless of whether there is a cross-border element. Indeed, it is probably fair to say that today there is no such requirement in relation to the vast majority of Community rules. It is not surprising that more recent research has been unable to confirm a causal relationship between cross-border trade and the number of preliminary references.[11] The cross-border trade factor also fails to explain why the number of references from Irish courts has remained rather low during the recent years of very considerable growth and increased cross-border trade with Ireland and also remains low when compared to references from eg Danish and Finnish courts.[12]

---

[10] A Stone Sweet and T Brunell, 'The European Court and National Courts: A Statistical Analysis of Preliminary References 1961–1995', Jean Monnet Working Paper, No 14/1997. See also B Rodger, *Article 234 and Competition Law* (2008) 35, according to whom one of the reasons for the high proportion of references from Dutch courts probably is that the Netherlands has traditionally had a particularly open economy.

[11] M Wind et al, 'The Uneven Legal Push for Europe, Questioning Variation when National Courts go to Europe' (2009) 10 European Union Politics 63, 69–72 and 81 with further references.

[12] See similarly E Fahey, *Practice and Procedure in Preliminary References to Europe* (2007) 67–8.

2.4. Level of compliance with Community law

A third factor that may partially explain the variation in the frequency of references is the difference in Member States' compliance with Community law. Both with regard to timely transposition and to application and compliance with Community law the Member States differ considerably. Where a Member State does not fulfil its Community law obligations the likelihood that its legislation will be challenged in the courts is presumably greater than if it duly complies with these obligations. Thus, there is less possibility for a national court to make a preliminary reference in States with a high performance rate compared to States which are less observant in living up to their Community obligations.[13]

There exists no single precise formula making it possible to establish the relative level of compliance of the various Member States. One way may be to look at the transposition deficit of each Member State. However, these figures only give an indication as to how many directives each State has reported to the Commission as being fully implemented. In contrast, they do not show whether the Commission considers the implementation to be correct or whether national legislation not purporting to implement Community directives is in conformity with Community law. Nor do they tell us whether in everyday administration Community law is applied in a correct manner.

A better way of measuring Member States' compliance with Community law is therefore the number of infringement cases that the Commission has opened against the Member States under Article 226 of the EC Treaty. This method not only takes account of belated implementation, but more broadly takes into account most types of infringements of Community law committed by national authorities. Admittedly, this approach is not without pitfalls either as not all violations of Community law result in infringement actions. First, the Commission does not have a full and detailed picture of all areas of national law and its knowledge about the actual application of Community law in the various Member States is even less complete. In practice the Commission is often relying on complainants to inform it about shortcomings in national legislation. Second, the Commission has considerable discretion as to whether to bring an infringement action. It can thus, for purely political reasons, decide not to bring such an action even if it is convinced that Community law has been infringed.[14] The number of

---

[13] See similarly T de la Mare, 'Article 177 in Social and Political Context' in P Craig and G de Búrca (eds), *The Evolution of EU Law* (1999) 215, 235, but contrast K Alter, *The European Court's Political Power* (2009) 291, who argues that countries with high reference rates are not necessarily less inclined to comply with Community law.

[14] Case 247/87 *Star Fruit* [1989] ECR 291, para 12; Case C-87/89 *Sonito* [1990] ECR I-1981, paras 6–9; Case C-107/95 P *Bundesverband der Bilanzbuchhalter* [1997] ECR I-947, para 19; Joined Cases T-479/93 and T-599/93 *Bernardi* [1994] ECR II-1115, paras 27–8; Case T-84/94 *Bilanzbuchhalter* [1995] II-101, paras 23–6; and Case T-575/93 *Koelman* [1996] ECR II-1, paras 71–2.

infringement cases must nevertheless be assumed to give a reasonably fair picture of the level of compliance in each Member State.

Tables 2.4–2.6 below list in the left hand column the number of open infringement cases at the Commission for each Member State. In order to determine to what extent there is indeed a correlation between the compliance level and the number of preliminary references from each Member State these figures are compared in the middle column with each Member State's average number of preliminary references, as found in Tables 2.1–2.3 above. Finally, the third column in Tables 2.4–2.6 looks at the ratio between the infringement cases of the Member State concerned and the average number of preliminary references from that State per 1 million inhabitants. In other words, in the third column we seek to ascertain to what extent it may be possible to explain the differences in the number of preliminary references by combining the population figures and the level of Community law compliance.

Table 2.4 Comparison of the number of references with number of infringement cases and population size, EU15

	No of open infringement cases as of 1 November 2008[15]	Ratio average references/no of open infringement cases	Ratio average no of references per 10 million inhabitants/no of open infringement cases
Austria	55	0.48	0.57
Belgium	78	0.23	0.21
Denmark	29	0.16	0.29
Finland	34	0.13	0.24
France	85	0.19	0.03
Germany	90	0.61	0.07
Greece	91	0.09	0.08
Ireland	56	0.03	0.06
Italy	112	0.35	0.06
Luxembourg	30	0.07	1.47
Netherlands	54	0.42	0.25
Portugal	70	0.05	0.05
Spain	103	0.13	0.03
Sweden	39	0.14	0.15
UK	59	0.31	0.05
EU15	65.7	0.23	0.24

[15] The Commission's 18th Internal Market Scoreboard, p 19, Figure 12. The figures include cases where the Commission presumes the transposition not to be in conformity with the directive it transposes and cases where the Commission presumes that the Internal Market rules (contained in the EC Treaty or in Internal Market Directives) are incorrectly applied and where a letter of formal notice has been sent to the Member State concerned. Cases of non-communication of transposition of directives are not included. The figure given in the EU15 bracket is the average number for the Member States concerned.

Table 2.5 Comparison of number of references with number of infringement cases and population size, EU10

	No of open infringement cases as of 1 November 2008	Ratio average references/no of open infringement cases	Ratio average no of references per 10 million inhabitants/no of open infringement cases
Cyprus	14	0.02	0.22
Czech Rep.	36	0.05	0.05
Estonia	25	0.04	0.30
Hungary	25	0.17	0.17
Latvia	30	0.03	0.11
Lithuania	22	0.06	0.17
Malta	40	0.00	0.00
Poland	65	0.05	0.01
Slovakia	33	0.02	0.03
Slovenia	21	0.00	0.00
EU10— total	31.1	0.04	0.11

Table 2.6 Comparison of number of references with number of infringement cases and population size, Bulgaria and Romania

	No of open infringement cases as of 1 November 2008	Ratio average references/ no of open infringement cases	Ratio average no of references per 10 million inhabitants/ no of open infringement cases
Bulgaria	20	0.03	0.03
Romania	13	0.04	0.02
Bulgaria and Romania—total	16.5	0.03	0.03

Tables 2.4–2.6 above do not display a clear correlation between the number of preliminary references from a Member State and that State's general level of compliance with Community law as expressed in the number of infringement proceedings open at the Commission. Nor is there such a clear correlation if at the same time one also takes account of differences in population figures, as has been done in the third column in the three Tables.

That is not to say that the level of compliance is not a relevant factor with regard to why some courts refer more than others. On the contrary, even if it is not possible to establish a clear correlation between the two figures for all Member States, the compliance level may still be a factor that influences the number of references so that it may still be relevant to take due account thereof when reading the figures.

The seemingly higher level of compliance of Denmark and Finland as compared with Belgium and the Netherlands may help to understand the lower number of preliminary references from the former two Member States as compared with the latter two. In contrast, the compliance factor does not explain why Austrian courts make so many preliminary references, nor can it explain why Irish and Portuguese courts are so reticent in this respect. Similarly, it does not explain the considerable differences in the number of preliminary references from the larger Member States, although it may partly explain why the number of preliminary references from Italy is higher than that of the UK. Indeed, considering the level of compliance, one would have expected more preliminary references from French and Spanish courts and fewer references from German courts.

2.5. Differences in litigation patterns

A low number of references need not be due to a reluctance to make preliminary references on the part of some Member States' courts. It might simply be due to the fact that in some Member States there is a relatively lower tendency to resolve disputes through the courts than by other means. Indeed, as already discussed above in Section 2.2 in relation to population figures, fewer national court cases necessarily means that there will be fewer cases which can form the basis of a preliminary reference.

That a high litigation rate generally tends to correlate with a high number of preliminary references has been confirmed by a couple of studies.[16] However, in order to evaluate the relative willingness of different courts to make use of the preliminary procedure, it is necessary to have data on the total number of cases raising issues of Community law before these courts as well as the proportion of those cases where a reference has been made. Such material is generally not available, however, inter alia because reported cases often represent only a fraction of all judicial rulings. The lack of reliable data is aggravated by the fact that the Court of Justice applies a Community notion of a 'court or tribunal' which implies that many quasi-judicial bodies that are not viewed as courts in the national legal system are nevertheless competent to make preliminary references.[17] Some of these quasi-judicial bodies may account for a very considerable number of cases raising Community law questions. Unfortunately this problem appears to characterise some of the few studies where scholars have sought to collect information on how many cases concerning Community law the national courts have been confronted with.[18]

---

[16] M Vink, M Claes, and C Arnold, 'Explaining the Use of Preliminary References by Domestic Courts in EU Member States: A Mixed-Method Comparative Analysis' Paper presented at the 11th Biennial Conference of the European Studies Association, April 2009. See also H Schepel and E Blankenburg, 'Mobilising the European Court of Justice' in G de Búrca and J Weiler (eds), *The European Court of Justice* (2001) 35.

[17] See below Ch 3.

[18] For example, J Golub, 'Modelling Judicial Dialogue in the European Community' EUI, Robert Schumann Working Paper 58/96, states that in the period 1984–93 Danish courts made

As already stated, it is submitted that knowledge of the amount of national litigation that gives rise to issues of Community law is a precondition for an in-depth understanding of the different numbers of preliminary references from the different Member States. It follows that, for example, the propensity in the different Member States to use legal redress and invoke Community law to challenge national legislation is also a factor that may affect how frequently national courts have occasion to consider use of the preliminary reference procedure.[19] Equally, the number of preliminary references might be influenced by the national rules on *locus standi* since in some Member States it may be appreciably easier to challenge national legislation than in others. Moreover, the establishment under national law of public agencies whose task it is to enforce Community law through litigation rather than through ordinary administrative supervision and enforcement may also stimulate an increase in the number of preliminary references. Or to put it differently: the existence of certain Member State institutional actors can itself lead to more litigation and thereby, other things being equal, to a higher number of preliminary references.[20]

Studies have shown that more than half of all preliminary reference proceedings involve a public authority.[21] Therefore, the behaviour of public bodies when faced with an argument based on Community law is of particular importance: in some Member States public authorities are ready to quickly settle such disputes if they consider that they have a weak case, thereby (intentionally or unintentionally) avoiding a preliminary reference. For instance, it has been suggested that public bodies in the Nordic countries are generally ready to settle cases they consider to be weak and that this is one of the reasons why Nordic courts have made relatively fewer references than eg Austrian courts.[22] In other Member States the public bodies are apparently more willing to fight to the bitter end, thereby increasing the likelihood that a preliminary reference will be made without this in itself meaning

---

preliminary references in 34 cases out of an overall 63 cases where issues of Community law arose before Danish courts. However, in that period the number of cases before Danish bodies covered by Art 234 was in fact many times higher.

[19] E Fahey, *Practice and Procedure in Preliminary References to Europe* (2007) 108–9, who demonstrates that a large proportion of all Irish references was spurred by actions taken by agricultural organisations.

[20] C Kilpatrick, 'Community or Community of Courts in European Integration? Sex Equality Dialogues between UK Courts and the ECJ' (1998) 4 European Law Journal 121, 133–6.

[21] C Harding, 'Who goes to Court in Europe?' (1992) 17 EL Rev 105, and J Weiler and R Dehousse, '*Primus inter Pares*, the European Court and National Court: Thirty Years of Cooperation', unpublished study (1992), 78, summarised in E Fahey, *Practice and Procedure in Preliminary References to Europe* (2006) 23–34.

[22] H P Graver, 'The Effects of EFTA Court Jurisprudence on the Legal Orders of the EFTA States' in C Baudenbacher, P Tresselt, and T Örlygsson (eds), *The EFTA Court—ten years on* (2005) 79, 84.

that the general level of national compliance with Community law is lower in those States than in the former, less litigious States.

2.6. Constitutional traditions

In the preceding sections, there was an examination of various factors that could influence the number of cases concerning Community law that are brought before the national courts, ie the first condition that must be fulfilled in order for a preliminary reference to be made, namely that a national court is faced with a dispute in which a Community law question arises. In this section and those which follow, another type of factor that might influence the number of preliminary references is considered, namely the attitude of national courts when faced with a dispute where it could be relevant to make a reference; in other words, theories that seek to explain why different Member States' courts react differently when exercising their discretion under Article 234 as to whether they should decide the case with or without the involvement of the Court of Justice.

Some scholars have suggested that the variations in preliminary references can be explained by differences in the Member State courts' perception of their role vis-à-vis the national legislator.[23] According to this theory, courts of Member States with an institutional legacy of so-called majoritarian democracy, with less intense judicial review of legislative acts, are more reluctant to make preliminary references than are courts coming from so-called constitutional democracies where in-depth judicial review of the national legislation is considered to be part and parcel of good democratic governance.

The theory reflects that it is probably a bigger step for a national court which rarely invalidates legislative acts by reason of non-constitutionality to set aside national legislation as being contrary to Community law than it is for a national court which is used to declaring legislative acts unconstitutional. Whilst at first glance that logic may appear attractive, on closer examination it appears somewhat doubtful whether differences in national judicial review as suggested constitute a factor that may be taken into account when explaining the variation in preliminary references amongst the different Member States.

Those supporting the theory that the difference in reference pattern may be explained by a difference between courts of majoritarian democracies and constitutional democracies have tried to substantiate the theory on statistical data. However, the proponents of the theory do not seem to have taken into account that the courts from the different Member States simply do not have the same possibility of making references since the number of cases before them where

---

[23] M Wind et al, 'The Uneven Legal Push for Europe, Questioning Variation when National Courts go to Europe' (2009) 10 European Union Politics 63, 71–72.

Community law issues arise differ appreciably.[24] Indeed, some of the proponents explicitly reject that both population size and the amount of intra-EU trade are relevant factors in this respect.[25] Nor do the proponents of the theory seem to recognise the relevance of other factors likely to influence the number of cases before the various Member State courts. Instead, they either assume that there is an equal number of cases involving Community law pending before eg Irish courts and German courts, or they appear to assume that is it is irrelevant to measure the willingness of a national court to make a reference in relation to the actual possibilities of making such references for these courts. Arguably, it follows that it is impossible to reliably demonstrate the alleged link by comparing the number of references from majoritarian democracies with the number of references from constitutional democracies. We simply do not know whether we are comparing comparable figures.

Indeed, if we try to take account of the various factors influencing the amount of litigation concerning Community law before the courts of the various Member States, we will readily see that the theory cannot be underpinned by statistics. As shown above in Tables 2.1–2.3 the number of preliminary references relative to population size made by courts in constitutional democracies such as Greece, Portugal, and Spain is in fact lower than the number of references by majoritarian democracies such as Denmark and Sweden. If account is also taken of the compliance level in the respective States the differences become even more striking, as is apparent from Tables 2.4–2.6. In fact, even if we only take account of the different compliance level, but not of the different population figures, the Danish and Swedish courts appear to be more willing to refer than do Greek, Portuguese, and Spanish courts. Other studies equally dismiss a systematic correlation between, on the one hand, the number of preliminary references and, on the other hand, the distinction between Member States with more or less intensive judicial review. Indeed, some studies have even indicated that courts from countries with less intensive judicial review are more prone to make preliminary references.[26]

It follows from the above that the theory does not appear to be founded on empirical data. The discussion will now therefore be centred upon the plausibility of the arguments and explanations that are brought forward in order to show the claimed link between, on the one hand, different national constitutional traditions and,

---

[24] See ss 2.2–2.5 above.

[25] M Wind et al, 'The Uneven Legal Push for Europe, Questioning Variation when National Courts go to Europe' (2009) 10 European Union Politics 63, 69–71 and 81–2.

[26] A Stone Sweet and T Brunell, 'The European Court and National Courts: A Statistical Analysis of Preliminary References 1961–1995', Jean Monnet Working Paper, No 14/1997, and M Vink, M Claes, and C Arnold, 'Explaining the Use of Preliminary References by Domestic Courts in EU Member States: A Mixed-Method Comparative Analysis', Paper presented at the 11th Biennial Conference of the European Studies Association, April 2009.

on the other hand, the variations in the number of references from the different Member States or whether it seems more likely that there is in fact no such link. In this respect, we would like to make the following three points.

First, as already stated it is probably a bigger step for a national court which rarely invalidates legislative acts by reason of non-constitutionality to set aside national legislation as being contrary to Community law than it is for a national court which is used to declaring legislative acts unconstitutional. That, however, does not necessarily speak in favour of assuming the existence of the suggested link. Indeed, the very effect of the Article 234 procedure is that it is not the national judges who alone will have to set aside national legislation; rather they can make the Court of Justice their accomplice by inviting the latter to rule on the matter, thereby in practice shifting the 'blame' to a body outside the national court structure. Therefore, one could just as well assume that a national judge who is not used to setting aside national legislation would be more prone to make a preliminary reference than would a national judge who is more accustomed to holding national legislation to be incompatible with a higher legal norm.

Second, as already indicated, the judicial review theory builds on an assumption that courts which perform an intense judicial review of legislative acts are more likely to accept the consequences of the judicial review inherent in the preliminary reference procedure. Moreover, as the theory thus seems to suggest that national courts from majoritarian democracies refrain from making preliminary references in order not to be forced into a situation where they will be obliged to set aside national legislation, it must also presuppose that in cases where they do not refer, such national courts do not themselves set aside national law as being contrary to Community law. However, no evidence has been brought forward to support these assumptions, and they certainly do not appear to be self-evident.[27]

Third, the theory rests on the assumption that that the purported fundamental difference between systems of majoritarian democracy and systems of constitutional democracy reflect a similar difference in how national courts tackle cases involving interpretation of international treaties. But why is that necessarily so? Member State legislation may also be set aside, for example, because it conflicts with the European Convention of Human Rights, and the premise of the above theory that courts of majoritarian democracies are unaccustomed to the setting aside of national legislation where this legislation conflicts with a superior norm does not fully mirror the realities.

---

[27] For examples of Swedish courts concluding that Community law necessitates an outcome that differs from the one which followed from Swedish law without having obtained a prior preliminary ruling see X Groussot et al, *Empowering National Courts in EU Law* (2009) 99–101.

Moreover, the assumed link between the attitude of courts in constitutional matters and cases concerning the relationship between national and internal law is not supported by other studies. Other scholars have discussed whether a national court's approach to using the preliminary reference procedure is related to how the national legal system views the place of international law in the national legal order. Again, the hypothesis was that countries used to setting aside national law as contrary to international law would be more open to using the preliminary reference procedure than would courts that are not used to performing a judicial review of national legislation based on an international norm. However, these scholars have not found that courts from countries with monist legal systems generally make more references than do courts from countries with dualist legal systems, and it can thus not on that basis be shown that courts which are more used to declaring national legislation invalid because of its being contrary to a higher international norm make more references.[28] This does not support the assumption that courts from Member States with a tradition of more intensive judicial review make more references.

2.7. Inter-court competition—circumventing the practice of higher courts

Some scholars have argued that preliminary references are regularly used by lower national courts as a means to increase their autonomy within their respective national legal systems and to circumvent the jurisprudence of higher courts. According to this theory, such lower courts are seen as independent actors in pursuit of a hidden agenda motivated by a self-interest in obtaining a higher standing in a kind of inter-court competition with the national supreme courts, a competition in which the Court of Justice operates similarly to a 'second parent' to lower courts who seek parental approval to ward off sanction from their national supreme courts.[29] It has even been argued that it 'is the difference in lower and higher court interests which provides a motor for legal integration to proceed'.[30] Others have argued along the same lines, suggesting more broadly that national judges engaged

---

[28] A Stone Sweet and T Brunell, 'The European Court and National Courts: A Statistical Analysis of Preliminary References 1961–1995', Jean Monnet Working Paper, No 14/1997; C Carrubba and L Murrah, 'Legal Integration and Use of Preliminary Ruling Process in the European Union' (2005) International Organization Vol 59, ss 399–418, and M Vink, M Claes, and C Arnold, 'Explaining the Use of Preliminary References by Domestic Courts in EU Member States: A Mixed-Method Comparative Analysis', Paper presented at the 11th Biennial Conference of the European Studies Association April 2009.

[29] K Alter, 'Explaining National Court Acceptance of European Court Jurisprudence: A Critical Evaluation of Theories of Legal Integration' in A Slaughter, A Stone Sweet, and J Weiler (eds), *The European Court and National Courts—Doctrine and Jurisprudence—Legal Challenge in Its Social Context* (1998) 227, 242–9.

[30] Ibid, 242. See also K Alter, 'The European Court's Political Power' (1996) West European Politics Vol 19, No 3 July 1996, 458, 466–7. See also S Nyikos, *The European Court and National Courts: Strategic Interaction within the EU Judicial Process* (2001) 21, 64, 65, and 71.

in the preliminary procedure are driven by three main goals: (1) judicial review; (2) prestige and power in relation to other national courts; and (3) the promotion of policy positions.[31]

It is, however, questionable whether it is justified to attribute such ulterior motives to national courts when describing the way the national courts apply the procedure in Article 234. The reality would seem to be much simpler: in nearly all cases national courts make use of the preliminary ruling procedure either because they need assistance in reaching the correct legal solution to a dispute brought before them or because they sit as a court of last instance and do not find that the Community law issue at stake qualifies as either *acte éclairé* or *acte clair*.[32]

Of course, some litigants try to act strategically within the preliminary reference procedure. In contrast, it would be quite surprising if most, or merely a significant part of, lower national courts had secret agendas to rebel against higher courts. Such suggestions hardly reflect how most judges think and act in daily life. Indeed, it has been pointed out that the proponents of these theories have underpinned their statements with only the most slender jurisprudential proof.[33]

This is not to say that there may not be examples of national courts which have only been prepared to set aside politically or economically important national legislation after having obtained the backing of the Court of Justice through a preliminary reference. However, that a national court seeks the backing of the Court of Justice does not necessarily mean that it is seeking this backing with a view to expanding its own competence; it might just as well reflect the very opposite, namely that the national court does not want to take such decisions on its own. In fact, assuming for a moment that national courts did indeed seek power and independence one could just as well imagine that they would have sought such empowerment by choosing to decide the cases themselves rather than by leaving an important part of the decision in the hands of the Court of Justice.

Finally, it is suggested that the theory fails to capture the typical preliminary reference case and therefore provides an incomplete picture of how national courts generally act when faced with the question of whether or not to make a preliminary

---

[31] W Mattli and A Slaughter, 'Revisiting the European Court of Justice' (1998) International Organization Vol 52, No 1 January 1998, ss 177–209; and similarly W Mattli and A Slaughter, 'The Role of National Courts in the Process of European Integration: Accounting for Judicial Preferences and Constraints' in A Slaughter, A Stone Sweet, and J Weiler (eds), *The European Court and National Courts—Doctrine and Jurisprudence—Legal Challenge in Its Social Context* (1998) 253, 258.

[32] See Ch 6, ss 3.3–3.4. As stated by J Korte, *Primus inter Pares: The European Court and National Courts. The follow-up by National Courts of Preliminary References ex. Art 177 of the Treaty of Rome: A Report on the Situation in the Netherlands* (1991) 94, most courts' principal interest is to obtain a clear-cut interpretation by the Court of Justice rather than to start a discussion about the most desirable interpretation of Community law.

[33] E Fahey, *Practice and Procedure in Preliminary References to Europe* (2007) 117–20.

reference. Indeed, as the theory focuses almost exclusively on constitutional themes it effectively ignores the day-to-day business of interpreting more technical and less controversial Community rules, which constitute the bulk of Community legislation relevant for citizens and businesses.[34]

2.8. The national court's policy preferences

It has also been argued that a national court's desire to shape specific policy outcomes influences its incentive to make use of the preliminary reference procedure. According to this theory a national court will be more prone to posing a preliminary question if it expects the answer by the Court of Justice to support an outcome which is in line with what the national court considers to constitute a proper substantive policy.[35] This theory has significant parallels to the theory on intercourt competition discussed above in Section 2.7 in that it is argued that the use of the preliminary reference procedure is driven, or at least influenced, by other objectives than merely upholding Community law. However, the theory relating to the national court's policy preferences does not argue that the national judge uses the preliminary reference procedure to gain autonomy in relation to higher national courts, but rather to advance a given political preference.

Judges do not operate in a complete vacuum and they are not blind to the consequences of a given judgment so it cannot be excluded that such factors might, more or less deliberately and consciously, play some role in marginal cases. It is, however, virtually impossible to either prove or disprove this theory. Indeed, how is one to identify the judicial preferences of each judge in any given case where the question of whether to make a reference arises, let alone establish some common denominators influencing national judges on the whole? It has been suggested that judges tend to support the policy of whatever government is in power when the case is being litigated.[36] In our opinion, it would be surprising if such a suggestion really reflected the behaviour of most judges who generally are influenced by a set of professional values that temper political instincts. Indeed other studies

---

[34] C Kilpatrick, 'Community or Community of Courts in European Integration? Sex Equality Dialogues between UK Courts and the ECJ' (1998) 4 European Law Journal 121, 124–6. Recently, one of the main proponents of the theory has, while still maintaining the theory in principle, acknowledged that the competition between courts argument has been overemphasised and that most cases do not raise questions concerning court competition, see K Alter, *The European Court's Political Power* (2009) 12.

[35] J Golub, 'The Politics of Judicial Discretion: Rethinking the Interaction between National Courts and the European Court of Justice' (1996) 19 West European Politics 360. For a variant of this thesis see G Tridimas and T Tridimas, 'National Courts and the European Court of Justice: A Public Choice Analysis of the Preliminary Reference Procedure' (2004) 24 International Review of Law and Economics 125.

[36] J Golub, 'The Politics of Judicial Discretion: Rethinking the Interaction between National Courts and the European Court of Justice' (1996) 19 West European Politics 360, 375–80.

show that there is no statistical support for a hypothesis that national courts apply the preliminary reference procedure in a manner that supports the national government's policies.[37] Without proof to the contrary, one must be allowed to assume that normally a judge's primary preference is to uphold the rule of law regardless of whether he personally favours another result.

2.9. Specialised judiciary vs non-specialised judiciary

Some scholars have argued that the more specialised national courts are the more inclined they will be to make preliminary references. The argument is that a highly specialised court will work more intensively with Community law in its respective field and, for that reason, be more likely to make a reference. This argument has been put forward as an explanation for the limited share of the total references from Denmark and Norway which the two countries' non-specialised supreme courts account for.[38] Other scholars have reached the same conclusion by arguing that non-specialised courts, although perhaps not well acquainted with Community law, are more accustomed to dealing with unknown areas of law and thus more ready to decide themselves any Community law question that may arise.[39]

It may well be that the level of specialisation of a Member State's judiciary is a factor that influences the courts' inclination to make preliminary references to the Court of Justice. Indeed, many specialised courts each make a considerable number of references. However, no studies appear to have shown that specialised courts make preliminary references in a higher proportion of those cases that involve Community law than do non-specialised courts. In this connection it is worth observing that certain types of specialised courts such as courts for customs matters are dealing almost exclusively with law that has been harmonised at Community level. It is also possible that specialised courts regularly dealing with Community law are better at spotting elements of Community law in a dispute which at first glance seems only to involve national law and for that reason make more preliminary references than do courts that are not equally acquainted with

---

[37] A Stone Sweet and T Brunell, 'The European Court and National Courts: A Statistical Analysis of Preliminary References 1961–1995', Jean Monnet Working Paper, No 14/1997.

[38] H P Graver, 'The Effects of EFTA Court Jurisprudence on the Legal Orders of the EFTA States' in C Baudenbacher, P Tresselt, and T Örlygsson (eds), *The EFTA Court—ten years on* (2005) 79, 85ff, with further references. See also A Stone Sweet and T Brunell, 'The European Court and National Courts: A Statistical Analysis of Preliminary References 1961–1995', Jean Monnet Working Paper, No 14/1997. As explained above in Ch 1, s 4, under the EEA Agreement Norway is subject to a reference system that in many respects mirrors the one found in Art 234.

[39] T de la Mare, 'Article 177 in Social and Political Context' in P Craig and G de Búrca (eds), *The Evolution of EU Law* (1999) 215, 234.

Community law.[40] On the other hand, it would not seem unreasonable to expect a specialised court which is thoroughly familiar with Community law and which presumably has better knowledge of the relevant case law of the Court of Justice to be more confident in solving the matter itself than a court which is not faced with many cases involving Community law.[41]

2.10. Special factors in the national judicial system

Special factors in the national judicial system may influence reference patterns. For example, if national courts are faced with several virtually identical cases where a preliminary reference on one and the same question should be made, many national courts prefer to make only one reference on a pilot case which will effectively cover all the national cases. In a few States such as Italy national courts are, however, required to make a reference for each of the national cases in order to enable all parties to the various cases to be able to present observations in the preliminary proceedings before the Court of Justice.[42] The result is a higher number of references concerning the same number of potential legal problems than is the case in most other Member States.[43]

Likewise, Dutch scholars have argued that since in the Netherlands the courts are paid on the basis of the number of judgments delivered each year there is a financial disincentive to make preliminary references, as a reference will normally mean a postponement of the final judgment for more than a year. It has been suggested that this circumstance constitutes one reason why lower courts in the Netherlands in recent years have shown reluctance when it comes to referring questions to the Court of Justice.[44]

2.11. The link between the use of Article 234 and the attitude to Community law by national courts

It is sometimes assumed that the operation of Article 234 provides an indicator of the degree to which Community law has de facto penetrated each domestic

---

[40] B Rodger, *Article 234 and Competition Law* (2008) 511, 531 where it is suggested that the low number of Portuguese references might be due to lack of awareness of Community competition law.

[41] Rodger argues (ibid, (2008) 28, 562) that the decrease in French references relating to competition issues may be partially due to French judges having become more familiar with competition law. Rodger also suggests that one of the reasons why Austrian courts—which are generally very open to making preliminary references—have only referred very few competition cases is that a concentration of competition law expertise within one specialised court has facilitated the development of competence sufficient to deal with complicated competition issues without the help of the Court of Justice.

[42] See below Ch 7, s 2.5.

[43] C Naomé, 'EU Enlargement and the European Court of Justice' in E Best et al, *The Institutions of the Enlarged European Union* (2008) 100, 112.

[44] S Prechal et al, *'Europeanisation' of the Law: Consequences for the Dutch Judiciary* (2005) 25.

legal system.[45] It may, however, be countered that one should not readily take for granted that the number of references from a given Member State tells us much about the degree to which national courts take account of Community law and to what extent they apply it in a *pro-communautaire* fashion.

Indeed, the preliminary reference procedure is not the only way in which national courts may protect Community rights. On the contrary, Community law builds on a decentralised system where the law is not only to be interpreted by the Court of Justice, but, in quantitative terms, first and foremost by national courts and administrative authorities. A low number of preliminary references is therefore not necessarily a reflection of national courts being reticent in applying Community law, nor is it in itself a sign of defiance or non-compliance. At least for national courts which are not under an obligation to make a preliminary reference,[46] it could just as easily indicate that the relevant courts are well versed in Community law and assume the responsibility of interpreting this law themselves, without needing the assistance of the Court of Justice for each and every interpretative issue they face.[47]

Conversely, a high number of references is neither proof of strong compliance nor of considerable expertise within Community law. It might simply reflect that national judges sometimes make preliminary references without having devoted sufficient time and effort to examining the Community law issue themselves. Indeed, a closer look at the individual references will show that often a preliminary question is either largely irrelevant for the resolution of the main proceedings or the result of a lack of understanding of Community law.[48] Moreover, as discussed above in Section 2.4, the better the compliance rate with Community law that a Member State has, the less reason there will be for litigation attacking national law as being contrary to Community law. Therefore, a high number of preliminary references may not be an indication that the relevant national legal system is particularly apt to apply Community law but rather it may be a reflection of the very opposite, namely that poor compliance has made it more necessary than otherwise for litigants to contest national legislation as being contrary to Community law. Indeed, as stated by Kilpatrick,

> by making Article [234] the measure of judicial co-operation, we cannot investigate whether failure to refer may sometimes represent not the nadir of judicial co-operation but its ape— like the relationship between an old married couple who do not need to talk to each other explicitly to know what the other requires.[49]

---

[45] J Golub, 'The Politics of Judicial Discretion: Rethinking the Interaction between National Courts and the European Court of Justice' (1996) 19 West European Politics 360.

[46] On this, see further Ch 6 below.

[47] See in this respect s 2.6 above.

[48] For examples see Ch 5 below.

[49] C Kilpatrick, 'Community or Community of Courts in European Integration? Sex Equality Dialogues between UK Courts and the ECJ' (1998) 4 European Law Journal 121, 126–8, 134–7,

2.12. Conclusion—why do some Member States make more preliminary references than others?

This chapter has examined a number of factors that might explain the variations in preliminary references between the different Member States. Whilst it is not possible to provide anything close to a formula explaining these variations, the analyses provide grounds for the following three conclusions:

1. None of the examined factors can on their own provide a comprehensive explanation for the variations. Rather the examinations appear to show that the variations are the product of several inter-related factors. Moreover, it is hardly possible to identify with certainty the relevant factors, not to mention their relative weight.

2. However, one overall factor stands out as almost certainly affecting the number of preliminary references, namely the number of cases before the national courts that potentially involve Community law. Therefore, the population size of each country is bound to become highly relevant: there are simply more cases pending before the courts in the larger than in the smaller Member States, and already for that reason a large Member State is likely to produce more preliminary references than is a small Member State. For the same reason, the level of cross-border activities, the individual Member State's level of compliance with Community law, and national differences in inclination to litigate are also likely to be factors that influence the amount of preliminary references. The extent to which each of these factors actually influences the number of references is, however, difficult to determine.

3. Amongst the factors examined there are a number of theories that attempt to establish a calculative frame for explaining how national judges act when faced with disputes where a preliminary reference may be made. As shown in the above analysis, these theories suffer from a common problem in that they seek to attribute certain (not always legitimate) objectives to all judges faced with the question of making preliminary references. Sometimes it is sought to underpin the theories by a statistical analysis of reference patterns from the various Member States. However, the statistics are normally not conclusive and do not take account of the factors mentioned above under (2). In any event, they fail to prove the asserted cause and effect relationship.

---

and 144–5. See also T de la Mare, 'Article 177 in Social and Political Context' in P Craig and G de Búrca (eds), *The Evolution of EU Law* (1999) 215, 244.

3

WHICH BODIES MAY REFER?

1. Who May Refer Preliminary Questions?

It is not every national body which, when confronted with a problem of Community law, has a right to refer a question about the problem to the Court of Justice for a preliminary ruling. According to Article 234, it is only 'a court or tribunal of a Member State' which has this right. The provision itself does not define in more detail what is meant by 'a court or tribunal' or 'of a Member State' and the Court does not by its own motion systematically examine whether a referring national body qualifies as 'a court or tribunal of a Member State'. Such examination is only made if the question is raised during the preliminary proceedings or if the Court itself entertains doubt in this respect.[1] Nevertheless, over the years the Court of Justice has considered these notions in a large number of cases.[2]

In the following, the definition of which bodies qualify as a 'court or tribunal' is approached from two different perspectives. First, Section 2 provides an analysis of the criteria which the Court of Justice uses to decide whether the referring body is a 'court or tribunal' within the meaning of Article 234. Next, Section 3 analyses a number of categories of bodies with a view to establishing which of these are regarded as a 'court or tribunal'. Thereafter, Section 4 deals with the question of when there is a court or tribunal 'of a Member State'. Section 5 considers those forms of preliminary references other than the ones made under Article 234 of the EC Treaty. Finally, Section 6 examines the situation where there is a restriction, under national law, on the right of national courts or tribunals to make references for preliminary rulings.

2. Criteria for Determining whether there is a 'Court or Tribunal' Entitled to Make a Reference

The decision of whether a given body constitutes a 'court or tribunal' entitled to make a reference must be made on the basis of a uniform and independent definition under Community law.[3] In other words, the definition does not refer to national law. This means, on the one hand, that it is not only bodies which are designated as courts or tribunals in national law that can make a reference for a preliminary ruling.[4] On the other hand, the mere fact that a body is designated as a 'court' or 'tribunal' in the national legal system does not in itself mean that this body is entitled to refer a question to the Court of Justice for a preliminary ruling.

In *Corbiau*, Luxembourg's *Conseil d'État* had ascribed the character of a court to the *directeur des contributions* under Luxembourg law. Nevertheless, the Court of Justice found that the *directeur des contributions* was not a national court for the purposes of Article 234.[5]

---

[1] C Naômé, *Le renvoi préjudiciel en droit européen* (2007) 84.
[2] See in this connection L P Moitinho de Almeida, 'La notion de juridiction d'un État membre (article 177 du traité CE)' in R Iglesias, O Due, R Schintgen, and C Elsen (eds), *Mélanges en hommage à Fernand Schockweiler* (1999) 463, 477.
[3] Advocate General Reichl's Opinion in Case 246/80 *Broekmeulen* [1981] ECR 2311 (2335–6).
[4] See s 3.2.2 below on administrative bodies which are regarded as national courts for the purposes of Art 234.
[5] Case C-24/92 *Corbiau* [1993] ECR I-1277, paras 15–16. See also para 4 of Advocate General Darmon's Opinion in this case. A summary of the judgment is given at s 3.2.1 below.

Whilst there is no abstract definition of a 'court or tribunal' in Article 234, it is nevertheless possible to deduce from the case law of the Court of Justice a number of organisational and functional criteria which are relevant for determining when a body can make a reference under that provision.

Below we offer a review of the criteria which are assessed according to the practice of the Court of Justice, and a description of the weighting which the Court gives to the different criteria.

2.1. Is the body established by law?

The Court of Justice has repeatedly held that, when deciding whether a body qualifies as a 'court or tribunal', it is relevant whether it has been established by law.[6] Thus, a body which is set up under an agreement or by a specific administrative decision cannot normally refer a question for a preliminary ruling. On the other hand, it makes no difference whether the body is established by primary or subordinate legislation. Similarly, it does not matter if the body is established by a law which at the same time restricts its jurisdiction to a particular kind of case.[7]

In *Dorsch Consult*, concerning the award of public service contracts, the Commission argued before the Court of Justice that the referring body had been set up under a framework budgetary law which did not give rise to rights or obligations for citizens as legal subjects. The Commission also pointed out that the body in question was confined to reviewing decisions made by review bodies. However, in the field of public service contracts, there was no competent review body at that time. Moreover, according to the Commission the body in question had no basis in law on which it could act. The Court of Justice merely noted that the body had been established by the framework budgetary law, and therefore found that its establishment by law could not be disputed. The fact that domestic legislation had not conferred powers on the body in the specific area of public service contracts was immaterial.[8]

Dorsch Consult thus suggests that the criterion that a body must be established by law in order to qualify as a national court is primarily a formal requirement. Indeed, there do not appear to be any decisions in which the Court of Justice has

---

[6] Case 61/65 *Vaassen-Göbbels* English special edition [1966] ECR p 261 (original reference: Rec 1966, 377) (273); Joined Cases C-110–147/98 *Gabalfrisa and others* [2000] ECR I-1577, para 34; Case C-416/96 *Nour Eddline El-Yassini* [1999] ECR I-1209, para 18; Case C-54/96 *Dorsch Consult* [1997] ECR I-4961, paras 24–5; and Joined Cases C-9/97 and C-118/97 *Jokela* [1998] ECR I-6267, para 19.

[7] Case 61/65 *Vaassen-Göbbels* English special edition [1966] ECR 261 (original reference: Rec 1966 377) (273). See, however, s 2.2 below, on those situations where a body is established with a view to resolving a specific existing dispute.

[8] Case C-54/96 *Dorsch Consult* [1997] ECR I-4961, paras 22–38.

refused to give a preliminary ruling solely on the grounds that the referring body was not established by law and therefore did not qualify as a 'court or tribunal' for the purposes of Article 234.

2.2. Does the body have a permanent character?

The Court of Justice also seems to attach importance to whether the body is of a permanent character.[9] However, there does not appear to have been a decision of the Court of Justice in which lack of permanence has been of decisive importance. In the great majority of cases the body in question has had a permanent character, and in the few cases where this has not been so, there have also been other criteria that have weighed against the recognition of the body in question being considered a court or tribunal for the purposes of Article 234.

The Court of Justice has not made clear precisely what the content is of the requirement for permanence. However, it is natural to assume that the Court will consider the requirement to be important, and not accept references for preliminary rulings from bodies which have been set up to resolve specific existing disputes.[10]

2.3. Is the body independent?

In assessing whether a given body can be regarded as a 'court or tribunal', the Court of Justice attaches weight to whether the legal basis for the body ensures that it has the necessary independence. This criterion is particularly significant in cases where there is a reference from a body which is not part of a Member State's ordinary court system (eg district court, high court, appeal court, etc) and whose characteristics place it somewhere in the grey zone between judicial and administrative bodies. Indeed, in these situations the Court of Justice may be expected to examine closely whether the referring court has jurisdiction under Article 234 of the EC Treaty.[11] For example, the Court has refused to accept references from appeal tribunals where it has found that these have been too closely connected with the administrative authority whose decisions the tribunal deals with. On the other hand, the Court does not seem to examine the personal independence of the members of the body in the actual case in connection with which a reference is made. Where the legal basis for a body does not ensure the necessary independence of the body in general, it will probably not be relevant whether or not in the actual case referred there is a problem of independence.

---

[9] Case 61/65 *Vaassen-Göbbels* English special edition [1966] ECR 261 (original reference: Rec 1966 377); Case 246/80 *Broekmeulen* [1981] ECR 2311, para 3; and Case C-54/96 *Dorsch Consult* [1997] ECR I-4961, para 26.

[10] See in this respect s 3.1.6 on the question of arbitration tribunals.

[11] Case C-246/05 *Häupl* [2007] I-4673, paras 15–21; and Case C-195/06 *Kommunikationsbehörde Austria* [2007] ECR I-8817, paras 18–22.

In *Schmid*, the Court of Justice declined to answer a preliminary question referred by an appeal chamber, as the Court found that the appeal chamber was insufficiently independent from the authority whose decisions the appeal chamber considered. There was both an organisational and a functional link between the appeal chamber and the regional finance authority which rendered the decisions that were contested before the appeal chamber. Thus, the appeal chamber could not be considered a 'court or tribunal' within the meaning of Article 234.[12]

In *Syfait*, a preliminary question was referred to the Court of Justice by the Greek Competition Commission (*Epitropi Antagonismou*). The Competition Commission was to decide on the cases on the basis of recommendations prepared by a secretariat and this secretariat was also responsible for the investigation of the cases. The chairman of the Competition Commission was the head of the secretariat, and was thus formally responsible for its management. The Competition Commission stated that the secretariat acted independently of the Competition Commission itself, but did not substantiate this with any reference to rules or procedures which ensured this independence. The Court of Justice found, inter alia, that there was a functional link between the Competition Commission and its secretariat which was responsible for dealing with the cases that were referred to the Competition Commission for its decision. This was one of the factors that led the Court to hold that the Competition Commission was not a court or tribunal within the meaning of Article 234.[13]

Further clarification of the independence criterion was given in *Wilson*, which concerned the interpretation of the term 'court or tribunal' in Directive 98/5/EC. When defining this term, the Court of Justice applied the practice established with regard to Article 234 and in this respect it was necessary to clarify the concept of independence. The Court observed that independence primarily involves an authority acting as a third party in relation to the authority which has adopted the contested decision. Moreover, the concept has two other aspects, one external and the other internal. The first aspect presumes that the body is protected against external intervention or pressure which may threaten the independent judgment of its members as regards proceedings before them. That essential freedom from such external pressure requires sufficient guarantees to protect those who have the task of adjudicating a dispute, such as guarantees against removal from office.

---

[12] Case C-516/99 *Schmid* [2002] ECR I-4573, paras 34–44. On this case see below s 3.2.1 as well as G Gori, 'La notion de juridiction d'un État membre au sens de l'article 234 CE' in N Fenger, K Hagel-Sørensen, and B Vesterdorf (eds), *Claus Gulmann Liber Amicorum* (2006) 155, 180ff; and T Tridimas, 'Knocking on Heaven's Door: Fragmentation, Efficiency and Defiance in the Preliminary Reference Procedure' (2003) 40 CML Rev 9, 32ff. See also Case C-53/03 *Syfait* [2005] ECR I-4609, paras 32–3; and Advocate General Jacobs's Opinion in Case C-465/03 *Kretztechnik v Finanzamt Linz* [2005] ECR I-4357, para 23.

[13] Case C-53/03 *Syfait* [2005] ECR I-4609, paras 30 and 37.

With regard to the second aspect the Court observed that independence is linked to impartiality and it is intended to ensure that there is a level playing field for the parties to the proceedings and their interests with regard to the subject matter of those proceedings. This aspect requires objectivity and the absence of any interest in the outcome of the proceedings apart from the strict application of the rule of law. Guarantees of independence and impartiality require rules, particularly as regards the composition of the body and appointments to it, length of service, and the grounds for abstention, rejection, and dismissal of its members, in order to remove any doubt as to the imperviousness of that body to external pressure and its neutrality with respect to the interests before it. In the actual case the Court found that the national body did not appear to have sufficient guarantees of impartiality.[14]

In *Pilato*, the Court of Justice found that the French *prud'homie de pêche de Martigues* did not enjoy such independence so as to qualify as a 'court or tribunal' within the meaning of Article 234. The Court particularly pointed to the fact that the members of the body were subject, at least for some of their activities, to supervision by the administration, that the members were required to swear an oath in which they promise, inter alia, to 'comply with the orders which they are given by their superiors', and that the process of dismissing a member of the body did not appear to be subject to specific guarantees which removed any reasonable doubt as to the imperviousness of the body to external factors.[15]

According to Advocate General Stix-Hackl it is not sufficient that there is a general principle that the members of a body which makes decisions should be independent. Thus, she has stated that in order to qualify as a 'court or tribunal' within the meaning of Article 234, it must be a condition that independence is secured by specific provisions concerning rejection or abstention of the members of the body with regard to a case.[16] In *Emanuel* the Court of Justice appears to have adopted a less strict rule, however.

In *Emanuel*, an 'Appointed Person' had been appointed by the Lord Chancellor. As long as the 'Appointed Person' carried out his functions, he was given the same guarantees of independence as judges in general. However, the 'Appointed Person' could be dismissed if certain specified conditions were fulfilled, and it was up to the Lord Chancellor to decide whether this was the case. In his Opinion in the case Advocate General Colomer expressed the view that the scope for making such a dismissal was exceptional and must be interpreted restrictively and he therefore found that there was no doubt that the 'Appointed Person' was independent.

---

14 Case C-506/04 *Wilson* [2006] ECR I-8613, paras 49–53.
15 Case C-109/07 *Pilato* [2008] ECR I-3503.
16 Para 50 in Advocate General Stix-Hackl's Opinion in Case C-506/04 *Wilson* [2006] ECR I-8613.

The Court of Justice did not even consider it necessary to address this issue itself, but instead went straight on to deal with the substantive question referred.[17]

2.4. Is the jurisdiction of the body compulsory?

The Court of Justice also considers it important that the jurisdiction of the body in question be compulsory. This criterion has three aspects: first, it means that the decision of the national body must be binding on the parties.[18] Second, the criterion of compulsion is fulfilled where the parties cannot themselves choose whether the case should be dealt with by the body in question.[19] Third, compulsory jurisdiction presumes that the parties cannot go to some other body to have the dispute settled.

An illustration of the last-mentioned aspect may be found in *Gabalfrisa and others*, where the decisions of the Spanish tax authority could be challenged before the administrative courts only after appeal proceedings had been brought before the Tribunales Económico-Administrativos. Hence, the jurisdiction of the Tribunales was compulsory.[20]

The ruling in *Gabalfrisa and others* may, however, be compared with the Court's ruling in *Emanuel* where the plaintiff had a choice between two national courts without this leading to a finding of inadmissibility,[21] and its ruling in *Broekmeulen* where in principle it was possible to challenge a given decision before the ordinary national courts, rather than before the referring appeals committee—though this had never happened in practice. The appeals committee was nevertheless considered to be a national court for the purposes of Article 234.[22] It therefore seems that—at least in borderline cases—the fact that the parties cannot go to some other body to settle a dispute may weigh in favour of considering the body a 'court or tribunal', but that it does not constitute an indispensable condition.

2.5. Does the body use an adversary procedure?

Where a national organ uses an adversary procedure this will usually be an argument in favour of the body being considered a national court.[23] The use of

---

[17] Case C-259/04 *Emanuel* [2006] ECR I-3089, para 24, and para 30 in the Advocate General's Opinion in the same case.

[18] Joined Cases C-110/98–147/98 *Gabalfrisa and others* [2000] ECR I-1577, para 36. See also Case C-161/03 *Samsung Electronics France* (ECJ 11 July 2003) para 15; and Case C-411/00 *Felix Swoboda* [2002] ECR I-10567, paras 24–8.

[19] Case 102/81 *Nordsee* [1982] ECR 1095, paras 7–16. A summary of the case is provided below at s 3.1.6.

[20] Joined Cases C-110/98–147/98 *Gabalfrisa and others* [2000] ECR I-1577, para 35.

[21] Case C-259/04 *Emanuel* [2006] ECR I-3089, paras 21–2.

[22] Case 246/80 *Broekmeulen* [1981] ECR 2311, para 15.

[23] Case 61/65 *Vaassen-Göbbels* English special edition [1966] ECR 261 (original reference: Rec 1966 377) at 273.

an adversary procedure is not an indispensable condition for a body to be allowed to make a reference for a preliminary ruling, however.

In *Simmenthal*, an undertaking had brought a case against the Italian authorities with a view to recovering previously paid fees. The case had been dealt with in summary proceedings, where judgment was given solely on the basis of the allegations presented by the plaintiff. Only if the other party raised objections to the decision would there have been adversarial proceedings. The Court of Justice ruled that Article 234 did not require that the preliminary ruling should be referred in connection with an adversarial procedure. It added, however, that it may prove to be in the interests of the proper administration of justice that a question should be referred for a preliminary ruling only after both sides have been heard.[24]

2.6. Does the body take its decisions on the basis of legal rules?

The Court of Justice has also emphasised that to qualify as a 'court or tribunal' within the meaning of Article 234 a body must make its decisions on the basis of legal rules.[25] Obviously, this criterion will be satisfied in the great majority of cases which are referred to the Court of Justice. However, there can be doubt in certain cases. This applies in particular where a body can decide according to what appears fair and reasonable.

In *Almelo*, a Dutch court had to consider an appealed arbitration award which had been decided according to what appeared fair and reasonable. According to Dutch law this meant that the referring court which had to decide the appeal also had to make its decision on the basis of what appeared fair and reasonable. Nevertheless, the Court of Justice held that the criterion that a decision has to be taken on the basis of legal rules was fulfilled. In support of this interpretation the Court of Justice argued that it followed from the principles of the primacy and uniform application of Community law together with the duty to take all appropriate measures to ensure fulfilment of the obligation arising out of Community law as laid down in the EC Treaty's Article 10, that even where it gives judgment on the basis of fairness, a national court to which an appeal against an arbitral award is made pursuant to national law must observe the rules of Community law, in particular those relating to competition.[26]

---

[24] Case 70/77 *Simmenthal* [1978] ECR 1453, paras 9–11. See similarly Joined Cases C-277/91, C-318/91, and C-319/91 *Ligur Carni* [1993] ECR I-6621, paras 15–16; Case C-54/96 *Dorsch Consult* [1997] ECR I-4961, para 31; and Case C-17/00 *De Coster* [2001] ECR I-9445, para 14. In Ch 7, s 4, below the question as to when it is most appropriate to make a preliminary reference during the procedure before the national court is considered.

[25] Joined Cases C-110/98–147/98 *Gabalfrisa and others* [2000] ECR I-1577, para 38.

[26] Case C-393/92 *Almelo* [1994] ECR I-1477, para 23.

The criterion, that a body must decide on the basis of legal rules, has also been considered where there was no doubt that the referring body would decide the *substance* of the main proceedings upon the basis of such rules, but where it was questioned whether the *procedural* rules, applied in reaching the substantive decision, could be qualified as legal rules.

In *Dorsch Consult*, the referring German Federal Public Procurement Awards Supervisory Board regulated the making of public service contracts. Procedure before the Federal Supervisory Board was governed by rules of procedure which it had itself adopted, which did not take effect in relation to third parties and which had not been published. The question therefore arose whether the criterion that a body must decide on the basis of legal rules was satisfied even under these circumstances. The Court of Justice noted that the Supervisory Board (also) applied the rules of Community law on the award of public service contracts, and that general procedural requirements laid down in national law (namely in *Verordnung über das Nachprüfungsverfahren für öffentliche Aufträge*) applied and the Court denied that the special circumstances surrounding the Supervisory Board's procedural rules were relevant.[27]

Rather than holding that in this situation the referring body was to decide on the basis of legal rules, the Court of Justice chose to examine the objection carefully and thereby implicitly accepted its relevance. In *Dorsch Consult* the objection was based on the fact that the referring body itself had adopted the rules of procedure in question, and that these rules of procedure did not take effect in relation to third parties and had not been published. The Court of Justice found that even in this situation the criterion that the referring body must decide on the basis of legal rules can be satisfied.

The significance of the criterion that the body must make its decisions on the basis of legal rules is not clear. The criterion will be fulfilled if the referring body is to decide the main proceedings on the basis of purely national rules and presumably also if the body is to decide the case on the basis of international rules. Similarly, the criterion will also be fulfilled if the referring body is to decide the main proceedings on the basis of Community rules. Indeed, a preliminary question is only admissible if it concerns the interpretation or validity of a Community rule that is to be applied in the national body's decision on the main proceedings.[28] This, it is submitted, presupposes that the referring body intends to take account of Community law, which must mean that it does not intend to decide the case on a purely equitable basis. In other words, it appears difficult to imagine a situation

---

[27] Case C-54/96 *Dorsch Consult* [1997] ECR I-4961, paras 32–3.

[28] On the particular situation where a preliminary reference concerns the interpretation of national law that has been modelled upon Community law, see Ch 4, ss 5.3.3 and 5.3.4.

where the referring body does not fulfil the criterion that its decision must be made on the basis of legal rules whilst at the same time it requires an interpretation of some Community rule in order to be able to decide the main proceedings. Nevertheless, the Court of Justice has referred to the criterion on several occasions.

2.7. Must the members of the referring body include lawyers?

As stated in Section 2.6 above, the Court of Justice attaches importance to whether the body takes its decisions on the basis of legal rules. However, it is less certain what importance (if any) the Court of Justice attaches to whether the body's members possess qualifications as lawyers or judges. There is no question that the Court of Justice does not require all the members of a body to have a legal background. Indeed, this criterion is rarely mentioned by the Court itself. The question remains, however, whether a body can qualify as a 'court or tribunal' if its rules do not require that at least some of its members are judges or other persons with legal qualifications.

In *Broekmeulen*, the Dutch Appeals Committee for General Medicine (*Commissie van Beroep Huisartsgeneeskunde*) referred a question to the Court of Justice. Three of the Appeals Committee's members, including the chairman, were appointed by two ministers, three members were appointed by the Dutch medical faculties, and three members by the Royal Netherlands Society for the Promotion of Medicine. There was no condition that the members of the Appeals Committee should be lawyers although, under the internal rules, it was laid down that the chairman preferably should be a high-ranking judge. The Court of Justice nevertheless found that the Appeals Committee constituted a national court for the purposes of Article 234.[29]

Even though, according to the ruling in *Broekmeulen*, there is no absolute requirement for the members of a referring body to be lawyers, it cannot be completely excluded that in cases of doubt the Court of Justice will be willing to take into account how many of the members have legal qualifications as lawyers or judges when deciding whether a body can be regarded as a 'court or tribunal' for the purposes of Article 234.[30]

2.8. Does the question arise in connection with the settlement of a dispute?

The purpose of Article 234 is that the Court of Justice should assist national courts with the interpretation of Community law in connection with the referring

---

[29] Case 246/80 *Broekmeulen* [1981] ECR 2311. See also Case C-416/96 *Eddline El-Yassini* [1999] ECR I-1209, (para 21 of the Advocate General's Opinion); and Case C-7/97 *Bronner* [1998] ECR I-7791 (two out of three of the referring body's members were not lawyers).
[30] Advocate General Jacobs in his Opinion in Case C-53/03 *Syfait* [2005] ECR I-4609, paras 26 and 33 proposed attaching importance to how many of the appointees of the body possess qualifications as lawyers.

bodies' decisions on disputes. For this reason, unless the case in question concerns the settlement of a dispute, the Court of Justice does not have jurisdiction under Article 234.[31] This applies regardless of whether, according to its organisational characteristics, the body is classified as a 'court or tribunal' according to the above criteria.[32]

2.9. Are there other judicial solutions to the conflict in question?

The preliminary ruling procedure is intended to give full effect to Community law in the Member States. The strength of the system lies in the fact that at least the more important disputes often—though far from always—find their way to the Member States' ordinary national courts at some point. If the dispute involves a question of a Community law character, this opens up the possibility of the question being referred to the Court of Justice.

However, in certain situations a dispute can in practice solely be brought before bodies which can only with difficulty be regarded as being a 'court or tribunal' within the meaning of Article 234. *Broekmeulen* is one such case, where there was in reality no possibility of appeal to the Member State's judicial organs. Here the Court showed itself willing to regard the decision-making body as being entitled to make a reference for a preliminary ruling. The alternative would be that the Court of Justice would not have the opportunity to decide on problems of Community law to which such cases might give rise.[33]

It remains to be seen how far the Court of Justice will stretch the *ratio* in *Broekmeulen*. We subscribe to the view of Advocate General Tesauro that '[i]f a body is not a judicial body, it does not become one simply because there is no better solution.'[34]

Moreover, where a case is dealt with by a body that qualifies as a national court, the fact that other conflict resolution bodies, such as an ombudsman or a mediator, could have handled the problem which the case concerns is irrelevant when it comes to the qualification of the body handling the case. This is so even if the alternative body would have been more appropriate. In this connection it is

---

[31] Case 138/80 *Borker* [1980] ECR 1975, para 4; Case 318/85 *Greis Unterweger* [1986] ECR 955, para 4; and Case C-256/05 *Telekom Austria* (ECJ 6 October 2005) paras 10–12.

[32] See further s 3.1.3 below.

[33] See Case 246/80 *Broekmeulen* [1981] ECR 2311, paras 16–17.

[34] Para 40 of the Opinion of Advocate General Tesauro in Case C-54/96 *Dorsch Consult* [1997] ECR I-4961. Compare however G Gori, 'La notion de juridiction d'un État membre au sens de l'article 234 CE' in N Fenger, K Hagel-Sørensen, and B Vesterdorf (eds), *Claus Gulmann Liber Amicorum* (2006) 155, 161ff. C Lewis, *Judicial Remedies in Public Law* (2008) 542 observes that 'the European Court has been influenced by the fact that there was no right of appeal from the body to the ordinary courts. If the individual was not able to properly invoke his rights under European Law, that body must be able to make references to the European Court.'

irrelevant whether the alternative body would itself have qualified as a court within the meaning of Article 234 and thus—hypothetically—could have made a reference for a preliminary ruling. The only thing that matters is whether the actual case is being dealt with by a body that qualifies as 'a court or tribunal'.

2.10. The Court's weighting of the different criteria

As stated above, there is no abstract definition of a 'court or tribunal' for the purposes of Article 234 and the Court of Justice has never expressed itself on the relative weighting of the criteria which are relevant in assessing whether a given body can refer a question for a preliminary ruling under Article 234.[35] Hence, it is not possible to derive an unambiguous definition from the Court's judgments.[36]

A rather harsh criticism of the fact that the Court of Justice has not given a clear definition of which types of bodies are entitled to make references for preliminary rulings has been given by Advocate General Colomer. In 2000 in his Opinion in *De Coster* he characterised the result of this as 'case-law which is too flexible and not sufficiently consistent, with the lack of legal certainty which that entails . . . The case-law is casuistic, very elastic and not very scientific, with such vague outlines that a question referred for a preliminary ruling by Sancho Panza as governor of the island of Barataria would be accepted.'[37]

While it is not possible to establish an unambiguous definition, the case law of the Court of Justice nevertheless suggests that some of the criteria referred to are more important than others.

Thus, the Court seems to work on the assumption that a referring body will be a 'court or tribunal' as long as it is part of a Member State's ordinary court system, and the reference is made as part of judicial proceedings which are intended to lead to the settlement of a dispute.[38] Where the Court cannot rely on this assumption, it will normally make a more detailed assessment of the organisational and functional criteria referred to above.[39] It is not clear whether these

---

[35] P Oliver, 'La recevabilité des questions préjudicielles: La jurisprudence des années 1990' (2001) 37 Cahiers de droit européen 15, 17; and G Gori, 'La notion de juridiction d'un État membre au sens de l'article 234 CE' in N Fenger, K Hagel-Sørensen, and B Vesterdorf (eds), *Claus Gulmann Liber Amicorum* (2006) 155, 167.

[36] T Tridimas, 'Knocking on Heaven's Door: Fragmentation, Efficiency and Defiance in the Preliminary Reference Procedure' (2003) 40 CML Rev 9, 27.

[37] Opinion in Case C-17/00 *De Coster* [2001] ECR I-9445, para 14. See also T Tridimas, 'Knocking on Heaven's Door: Fragmentation, Efficiency and Defiance in the Preliminary Reference Procedure' (2003) 40 CML Rev 9, 31ff.

[38] G Gori, 'La notion de juridiction d'un État membre au sens de l'article 234 CE' in N Fenger, K Hagel-Sørensen, and B Vesterdorf (eds), *Claus Gulmann Liber Amicorum* (2006) 155, 183.

[39] Case C-192/98 *ANAS* [1999] ECR I-8583, paras 2–25; and Case C-440/98 *RAI* [1999] ECR I-8597, paras 11–16.

criteria constitute an exhaustive list, or whether it is possible that further criteria may be included.

The Court of Justice gives special weight to whether the reference is made as part of judicial proceedings which are to lead to the settlement of a dispute.[40] If this is not the case, it can be expected that the Court of Justice will refuse to accept the reference.

If the reference is made as part of judicial proceedings which are to lead to the settlement of a dispute, but the referring body is not part of a Member State's ordinary court system, it will be particularly important whether the body is independent,[41] and whether it has compulsory jurisdiction. Correspondingly, it is to be expected that the Court of Justice will reject references from bodies that are only set up with a view to resolving a particular individual dispute, or which are not established by law.

The criteria concerning the adversarial nature of the procedure—that the body should make its decisions on the basis of legal rules, and that there should not be any other possibility for resolving the dispute in question—have all been given less weight and seem only to play a role in cases where the other criteria do not point in a particular direction. The last criterion, on the extent to which the members of the body are lawyers, has hitherto only been proposed by an Advocate General, but not by the Court of Justice itself. As observed above, it therefore remains unclear whether the Court will follow its Advocate General and attach any weight to this at all.[42]

3. Which Bodies Qualify as a 'Court or Tribunal'?

In Section 2 above we analysed the different criteria that determine whether a body can refer a question for a preliminary ruling under Article 234 as well as examining the weighting of the different criteria. In this section the same question, namely what bodies qualify as a 'court or tribunal', is approached from a

---

[40] G Gori, 'La notion de juridiction d'un État membre au sens de l'article 234 CE' in N Fenger, K Hagel-Sørensen, and B Vesterdorf (eds), *Claus Gulmann Liber Amicorum* (2006) 155, 173; and T Tridimas, 'Knocking on Heaven's Door: Fragmentation, Efficiency and Defiance in the Preliminary Reference Procedure' (2003) 40 CML Rev 9, 28.

[41] G Anagnostaras, 'Preliminary problems and jurisdiction uncertainties: the admissibility of questions referred by bodies performing quasi-judicial functions' (2005) 30 EL Rev 878, 883.

[42] The independence criterion, which is now given considerable weight, was originally put forward by Advocate General Gand in 1966 in Case 61/65 *Vaassen-Göbbels* English special edition [1966] ECR 261 (original reference: Rec 1966 377) at 281. It was not until 1987—ie more than 20 years later—that the Court of Justice itself referred to this criterion in Case 14/86 *Pretore di Salò* [1987] ECR 2545, para 7. See also in this regard Advocate General Colomer's Opinion in Case C-17/00 *De Coster* [2001] ECR I-9445, para 17.

different perspective, ie by examining which bodies the Court of Justice regards as being entitled to make references and which are not so entitled. The examination is divided into three parts. Section 3.1 looks at judicial bodies; Section 3.2 looks at other public bodies; and Section 3.3 looks at various private bodies.

3.1. Judicial bodies

3.1.1. *Ordinary national courts*

A national district court, high court, or supreme court settling disputes is regarded as a national court for the purposes of Article 234 regardless of whether the dispute is of a private law, criminal law, or administrative law character. The same applies to courts which are not included in the ordinary court system (ie extraordinary courts which fulfil the requirements identified in Section 2 above).[43] Courts martial are also included if they otherwise meet the criteria. On the other hand, public prosecutors are not bodies entitled to make a reference.

In *Criminal proceedings against X*, the public prosecutor's office in Turin made a reference to the Court of Justice for a preliminary ruling. Shortly afterwards the national Italian court hearing the case decided to refer the same questions, in case the Court of Justice were to decide that the public prosecutor was not entitled to refer the questions for a preliminary ruling. The Court of Justice ruled that the Italian public prosecutor could not be regarded as a 'court or tribunal' for the purposes of Article 234, but since the national court had also referred the questions for a preliminary ruling the Court of Justice nevertheless went on to give an answer.[44]

3.1.2. *International courts and courts with jurisdiction in more Member States*

It has not been definitively settled whether international courts, such as the European Court of Human Rights, can make references under Article 234. Nevertheless, only 'a court or tribunal of a Member State' is entitled to make a reference—and international courts are not part of the court systems of the Member States. Consequently, they must be regarded as prevented from making references for preliminary rulings under Article 234.[45]

In comparison, a court which is an integrated part of the national court systems of more than one Member State can make references for preliminary rulings. So long as that court is only part of the court systems of Member States, and is not also part of the court system of a third country, the referring multi-State court as well as the

---

[43] Case 287/86 *Ny Mølle Kro* [1987] ECR 5465.

[44] Joined Cases C-74/95 and C-129/95 *Criminal proceedings against X* [1996] ECR I-6609.

[45] T C Hartley, *The Foundations of European Community Law* (2007) 282; and P Oliver, 'Recevabilité des questions préjudicielles: La jurisprudence des années 1990' (2001) 37 Cahiers de droit européen 15, 24.

national courts of those States that are covered by the multi-State court will be bound by the ruling of the Court of Justice.[46] In this situation it will be difficult to argue that it is not a court or tribunal of a Member State as required in Article 234.[47]

The three Benelux countries adopted a 'Uniform Benelux Law on Trade Marks'. With a view to ensuring the uniform interpretation of this law, the three countries set up a common Benelux Court. In *Parfums Christian Dior*, the question arose as to whether the Benelux Court was entitled to make a reference to the Court of Justice for a preliminary ruling. The Court of Justice found that there was no reason why a court that was common to more than one Member State could not make such a reference in the same way as the national courts of any of those Member States. The Court of Justice recognised that the Benelux Court had the task of ensuring the uniform application of the common rules of the Benelux States, and that cases were brought before the Benelux Court as a part of the proceedings before the national courts leading to definitive interpretations of common Benelux legal rules. In other words, it was in line with the aims of Article 234 to admit references from the Benelux Court.[48]

3.1.3. *Activities which do not lead to decisions of a judicial nature*

Questions of the more specific definition of when a reference for a preliminary ruling can be made do not only arise where commercial or administrative bodies exercise judicial functions. These questions also arise with regard to bodies which are unquestionably 'courts or tribunals' in a national judicial system, in those situations where they perform tasks other than deciding disputes.

It was previously assumed that judicial bodies were entitled to refer questions to the Court of Justice for a preliminary ruling, even when the question was not prompted by a judicial decision for the settlement of a dispute but arose, for example, in connection with a notarial function. Thus, under this earlier case law the Court had ruled that it had jurisdiction to give preliminary rulings in all cases where the reference was made by a body which fulfilled the organisational criteria discussed in Section 2 above for constituting a national court. In this connection it made no difference whether the tasks of the 'court or tribunal' within the meaning of Article 234 in the case referred related to a decision in a dispute or to other non-contentious tasks within the scope of its responsibilities.[49]

---

[46] Para 27 (implicitly) in Advocate General Jacobs' Opinion in Case C-337/95 *Parfums Christian Dior* [1997] ECR I-6013. See also Opinion 1/91, first Opinion on an EEA Agreement [1991] ECR I-6079, paras 58–65.

[47] See further below in s 4.

[48] Case C-337/95 *Parfums Christian Dior* [1997] ECR I-6013. In Case C-265/00 *Campina Melkunie* [2004] ECR I-1699, the Benelux Court for the first time made a preliminary reference.

[49] Case 14/86 *Pretore di Salò* [1987] ECR 2545, para 7.

This purely organisational approach has since been abandoned. According to the more recent practice of the Court of Justice, only questions related to truly judicial activities can be referred.

The change to the case law was introduced with *Job Centre*, where an Italian court had referred a question to the Court of Justice within the framework of the special Italian non-contentious proceedings (*giurisdizione volontaria*). This form of administration of justice is used in cases which do not lead to a decision on a dispute. The Court of Justice held that a reference of a question in accordance with Article 234 can only be made if there is a dispute before the national court and if the reference is made with a view to making a decision on that legal dispute. In the main proceedings in *Job Centre*, the Italian court had to consider whether to approve the articles of association of a company with a view to its registration. The Court of Justice found that the Italian court did not thereby exercise a judicial function, but on the contrary was acting as an administrative authority, without having to decide on a dispute. It therefore declined to give a preliminary ruling.[50]

In *Standesamt Stadt Niebüll* the Registry Office in Germany refused to recognise the surname of the child of a couple of German nationality as it had been determined in Denmark where the child and his parents were living. Without having taken, or been able to take, a decision on the matter, the Registry Office brought the matter before the *Familiengericht*, which exercised administrative authority, without at the same time being called on to decide a dispute. Therefore, the *Familiengericht* could not be regarded as exercising a judical function and so the Court of Justice ruled that it did not have jurisdiction to answer the question referred.[51]

A request for a preliminary ruling can be admissible even if the referring national court asks the question as part of a preliminary examination, as long as that preliminary examination is to result in the national court taking a judicial decision.[52]

In *Züchner*, a German court made a preliminary reference in proceedings relating to an application for legal aid. Observing that the legal aid depended on the main

---

[50] Case C-111/94 *Job Centre* [1995] ECR I-3361, paras 9–11. The *Job Centre* decision has since been followed in a large number of other cases: see Case C-182/00 *Lutz et al* [2002] ECR I-547, paras 13-17; Case C-192/98 *ANAS* [1999] ECR I-8583, para 24; Case C-178/99 *Salzmann* [2001] ECR I-4421, paras 11–22; Case C-447/00 *Holto* [2002] ECR I-735, paras 17–23; Case C-86/00 *HSB-Wohnbau* [2001] ECR I-5353, paras 11–17; Case C-248/01 *Hermann Pfanner Getränke et al* (ECJ 14 June 2002) paras 16–19; Case C-424/01 *CS Austria* [2003] ECR I-3249, paras 21–5; Case C-165/03 *Längst* [2005] ECR I-5637, paras 24–8; and Case C-105/03 *Pupino* [2005] ECR I-5285, para 22.
[51] Case C-96/04 *Standesamt Stadt Niebüll* [2006] ECR I-3561, para 17.
[52] Case C-60/02 *X* [2004] ECR I-651, paras 25–9.

action having a sufficient prima facie prospect of success, and as no further appeal would lie against a refusal of legal aid in the appeal in question, and as the national court that had to determine the application had found it necessary to submit the preliminary questions concerning the interpretation of a directive, the Advocate General found that the Court of Justice should answer the preliminary questions. The Court itself did not comment on the matter, but instead went straight on to answering the questions.[53]

In contrast, national courts will not, for example, be able to refer a question for a preliminary ruling in connection with the registration of real property transactions in the land register.[54]

In *Victoria Film*, the Swedish Revenue Law Commission (*Skatterättsnämnden*) had to give binding preliminary decisions on whether there was a duty to pay VAT in certain circumstances. Victoria Film argued that the Swedish rules were contrary to the Community rules, and the Revenue Law Commission therefore referred this question to the Court of Justice. The Court of Justice declined jurisdiction to answer the preliminary question. Whilst there were circumstances which indicated that the Revenue Law Commission performed a judicial function, it did not have the task of examining the legality of the tax authorities' decisions. On the contrary, it had to take the initial decision on the taxation of certain transactions. Therefore, in the case in question the Revenue Law Commission exercised a non-judicial function which, in other Member States, is exercised by the tax authorities themselves.[55]

Where a non-judicial decision is appealed to a higher court, the higher court will be faced with a dispute within the meaning of Article 234. Consequently, the higher court can refer a question to the Court of Justice.

In *X AB and Y AB*, the Court of Justice held that the Swedish Supreme Administrative Court could refer a question for a preliminary ruling as long as a decision of the Swedish Revenue Law Commission (which in such cases did not exercise a judicial function and therefore was not entitled to make a reference) was brought before the Supreme Administrative Court for trial.[56]

---

[53] Para 15 in the Advocate General's Opinion in Case C-77/95 *Züchner* [1996] ECR I-5689.

[54] For similar examples, see Case C-178/99 *Salzmann* [2001] ECR I-4421, paras 14–18; Case C-440/98 *RAI* [1999] ECR I-8597, paras 12–15; and Case C-424/01 *CS Austria* [2003] ECR I-3249, paras 21–5.

[55] Case C-134/97 *Victoria Film* [1998] ECR I-7023, paras 12–19.

[56] Case C-200/98 *X AB and Y AB* [1999] ECR I-8261; and Case C-436/00 *X and Y* [2002] ECR I-10829. See also Case C-300/01 *Salzmann II* [2003] ECR I-4899, para 14; Case C-178/99 *Salzmann I* [2001] ECR I-4421, para 17; Case C-411/03 *SEVIC Systems* [2005] ECR I-10805, paras 6–8; and Case C-117/06 *Möllendorf* [2007] ECR I-8361, paras 27–31.

A higher court may even make a preliminary reference following an appeal of a non-judicial decision where the proceedings before the higher court are not *inter partes*.[57]

In its case law, starting with the decision in *Job Centre*, the Court of Justice has tightened up its requirements for when a national court can make a reference for a preliminary ruling. At the same time, however, the Court has adopted a relatively wide interpretation for when a dispute will be found to exist.

In *Déménagements-Manutention Transport*, the Belgian *Tribunal de commerce de Bruxelles* referred a question in a situation where, *ex officio*, it should decide whether an undertaking was insolvent and should therefore be declared bankrupt. The investigation into the possible insolvency of an undertaking was initially carried out by an investigating judge. If the investigating judge had information which indicated that an undertaking was insolvent, the case should be referred to the *Tribunal de commerce*. The Court of Justice found that it only had jurisdiction to answer a preliminary question if there were a dispute before the national court, and if the reference of the question were made with a view to deciding on a legal dispute. In the circumstances of the case, the Court of Justice found that it did have jurisdiction.[58]

A national court is not prevented from making a reference for a preliminary ruling in cases where the procedure before the national court has elements which are more in the nature of giving an advisory opinion, as long as the procedure leads to a decision that is judicial in character and binding on the parties.

In *Österreichischer Gewerkschaftsbund*, an Austrian trade union submitted a request to the Austrian Supreme Court (*Oberster Gerichtshof*) in accordance with a provision in Austrian law giving associations of employees and employers the possibility of requesting the Supreme Court to establish the existence or non-existence of rights or legal relationships. There were thus clearly conflicting interests between the two parties. In order to be admissible, the request would have to concern a substantive question of labour law, and to be relevant for at least three employers or employees. The respondent—as well as other trade associations—were offered the opportunity of submitting comments before the Supreme Court made its decision. This decision would rely on the factual circumstances submitted by the applicant, without trying the facts. In the actual case the Supreme Court had had a question referred to it which involved Community law. The Supreme Court therefore made a reference to the Court of Justice for a preliminary ruling, but at the same time it commented that the case did not correspond to the conventional

---

[57] Case C-210/06 *Cartesio* (ECJ 16 December 2008) paras 61 and 63.
[58] Case C-256/97 *Déménagements-Manutention Transport* [1999] ECR I-3913, paras 4 and 9; and paras 15–17 of the Advocate General's Opinion on the case.

view of litigation, but rather was a matter of giving an advisory opinion on the law with the appearance of a judicial decision. The Court of Justice held that, 'from an institutional point of view', the Austrian Supreme Court had the characteristics which defined a national court for the purposes of Article 234. As for the special procedures which applied to the actual case, the Court of Justice found that most of these were typical of judicial proceedings. The Austrian Supreme Court thus acted as a national court of compulsory jurisdiction in the sense that both parties to a dispute could bring a case, irrespective of the objections of the other party. Moreover, the procedure was regulated by legal rules, was adversarial, and did not allow for the reference of purely hypothetical questions to the Supreme Court. At the same time the Court of Justice acknowledged that the Austrian procedure also had certain aspects which were less characteristic of judicial proceedings—in particular, that the Supreme Court did not resolve disputes which concerned the specific case, involving identified persons; that the legal assessment relied on facts alleged by the applicant without further examination; that the decision was declaratory; and that the right to bring proceedings was exercised collectively. Nevertheless, the aim of the proceedings was to arrive at a decision that was judicial in character. In this connection, the Court of Justice emphasised that the final decision was binding on the parties, who could not submit a further request with a view to getting a declaratory judgment concerning the same factual circumstances and raising the same legal questions. Furthermore, the decision was intended to have 'persuasive authority for parallel proceedings concerning individual employers and employees'. The Court of Justice therefore considered that the Austrian Supreme Court's reference was admissible.[59]

In *Gourmet Classic*, the Court of Justice was asked to consider a question submitted by the Swedish Supreme Administrative Court. The case arose because the company Gourmet Classic had applied for a preliminary opinion from the Swedish Revenue Law Commission in order to have firm knowledge about how it would be taxed when it started to market a specific product in Sweden. Neither Gourmet Classic nor the Swedish tax administration disputed the decision rendered by the Revenue Law Commission, but the tax administration chose to make use of the possibility of seeking confirmation of the preliminary opinion from the Supreme Administrative Court which in turn made a preliminary reference. Contrary to the Opinion of its Advocate General, the Court of Justice found that the Supreme Administrative Court was carrying out a judicial function since it was reviewing the legality of an opinion which, once it became definitive, would bind the tax authorities and would serve as the basis for the assessment to tax if and to the extent Gourmet Classic continued with the action envisaged in its application.

---

[59] Case C-195/98 *Österreichischer Gewerkschaftsbund* [2000] ECR I-10497, paras 21–32.

Hence, the Court of Justice had jurisdiction to reply to the question posed by the Supreme Administrative Court.[60]

A fact-finding committee which is set up with a view to examining a specific and already known factual situation will not satisfy the criteria of being of a permanent character, and will, for this reason alone, not qualify as a 'court or tribunal'.[61] Moreover, such a body will usually only give a view on the facts, without giving a judicial decision on them. For this reason too, such a body will not qualify as a 'court'.

3.1.4. The function as a judicial body is combined with other functions

In certain Member States the function as a judicial body is combined with other functions. For example, this is the case in Italy where in certain procedures some judges act as prosecution authorities and as investigating authorities. Back in 1987 the Court of Justice had held that it was not prevented from giving preliminary rulings on questions referred by such judges, even though the questions were asked in connection with the exercise of a function which would not in itself result in a judicial decision.[62] Similarly, the Court of Justice has previously accepted questions referred by French examining magistrates in criminal cases.[63]

In light of the change of practice which was introduced in *Job Centre*,[64] it is natural to assume that in cases where the referring judge has both judicial functions and other functions, the Court of Justice only has jurisdiction to answer preliminary questions that are referred in connection with the judge's exercise of the judicial function.

In *Criminal proceedings against X*, which concerned trade mark counterfeiting, an Austrian court referred a question for a preliminary ruling in connection with an investigation, the purpose of which was to make an initial examination of the allegations of a criminal offence and to clarify the facts to the extent necessary to uncover any evidence likely to result in the discontinuance of the criminal proceedings or in their prosecution. The Court of Justice admitted the reference, observing that the national court would in any event adopt a decision of a judicial nature, whether or not that decision related to the possible application of criminal penalties, to the confiscation and destruction of the goods suspected of being counterfeit, or to an acquittal or an order that no further action be taken.[65]

---

60 Case C-458/06 *Gourmet Classic* [2008] ECR I-4207. See also Ch 5, s 4.1, below.
61 See the discussion on this in s 2.2 above.
62 Case 14/86 *Pretore di Salò* [1987] ECR 2545, paras 6–7.
63 Case 65/79 *Chatain* [1980] ECR 1345; and Case 54/80 *Wilner* [1980] ECR 3673.
64 See s 3.1.3 above.
65 Case C-60/02 *Criminal proceedings against X* [2004] ECR I-651, para 27.

In *Déménagements-Manutention Transport*, a Belgian court made a reference in connection with its conduct of some insolvency proceedings concerning a company. These insolvency proceedings were divided into two steps. Initially an investigation into the possible insolvency of an undertaking was carried out by the investigating judge who thereupon referred the matter to a chamber of the same court for a decision. It was possible to make use of the Article 234 procedure, at least after the case had been referred to the chamber for a decision.[66]

Whilst today the Court of Justice will normally only answer preliminary questions that are referred in connection with the exercise of a judge's judicial function, it has not been fully consistent in this regard. Thus, in a ruling from 2004 it held that a judge who makes a criminal examination is a 'court or tribunal' within the meaning of Article 234.[67]

3.1.5. *Summary proceedings*

The fact that a national court uses summary proceedings does not in itself mean that a reference for a preliminary ruling is inadmissible under Article 234.[68] This will presumably be particularly relevant in cases concerning arrests, injunctions, and other interim measures.

At the same time a national court can only make a preliminary reference if it can itself apply the Court of Justice's ruling in the main proceedings that have given rise to the reference. This means that a national court cannot make a reference for a preliminary ruling if, having made a decision on interim measures, it loses jurisdiction over both the final decision and over a possible amendment of the interim measures.[69]

3.1.6. *Arbitration tribunals*

Arbitration tribunals are treated in the same way as other bodies.[70] An arbitration tribunal will therefore be regarded as a national court for the purposes of Article 234, provided that it is permanent, that it is established by law, that its jurisdiction does not require the consent of the parties (meaning that each of the parties can bring a case before the tribunal without the other party being able to resist the

---

[66] Case C-256/97 *Déménagements-Manutention Transport* [1999] ECR I-3913, para 9. See also Case C-411/00 *Felix Swoboda* [2002] ECR I-10567, paras 24–8.

[67] Case C-235/02 *Saetti* [2004] ECR I-1005. Regarding this case, see also C Naômé, *Le Renvoi préjudiciel en droit européen* (2007) 89.

[68] Case 29/69 *Stauder* [1969] ECR 419 (see in particular the Advocate General's Opinion at 428); Case 78/70 *Deutsche Grammophon* [1971] ECR 487 (see in particular the Advocate General's Opinion at 505); Case 107/76 *Hoffmann-La Roche/Centrafarm* [1977] ECR 957, para 4; and Joined Cases 35/82 and 36/82 *Morson and Jhanjan* [1982] ECR 3723, para 10 (implicitly).

[69] See Ch 5, s 3.

[70] Case 61/65 *Vaassen-Göbbels* English special edition [1966] ECR 261 (original reference: Rec 1966 377) (273), together with the Advocate General's Opinion at 281.

tribunal's jurisdiction), and that the parties are not free to determine the composition of the tribunal.

In *Handels- og Kontorfunktionærernes Forbund*, as well as in *Royal Copenhagen*, the Danish Industrial Arbitration Board referred some questions to the Court of Justice for preliminary rulings. Under Danish law, if the parties to a collective agreement have not adopted rules for the settlement of trade disputes, disputes are subject to the Agreed Standard Rules adopted by the Employers' Association and Employees' Union. The Danish Industrial Arbitration Board decided such disputes as the forum of last instance. There was compulsory jurisdiction, as either party could bring a case before the Arbitration Board, regardless of the consent of the other party to this. Finally, the Law on the Labour Court governed the composition of the Board, including the number of members who must be appointed by the parties and the way in which the umpire must be appointed. The composition of the Arbitration Board was thus not within the parties' discretion. On this basis the Court of Justice found that the Industrial Arbitration Board was entitled to refer questions for preliminary rulings in accordance with Article 234.[71]

In contrast to the above, an arbitration tribunal cannot make a preliminary reference *where* the parties to an agreement are neither legally nor actually obliged to have their dispute decided by arbitration, and *where* the authorities of the Member State in question are neither involved in the decision to use arbitration, nor required to intervene automatically in the proceedings before the arbitration tribunal.[72] In this connection it is not enough that the arbitral award is binding, as between the parties, and can be enforced in the same way as the decisions of the ordinary courts. In view of this, the main rule seems to be that arbitration tribunals are not in a position to request the Court of Justice to give a preliminary ruling.[73]

In *Nordsee*, a German arbitration tribunal made a preliminary reference to the Court of Justice. The Court found that the work of the arbitration tribunal was comparable with that of an ordinary court or tribunal on certain points. Thus, arbitration proceedings were provided within the framework of the law, the

---

[71] Case 109/88 *Handels- og Kontorfunktionærernes Forbund* [1989] ECR 3199, paras 7–9; and Case C-400/93 *Royal Copenhagen* [1995] ECR I-1275.

[72] Case 102/81 *Nordsee* [1982] ECR 1095, paras 10–12; and Case C-125/04 *Denuit* [2005] ECR I-923, paras 13–17. For a critical assessment of the *Nordsee* judgment, see G Bebr, 'Arbitration Tribunals and Article 177 of the EEC Treaty' (1985) 22 CML Rev 489 and S Prechal, 'Community Law in National Courts: The Lessons From Van Schijndel' (1998) 35 CML Rev 681, 695–7. According to Prechal, at 697, the Court's case law on arbitration tribunals creates problems and she argues that one way of remedying this is to open up the preliminary procedure to arbitrators. In this regard, see also Advocate General Saggio at para 32 (with footnote 18) of his Opinion in Case C-126/97 *Eco Swiss* [1999] ECR I-3055.

[73] Case C-126/97 *Eco Swiss* [1999] ECR I-3055, para 40.

arbitration tribunal had to decide the case in accordance with the law, the award of the tribunal had, as between the parties, the force of *res judicata*, and it could be enforceable if leave to issue execution was obtained. Nevertheless the Court of Justice found that the arbitration tribunal did not qualify as a 'court or tribunal' within the meaning of Article 234. It emphasised that, at the time of entering into the agreement which gave rise to the dispute, the parties were free to choose whether to have any disputes referred to the ordinary courts or to refer them to arbitration by including a clause to this effect in the contract. Moreover, the German authorities were not involved in the decision to opt for arbitration nor were they called upon to intervene automatically in the proceedings before the arbitrator. The German State had not entrusted or left to private individuals the duty of ensuring that such obligations were complied with in the sphere at issue in the case.[74]

In certain Member States a decision of an arbitration tribunal can be referred to the ordinary national courts, for example with a view to the enforcement of an arbitral award or for taking evidence. In this situation the ordinary national courts will be able to make a reference for a preliminary ruling under Article 234, as it is only the circumstances of the referring body that are taken into account.[75] The same applies where an arbitration tribunal requests the ordinary national courts 'to interpret the law applicable'.[76] In Denmark, the legislator has made use of this possibility in the Law on Arbitration, s 27(2), which states that, if an arbitration tribunal considers that a decision on a question of Community law is necessary to enable it to make an award, the arbitration tribunal may request the Danish courts to ask the Court of Justice to give a preliminary ruling thereon.[77] If an arbitration tribunal makes such a request, it is the Danish court which has competence to decide whether to make a reference for a preliminary ruling, and how to formulate the questions.

A national court which acts as a court of appeal in an arbitration case constitutes a 'court or tribunal' for the purposes of Article 234. This is so because the national court is obliged to comply with Community law, even if the arbitration agreement requires the court to make its decision on an equitable basis. This follows from the principles of supremacy of Community law and of its uniform application in conjunction with the Member States' duty of loyal cooperation, laid down in Article 10 of the EC Treaty.[78]

---

[74] Case 102/81 *Nordsee* [1982] ECR 1095, paras 7–16.
[75] Ibid, paras 14–15.
[76] Ibid, para 14.
[77] K Hertz, *Danish Arbitration Act 2005* (2005) 134ff.
[78] Case C-393/92 *Almelo* [1994] ECR I-1477, para 23. A summary of the judgment is given above at s 2.6.

The above considerations apply to private arbitration. At least in principle the same considerations apply where two or more Member States choose to settle a dispute through an international arbitration tribunal. In practice such an international arbitration tribunal is unlikely to qualify as a 'court or tribunal' under Article 234, however. This is so in particular because the international arbitration tribunal must be permanently established[79] and must be part of one or more Member State judicial systems without at the same time also being part of the court system of non-Member States.[80]

Moreover, the likelihood is very slim that an international arbitration tribunal will have to decide a case between two Member States on the basis of Community law. Under Article 292 of the EC Treaty the Member States are bound not to submit a dispute concerning the interpretation or application of the EC Treaty to any method of settlement other than those provided for in the Treaty.[81] It cannot be completely excluded that such a situation may arise, however. Indeed, Article 292 can hardly preclude Member States from submitting a dispute of international law to an international arbitration tribunal even if this dispute also raises an issue of Community law, provided that the Court of Justice would not have been competent to hear the case and the issue of Community law could not reasonably have been brought separately before the Court of Justice.

3.1.7. *Courts that do not have jurisdiction to decide on the main action*

As described above, the Court of Justice examines whether a reference for a preliminary ruling has been made by a 'court or tribunal' within the meaning of Article 234. On the other hand, the Court of Justice has consistently denied that it has jurisdiction to examine whether the referring court has jurisdiction to deal with the case according to the applicable national law, nor does the Court of Justice examine whether the decision to make a reference has been made in accordance with national procedural rules.[82]

In *WWF*, it was argued that the referring court was not competent to decide on the substantive issue in the main proceedings. On this the Court of Justice observed that, in view of the distribution of functions between itself and the national courts, it was not for the Court of Justice to determine whether the decision whereby a matter is brought before it has been taken in accordance with the rules of national law governing the organisation of the national courts and their procedure.[83]

---

[79] s 2.2 above.
[80] s 3.1.2 above.
[81] Case C-459/03 *Commission v Ireland* [2006] ECR I-4635.
[82] Case C-116/00 *Laguillaume* [2000] ECR I-4979, para 10; Joined Cases C-51/96 and C-191/97 *Deliège* [2000] ECR I-2549, para 29; Case C-143/99 *Adria-Wien Pipeline* [2001] ECR I-8365, para 19; and Case C-238/05 *ASNEF-EQUIFAX* [2006] ECR I-11125, paras 12–14.
[83] Case C-435/97 *WWF* [1999] ECR I-5613, para 33.

The Court of Justice is thus bound by a referring court's decision to refer a preliminary question, as long as this decision has not been overturned by an appeal under national law.[84]

In *Balocchi*, the Italian authorities' collection of VAT was challenged before an Italian court. The Italian government disputed that the Court of Justice could admit the reference from the referring national court, since the latter did not have jurisdiction over questions of tax. The Court of Justice rejected the objection on the grounds that the argument made was a matter of national law.[85]

Similarly, the Court of Justice does not have jurisdiction to examine whether the referring court has jurisdiction in the main action under international law, including the private international law rules on choice of forum.[86]

In *Celestini*, concerning a dispute between an Italian and a German company, the Commission and the German government argued that the referring Italian court's request for a preliminary ruling was inadmissible, among other things because the Italian courts did not have the necessary international jurisdiction. In relation to this, the Court of Justice stated that, just as it was not for the Court of Justice to examine whether the decision to make a reference was taken in accordance with the national law governing the organisation of the national courts and their procedure, it was also not a matter for the Court of Justice to examine whether the decision to make a reference was taken in accordance with the referring national court's international jurisdiction.[87]

In *Centrosteel*, an Italian company had brought proceedings before an Italian court against an Austrian company. The Commission raised objections to this, arguing that the Italian court's request for a preliminary ruling was inadmissible, because the Italian courts did not have jurisdiction, under private international law, to decide the dispute in the main proceedings. In his Opinion on the case, the Advocate General rejected this argument, as the jurisdiction of the Court of Justice was not dependent on whether the private international law rules on choice of

---

[84] Case 65/81 *Reina* [1982] ECR 33, paras 6–8; Joined Cases C-13/91 and C-133/91 *Debus* [1992] ECR I-3617, para 8; Joined Cases C-322/92, C-333/92, and C-335/92 *Eurico Italia* [1994] ECR I-711, paras 12–13; Case C-472/93 *Luigi Spano* [1995] ECR I-4321, para 16; Case C-33/99 *Fahmi and Esmoris Cerdeiro-Pinedo Amado* [2001] ECR I-2415, para 28; Case C-343/96 *Dilexport* [1999] ECR I-579, para 19; Case C-39/94 *SFEI et al* [1996] ECR I-3547, para 24; and Case C-309/02 *Radlberger Getränkegesellschaft* [2004] ECR I-11763, paras 25–9. On appeals against a national court's decision to refer, see Ch 9, s 2.

[85] Case C-10/92 *Balocchi* [1993] ECR I-5105, paras 15–17.

[86] Case C-213/04 *Burtscher* [2005] ECR I-10309, paras 27 and 31. Obviously, the above does not apply where the referring national court has asked for a preliminary ruling on whether it has jurisdiction to deal with the main action under the Brussels I Regulation or other Community rules.

[87] Case C-105/94 *Celestini* [1997] ECR I-2971, paras 19–20.

forum are fulfilled. This question of jurisdiction was a matter for the national courts which ultimately had responsibility for deciding the main proceedings. The Court of Justice agreed and found the question referred to be admissible under Article 234.[88]

3.2. Administrative authorities and ombudsmen

3.2.1. General observations

As a clear general rule, administrative authorities do not have a right to refer questions for preliminary rulings under Article 234 of the Treaty.

A superior administrative body cannot be regarded as a 'court or tribunal' in relation to the assessment of decisions which are taken by a subordinate administrative body, and where the superior body would itself be a party to the case if its decision were later to be brought before a national court. This applies even if the superior body is regarded as a court or tribunal in the Member State's court system.

In *Corbiau*, the question arose as to whether the Luxembourg *directeur des contributions* constituted a national court for the purposes of Article 234. On the one hand, the *directeur* was regarded as a court under Luxembourg law. Furthermore, the *directeur* exercised his functions within the framework of a national law. The requirement for the body to have a permanent character was also satisfied. On the other hand, the *directeur* was under the immediate authority of the Minister for Finance. The task of the *directeur* was to decide disputes between the administration, of which he was the head, and taxpayers who challenged the decisions which one of his officers had made. If a taxpayer were to choose to appeal against the decision of the *directeur* to the *Conseil d'État*, in many cases it would be the *directeur* who would plead before the *Conseil d'État* in support of the administration of which he was head. In particular the fact that the *directeur* was head of the authority which had taken the decision that was the subject of the appeal led the Court of Justice to the finding that the *directeur* could not be regarded as being impartial in relation to this authority. The Court of Justice therefore held the reference to be inadmissible.[89]

In *Schmid*, a taxpayer had appealed against the Austrian tax authorities' assessment of his tax. The appeal chamber which was to hear the appeal consisted of five members. Two of these members came from the tax authority whose decision was the subject of the appeal. One of these two members was the president of the tax authority, and according to Austrian law, that person should act as chairman for

---

[88] Case C-456/98 *Centrosteel* [2000] ECR I-6007, para 12, together with para 15 in the Advocate General's Opinion.
[89] Case C-24/92 *Corbiau* [1993] ECR I-1277, paras 14–17.

the appeal chamber. The other of these two members still carried out his activities in the tax authority and to this extent was subject to the directions of his hierarchical superior. Furthermore, it was the president of the tax authority who appointed the members of the appeal chambers, and there were no legal provisions to prevent him from changing the composition of an appeal chamber at his discretion with a view to the handling of each appeal, or even during the course of an appeal hearing. The Court of Justice stated that, in the absence of express legislative provisions determining the length of the mandate of appeal chamber members and specifying the conditions of removal, the members could not be said to enjoy sufficient safeguards against undue intervention or pressure on the part of the executive. It also pointed out that the president of the tax authority could bring an appeal against a decision of the appeal chamber, and in so doing defend a different point of view than that of the appeal chamber for which he was chairman. In this situation the president would be subject to directions from the Minister for Finance. In those circumstances, the Court of Justice held, the legal prohibition 'against receiving directions in the exercise of the functions of an appeal chamber member, the fact that, in practice, the President of the [tax] authority does not himself, as, in law, he may, assume the presidency of the appeal chamber and nominates for that purpose another member of the tax authority, and the fact that the second member of the chamber belonging to the tax authority does not intervene on the questions and procedures with which he is usually involved within that administrative authority do not suffice to guarantee the independence of an appeal chamber'. As a consequence, the Court of Justice held that it did not have jurisdiction to give a preliminary ruling on the question referred.[90]

In *Giant*, an undertaking had appealed to the Belgian *Bestendige Deputatie van de Provincieraad van Brabant* on the levying of a tax by a local government authority. This type of body was established by each Belgian provincial council electing from among its members *bestendige deputatie* to act under the chairmanship of the Governor of the province, who was appointed by the King. The role of the *bestendige deputatie* was mainly administrative, but for historical reasons it also had jurisdiction to decide on disputes concerning local taxes. This jurisdiction was laid down by law and was exercised at public hearings in accordance with an adversarial procedure. Reasons for the decisions had to be given, and the decisions could be brought before an appeal court or the Belgian *Cour de cassation*. Without any express argumentation the Court of Justice gave a preliminary ruling on the question referred by the *Bestendige Deputatie van de Provincieraad van Brabant*.[91]

---

[90] Case C-516/99 *Schmid* [2002] ECR I-4573, paras 34–44.
[91] Case C-109/90 *Giant* [1991] ECR I-1385.

In *Syfait*, the Greek Competition Commission (*Epitropi Antagonismou*) referred a question for a preliminary ruling. The Competition Commission was permanently established by law, it made judicial decisions on the basis of legal rules, and it had sole competence to impose penalties for infringements of Greek competition law. The Competition Commission had nine members, appointed for three-year periods. Four members were appointed on the nomination of trade union and commercial organisations, one was required to be an academic economist, one was required to be an academic lawyer, one was to be from the Greek State's court service, and the last two were to be persons of recognised reputation and relevant experience. The law laid down that the members were to benefit from independence in their work for the Competition Commission. There was a secretariat associated with the Competition Commission. This secretariat was responsible for the investigation of cases, and the preparation of recommendations to the Competition Commission for its decisions. The chairman of the Competition Commission was the head of the secretariat, and was thus formally responsible for its management. In its reference to the Court of Justice, the Competition Commission stated that the secretariat acted independently of the Competition Commission itself, but no reference was made to rules or procedures which ensured this independence. The Court of Justice found that the Competition Commission did not qualify as a 'court or tribunal' within the meaning of Article 234. In support of this finding it referred to four factors of which three concerned the Competition Commission's independence. First, that the Greek Minister for Development was empowered to review the lawfulness of the decisions of the Competition Commission. Second, there were no particular safeguards in respect of the dismissal or the termination of the appointment of the members of the Competition Commission. Third, there was a functional link between the Competition Commission and its secretariat, so it was not a clearly distinct third party in relation to the State body which, by virtue of its role, may be akin to a party in the course of competition proceedings. As the fourth factor, the Court of Justice observed that the European Commission had powers to remove the jurisdiction of the Greek Competition Commission in a given case so that the proceedings initiated before that authority would not lead to a decision of a judicial nature. The Court of Justice therefore declined to answer the preliminary question.[92]

The Court's reasoning in *Syfait* seems to indicate a certain tightening up of the requirements for national bodies which can use the procedure in Article 234.[93]

---

[92] Case C-53/03 *Syfait* [2005] ECR I-4609, paras 29–37, but compare this with paras 26–32 in the Advocate General's Opinion.

[93] Advocate General Colomer's Opinion in Case C-259/04 *Emanuel* [2006] ECR I-3089, para 26; and G Anagnostaras, 'Preliminary problems and jurisdiction uncertainties: the admissibility of questions referred by bodies performing quasi-judicial functions' (2005) 30 EL Rev 878, 890.

In the following section we examine the limited number of situations in which administrative bodies will be able to make a reference for a preliminary ruling.

3.2.2. *Administrative appeal boards*

Administrative appeal boards can satisfy the conditions for being considered a 'court or tribunal' for the purposes of Article 234, even if they are considered administrative bodies under national law.[94] For instance, on several occasions the Court of Justice has given preliminary rulings on questions referred by Member States' public procurement appeal boards.[95]

In order to establish whether an administrative appeal board qualifies as a 'court or tribunal', the Court of Justice makes a factual assessment of whether there is the necessary independence. Here it is the totality of the national rules for securing this independence that is decisive. In contrast, it is not important whether the rules are laid down in one law or another.[96]

In practice it may be difficult to determine whether an administrative appeal board has such independence that it can be regarded as a 'court or tribunal' for the purposes of Article 234. Moreover, even minor changes in the rules of procedure for an already established board can mean that it either gains or loses the right to make references for preliminary rulings. Likewise, if an administrative appeal board changes from being responsible for both processing cases and making decisions, to only making review decisions, it may thereby become entitled to make references.

Köllenberger and Atzwanger illustrates how difficult it can be to establish whether an administrative appeal board has the necessary independence to qualify as a 'court or tribunal'. Here Advocate General Saggio reviewed the rules which regulated the independence of the members of the Public Procurement Office of the

---

As pointed out by C Naômé, *Le Renvoi préjudiciel en droit européen* (2007) 88, the importance of the ruling in *Syfait* should not be underestimated. The case prompted discussion in the legal literature, see A Komninos, 'Article 234 EC and National Competition Authorities in the Era of Decentralisation' (2004) 29 EL Rev 106.

[94] Case C-416/96 *Eddline El-Yassini* [1999] ECR I-1209, paras 16–22; Joined Cases C-9/97 and C-118/97 *Jokela* [1998] ECR I-6267, paras 17–24; Joined Cases C-110/98–147/98 *Gabalfrisa and others* [2000] ECR I-1577, paras 33–41; Case C-407/98 *Abrahamson* [2000] ECR I-5539, paras 28–38; and implicitly Case C-361/97 *Nour* [1998] ECR I-3101. With particular regard to EEA law, see Case E-1/94 *Restamark* [1994–95] EFTA Court Report 17, concerning a request for a preliminary ruling from the Appeals Committee at the Finnish Board of Customs (*Tullilautakunta*).

[95] Case C-275/98 *Unitron Scandinavia* [1999] ECR I-8291 (the Danish Procurement Review Board); Case C-54/96 *Dorsch Consult* [1997] ECR I-4961 (the German Federal Public Procurement Awards Supervisory Board); Case C-92/00 *HI* [2002] ECR I-5553 (the Public Procurement Review Chamber of the Vienna Region); and Case C-411/00 *Felix Swoboda* [2002] ECR I-10567 (the Austrian Federal Public Procurement Office).

[96] Case C-54/96 *Dorsch Consult* [1997] ECR I-4961, para 34.

Land of Tyrol. The Advocate General found that the national rules were so vague that they did not sufficiently protect the members of the office from undue interference. This led the Advocate General to conclude that the body did not have such independence as to enable it to be classified as a 'court or tribunal'. The Court of Justice arrived at the opposite conclusion. It first made a review of the provisions that were relevant to the members' independence and found that these provisions taken together could not support the conclusion reached by the Advocate General. As for the possibility of improper interference, the Court of Justice added that it is not for it to infer that the provisions for the removal of the members of a body, such as the Public Procurement Office of the Land of Tyrol, would be applied in a manner contrary to the Austrian constitution and the principles of a State governed by the rule of law.[97]

The judgment in *Köllenberger and Atzwanger* illustrates that, in relation to the independence criterion, there appears to be an assumption that a Member State will respect the independence of an administrative appeal board.[98] There are thus limits as to how closely the Court of Justice will examine the provisions which may be relevant to formal independence.[99]

In *Dorsch Consult*, the German Federal Public Procurement Awards Supervisory Board was linked to the organisational structure of the Federal Cartel Office (*Bundeskartellamt*), which in turn was subject to supervision by the Ministry for Economic Affairs. The terms of office of the chairman and the official assessors were not fixed, and the provisions for guaranteeing impartiality only applied to lay members. The Court of Justice did not find these factors decisive in assessing the independence of the body, as there were other rules which secured this satisfactorily.[100]

3.2.3. *Advisory bodies*

An advisory body, which only has the task of giving its opinion as part of an administrative process, does not constitute a 'court or tribunal' of a Member State. This is so regardless of whether the members of the body are representatives of public or private interests, regardless of whether they have legal training, or may even act as judges in other situations, and regardless of whether the members of the body are given absolute independence in carrying out their tasks.

---

97 Case C-103/97 *Köllensperger and Atzwanger* [1999] ECR I-551, paras 19–24.
98 T Tridimas, 'Knocking on Heaven's Door: Fragmentation, Efficiency and Defiance in the Preliminary Reference Procedure' (2003) 40 CML Rev 9, 29, who describes the judgment in *Köllensberger and Atzwanger* as being a relaxation in relation to previous practice.
99 Case C-407/98 *Abrahamson and Anderson* [2000] ECR I-5539, paras 36–7.
100 Case C-54/96 *Dorsch Consult* [1997] ECR I-4961, para 34.

In *Greis Unterweger*, the Italian Consultative Commission for Currency Offences (*Commissione Consultiva per le Infrazioni Valutarie*) referred a number of questions to the Court of Justice. The job of the Consultative Commission was to give reasoned advisory opinions to the Italian Treasury Minister on the sanctions which could be imposed on persons who breached the Italian foreign currency regulations. Since the Consultative Commission did not resolve disputes, the Court of Justice declined to answer the questions.[101]

In certain situations the Court of Justice has, however, been willing to regard a body as being covered by Article 234 if, while formally the body only gives advisory opinions, in fact its opinions are normally relied upon, so that it does in reality resolve the given dispute.

In *Garofalo*, a group of doctors brought an 'extraordinary petition' against an administrative decision. The petition was made to the Italian Minister for Health, who asked the Italian Council of State (*Consiglio di Stato*) for its opinion. With a view to giving such an opinion, the Council of State referred some questions to the Court of Justice, but the Council of State was in doubt about whether it qualified as a 'court or tribunal' for the purposes of Article 234. The Council of State had two different functions. First, it gave rulings in second and final instance on appeals against judgments of regional administrative courts in proceedings concerning administrative acts. In respect of this function it was not disputed that the Council of State could make references for preliminary rulings. Second, the Council of State gave opinions in relation to extraordinary petitions. It was as part of the last-mentioned function that it referred the preliminary questions to the Court of Justice. The Court of Justice found that the proceedings of the Council of State in dealing with cases in connection with extraordinary petitions corresponded in all important respects to the proceedings of the ordinary courts. As far as extraordinary petitions were concerned, a reference to the Council of State was compulsory and its opinion, based solely on the application of rules of law, formed the basis for a decision which was formally adopted by the President of the Italian Republic. Such an opinion was an integral part of a procedure which was the only one capable of resolving a dispute between private individuals and the administration. A decision which did not conform to the opinion of the Council of State could be adopted only after deliberation within the Italian Council of Ministers and had to be duly reasoned. On this basis the Court of Justice found that the Council of State qualified as a national court for the purposes of Article 234.[102]

---

[101] Case 318/85 *Greis Unterweger* [1986] ECR 955, para 4.
[102] Joined Cases C-69/96–79/96 *Garofalo* [1997] ECR I-5603, paras 17–27. See also P Lasok, *The European Court of Justice—Practice and Procedure* (1994) 556.

Nederlandse Spoorwegen concerned a reference for a preliminary ruling by the Netherlands Council of State (*Raad van State*). Formally, this was only an advisory body for the Crown (ie the Netherlands head of state) in the area of administrative cases, which was the area concerned in the case in question. Nevertheless, the Court of Justice chose to give a preliminary ruling without even addressing the question of whether the Netherlands Council of State was entitled to refer questions for preliminary rulings. In contrast, in his Opinion the Advocate General argued that the procedural guarantees and the powers of the referring department of the Council of State and the Crown, and the powers to annul administrative acts, must lead to the conclusion that the body was in effect a 'court or tribunal' for the purposes of Article 234.[103]

Garofalo and *Nederlandse Spoorwegen* indicate that the Court of Justice is prepared to allow the highest national constitutional bodies to make references for preliminary rulings where in fact they give binding rulings.[104] On the other hand, if a preliminary question arises in a case where it is obvious that such body is not giving a binding ruling, it does not seem likely the Court of Justice will be willing to answer.[105] In any event, there are reasons to be cautious about applying the Court of Justice's reasoning in the two above cases to other national bodies which do not have a similar supreme position in constitutional law.[106]

3.2.4. Ombudsmen

It is a general characteristic of the Member States' ombudsmen that they can make critical assessments and issue recommendations whereas they cannot issue binding orders. Thus, if a citizen files a complaint against a public authority with the national ombudsman, the public authority is not legally obliged to comply with the ombudsman's subsequent opinion in the case.[107] Neither can the successful complainant require the Member State's judiciary to enforce the opinion. If a public authority does not comply with an ombudsman's opinion, the only legal remedy will therefore be to bring legal proceedings against the public authority

---

[103] Case 36/73 *Nederlandse Spoorwegen* [1973] ECR 1299 (see in particular the Advocate General's Opinion, pp 1317–20).

[104] An overview of the relation between the constitutional courts of the Member States and Art 234 is provided by H Kanninen, Association of the Councils of State and Supreme Administrative Jurisdiction of the European Union, 18th Colloquium 2002, General Report on the Colloquium subject 'The Preliminary Reference to the Court of Justice of the European Communities', 19ff.

[105] For an example of this distinction, see the account provided by P Gilliaux, *Le renvoi préjudiciel à la Cour de justice des Communautés européennes—Rapport belge* (2002) 4.

[106] See in this respect *Re Czech Sugar Quotas* [2006] 3 CMLR 15 at paras 47–9, where the Czech Constitutional Court observes that it is unclear whether it constitutes a 'court or tribunal' within the meaning of Art 234. In this respect it points to a rather inconclusive practice amongst other Member State constitutional courts.

[107] The importance of this criterion was stressed in Case C-161/03 *Cafom and Samsung* (ECJ 11 July 2003) reported by C Naômé, *Le Renvoi préjudiciel en droit européen* (2007) 86.

(or possibly the ombudsman) before the ordinary courts in order to have the latter decide the case. It follows that ombudsmen will not be competent to refer preliminary questions to the Court of Justice.[108]

Nevertheless, in some respects the workings of ombudsmen resemble those of an administrative court and generally speaking public authorities comply with the opinions of the ombudsman. This means that the national ombudsmen have a legitimate need for authoritative advice on the correct interpretation of Community law. To some extent this need may be met by the possibility of making a query in order to obtain a report from the European Ombudsman.[109] Normally, the European Ombudsman simply forwards the opinion produced by the relevant Community institution and his reports do not have the same legal authority as does a preliminary ruling. It has therefore been argued, *de lege ferenda*, that ombudsmen should be allowed the possibility of making preliminary references to the Court of Justice.[110]

3.3. Private bodies

3.3.1. *Private disciplinary bodies*

The question of defining a 'court or tribunal' also arises in connection with industry or professional bodies which have disciplinary authority over those who carry on business in a given commercial sector, and to whom a Member State's public authorities have assigned the task of implementing and/or administering Community law rules. At least to the extent that such bodies do not make decisions on the rights and obligations of individual members of the group concerned, they cannot refer questions for preliminary rulings under Article 234.

In *Borker*, a member of the Paris bar had asked the Bar Council of the *Cour de Paris* to determine the conditions for the pursuit of his activities as a lawyer by way of provision of services before any of the courts of a Member State. With a view to being able to answer this question, the Bar Council decided to make a reference to the Court of Justice for a preliminary ruling. The Court of Justice held that it can only be requested to give a preliminary ruling under Article 234 by a national court which is called upon to give judgment in proceedings intended to lead to a

---

[108] However, compare with H Rasmussen, *FIDE 1980, vol 1* (1980) 313. D Anderson and M Demetriou, *References to the European Court* (2002) 45, refer to ombudsman institutions as 'borderline cases'.

[109] See Ch 1, s 5.2.

[110] M Broberg, 'Preliminary References by Public Administrative Bodies: When Are Public Administrative Bodies Competent to Make Preliminary References to the European Court of Justice?' (2009) 15 European Public Law 207, 220ff.

decision of a judicial nature. This was not the situation in this case, as the Bar Council did not have before it a case which it was under a legal duty to try.[111]

Where a body under normal circumstances does not make decisions of a judicial character, but exceptionally in the actual case it is to make a judicial decision, it can ask for a preliminary ruling according to the procedure in Article 234 provided that it fulfils the organisational criteria for being considered a 'court or tribunal'.

This seems to have been the situation in *Bauer* where the Belgian Francophone Appeals Committee of the Association of Architects made a reference for a preliminary ruling.[112]

3.3.2. *Private professional bodies*

Sometimes a Member State entrusts a private professional body with the task of implementing Community rules, and in conjunction with the public authorities this body creates an appeal procedure which can affect the rights granted by Community law.

This was the situation in *Broekmeulen*. Here the Dutch General Practitioners Registration Committee had refused an application from a doctor of Dutch nationality for registration as a general practitioner. The Committee was appointed by the Royal Netherlands Society for the Promotion of Medicine, and registration by the Committee was effectively a pre-requirement for practising as a general practitioner in the Netherlands. In principle, the applicant could appeal to the ordinary Dutch courts against the refusal, but there had never previously been such an appeal. Instead, all appeals had been referred to the Appeals Committee for General Medicine, which was also appointed by the Royal Netherlands Society for the Promotion of Medicine. According to the Netherlands government, the decisions of this Appeals Committee had not been tried in the ordinary courts either. The Court of Justice found that it could give preliminary rulings on questions referred by a professional body where: (1) under the legal system of the Member State, the body must implement provisions made by Community institutions under a degree of governmental supervision; and (2) the body, together with the public authorities, creates appeal procedures which may affect the exercise of rights granted by Community law. In the absence, in practice, of any right of appeal to the ordinary Dutch courts, in a matter involving the application of

---

[111] Case 138/80 *Borker* [1980] ECR 1975, para 4. Compare with Case C-447/93 *Dreesen* [1994] ECR I-4087 (French Language Appeals Committee of the Architects' Association, Liège, Belgium), and Case C-55/94 *Gebhard* [1995] ECR I-4165 (National Council of the Bar of Milan).

[112] Case C-166/91 *Bauer* [1992] ECR I-2797. See similarly Case 14/86 *Pretore di Salò* [1987] ECR 2545, para 7.

Community law the Appeals Committee was entitled to refer questions for preliminary rulings under Article 234.[113]

In other words, the Court of Justice took the position that to ensure that the provisions adopted by the Community institutions were implemented in their entirety, a private professional body could be entitled to make a reference for a preliminary ruling, as long as there was no possibility of bringing the case before the ordinary courts so that the decision of the body had to be regarded as final. Whilst the ruling in *Broekmeulen* has not been overturned in the Court's subsequent case law, it does not sit comfortably with the Court's more recent practice.[114] Therefore, when applying the ruling considerable caution should be exercised.[115]

3.3.3. *Management and Labour (social partners)*

The EC Treaty in Articles 138 and 139 has established a procedure whereby management and labour are given a key role in the drafting of new Community legal measures in the field of social policy. Essentially, where the Commission initiates new legislation in the social policy field, European management and labour organisations are given the possibility of taking over this initiative and jointly deciding how to regulate the matter in question. If management and labour conclude such an agreement at Community level, it may be implemented either by management and labour and the Member States, or by 'a Council Decision'; in practice it will generally be implemented by a Council directive to which the agreement is annexed.[116] For example, in the Nordic Member States interpretation of such a directive (the annexed agreement) will primarily lie with the national social partners and only rarely are questions of interpretation likely to be brought before the national courts or industrial arbitration tribunals. Nevertheless, management and labour organisations do not qualify as 'a court or tribunal' within the meaning of Article 234 and therefore they are not competent to make preliminary references.

4. The Term 'of a Member State'

Not every body which satisfies the criteria referred to above, and as such may be considered a 'court or tribunal' for the purposes of Article 234, can refer questions to the Court of Justice for preliminary rulings. This right only applies to courts or tribunals 'of a Member State'. The Court of Justice will of its own motion examine

---

[113] Case 246/80 *Broekmeulen* [1981] ECR 2311.

[114] See Case C-24/92 *Corbiau* [1993] ECR I-1277; and K Lenaerts et al, *Procedural Law of the European Union* (2006) 37–9.

[115] See also s 2.9 above.

[116] Art 139(2) of the EC Treaty. See also Ch 4, s 3.2.2.

whether the referring body satisfies this condition.[117] Hence, if for example two undertakings enter into a commercial agreement and in this connection agree that disputes shall be decided according to English law, and that the forum to decide any such dispute shall be a court of a third country, any questions of Community law which may arise from the case cannot be referred to the Court of Justice by the court of that third country under Article 234.

It is for the Member States to define the extent of their territories. Article 234 applies to bodies whose jurisdiction covers a whole Member State or parts thereof. The Court of Justice has accepted references from national courts which are not located in the territory of the Member State, but where the EC Treaty applies in whole or in part. It is not fully clear from these judgments how the boundaries are to be drawn, but the Court of Justice has given weight to the need to ensure the uniform application of Community law rules.[118] This suggests that Article 234 must apply to national courts in all cases where all or part of the Treaty applies, regardless of the geographic location of the court.[119] Indeed, the Court of Justice appears to have adopted a wide interpretation of what is meant by 'of a Member State', where the most important factor is trying to ensure the uniform interpretation and application of Community law.[120]

National courts in overseas countries or territories that are associated with the Community are covered by the term 'court or tribunal of a Member State'. The Court of Justice thus has jurisdiction to give rulings on questions from such national courts, to the extent that the questions concern Community law rules which apply in the overseas countries or territories concerned.[121]

---

[117] Case 65/81 *Reina* [1982] ECR 33, para 7.

[118] Case C-355/89 *Barr and Montrose Holdings* [1991] ECR I-3479, paras 9–10. A summary of the judgment is given immediately below.

[119] See in support of this the Opinion of Advocate General Jacobs in Case C-355/89 *Barr and Montrose Holdings* [1991] ECR I-3479, para 18. The geographic scope of application of the EC Treaty is laid down in Art 299 of the Treaty.

[120] T C Hartley, *The Foundations of European Community Law* (2007) 277. See also C Barnard and E Sharpston, 'The Changing Face of Article 177 References' (1997) 34 CML Rev 1113, 1135. A Arnull, 'The evolution of the Court's jurisdiction under Article 177 EEC' (1993) 18 EL Rev 129, 133 identifies four categories where courts located outside the European Union have a right to make references: (1) The French overseas territories of Guadeloupe, French Guyana, Martinique, Réunion, and Saint-Pierre and Miquelon; (2) the overseas countries and territories listed in Annex II to the EC Treaty (Art 299(3)); (3) European territories for whose external relations a Member State is responsible (Art 299(4)); and (4) the Channel Islands and the Isle of Man (Art 299(5)(c)). On this basis, Arnull concludes that, among others, the courts of Monaco, San Marino, the Vatican State, and Andorra are not entitled to make references.

[121] Joined Cases 100/89 and 101/89 *Kaefer* [1990] ECR I-4647, paras 6–10; and Case 260/90 *Leplat* [1992] ECR I-643, paras 7–9.

With regard to a national court in a new Member State, the right to make a reference depends on whether the State in question was a Member State of the EU at the time when the reference is made to the Court of Justice for a preliminary ruling.[122] The same must apply if a Member State or a territory of a Member State leaves the EU.

A court in a third country which has an association agreement with the EU is not entitled to make a reference under Article 234, even if the question for a preliminary ruling concerns the interpretation or validity of the association agreement.[123] However, there is nothing to prevent such association agreements from providing that the courts in the third country in question shall have the right to make references to the Court of Justice for preliminary rulings, provided that the Court of Justice's rulings will be binding on the referring courts.[124]

If a country which has entered into an association agreement with the EU subsequently becomes a Member State, there may be situations where that country's courts wish to make preliminary references on the interpretation or validity of the association agreement. Even though association agreements constitute part of Community law in the Member States, this is not the case in the associated State before that State accedes to the EU. The Court of Justice only has jurisdiction to interpret association agreements in connection with a preliminary ruling in respect of the application of such an agreement to situations which are subject to the legal system of the Community. This means that the Court's jurisdiction to interpret Community law, in relation to its application to a new Member State, only arises from the date of that Member State's accession.

In *Salzmann II*, an Austrian court asked the Court of Justice to give an interpretation of a part of the EEA Agreement. If the Court answered the question, it would rule on that agreement's effects, within the Austrian legal system, during the period prior to Austria's accession to the European Union. Even though the EEA Agreement forms an integral part of Community law so that it comes within the jurisdiction of the Court of Justice as regards the Agreement's application in the new Member States, this only takes effect from the date of their accession. Since the relevant provision of the EEA Agreement would apply to facts that had arisen prior to Austria's accession to the Community, the Court had no jurisdiction to answer the question submitted.[125]

---

[122] Here there is only a consideration of the question when a referring body qualifies as a court 'of a Member State'. A different question is which matters can be referred to the Court of Justice. The Court of Justice cannot consider questions relating to factual circumstances which arose before the State in question acceded to the EU, so that the facts concerned were not subject to Community law on the material date. See further below Ch 4, s 5.4.

[123] T C Hartley, *The Foundations of European Community Law* (2007) 277 with footnote 70.

[124] Opinion 1/91 *EEA Agreement* [1991] ECR I-6079, paras 54–65.

[125] Case C-300/01 *Salzmann II* [2003] ECR I-4899, paras 68–9.

Even if a given territory is not covered by an association agreement, its national courts are not entirely prevented from making a preliminary reference. Hence, it appears that such a reference can be made where the national court asks a question about the interpretation of a Community act which regulates relations between the Community and the territory, or the interpretation of Community provisions to which the Community act refers, as well as acts of Community institutions adopted on the basis thereof.

In *Barr and Montrose Holdings*, a prosecution was brought before the Deputy High Bailiff's Court in Douglas in the Isle of Man against an employee and an employer for breach of a number of provisions laid down by Tynwald (the Parliament of the Isle of Man). The defendants argued that they should be found not guilty, because the legislation in question was contrary to Protocol No 3 to the Act concerning the Conditions of Accession of the United Kingdom of Great Britain and Northern Ireland to the European Communities. The Deputy High Bailiff's Court therefore referred the question to the Court of Justice for a preliminary ruling. Before the Court of Justice could consider the question, it first had to decide whether the Deputy High Bailiff's Court was entitled to make such a reference, even if it did not form part of the United Kingdom court system. The Court of Justice noted first that, according to Article 299(6)(c) of the EC Treaty, the Treaty's provisions are only applicable to the Channel Islands and the Isle of Man to the extent provided for by Protocol No 3. Moreover, according to Article 1(3) of the Treaty of Accession, the provisions concerning the powers and jurisdiction of the institutions of the Communities are to apply in respect of Protocol No 3. Accordingly, the jurisdiction in preliminary ruling proceedings conferred on the Court of Justice by Article 234 of the Treaty extends to Protocol No 3. In addition to this, it would be impossible to ensure the uniform application of Protocol No 3 in the Isle of Man if its courts were unable to refer questions to the Court of Justice concerning the interpretation of that protocol, the interpretation and validity of the Community legislation to which that protocol refers, and the interpretation and validity of measures adopted by the Community institutions on the basis of Protocol No 3. In order to ensure the uniform application of that protocol, the Deputy High Bailiff's Court had to be regarded as a national court under Article 234 of the Treaty.[126]

If a national court is located in an overseas country or territory that is not associated with the European Union, and where Community law does not otherwise

---

[126] Case C-355/89 *Barr and Montrose Holdings* [1991] ECR I-3479, paras 6–10. See similarly para 24 of the Advocate General's Opinion in Case C-171/96 *Pereira Roque* [1998] ECR I-4607; and Case C-293/02 *Jersey Produce Marketing Organisation* [2005] ECR I-9543 (implicitly).

apply, it must be assumed that such courts will not be able to make references for preliminary rulings.[127]

International courts, such as the European Court of Human Rights, must be regarded as prevented from making a reference irrespective of whether they are situated in a Member State or not. On the other hand, national courts that are an integrated part of the national court systems of more than one Member State can make references for preliminary rulings, as long as the national court is not also part of the court system of a third country.[128]

5. Other Forms of Preliminary References

5.1. Overview

In Chapter 1, Section 3, it was shown that preliminary references to the Court of Justice may be made on legal bases other than Article 234. Below we examine which courts are competent to make preliminary references under the Euratom Treaty (Section 5.2), in the field of justice and home affairs (Section 5.3), and under those conventions that provide for the possibility of making preliminary references (Section 5.4).

5.2. Euratom Treaty

Just like Article 234 of the EC Treaty, Article 150 of the Euratom Treaty refers to 'any court or tribunal of a Member State'. The identical formulations are to be construed in the same way.

5.3. Justice and Home Affairs

5.3.1. Article 68 of the EC Treaty

Article 68 of the EC Treaty lays down that Article 234 shall apply to the EC Treaty's Title IV on visas, asylum, immigration, and other policies related to free movement of persons. Article 68 goes on to establish that only those courts or tribunals 'against whose decisions there is no judicial remedy under national law' may make a preliminary reference under that provision.[129] This means that only courts of last instance as defined in Article 234 are competent to make preliminary

---

[127] However, for a somewhat more sceptical view see P Oliver, 'Recevabilité des questions préju-dicielles: La jurisprudence des années 1990' (2001) 37 Cahiers de droit européen 15, 23.

[128] See further s 3.1.2 above.

[129] Case C-51/03 *Georgescu* [2004] ECR I-3203, paras 29–30; Case C-555/03 *Warbecq* [2004] ECR I-6041, paras 12–13; and Case C-2 24/02 *Marseille Fret* [2002] ECR I-3383, paras 14–15, where, in connection with references from national lower courts for preliminary rulings under Art 68 of the EC Treaty, the Court of Justice rejected the references and in so doing only decided on

references under Article 68. In this respect, the Court of Justice will admit the reference if the referring court indicates in its reference for a preliminary ruling that the decision it will deliver in the main proceedings will be final and that it is not possible to appeal against it.[130]

Where a preliminary reference is received from a court that is not one of last instance the Court of Justice will only be competent to answer those of the questions on the EC Treaty which do not concern that Treaty's Title IV.[131]

5.3.2. *Article 35 of the EU Treaty*

Article 35 of the Treaty on European Union provides that the Court of Justice shall have jurisdiction to give preliminary rulings with respect to legal measures established under that Treaty's Title VI on police and judicial cooperation in criminal matters. However, the provision only gives national courts competence to make a preliminary reference if the Member State in question has made a declaration accepting the jurisdiction of the Court of Justice.[132] Such declaration may either confer competence to make references on any of a Member State's courts or only on its courts of last instance.[133] In either case Article 234's definition of 'court or tribunal' applies.[134]

Where a reference is made under Article 35 of the EU Treaty, the system in Article 234 of the EC Treaty will be applicable, subject to the conditions laid down in the former provision. Moreover, the Court of Justice's practice concerning the procedures for questions referred for preliminary rulings under Article 234 of the EC Treaty can in principle be applied to requests for preliminary rulings made under Article 35 of the EU Treaty.[135] This means that the definition under Article 234 of the EC Treaty of 'a court or tribunal' competent to make a preliminary reference equally applies vis-à-vis Article 35 of the EU Treaty.[136]

---

the question of whether it was competent to give preliminary rulings. See also Advocate General Colomer at paras 33–6 in Case C-14/08 *Roda Golf & Beach Resort* (ECJ 25 June 2009).

[130] Case C-14/08 *Roda Golf and Beach Resort* (ECJ 25 June 2009), paras 24–30.

[131] Case C-228/06 *Soysal* (ECJ 1 19 February 2009), paras 38–42.

[132] Case C-66/08 *Kozlowski* (ECJ 17 July 2008), para 12; and Case C-404/07 *Katz* (ECJ 9 October 2008), para 27.

[133] At times close examination of the declaration(s) made by a Member State is necessary to determine both the type of the declaration and the time when it was made. See for example Advocate General Kokott in her Opinion in Case C-404/07 *Katz* (ECJ 9 October 2008), paras 16–21.

[134] See further Ch 1, s 3.3.

[135] S Peers, 'Who's Judging the Watchmen? The Judicial System of the "Area of Freedom Security and Justice"' in P Eeckhout and T Tridimas (eds), *Yearbook of European Law 1998* (1999) 337, 380 observes that it is logical to transpose the case law on Art 234 of the EC Treaty to Art 35 of the EU Treaty.

[136] Case C-105/03 *Pupino* [2005] ECR I-5285, paras 19 and 28–9.

5.3.3. *Criticism of the regimes applying to justice and home affairs*

The different regimes which apply depending on whether a measure has been adopted under the third pillar (justice and home affairs) or the first pillar (Community matters other than those covered by Title IV of the EC Treaty) have been criticised. Thus, the various rules surrounding the Court's jurisdiction have been held to result in a patchwork system that is widely regarded as opaque, incoherent, and generally unsatisfactory,[137] and Title IV of the EC Treaty has been said to represent the most severe threat in the history of the Community to the uniformity of Community law.[138] Moreover, it has been argued that among the many problems associated with the limitations of Article 68 EC and Article 35 EU, their detrimental effects for the rule of law are paramount.[139] Thus, it has been held that

> [i]n particular, with the conversion of the Brussels Convention into a Community instrument, the interpretation of the 'Brussels I' Regulation fell within Article 68 EC with anomalous results: the scope of the ECJ was narrowed to receiving references from the highest courts only, in contrast to its Convention format under which national appellate courts were also included.[140]

Indeed, the criticism of the fragmentation of the preliminary reference scheme has been overwhelming in the legal literature.[141]

---

[137] House of Lords, European Union Committee, 10th Report of Session 2007–08, The Treaty of Lisbon: an impact assessment, p 124. See likewise D M Curtin and R H van Ooik, 'Revamping the European Union's enforcement systems with a view to eastern enlargement', WRR Working Documents no W110, The Hague 2000, p 93.

[138] S Peers, 'Who's Judging the Watchmen? The Judicial System of the "Area of Freedom Security and Justice"' in P Eeckhout and T Tridimas (eds), *Yearbook of European Law 1998* (1999) 337, 356–7.

[139] K Lenaerts, 'The Unity of European Law and the Overload of the ECJ—The System of Preliminary Rulings Revisited' in I Pernice, J Kokott, and C Saunders (eds), *The Future of the European Judicial System in a Comparative Perspective* (2006) 211, 216.

[140] Ibid, 214.

[141] Similar criticisms have been adduced by P J G Kapteyn, 'Administration of Justice' in P J G Kapteyn et al (eds), 'The Law of the European Union and the European Communities' (2008) 500; S Peers, 'Who's Judging the Watchmen? The Judicial System of the "Area of Freedom Security and Justice"' in P Eeckhout and T Tridimas (eds), *Yearbook of European Law 1998* (1999) 337, 351; K Lenaerts et al, *Procedural Law of the European Union* (2006) 513; T Tridimas, 'Knocking on Heaven's Door: Fragmentation, Efficiency and Defiance in the Preliminary Reference Procedure' (2003) 40 CML Rev 9, 14; A Albors-Llorens, 'Changes in the Jurisdiction of the European Court of Justice under the Treaty of Amsterdam' (1998) 35 CML Rev 1273, 1288; M Petite, 'La Cour de justice dans la coopération judiciaire: réalités et perspectives?' speech given at Seminar of the members of the European Union Supreme Judicial Courts Network and representatives of the European Union institutions, Tuesday 22 November 2005, Brussels, pp 8–9 (available at <http://www.rpcsjue.org/IMG/pdf/petite.pdf>) and by the Commission in Communication from the Commission to the European Parliament, the Council, the European Economic and Social Committee, the Committee of the Regions and the Court of Justice of the European Communities—Adaptation of the provisions of Title IV of the Treaty establishing the European Community relating to the jurisdiction of the Court of Justice with a view to ensuring more effective judicial protection of 28 June 2006 (COM(2006) 346 (final)), pp 7–8.

Whilst it is difficult not to agree that the limitations on the access to make preliminary references are detrimental to the rule of law, it appears to us to be less obvious
that in every respect Article 68 of the EC Treaty constitutes a step backwards.

Under the Brussels Convention supreme courts and courts 'sitting in an appellate
capacity' were competent to make preliminary references. In contrast, Article 68
provides that only a court of last instance will be competent to refer. Thus, on the
one hand Article 68 limits the right to refer of courts which hear a case on appeal,
but which are not sitting as courts of last instance. On the other hand, where a case
is heard by only a single instance court (other than a supreme court) without a
right of appeal, Article 68 signifies an increased access to make preliminary references as compared with what applied under the Brussels Convention. In the latter
situation under the Brussels Convention there would be no possibility of making
a preliminary reference as part of the main proceedings. In contrast, there will
always be a possibility of making a preliminary reference with regard to a national
case covered by Article 68. In our opinion, this improvement must be taken into
account when comparing the system under Article 68 with that which applied
under the Brussels Convention.

The picture becomes even more opaque if we compare the access to make preliminary references under Article 68 of the EC Treaty with Article 35 of the EU Treaty.
Of those Member States which have made a declaration allowing their courts to
make preliminary references under Article 35, all but one have chosen to allow
any of their courts to make such a reference. Hence, in this situation Article 68
appears as a retrograde step when compared with Article 35. A number of Member
States have not made a declaration, however. The courts in these Member States
therefore cannot make preliminary references under Article 35 and so the limited
access provided under Article 68 may appear to be an improvement.[142]

5.4. Conventions

In Chapter 1, Section 3.5, above, a number of Community conventions were
listed. These conventions provide for the possibility of making preliminary
references to the Court of Justice. A few of these conventions limit access to make
preliminary references to the highest national courts and to courts which are hearing cases on appeal.[143] Most of the conventions, however, allow the Member States

---

[142] Art 42 of the EU Treaty (the so-called 'grande passerelle' clause) allows for a transfer of areas
falling under Title VI of the EU Treaty to Title IV of the EC Treaty. Such transfer may increase the
competence of some national courts, but may restrict the competence of other such courts, cf A
Jour-Schröder and C Konow, 'Die Passerelle des Art. 42 EU-Vertrag' (2006) 18 Europäische
Zeitschrift für Wirtschaftsrecht 550, 553. So far Art 42 has not been used.
[143] Brussels Convention on Jurisdiction and Enforcement of Judgments in Civil and Commercial
Matters together with Protocol concerning the interpretation by the Court of Justice of the
Convention of 27 September 1968 on jurisdiction and the enforcement of judgments in civil and

a certain choice as to what national courts shall be competent to make preliminary references regarding the convention in question.[144]

6. References from a National Court that May not Make a Reference under National Law

Situations can arise where, under national law, a national court may not make a reference for a preliminary ruling. This situation may exist where the national court is prevented from making a reference under national law, or where a higher national court has previously held that a disputed national provision complies with Community law. These two situations are examined in the following section.

---

commercial matters—signed in Luxembourg on 3 June 1971 [1975] OJ L204/28, Art 2; Convention on the law applicable to contractual obligations together with First Protocol on the interpretation by the Court of Justice of the European Communities of the Convention on the law applicable to contractual obligations, opened for signature in Rome on 19 June 1980 [1989] OJ L48/1, Art 2; Convention on the service in the Member States of the European Union of judicial and extrajudicial documents in civil or commercial matters together with Protocol, drawn up on the basis of Art K.3 of the Treaty on European Union, on the interpretation, by the Court of Justice of the European Communities, of the Convention on the service in the Member States of the European Union of judicial and extrajudicial documents in civil or commercial matters [1997] OJ C261/18, Art 2(1). For an example where a lower court was not competent to make a preliminary reference concerning the Brussels Convention, see Case C-24/02 *Marseille Fret* [2002] ECR I-3383.

[144] See Convention on the establishment of a European Police Office together with protocol drawn up on the basis of Art K.3 of the Treaty on European Union, on the interpretation, by way of preliminary rulings, by the Court of Justice of the European Communities of the Convention on the establishment of a European Police Office [1996] OJ C299/2, Art 2(2); Convention on the protection of the European Communities' financial interests and the Protocol to that Convention drawn up on 27 September 1996 together with Council Act of 29 November 1996 drawing up, on the basis of Art K.3 of the Treaty on European Union, the Protocol on the interpretation, by way of preliminary rulings, by the Court of Justice of the European Communities of the Convention on the protection of the European Communities' financial interests [1997] OJ C151/1, Art 2(2); Convention on the use of information technology for customs purposes together with Council Act of 29 November 1996 drawing up, on the basis of Art K.3 of the Treaty on European Union, the Protocol on the interpretation, by way of preliminary rulings, by the Court of Justice of the European Communities of the Convention on the use of information technology for customs purposes [1997] OJ C151/15, Art 2(2); Convention drawn up on the basis of Art K.3(2)(c) of the Treaty on European Union on the fight against corruption involving officials of the European Communities or officials of Member States of the European Union [1997] OJ C195/2, Art 12(5); Convention drawn up on the basis of Art K.3 of the Treaty on European Union, on mutual assistance and cooperation between customs administrations [1998] OJ C24/2; Convention drawn up on the basis of Art K.3 of the Treaty on European Union on Driving Disqualifications [1998] OJ C216/2, Art 26(5); and Convention on Jurisdiction and the Recognition and Enforcement of Judgments in Matrimonial Matters together with Protocol drawn up on the basis of Art K.3 of the Treaty on European Union, on the interpretation by the Court of Justice of the European Communities of the Convention on Jurisdiction and the Recognition and Enforcement of Judgments in Matrimonial Matters [1998] OJ C221/20, Art 2.

6.1. The national court is prevented from setting aside a disputed national provision

Member State legislation may not prevent a national court from making preliminary references. This situation is particularly relevant where a national court has to consider whether a national provision is unconstitutional, since there is a requirement in several Member States that such a question first be laid before the country's constitutional court. Where the case also involves aspects of Community law, the Court of Justice has stated that such an obligation to lay the case before a constitutional court does not prevent the national (lower) court from making a reference for a preliminary ruling. This is so since it is only the national court before which a case is brought that has jurisdiction to determine whether there should be a reference to the Court of Justice.[145]

In *Simmenthal*, an Italian court had referred a number of questions to the Court of Justice. On the basis of the ruling received, it was clear that various Italian laws were in conflict with Community law. However, under Italian law it was only the Italian constitutional court which could declare that Italian law was inapplicable. The referring Italian lower court was thus, under Italian law, prevented from setting aside the Italian provisions solely on the basis of the judgment of the Court of Justice. The Italian court therefore referred some further questions to the Court of Justice for preliminary rulings, including asking whether national law could prevent it from immediately setting aside the national laws which were in breach of Community law. The Court of Justice held that a national court both could and should set aside national law purely on the basis of the decision of the Court of Justice. Thus, Community law prevented a provision in national law that would hinder a national court in referring a question to the Court of Justice about the compatibility of national provisions with Community law.[146]

In *Mecanarte*, according to Portugal's constitutional system, international law had priority over national law, and it would be contrary to the constitution for a national provision to conflict with Community law. Moreover, under the constitution the question of whether a Portuguese law was unconstitutional had to be referred to the Portuguese constitutional court. This gave rise to the question of whether only the Portuguese constitutional court could make references to the Court of Justice in cases where the finding could lead to a Portuguese legal provision being found to be contrary to Community law. The Court of Justice ruled that Article 234 required that national courts should have the widest possible powers to refer questions to the Court of Justice if they consider that an interpretation of Community law is necessary in a case before them. If the right to make a reference were to be

---

[145] See below Ch 9, s 2, concerning the possibility of appealing a court decision to make a preliminary reference.

[146] Case 106/77 *Simmenthal* [1978] ECR 629, para 24.

restricted, the effectiveness of Community law would be in jeopardy. The lower Portuguese court could thus make a reference for a preliminary ruling.[147]

The problem can also arise as a result of national procedural requirements on the barring of arguments in proceedings before the national court.

In *Peterbroeck*, a Belgian court had to consider a tax dispute between the Belgian tax authorities and a limited liability partnership. When the case was brought before the Belgian court, the limited liability partnership argued, as a new argument, that the way in which the Belgian authorities applied the tax rules was contrary to Community law. The Belgian authorities responded by claiming that under the Belgian Income Tax Code, arguments should either be made in the claim to the tax authorities (ie prior to the case coming before the national court), should be included by the tax authorities on their own initiative (again, prior to the case being brought before the national court), or should be stated in the writ or in a written plea to the national court by a given short time limit. As the new argument based on Community law had not been made in due time, it could not be taken into consideration. The Belgian court agreed that the national procedural rules precluded the acceptance of the new argument, but found that on the one hand the procedural rules limited its ability to examine whether the national provisions were compatible with Community law, and on the other hand they restricted the Belgian court's scope for requesting the Court of Justice for a preliminary ruling under Article 234 on the interpretation of Community law. The Belgian court therefore sought to ascertain whether Community law precluded the application of a domestic procedural rule whose effect, in circumstances such as those in the main proceedings, was to prevent the national court from considering of its own motion whether a measure of domestic law was compatible with Community law, when such argument has not been invoked by the litigant within a certain period. The Court of Justice found that there was no reason in principle to criticise the Belgian time limit. At the same time it noted: *first*, that the referring national court was the first national court which could make a reference to the Court of Justice for a preliminary ruling; *second*, that the period during which new pleas could be raised by the appellant had expired by the time the national court held its hearing so that that court was denied the possibility of considering the question of compatibility; *third*, that no other national court in subsequent proceedings could, of its own motion, consider the question of the compatibility of a national measure with Community law; and *fourth*, the impossibility for national courts to raise points of Community law of their own motion did not appear to be reasonably justifiable by principles such as the requirement of legal certainty or the proper conduct of procedure. Thus, the Belgian procedural rule restricted the right of the Belgian court to make a reference for a preliminary ruling, and the

---

[147] Case C-348/89 *Mecanarte* [1991] ECR I-3277, paras 41–46.

Court of Justice therefore concluded that in the case in question this rule was contrary to Community law.[148]

Thus, in principle, the Court of Justice accepts national procedural rules. Only where the formulation of the procedural rules effectively prevents a national court from making a reference for a preliminary ruling will the Court of Justice set them aside.

6.2. A superior court has declared the contested national provision to be compatible with Community law

A national rule under which a lower court is bound by a superior court's interpretation of Community law cannot of itself deprive the lower court of the possibility of making a reference to the Court of Justice for a preliminary ruling. If the lower court were bound in this way, and thus prevented from making a reference for a preliminary ruling, this would undermine the Court of Justice's ability to ensure the uniform application of Community law at all levels of the national legal systems.

In *Rheinmühlen*, an action was brought before a German Fiscal Court (*Finanzgericht*). The Fiscal Court had given judgment, whereafter the case was appealed to the Federal Fiscal Court (*Bundesfinanzhof*). On appeal the first judgment was overturned and the case was sent back to the Fiscal Court to be retried. However, the Fiscal Court was of the view that the arguments which the Federal Fiscal Court had relied on when overturning the first judgment were contrary to Community law. The Fiscal Court thus faced a dilemma; on the one hand it was obliged to apply the interpretation which had been given by the Federal Fiscal Court, and on the other hand the Fiscal Court believed that this interpretation was contrary to Community law. On the grounds of ensuring the full effect of Community law, the Court of Justice held that a rule under national law which obliges national courts which are not national courts of last instance to follow the judgments of superior national courts cannot deprive the lower national courts of the possibility to make references to the Court of Justice on questions of the interpretation of Community law that are the subject of such a legal ruling.[149]

Even where a superior national court has ruled on the necessity of making a reference for a preliminary ruling in another case concerning the same problem, and has denied that a reference was necessary, a lower national court will not be bound by this.[150]

---

[148] Case C-312/93 *Peterbroeck* [1995] ECR I-4599, paras 11–21.

[149] Case 166/73 *Rheinmühlen* [1974] ECR 33, paras 3–11. See also Case 146/73 *Rheinmühlen* [1974] ECR 139; F Jacobs, 'The Role of the European Court of Justice in the Development of European Law' in N Jareborg (ed), *De Lege, Juridiska Fakulteten Uppsala Årsbok 1995* (1995) 205, 208; and S Prechal, 'Community law in national courts: the lessons from van Schijndel' (1998) 35 CML Rev 681, 694.

[150] On the possibility of appealing against a national court's decision to make a preliminary reference, see below Ch 9, s 2.

4

WHAT QUESTIONS CAN BE REFERRED?

1. Introduction

Not every question from a body that fulfils the conditions for being categorised as a court or tribunal of a Member State in accordance with Article 234 can be accepted for a preliminary ruling. The categories of questions that can be referred for a preliminary ruling are listed in Article 234(1)(a)–(c). According to these provisions the Court of Justice only has jurisdiction to give preliminary rulings on the interpretation of the EC Treaty, and on the validity and interpretation of legal acts issued by the institutions of the Community and by the European Central Bank (ECB) as well as the interpretation of the statutes of bodies established by an act of the Council, where those statutes so provide. On the other hand, it does not have jurisdiction to rule on the interpretation or validity of international law or national laws. Likewise, the Court of Justice is prevented from giving a binding ruling on the facts that are put before a national court.

In this chapter, Section 2 looks at what the reference to 'this Treaty' in Article 234(1)(a) means. Next, in Section 3 the meaning of 'acts', 'institutions', and 'validity' is established. In Section 4 we consider what 'interpretation of the statutes of bodies established by an act of the Council' covers; cf Article 234(1)(c). Finally, in Section 5 there is a review of the extent to which the Court of Justice can give its opinion on the facts or the content of national law in connection with a reference for a preliminary ruling.

2. Article 234(1)(a) on 'the interpretation of this Treaty'

2.1. Questions on validity of the EC Treaty

According to Article 234(1)(a), any question on the interpretation of the EC Treaty can be referred to the Court of Justice for a preliminary ruling. Hence, it seems natural to conclude, *a contrario*, that the Court of Justice does not have jurisdiction to answer questions on the validity of the Treaty itself. It cannot fully be excluded that in quite exceptional circumstances the Court would set aside a Treaty provision as being invalid, for example because the provision in question is clearly contrary to the fundamental principles of Community law, or has been included by an amendment to the Treaty which has been carried out in a manner which is indisputably contrary to the Treaty.[1] Whether it is conceivable that the Court of Justice would do this in practice is, however, an open question. Indeed, not only does the wording of Article 234 militate against such a step; since the Treaties form the constitution of the Community, the natural starting point also is that they cannot be challenged within the framework of the Community's legal order, since the legal order derives its legitimacy from that constitutional basis.[2]

The Court of Justice has not yet had a reference of a question requiring it to consider the validity of a Treaty provision. However, the EFTA Court, which to a considerable extent has been modelled on the Court of Justice, has had to consider a similar question in *CIBA*.

In *CIBA*, the Oslo City Court referred a question to the EFTA Court as to whether the EEA Joint Committee had the necessary authority to adopt a Joint Statement. The Norwegian State, which was the defendant in the main proceedings, argued

---

[1] In this regard, see also Art 46(a) and (f) of the Treaty on European Union.

[2] T C Hartley, *The Foundations of European Community Law* (2007) 266; and H Schermers and D Waelbroeck, *Judicial Protection in the European Union* (2001) 286.

that the reference for a preliminary ruling meant that the EFTA Court had to decide on the validity of a decision taken by the EEA Joint Committee. In the opinion of the Norwegian State the EFTA Court did not have the authority to make such a decision so that the case should be dismissed. The EFTA Court acknowledged that, in contrast to the Court of Justice, it did not have jurisdiction to decide on the validity of acts issued by EEA bodies. It nevertheless chose to consider the question, and, in so doing, made a fine distinction between, on the one hand, questions of the validity of the disputed legal act, and, on the other hand, questions of the interpretation of the higher legal principles which determined whether the Joint Statement (ie the legal act) could be regarded as valid. By using this approach the EFTA Court was able to express a view on the question of validity without directly passing judgment on it.[3]

Were the Court of Justice to have a question referred to it on the validity of a Treaty provision, it is natural to assume that it would adopt the same approach as the EFTA Court took in *CIBA*.

2.2. What is covered by 'this Treaty'?

The words 'this Treaty' include not only the EC Treaty in its original form, but also all subsequent amendments to it and the various accession treaties.[4] The term also covers the annexes and protocols to the EC Treaty, as these documents are an integral part of the legal acts which have created the Community.[5] Conversely, the term is unlikely to include those non-binding unilateral declarations which the Member States may have associated with the Treaty.

The reference to 'this Treaty' also covers all of the EC Treaty including its Title IV which, however, in Article 68 lays down particular conditions which must be met where a national court wants to make a preliminary reference with regard to that Title. Exempt from the Court's jurisdiction are measures and decisions taken pursuant to Article 62(1) of the EC Treaty relating to the maintenance of law and order and the safeguarding of internal security.[6]

---

[3] Case E-6/01 *CIBA* [2002] EFTA Court Report 281, paras 20–1. For a somewhat similar line of reasoning, see Case C-303/05 *Advocaten voor de Wereld* [2007] ECR I-3633, para 18. A summary of the latter case is given in s 2.3.3 below.

[4] Joined Cases 3, 4, and 6/76 *Kramer* [1976] ECR 1279.

[5] Case C-355/89 *Barr and Montrose Holdings* [1991] ECR I-3479, para 8. A summary of the judgment is given in Ch 3, s 4 above.

[6] Art 68(2). It has been argued that, from the point of view of uniformity of the law and judicial protection, this provision is highly regrettable, cf P J G Kapteyn, 'Administration of Justice' in P J G Kapteyn et al (eds), *The Law of the European Union and the European Communities* (2008) 421, 501.

Moreover, the Court of Justice has jurisdiction to give preliminary rulings on the interpretation of the Merger Treaty and in relation to the protocols of the Merger Treaty.[7]

2.3. Questions concerning the EU Treaty

2.3.1. Overview

Article 234's reference to 'this Treaty' only covers the Treaty on the establishment of the European Community (the EC Treaty). Article 234 in itself therefore does not vest in the Court of Justice the power to answer preliminary questions concerning the Treaty on European Union (the EU Treaty).

In *Grau Gomis,* a Spanish court made a reference under Article 234 to the Court of Justice concerning, inter alia, the interpretation of Article 2 of the EU Treaty. The Court of Justice declared that it clearly had no jurisdiction to reply to interpret that article in the context of such proceedings.[8]

Under Article 234 the Court therefore does not have competence to rule on matters concerning the common foreign and security policy of the European Union, or on police and judicial cooperation in criminal matters.

The EU Treaty, however, gives the Court of Justice some—limited—competence to answer preliminary references regarding EU Treaty provisions. Thus, Article 46 of the EU Treaty lays down that the provisions of the EC Treaty and of the Euratom Treaty concerning the powers of the Court of Justice and the exercise of those powers shall apply (only) to the following provisions of the EU Treaty:

1. Provisions amending the EC Treaty, the ECSC Treaty and the Euratom Treaty;
2. Provisions in Title VI of the EU Treaty, on Police and Judicial Cooperation in Criminal Matters, under the conditions provided in Article 35 in that Treaty;
3. Provisions in Title VII of the EU Treaty, on enhanced cooperation, under the conditions provided in Article 40 of the EU Treaty and Article 11 of the EC Treaty;
4. Article 6(2) of the EU Treaty, on fundamental rights with regard to action of the institutions, insofar as the Court of Justice has jurisdiction under the EU Treaty or the EC Treaty;
5. The purely procedural stipulations in Article 7 of the EU Treaty, on sanctions in connection with a Member State's breach of human rights; and
6. The final provisions of the EU Treaty laid down in its Articles 46–53.

---

[7] Art 30 of the Treaty establishing a Single Council and a Single Commission of the European Communities (Merger Treaty) [1967] OJ 152/1.
[8] Case C-167/94 *Grau Gomis* [1995] ECR I-1023.

Failure to invoke the correct legal basis for the preliminary reference—for example invoking Article 234 of the EC Treaty instead of Article 35 of the EU Treaty—will not, in itself, lead to the rejection of a request for a preliminary ruling. What matters is whether the referring court is in fact competent to make the preliminary reference and not whether the correct legal basis had been invoked.[9]

Below we first consider the Court of Justice's competence to review possible conflicts between the EU Treaty and the EC Treaty and/or the ECSC Treaty and/or the Euratom Treaty (Section 2.3.2). Next we examine what references can be made under Article 35 of the EU Treaty (Section 2.3.3). We then look at the Court's competence where some of the Member States enter into so-called enhanced cooperation (Section 2.3.4). Following this we turn to the Court's jurisdiction with regard to the EU Treaty's Article 6(2) on fundamental rights (Section 2.3.5). Next we consider the Court's competence regarding Article 7 of the EU Treaty, on sanctions in connection with a Member State's breach of human rights (Section 2.3.6). The final provisions of the EU Treaty constitute the last area listed under Article 46 to be examined (Section 2.3.7). Finally, we consider the Schengen Agreement (Section 2.3.8) followed by the Treaty of Lisbon (Section 2.3.9).

2.3.2. *Provisions amending the EC Treaty, the ECSC Treaty, or the Euratom Treaty*

The EU Treaty in Articles 8–10 (Titles II–IV) amends the EC, the ECSC,[10] and the Euratom Treaties. It follows from Article 46(a) of the EU Treaty that the Court of Justice is competent to rule on preliminary references regarding these provisions.

2.3.3. *References under Article 35 of the EU Treaty*

With the entry into force in 1999 of the Treaty of Amsterdam, Article 35 was introduced into the EU Treaty. Article 35 gives the Court of Justice competence in preliminary references on questions regarding the EU Treaty's Title VI which sets out 'Provisions on Police and Judicial Cooperation in Criminal Matters'. The relevant parts of Article 35 provide that:

> 1. The Court of Justice of the European Communities shall have jurisdiction, subject to the conditions laid down in this Article, to give preliminary rulings on the validity and interpretation of framework decisions and decisions, on the interpretation of conventions established under the Title and on the validity and interpretation of the measures implementing them.
>
> . . .

---

[9] Case C-467/05 *Dell'Orto* [2007] ECR I-5557, paras 34–6; and Case C-296/08 PPU *Goicoechea* [2008] ECR 1–6307 para 36.

[10] The Treaty establishing the European Coal and Steel Community expired on 23 July 2002.

5. The Court of Justice shall have no jurisdiction to review the validity or proportionality of operations carried out by the police or other law enforcement services of a Member State or the exercise of the responsibilities incumbent upon Member States with regard to the maintenance of law and order and the safeguarding of internal security.

. . .

The Court of Justice has held that the system in Article 234 of the EC Treaty is capable of being applied to Article 35 of the EU Treaty, subject to the conditions laid down in that provision. Hence, its practice regarding the procedures for questions for preliminary rulings under Article 234 can in principle be applied to requests for preliminary rulings made under Article 35 of the EU Treaty.

The *Pupino* case was the first preliminary reference requesting an interpretation of a framework decision under Article 35 of the EU Treaty. The case arose from a criminal prosecution of Maria Pupino for mistreating children under the age of five. Because of the young ages of the victims, the prosecution authorities wanted to exercise particular care in taking evidence. The procedure was contrary to Italian law, but there was support for it in a Council framework decision issued under the authority of the EU Treaty. On this basis the Italian court decided to refer the question to the Court of Justice for a preliminary ruling in accordance with Article 35 of the EU Treaty. In this connection the Italian court observed that it was obliged to interpret its national law in the light of the letter and the spirit of Community provisions, and since it had doubts as to the Italian law's compatibility with the framework decision, it decided to ask the Court of Justice to rule on the scope of the relevant provisions of the framework decision. The Court of Justice held that the system in Article 234 of the EC Treaty is capable of being applied to Article 35 of the EU Treaty, subject to the conditions laid down in that provision. It also held that its practice concerning the procedures for questions referred for preliminary rulings under Article 234 of the EC Treaty can in principle be applied to requests for preliminary rulings made under Article 35 of the EU Treaty.[11]

According to Article 35(1) of the EU Treaty the Court of Justice shall have jurisdiction to give preliminary rulings on the validity and interpretation of framework decisions and decisions, on the interpretation of conventions established under Title VI, and on the validity and interpretation of the measures implementing them. Based on a literal reading of the provision the Court would therefore appear not to be competent to interpret the provisions of Title VI of the EU Treaty. On the other hand, in order to give a meaningful interpretation of the legislative

---

[11] Case C-105/03 *Pupino* [2005] ECR I-5285, paras 28–9. See also M G Garbagnati Ketvel, 'Almost, but not quite: The Court of Justice and judicial Protection of Individuals in the Third Pillar' (2007) 6 European Law Reporter 223, 235.

measures adopted on the basis of Title VI it will often be necessary also to interpret the Treaty provisions as such. Faced with this dilemma the Court has held
that even if there is no express provision giving it the power to interpret provisions
of Title VI of the EU Treaty, it necessarily had this power.

In *Advocaten voor de Wereld*, a Belgian court asked, inter alia, whether a specific
framework decision was compatible with Article 34(2)(b) of the EU Treaty. One
of the Member States submitting observations in the case argued that this
question was inadmissible on the ground that it required the Court to examine
Article 34(2)(b), and that as a provision of primary law it was not reviewable by
the Court. The Court rejected this argument, holding that under Article 35(1) of
the EU Treaty it had jurisdiction, subject to the conditions laid down in that article, to give preliminary rulings on the interpretation and validity of, inter alia,
framework decisions. This necessarily implied that the Court could, even if there
was no express power to that effect, be called upon to interpret provisions of primary law, such as Article 34(2)(b), where the Court was being asked to examine
whether a framework decision had been properly adopted on the basis of that
latter provision.[12]

The Court of Justice has ruled that its jurisdiction to answer preliminary references regarding the EU Treaty must be construed in the light of the fundamental
right to effective judicial protection. Therefore, subject to the conditions fixed by
Article 35 of the EU Treaty, it is possible to make a reference for a preliminary
ruling in respect of all measures adopted by the Council, whatever their nature or
form, provided these measures are intended to have legal effects in relation to
third parties.

In *Gestorias Pro Amnistia,* the Community had adopted a common position as
part of the 'fight against terror'. The basis of the common position was Article 15
of the EU Treaty's Title V (entitled 'Provisions on a common foreign and security
policy'), and Article 34 of the EU Treaty's Title VI (entitled 'Provisions on police
and judicial cooperation in criminal matters'). Amongst the groups which were
listed in the common position was the Basque Gestorias Pro Amnistia. Finding
that the inclusion in the list was incorrect, Gestorias Pro Amnistia instituted proceedings before the Court of First Instance to have the Council pay compensation. The Court of First Instance dismissed the action on the basis that Title VI of
the EU Treaty did not provide any judicial remedy to allow for an order for
damages. Gestorias Pro Amnistia appealed the ruling to the Court of Justice. The
Court of Justice considered Gestorias Pro Amnistia's argument that the Court of
First Instance had disregarded the right to effective judicial protection. It first

---

[12] Case C-303/05 *Advocaten voor de Wereld* [2007] ECR I-3633. See also the Opinion of Advocate
General Colomer in the case, in particular para 34 thereof.

observed that a common position is not supposed to produce of itself legal effects in relation to third parties. Therefore there was no need for a judicial remedy against common positions—and this was reflected, inter alia, in the fact that the Court's jurisdiction, as defined by Article 35(1) of the EU Treaty, to give preliminary rulings did not also extend to common positions but was limited to rulings on the validity and interpretation of framework decisions and decisions on the interpretation of conventions established under Title VI of the EU Treaty and on the validity and interpretation of the measures implementing them. Since Article 35(1) did not enable national courts to refer a question to the Court of Justice for a preliminary ruling on a common position but only a question concerning the acts listed in that provision, the provision treated as acts capable of being the subject of such a reference for a preliminary ruling all measures adopted by the Council and intended to produce legal effects in relation to third parties. Given that the procedure enabling it to give preliminary rulings is designed to guarantee observance of the law in the interpretation and application of the Treaty, it would run counter to that objective to interpret Article 35(1) narrowly. It followed that the right to make a preliminary reference exists in respect of all measures adopted by the Council, whatever their nature or form, which are intended to have legal effects in relation to third parties. As a result, it had to be possible to make subject to review by the Court a common position which, because of its content, had a scope going beyond that assigned by the EU Treaty to that kind of act. It followed that where a national court heard a dispute that indirectly raised the issue of the validity or interpretation of a common position adopted on the basis of Article 34 of the EU Treaty and where that court entertained serious doubts whether that common position was really intended to produce legal effects in relation to third parties, then the national court would be able, subject to the conditions fixed by Article 35 of the EU Treaty, to ask the Court of Justice to give a preliminary ruling. It would then fall to the Court to find, where appropriate, that the common position was intended to produce legal effects in relation to third parties, to accord it its true classification, and to give a preliminary ruling.[13]

Article 35(5) lays down that the Court of Justice may not review the validity or proportionality of operations carried out by the police or other law enforcement services of a Member State or the exercise of the responsibilities incumbent upon

---

[13] Case C-354/04 P *Gestorias Pro Amnistía* [2007] ECR I-1579, in particular paras 53–4. See also Case C-355/04 P *Segi* [2007] ECR I-1657, in particular paras 53–4. In the legal literature several authors have taken a critical approach to the two judgments, finding that the Court's protection of the individual is inadequate. See for example A Berramdane, 'Les limites de la protection juridictionnelle dans le cadre du titre VI du traité sur l'Union européenne' (2007) 2 Revue du Droit de l'Union Européenne 433, 440–6 and M G Garbagnati Ketvel, 'Almost, but not quite: The Court of Justice and judicial Protection of Individuals in the Third Pillar' (2007) 6 European Law Reporter 223.

Member States with regard to the maintenance of law and order and the safe-guarding of internal security.[14]

2.3.4. Enhanced cooperation

Articles 40–45 of the EU Treaty and Articles 11 and 11a of the EC Treaty provide for so-called enhanced cooperation, meaning that some (but not all) of the Member States decide to jointly establish closer cooperation between themselves in a specific area covered by the EU or EC Treaty.[15] If some Member States enter into such enhanced cooperation, arguably Article 46 of the EU Treaty gives the Court of Justice the same jurisdiction regarding this enhanced cooperation as it enjoys with regard to the EC regime on judicial protection with regard to the framework of procedures in which a decision is taken on the basis of Article 11 of the EC Treaty or Articles 40–40b of the EU Treaty.[16] However, with regard to enhanced cooperation in the field of police and judicial cooperation in criminal matters the Court's jurisdiction regarding the actual measures of enhanced coop-eration enacted by the Council cannot be wider than what is provided under Article 35 of the EU Treaty.[17]

2.3.5. Article 6(2) of the EU Treaty, on fundamental rights

Article 6(2) provides that the Union shall respect fundamental rights, as guaran-teed by the European Convention on Human Rights and as they result from the constitutional traditions common to the Member States, as general principles of Community law. Article 46(d) goes on to provide that the Court of Justice has jurisdiction with regard to Article 6(2) of the EU Treaty 'with regard to action of the institutions, insofar as the Court has jurisdiction under the Treaties establishing the European Communities and under this Treaty'.

It follows that the Court of Justice's jurisdiction is limited to examining only the actions of the institutions and that it can only make this examination within those limits on its jurisdiction which have been laid down in other provisions of the treaties.[18] Hence, Article 46(d) does not provide for uniform protection of human

---

[14] This restriction has been characterised as 'unsatisfactory' by P J G Kapteyn, 'Administration of Justice' in P J G Kapteyn et al (eds), *The Law of the European Union and the European Communities* (2008) 421, 501.

[15] This is sometimes also referred to as differentiated integration.

[16] C Timmermans, 'General Aspects of the European Union and the European Communities' in P J G Kapteyn et al (eds), *The Law of the European Union and the European Communities* (2008) 53, 108–9.

[17] Ibid, 109 and K Lenaerts and P Van Nuffel, *Constitutional Law of the European Union* (2005) 54–5 and 377. See also H G Schermers and D F Waelbroeck, *Judicial Protection in the European Union* (2001) 224.

[18] K Lenaerts and P Van Nuffel, *Constitutional Law of the European Union* (2005) 808 observe that under Art 46(d) the Court is competent in the field of police and judicial cooperation in crimi-nal matters whilst these authors leave it open whether the Court is also competent in the field of the

rights against any measure affecting union citizens where they exercise their right of free movement or freedom to provide services.[19] It has, however, been argued that when interpreting acts issued within the EU Treaty's area of police and judicial cooperation in criminal matters the Court might be prepared to indicate how such interpretation and application can be kept compatible with fundamental rights.[20]

2.3.6. *Article 7 of the EU Treaty, on sanctions in connection with a Member State's breach of human rights*

Article 7 of the EU Treaty lays down that if a Member State commits a serious and persistent breach of the principles of liberty, democracy, respect for human rights and fundamental freedoms, and the rule of law, the Council may decide to suspend certain of that Member State's rights deriving from the application of the EU and the EC Treaties. According to Article 46(e) the Member State concerned may request the Court of Justice to review the purely procedural stipulations laid down in Article 7 of the EU Treaty. Thus, this provision does not vest in the Court jurisdiction to answer preliminary references.

However, the Court of Justice is not completely barred from considering actions taken against a Member State under Article 7 of the EU Treaty. This is so since Article 7 of the EU Treaty has a counterpart in Article 309 of the EC Treaty regarding the measures which may be taken where a decision has been taken to suspend the voting rights of the representative of the government of the Member State in accordance with Article 7 of the EU Treaty. Under Article 234, the Court of Justice is competent to answer preliminary references regarding this provision.

2.3.7. *The final provisions of the EU Treaty*

Article 46(f) lays down that the Court of Justice is competent to rule on Articles 46–53 of the EU Treaty (Title VIII—final provisions). In this respect Article 47 is of particular relevance since it provides that 'nothing in this Treaty shall affect the Treaties establishing the European Economic Communities or the subsequent Treaties and Acts modifying or supplementing them'. In a few direct actions the

---

common foreign and security policy. R H Lauwaars, 'Institutional Structure' in P J G Kapteyn et al (eds), *The Law of the European Union and the European Communities* (2008) 175, 250, and 251 and P J G Kapteyn, 'Administration of Justice' in P J G Kapteyn et al (eds), *The Law of the European Union and the European Communities* (2008) 421, 432 both appear to be of the view that Art 46(d) does not vest in the Court jurisdiction in the latter field.

[19] On such broad jurisdiction see Advocate General Jacobs at para 46 of his Opinion in Case C-168/91 *Konstandinidis* [1993] ECR I-1191; and K Lenaerts and P Van Nuffel, *Constitutional Law of the European Union* (2005) 726.

[20] K Lenaerts and P Van Nuffel, *Constitutional Law of the European Union* (2005) 726.

Court has held that where it is disputed whether an act shall be based on the EU Treaty or on the EC Treaty, it is competent to decide the matter.

In *Commission v Council (airport transit visas)*, the Commission sued the Council for breach of the EC Treaty arguing that an act adopted by the Council on the basis of the EU Treaty should rightly have been based on the EC Treaty. As part of the procedure it was argued that the Court of Justice was not competent to hear and determine the Commission's application since the act was not a measure that could be challenged under the EC Treaty. The Court dismissed the argument. It held that it was its task to ensure that acts which, according to the Council, fall within the scope of the Treaty on European Union do not encroach upon the powers conferred by the EC Treaty on the Community. It followed that the Court had jurisdiction to review the content of the act in the light of the EC Treaty in order to ascertain whether the act affected the powers of the Community under that Treaty and to annul the Act if it appeared that it should have been based on the EC Treaty.[21]

It seems arguable that the reasoning of the Court in the *Airport transit visa case* also applies to acts within the field of the Common Foreign and Security Policy.[22] Whilst this judgment concerned a direct action it is submitted that the Court of Justice would take the same approach if the matter were raised as part of a preliminary ruling.

2.3.8. *The Schengen Agreement*

When the Schengen Agreement was concluded, it did not come within the scope of the European Union as such. With the Treaty of Amsterdam the Schengen Agreement was integrated into the European Union.[23] However, the Schengen Agreement covers both civil and criminal matters so that parts of the Agreement fall within the EC Treaty whilst other parts fall within the EU Treaty. The consequence is that preliminary questions regarding criminal matters falling within Article 35 of the EU Treaty can only be asked by those national courts whose Member State has made a declaration to this effect in accordance with that provision.[24] Likewise, questions on civil matters can only be asked by national courts of last instance in accordance with Article 68 of the EC Treaty.[25] It follows that in

---

[21] Case C-170/96 *Commission v Council* [1998] ECR I-2763, paras 12–18, on an arrangement for airport transit visas; and Case C-176/03 *Commission v Council* [2005] ECR I-7879, paras 38–40, on criminal sanctions for environmental protection.

[22] R H Lauwaars, 'Institutional Structure' in P J G Kapteyn et al (eds), *The Law of the European Union and the European Communities* (2008) 175, 252 with further references.

[23] Protocol (No 2) integrating the Schengen *acquis* into the framework of the European Union (1997) [2006] OJ C321E/191.

[24] See further Ch 1, s 3.3. For an example, see Case C-150/05 *van Straaten* [2006] ECR I-9327.

[25] See further Ch 1, s 3.2. For an example, see Case C-241/05 *Bot* [2006] ECR I-9627.

order for a national court to establish whether it can make a preliminary reference with regard to the Schengen Agreement, it may be necessary to first establish which provision of the Agreement the preliminary reference concerns. In a Decision the Council has specified which parts of the Schengen *acquis* fall within one or the other of the two treaties.[26]

2.3.9. The Treaty of Lisbon

If the Treaty of Lisbon enters into force, the European Union's present pillar structure will be abandoned. This will affect those acts which will be adopted on the basis of the subsequent Treaty structure. The existing acts which have been based upon the EU Treaty will continue to be in force—and to the extent that they fall outside the scope of Article 234 today, this will also continue to be the case after the (possible) entry into force of the Treaty of Lisbon.

In contrast, following the entry into force of the Treaty of Lisbon, new acts in the field of justice and home affairs will come within the Court's jurisdiction so that in this respect it may answer preliminary questions in the field from any Member State court. The objective is that over a short time-span the existing acts based on the EU Treaty shall be replaced by new acts based on the future Treaty structure.[27]

2.4. Mixed jurisdiction

Situations might arise where a preliminary reference concerns acts that span two or more of the three different legal bases; namely Title VI of the EU Treaty, Title IV of the EC Treaty, and the EC Treaty except Title IV. If the referring court is competent to make preliminary references under all the relevant legal bases no problem arises. If this is not the case the Court of Justice will have to consider to what extent the preliminary questions can be admitted.

Where the Court of Justice can meaningfully answer those parts of the preliminary reference which the referring court is competent to refer while declining to answer the other questions, the Court must be expected to limit its answer to only the former parts.[28] However, situations may also arise where it is not possible to

---

[26] Council Decision 1999/435 of 20 May 1999 concerning the definition of the Schengen *acquis* for the purpose of determining, in conformity with the relevant provisions of the Treaty establishing the European Community and the Treaty on European Union, the legal basis for each of the provisions or decisions which constitute the *acquis* [1999] OJ L176/1 and Council Decision 1999/436 of 20 May 1999 determining, in conformity with the relevant provisions of the Treaty establishing the European Community and the Treaty on European Union, the legal basis for each of the provisions or decisions which constitute the Schengen *acquis* [1999] OJ L176/17.

[27] On the Treaty of Lisbon, see further Ch 1, s 3.7.

[28] T Tridimas, 'Knocking on Heaven's Door: Fragmentation, Efficiency and Defiance in the Preliminary Reference Procedure' (2003) 40 CML Rev 9, 15, points out that where a lower court is faced with a dispute giving rise to issues pertaining both to the interpretation of Title IV of the EC Treaty and to other articles of the EC Treaty arguably the preclusion of lower courts under Art 68 of

meaningfully make a distinction between those parts of the preliminary reference which the referring court is competent to refer and those parts which fall outside the referring court's competence. If the Court of Justice were to completely decline jurisdiction in the latter situations, arguably it would amount to a denial of the referring court's right to make a preliminary reference. Therefore, it is submitted that the Court of Justice should apply a 'most favourable jurisdiction' approach in this situation and thus consider such preliminary references admissible in full.[29] This approach would be in line with the Court's approach in comparable situations where it has ruled that its jurisdiction to answer preliminary references must be interpreted in the light of the fundamental right to effective judicial protection.[30]

3. Article 234(1)(b) on 'the validity and interpretation of acts of the institutions of the Community and of the ECB'

According to Article 234(1)(b), all questions concerning the validity and interpretation of acts of the institutions of the Community and of the ECB can be referred. If the Treaty of Lisbon enters into force the preliminary ruling procedure will be extended to acts of European Union bodies, offices or agencies, which will thus be incorporated into the law of the Union which can be interpreted and the validity of which can be reviewed by the Court of Justice.[31]

3.1. The meaning of 'the institutions of the Community'

The institutions of the Community are exhaustively listed in Article 7 of the EC Treaty. According to this provision, the institutions of the Community consist of the European Parliament, the Council, the Commission, the Court of Justice, and the Court of Auditors. In other words, not all the bodies which issue or apply Community legal acts are covered by the term 'institutions'.[32]

In relation to Article 234 the clear point of departure must be that in principle the reference to 'institutions' should be understood in accordance with the definition given in Article 7 of the EC Treaty. This interpretation is supported by the fact that 'and of the ECB' has been included in Article 234(1)(b). This reference would have been unnecessary if all the bodies which issue or apply Community acts were

---

the EC Treaty may tempt these courts not to make a reference on those issues on which they are competent and instead leave the possibility of a preliminary reference to a higher court.

[29] See also S Peers, 'Who's Judging the Watchmen? The Judicial System of the "Area of Freedom Security and Justice"' in P Eeckhout and T Tridimas (eds), *Yearbook of European Law 1998* (1999) 337, 397–9.

[30] See above s 2.3.3.

[31] Article 267(1)(6) of the Treaty on the Functioning of the European Union.

[32] See the Opinion of Advocate General Slynn in Case 44/84 *Hurd* [1986] ECR 29 (at 36).

covered by the term 'institutions'.[33] Nevertheless, the possibility cannot be entirely excluded that the Court of Justice will deal with requests for preliminary rulings concerning legal acts issued by bodies not covered by the definition of Community institutions in Article 7. For example, the aim of Article 234 suggests that the Structural Funds ought to be covered.[34] This applies in particular when the nature of the rules which they have powers to issue is taken into account. Likewise, the possibility cannot be excluded that decisions taken within the framework of the European Investment Bank (EIB) may be subject to preliminary rulings.

Finally, it is not yet clear whether legal acts adopted by the Member States' representatives in the Council are to be regarded as being covered by Article 234. Regardless of whether these legal acts are adopted within the institutional framework of the Council, they are not adopted by the Council as a Community institution, but by the Member States' representatives outside Community law. It therefore seems most natural to regard such legal acts as *not* being 'acts of the institutions of the Community' within the meaning of Article 234.

Where a legal act of the Community allows one or more Member States to enter into agreements or otherwise issue legal acts, these will not be regarded as having been issued by the institutions of the Community. The Court of Justice thus does not have jurisdiction to interpret such acts in connection with a reference for a preliminary ruling.[35] On the other hand, the Court of Justice will have jurisdiction if the referring national court requests an interpretation of a Community act with a view to itself applying the Court of Justice's interpretation of the Community act to interpret an agreement entered into between Member States.[36]

3.2. The meaning of 'acts'

3.2.1. Acts adopted on the basis of the EC Treaty

Article 230 of the EC Treaty, on the legality of acts, defines the Community acts which the Court of Justice can review in direct proceedings. There are no corresponding limitations to the jurisdiction of the Court of Justice under Article 234.[37]

---

[33] Only since 1 January 1999, when the third stage of Economic and Monetary Union started, has the ECB been able to issue binding legal acts in accordance with Art 110 of the EC Treaty. Art 117(9) of the EC Treaty states, however, that during 'the second stage, the term "ECB" used in Articles ... 234 ... shall be read as referring to the EMI.' The EMI (European Monetary Institute) did not issue binding legal acts. The provision in Art 117(9) therefore seems to assume that it is possible to make preliminary rulings in relation to the non-binding legal acts of the EMI.

[34] The European Agricultural Guidance and Guarantee Fund, Guidance Section; the European Social Fund; and the European Regional Development Fund—see Arts 159–62 of the EC Treaty.

[35] Case C-162/98 *Hartmann* [1998] ECR I-7083, paras 10–11. See also C Naômé, *Le renvoi préjudiciel en droit européen* (2007) 80.

[36] Case C-193/98 *Pfennigmann* [1999] ECR I-7747, paras 16–22. See further s 3.3.7 below.

[37] Case 322/88 *Grimaldi* [1989] ECR 4407, para 8.

Indeed, any such limitation would be contrary to the purpose of preliminary rulings, which is to ensure that Community law is applied and interpreted uniformly in all Member States and in accordance with the Treaty. This means that the Court of Justice not only has jurisdiction to give rulings on regulations, directives, and decisions, it also has jurisdiction to give rulings on non-binding acts, including Council resolutions, as well as recommendations, statements, and notices adopted on the basis of the EC Treaty.[38]

In *Grimaldi* the Court of Justice was asked to interpret some recommendations which, according to Article 249 of the EC Treaty, are not binding. The Court considered itself competent to deal with the reference for a preliminary ruling as Article 234 gives it jurisdiction to give preliminary rulings on the validity and interpretation of all acts of the institutions of the Community, without exception.[39]

The Court's own Statute and its Rules of Procedure can also be subject to a review of their interpretation and validity through a preliminary ruling.[40] Similarly, legal acts which are *sui generis* and not referred to in Article 249 of the EC Treaty—for example Council resolutions which are intended to have binding effect—are covered by the term 'acts' in Article 234.[41] The same applies to individual decisions which are addressed to natural or legal persons.

3.2.2. *Community acts which refer to non-Community act*

The Court of Justice is not competent to give rulings on acts of the Member States. If, however, a Community act makes reference to certain non-Community acts (including acts that are to be adopted by the Member States) the Court is competent to interpret the Community act including the Community act's reference to the non-Community acts.

In *Fazenda Pública,* the Court of Justice was asked to rule on the concept of 'an act that could give rise to criminal court proceedings' contained in a Community regulation. The Advocate General pointed out that the concept was closely connected with the substance or procedure of criminal law and so it could be argued that it fell within the interpretative authority of national courts and outside the

---

[38] Case 113/75 *Frecasetti* [1976] ECR 983, paras 8–9; Case 90/76 *Van Ameyde* [1977] ECR 1091, paras 14–15; Case C-188/91 *Deutsche Shell* [1993] ECR I-363, paras 18–19; and Case C-312/07 *JVC France* [2008] ECR I-4165, paras 33–7.

[39] Case 322/88 *Grimaldi* [1989] ECR 4407, paras 7–9.

[40] Case C-472/99 *Clean Car II* [2001] ECR I-9687, paras 12–22.

[41] D Anderson and M Demetriou, *References to the European Court* (2002) 63. In support of this view the authors refer to three cases concerning direct actions, namely Case 22/70 *Commission v Council (ERTA)* [1971] ECR 263; Case C-366/88 *France v Commission* [1990] ECR I-3571; and Case C-327/91 *France v Commission* [1994] ECR I-3541.

competence of the Court of Justice. In its judgment the Court did not enter this discussion, but simply provided an interpretation of the concept.[42]

On the other hand, the Court of Justice does not have jurisdiction under Article 234 to interpret agreements under private law which are entered into without the involvement of a Community institution or other organ. This applies regardless of whether a secondary Community legal act refers to the agreement, and regardless of whether the entry into the agreement under private law is made a condition for the entry into force of a secondary Community legal act. It is likewise irrelevant whether the period of validity of this secondary Community legal act is conditional on the period of validity of an agreement under private law.

In *Demouche*, a question was referred to the Court of Justice on the interpretation of a standard agreement, and a supplementary agreement associated with it, which had been entered into between a number of insurance bureaux. The standard agreement in private law introduced a cooperative arrangement for the payment of compensation in connection with car accidents which occurred while driving abroad. The arrangement had since been supplemented by a Council directive on the approximation of the laws of the Member States relating to insurance against civil liability in respect of the use of motor vehicles. This directive provided that its entry into force depended on the making of a supplementary agreement under private law to the standard agreement. Moreover, the period of validity of this supplementary agreement determined the period of validity of the directive. In other words, the purpose of the directive could not have been achieved without the agreement being made under private law. Nevertheless, the Court of Justice found that it did not have jurisdiction to interpret the agreement, since no Community institution or agency took part in its making. The fact that the conclusion of the agreement was a pre-condition for the entry into force and period of validity of the directive did not affect the nature of the supplementary agreement as a measure adopted by private associations.[43]

It follows that the Court of Justice does not have jurisdiction to rule on the interpretation or validity of an agreement 'concluded at Community level' between management and labour in accordance with Article 139 of the EC Treaty.

In *Polier*, a French court asked the Court of Justice to rule on the validity and interpretation of a specific French 'ordonnance' concerning work contracts. The Court declined to give such ruling, observing inter alia that even though under

---

[42] Case C-62/06 *Fazenda Pública* [2007] ECR I-11995, paras 18–31 and the Opinion of the Advocate General, paras 29–38.
[43] Case 152/83 *Demouche* [1987] ECR 3833, paras 15–21.

Article 136 of the EC Treaty the Community legislator was competent to adopt legislation in the field in question, an 'act' would only come within the scope of Community law if it were adopted on the basis of Articles 136 and 137.[44]

It appears to follow from the ruling in *Polier* that, *a contrario,* an agreement may form the basis of a reference if it is implemented by 'a Council Decision' in accordance with Article 139(2). In practice these agreements are implemented by the adoption of a Council directive to which the agreement is annexed.

3.2.3. *The act must have been adopted, but not necessarily have entered into force*

An 'act' requires that an act has been adopted. This means that the Court of Justice does not have jurisdiction to answer if a national court asks it to rule that an institution has failed to act.[45] Moreover, the content of the act should be sufficiently established for the Court of Justice to have a basis for ruling on its validity or interpretation.

In *Mattheus*, the Court of Justice was asked to rule on whether Community law was a hindrance to the accession of Spain, Portugal, and Greece to the European Communities in the foreseeable future. The Court of Justice found that it could not give such a preliminary ruling because the legal conditions for such accession had to have been defined in the context of the procedure for the admission of new Member States. It was not possible for the Court of Justice to determine the content of the conditions of accession in advance.[46]

There is no requirement that the adopted act has also entered into force.[47] The fact that an act has been annulled does not in itself mean that the Court of Justice is prevented from interpreting it, if the interpretation can be relevant for the decision of the main proceedings.[48]

In *Pfennigmann*, the Court of Justice was asked to interpret a provision in a directive which it had previously annulled for infringement of significant procedural requirements. However the Court had maintained the legal effect of the directive until new provisions were adopted in the area. The Court could interpret the annulled directive's provisions.[49]

---

[44] Case C-361/07 *Polier* [2008] ECR 1–6, para 13.

[45] Case C-68/95 *Port* [1996] ECR I-6067, para. 53. See also below Ch 8, s 3.2.2.

[46] Case 93/78 *Mattheus* [1978] ECR 2203. See in this regard W Alexander, 'La recevabilité des renvois préjudiciels dans la perspective de la réforme institutionnelle de 1996' (1995) 31 Cahiers de droit européen 561, 573; and H Rasmussen, 'Issues of Admissibility and Justiciability in EC Judicial Adjudication of Federalism Disputes under Article 177 EEC' in H Schermers et al (eds), *Article 177 EEC: Experiences and Problems* (1987) 379, 388ff.

[47] See further Ch 5, s 4.9.

[48] See further Ch 5, s 4.7.

[49] Case C-193/98 *Pfennigmann* [1999] ECR I-7747.

3.2.4. *The act does not have direct effect*

The Court of Justice's jurisdiction to make preliminary rulings does not depend on whether the disputed legal act has direct effect.

In *Mazzalai*, an Italian court referred a question on the correct interpretation of a directive. In the pleadings the Italian government argued that the Court of Justice could not give a ruling on the question because the Community rule was not directly applicable and therefore did not have direct effect. The Court of Justice rejected this objection and stated that, under Article 234, it has jurisdiction to give preliminary rulings on the interpretation of legal acts adopted by the institutions of the Community, regardless of whether they are directly applicable.[50]

3.2.5. *The act has previously been the subject of a preliminary ruling*

The Court of Justice can also interpret a Community law provision, even if it has previously been the subject of a preliminary ruling. Here it might appear that the Court is interpreting—or distinguishing—the earlier preliminary ruling.[51] However, the Court cannot examine the validity of a previous preliminary ruling.

In *Wünsche*, a German court asked the Court of Justice to rule on the validity of a preliminary ruling. The background to the case was that the national court had previously referred a question to the Court of Justice for a preliminary ruling on the validity of a regulation. In the earlier case the Court of Justice had stated that the regulation in question was valid. After having received the preliminary ruling the national court asked the plaintiff in the main proceedings to submit a statement on the ruling. The plaintiff contended that the Court of Justice's ruling was vitiated by serious breaches of law and that those breaches deprived it of all binding force. The national court then requested the Court of Justice to consider whether the first preliminary ruling should be considered invalid. The Court of Justice stated that the authority of a preliminary ruling does not preclude the national court from making a further reference to the Court of Justice if it encounters difficulties in understanding or applying the ruling, as long as it refers a fresh question of law to the Court of Justice, or submits new considerations. However, it is not permissible to contest the validity of a judgment delivered previously, as this would call in question the allocation of jurisdiction between national courts and the Court of Justice under Article 234 of the EC Treaty.[52]

---

[50] Case 111/75 *Mazzalai* [1976] ECR 657, paras 6–7; and Case C-373/95 *Maso* [1997] ECR I-4051, para 28.

[51] See further Ch 5, s 4.7, and Ch 12, s 6.

[52] Case 69/85 *Wünsche* [1986] ECR 947, paras 10–16.

3.3. The distinction between 'acts of the institutions of the Community' and agreements under international law outside the jurisdiction of the Court of Justice

3.3.1. Overview

It is not only the classic acts of Community institutions referred to above that are covered by the Court of Justice's jurisdiction under Article 234. There are also a number of international agreements that constitute acts of the institutions of the Community which fall within the jurisdiction of the Court of Justice to interpret or rule on their validity. What is decisive for the Court's jurisdiction is the nature of the disputed act, and not the categories of parties involved.

In *Eurocontrol*, a Belgian court referred a question in connection with a case between a German airline company and the European Organisation for the Safety of Air Navigation (Eurocontrol). Eurocontrol is an international organisation with its headquarters in Brussels. Among its Contracting States are countries which are Member States of the EU and countries which are not members of the EU. In the hearing on the preliminary ruling, Eurocontrol argued that, as an international organisation whose relations with the Community are governed by the rules of public international law, it was outside the jurisdiction of the Court of Justice. The Court of Justice rejected this argument. The national court had referred a question to the Court of Justice which neither concerned the interpretation of the Convention setting up Eurocontrol, nor the Multilateral Agreement relating to the Collection of Route Charges, but rather the interpretation of Articles 82 and 86 of the EC Treaty. The question of whether the rules of Community law could be relied upon as against Eurocontrol was connected with the substance of the case and had no bearing on the jurisdiction of the Court of Justice.[53]

In the next section we first examine the Court's competence regarding agreements between the Community and third countries (Section 3.3.2). Next we analyse the Court's jurisdiction vis-à-vis so-called mixed agreements, ie international agreements which both the Community and the Member States have competence to enter into, and where the Community and the Member States have decided 'internally' to exercise this competence together (Section 3.3.3). We then turn to consider acts of organs set up by an international agreement to which the Community is party (Section 3.3.4) followed by an examination of the Court's competence with regard to international agreements to which the Community is not party, but which are an integral part of Community law (Section 3.3.5). We also look at the extent to which the Court is competent to answer preliminary

---

[53] Case C-364/92 *Eurocontrol* [1994] ECR I-43, paras 8–11.

references concerning international law that does not qualify as Community law, but that may affect the validity of Community law (Section 3.3.6). In the following section we consider the Court's jurisdiction with respect to questions on international agreements to which the Community is not a party (Section 3.3.7). Finally, we briefly look at other international agreements which give the Court of Justice jurisdiction to interpret (Section 3.3.8).

3.3.2. Agreements between the Community and third countries

Agreements between the Community and third countries constitute part of the Community's legal foundation. The requirement for uniform interpretation and application of Community law therefore also exists in this context. On this basis the Court of Justice has established that such agreements must be regarded as acts of the institutions of the Community in accordance with Article 234(1)(b), and the Court can therefore give preliminary rulings on the interpretation of such agreements.

In *Haegeman*, the Court of Justice was asked to interpret some of the provisions in the Agreement of Association with Greece, before Greece joined the Community. The Court found that the Association Agreement had been entered into by the Council in accordance with the provisions of the EEC Treaty which are now found in Articles 228 and 238 of the EC Treaty. There was therefore an act of a Community institution within the meaning of Article 234(1)(b). Furthermore, from the date of entry into force of the Agreement, its terms were an integral part of Community law. The Court therefore had jurisdiction to give preliminary rulings on the interpretation of the Agreement.[54]

In *Kupferberg*, a German court referred a question concerning the correct interpretation of a free trade agreement between the Community and Portugal, before Portugal became a Member State. The Court of Justice stated that the obligations which flowed from such an agreement bound the Member States not only in relation to the third country concerned, but also in relation to the Community, which had taken on responsibility for the correct implementation of the agreement. It also stated that, due to the Community law character of the provisions in question, they must be given uniform effect throughout the Community. It was therefore within the Court's jurisdiction to interpret the provisions.[55]

Correspondingly, in connection with a preliminary ruling, the Court of Justice must be able to declare invalid a Community legal act whereby such an agreement is entered into, for example because the Community lacks the competence to

---

[54] Case 181/73 *Haegeman* [1974] ECR 449, paras 2–6.
[55] Case 104/81 *Kupferberg* [1982] ECR 3641, paras 13–14.

enter into the agreement. In such a case the agreement will not be applicable in the Community.[56]

The Court of Justice's jurisdiction to interpret a provision in an international agreement does not depend on whether the provision has direct effect. Where this is not the case the Court often examines whether the provision could be relevant to the decision in the main proceedings. If not, a preliminary ruling will normally be superfluous to the referring national court's decision in the main proceedings, and on this basis the Court of Justice may refuse to make a substantive ruling on the question referred.[57] On the other hand, if a ruling is relevant for deciding the dispute in the main proceedings, the Court of Justice will give a ruling, even if the provision does not have direct effect.[58]

3.3.3. *Mixed agreements*

3.3.3.1. Overview—the four situations.   A mixed agreement is an international agreement which both the Community and the Member States have competence to enter into, and where the Community and the Member States have decided 'internally' to exercise this competence together. Mixed agreements thus stand in contrast to agreements which fall entirely outside the competence of the Community, and agreements which are entirely within the exclusive competence of the Community.

If the Lisbon Treaty enters into force Articles 3 and 4 of the new Treaty on the Functioning of the European Union will lay down in what areas the Union has exclusive competence and in what areas the Union and the Member States have shared competence. With particular regard to international agreements, Article 3(2) provides:

> The Union shall . . . have exclusive competence for the conclusion of an international agreement when its conclusion is provided for in a legislative act of the Union or is necessary to enable the Union to exercise its internal competence, or in so far as its conclusion may affect common rules or alter their scope.

In a number of cases questions have been referred to the Court of Justice for preliminary rulings on the interpretation of provisions in mixed agreements. The practice which has arisen in connection with this is far from clear and it does not appear to be coherent.[59]

---

[56] R Holdgaard, 'Principles of Reception of International Law in Community Law' in P Eeckhout and T Tridimas (eds), *Yearbook of European Law 2006* (2007) 263, 271ff. See also Joined Cases C-317/04 and C-318/04 *Parliament v Council and Commission* [2006] ECR I-4721, paras 67–70.

[57] Joined Cases 21–24/72 *International Fruit Company* [1972] ECR 1219, paras 3, 8, and 27–8.

[58] Case C-89/99 *Schieving-Nijstad vof* [2001] ECR I-5851, paras 51–5.

[59] P Koutrakos, 'The Interpretation of Mixed Agreements under the Preliminary Reference Procedure' (2002) 7 European Foreign Affairs Review 25; A Dashwood, 'Preliminary Rulings on the

However, it seems to be accepted that the question as to whether the Court of Justice can interpret a mixed agreement in connection with a reference for a preliminary ruling cannot be answered generally for the agreement in question, but requires an analysis of the jurisdiction in relation to the agreement's specific provision of which interpretation is required.[60] In determining when the Court of Justice considers itself to have jurisdiction to interpret provisions in mixed agreements, it is appropriate to distinguish between four situations:

- Interpretation of provisions which belong to the Community's exclusive competence.

- Interpretation of provisions in areas where the Community has competence, but where this competence is not exclusive, and where the Community has legislated in the area to which the provision under consideration applies.

- Interpretation of provisions in areas where the Community has competence, but where this competence is not exclusive, and where the Community has not legislated in the area to which the provision under consideration applies.

- Interpretation of provisions which fall outside the area of the Community's competence.

3.3.3.2. Provisions covered by exclusive competence.   In the first situation, where a provision in a mixed agreement falls within the Community's exclusive competence, the Court of Justice has jurisdiction to interpret the provision in a preliminary ruling.

3.3.3.3. Provisions covered by non-exclusive competence and where the Community has legislated.   The Court of Justice also has jurisdiction in the second situation,[61] and this jurisdiction is not dependent upon whether the interpretation is to be used for the application of Community rules or national rules. In support of this, the Court has emphasised that it is in the Community's interest that provisions in mixed agreements should be interpreted uniformly, regardless of whether they apply in situations governed by national law or by Community law.

Interpretation of Mixed Agreements' in D O'Keeffe and A Bavasso (eds), *Judicial Review in European Union Law. Liber Amicorum in Honour of Lord Slynn of Hadley, Vol 1* (2000) 167, 167–8; and J Heliskoski, 'The Jurisdiction of the European Court of Justice to Give Preliminary Rulings on the Interpretation of Mixed Agreements' (2000) Nordic Journal of International Law Vol 69, No 4, 2000, ss 395–412.

[60]   The Court of Justice's jurisdiction to interpret international agreements is thus not co-extensive with the Community's competence to enter into treaties.

[61]   Case C-89/99 *Schieving-Nijstad vof* [2001] ECR I-5851, para 30.

Hermès concerned the interpretation of a provision in the TRIPS Agreement (on trade-related aspects of intellectual property rights). The TRIPS Agreement is contained in an annex to the WTO Agreement, which is a mixed agreement. In this case several Member States argued that the Court of Justice lacked jurisdiction to give a preliminary ruling. It was pointed out that the Court of Justice had itself previously held that, among other things, the specific provision in the TRIPS Agreement which the Court of Justice was called upon to interpret primarily fell within the competence of the Member States. The Court of Justice considered that it had jurisdiction to give a ruling since Community legislation had been issued in the area. The enforcement of these Community measures was the responsibility of the authorities of the Member States, using national legal systems and national procedural rules. When Member States' authorities enforce Community measures, they are obliged to comply with the provision of the TRIPS Agreement which the national court had referred to the Court of Justice for interpretation. Since the provision could be relevant for the enforcement of Community rules, the Court of Justice had jurisdiction to interpret it. That the actual case did not concern the enforcement of Community rules did not alter this fact. First, it was up to the national court to decide whether a preliminary ruling was necessary. Next, it was in the Community's interest that there should be uniform interpretation of the provision, regardless of whether it was applicable in a situation covered by national law or a situation covered by Community law.[62]

Some authors have assumed that the judgment should be interpreted as not only covering the provision referred, but the whole of the mixed agreement (ie in this case the TRIPS Agreement).[63] According to these authors, in the *Hermès* case the Court of Justice established that it has jurisdiction to interpret all the provisions in the TRIPS Agreement which are covered by the Community's competence (both exclusive and non-exclusive).[64] However, others have argued that in the *Hermès* case the Court of Justice only decided on the possibility of interpreting an individual provision in a mixed agreement, where this provision applies in an area where the Community has legislated—regardless of the fact that in the main

---

[62] Case C-53/96 *Hermès* [1998] ECR I-3603, paras 22–33.

[63] A Dashwood, 'Preliminary Rulings on the Interpretation of Mixed Agreements' in D O'Keeffe and A Bavasso (eds), *Judicial Review in European Union Law: Liber Amicorum in Honour of Lord Slynn of Hadley, Vol 1* (2000) 167, 173; and A Rosas, 'The European Union and Mixed Agreements' in A Dashwood and C Hillion (eds), *External Relations Law of the European Community* (2000) 200, 215.

[64] P Eeckhout, *External Relations of the European Union—Legal and Constitutional Foundations* (2004) 240, finds it difficult to measure the precise implication of the Court of Justice's reasoning on this point.

proceedings the provision is not to be used in relation to Community legislation.[65] Indeed, this position, which the present authors share, appears to find support in the more recent ruling in *Merck Genéricos*.[66]

3.3.3.4. Provisions covered by non-exclusive competence and where the Community has not legislated.

The third of the four situations set out above is the most complex. Here the provision which is referred for a preliminary ruling applies in an area where the Community has non-exclusive competence. In contrast to the second situation discussed above, where the Community had legislated within the area, the third situation is characterised by the fact that the Community has not legislated within the area.

In *Dior*, the Court of Justice was asked to give an interpretation of a provision in the TRIPS Agreement. The case concerned two preliminary references which were joined, one of which concerned the protection of an industrial design, an area in which, at the material time, the Community had not legislated. This led the national court to refer the question as to whether in these circumstances the Court of Justice had jurisdiction to give a preliminary ruling on the interpretation of the TRIPS Agreement. In answer to this the Court of Justice noted that the provision in the TRIPS Agreement which it had been asked to interpret not only applied to industrial designs, but also to trade marks. The provision in question thus not only applied in the area where at the material time the Community had not (yet) legislated, but also where the Community had legislated. In order to ensure uniform interpretation of the provision, the Court of Justice therefore had to interpret the provision, even though the main proceedings were outside the area where the Community had legislated. The Court of Justice thus concluded that it had jurisdiction to give a preliminary ruling on the question referred.[67]

It follows from the decision in *Dior* that the Court of Justice has jurisdiction to interpret a provision in a mixed agreement where this provision applies in an area for which the Community has legislated. This is so even if in the actual main proceedings the specific provision of the agreement is to apply to an area where the Community has not yet legislated.[68] What this means—including the exact meaning of the term 'area'—is not stated in the judgment.[69] Possibly the most

---

[65] J Heliskoski, 'The Jurisdiction of the European Court of Justice to Give Preliminary Rulings on the Interpretation of Mixed Agreements' (2001) Nordic Journal of International Law Vol 69, No 4, 2000, ss 395–412; and N Fenger and M Broberg, *Præjudicielle forelæggelser for EF-domstolen* (2008) 79–80.

[66] Case C-431/05 *Merck Genéricos* [2007] ECR I-7001.

[67] Joined Cases C-300/98 and C-392/98 *Dior* [2000] ECR I-11307, paras 32–40.

[68] It is not clear what precisely the Court of Justice means by 'legislated'; cf P Koutrakos, 'The Interpretation of Mixed Agreements under the Preliminary Reference Procedure' (2002) European Foreign Affairs Review Vol 7, 25, 45.

[69] In *Hermès* the English version of the judgment refers to 'area' whereas in the *Dior* case it refers to 'field'. The judgments were originally drafted in French, and in the French versions the term

important difference between the second and the third situation is that in the former situation (where the Community has legislated) the question of direct effect of the international agreement is decided in accordance with Community law. In contrast, in the third situation, the Court of Justice is unable to rule on the way in which the provisions in the international agreement shall be applied in the national legal order. Hence, it is left to national law to decide whether the provisions should have direct effect in and take precedence over national law.[70]

The judgment in *Dior* does not give a clear answer as to where the boundaries to the Court of Justice's jurisdiction may be presumed to lie.[71] On the one hand the judgment can be understood as saying that the Court of Justice only has jurisdiction to interpret the provision of a mixed agreement where this interpretation may be relevant to the application of the provision within an area where the Community has in fact legislated. In other words, according to this understanding of the judgment, where a provision in a mixed agreement applies both in area A (eg trademark law) and in area B (eg patent law), and where the Community has legislated only in area A, the Court of Justice would have competence to establish the interpretation of the provision if the reference from the national court concerns area A. By contrast, if the reference from the national court concerns area B, Community law will leave it to the national court to determine what effects the provision shall have within the national legal order.[72]

On the other hand, in its decision the Court of Justice took care to explain that it has jurisdiction to interpret the referred provision 'in order to forestall future differences of interpretation'.[73] Future differences of interpretation do not require

---

domaine is used in both judgments. It must be presumed that the two terms applied in the English versions are intended to have identical meanings. For further discussion of the *Dior* case see R Holdgaard, 'Principles of Reception of International Law in Community Law' in P Eeckhout and T Tridimas (eds), *Yearbook of European Law 2006* (2007) 263, 296ff.

[70] R Holdgaard, 'Case note on Case C-431/05 *Merck Genéricos* [2007] ECR I-7001' (2008) 45 CML Rev 1233, 1241–2.

[71] P Eeckhout, *External Relations of the European Union—Legal and Constitutional Foundations* (2004) 242, puts forward fundamental criticisms of the Court of Justice's practice in this area.

[72] See in support of this interpretation Case C-431/05 *Merck Genéricos* [2007] ECR I-7001, paras 34–5 and 46–7.

[73] Joined Cases C-300/98 and C-392/98 *Dior* [2000] ECR I-11307, para 35. The reference to 'future differences of interpretation' is taken from Case C-53/96 *Hermès* [1998] ECR I-3603, para 32. G Bontinck, 'The TRIPs Agreement and the Court of Justice: A New Dawn?—Some Comments About Joined Cases C-300/98 and C-392/98 *Parfums Dior* and *Assco Gerüste*'. Jean Monnet Working Paper 16/01, p 14, speculates as to whether the judges of the Court of Justice had kept themselves informed via the Internet about the ongoing negotiations which led to the Nice Treaty (and the consequent amendment to Art 133 of the EC Treaty), and whether the judgment in *Dior* (which was given before the Nice Treaty was signed) was influenced by this. This, however, seems improbable.

that the Community has legislated already, but equally apply where Community competence remains purely potential.[74]

3.3.3.5. Provisions not covered by the Community's competence. The fourth and last of the situations listed above concerns cases where a national court makes a reference for a preliminary ruling on a provision in an international agreement, and the provision falls outside the Community's competence. It appears that the Court of Justice—in a direct action—has established that it is competent to assess compliance with obligations stemming from mixed agreements where the provision in question falls outside the Community's competence if the provisions of a mixed agreement cover an area which comes in large measure within the scope of Community competence, and these provisions create rights and obligations in areas covered by Community law, if the provisions of the mixed agreement, that are referred to the Court of Justice for interpretation, are inextricably linked to those parts of the mixed agreement that unquestionably fall within the scope of Community competence, and if the Community has assumed responsibility for the due performance of the agreement. This is so even if it means that the Court must interpret a provision of the mixed agreement which, strictly speaking, falls outside the Community's competence.[75]

In other words, if the Community's adherence to the mixed agreement can only be understood as the consequence of adherence to the agreement in its entirety, given the indivisibility of the obligations it lays down, the Court of Justice may be competent. Arguably, this approach may be transposed to preliminary references as well. At the same time it is submitted that if the mixed agreement is not indivisible, the Court of Justice shall not have jurisdiction to rule on the interpretation of provisions falling outside the Community's competence. This finds support in a number of cases in which the Court of Justice has gone to great lengths to show that a provision in an international agreement falls within the Community's competence and for that reason gives it jurisdiction to answer a preliminary reference.[76] These efforts would seem to be superfluous if the Court of Justice would have had jurisdiction under any circumstance in the fourth situation.[77]

---

[74] A Dashwood, 'Preliminary Rulings on the Interpretation of Mixed Agreements' in D O'Keeffe and A Bavasso (eds), *Judicial Review in European Union Law: Liber Amicorum in Honour of Lord Slynn of Hadley, Vol 1* (2000) 167, 173. A practicable example would be where a legislative proposal has been tabled by the Community in the area in question and this proposal is expected to be adopted in the near future.

[75] See in support of this Case C-13/00 *Commission v Ireland* [2002] ECR I-2943, in particular paras 15, 19, and 20. See also Advocate General Mischo's Opinion in the same case, paras 48 and 50.

[76] Illustrative examples are Joined Cases C-300/98 and C-392/98 *Dior* [2000] ECR I-11307 and Case C-53/96 *Hermès* [1998] ECR I-3603.

[77] D Anderson and M Demetriou, *References to the European Court* (2002) 67. See also T C Hartley, *The Foundations of European Community Law* (2007) 271.

3.3.4. *Acts of organs set up by an international agreement to which the Community is party*

Where the Community is a party to an international agreement which involves the setting up of an organ that can take decisions giving effect to the agreement, these decisions form an integral part of the agreement. The Court of Justice therefore has jurisdiction to give preliminary rulings on the interpretation of such decisions.

In *Sevince*, a Turkish citizen was refused an extension of his residence permit to stay in the Netherlands causing him to bring a case against the Dutch authorities. The matter was governed by the Agreement establishing an Association between the Community and Turkey. This Agreement set up a Council of Association which had made several decisions that were relevant to the case. The Dutch court wanted an interpretation of these decisions, but was in doubt about whether it could make a reference for a preliminary ruling on them. The Court of Justice held that the provisions in the Association Agreement constituted an integral part of Community law, and as the decisions of the Council of Association were directly linked to the Association Agreement, these decisions equally formed an integral part of Community law. Since the Court could give preliminary rulings on the Association Agreement itself, it also had jurisdiction to decide on the interpretation of decisions taken by an organ which was set up in accordance with the Agreement and which had the task of implementing it.[78]

The Court of Justice's jurisdiction to give preliminary rulings extends to non-binding legal acts.

In *Deutsche Shell*, a German court had to decide on some questions which required the interpretation of a convention entered into between the Community and some third countries. Under the convention an organ was set up which could make recommendations. As these recommendations were directly linked to the convention, not only the convention but also the recommendations formed part of Community law. Since, according to the established practice of the Court of Justice, non-binding acts may be the subject of preliminary references,[79] the Court had jurisdiction to give preliminary rulings on the interpretation of the recommendations.[80]

Unless otherwise provided for in the agreement between the Community and a third country a preliminary ruling concerning an agreement is only binding on

---

[78] Case C-192/89 *Sevince* [1990] ECR I-3461, paras 9–11. See also Case C-237/91 *Kus* [1992] ECR I-6781, para 9.

[79] See further above s 3.2.1.

[80] Case C-188/91 *Deutsche Shell* [1993] ECR I-363, paras 17–18.

the Community and not on the third country.[81] The same applies to preliminary rulings on decisions taken by organs set up under such agreements.

3.3.5. *International agreements to which the Community is not party, but which are an integral part of Community law*

In certain situations the Court of Justice has jurisdiction to interpret international agreements to which the Community is not party, because the agreements in question are nevertheless an integral part of Community law.

These situations concern agreements which were originally entered into by the Member States but which subsequently in whole or in part have come under the competence of the Community (sometimes even its exclusive competence). In such a situation the Community can take over the rights and duties of the Member States and thereby—under Community law—it can be bound by the agreement. Thus, even if the Community has neither negotiated nor signed the agreement in question, the Court of Justice nevertheless has jurisdiction to interpret it in accordance with Article 234, to the extent that the agreement has become part of Community law.[82]

Where rules of international law prevent the Community from entering into an international agreement or participating in an international organisation, the Community can require that, in areas where the Community has competence (perhaps exclusive competence), the Member States should act in the interests of the Community and on its behalf. Also in these situations the Court of Justice will have jurisdiction to interpret the agreement and the acts of the international organisation in question.

In *Cipra and Kvasnicka*, it had been laid down in a regulation that, from the date of the regulation's entry into force, it fell within the competence of the Community to negotiate and enter into the AETR Agreement on road transport. It was also clear from the regulation that, in ratifying the Agreement, the Member States acted in the interests of the Community and on its behalf. The regulation also stated that in certain situations it should give way to the Agreement. On this basis the Court of Justice found that the Agreement was part of Community law, and that it had jurisdiction to interpret the Agreement.[83]

---

[81] R Grass, 'L'article 177 du Traité de C.E.E.' in J Chauvin and F Trubert (eds), *Le Droit Communautaire & International devant le juge du commerce* (1989) 81, 84.

[82] R Holdgaard, 'Principles of Reception of International Law in Community Law' in P Eeckhout and T Tridimas (eds), *Yearbook of European Law 2006* (2007) 263, 281–6; Joined Cases 21–24/72 *International Fruit Company* [1972] ECR 1219, paras 4–7 and 10–18; and Joined Cases 267/81 and 269/81 *SPI and SAMI* [1983] ECR 801, paras 15 and 19 (the GATT rules).

[83] Case C-439/01 *Cipra and Kvasnicka* [2003] ECR I-745, paras 23–4.

3.3.6. *International law that does not qualify as Community law, but that may affect the validity of Community law*

Apart from in the situations referred to in Sections 3.3.2—3.3.5 above, the Court of Justice does not have jurisdiction to accept references for preliminary rulings on international agreements. Consequently, the Court of Justice does not have jurisdiction to interpret measures under international law which bind the Member States outside the framework of Community law. This is so even where these measures concern areas that are also regulated by Community law.

In *Vandeweghe*, a German court referred a question to the Court of Justice for a preliminary ruling on the correct interpretation of a provision in an agreement between Belgium and Germany. The Court of Justice stated that it did not have jurisdiction to make decisions on the interpretation of provisions under international law that were binding on the Member States outside the framework of Community law.[84] Instead, the Court of Justice chose to interpret the relevant parts of a Community act which the referring court believed could be relevant to the interpretation of the international agreement in question.[85]

Nevertheless, in certain particular situations the Court of Justice may find it necessary to engage in an interpretation of an international law agreement which— strictly speaking—does not qualify as Community law. This is so since the Court's jurisdiction covers all the grounds for invalidity to which an act can be subject. Thus, since a Community act can be invalid, among other reasons, because it is contrary to international law, it is sometimes necessary for the Court to interpret an international agreement in order to be able to give a preliminary ruling on the interpretation or validity of a Community act.[86]

In *Orkem* and *Hoechst*, the Court of Justice had to decide whether some Community acts entailed a breach of certain fundamental rights. In this connection the Court of Justice chose to look at the protection which the European Convention on Human Rights provides in the area in question. At the time when the two cases were heard there were only few relevant precedents from the European Court of

---

[84] On this point see also Case C-87/97 *Käserei Champignon* [1999] ECR I-1301, para 36; Case C-141/99 *AMID* [2000] ECR I-11619, para 18; and the Opinion of Advocate General La Pergola in Case C-293/98 *Entidad de Getstión de Derechos de los Productores Audiovisuales* [2000] ECR I-629, para 16.

[85] Case 130/73 *Vandeweghe* [1973] ECR 1329, paras 2–4. See also Case C-193/98 *Pfennigmann* [1999] ECR I-7747, paras 16–22; and Case C-302/06 *Koval'Ský* [2007] ECR I-11, according to which the Court of Justice does not have jurisdiction to interpret the European Convention on Human Rights, other than in cases where Community law applies. Below, in s 5.3, there is a review of the Court of Justice's jurisdiction to interpret Community acts where such interpretation has to take account of factors which lie outside the scope of Community law.

[86] Case C-162/96 *Racke* [1998] ECR I-3655, paras 25–8. See also Case C-286/90 *Peter Michael Poulsen and Diva Navigation Corp* [1992] ECR I-6019, para 9.

Human Rights (and the European Commission on Human Rights), so the Court of Justice itself had to interpret the Convention.[87]

Such 'supplementary interpretation' of an international agreement does not constitute an authoritative interpretation for the purposes of international law, but merely means that the Court of Justice establishes the necessary basis for being able to give a preliminary ruling on the validity of a given Community act. The Court's decision will therefore only be relevant to the validity of the Community act in question.[88]

3.3.7. *International agreements to which the Community is not a party*

The fact that an agreement under international law is entered into in connection with the tasks of the Community does not in itself mean that it should be considered part of Community law.[89] Therefore, the Court of Justice does not, on these grounds alone, have jurisdiction to give preliminary rulings on the interpretation of such agreements.

In *Hurd*, an English court referred a question on the interpretation of the Statute of the European School and the Protocol on the setting up of the European Schools. The Court of Justice held that it did not have jurisdiction to give a ruling, since the agreements, instruments, measures, and decisions of organs of the European School adopted on the basis of its Statute and the Protocol do not fall within any of the categories of measures covered by Article 234. The mere fact that those agreements are to a certain degree linked to the Community and to the functioning of its institutions does not mean that they must be regarded as an integral part of Community law.[90]

In *Peralta*, the captain of a ship had discharged waste water from his ship within Italian territorial waters, and the Italian authorities had brought a criminal prosecution against him. In this connection a question was referred to the Court of Justice as to whether the Italian law was in accordance with the Marpol Convention on maritime pollution. In reply the Court of Justice noted that the Community

---

[87] Case 374/87 *Orkem* [1989] ECR 3283, paras 30–1 (self-incrimination); and Case 46/87 *Hoechst* [1989] ECR 2859, para 18 (respect for private life—undertakings). When later the European Court of Human Rights was called upon to consider the same legal questions it arrived at interpretations that were at variance with those applied by the European Court of Justice. In its subsequent case law, the European Court of Justice has—in principle—followed the interpretations provided by the European Court of Human Rights. On this, see further M Broberg, 'The preliminary reference procedure and questions of international and national law' in P Eeckhout and T Tridimas (eds), *Yearbook of European Law 2009* (forthcoming).

[88] However, the judgment can very well expressly refer to the Court of Justice's interpretation of the international law measure; see eg Case C-305/05 *Ordre des barreaux francophones et germanophone and others v Council* [2007] ECR I-5305.

[89] Case C-162/98 *Hartmann* [1998] ECR I-7083, paras 9–12.

[90] Case 44/84 *Hurd* [1986] ECR 29.

was not a party to the Marpol Convention and that the Community had not assumed the powers that had previously been exercised by the Member States in the area of application of the Marpol Convention. The Community was thus not bound by the Convention and so the Court of Justice refused to answer the preliminary question.[91]

Even where one of the Community's acts contains an express reference to a bilateral agreement entered into by Member States and where this agreement concerns the same area of law as the Community act, such an agreement cannot be the subject of a preliminary ruling.

In *Torrekens*, a French court referred a question to the Court of Justice on the right of a Belgian citizen to receive an old-age pension in France. The question concerned the correct interpretation of a number of provisions in a regulation. One of these provisions referred to an annex to the regulation, and this annex referred further to an agreement between France and Belgium. The Court of Justice held that an interpretation of the Franco-Belgian agreement lay outside its jurisdiction under Article 234.[92]

Also, the Court of Justice does not have jurisdiction under Article 234 to interpret international agreements of a private law character. In this connection it will not be sufficient if there is a reference to Community secondary legislation in the agreement, or that the making of the agreement is a condition for the entry into force of a Community legal act. Nor is it sufficient that the period of validity of a Community legal act is conditional on the period of validity of a private law agreement.[93]

Article 307 of the EC Treaty states that the provisions of the Treaty do not affect the rights and obligations that arise from agreements concluded before the entry into force of the Treaty between one or more Member States on the one hand, and one or more third countries on the other. The same may be assumed to be the case in relation to an international agreement which a Member State has entered into after accession to the Community and where the Community has only subsequently assumed responsibility for regulating the area which is covered by such international agreement. Where one of the two situations referred to here occurs, it is outside the jurisdiction of the Court of Justice to decide, in connection with a preliminary ruling, the extent of the obligations of the Member State under the international agreement in question. This falls within the jurisdiction of the

---

[91] Case C-379/92 *Peralta* [1994] ECR I-3453, paras 15–17.
[92] Case 28/68 *Torrekens* [1969] ECR 125.
[93] Case 152/83 *Demouche* [1987] ECR 3833, paras 15–21, summarised above at s 3.2.2.

national court which must itself decide the extent to which the obligations prevent the application of Community law.[94]

In *Levy*, an action was brought against a French undertaking which employed women to carry out night work. In France there was a prohibition on employing women for night work, and this prohibition had been introduced with a view to complying with an ILO convention which France had ratified in 1953, ie before the foundation of the Community. The referring national court sought clarification as to whether the French rule was contrary to Community law which prohibited sex discrimination. The Court of Justice held that it did not have jurisdiction to give a preliminary ruling on the obligations of a Member State under an earlier international convention.[95]

In *R v Secretary of State for the Environment, Transport and the Regions, ex parte International Air Transport Association* the applicant requested that the English High Court (Queen's Bench Division) made a preliminary reference to the Court of Justice regarding the validity of a Community regulation. According to the applicant the regulation was invalid for breach of the Member State's obligations to third parties under the Warsaw Convention. The High Court refused this request holding that although only the Court of Justice could declare Community acts invalid, its jurisdiction under Article 234 was limited to rulings concerning the validity and interpretation of Community acts and therefore did not extend to the interpretation of other international measures, such as the Warsaw Convention. Moreover, Article 307 of the EC Treaty provided that international obligations concluded prior to entry into force of the EC Treaty were not affected by it. According to the High Court, the Court of Justice had interpreted this as implying a duty on the part of the Community institutions not to impede the performance of the obligations of Member States which stemmed from a prior agreement, although this did not bind the Community as regards non-Member States. However, this did not bring the Warsaw Convention within the jurisdiction of the Court of Justice.[96]

Similarly, the Court of Justice does not have jurisdiction to interpret international agreements which, at the time when the circumstances in the main proceedings arose, did not fall within Community law. This is, for example, relevant where there has been an association agreement such as the EEA Agreement. These agreements

---

[94] Case C-324/93 *Evans Medical* [1995] ECR I-563, para 29; and Case C-124/95 *Centro-Com Srl* [1997] ECR I-81, para 58. At the same time, the Court of Justice has established that the national court must, as far as possible and while complying with international law, seek to interpret the Member State's international agreements in accordance with Community law; see Case C-216/01 *Budvar* [2002] ECR I-13617, paras 168–70.

[95] Case C-158/91 *Levy* [1993] ECR I-4287, para 21.

[96] [1999] 1 CMLR 1287.

are part of Community law in the Member States, but not in the third countries which have entered into such agreements with the Community. The Court of Justice will therefore not have jurisdiction to give a ruling on a question from a national court in a new Member State if that question concerns the interpretation of such an agreement in relation to factual circumstances that arose before that State became part of the Community.[97]

The fact that a decision of the Court of Justice can have implications for international agreements which lie outside the scope of Community law does not, in itself, mean that the Court of Justice is prevented from giving a preliminary ruling on a Community act.

Asjes concerned the question of whether it was compatible with the competition rules in the EC Treaty that under French law air tariffs were subject to a compulsory approval procedure. The area was regulated by a number of international measures and the French government argued that it must be taken into account that the French legislation and rules at issue in the main proceedings were part of a system of international agreements. The Court of Justice noted that it could not be assumed that the international agreements required the Member States which signed up to them *not* to comply with the Treaty's competition rules. On this basis the Court of Justice did not consider that it was prevented from giving a preliminary ruling on the question.[98]

3.3.8. *Other international agreements which give the Court of Justice jurisdiction to interpret*

The Member States have entered into a number of agreements which do not fall under the heading of 'acts of the institutions of the Community' in Article 234(1)(b). Some of these agreements give the Court of Justice jurisdiction to give preliminary rulings on the correct interpretation of the agreement.[99] Examples of such agreements include the Convention on the Mutual Recognition of Companies and Bodies Corporate of 29 February 1968.[100]

3.4. The meaning of 'validity'

According to Article 234(1)(a), the Court of Justice has jurisdiction to interpret the EC Treaty, but it cannot make decisions concerning the validity of the Treaty.[101]

---

[97] See s 5.4 below.
[98] Joined Cases 209–213/84 *Asjes* [1986] ECR 1425, paras 18–26.
[99] H Schermers and D Waelbroeck, *Judicial Protection in the European Union* (2001) 225ff.
[100] Protocol concerning the Interpretation by the Court of Justice of the Convention of 29 February 1968 on the Mutual Recognition of Companies and Legal Persons. Signed at Luxembourg on 3 June 1971. Bulletin of the European Communities, Supplement 4/71, p 6ff. See further above Ch 1, s 3.5.
[101] See s 2.1 above.

On the other hand, in the case of acts issued by the institutions of the Community or the ECB (ie derived or secondary law), the Court of Justice has jurisdiction to make decisions on both interpretation and validity. The reason why Article 234 has given national courts the possibility of referring questions on validity is that secondary Community acts are not only applied by the institutions of the Community, but are in fact primarily administered by the authorities of the Member States. Together with Articles 230 and 241 of the Treaty, Article 234 has established a complete system of legal remedies and procedures which allow the Court of Justice to control the validity of the acts issued by the institutions of the Community, regardless of which organ applies the provisions.[102] Where a decision is applicable to a legal or natural person (so the person is directly and individually concerned by the decision), such a decision can be tried directly by the Court of Justice in accordance with Article 230. If instead there is an act of general application, legal and natural persons are in principle prevented from making use of Article 230. However, it will be possible to try the act under Article 234. When the administrative authorities of a Member State apply a general Community act, legal and natural persons can challenge the validity of the act before the national courts and may thereby succeed in provoking a reference to the Court of Justice for a preliminary ruling on the question.[103]

The fact that the Court of Justice may previously have considered the correct interpretation of a Community act does not mean that it is subsequently prevented from considering its possible invalidity.[104] On the face of it, it seems reasonable to expect the Court of Justice not to give interpretations of acts that are in fact invalid, and that the Court should therefore, on its own initiative, examine the validity of an act before it interprets it. However, in practice it is not possible for the Court to undertake a full examination of the legal acts involved when giving a preliminary ruling. If the Court did not reserve the right to declare a Community act invalid, even though it may previously have interpreted it, the consequence would be that the Court would be prevented from declaring such acts invalid, even where it was absolutely clear that this was necessary.

With the exception of the Court of Justice's own decisions, this jurisdiction to assess validity applies to all the acts of the institutions of the Community and the ECB. The Court of Justice is not prevented from considering the validity of an act in connection with a reference for a preliminary ruling merely because the act in question does not have direct effect. However, there does not seem to be much

---

[102] Case 294/83 *Les Verts* [1986] ECR 1339; and Case C-212/94 *FMC* [1996] ECR I-389, para 56.
[103] See further below Ch 6, s 4.2.
[104] Joined Cases C-393/99 and C-394/99 *Inasti* [2002] ECR I-2829, para 27, and see further below Ch 11, s 2.6.

point in considering the validity of a non-binding act. If a question is referred on this, the Court will reformulate the question so that it will instead consider whether the non-binding rule is in accordance with binding rules in the same area.[105]

To the extent that the Community is bound by a provision of international law, in connection with a reference for a preliminary ruling, the Court of Justice can assess whether the Community provision may be invalid because it is contrary to the provision of international law.[106]

4. Article 234(1)(c), 'the interpretation of the statutes of bodies established by an act of the Council'

According to Article 234(1)(c), the third category of questions which can be subject to a reference for a preliminary ruling concerns questions of 'the interpretation of the statutes of bodies established by an act of the Council, where those statutes so provide'. Sub-paragraph (c) refers only to 'interpretation', while the question of validity is not included. By their very nature, statutes of the Council constitute acts of an institution of the Community so in this situation the validity of the statutes can in any case be tried under Article 234(1)(b). According to certain authors Article 234(1)(c) may originally have been based on a distinction between, on the one hand, the act whereby the Council established the body in question and, on the other hand, the statute which the Council conferred upon it. While the establishing act was covered by Article 234(1)(b), the statutes should be covered by sub-paragraph (c). At the same time, these authors note that the Court's wide interpretation of sub-paragraph (b) has made such a distinction superfluous.[107]

It follows from the above that Article 234(1)(c) only has independent significance for a body which is established by the Council, but where that body's statutes are not laid down by the Council (or another institution of the Community or the ECB). It would be extremely rare for such statutes not to be laid down in a Regulation, so that the act comes within the scope of Article 234(a)(b). The Court of Justice has therefore not yet received any question under the heading of sub-paragraph (c).[108]

---

[105] Case C-94/91 *Wagner* [1992] ECR I-2765, para 17.
[106] Joined Cases 21–24/72 *International Fruit* [1972] ECR 1219, para 8; and Case 9/73 *Schlüter* [1973] ECR 1135, para 27.
[107] D Anderson and M Demetriou, *References to the European Court* (2002) 64ff.
[108] E Traversa, 'Les voies de recours ouvertes aux opérateurs économiques: le renvoi préjudiciel au titre de l'article 177 du traité CEE' (1992) 2 Revue du Marché Unique Européen 51, 56.

5. Questions which Fall Outside the Jurisdiction of the Court of Justice

5.1. Overview

The right to refer a question to the Court of Justice for a preliminary ruling does not cover questions on the validity or interpretation of national law, international law, or agreements under private law. Similarly, the provision cannot be used to refer to the Court of Justice questions on the specific application of Community law in the main proceedings, or on the evaluation of proof regarding the facts which are laid before the national court.

In Section 3.3 above we reviewed the distinction between, on the one hand, questions of international law which are outside the Court of Justice's jurisdiction, and on the other hand, questions of Community law which are within its jurisdiction. In the following sections there is a review of the limits to the Court of Justice's jurisdiction in relation to national law (Section 5.2), in relation to Community rules which do not apply to the main proceedings (Section 5.3), in relation to circumstances arising in a Member State before its entry into the European Community (Section 5.4), in relation to the facts of the main proceedings (Section 5.5), and in relation to the actual application of Community law to the facts of the case (subsumption) in the main proceedings (Section 5.6).

5.2. National law

Article 234 does not give the Court of Justice jurisdiction to decide on the validity of the laws of the Member States. Likewise, under Article 234 the Court cannot interpret the laws of a Member State with binding effect for the national court.[109] In this context it is irrelevant whether the national legislation in question is intended to implement a directive in national law, and that the authorities of the Member State are under an obligation to interpret the rule in conformity with the directive.

In *Vanacker and Lesage*, two Belgian citizens had been prosecuted for breaching some French rules on the collection and disposal of waste oil. According to the French government these rules were issued with a view to implementing the

---

[109] Case C-212/04 *Adeneker* [2006] ECR I-6057, para 103; Case C-424/97 *Haim* [2000] ECR I-5123, paras 55–6; Case C-19/00 *SIAC Construction* [2001] ECR I-7725, para 30; Case C-390/99 *Canal Satélite Digital* [2002] ECR I-607, para 24; Case 54/72 *F.O.R.* [1973] ECR 193, para 8; Case 152/79 *Lee* [1980] ECR 1495, para 11; Case C-269/89 *Bonfatti* [1990] ECR I-4169, para 8; Case C-328/04 *Vajnai* (ECJ 6 October 2005), para 13; Case C-287/08 *Crocefissa Savia* [2008] ECR I-136; and Case C-511/03 *Ten Kate Holding and others* [2005] ECR I-8979, para 25.

directive which governed the area. The national court referred a question to the Court of Justice consisting of two parts. While the second part concerned the interpretation of the directive, the first part concerned the interpretation of the French implementing provisions. The Court of Justice explained that under the provisions of Article 234 it is for the national courts to interpret national rules. The Court of Justice therefore only ruled on the question concerning the interpretation of the directive.[110]

This delimitation of jurisdiction does not prevent the Court of Justice from helping the referring national court solve the problem in the main proceedings so that the latter is able to decide on the legal questions relating to the main proceedings.[111] This does not imply that the referring court should refrain from giving information about the content and form of the relevant national rules. On the contrary, in the Court of Justice's consideration of the preliminary question the national law constitutes part of the facts of the case, rather than a part of the law. The Court of Justice thus usually takes account of the national law when giving a preliminary ruling.[112]

The sole jurisdiction of the national court to apply Community law in the main proceedings also means that the Court of Justice is prevented from making preliminary rulings on the classification of a payment which is granted in accordance with the law in one Member State, but which is to be assessed under the law in another Member State.

In *Adlerblum*, the question arose as to whether a regular German payment awarded as compensation to a woman who was resident in France should be categorised as a pension or as a social assistance benefit. The answer was crucial for whether the woman's husband could receive an increase in his old-age pension in respect of his dependent spouse. The French court which had to decide the main proceedings asked the Court of Justice to decide this in the form of a preliminary ruling. However, the Court of Justice refused to do so, as it pointed out that the question in dispute only concerned national law and thus fell outside its jurisdiction.[113]

---

[110] Case C-37/92 *Vanacker and Lesage* [1993] ECR I-4947, para 7.
[111] Case C-28/99 *Verdonck* [2001] ECR I-3399, para 28; Case C-355/97 *Beck* [1999] ECR I-4977, paras 25–7; Case C-302/97 *Konle* [1999] ECR I-3099, para 27; Case 111/76 *Van den Hazel* [1977] ECR 901, para 4; Case C-369/89 *Piageme* [1991] ECR I-2971, para 7; and Case C-153/93 *Delta* [1994] ECR I-2517, para 11.
[112] See below Ch 8, s 3.2.4, Ch 10, s 3.3.3.4, and Ch 11, s 2.4.
[113] Case 93/75 *Adlerblum* [1975] ECR 2147, para 4.

5.3. Interpretation of Community acts which do not apply in the main proceedings

5.3.1. Overview

Sometimes a national court refers a question for a preliminary ruling in a case where the Community act in question does not apply directly, but where the national court nevertheless believes that an interpretation will be relevant to the decision in the main proceedings. In principle the Court of Justice only has jurisdiction to interpret Community provisions where they are in fact applicable to the main proceedings.[114] In a limited number of situations Community law may nevertheless prove to be of considerable importance for deciding the proceedings and in some of these situations the Court of Justice has been ready to rule on preliminary references. Four categories of this type of case may be identified, namely (i) procedural matters, (ii) application of Community law outside Community law's scope of application, (iii) national law that has been modelled upon Community law, and (iv) regarding a national prohibition of 'reverse discrimination' within the field of the four freedoms. These four categories are examined in turn.

5.3.2. Preliminary rulings on procedural questions in the main proceedings

The first situation concerns cases where a question of procedure or of jurisdiction in the main proceedings requires the classification of a Community act. For example, these are situations where a national administrative authority's or court's competence to decide the case in question depends on whether the case is classified as a tax case or as an agricultural case under Community law. Even if the Court of Justice does not have jurisdiction to rule on the question of national procedure or jurisdiction, it may nevertheless give a preliminary interpretation of the Community act in order to help the national court clarify this kind of question.

In *Bozzetti*, an Italian farmer had brought an action before the *Pretura di Cremona*, with a claim for the repayment of a tax which the Italian authorities had imposed in accordance with a Community regulation. The jurisdiction of the *Pretura di Cremona* to decide the main proceedings depended on whether the co-responsibility levy in question was to be defined as a tax. The Court of Justice noted that it was not for it to intervene in order to resolve any questions of jurisdiction which might arise within a national judicial system, but it could give information on Community law which could help the national court solve the problem of jurisdiction with which it was faced.[115] The Court of Justice answered the preliminary question on this basis.

---

[114] See for example Case C-309/96 *Annibaldi* [1997] ECR I-7493, paras 13 and 24.

[115] Case 179/84 *Bozetti* [1985] ECR 2301, paras 17–18. See also Case C-446/93 *SEIM* [1996] ECR I-73, paras 31–3; Joined Cases C-10–22/97 *IN.CO.GE'90 et al.* [1998] I-6307, paras 13–17; and Case C-470/99 *Universale-Bau* [2002] ECR I-11617, paras 41–5.

5.3.3. *Application of Community law outside the scope of Community law*

The second category concerns cases where national law or private contracts state that Community law shall apply, even though the circumstances do not fall within the scope of application of Community law. This situation particularly arises where Member States choose to make their implementing provisions for directives more widely applicable than is prescribed by the directive in question.

In these situations the Court of Justice has accepted references for making preliminary rulings on Community law rules, even though, strictly speaking, the Community rules do not apply in the actual case.

Andersen og Jensen ApS concerned the Danish law on the taxation applicable to mergers. According to the preparatory documentation to the Danish legislation, it was intended to implement changes in the Danish tax legislation that were necessary to comply with the Merger Directive. However, the Danish law also implemented rules corresponding to those in the Merger Directive outside the scope of application of the directive, namely rules for divisions, transfers of assets, and exchanges of shares in companies which were all registered in Denmark. The main proceedings in *Andersen og Jensen ApS* fell outside the scope of application of the Merger Directive, but it was covered by the Danish extension of the directive's scope. The Court of Justice had jurisdiction to give a ruling.[116]

The Netherlands also chose to extend the scope of the Merger Directive, so that certain of the directive's rules also applied to mergers involving only companies established in the Netherlands. In order to cover such purely internal situations, when implementing the directive's definition of a merger the Dutch authorities therefore added a provision that was effectively identical to that of the directive. In *Leur-Bloem* a dispute then arose about the correct understanding of the merger definition. The dispute concerned a transaction between Dutch companies, so the directive itself was not applicable. The Dutch court hearing the main proceedings referred a question to the Court of Justice on the correct interpretation of the directive. The Court of Justice found that it had jurisdiction to interpret Community law even where this did not directly govern the circumstances in the case where, in transposing the provisions of the directive into domestic law, the national legislator had chosen to apply the same treatment to purely internal situations and to those governed by the directive, so that it had aligned its domestic legislation with Community law. At the same time the Court of Justice made it clear that it was decisive that the national court was bound by the Court of Justice's interpretation of Community law, and that Community law was not merely used as a partial model.[117]

---

[116] Case C-43/00 *Andersen og Jensen ApS* [2002] ECR I-379, paras 12 and 14–19.
[117] Case C-28/95 *Leur-Bloem* [1997] ECR I-4161, paras 23–34.

In *Kofisa Italia*, a question was referred to the Court of Justice on the interpretation of the Community Customs Code (a regulation), whose procedural provisions on the right of appeal had been given general applicability in Italian law, beyond the direct scope of application of the Code. The dispute in the main proceedings apparently concerned VAT levied on importation and not customs duties, and according to the Commission the relevant Italian procedural rules in the area of customs duties were inspired by the system applicable in direct and indirect taxation. In other words, it was national law which inspired the procedural rules in the area regulated by Community law, and not the other way round. The Court of Justice found that the referring national court had affirmed that the dispute should in fact be decided on the basis of Italian customs law and thereby indirectly on the basis of the rules in the Community Customs Code. On this basis the Court of Justice held that it had jurisdiction to give a preliminary ruling on the question referred, noting that its jurisdiction could not be called in question merely because the competent administrative authorities in the case were other than those which decided in customs cases.[118]

In *Gmurzynska*, the owner of a German art gallery had bought a work of art in the Netherlands. When importing the work into Germany a turnover tax on importation was payable. The amount of the tax was determined by the German rules and depended on the classification of the work of art. On this point the German rules referred to the Community's nomenclature used in the Common Customs Tariff. In other words, the case had to be decided under German law, but it depended on the correct classification of the work of art under Community law. The Court of Justice held that, neither according to the wording of Article 234 of the EC Treaty nor the purpose of the procedure introduced by this Article, was it apparent that the Treaty's draftsmen intended to deprive the Court of Justice of jurisdiction over references for preliminary rulings on questions of Community law provisions in the special instances where a Member State's legislation refers to the content of such provisions in order to determine the provisions that apply to a purely domestic matter in the Member State in question. On this basis the Court of Justice gave a preliminary ruling.[119]

Where in this situation the Court of Justice has taken jurisdiction, it has generally emphasised the importance of avoiding the risk of differences of interpretation of Community law even where it is not directly applicable.[120] In this connection it is

---

[118] Case C-1/99 *Kofisa Italia* [2001] ECR I-207.
[119] Case C-231/89 *Gmurzynska* [1990] ECR I-4003.
[120] Case C-447/04 *Ostermann* [2005] ECR I-10407, paras 19–20; Case C-222/01 *British American Tobacco Manufacturing* [2004] ECR I-4683, paras 39–42; Case C-130/95 *Giloy* [1997] ECR I-4291, para 28; Case C-247/97 *Schoonbroodt* [1998] ECR I-8095, paras 13–16; and Case C-267/99 *Adam* [2001] ECR I-7467, paras 21–32 (but compare with the Opinion of Advocate General Tizzano in the same case, paras 22–35).

not necessary for there to be a verbatim implementation of the Community law provisions in the national law or contract.[121] On the other hand, it is a requirement that the national law provisions which are applicable in the main proceedings should in fact be based on the Community law provisions for which interpretation is requested. If this is not the case, the Court of Justice's interpretation of the Community law provisions will not be relevant to the application of the national rules, and the Court of Justice will decline jurisdiction to give a ruling.[122]

The Court of Justice has adopted the same approach as the one set out above where the application of Community rules outside the scope of their application is based on an agreement under contract law.

In *Federconsorzi*, the Italian intervention authority entered into a contract by public tender with Federconsorzi to undertake interventions in the olive oil sector. The contract contained a provision that 'the contractor shall be liable ... for any losses for which he is responsible to the amount stipulated by the Community legislation in force'. There was thus a direct application of Community rules, but this was outside their scope of application under Community law. The national court referred a question to the Court of Justice as to how the Community rules determined the value of the stolen goods. The Court of Justice noted that, for the Community's legal order, there was a clear interest in all Community law provisions being interpreted uniformly, regardless of the circumstances under which a provision might be applied, in order to forestall future differences of interpretation. Since the contractual term in the main proceedings referred to the Community rules with a view to establishing the parties' financial liabilities, the Court of Justice could interpret these rules by giving a preliminary ruling. However, at the same time the Court of Justice made clear that its jurisdiction was limited to a review of the Community rules in question. It was therefore neither possible to consider the scheme of the contract nor the provisions of national law which could determine the extent of the contractual obligations.[123]

5.3.4. Community law has been the model for national law

The third category of situations includes those cases where, other than in the context of an obligation under Community law to implement or enforce a Community act in national law, a Member State has chosen to model purely national legislation

---

[121] Case C-306/99 *BIAO* [2003] ECR I-1, paras 19, 30, and 91–4.

[122] Case C-2/97 *IP* [1998] ECR I-8597, paras 58–62. This approach to some extent is mirrored in the Court of Justice's Opinion 1/91, [1991] ECR I-6079, paras 13–29, according to which the fact that provisions in an agreement between the Community and its Member States on the one hand and some third countries on the other were worded identically to Community provisions did not mean that they must necessarily be interpreted identically. What was important was the wording in combination with the objectives of the provisions in question.

[123] Case C-88/91 *Federconsorzi* [1992] ECR I-4035, paras 6–10.

upon Community law provisions. While the situation discussed in Section 5.3.3 above concerns cases where the Community rules are given a wider application than required under Community law, in this third situation the link to Community law is weaker. Here the Community rules have only been used as a model or source of inspiration for the national rules. Often it will be made clear in the legislation's *travaux préparatoires* that the national rules must be interpreted in the light of their Community law model. This practice is particularly widespread in relation to the Member States' competition rules,[124] but it also exists in other areas.[125] In principle Community law does not apply here, so that an interpretation of Community law will only very indirectly have significance for the correct solution to the main proceedings.

There has been some debate about whether the Court of Justice can—and should—give preliminary rulings on such questions. On the one hand, formally speaking, Community law is not applied in the main proceedings; it is merely one among several aids to interpretation. Moreover, the risk that the lack of a preliminary ruling will give rise to a practice that is unsustainable in situations regulated by Community law is less pronounced in the situations covered by the present category than in the situations described in Section 5.3.3 regarding cases of direct application of Community law outside the scope of Community law. On the other hand, the Court's interpretation of Community law where this law has served as a model for national law will often be highly relevant for the actual decision in the main proceedings.

Up until the mid 1990s the Court of Justice accepted references of questions related to such national rules, without attaching any conditions to the referring national court's subsequent application of the preliminary ruling.[126]

In *Fournier*, a French court had to consider the interpretation of a Council directive which harmonised the Member States' laws on insurance against civil liability in respect of the use of motor vehicles. In connection with a traffic

---

[124] Likewise, the new Member States, prior to their accession to the EU, have largely modelled their competition laws on the Community's competition rules. The fact that this 'copying' took place prior to accession can hardly, in itself, be assumed to have general significance for whether the Court of Justice will consider itself to have jurisdiction if a national court in one of these Member States were to refer a question in relation to the national competition rules, provided that the facts of the case relate to the time after the accession to the Community of the Member State in question.

[125] eg the Brussels Convention (which has now almost entirely been replaced by Council Regulation (EC) No 44/2001 on jurisdiction and the recognition and enforcement of judgments in civil and commercial matters, generally known as the Brussels I Regulation) lays down rules on the choice of forum whereby in civil cases it is decided which courts of a Member State have jurisdiction. The United Kingdom, which consists of different jurisdictions (England and Wales, Scotland, and Northern Ireland), has in part copied these rules in its national legislation.

[126] Case 166/84 *Thomasdünger* [1985] ECR 3001, para 11.

accident, the French court had to determine whether compensation was due from a French, a Dutch, or a German insurance bureau. In this connection the French court had to interpret an agreement between the national bureaux. There was thus a private contract which was nevertheless closely linked to the directive. However, during the preliminary ruling procedure it was argued that one of the several possible interpretations of the directive would produce unsatisfactory consequences. On this the Court of Justice stated that this argument was irrelevant, even though the national court had put its question for a preliminary ruling with regard to the agreement between the national bureaux, in order to determine which bureau had liability to pay compensation to the victim. This was so because the rules in the agreement for which bureau was liable to pay compensation were part of an area which was not covered by the directive. Therefore, the terms used in the agreement should not necessarily be given the same meanings as the terms used in the directive. On this basis the Court of Justice concluded that it was up to the national court, which alone had jurisdiction to interpret the agreement between the national bureaux, to give such meanings to the terms used in the agreement as the national court found appropriate. In this connection the national court was not bound by the meanings which must be attributed to the corresponding terms used in the directive.[127]

However, in the mid 1990s the Court of Justice qualified this practice and refused to consider preliminary questions in cases where the national legislator has not determined, with binding effect for the national courts, that the relevant national provisions must be interpreted in the same way as the Community rule which forms the basis of the reference for a preliminary ruling.

In *Kleinwort Benson*, an English court made a reference for a preliminary ruling on the interpretation of the Brussels Convention. The United Kingdom consists of three jurisdictions (England and Wales, Scotland, and Northern Ireland), and there is therefore a need for rules within the United Kingdom for the allocation of jurisdiction between the different legal systems. Upon the implementation in the United Kingdom of the Brussels Convention, on the allocation of jurisdiction between the different Member States' national courts, it was therefore decided at the same time to establish rules on the internal allocation of jurisdictions between the different UK legal systems. In *Kleinwort Benson* a dispute arose between a party in England and a party in Scotland. The dispute was brought before an English court, but the Scottish party argued that the case should be dealt with by a Scottish court. The English court found that a decision of the issue depended on the scope of application of two of the provisions in the UK legislation. These provisions had essentially the same wording as two provisions in the Brussels Convention.

---

[127] Case C-73/89 *Fournier* [1992] I-5621, paras 22–3.

At the time when the case was heard the Court of Justice had not yet given its interpretation of these two provisions of the Convention, and the English court therefore referred a question to the Court of Justice for a preliminary ruling on the correct interpretation. The Court of Justice refused to answer the question: The UK legislation did not make a direct and unconditional *renvoi* to Community law, so as to incorporate it into the domestic UK legal order. On the contrary, the legislation merely used the Convention as a model and only partially reproduced the provisions of the Convention. Even though a number of the Convention's provisions were reproduced word for word, other provisions of the UK legislation departed from the wording of the corresponding provisions in the Convention. In addition to this, the UK legislation expressly gave the authorities powers to make amendments which were 'designed to produce divergence' between the provisions of the law on the internal UK legal systems and the corresponding provisions in the Convention, as interpreted by the Court of Justice. Finally, the UK legislation did not absolutely and unconditionally bind the national courts to apply the Court of Justice's interpretations of the Convention when deciding on cases brought before them. The national courts were thus only required to have regard to the Court of Justice's case law. On this basis the Court of Justice found that the referring national court was free to decide whether the Court of Justice's interpretations should apply under the national law which was modelled on the Convention. The Court of Justice found that this meant that it did not have jurisdiction to give a preliminary ruling on the question.[128]

Hence, in *Kleinwort Benson* the Court of Justice based its refusal to give a preliminary ruling on the following three grounds:

- First, there was no direct and unconditional reference to Community law.
- Next, according to the relevant provisions, the UK authorities had powers to make amendments which could lead to the national rules diverging from the Community rules.
- Third, the UK law did not absolutely and unconditionally bind the national courts to use the Court of Justice's interpretations when deciding the main proceedings.

Subsequent practice has shown that the first of these three grounds is not applied strictly. Thus, it is not a requirement that there should be complete identity between the wording of the Community provisions and the wording of the provisions which only apply to national circumstances. Indeed, as already referred to in Section 5.3.3, the Court of Justice does not demand there to be absolute identity in the wording of the provisions in relation to cases where the Community rule in

---

[128] Case C-346/93 *Kleinwort Benson* [1995] ECR I-615, paras 16–25.

question is to be interpreted in order for the referring national court to decide a dispute concerning a national implementing provision in a situation where the underlying Community rule does not apply.

In *BIAO*, the Court of Justice found it sufficient to consider the questions referred admissible that the national legislator had wanted cases falling outside the scope of application of Community law to be treated in the same way as cases within the scope of application of Community law.[129]

In *Adam*, Advocate General Tizzano pointed out that the national legislation did not even contain an indirect reference to the Community legislation in question. Nevertheless, the Court of Justice replied to the preliminary questions.[130]

The second of the grounds which the Court of Justice put forward in *Kleinwort Benson* does not seem to be well suited for distinguishing cases where the Court of Justice does not have jurisdiction. Here the Court of Justice pointed out that, according to the UK rules, the UK authorities had powers to make amendments which could lead to the national rules diverging from the Community rules. However, vis-à-vis Community law, national legislators always have this competence outside the scope of application of Community law.[131] It would give rise to considerable legal uncertainty if the Court of Justice's jurisdiction were dependent on whether, in a given case, the national legislator had stated that it was prepared to make such amendments. Unsurprisingly, the second of the grounds on which the refusal in *Kleinwort Benson* was based has not been found significant in the Court's subsequent practice.

On the other hand, at least in principle the third ground given in *Kleinwort Benson*, that there can only be a reference for a preliminary ruling if the national courts have an absolute and unconditional obligation to apply the Court of Justice's interpretation of Community rules, has been maintained in subsequent cases.[132] Indeed, this approach is in line with the Court of Justice's Opinion 1/91 in which it observed that it would be unacceptable if the preliminary rulings which it was supposed to give to EFTA State courts were 'to be purely advisory and without any binding effects. Such a situation would change the nature of the function of the Court of Justice as it is conceived by the EEC Treaty, namely that of a court whose judgments are binding.'[133]

---

[129] Case C-306/99 *BIAO* [2003] ECR I-1, paras 19, 30, 81, and 91–4.

[130] Case C-267/99 *Adam* [2001] ECR I-7467, paras 27–9 in the Advocate General's Opinion.

[131] Betlem, Case note to Case C-346/93 Kleinwort Benson Ltd v City of Glasgow District Council [1995] ECR I-615' (1996) CML Rev Vol 33, 137, 145.

[132] Case C-217/05 *Confederación Española de Empresarios de Estaciones de Servicio* [2006] ECR I-11987, paras 21–2; and Case C-306/99 *BIAO* [2003] ECR I-1, para 93.

[133] Opinion 1/91 [1991] ECR I-6079, para 61.

Nevertheless, the above view may be contrasted with the observation by Advocate General Sharpston in *Les Vergers du Vieux Tauves* that 'the judgment of the Court in the present case could be regarded in a sense as purely advisory—it will be open to the Member State to amend its legislation or simply disregard the ruling'. She continued by observing that this would always be the case in those situations where Community law has been the model for national law and that this is of the essence of the Court's case law in the field, and still it has not prevented the Court from ruling those cases admissible.[134] Thus, in practice, the Court of Justice seems to apply a presumption that if a national court has made a preliminary reference, it will regard itself as bound to follow the Court of Justice's interpretation of the Community rules.[135] Even if the Member State government, responsible for applying the relevant national legislation, argues that this legislation was not intended to transpose the Community rule in question for domestic situations this may not suffice to rebut the presumption.[136] Only if this presumption is rebutted will the Court of Justice refuse to give a preliminary ruling.[137]

In *ETI*, an Italian court requested the interpretation of Article 81 of the EC Treaty and of the general principles of Community law. The main proceedings concerned the application of Italian competition law which was to be interpreted on the basis of the principles of Community competition law. In its intervention before the Court of Justice the Commission argued that the preliminary questions should be declared inadmissible because the Italian law did not specify that the national courts must apply the interpretations of the Court of Justice absolutely and unconditionally. In assessing whether it had jurisdiction to give a preliminary ruling in the case, the Court of Justice noted that, in accordance with its established practice, it did have jurisdiction to give preliminary rulings on Community law in cases where national law refers to it. At the same time, the Court of Justice noted that there was no suggestion in the wording of the relevant Italian provision, the order for reference, or the other documents before the Court that the reference to Community law in that provision was subject to any condition whatsoever. There was thus nothing to suggest that the national court would *not* consider itself bound to apply the Court of Justice's interpretation of Community rules, so the Court of Justice answered the questions.[138]

---

[134] Case C-48/07 *Les Vergers du Vieux Tauves* (ECJ 22 December 2008), at para 37 of the Opinion.
[135] Case C-48/07 *Les Vergers du Vieux Tauves* (ECJ 22 December 2008), para 25.
[136] ibid, paras 22 and 25.
[137] Regarding the binding effect of a preliminary ruling rendered in these situations see Ch 12, s 3.1 below.
[138] Case C-280/06 *ETI* [2007] ECR I-10893, paras 19–29. See also Case C-170/03 *Feron* [2005] ECR I-2299, paras 10–11.

It thus appears from the above that what is decisive is whether the national legislator has (1) decided to deal with situations outside the scope of application of Community law in the same way as situations which fall under Community law,[139] and (2) whether the national courts may be presumed to be obliged to apply the Court of Justice's interpretations of Community rules. In practice this means that there is no real difference between the situations discussed above in Section 5.3.3 and the situations dealt with in this section.

The Court of Justice's approach in this area is controversial and it has been criticised in the legal literature.[140] Likewise, some of the Advocates General have expressed scepticism about the practice of the Court of Justice.[141] From a formal point of view it also seems problematic that the Court of Justice is willing to give preliminary rulings in situations where Community law is not applicable in the main proceedings. Conversely, it can have practical significance that the Court of Justice is willing to assist the national courts in such cases. This significance will increase as more Member States draw inspiration from Community law when framing their national rules.[142]

The considerations that apply in relation to national law also apply to international agreements that are modelled on Community rules, but where there is no right to make a reference for a preliminary ruling. An example of this is the Lugano Convention, which is modelled on the Brussels Convention. It is not clear whether the Court of Justice can give rulings on the interpretation of provisions in the Brussels Convention (or the Brussels I Regulation) where the main proceedings concern the application of parallel provisions in the Lugano Convention. If the referring national court is obliged to apply the Court of Justice's interpretation of

---

[139] Case C-267/99 *Adam* [2001] ECR I-7467, para 29.

[140] K Lenaerts, 'Form and Substance of the Preliminary Ruling Procedure' in D Curtin and T Heukels (eds), *Institutional Dynamics of European Integration, Vol II, Essays in Honour of Henry G. Schermers* (1994) 355, 359; V Hatzopoulos, 'De l'arrêt Foglia-Novello à l'arrêt TWD Textilwerke' (1994) Revue du Marché Unique Européen Vol 3, 195, 216ff; D Simon, 'Questions préjudicielles' (1991) Journal de droit international Vol 118, 455, 457; and N Fenger, 'Article 177' in H Smit and P Herzog (eds), *The law of the European Community: a commentary on the EEC Treaty* (1997) 5, 5–466.

[141] Joined Opinion of Advocate General Jacobs in Case C-28/95 *Leur-Bloem* [1997] ECR I-4161 and Case C-130/95 *Giloy* [1997] ECR I-4161, paras 47–50; the Opinion of Advocate General Tesauro in Case C-346/93 *Kleinwort Benson* [1995] ECR I-615, para 27; the Opinion of Advocate General Colomer in Case C-1/99 *Kofisa Italia* [2001] ECR I-207, para 22; the Opinion of Advocate General Mancini in Case 166/84 *Thomasdünger* [1985] ECR 3001, para 2; and the Opinion of Advocate General Tizzano in Case C-267/99 *Christiane Adam* [2001] ECR I-7467, paras 28–35.

[142] T Tridimas, 'Knocking on Heaven's Door: Fragmentation, Efficiency and Defiance in the Preliminary Reference Procedure' (2003) 40 CML Rev 9, 36, has explained the practice as an expression that the Court of Justice sees itself as the Supreme Court of the Union and views the national and the Community legal orders as a unitary system.

the Community provisions it would seem natural to assume that the Court of Justice would give a preliminary ruling.[143]

5.3.5. *Internal situations*

The fourth and final category of situations, where the Court of Justice has been willing to answer preliminary references even though no Community act applies in the main proceedings, concerns cases where, according to the law of a Member State, the protection of the citizens may not be weaker in situations which are not governed by Community law than in situations which are so governed. In such cases the national courts may therefore want clarification as to what rights Community law would have allowed the parties if there had been the necessary cross-border element.

In *Guimont*, a criminal prosecution was brought against Jean-Pierre Guimont for possessing, with a view to selling or offering for sale, Emmenthal cheese with deceptive labelling. Guimont's defence was that the French provisions were contrary to the EC Treaty's provisions on the free movement of goods. On the face of it this argument did not seem strong, since the facts in the main proceedings seemed to concern a situation which, according to the practice of the Court of Justice, would only be covered by the provisions of the Treaty if there were a link to imported goods, and this was not the situation in this case. Nevertheless the Court of Justice considered that it had jurisdiction to give a ruling. A ruling could be useful to the national court where the national law required that a domestic producer should have the same rights as those which a producer from another Member State would be able to rely on in a corresponding situation.[144]

Salzmann also concerned a reference for a preliminary ruling where all the elements of the main proceedings concerned a single Member State. The Court of Justice stated that there is a presumption that questions submitted by national courts are relevant. Only in exceptional circumstances can the Court of Justice refrain from giving a preliminary ruling. However, where national law requires that a national be allowed to enjoy the same rights as those which nationals of other Member States would derive from Community law in the same situation, this would not correspond to such exceptional circumstances. In the case in question, the Austrian court considered that Austrian citizens could claim such equal treatment. Thus a preliminary ruling could be given.[145]

---

143 Contrast with J Hill, *International Commercial Disputes* (2005) 58ff.
144 Case C-448/98 *Guimont* [2000] ECR I-10663, paras 13–24. See likewise Case C-281/98 *Angonese* [2000] ECR I-4139, paras 15–20.
145 Case C-300/01 *Salzmann* [2003] ECR I-4899, paras 23–35.

In a consistent line of rulings beginning as early as 1990 the Court of Justice seems to have made it a general rule to accept references relating to the four Treaty-based freedoms, even where the actual case before the national court does not concern a situation with links to other Member States.[146] In this situation the Court of Justice does not require the referring court to substantiate or even merely to state that national law contains a principle of equal treatment. Rather the Court of Justice limits itself to observing that a ruling on the question referred might in fact affect the decision in the main proceedings if such a principle of equal treatment were to exist, and that the mere possibility of this is sufficient to warrant a full examination of the referred questions.

5.4. Circumstances arising before entry into the European Community

The Court of Justice does not have jurisdiction to give preliminary rulings if the facts in the main case giving rise to the preliminary questions all relate to a period prior to the accession of a Member State to the Community.[147]

In *Ceramika Paradyz*, a Polish court referred a question on the interpretation of the First and Sixth VAT Directives. The Court of Justice found that the factual circumstances in the main proceedings related to the period prior to Poland's entry into the Community. The Court therefore held that it did not have jurisdiction to give a preliminary ruling in the case.[148]

In *Rechberger*, an Austrian court had to consider claims from a number of purchasers of package holidays from a package tour operator. This gave rise to questions on the interpretation of the Directive on package travel, package holidays, and package tours which Austria should already have implemented on the basis of the EEA Treaty, to which Austria was signatory, before its accession to the Community. Some of the cases had arisen immediately before Austria acceded to the Community, while other cases had arisen after the date of accession. The Court of Justice held that it only had jurisdiction to give a ruling on Austria's implementation of

---

[146] The first judgment appears to be Joined Cases C-297/88 and C-197/89 *Dzodzi* [1990] ECR I-3763. The view has been put forward that this development might be part of a wider transformation of the European Union where eventually all 'Union citizens' shall have the same rights under Community law, see further M Broberg, 'The preliminary reference procedure and questions of international and national law' in P Eeckhout and T Tridimas (eds), *Yearbook of European Law 2009* (forthcoming).

[147] Case C-321/97 *Andersson and Wåkerås-Andersson* [1999] ECR I-3551, paras 23–33; and Case C-300/01 *Salzmann* [2003] ECR I-4899, para 68. See also C Naômé, *Le renvoi préjudiciel en droit européen* (2007) 80–3 who also provides references to unpublished cases. Concerning preliminary references and lack of relevance *ratione temporis,* see further Ch 5, ss 4.9 and 4.10.

[148] Case C-168/06 *Ceramika Paradyz* [2007] ECR I-29, paras 20–5. For a critical comment on this case, see N Póltorak, '*Ratione Temporis* Application of the Preliminary Rulings Procedure' (2008) 45 CML Rev 1357, 1372–5.

the directive in relation to the period following Austria's accession to the Community.[149]

The approach of the Court of Justice is not always fully consistent, however.

In *Beck*, concerning an Austrian case, it was objected that the facts in the main proceedings related to the time prior to Austria's membership of the EU. The Court of Justice dismissed this objection, stating that it was not for it to examine the factual or legal basis of a reference for a preliminary ruling.[150]

The same reasoning can be applied in cases where the Court of Justice has a question referred to it concerning an area which, at the time when the facts arose, was regulated by the EU but without falling within the jurisdiction of the Court of Justice. It is natural to assume that in such a case the Court of Justice would refuse to give a preliminary ruling, even if the area in question had subsequently come within its jurisdiction.

In *Bourquain*, a German court made a preliminary reference concerning the interpretation of a provision in the Convention implementing the Schengen Agreement which was signed in 1990. The main proceedings related to a criminal act which Mr Bourquain was held to have committed while a member of the French Foreign Legion. For this he was sentenced *in absentia* by a French court in 1961. Mr Bourquain managed to hide in Eastern Germany, but was discovered in 2001. In 2002 he was charged by the German public prosecutor before the German courts. The German court hearing the case was faced with the question whether Mr Bourquain could invoke the principle of *ne bis in idem* as laid down in the Convention implementing the Schengen Agreement. The Court of Justice held that it did have jurisdiction to answer the question: Although the Convention implementing the Schengen Agreement was not yet in force in France at the time when Mr Bourquain's first conviction was pronounced by a competent French judicial authority, it was, however, in force in France and Germany when the court before which the second proceedings were brought considered the conditions governing the applicability of the *ne bis in idem* principle, which prompted the reference for a preliminary ruling.[151]

Arguably, it follows from *Bourquain* that the Court of Justice only considered itself competent to hear the case because the preliminary question related to facts

---

[149] Case C-140/97 *Rechberger* [1999] ECR I-3499, paras 38 and 40.

[150] Case C-355/97 *Beck* [1999] ECR I-4977, paras 18–27. See also para 7 of the Opinion of the Advocate General.

[151] Case C-297/07 *Bourquain* (ECJ 11 December 2008), para 28. See also Case C-491/07 *Turanský* (ECJ 22 December 2008), para 27 and Case C-367/05 *Kraaijenbrink* [2007] ECR I-6619, para 22.

that arose after the matter had become regulated by the EU, namely to the second proceedings against Mr Bourquain and not to the first proceedings against him.

In general, a Community provision will apply to the effects of a situation which has arisen before the provision takes effect, but where the effects of the situation arise after this time [152] Therefore, if there is a reference for a preliminary ruling that relates to a situation in the main proceedings which arose before a Member State's accession to the Community, but where this situation continues to produce effects following the accession, the Court of Justice will have jurisdiction to give a ruling with regard to these latter effects. In its more recent case law the Court of Justice has applied a rather strict interpretation of the requirement that the situation must continue to produce effects following the accession in order for the Court to have jurisdiction to give a preliminary ruling.[153] Indeed, it has been argued that the Court's most recent practice may be interpreted as meaning that it does not have jurisdiction under these circumstances either.[154]

5.5. The facts in the main proceedings

A national court cannot refer a question to the Court of Justice about the correct interpretation of the facts in the main proceedings. Such a question will either be rejected or, if the purpose of the question is to obtain an interpretation of Community law for application in the case in question, it will be reformulated.[155]

In *Ecologistas en Acción-CODA*, a Spanish court referred a question as to whether some administrative records 'complied with the obligations' arising from a specific Directive. The Court of Justice answered that any assessment of the facts in the case was a matter for the national court and therefore declined to answer the question.[156]

Likewise, the Court of Justice cannot judge the correctness of an expert opinion,[157] nor can it resolve differences about the factual circumstances of the main proceedings.[158] Such matters are under the sole jurisdiction of national courts.[159]

---

[152] Case C-162/00 *Pokrzeptowicz-Meyer* [2002] ECR I-1049, para 50.
[153] See in particular Case C-168/06 *Ceramika Paradyz* [2007] ECR I-29.
[154] See—for a critical view—N Póltorak, '*Ratione Temporis* Application of the Preliminary Rulings Procedure' (2008) 45 CML Rev 1357–81, K Herrmann, 'Gebrauchtwagenhandel—Wie Richter aus neuen EU-Mitgliedstaaten den Dialog mit dem EuGH aufnehmen' (2007) 18 Europäische Zeitschrift für Wirtschaftsrecht 385; and M Bobek, 'Learning to Talk: Preliminary Rulings, The Courts of the New Member States and the Court of Justice' (2008) 45 CML Rev 1611, 1616–20.
[155] Case C-451/03 *Servizi Ausiliari Dottori Commercialisti* [2006] ECR I-2941, para 69; and Case C-282/00 *RAR* [2003] ECR I-4741, para 47.
[156] Case C-142/07 *Ecologistas en Acción-CODA* [2008] ECR I-6097, paras 47–51.
[157] Case C-332/88 *Alimenta* [1990] ECR I-2077, para 21.
[158] Case 51/74 *Hulst* [1975] ECR 79, para 12.
[159] Case 36/79 *Denkavit* [1979] ECR 3439, para 12.

In the interpretation of Community law the Court of Justice relies on the facts presented by the national court. However, depending on the circumstances, the Court of Justice will supplement—and in very special circumstances even correct—the understanding of the facts expressed by the national court with a view to giving an interpretation of Community law that is both correct and relevant for the resolution of the dispute in the main proceedings.[160]

5.6. Application of Community law in the main proceedings

Article 234 distinguishes between the interpretation of Community law and its application in the actual case before the national court (the legal classification of facts or 'subsumption'). While the Court of Justice has jurisdiction to interpret Community law, it is for the national court to apply the Court of Justice's interpretation in the main proceedings.[161] In other words, within the framework of the procedures for preliminary rulings, it is for the national court to decide whether Community law applies in the case before it, and whether a given national law provision is in accordance with Community law.[162]

On this basis, references to the Court of Justice for preliminary rulings should be formulated so that the Court of Justice is not requested to make a specific application of the law to the case. Instead, the formulation of the question should ensure that the Court of Justice can make an, in principle, abstract interpretation of the relevant Community rule.[163]

Nevertheless, an abstract question may be formulated in such a way that it relates to the factual circumstances of the main proceedings.[164] The Court of Justice for example is frequently asked to rule on whether a trade restriction is proportionate. In this respect the referring court is free to invite the Court of Justice to give an interpretation that takes due account of the facts in the main proceedings so that whilst formulated in abstract terms, in reality the legal classification of the facts is

---

[160] See further below Ch 10, s 3.3.3, and Ch 11, s 2.4.

[161] Case C-220/06 *Asociación Profesional de Empresas de Reparto y Manipulado d Correspondencia* [2007] ECR I-12175, para 36; and Case C-162/06 *International Mail Spain* [2007] ECR I-9911, para 24.

[162] Case C-279/06 *CEPSA* (ECJ 11 September 2008), paras 27–30. If a national court considers that a specific provision of Community law applies in the main proceedings, the Court of Justice will normally accept this, at least in cases where there is no information about the facts of the case which give grounds for questioning this view; cf Case C-9/02 *Hughes de Lasteyrie du Saillant* [2004] ECR I-2409, para 41. See also, in relation to the jurisdiction of the EFTA Court under Art 34 of the Agreement between the EFTA States on the Establishment of a Surveillance Authority and a Court of Justice, Case E-8/00 *LO and NKF* [2002] EFTA Court Report 114, para 48.

[163] See also below Ch 8, s 3.2.2.

[164] See below ibid.

made in the preliminary ruling.[165] Indeed, the doctrine that under Article 234 the Court of Justice does not have jurisdiction to rule on whether a given national law or administrative decision complies with Community law does not preclude the Court of Justice showing in the preliminary ruling how the Community rule will apply to a situation such as the one in the main proceedings. Where a preliminary ruling contains such guidance, de facto it amounts to the Court of Justice applying Community law to the facts and national law aspects in the main proceedings.[166] Hence, to a fair extent the distinction between interpretation and application, where the former falls within the Court's competence whereas the latter is a matter solely for the referring court, is more a question of form than a substantive delimitation of the Court's competence.

When a national court invites the Court of Justice to rule directly and explicitly on the application of Community law in a particular factual situation, the Court will not normally decline jurisdiction and hold the question to be inadmissible. Instead it will reformulate the preliminary question so that it fulfils the formal requirements whereupon it will answer the reformulated question.[167] The extent to which the Court will give a general or fact specific answer depends on a range of factors including the subject matter of the dispute, the information contained in the reference as well as in the observations presented to the Court during the preliminary proceedings, the certainty with which the consequences of the ruling can be foreseen, and how unanimous the participating judges are about the answer to the preliminary question.[168]

---

[165] G Davies, 'Abstractness and concreteness in the preliminary reference procedure: implications for the division of powers and effective market regulation' in N N Shuibhne (ed), *Regulating the Internal Market* (2006) 210, 218–25 provides a number of examples of specificity by the Court of Justice in preliminary rulings.

[166] K Lenaerts et al, *Procedural Law of the European Union* (2006) 187, and K Lenaerts, 'Form and Substance of the Preliminary ruling Procedure' in D Curtin and T Heukels (eds), *Institutional Dynamics of European Integration, Vol II, Essays in Honour of Henry G Schermers* (1994) 355, 364–70.

[167] See below Ch 11, ss 2.1 and 2.2.

[168] See below Ch 11, s 3.

5

WHEN CAN A REFERENCE FOR A PRELIMINARY RULING BE MADE?

1. Overview

According to both the second and third paragraphs of Article 234 of the EC Treaty, the preliminary reference procedure applies whenever a question concerning Community law is raised before a national court or tribunal. Furthermore, according to the second paragraph of Article 234, the national court or tribunal must consider 'that a decision on the question is necessary to enable it to give judgment'. In other words, the answer of the Court of Justice to the question referred must be relevant to the decision in the main proceedings, whereas it is not the task of the Court to rule on hypothetical questions. According to the wording of the third paragraph of the provision, there is no corresponding requirement for the relevance of decisions that cannot be appealed to a higher instance. This paragraph only states that '[w]here any such question is raised in a case pending before a court or tribunal of a Member State against whose decisions there is no judicial remedy under national law, that court or tribunal shall bring the matter before the Court of Justice.' The formulation notwithstanding, a party to the main proceedings cannot, merely by appealing to the highest instance, use Article 234(3) to force a national court to make a reference to the Court of Justice concerning a matter that is not relevant for the resolution of the dispute.[1] Indeed, as will be shown in this chapter, it is the established practice of the Court to reject such a reference.

The first part of the chapter analyses the practical application of the principle to hypothetical questions. First, we highlight, in Section 2, some general points regarding the referring court's margin of discretion to decide on the relevance of the question referred. Next, we analyse, in Section 3, the requirement that the Court of Justice's ruling is relevant for the specific court that has referred the question. We then examine when a preliminary ruling must be assumed to be irrelevant to the decision in the main proceedings, see Section 4. Further, we discuss, in Section 5, the so-called *Foglia* principle according to which the Court declines jurisdiction to reply to questions of interpretation which are submitted to it within the framework of procedural devices arranged by the parties in order to induce the Court to give its views on problems of Community law which do not correspond to an objective requirement inherent in the resolution of a dispute (contrived cases). Next, we turn to the question as to when a preliminary reference is precluded because the same issue is, has been, or could be subject to a direct action before the Court of Justice. In this respect, Section 6 examines the relationship between, on the one hand, the preliminary procedure and, on the other hand,

---

[1] Opinion of Advocate General Mischo in Case C-81/98 *Alcatel Austria* [1999] ECR I-7671; and D Anderson and M Demetriou, *References to the European Court* (2002) 95.

Articles 226 and 227 of the EC Treaty concerning infringement proceedings. Finally, Section 7 analyses the relationship between the preliminary procedure and Article 230 concerning actions for annulment before the Court of Justice (Court of First Instance).

The analysis will focus on the preliminary procedure as laid down in Article 234. That being said, the very same principles apply to the system of preliminary references under Article 35 of the EU Treaty.[2]

2. General Considerations

2.1. Who has jurisdiction to decide the relevance of a preliminary question?

According to the wording of Article 234(2), it is for the national court or tribunal to decide whether it is necessary to make a reference for a preliminary ruling in order to give judgment. This jurisdiction is naturally linked to the fact that it is the national court which is seized of the substance of the dispute and which must bear the final responsibility for the decision to be taken. The division of roles between the national courts and the Court of Justice provided for in Article 234 thus means that, in principle, the latter does not have jurisdiction to question the reasons for a decision to make a reference. Hence, the clear starting point is that the Court of Justice has to give a ruling whenever the question which is referred by a national court or tribunal concerns the validity or the interpretation of acts of the institutions of the Community.[3]

This allocation of roles, however, neither can nor should be used to refer questions where the reference has no purpose in relation to the main proceedings. In exercising its power of appraisal the national court in collaboration with the Court of Justice fulfils a duty entrusted to them both of ensuring that in the interpretations and application of the Treaty the law is observed. Whilst the spirit of cooperation, which must govern the performance of the duties assigned by Article 234 to the national courts on the one hand and the Court of Justice on the other, requires the latter to have regard to the national court's proper responsibilities, it also implies that, in the use which it makes of Article 234, the national court should equally have regard to the proper functioning of the Court of Justice in this field. Moreover, Article 234 does not give the latter jurisdiction to answer hypothetical questions, but only to contribute to the solution of actual legal disputes in the Member States.[4]

---

[2] Case C-105/03 *Pupino* [2005] ECR I-5285, para 30; Case C-467/05 *Dell'Orto* [2007] ECR I-5557, para 40; and Case C-404/07 *Katz* (ECJ 9 December 2008), para 31.

[3] Case C-231/89 *Gmurzynska-Bscher* [1990] ECR I-4003.

[4] Case 244/80 *Foglia II* [1981] 3045, paras 16 and 20.

Therefore, with a view to verifying its own jurisdiction to give a ruling, the Court of Justice has assumed the jurisdiction to examine the circumstances under which a question has been referred to it. In principle, Article 234 permits the Court of Justice neither to assess the facts of the case nor to review the grounds on which the question submitted for a preliminary ruling is based. Nonetheless, it is for the Court to set the measure whose validity is contested in a Community law context and to examine the criteria for interpretation established by Community law in order to be able to give the national court an adequate answer for the purpose of resolving the dispute in the main proceedings. If this examination shows that the Community law provision which the Court of Justice has been asked to consider is not relevant for deciding the dispute in the main proceedings, the Court of Justice will hold that it is not necessary to give a ruling on the provision.[5] For the same reason, the Court tries to restrict its interpretation of Community law to the factual situation before the national court, without venturing into other issues the resolving of which is not necessary for the resolution of the case before the national court.[6]

2.2. The margin of discretion of the national courts

In recent years, the Court of Justice has intensified its examination of whether it has jurisdiction to rule on preliminary questions that have no bearing on the resolution of the dispute in the main proceedings. However, the Court only refuses to treat the question as admissible 'if it is *quite obvious* that the interpretation of Community law or the examination of the validity of a rule of Community law sought by that court bears no relation to the actual nature of the case or the subject-matter of the main action'.[7]

It therefore frequently happens that the Court of Justice accepts the admissibility of a question even if it can be difficult to see the relevance of a preliminary ruling for the judgment in the main proceedings. As long as the Court cannot exclude the possibility that a preliminary ruling may be relevant, it will answer the question.

---

[5] Case 172/84 *Celestri* [1985] ECR 963, paras 12–16.

[6] Case C-319/94 *Dethier Equipment* [1998] ECR I-1061, paras 18–20; Case C-412/93 *Leclerc-Siplec* [1995] ECR I-179, paras 8 and 15–16; Joined Cases 196/88–198/88 *Cornee* [1989] ECR 2309, para 19; and Case 149/82 *Robards* [1983] ECR 171, paras 18–19.

[7] Case C-62/93 *BP Soupergaz* [1995] ECR I-1883, paras 9–11 (emphasis added). See also Case C-368/89 *Crispoltini I* [1991] ECR I-3695, para 11; Case C-67/91 *Asociatión Espanola de Banco Privada* [1992] ECR I-4785, paras 24–6; Case C-129/94 *Ruiz Bernaldez* [1996] ECR I-1829, para 7; Case C-143/94 *Furlanis Costruzioni* [1995] I-3633, paras 11–12; Joined Cases C-215/96 and C-216/96 *Bagnasco* [1999] ECR I-135, para 20; Case C-399/98 *Odine degli Architetti* [2001] ECR I-5409, para 41; Case C-33/99 *Fahmi and Esmoris Cerdeiro-Pinedo Amado* [2001] ECR I-2415, para 29; and Case C-414/07 *Magoora* (ECJ 22 December 2008), paras 21–5. See also Joined Cases C-462/03 and C-463/03 *Strabag and Kostmann* [2005] ECR I-5397, para 30, where it was not 'obvious' that the question had no relevance for the referring court, so that it was accepted for a substantive hearing.

When faced with such a situation the Court often comments that the presumption of relevance associated with references for preliminary rulings has not been overturned in the actual case and that this presumption can only be denied in exceptional cases.[8]

In *Ecotrade*, the Court of Justice found it doubtful whether the facts of the case were really such that the resolution of the dispute before the referring court would depend on the manner in which the Court answered the preliminary question. However, it answered the question referred.[9] The Ecotrade case was followed by *Piaggio* where Advocate General Colomer—in relation both to the earlier case and the case which was the subject of his Opinion—disputed that the Italian rules in question were framed in such a way that an interpretation of Community law could be relevant for the referring court. However, the Court of Justice repeated that there was room for doubt and found the questions admissible.[10]

In other words, in contrast to the *certiorari* principle known in US law, the Court of Justice does not use this practice to establish some form of sorting of cases, whereby it decides itself whether a case has sufficient interest to be given a substantive hearing.[11]

There are good reasons for this reticence in rejecting references for preliminary rulings. As the Court of Justice has emphasised, Article 234 is based on a distinct separation of functions between national courts and the Court of Justice.[12] In the first instance the test in Article 234 is first and foremost subjective, as the wording of the provision does not require a reference to be objectively necessary, but merely that the national court should 'consider' a reference to be necessary. Moreover, in contrast to the Court of Justice, the national court has direct knowledge of the facts of the case and the national law and must therefore be assumed to be in the better position to assess the relevance of a given question.

---

[8] Case C-355/97 *Beck and Bergdorf* [1999] ECR I-4977, paras 18–22, where not only the Austrian government and the Austrian authority which was a party to the case, but also the Commission as well as Advocate General la Pergola argued that a preliminary ruling would be of no use whatsoever in resolving the dispute in the main proceedings. In Joined Cases 98/85, 162/85, and 258/85 *Bertini* [1986] ECR 1885, para 8, the Court of Justice gave a ruling on the question referred, but at the same time it stated: 'It is difficult to see how the answers which the Court is asked to give can influence the decision in the main proceedings.' See also Case C-429/05 *Rampion and Godard* [2007] ECR I-8017, paras 17–26; Case C-286/02 *Bellio* [2004] I-3465, paras 26–9; Case C-247/02 *Sintesi* [2004] ECR I-9215, paras 18–24; and Case C-408/95 *Eurotunnel* [1997] ECR I-6315, paras 23–5.

[9] Case C-200/97 *Ecotrade* [1998] ECR I-7909, paras 23–7.

[10] Case C-295/97 *Piaggio* [1999] ECR I-3735.

[11] T Tridimas, 'Knocking on Heaven's Door: Fragmentation, Efficiency and Defiance in the Preliminary Reference Procedure' (2003) 40 CML Rev 9, 22. See also Ch 1, s 6.4.

[12] Case 126/80 *Salonia* [1981] ECR 1563, para 6.

However, the increasingly intense examination of the relevance of questions and the many decisions that now exist where the Court of Justice has refused to give a preliminary ruling means that it has become quite normal for one of the parties to the main proceedings to argue that the question should be rejected as irrelevant, even in cases where there is not much doubt that the referring court will actually apply the ruling of the Court of Justice in the case in question.[13]

According to Article 104 of the Court's Rules of Procedure, the Court may request clarification from the national court as to why it considers the question referred to be relevant for the decision in the main proceedings. The Court does not, however, consider itself obliged to obtain such clarification before deciding whether the question should be declared inadmissible on the grounds of a lack of connection with the dispute in the main proceedings.[14]

It is not fully clear whether the complexity and controversial character of a dispute has any bearing on whether the Court of Justice will refuse to consider an apparently irrelevant question. In an early case the Court regretted that the national court had not supplied any grounds for its orders requesting a preliminary ruling, particularly since it was impossible to determine, both from the documents submitted and from the facts of the case, what value an answer to the questions raised would have for the resolution of the case in the main proceedings. Nevertheless, the Court did not decline to reply to the questions submitted since a refusal 'would not be in the interests of procedural economy'.[15] It is unlikely that the Court would express itself in such terms today. However, it might occasionally be tempting for the Court to choose to answer an easy question rather than to tackle a difficult and confrontational assessment of whether the national court has referred an irrelevant question and thereby wasted the time and money of the parties. It has, however, also been argued that where a preliminary question appears to be interesting or concerns an important legal problem the Court of Justice seems less inclined to examine whether the question is of a hypothetical character.[16] If that is true, such an approach would make it difficult for parties and their legal advisers

---

[13] Case C-412/06 *Hamilton* [2008] ECR I-2383, paras 21–5; Case C-212/06 *Government of Communauté française* [2008] ECR I-1683, paras 25–31; Case C-439/06 *Citiworks* [2008] ECR I-391, paras 31–6; Case C-425/06 *Part Service* [2008] ECR I-897, paras 33–9; Case C-450/06 *Varec* [2008] ECR I-581, paras 22–5; Joined Cases C-223/99 and C-260/99 *Agorà and Excelsior* [2001] ECR I-3605, paras 17–21; Case C-373/00 *Adolf Truley* [2003] ECR I-1931, paras 19–26; Case C-255/00 *Grundig Italiana* [2002] ECR I-8003, paras 29–32.

[14] R Lane, 'Article 234: A few Rough Edges Still' in M Hoskins and W Robinson (eds), *A True European, Essays for Judge David Edward* (2003) 327, 335.

[15] Joined Cases 98/85, 162/85, and 258/85 *Bertini* [1986] ECR 1885, paras 4–9.

[16] C Barnard and E Sharpston, 'The Changing face of Article 177 References' (1997) 34 CML Rev 1113, 1144.

to know when the Court of Justice will admit a case for a substantive hearing.[17] Similarly, it has been argued that the Court of Justice will be less likely to dispute the relevance of a reference for a preliminary ruling from the supreme court of a Member State than a reference from a lower court.[18]

3. The Referring Court Must be Able to Apply the Court of Justice's Ruling to the Main Proceedings

As described above in Chapter 3, Section 3.1.7, it is in the sole competence of the national court to determine its jurisdiction under national law. The Court of Justice will therefore not decline the admissibility of a preliminary question on the grounds that the decision to refer has not been taken in accordance with the rules of national law governing the organisation of courts and their procedure.[19]

That being said, the power to seek a preliminary ruling is conferred on the national courts solely in order to enable them to resolve disputes before them by taking account of the elements of Community law clarified by the Court of Justice. It follows from both the wording and the scheme of Article 234 that a national court may only refer a question for a preliminary ruling if the Court of Justice's answer is 'necessary to enable it to give judgment'. That right is therefore limited to a national court which considers that a case pending before it raises questions of Community law requiring a decision on its own part. It is thus a condition that in the main proceedings the referring court is called upon to give a decision capable of taking into account the preliminary ruling. Indeed, the Court of Justice has no jurisdiction to admit a reference for a preliminary ruling when, at the time it is made, the procedure before the national court making the reference has already been terminated.

In contrast, it is not decisive whether the main proceedings have been reserved for judgment, as long as this does not preclude the national court from applying the preliminary ruling in its decision.

---

[17] See G Vandersanden, 'La procédure préjudicielle: À la recherche d'une identité perdue' in M Dony (ed), *Mélanges en hommage à Michel Waelbroeck, vol I* (1999) 619, 630. In the view of Vandersanden, the Court's margin for discretion in assessing whether a question is sufficiently linked to the dispute in the main proceedings makes it very difficult to predict when a question will be accepted.

[18] See D Anderson, 'The Admissibility of Preliminary References' in A Barav and D Wyatt (eds), *Yearbook of European Law 1994* (1996) 179, 187.

[19] Case C-309/02 *Radlberger Getränkegesellschaft* [2004] ECR I-11763, para 25, where the Court of Justice accepted the admissibility of a question referred by a court in a German state, even though one of the parties to the main proceedings argued that the question of the legality of a federal German law should be brought before a federal court.

In *Grogan*, the High Court in Dublin referred three questions for a preliminary ruling before deciding on a request for an injunction applied for by the plaintiff. An appeal was brought against that decision to the Supreme Court which granted the injunction applied for but did not overturn the High Court's decision to make a preliminary reference. Moreover, each of the parties was given leave to apply to the High Court in order to vary the decision of the Supreme Court in the light of the preliminary ruling to be given by the Court of Justice. The Court of Justice ruled that it had jurisdiction to answer the preliminary questions. Even though these had been referred as part of the proceedings on whether to impose the injunction, the Irish Supreme Court had expressly authorised the referring court to vary the injunction granted in the light of the preliminary ruling to be given by the Court of Justice. Hence, the Irish court making the reference was called upon to give a decision which could take into account the preliminary ruling.[20]

In *Siemens AG Österreich*, on the basis of a suit brought by the tenderer Siemens, the *Bundesvergabeamt* (Austrian Federal Procurement Office), had annulled a decision of a contracting authority not to revoke the procedure by which a contract had been awarded. In spite of this decision, the contracting authority decided to award the contract to another tenderer without going through a new public procurement process. In this connection the contracting authority took the view that the *Bundesvergabeamt* had not taken a legally binding decision that the contracting authority's decision to award the contract to the tenderer which had submitted the lowest tender was invalid or ought to have been annulled. Furthermore, the contracting authority appealed the decision of the *Bundesvergabeamt* to the *Verfassungsgericht* (Austrian Constitutional Court). The *Verfassungsgericht* annulled the decision of the *Bundesvergabeamt* on the grounds that it was a logical impossibility to annul a decision that an action should not be taken. Siemens then submitted a new complaint to the *Bundesvergabeamt* claiming the annulment of the contracting authority's decision to award the contract to the other tenderer. As part of the proceedings in this case, the *Bundesvergabeamt* referred a number of questions to the Court of Justice for preliminary rulings, which in effect concerned the clarification of whether the procedural rules in Austrian law were sufficient to ensure the effective fulfilment of the decisions taken by the *Bundesvergabeamt*. The Court of Justice stated that it was a requirement for questions to be admissible that they should still be relevant for the solution of the dispute in the main proceedings. In the present case, the request for a preliminary ruling was essentially based on the fact that the annulment decision of the *Bundesvergabeamt* could not be enforced. However, as the *Verfassungsgericht* had annulled the decision of the *Bundesvergabeamt*, the questions referred had become

---

[20] Case C-159/90 *Grogan* [1991] ECR I-4685, para 12. See also Case C-176/96 *Lehtonen* [2000] ECR I-2681, paras 19–20.

hypothetical. Nevertheless, the Court of Justice could not exclude the possibility that an answer to one of the questions—which concerned the right to use a sub-contractor—could still be of interest for the resolution of the dispute in the main proceedings. This would be the case if the dispute were to be continued before the civil courts which, under Austrian law, had jurisdiction to rule on a claim for compensation following the award of a contract.[21]

A reference does not become inadmissible simply because the composition of the judges of the referring court changes between the submission of the reference and the giving of the preliminary ruling, as long as it is still the same court that is to make the decision in the main proceedings. In contrast, the Court of Justice will not have jurisdiction in cases where the main proceedings have been referred to another court so that the referring court will not be able to apply the preliminary ruling.

In *Pardini*, an Italian court had referred four questions for a preliminary ruling in a case on interlocutory proceedings and at the same time it had granted interim relief. Proceedings on the substance of the case had not yet been initiated, and when they were to be initiated, the case would have been heard by another court. Hence, the purpose of seeking a preliminary ruling was apparently not to enable the referring court itself to arrive at a judicial decision. The starting point was therefore that the reference was inadmissible. However, both the plaintiff in the main proceedings and the Italian government had explained that the case had a special feature since, having granted the interim relief, the referring court had failed to set a date for the appearance of all parties. Under Italian law this meant that the case was still pending before the referring court, which could therefore still summon the parties with a view to confirming, amending, or revoking the interim relief, as long as the substantive proceedings had still not commenced. Accordingly, the Court of Justice had jurisdiction to answer the preliminary questions.[22]

---

[21] Case C-314/01 *Siemens AG Österreich* [2004] ECR I-2549, paras 31–9. One might ask whether it was correct to declare the question admissible on the grounds set out in the judgment. Indeed, the case before the *Bundesvergabeamt* did not concern a claim for compensation (it only concerned a claim for annulment) and the *Bundesvergabeamt* had no jurisdiction itself to decide on any future claim for compensation in the same case.

[22] Case 338/85 *Pardini* [1988] ECR 2041, paras 7–14, and see further C Naômé, *Le renvoi préjudiciel en droit européen* (2007) 95–6. As argued by R Gordon, *EC Law in Judicial Review* (2007) 120, where the English Court of Appeal grants permission to apply for judicial review on a renewed permission hearing but remits the case to the High Court, the Court of Appeal ought not to request a preliminary ruling. For the same reason Gordon argues that if the Court of Appeal considers that a preliminary ruling should be requested the safest course is for that court, when granting permission, to assume jurisdiction to hear the substantive application for judicial review.

In *Monin II*, the supervising judge in winding-up proceedings had referred several questions concerning Community law rules which the judge was not required to apply in the winding-up proceedings in question. The company which was subject to the proceedings argued that the judge could not make a decision to wind up the company before it had been decided whether the reasons behind the suspension of payments included conduct in breach of the EC Treaty by the French government. On this basis the supervising judge found that it could be relevant to find out whether the French government had disregarded its obligations under Community law, since the answer to this would enable him to assess the relevance of the arguments which the company had put forward to ensure its survival until the winding-up procedure had been completed. The Court of Justice noted that the supervising judge's interest in the answers to the questions referred essentially concerned the question of the chances which the company had to obtain a favourable ruling in proceedings against the French government for compensation, as well as in a case against the French competition authority. However, neither of these cases had been brought before the supervising judge, nor could they be brought before him. On these grounds the Court of Justice refused to give a preliminary ruling.[23]

If, after a reference has been made, it is evident that a preliminary ruling is no longer needed—for example because a settlement has been reached in the main proceedings—then the referring court should withdraw the reference on its own initiative, and thereby save the Court of Justice the time and the expense associated with giving preliminary rulings. In contrast, if the national court considers that it is still seized of the case in the main proceedings, the Court of Justice has normally not challenged this view.[24] In this respect, a preliminary ruling does not necessarily lose its relevance for the main proceedings just because the defendant in the proceedings admits the plaintiff's claims and meets his demands. The Court of Justice will maintain its jurisdiction if the national court upholds its request and if the main proceedings have not yet been concluded in a manner which excludes the possibility of the national court applying the preliminary ruling in its judgment.

In *Bernini*, the Court of Justice had been asked a number of questions concerning the right of an Italian citizen to receive student support in the Netherlands. After making the reference, the national court informed the Court of Justice that, following the latter's decision in *Di Leo*,[25] the Dutch government had now acknowledged the student's claims and that, moreover, the student had received the aid that she sought. However, the national court also said that it wished to

---

[23] Case C-428/93 *Monin II* [1994] ECR I-1707, paras 12–16.
[24] See also Ch 3, s 3.1.7 above, on admissibility objections based on the argument that the national court did not have jurisdiction under national law.
[25] Case C-308/89 *Di Leo* [1990] ECR I-4185.

receive as complete a reply as possible on the remaining unanswered questions. The Court of Justice noted that although the finance applied for had been granted, neither the letter from the referring court nor the observations submitted at the hearing gave reason to believe that the student had withdrawn her application. Accordingly, a dispute remained pending before the referring court, in the context of which that court was called upon to give a decision capable of taking into account a preliminary ruling. Furthermore, the referring court had re-evaluated the relevance of the questions referred following the *Di Leo* case and had found that the answers to only two of its five questions could be deduced from that judgment. On this basis the Court of Justice found that it did have jurisdiction to rule on the three remaining questions.[26]

In *Martinez*, following the national court's preliminary reference, the relevant national legislation was changed with the result that the plaintiff in the main proceedings was granted the right to child allowance claimed by him with retroactive effect. However the referring court had acquiesced to the plaintiff's argument that he nevertheless had a legal interest in the outcome of the case. A case thus remained pending before the referring court which could still take the Court of Justice's rulings into account. On this basis the Court of Justice found that it had jurisdiction.[27]

In *Arduino*, a judge in an Italian criminal court had fined the defendant for a traffic offence which had resulted in a collision with another car. The defendant had also been required to pay the litigation costs of the other driver. However, the Italian court refused to approve the fee charged by the other driver's lawyer, regardless of the fact that it was based on the rates which had been approved by a ministerial decree laying down fixed rates for the professional services of lawyers. This decision concerning the lawyer's fee was reversed on appeal and referred back for a new decision based on the decree. Thereafter the criminal court referred two questions to the Court of Justice concerning the compatibility of the decree with Article 81 of the EC Treaty on agreements which distort competition. The Italian government argued that the question was inadmissible. Indeed, the defendant's insurance company had paid the other driver's litigation costs after the appeal court had given its decision, and in light of this payment the other driver had

---

[26] Case C-3/90 *Bernini* [1992] ECR I-1071. In a case note on this judgment in (1992) CML Rev Vol 29, No 6, 1215, 1228, D O'Keeffe adds that the Court's answers to the questions were also relevant to other pending cases. However, this circumstance is irrelevant when assessing the admissibility since a question is only admissible if the answer can be used in the particular case in which it has been posed, see s 4.1 below.

[27] Case C-321/93 *Martinez* [1995] ECR I-2821, para 17. See also Case C-137/00 *Milk Marque* [2003] ECR I-7975, paras 32–41, where a company had initially voluntarily accepted the decision of the national competition authorities that it should be split up into smaller units, but shortly afterwards brought a case challenging the lawfulness of that decision; and Case C-336/05 *Echouikh* [2006] ECR I-5223, paras 27–33, where there was an outstanding question concerning payment of default interest.

withdrawn from the remainder of the proceedings. Moreover, the defendant's lawyer requested the referring court to order that the case should not proceed to judgment. In the view of the Italian government, the dispute in the main proceedings had therefore become devoid of purpose. In response to this, the Court of Justice noted that according to the documentation on the main proceedings, the case was still pending before the criminal court, and the government had not presented evidence of an agreement between the parties on the question of costs so as to bring the case to a close. The questions were therefore admissible.[28]

As the Court's jurisdiction is dependent on the continued existence of an action in the main proceedings the Court may also verify it of its own motion.[29] If circumstances arising after the submission of a request for a preliminary ruling indicate that the dispute in the main proceedings might have lapsed, the Court of Justice will often ask the referring court to confirm that the case is still pending and that a preliminary ruling is still needed. Normally that answer will be binding upon the Court of Justice. Indeed, since it is for the national courts to assess the need for a preliminary ruling, the Court of Justice cannot decline jurisdiction merely on the grounds that the national court has not convincingly shown that a preliminary ruling is still required.

In *Esso Española*, a Spanish court raised a number of questions in order to assess the relationship between Community law and a decree concerning the regulation of the business of a wholesaler of oil products in the Canary Islands. After the reference was made, another Spanish court annulled the decree. On this basis the plaintiff in the main proceedings requested the referring court to withdraw the request for a preliminary ruling. The referring court refused this request arguing that a ruling of the Court of Justice would be of major interest, not only to the Canary Islands, but for the whole of the Spanish national territory. Thereafter the Court of Justice wrote to the referring court and asked whether the case in question had not become devoid of purpose. However, the national court maintained its question and in this connection gave a different reason from that given to the plaintiff, namely that there had been an appeal to examine the judgment whereby the decree had been annulled. Furthermore, it stated that the annulment had not been made on the basis of the Community rules which were the subject of the request for a preliminary ruling. Lastly, it stated that if conflicting judgments were to be delivered, an action to harmonise them could be brought before the Tribunal Supremo. The Court of Justice thereafter found the questions to be admissible.[30]

Sometimes the national court's desire to maintain its request for a preliminary ruling is based on a misunderstanding of the procedure laid down in Article 234.

---

[28] Case C-35/99 *Arduino* [2002] ECR I-1529, paras 19–27.
[29] Joined Cases C-428/06–434/06 *UGT-Rioja* [2008] ECR I-6747, para 40.
[30] Case C-134/94 *Esso Española* [1995] ECR I-4223, paras 5–10.

It has, for example, happened that the referring court wrongly believed that Community law did not allow it to withdraw its request for a preliminary ruling. There have also been situations where the referring court wrongly assumed that even where it had taken a final decision in the main proceedings, the Court of Justice continued to have jurisdiction to make a ruling if the question was of general interest. Where there is such a misunderstanding, the Court of Justice declines to accept jurisdiction until the national court has confirmed that the main proceedings remain undecided under national law.

In *Zabala Erasun*, after a reference to the Court of Justice for a preliminary ruling, the Spanish government acceded to the claims of the plaintiff and paid the unemployment benefits claimed by the latter. Furthermore, the government declared that the payment, with retrospective effect, should be regarded as being covered by the scope of the relevant rule in Community law, as the plaintiff had argued in the main proceedings. Finally, the government submitted that the preliminary reference should be withdrawn as the dispute no longer existed. As a result of this the Court of Justice asked the referring court whether it maintained its request for a preliminary ruling. The national court replied in the affirmative. It explained that it could not accept the government's acquiescence, hold that the case had been terminated, and withdraw the questions referred for a preliminary ruling. This was so, first because the case was no longer pending before the court itself but had been referred to the Court of Justice, and secondly because the questions were of such importance that they went beyond the dispute between the parties in so far as the interpretation which the Court would give would have general scope. The Court of Justice held that these two points of reasoning did not fall under national law, but related to the interpretation of Article 234. On the first point, it followed from Article 234 that where a case is referred for a preliminary ruling, only the request for interpretation or a decision on validity is addressed to the Court; the case itself is not transferred. Consequently, the national court remains seised of the case, which is still pending before it. Only the procedure before that court is suspended until the Court of Justice has delivered its ruling on the reference. As for the second point, the Court of Justice noted that the purpose of the preliminary rulings procedure was not to enable it to give answers to general or hypothetical questions, but rather to help in the resolution of concrete legal disputes. Accordingly, Community law did not preclude a national court which had made a preliminary reference from finding that in national law the claims of the appellants had been acceded to and, where appropriate, that the main proceedings were thereby terminated. On this basis the Court of Justice declared that it did not have jurisdiction as long as the Spanish court had not confirmed that, under Spanish law, the proceedings continued to be pending.[31]

---

[31] Joined Cases C-422/93–424/93 *Zabala Erasun* [1995] ECR I-1567.

Where it is obvious that the national court does not in fact need an answer to the question referred, but is merely prevented by national law from withdrawing the question because the plaintiff has not taken the necessary steps to end the case the Court of Justice will, however, set aside the assessment of the referring court.

In *Djabali*, after the national court had made a reference for a preliminary ruling, the French government paid the plaintiff the amount that she had claimed and requested her to terminate the case. However, the plaintiff did not do so and the national court informed the Court of Justice that under the national rules of procedure it had no power to withdraw a question duly referred to the Court for a preliminary ruling. The Court of Justice held that since the claims of the plaintiff had been satisfied in full, the case pending before the national court no longer had any purpose. In those circumstances, for the Court to reply to the question referred would be of no avail for the referring court. Hence, it was unnecessary to give a ruling.[32]

A recent decision raises doubt about whether the Court of Justice continues to apply this approach or whether the Court is in the process of making the requirements for admissibility stricter in the sense that it is itself prepared to perform the assessment of whether an answer to the questions referred may really be of use for the national court.

In *García Blanco*, a Spanish court had referred several questions in connection with a dispute between Garciá Blanco and the Spanish social authorities. Garciá Blanco died two months later. Referring to *Zabala* and *Djabali*, the Court of Justice stated that a national court could only make a reference for a preliminary ruling if it were to give a judgment in which it could take the preliminary ruling into account. The Court also noted that, after the case had been referred to it, the Spanish authorities had granted García Blanco the pension she had claimed. Furthermore, her heirs had been given the choice between two different pension schemes which could not be granted simultaneously, without having raised objections to this. On this basis the Court of Justice asked the national court to assess whether it maintained its request for a preliminary ruling. The national court answered in the affirmative, as it believed that a ruling could be relevant for other cases pending before the same court. This led the Court of Justice to inform the national court that a reference for a preliminary ruling could be made to the Court only in proceedings pending before that same national court. Moreover, the Court of Justice observed that it was open to the referring court to refer the same questions for a preliminary ruling in other pending proceedings. In answer to this, the national court stated that the main proceedings were in fact not concluded, in that, in particular, the deceased's successor had not discontinued the action and

---

[32] Case C-314/96 *Djabali* [1998] ECR I-1149, paras 15–25.

the defendants had not formally revoked the original decision refusing a pension against which the main action had been brought. Notwithstanding this, the Court of Justice refused to answer the question as it could not see how a preliminary ruling could be of assistance to the Spanish court.[33]

Nevertheless, in a more recent judgment handed down by the Grand Chamber, the Court reverted to its traditional approach.

In *Commune de Mesquer*, an oil tanker had caused pollution of the Atlantic coast of France. The municipality of Mesquer brought proceedings before the French courts against the relevant company seeking a ruling that the company should be liable for the consequences of the damage caused by the waste which had spread across the territory of the municipality. The French *Cour de cassation* made a reference to the Court of Justice. Before the Court, the potentially liable company submitted that the reference for a preliminary ruling should be declared inadmissible in so far as the municipality had already received compensation from the International Oil Pollution Compensation Fund and consequently had no legal interest in bringing proceedings. In these circumstances the request for a preliminary ruling was, the company submitted, hypothetical. The Court of Justice noted that it did indeed transpire from the documents in the case that the municipality had received payments from the fund and that those payments were the subject of settlements by which the municipality expressly agreed not to bring any actions or proceedings, on pain of having to repay the sums received. However, it also transpired from the documents that, at the time of making the reference, the referring court had that information before it, but nonetheless did not consider that the dispute in the main proceedings had ceased or that the municipality had lost its legal interest in bringing proceedings. In these circumstances the Court chose to answer the questions referred.[34]

4. Questions not Related to the Facts and Circumstances of the Main Proceedings

4.1. The Court's answer will only be relevant for future cases

In its earlier decisions the Court of Justice did not declare a question inadmissible, regardless of the fact that it was not relevant to the solution of the dispute in connection with which the question was raised, as long as the referring court indicated that the answer would be relevant to other pending or subsequent cases.

---

[33] Case C-225/02 *Garciá Blanco* [2005] ECR I-523, paras 29–32. See also Case C-306/03 *Alonso* [2005] ECR I-705, paras 39–45.
[34] Case C-188/07 *Commune de Mesquer* [2008] ECR I-4501, paras 29–34. See also Joined Cases C-428/06–434/06 *UGT-Rioja* [2008] ECR I-6747, para 40.

For example, this could be the situation if the main proceedings were a test case for a series of later cases and a ruling on a question which was not relevant for the actual main proceedings would mean that it would not be necessary to make further references in these later cases.[35] Such questions will, however, no longer be found admissible. According to the current practice, it is a condition for the admissibility of a reference for a preliminary ruling that it relates to the actual circumstances of the case and to an existing dispute. Thus, it is no longer sufficient that the question might be relevant to other subsequent cases.[36]

In *Saddik*, the referring court had asked the Court of Justice to give a ruling on whether the EC Treaty prevented legislation which imposed penalties for contraventions of the Italian rules on processed tobacco sales. It was clear from the order for reference that such criminal proceedings had not been initiated, but that this could later be the case. The Court of Justice refused to give a ruling on the question.[37]

In *Nour*, a German social security appeal tribunal had referred a number of questions concerning the general principles of Community law in connection with a case about a doctor's right to terminate various agreements on fees. It was not clear from the reference how the principles in question could be applicable to the actual case, which did not involve any cross-border elements. This situation was not altered by the fact that the referring court had stated that doctors who were citizens of other Member States could be involved in similar disputes in the future. The Court ruled that a hypothetical possibility of exercising Treaty-based rights did not of itself create such a link with Community law as to justify its application. Thus, it declined jurisdiction to answer the questions.[38]

This practice is praiseworthy even if it will sometimes entail that subsequent cases take longer to decide. This is particularly so because the Court of Justice will often not receive submissions from the parties in the main proceedings (who will not necessarily have an interest in the answer to the questions raised by the referring court). Moreover, the order for reference will often not contain sufficient information for the Court to have enough knowledge about the factual situation to which the Court's answer might be applied in the future. Finally, the situation can be complicated if the facts in the subsequent cases turn out not to correspond entirely with those which were assumed in the preliminary question.

---

[35] See G Bebr, 'The Existence of a Genuine Dispute: An Indispensable Precondition for the Jurisdiction of the Court under Article 177 EEC Treaty' (1980) CML Rev Vol 7, ss 525–537, with references to the relevant judgments.

[36] See also Ch 7, s 2.5 below.

[37] Case C-458/93 *Saddik* [1995] ECR I-511, para 17. See also Case C-225/02 *Garciá Blanco* [2005] ECR I-523, paras 29–32, referred to above in s 3.

[38] Case C-361/97 *Nour* [1998] ECR I-3101.

The requirement that a question should concern a pending dispute does not prevent a national court from referring a question for a preliminary ruling in connection with a judgment of a preliminary opinion ('avis préalable'/'Vorbescheid'). This is so even if the preliminary opinion will often relate to actions which have not yet been carried out and that, for example, certain tax dispositions may not have been made at the time when the reference for a preliminary ruling is made to the Court of Justice.[39] Indeed, the subsequent carrying out of such actions may well depend upon the outcome of the preliminary opinion procedure.

In the same manner, the Court of Justice will accept references for preliminary rulings that are made in connection with declaratory judgments. A suit for a declaratory judgment can be an important means for ensuring the effective protection of rights. A national court that has to deal with such a suit must therefore be able to make a reference for a preliminary ruling on the relevant Community law provisions. Only in very special cases should the Court of Justice set indirect limits on national procedural autonomy, including in relation to proceedings that are intended to clarify the legality of some given future conduct. In general it must be assumed that the restrictions in national law on the right to bring proceedings relating to uncertain future events take sufficient account of the fact that the procedure for making references for preliminary rulings is intended to contribute to the administration of justice and that it should not have the character of providing answers to abstract questions. The linking of a question to the substance of a case must be determined on the basis of the claims of the plaintiff. Where these claims are admitted to substantive proceedings under national rules, it is difficult for the Court of Justice to reject a question as being hypothetical in relation to the issue pending before the national court.

In *Bosman*, the relevant heads of claim had been held admissible in the main proceedings on the basis of a procedural provision in Belgian law permitting an action to be brought, albeit for declaratory purposes only, to prevent the infringement of a right which is seriously threatened. One of the questions concerned the legality of certain 'nationality clauses' according to which football associations mutually voluntarily restricted their rights to employ players of foreign nationality. At the time when the case was brought and considered by the national court, the plaintiff Bosman, a Belgian footballer, was employed by a Belgian club, but he had previously played for and negotiated with foreign clubs. The national court had accepted the case concerning the nationality clause on the grounds that it was possible that, after the expiry of his contract with the Belgian club, Bosman would seek employment with a club outside Belgium. Advocate General Lenz acknowledged that the

---

[39] Case C-200/98 *X and Y* [1999] ECR I-8261, paras 18–23; and Case C-458/06 *Gourmet Classic* [2008] ECR I-4207.

nationality clause had not hitherto prevented Bosman from playing for a foreign club and that the possibility that such a clause would in future cause problems for Bosman was highly doubtful and of a hypothetical nature. Nevertheless he suggested that the question be accepted for a hearing since, in connection with the examination of whether the case could be brought under national law, the referring court had judged that the rights which Bosman claimed to have under Community law were in fact threatened. The Court of Justice reached the same conclusion, noting that it was not for it to challenge this finding of the referring court. Moreover, questions submitted by a national court called upon to decide on declaratory actions seeking to prevent the infringement of a right which was seriously threatened were to be regarded as meeting an objective need for the purpose of settling the dispute brought before that court, even though they were necessarily based on hypotheses which were, by their nature, uncertain, if it holds them to be admissible under its interpretation of its national law. The questions referred were therefore not regarded as being hypothetical in relation to the dispute on which the national court had to pass judgment.[40]

In *Omega Spielhallen*, the German company Omega had begun the operation of a 'laserdrome' in which customers shot at targets with laser pistols. After finding out that one of the games involved hitting targets that were placed on other players, the German police prohibited Omega from continuing to offer this game, which the police believed was contrary to public order and morals. Omega then brought a case before the German courts in which, among other things, it claimed that the prohibition was contrary to the right to offer cross-border services, as the game used equipment and technology provided by an English company. When the case was referred to the Court of Justice for a preliminary ruling, the German police queried the admissibility of the question referred as the prohibition had not affected any cross-border transaction. At the date on which the order was adopted, the equipment which the English company had offered to Omega had not yet been delivered. In fact, Omega had not even concluded a binding contract with the supplier. Notwithstanding this, the Court of Justice found the questions admissible, referring to the fact that the contested order was of a forward-looking nature and capable of restricting the future development of contractual relations between Omega and the English supplier.[41]

The fact that a final administrative decision has not yet been taken does not prevent a reference being made for a preliminary ruling on a declaratory judgment against a Member State's administrative authorities on the same question.

---

[40] Case C-415/93 *Bosman* [1995] ECR I-4921, paras 55–67.
[41] Case C-36/02 *Omega Spielhallen* [2004] ECR I-9609, paras 18–22.

Some Danish freelance interpreters working at the EC had brought a case against the Danish Ministry of Taxation with a claim that the Ministry should recognise that the interpreters' fees were exempt from national taxation. The Danish Supreme Court found that the fact that the Danish tax authorities had not made a final tax assessment of the interpreters' income did not prevent the case from being the subject of court proceedings, including the making of a reference to the Court of Justice for a preliminary ruling.[42]

4.2. Questions concerning factual circumstances which differ from those in the main proceedings

Increasingly, the Court of Justice examines whether a question referred for a preliminary ruling concerns the factual situation which, according to the referring court's own information, exists in the main proceedings. Where this is not the case—and a ruling on the question will not even be indirectly relevant to the decision in the main proceedings—the Court of Justice holds the preliminary reference inadmissible on the grounds that an answer to the question referred will not be material for the actual case with which the national court is presented.

For example, a question concerning the proportionality of criminal sanctions will not be accepted for a substantive hearing if it is made in connection with a civil action between two private parties.[43] Similarly, in a case concerning the validity of a national law which prohibits advertisements, a ruling will only be given in relation to the form of advertisement or type of product which is in fact involved in the case. Thus, if the main proceedings only concern the lawfulness of advertisements for an undertaking which is only active in the distribution sector, the Court of Justice will refuse to give a ruling that relates to other business sectors.[44]

Safety Hi-Tech concerned a reference for a preliminary ruling on the validity of a regulation as a whole. However, the main proceedings only concerned the regulation's prohibition of the use of certain materials for fire-fighting. Since the dispute in the main proceedings neither covered the regulation's provisions on other materials nor the regulation's provisions on other uses of the materials in question, the Court of Justice did not consider the validity of these provisions in its ruling, but only ruled in relation to the facts in the main proceedings.[45]

That a question relates to facts that differ from those in the main proceedings is the most frequently used ground for holding requests for preliminary

---

[42] UfR 1984 p 1059 H.
[43] Case C-2/97 *IP* [1998] ECR I-8597, para 51.
[44] Case C-412/93 *Leclerc-Siplec* [1995] ECR I-179, paras 8–16.
[45] Case C-284/95 *Safety Hi-Tech* [1998] ECR I-4301, para 19.

rulings inadmissible.[46] The practice of the Court of Justice thus illustrates that there are limits to how far the preliminary ruling procedure can be used for a more general challenge to national law.

In a number of cases concerning the validity of progressive taxation of motor vehicles based on horsepower or cylinder capacity, the Court of Justice has refused to rule on possible questions of tax discrimination which did not concern the actual imposition of tax that was disputed in the main proceedings. In *Tarantik*, two of the three questions concerned French tax rules concerning individually approved vehicles. The Court of Justice noted that the plaintiff in the main proceedings had given information that his vehicle had been type-approved. On this basis the Court of Justice refused to answer these two questions.[47] In *Lourenco Dias*, a Portuguese court had referred a number of questions which in reality asked the Court of Justice to pass judgment in abstract terms on the entire Portuguese system of taxation of motor vehicles. Thus, one of the questions concerned the tax on second-hand cars, even though the vehicle which was the subject of the disputed tax was new. Furthermore, other questions concerned other cylinder capacities than those that characterised the motor of the vehicle in question.[48]

SONAE concerned various questions on indirect taxation of the raising of capital. In one of its questions the referring court wanted the view of the Court of Justice on whether Community law required an amendment to a Portuguese law to be given retroactive effect. According to the preliminary reference, this amendment meant that there was a maximum taxation of PTE 15 million. The Court of Justice noted that the plaintiff in the main proceedings had only paid a little over PTE 7.6 million. The answer to the question was therefore not relevant to the resolution of the case pending before the referring court, regardless of whether Community law required the amendment to be given retroactive effect. Consequently the Court of Justice refrained from answering the question.[49]

---

[46] Case C-313/07 *Kirtruna* (ECJ 16 October 2008), paras 24–32, Case C-62/06 *ZF Zefeser* [2007] ECR I-11995, paras 12–17; Case C-6/05 *Medipac* [2007] ECR I-4557, paras 28–36; Case C-467/04 *Gaspari* [2006] I-9199, paras 38–46; Joined Cases 196/88–198/88 *Cornée* [1989] ECR 2309, paras 18–19; Case C-18/92 *Bally* [1993] ECR I-2871, paras 19–21; Case C-18/93 *Corsica Ferries* [1994] ECR I-178, paras 14–16; Case C-297/93 *Grau-Hupka* [1994] ECR I-5535, paras 11–19; Case C-96/94 *Centro Servizi Spediporto* [1995] ECR I-2883, paras 43–6; Case C-299/94 *Anglo Irish Beef Processors International* [1996] ECR I-1925, paras 37–9; Case C-375/96 *Zaninotto* [1998] ECR I-6629, paras 74–80; Case C-389/99 *Yorkshire Co-operatives* [2003] ECR I-427, paras 13–15; Case C-283/01 *Shield Mark BV* [2003] ECR I-14313, paras 51–4; Case C-421/01 *Traunfellner* [2003] ECR I-11941, paras 35–9; Case C-281/02 *Owusu* [2005] ECR I-1383, paras 47–52; Case C-152/03 *Ritter-Coulais* [2006] ECR I-1711, paras 11–17; and Case C-459/07 *Elshani* (ECJ 2 April 2009), paras 39–46.

[47] Case C-421/97 *Tarantik* [1999] ECR I-3633, paras 33–7.

[48] Case C-343/90 *Lourenco Dias* [1992] ECR I-4673, paras 11–42.

[49] Case C-206/99 *SONAE* [2001] ECR I-4679, paras 44–7.

In *Alabaster*, a question was referred to the Court of Justice about the legal effects of sex discrimination. One part of the question concerned whether, in calculating the pay that was due to the person discriminated against, account should be taken of any decrease in the person's pay during a given period. The Court of Justice stated that it appeared from the order for reference that the dispute in the main proceedings related exclusively to a refusal to take account of a pay rise, there being no question of any pay decrease. A ruling on the part of the question that concerned pay reduction was therefore not relevant to the dispute in the main proceedings, and this part of the question was thus declared inadmissible.[50]

The main proceedings in *My* concerned a dispute about whether Mr My fulfilled the conditions for a Belgian early retirement pension requiring that he had completed 35 years of employment. In this connection, the principal question in the main proceedings was whether Mr My's 27 years of service as an EU official should be taken into account in respect of his entitlement to an early retirement pension under Belgian law. In a reference for a preliminary ruling the Court of Justice was asked, among other things, to rule on various questions about the transfer of pension rights between the pension scheme for EU officials and the pension scheme for Belgian public employees. The Court of Justice refused to give a ruling on these questions because Mr My had never requested a transfer to the Belgian pension scheme of pension rights that he had acquired under the Community scheme, but had merely requested an early retirement pension, and in this connection had challenged the Belgian authorities' refusal to take into account the years he had worked as a Community official.[51]

The situation is different in cases where, in a narrow sense, a question does not concern the dispute which is before the national court, but where the answer to that question can nevertheless be relevant to the formulation and extent of the judgment which is to be given by the national court. The Court of Justice has accepted such questions.

In *Inspire Art*, the parties to the main proceedings disagreed about whether the Inspire Art company should be registered in the Netherlands as a Dutch company or as a foreign company. On this basis the national court referred a question to the Court of Justice, while at the same time requesting an assessment of a number of provisions in Dutch law which did not directly concern the question of registration, but rather the legal effects associated with registration. The Commission, the Netherlands government, and the Netherlands Chamber of Commerce argued that the preliminary ruling should be limited to whether Community law precluded the Netherlands provisions which regulated the right to be registered as a

---

[50] Case C-147/02 *Alabaster* [2004] ECR I-3101, paras 51 and 54–5.
[51] Case C-293/03 *My* [2004] ECR I-12013, paras 23–8.

Netherlands company. In response to this, the Court of Justice stated that the national court had found that the possible problems in relation to Community law also related to various provisions concerning the obligations of registered companies, and that these obligations were imposed on registered companies as a legal consequence of registration. In order to give the referring court an answer which it could use in framing its judgment in the main proceedings it was therefore necessary to examine the compatibility with Community law of these Netherlands provisions.[52]

Sometimes developments in the main proceedings after the reference has been submitted beg the question as to whether a preliminary ruling can still be of use to the referring court.

In *Unitron Scandinavia A/S*, the Danish Ministry for Food, Agriculture and Fisheries argued that the Court of Justice should refuse to give a preliminary ruling on a question from the Danish Public Procurement Review Board, as a new tendering procedure had taken place in the meantime so that any infringement of the tendering rules was made good. The Court of Justice nevertheless accepted the question for a ruling, as it was not for the Court to assess the possible consequences under Danish law of the fact that a new tendering procedure in accordance with the relevant procurement directive had taken place after the main proceedings had been brought. The Court added that it was not impossible that the answers to the questions referred might cause the Procurement Review Board to annul the tendering procedure at issue in the main proceedings or to hold that it was irregular.[53]

In *Alcatel Austria*, as part of a case on the prohibition of the fulfilment of a public procurement contract, the Court of Justice was requested to assess when a tendering procedure could be annulled. Before the Court of Justice, the Austrian government contended that, in so far as the contract had already been performed in its entirety, there was in reality no longer a dispute in the main proceedings. An answer to the preliminary questions would therefore be irrelevant since the applicants in the main proceedings could only obtain damages at this stage. The Court of Justice nevertheless found the questions admissible, stating that the referring court had informed it that, under domestic law, the question had arisen whether the national court was entitled or even required under Community law to set aside a previous decision terminating the first award procedure on the grounds that the contract had not been awarded to the tenderer which had made the best offer. In the light of that procedural issue, the questions referred to the Court for

---

[52] Case C-167/01 *Inspire Art* [2003] ECR I-10155, paras 40–51.
[53] Case C-275/98 *Unitron Scandinavia A/S* [1999] ECR I-8291, paras 15–20.

a preliminary ruling seemed to remain pertinent even if the award procedure in question had in the meantime been settled.[54]

4.3. The question is based on unverified alternative views of the facts

The Court of Justice distinguishes between, on the one hand, questions based on artificial facts or which are unrelated to the facts of the case and, on the other hand, questions which are related to the facts of the case but might prove not to be determinative of its final outcome. Only the former group of questions are treated as inadmissible. Thus, the principle that rulings should not be given on hypothetical questions does not prevent a national court from referring several questions, each of which is based on different hypothetical views of the facts of the case, as long as the national court has not yet decided which view it will take.[55] For the same reason, a question which is based on an as yet unverified view of the facts will usually not be rejected.[56] In other words, a question can be regarded as 'necessary' within the meaning of the second paragraph of Article 234, even if the later establishment of the facts will show the opposite. It is thus sufficient that the question might turn out to be relevant for the resolution of the dispute in the main proceedings.

In *Enderby*, the English Court of Appeal referred a question as to whether the principle of equal pay for men and women requires the employer to prove that a difference in pay between two jobs assumed to be of equal value, of which one is carried out almost exclusively by women and the other predominantly by men, does not constitute sex discrimination. The German government argued before the Court of Justice that the question could not be answered before it had been decided whether the two occupations should be regarded as equivalent. In the view of the government this was not the case, so that it was irrelevant whether or not the differences in pay could be objectively justified. The Court of Justice rejected this argument, noting that the Court of Appeal, in accordance with the UK law and with the agreement of the parties, had decided to deal with the

---

[54] Case C-81/98 *Alcatel Austria* [1999] ECR I-7671, paras 25–8. See also Case C-15/04 *Koppensteiner* [2005] ECR I-4855, paras 23–8.

[55] Case C-297/89 *Ryborg* [1991] ECR I-1943, para 6; and Case C-209/98 *Sydhavnen Sten & Grus* [2000] ECR I-3743, para 33.

[56] Case C-279/06 *CESPA* [2008] ECR I-6681, paras 26–32; Case C-66/96 *Høj Pedersen* [1998] ECR I-7327, paras 43–6 (but compare with paras 26–30 in Advocate General Colomer's Opinion); and Case C-116/02 *Gasser* [2003] ECR I-14693, paras 21–7. Indeed, the existence of a contingent element is not special and does not lead to inadmissibility. As emphasised by Advocate General Maduro in para 13 of his Opinion in Case C-210/06 *Cartesio* (ECJ 16 December 2008), the Court can never be absolutely certain that the answer it is providing will, in fact, be relevant to the outcome of the dispute in the main proceedings. The national court may, for example, end up deciding the main proceedings on the basis of a national procedural point of law without applying the Community law answer provided by the Court of Justice.

question of whether the differences in pay were objectively justified, before deciding whether the occupations in question were of equal value, since this could require more complex investigations. The preliminary questions had thus been referred on the assumption that the occupations in question were of equal value. The questions were not clearly unconnected with the actual situation or the dispute in the main proceedings, and the Court of Justice could therefore answer them without itself considering the validity of a hypothesis which it was a matter for the referring court to subsequently verify, should that prove to be necessary.[57]

That being said, it might often be most appropriate to wait to make a reference for a preliminary ruling until the facts of the case and the national legal context have been established. This ensures that questions are not referred which are subsequently found to be irrelevant to the case. Moreover, it is frequently at this stage that it is possible to draft for the first time a preliminary reference containing the requisite information about the main proceedings so as to enable the Court of Justice to address its preliminary ruling to the concrete circumstances of the case and thus be of genuine help to the national court.[58]

4.4. The question concerns legal questions which cannot be relevant to the main proceedings

A related issue arises where the relevant Community rules mean that a preliminary ruling cannot be applicable to the judgment in the main proceedings if the referring court's own understanding of the national law and the subject of the dispute is correct. In such cases the Court of Justice declines to give a ruling.

In *EKW*, the Court of Justice refused to answer a question about whether, under Austrian law, an exemption from payment of the beverage duty in the case of direct sales of wine to the end consumer constituted State aid incompatible with Community law. The Court of Justice found that this question was wholly irrelevant to the resolution of the dispute in the main proceedings. Indeed, those proceedings concerned the obligation on a company to pay duties in respect of supplies of beverages and ice cream made for consideration, and not the question of whether exemption from payment of such a duty on wine sold directly at the place of production constituted State aid incompatible with the Treaty.[59]

---

[57] Case C-127/92 *Enderby* [1993] I-5535, paras 11–12.

[58] See further Ch 7, s 4 below.

[59] Case C-437/97 *EKW and Wein & Co* [2000] ECR I-1157, paras 51–4. See similarly Case C-36/99 *Idéal Turisme* [2000] ECR I-6049, paras 26–9; and Joined Cases C-430/99 and C-431/99 *Sea Land Service* [2002] ECR I-5235, paras 45–7, where in relation to a similar situation the Court of Justice added that the question of State aid was not relevant, since the main proceedings concerned two companies' obligation to pay a tax, and the persons liable to pay the tax could not avoid paying by reference to the fact that the exemption that applied to others constituted unlawful State aid. In Joined Cases C-393/04 and C-41/05 *Air Liquide Industrie Belgium* [2006] ECR I-5293,

In *Helmut Horn*, Mr Schelling had requested Advocate Horn to prepare a law suit before the Austrian courts against the German State for the loss which Schelling claimed to have suffered as a result of the reaction in January 2001 of the then 14 other Member States against the result of the Austrian election. Advocate Horn, however, wrote to Schelling and advised him against bringing proceedings, as the chances of winning such a suit were very slim. At the same time Horn presented his invoice to Schelling who refused to pay. In connection with the subsequent legal proceedings on this the parties jointly requested the Austrian court to refer to the Court of Justice the question of the lawfulness of the actions of the 14 Member States against Austria, since the parties agreed that an answer to this question was decisive for whether Horn's invoice could be regarded as reasonable. The Court of Justice refused to answer this question. Horn's claim to a fee was not dependent on the lawfulness of the actions of the 14 Member States.[60]

In *Grado and Bashir*, the Court of Justice was asked to decide whether it was compatible with Community law for a Public Prosecutor to refuse to use the German courtesy title 'Herr' (ie Mr) to designate the accused in an application, which the prosecutor had drafted and subsequently placed before the court for signature, for a summary punishment order in the case of a foreign worker from another Member State of the European Union, particularly where this was contrary to the prosecutor's own usual practice. The Court declared this question inadmissible, inter alia, because even if this manner of proceeding were shown to discriminate against nationals of other Member States, it would have no bearing on the main proceedings.[61]

In *Schneider*, an Austrian judge had originally brought a case against the Austrian State in the civil courts, claiming compensation for the loss he claimed to have suffered through not being promoted. In support of this claim he argued that the position he had applied for had instead been given to a female applicant who had less seniority, and that he had not been promoted because the quota for the promotion of women had not yet been fulfilled. The Austrian civil courts found that Community law had been infringed by the Austrian measure to promote women, since the measure did not provide for any possibility to derogate from the preferential treatment. However, the case was dismissed as there was no causal connection between that violation of Community law and the claimed loss. As a supplement to the suit before the civil courts, Schneider also brought a claim for compensation based on the same facts before the Austrian Administrative Court.

---

paras 20–5, the Court of Justice accepted a reference for a preliminary ruling in an apparently corresponding context, noting that even though the plaintiff sought repayment of the disputed tax, the plaintiff also challenged the validity of the law by which the tax had been imposed. See also Case C-333/07 *Regie Networks* (ECJ 22 December 2008), paras 43–52.

   [60] Case C-44/03 *Helmut Horn* (ECJ 24 July 2003).
   [61] Case C-291/96 *Grado and Bashir* [1997] ECR I-5531.

In this connection he argued that the trial which took place before the Administrative Court did not satisfy the requirements of judicial protection laid down in Directive 76/207 on the implementation of the principle of equal treatment for men and women as regards access to employment, vocational training and promotion, and working conditions. The Administrative Court then requested the Court of Justice to give a preliminary ruling on whether the directive had been incorrectly implemented and whether 'the possibility required by [the directive] of pursuing claims (in the present case, a claim for compensation) by judicial process was not adequately satisfied by the Austrian *Verwaltungsgerichtshof* (Administrative Court) alone, in view of that court's legally limited powers (a court which hears appeals on points of law only with no fact-finding powers)?' The Court of Justice noted that it appeared from the order for reference that it was possible in Austria to bring a normal case for compensation against the State before the civil courts, and there was a normal appeal process whereby the facts and law of the case could be tried before the civil courts at three levels of judicial review. Such court proceedings unquestionably fulfilled the requirements in the directive for adequate and effective judicial protection. The requirements of the directive were therefore fully satisfied by the right to bring a case before the civil courts, as had happened in the actual case. Thus, the question of whether the procedure before the Administrative Court fulfilled the requirements of the directive was hypothetical, and the Court of Justice therefore did not have jurisdiction to consider the question.[62] It is remarkable that the above-quoted question of the referring court, seemingly in contradiction to the Court of Justice's reasoning, stated that a claim for compensation for a breach of the rules on equal treatment could only be made before the Administrative Court. The Court of Justice does not normally regard itself as competent to make such an interpretation of national law, even if its interpretation of the Austrian law has been corroborated by statements made by the Austrian government.[63] It was presumably a contributing factor that Judge Schneider's case had in fact been heard by the civil courts.

4.5. The referring court's interpretation of the facts or national law is being disputed

The situation is different from that described above when the question referred for a preliminary ruling must be regarded as relevant if the information from the referring court is relied on, but when a party to the main proceedings or others entitled to submit observations before the Court of Justice dispute the correctness of the information, and the question must be regarded as irrelevant if the understanding of that party is relied on. The same applies to cases where the referring

---

[62] Case C-380/01 *Schneider* [2004] ECR I-1389.
[63] See Ch 4, s 5.2, and Ch 10, s 3.3.3.4.

court interprets national law in such a way that a connection with Community law can be established, but where such interpretation of national law is challenged before the Court of Justice.

In the procedure for preliminary rulings, the Court of Justice cannot with binding effect establish the actual facts of the main proceedings, nor can it interpret national law as this lies with the referring court.[64] Therefore, the Court cannot reject a request for a preliminary ruling on the grounds that the question is hypothetical and thus not necessary for the decision in the main proceedings because it is based on an incorrect evaluation of the facts or interpretation of national law.[65] Or to put in the terms of a recent judgment: when examining whether a question is inadmissible, despite the presumption of relevance that any preliminary question enjoys, the Court of Justice will take as its basis the factual and legislative context which the referring court is responsible for defining and the accuracy of which is not a matter for the Court to determine.[66]

In *Centrosteel*, it was argued that a reference from an Italian court for a preliminary ruling should be declared inadmissible, among other things: because it was based on a misunderstanding of the facts; because, contrary to Italian procedural rules, the referring court had included Community rules which had not been referred to by the parties in the main proceedings; because under private international law the Italian courts did not have jurisdiction to decide the dispute in the main proceedings, since only the Austrian courts were competent in that respect; and because the case should have been decided under Austrian law rather than under Italian law, which meant that it was not relevant for the decision in the case whether Italian law was compatible with Community law. The Court of Justice rejected these arguments on the grounds that it was not for the Court to examine whether the national court had correctly established the facts of the case, nor

---

[64] See Ch 4, ss 5.2 and 5.5.

[65] Case C-313/07 *Kirtruna* [2008] ECR I-7907, paras 32–5, Case C-11/07 *Eckelkamp* [2008] ECR I-6845, paras 25–35; Case C-500/06 *Corporación Dermoestética* [2008] ECR I-5785, paras 26–8; Case C-347/06 *ASM Brescia* [2008] ECR I-5641, paras 21–30; Joined Cases C-222/05–225/05 *van der Weerd* [2007] ECR I-4233, paras 21–5; Case C-347/89 *Eurim Pharm* [1991] ECR I-1747, paras 14–17; Case C-152/94 *van Buynder* [1995] ECR I-3981, paras 7–9; Case C-249/97 *Grube* [1999] ECR I-5275, paras 17–18; C-379/98 *PreussenElektra* [2001] ECR I-2099, para 40; Case C-390/99 *Canal Satélite Digital* [2002] ECR I-607, paras 17–21; Case C-326/00 *IKA* [2003] ECR I-1703, paras 25–9; Case C-153/02 *Neri* [2003] ECR I-13555, para 33; Case C-28/04 *Tod's and Tod's France* [2005] ECR I-5781, paras 13–16; Case C-222/04 *Cassa di Risparmio di Firenze* [2006] ECR I-289, paras 61–5; Case C-346/05 *Chateignier* [2006] ECR I-10951, paras 17 and 22; Joined Cases C-94/04 and C-202/04 *Cipolla* [2006] ECR I-11421, paras 21–8 and 33–43; and Case C-220/05 *Auroux* [2007] ECR I-389, paras 21–7. See similarly concerning the jurisdiction of the EFTA Court under Art 34 of the EFTA Surveillance and Court Agreement, Case E-10/04 *Piazza* [2005] EFTA Court Report 76, para 22.

[66] Case C-248/07 *Trespa International* (ECJ 6 November 2008), paras 31–8, and similarly Case C-379/05 *Amurta* [2007] ECR I-9569, paras 63–7.

could it examine the jurisdiction of the national court under the private international law rules on the correct forum.[67]

In *Klughardt*, the Court of Justice was asked to consider whether the meat of a wild buffalo was covered by a common market organisation under a specific Community regulation, and if so whether the regulation was invalid on the ground that it did not state the reasons on which it was based. Both the Council and the Commission contended that the questions were based on an erroneous premise. According to the two institutions, the main proceedings concerned Australian buffalo which were descended from the Asiatic buffalo: and that type of buffalo should be regarded as being an animal of a domestic species which was already covered by the common organisation of the market in beef and veal before the entry into force of the regulation in question. The Court of Justice replied that the questions referred by the national court concerned meat from wild buffalo, and that it was for the referring court to determine whether the main action in fact concerned such a product.[68]

In *Butterfly Music*, one of the parties to the main proceedings argued that the Court of Justice should decline to answer a preliminary question on the validity of a reinstatement of intellectual property rights as a result of a Community directive which extended the copyright in musical recordings. In fact, the parties had signed an agreement according to which the manufacture of the compact disc in question was to stop several years before the introduction of the supplementary period of protection under the directive. Moreover, all copies of the compact disc had already been sold before this supplementary period. The Court of Justice denied that it had thereby been established that the requested interpretation of the directive had no connection with the actual circumstances of the main proceedings.[69]

That being said, if a national court's interpretation of national law differs significantly from the one which is being put forward in the observations before the Court of Justice, the latter might be so much in doubt as to the context and character of the dispute that it will have difficulties in giving a ruling that contains useful guidance for how the dispute before the referring court must be solved. In the same way, the description of national law in observations presented during the preliminary procedure might have a bearing on how the Court of Justice frames its judgment.[70]

---

[67] Case C-456/98 *Centrosteel* [2000] ECR I-6007, paras 11–12.
[68] Case 309/81 *Klughardt* [1982] ECR 4281, paras 4–6.
[69] Case C-60/98 *Butterfly Music* [1999] ECR I-3939, paras 12–14. Similarly see Case C-291/05 *Eind* [2007] ECR I-10719, paras 16–19.
[70] See Ch 10, s 3.3.3.4, and Ch 11, s 3.3.

In a more recent decision, the Court has, on this basis, departed from its traditional standpoint set out above and refrained from giving a preliminary ruling since all those presenting observations to the Court agreed that the question asked concerned a legal problem which did not arise in national law, and since the referring court, furthermore, had not given reasons for why it found the question relevant.

In *Lenz*, the Court of Justice was asked, inter alia, to what extent the rules on free flow of capital in the EC Treaty precluded tax legislation which allowed taxpayers who lived in Austria, and received revenue from capital originating in another Member State, to deduct *pro rata* from their income tax the corporation tax paid by the company in which they had a holding. The plaintiff in the main proceedings, the Austrian government, and the Commission all admitted that the question concerned a different tax system than that which was applicable in Austria at the relevant time. The Court of Justice concurred and held that the provisions referred to in the order for reference did not provide for the possibility of deducting in Austria corporation tax which had been paid in another Member State. Hence, there was no reason to answer that question.[71]

Whilst illustrating the increasingly intense examination of the relevance of a question which has characterised the case law of the Court of Justice in recent years, the judgment in *Lenz* marks a departure from the Court's previous case law and has not been followed in later decisions. It therefore does not appear likely that the Court of Justice in future cases will substitute the referring court's interpretation of national law with its own in order to determine the relevance of a preliminary question. It still seems to be good law that the Court of Justice will only reject a question where the explanation given by the referring court itself indicates that the question does not raise any legal problems that are relevant to the decision in the main proceedings. For this reason, it is important that the national court gives detailed reasons for why it raises a given question.[72] Where the referring court fails to explain adequately the background to a question, an alternative approach could be for the Court of Justice to seek clarification of the relevance of the question by inviting the referring court to provide clarity on the issue before refusing to answer the question.

4.6. The answer can already be given on the basis of national law

It is sometimes argued that a preliminary ruling is unnecessary for the resolution of the dispute in the main proceedings, since the alleged right or obligation in any case already follows from national law. The Court of Justice has, however, always

---

[71] Case C-315/02 *Lenz* [2004] ECR I-7063, paras 51–5.
[72] See further in Ch 8, s 3.2.2. The judgment is further discussed below in Ch 10, s 3.3.3.4.

maintained that such a circumstance cannot imply that a preliminary question is inadmissible. This is so, first, because it is not for the Court of Justice to determine the scope of national law and, second, because a national court can have a proper interest in having the position clarified as to whether the right or obligation in question follows directly from Community law.

In *Baumbast*, an English court referred a number of questions concerning the significance of Community law for the residence permits of foreigners. In the period between the initiation of the main proceedings and the reference for a preliminary ruling, the persons concerned had obtained indefinite residence permits for the United Kingdom. The Court of Justice did not find that this was a reason for refusing to answer the questions referred, as the permits had been granted under English law and as the question of the rights conferred under Community law on the persons concerned therefore had not been resolved definitively.[73]

Nor will a reference be rejected as inadmissible when the referring court has not yet itself determined whether the dispute can be decided exclusively on the basis of national law. Thus, a national court does not have a duty to seek to decide a case on the basis of the Member State's own legal system before seeking a preliminary ruling.

In *Jiménez Melgar*, both the Spanish government and the Commission argued that some questions about the Community rules on sex discrimination were irrelevant to the decision on a case of unfair dismissal, since the case could be decided directly on the basis of a provision in Spanish law on the use of contracts for a limited period. In its order for reference the Spanish court had itself found that this could be the case. Nevertheless the referring court had preferred not to examine this more closely, reserving the right to return to the question once the Court of Justice had assessed whether the dismissal was unlawful on the basis of sex discrimination. The Court of Justice stated that the national court had explained the relevance of the questions and answered the questions submitted.[74]

In *Oscar Bronner*, the Court of Justice found admissible a preliminary question from an Austrian court before which a dispute had been brought in accordance with national competition law. In this connection the Court of Justice noted that the same facts could be covered both by Community law and by national law.

---

[73] Case C-413/99 *Baumbast* [2002] ECR I-7091, paras 29–38. See also Case C-348/89 *Mecanarte* [1991] ECR I-3277, where the Court of Justice accepted a reference even though the national legal provision had been declared unconstitutional.

[74] Case C-438/99 *Jiménez Melgar* [2001] ECR I-6915, paras 26–30. See also Joined Cases C-502/01 and C-31/02 *Gaumain-Cerri* [2004] ECR I-6483, paras 14–15; and Case C-228/96 *Aprile* [1998] ECR I-7141, paras 10–11.

In such circumstances, the fact that the national court was dealing with a dispute involving Austrian law and not Community law did not prevent the national court from making a reference, when it considered that a conflict between Community law and national law was capable of arising.[75]

Similarly, a question does not become inadmissible in the reverse situation where a party entitled to intervene before the Court of Justice argues that national law, on grounds that are unquestionably not contrary to Community law, in any case prevents a party being accorded the right in question.

In *ICI*, the UK House of Lords referred a question concerning the relationship between the EC Treaty's rules on the right of establishment and a provision in UK law on tax relief for corporate groups. The UK government argued that a preliminary ruling would have no bearing on the decision in the main proceedings. Regardless of the ruling of the Court of Justice, the company concerned could not obtain tax relief because this was excluded on other grounds. The Court of Justice noted that the House of Lords had observed that the correct interpretation of the disputed provision in English law had not yet been resolved. It was presumably correct that a preliminary ruling would not be relevant if one of the interpretations of the English law which had been put forward in the main proceedings was accepted. However, the House of Lords had stated that there was another possible interpretation of the English provision, and this interpretation required an examination of whether the provision was in accordance with the EC Treaty's rules on the right of establishment. On this basis, the Court of Justice found it necessary to consider the questions referred by the House of Lords.[76]

The fact that a directive has been implemented in national law does not in itself mean that a preliminary ruling on the interpretation of the directive becomes unnecessary. On the contrary, a preliminary ruling on the correct interpretation of the directive in question can be necessary to enable the national court to ensure that the national implementing provisions are interpreted and applied in accordance with the directive.[77] Nor can the relevance of such a question be denied on the grounds that the main proceedings concern a dispute between two private parties and that the directive cannot therefore have direct effect in the main proceedings. Both the duty to interpret national law in conformity with Community law and the possibility of a subsequent action against the State can make such a question relevant.[78]

---

[75] Case C-7/97 *Oscar Bronner* [1998] ECR I-7791, paras 12–20.

[76] Case C-264/96 *ICI* [1998] ECR I-4695, paras 14–17. See also Case C-296/03 *GlaxoSmithKline* [2005] ECR I-669, paras 21–4.

[77] Case C-331/92 *Gestion Hotelera International* [1994] ECR I-1329, paras 11–13; and Case C-62/00 *Marks & Spencer* [2002] ECR I-6325.

[78] Case C-472/93 *Spano* [1995] ECR I-4321, paras 14–19; and Case C-343/98 *Collino and Chappero* [2000] ECR I-6659, paras 19–25. See also Ch 4, s 3.2.4. The situation is different where

In *Quelle*, it was argued that the question referred for a preliminary ruling was not admissible, given that the referring court had stated that the provisions of national law implementing a directive were open to only one interpretation and that German constitutional law prohibited the referring court from espousing an interpretation *contra legem*. In consequence, if the Court of Justice were to place a different construction on the directive in question, the referring court would not be able to take account of the Court's answer. The Court of Justice did not agree that the reference was inadmissible as the uncertainty as to whether the national court could interpret national law in the light of the answer given by the Court of Justice could not affect the Court's obligation to rule on the referred question. As noted by the Court, any other approach would be incompatible with the very aim of the powers given to the Court by Article 234, which are intended, in essence, to ensure the uniform application of Community law by the national courts.[79]

Where a reference for a preliminary ruling made in connection with a national criminal case is merely intended to clarify whether an interpretation of the national law in accordance with the directive means that the accused has committed a criminal offence, the Court of Justice has sometimes notified the referring court that a directive cannot be used to create criminal liability rather than giving an interpretation of the directive in question.[80]

Moreover, the fact that a directive is only a minimum harmonisation directive cannot justify a refusal to interpret one of its provisions on the grounds that stricter national rules would in any case be compatible with the directive. This is so as the principle that national law must as far as possible be interpreted in conformity with Community law might also be relevant in such a situation, just as it is possible that the authorising provisions in national law only allow for the possibility of adopting rules to the extent required in order to fulfil the Community requirements. In such a case the question can have a bearing on the validity of the implementing provisions under national law.[81]

---

a party in the main proceedings is in fact covered by the concept of the State, and can therefore be subject to the direct effect of the directive, and the Court of Justice wishes to positively confirm the relevance of the question; see Case C-53/04 *Marrosu* [2006] ECR I-7213, paras 26 and 29–30; and Case C-180/04 *Vasallo* [2006] ECR I-7251, paras 24–7.

[79] Case C-404/06 *Quelle* [2008] ECR I-2685, paras 18–23.

[80] Case C-311/99 *Caterino* (ECJ 29 May 2001); and Case C-80/06 *Carp* [2007] ECR I-4473, paras 18–23. See also Case C-105/03 *Pupino* [2005] ECR I-5285, paras 31–48, where, with a view to showing the relevance of the question, the Court of Justice stated that the limits to interpretation in conformity with a directive did not, in the case at hand, make the question hypothetical.

[81] Joined Cases C-320/94, C-328/94, and C-337/94–339/94 *RTI* [1996] ECR I-6471, paras 17–24, (and see in more detail Advocate General Jacob's Opinion on the case, at paras 15–16); and Case C-491/01 *British American Tobacco* [2002] ECR I-11453, paras 28–41.

4.7. The question has already been answered

The authority of a preliminary ruling[82] does not prevent the national court to which the ruling is addressed from making a new reference to the Court of Justice before giving judgment in the main proceedings. For example, such a reference might be appropriate when the referring court encounters difficulties in understanding or applying the earlier preliminary ruling, when it refers a fresh question of law to the Court, or again when it submits new considerations which might lead the Court to give a different answer to a question submitted earlier.[83]

Other national courts are prevented even less from referring questions for preliminary rulings about problems which the Court of Justice has already clarified.[84] For example, there can be an interest in having a new decision if there are outstanding questions about the reasons for, the extent of, or the consequences of a previous ruling of invalidity.[85] Similarly, the courts in question might wish to persuade the Court of Justice to change its case law.[86] New facts or new developments in legal practice, for example, can justify making a new reference.[87] In the same way, the Court of Justice will not reject a reference purely on the grounds that it has already found the relevant national provision to be incompatible with Community law in infringement proceedings under Article 226 of the EC Treaty.[88]

Where a reference is assumed to be due to the fact that the referring court is not aware of previous rulings which, on the face of it, appear to provide an answer to the question put, the Registry of the Court of Justice will draw the attention of the referring court to the rulings in question. In most cases the referring court will thereafter either withdraw its reference or reformulate it and give a more precise explanation of the background to the reference.[89]

---

[82] See Ch 12, s 2 below.

[83] Case C-466/00 *Kaba* [2003] ECR I-2219, para 39. See also K Riechenberg, 'Note concernant les renvois préjudiciels qui réinterrogent la Cour' in V Christianos (ed), *Evolution récente du droit judiciare communautaire, vol I* (1994) 99.

[84] Joined Cases 28/62–30/62 *Da Costa* [1954-64] ECR 395; Joined Cases 332/92, 333/92, and 335/92 *Eurico Italia* [1994] ECR I-711, paras 14–15; Case C-155/99 *Busolin* [2000] ECR I-9037, paras 9–11; and Case C-260/07 *Pedro IV Servicios* (ECJ 2 April 2009), paras 26 and 30. In such cases the Court of Justice sometimes gives preliminary rulings in the form of a reasoned order rather than by a judgment, see further below in Ch 11, s 1.

[85] Case 66/80 *International Chemical Corporation* [1981] ECR 1191, para 14.

[86] Case C-297/92 *Baglieri* [1993] ECR I-5228, paras 5–8; and Case C-255/00 *Grundig Italiana* [2002] ECR I-8003, para 20.

[87] Joined Cases C-393/99–394/99 *Hervein* [2002] ECR I-2829, paras 26–8. For a review of the cases in which renewed references have prompted the Court of Justice to alter its previous practice, see T Tridimas, 'Knocking on Heaven's Door: Fragmentation, Efficiency and Defiance in the Preliminary Reference Procedure' (2003) 40 CML Rev 9, 39ff.

[88] See also Ch 4, s 3.2,5; Ch 6, s 4.2.3; and Ch 12, s 2.1.

[89] D Edward, 'Reform of Article 234 Procedure: The Limit of the Possible' in D O'Keeffe, Gordon Slynn, and A Bavasso (eds), *Judicial Review in European Union Law, vol I* (2000) 119, 121ff. Due to a misunderstanding of Community law, there have been cases where the referring court has

In the same way, if, after a reference is made, the Court of Justice decides on a corresponding question in another case, its established practice is to send the referring court the new ruling and ask whether it maintains its request for a preliminary ruling.[90] The referring court will often withdraw its reference in whole or in part or reformulate its questions so as to take account of any remaining issues in doubt.[91] Where a request for a preliminary ruling is maintained, the Court of Justice will be able to restrict its answers to the outstanding issues which are the reasons why the referring court decided that the case before it could not be decided solely on the basis of the ruling in the earlier case.[92]

In *Royscott Leasing Ltd and others v Commissioners of Customs and Excise*, in connection with Directive 77/388, the English Court of Appeal refused to withdraw a request for a preliminary ruling which it had made to the Court of Justice despite an intervening ruling by the latter in another case, but relating to the same directive. In the opinion of the Court of Appeal there was only reason to withdraw a reference if it was clear that a ruling on the question posed had become entirely without interest. That condition was not met in the instant case. Indeed, as the Court of Justice had not suggested that the request for a preliminary ruling should be withdrawn, it apparently did not itself find that the issue had already been decided in the other case. Moreover, the proceedings before the Court of Justice were at an advanced stage as the hearing was imminent and the Advocate General was to deliver his conclusions in about two months' time. Hence, to withdraw the reference would not entail a substantial reduction of the length of the national proceedings. Rather to the contrary, at this advanced stage of proceedings withdrawing the reference for a preliminary ruling could unduly prolong the case as a whole.[93]

4.8. The relationship between issues of admissibility and issues of substance

Often, the relevance of a request for a preliminary ruling will depend on how the Court of Justice interprets the relevant Community act. In observations to the Court of Justice it is regularly argued that a preliminary ruling will not be relevant to the decision in the main proceedings because the Community provision that

---

been of the view that it was not entitled to withdraw its preliminary question without the consent of the parties to the main proceedings, cf C Naômé, *Le renvoi préjudiciel en droit européen* (2007) 22, with further references.

[90] Where the other case is already at an advanced stage, the Court may choose to suspend its dealing with the new reference until the other case has been decided.

[91] Case C-320/96 *Ferreiro Alvite* [1999] ECR I-951, paras 9–13 and 15.

[92] Case C-186/96 *Demand* [1998] ECR I-8529, paras 25–9. See also Case C-201/05 *Test Claimants* [2008] ECR I-2875, paras 31–4.

[93] Court of Appeal (England and Wales), 5 November 1998, *Royscot Leasing Ltd and others v Commissioners of Customs and Excise* [1999] 1 CMLR 903–6.

the referring court seeks to have interpreted clearly cannot be used in support of the claim that has been presented before the national court. The Court of Justice has, however, consistently rejected such arguments and has stated that the issue as to whether the Community rule in question is applicable to the facts before the referring court is a question of the correct interpretation of that provision. Hence it is not something that should be dealt with when examining the admissibility of the preliminary reference, but rather it is a question relating to the substance of the case.

The Court of Justice will therefore not decline jurisdiction to answer a preliminary question if its relevance depends on which interpretation of some Community provision is applied. Indeed, the very purpose of a preliminary reference in these cases is to obtain the opinion of the Court of Justice as to whether Community law is of relevance for the resolution of the dispute in the main proceedings.[94]

In *Testa and Lazzeri*, the Court of Justice was asked to rule on whether it was compatible with Community law to implement in national law a definition in Directive 93/22 on investment services in the securities field by using a broader definition than that given in the directive. The Italian government argued that the question was irrelevant, since the parties in the main proceedings did not carry on activities which fell within the scope of the directive. The Court of Justice, however, found the question admissible, noting that the parties in the main proceedings had been penalised for carrying on the form of unlawful undertaking that was covered by the Italian provision implementing the directive. It was therefore relevant for the referring court to know whether the definition in the directive could lawfully be broadened when implemented into national law. In its answer to the referred question, the Court of Justice stated that there was nothing to prevent national law giving a broader application of the directive's provisions to transactions that were not covered by the directive, as long as it was made clear that the national provisions in question were not an implementation of the directive, but an expression of the will of the national legislators.[95]

---

[94] Case C-412/06 *Hamilton* [2008] ECR I-2383, paras 21–5; Case C-446/05 *Doulamis* [2008] ECR I-1377, paras 12–17; Case C-238/05 *ASNEF-EQUIFAX* [2006] I-11125, para 22; Case C-104/95 *Kontogeorgas* [1996] ECR I-6642, paras 10–13; Case C-125/96 *Simon* [1998] ECR I-145, paras 14–17; Joined Cases C-215/96 and C-216/96 *Bagnasco* [1999] ECR I-135, paras 19–22; Case C-107/97 *Rombi and Arkopharma* [2000] ECR I-3367, paras 21–4; Case C-379/98 *PreussenElektra* [2001] ECR I-2099, paras 50–1; Case C-268/01 *Agrargenossenschaft Alkersleben* [2003] ECR I-4353, paras 44–8; Joined Cases C-295/04–298/04 *Manfredi* [2006] ECR I-6619, para 30; and Case C-466/03 *Reiss* [2007] ECR I-5357, paras 33–7. Compare, however, Case C-233/98 *Lensing & Brockhausen* [1999] ECR I-7349, paras 19–22, where, in deciding on the admissibility issue, the Court of Justice ruled on the correct interpretation of the Community regulation that was the subject of the preliminary question and stated that a correct interpretation of the regulation showed that the question was indeed relevant.
[95] Case C-356/00 *Testa and Lazzeri* [2002] ECR I-10797, paras 26–9 and 46.

In *Christelle Deliège*, a number of questions were referred for a preliminary ruling on whether it was contrary to Articles 49, 81, and 82 of the EC Treaty that semi-professional sportspeople had to be authorised by their federation in order to be able to participate in international sports competitions which did not involve national teams competing. In most of the observations submitted to the Court of Justice it was argued that the questions should be dismissed on the ground that they were of a hypothetical nature as they concerned amateur sport that fell outside the scope of Community law. The Court of Justice held that whether a preliminary question concerned matters unconnected with Community law did not concern the admissibility of the question, but instead related to the substance of the case. Thus, the Court was competent to answer the questions referred.[96]

The Court of Justice has adopted a similar approach in cases where there is doubt about the relevance of a question because the national court appears to have overlooked a given condition which must be fulfilled before the Community rule it wishes to have interpreted becomes applicable. In such situations the Court of Justice normally accepts the question as admissible. At the same time the Court draws the referring court's attention to the conditions which must be fulfilled in order for the Community provision to be applicable to the facts in the main proceedings.[97] It is then for the national court to judge whether directly or indirectly Community law does in fact apply to the case before it and, if so, to apply the preliminary ruling. This practice is particularly relevant to so-called internal situations, where all the factual elements of the main proceedings relate to a single Member State, so that the case does not appear to give rise to the cross-border issues which are necessary for the rules on freedom of movement in the EC Treaty to be applicable.[98]

The same principles apply when a question relates to the interpretation of Article 307 of the EC Treaty concerning the interplay between Community law and obligations that the State in question has taken upon itself in relation to third countries. In this situation the question of the correct interpretation of this provision forms part of the substance of the case and so the relevance of a question about the relationship between Community law and such an international agreement cannot be rejected on the ground that the correct interpretation of Article 307 makes the question raised irrelevant.[99]

---

[96] Joined Cases C-51/96 and C-191/97 *Christelle Deliège* [2000] ECR I-2549, paras 25 and 28. See also Case C-350/96 *Clean Car Autoservice I* [1988] ECR I-2521; and Case C-454/98 *Schmeink & Cofreth and Strobel* [2000] ECR I-6973, paras 34–42.

[97] Case C-473/00 *Codifis* [2002] ECR I-10875, paras 17–26; see also Ch 10, s 3.3.3.3.4, and Ch 11, s 2.4.

[98] See Ch 4, s 5.3.5.

[99] Case C-216/01 *Budvar* [2003] ECR I-13617, paras 48–9.

4.9. The question concerns a Community act which was not in force at the relevant time

Doubt about the relevance of a question can also arise if the question concerns a Community act which has either not yet entered into force or has ceased to be in force. According to the practice of the Court of Justice, a question about the validity of a Community act can be submitted for a preliminary ruling even if the act in question has not yet entered into force.[100] Citizens and undertakings need certainty about the rights and obligations which will apply to them in the near future. Indeed, in some situations they might need to adopt operational measures before the Community act enters into force.

In *British American Tobacco*, the Commission and the French government argued that the Court of Justice should refuse to give a preliminary ruling on a question from an English court on the validity of a directive on tobacco products. First, the deadline for implementing the directive had not yet expired. And second, no UK implementing legislation had been adopted. The French government and the Commission referred to the fact that a directive cannot create rights prior to the expiry of the deadline for its implementation, and that an answer to the preliminary question would lead to the circumvention of Article 230 of the EC Treaty on annulment proceeding directly before the Community courts. The Court of Justice replied that an adopted directive was an act within the meaning of Article 234, regardless of whether the deadline had expired. In the case before it, under English law it was possible to seek judicial review of the legality of the intention and/or obligation of the UK government to implement the directive even though, when that application was made, the period prescribed for implementation of the directive had not yet expired and the government had adopted no national implementation measures. Moreover, the plaintiffs in the main proceedings had argued that the UK government could only use the authority under UK law to implement Community rules if the Community rules in question were valid. Finally, the argument on the connection with Article 230 could not lead to any other conclusion. The opportunity open to individuals to plead the invalidity of a Community act of general application before national courts was not conditional upon that act actually having been the subject of implementing measures adopted pursuant to national law. In that respect, it was sufficient if the national court was called upon to hear a genuine dispute in which the question of the validity of such an act was raised indirectly.[101]

---

[100] Case C-308/06 *Intertank O* [2008] ECR I-4057, paras 30–5; Joined Cases C-27/00 and C-122/00 *Omega Air* [2002] ECR I-2569; and Case C-306/93 *SMW Winzersekt* [1994] ECR I-5555, paras 12–16.

[101] Case C-491/01 *British American Tobacco* [2002] ECR I-11453, paras 28–41. On the relation between Arts 230 and 234 of the EC Treaty, see further below in s 7.

In *Pêcheurs de l'Étang de Berre*, the Court of Justice ruled that it had jurisdiction to answer some preliminary questions about amendments to an international agreement which the Community was party to and which had not yet entered into force, noting that it was possible that the amendments could have entered into force prior to the date of the national court's final judgment.[102]

In contrast, a question concerning the validity of a Community rule will be dismissed if the dispute in the main proceedings relates solely to the legal assessment of an activity which has been completed in all respects prior to the entry into force of the Community rule.

CBA Computer concerned a situation where the plaintiff in the main proceedings had in July 1997 imported sound cards from Taiwan. In connection with a dispute about the customs treatment of the sound cards, the Court of Justice was requested to decide on the validity of a Commission regulation which allocated sound cards to a particular tariff heading. The Court noted that the regulation in question had entered into force on 1 January 1998 and thus after the circumstances in the main proceedings had taken place. Moreover, the Commission regulation did not have retroactive effect. The question therefore had no bearing on the decision in the main proceedings and it was thus not necessary to rule on it.[103]

The same applies in cases where the validity of a Community act is raised in connection with a case where all the relevant facts of the case had occurred at a time where that act, according to its own terms, had ceased to be in force.[104]

The situation is less clear-cut if the question does not concern the validity of a Community act, but its correct interpretation. In a number of situations the Court of Justice has accepted questions on the interpretation of a Community rule where the issue in the main proceedings has been to establish whether the plaintiff could lawfully carry on some current or future activity and the national court therefore has to take into account provisions that apply at the time when it has to make its decision.[105] The same applies when, under national law, a criminal act cannot be prosecuted if a subsequent legal act makes the same

---

[102] Case C-213/03 *Pêcheurs de l'Étang de Berre* [2004] ECR I-7357, paras 26–30.
[103] Case C-479/99 *CBA Computer* [2001] ECR I-4391, paras 29–32.
[104] Case C-369/95 *Somalfruit* [1997] ECR I-6619, paras 55–6.
[105] Case C-210/96 *Gut Springenheide* [1998] ECR I-4657, paras 16–19. Presumably the same thinking lies behind Case C-61/97 *Laserdisken* [1998] ECR I-5171, para 19, just as the acceptance of the questions in Joined Cases C-253/96–258/96 *Kampelmann* [1997] ECR I-6907 may have been due to the fact that the disputed lawfulness of a refusal to promote the applicants in the main proceedings should not only be judged on the basis of the rules at the time of the refusal but also on the basis of the rules of a subsequent directive since the applicants had still not been promoted at the date when the directive should have been transposed into national law. See also Case C-53/04 *Marrosu* [2006] ECR I-7213, paras 28 and 36.

conduct lawful.[106] Finally, a question will be relevant where the events which gave rise to the main proceedings took place in the period between the adoption of a directive and the deadline for its implementation, but where the national implementation measure had already entered into force at the time where the relevant facts took place.[107] Indeed, in such cases it might be natural, although not required by Community law, to interpret the national implementing provision in conformity with the directive even if that directive has not yet entered into force.[108]

Where the relevance of a question cannot be justified on the basis of the above considerations, and is not otherwise demonstrated by the referring court, the Court of Justice has been increasingly unwilling to answer questions of interpretation of a Community rule that has neither entered into force nor been implemented in national law before the deadline for its implementation. The assumption now is that the Court of Justice will dismiss the question.[109]

In *Pascoal and Filhos*, the referring court requested an interpretation of a regulation that had not yet entered into force. The Court of Justice noted that the regulation re-enacted in large measure the Community legislation in force prior to its adoption. However, the question related to a new provision. Hence, an answer to the question of how this provision should be interpreted would have no connection with the facts or subject matter of the dispute, and the Court refused to answer the question.[110]

On this basis it is doubtful to what extent the earlier practice continues to provide guidance.[111]

Occasionally, it happens that the reason why a national court refers to a Community provision that has not yet entered into force is because of a misunderstanding about the applicability *ratione temporis* of that provision to the circumstances in

---

[106] Joined Cases C-358/93 and C-416/93 *Bordessa* [1995] ECR I-361, paras 8–10; Joined Cases C-163/94, C-165/94, and C-250/94 *Sanz de Lera* [1995] ECR I-4821, paras 13–15; Case C-183/94 *Skanavi* [1996] ECR I-929, paras 16–18; Case C-230/97 *Awoyemi* [1998] ECR I-6781, paras 33–8; Case C-319/97 *Kortas* [1999] ECR I-3142, paras 15–17; and Joined Cases C-369/96 and C-376/96 *Arblade* [1999] ECR I-8453, para 29.

[107] Case C-66/96 *Høj Pedersen* [1998] ECR I-7327, paras 30–1.

[108] Case C-212/04 *Adelener* [2006] ECR I-6057.

[109] Case C-165/98 *Mazzoleni and ISA* [2001] ECR I-2189, paras 16–18; Joined Cases C-49/98, C-50/98, C-52/98–C-54/98, and C-68/98–71/98 *Finalarte* [2001] ECR I-7831, paras 24–5; Case C-164/99 *Portugaia Construcoes* [2002] ECR I-787, para 14; Case C-159/00 *Sapod Audic* [2002] I-5031, paras 19–20; and Joined Cases C-421/00, C-426/00, and C-16/01 *Sterbenz* [2003] ECR I-1065.

[110] Case C-97/95 *Pascoal and Filhos* [1997] ECR I-4209, paras 25–6. See also Case C-228/05 *Stradasfalti* [2006] ECR I-8391, paras 39, 48, and 64–5, where the Court of Justice in assessing the relevance of the questions referred put more emphasis on the facts of the case rather than on its formalities.

[111] Case 126/86 *Giménez Zaera* [1987] ECR 3697, paras 6–7, and Case C-297/89 *Ryborg* [1991] ECR I-1943, paras 8–10.

the main proceedings. In such cases the Court of Justice will often rephrase the question, and instead consider the situation referred to in the question on the basis of the Community rules actually applicable at the relevant date for the main proceedings.[112]

4.10. Relevance *ratione temporis* and national law

Where questions of the applicability *ratione temporis* arise in relation to national law, the Court of Justice is generally more reticent in dismissing the relevance of a question. Indeed, in such situations it is more difficult for the Court of Justice to be certain that an answer to a question will not have a bearing on the decision in the main proceedings. Moreover, the Court does not have the jurisdiction to overrule the referring court's own assessment of the applicability of the national rules.

A reference for a preliminary ruling is, for example, not necessarily hypothetical merely because it concerns the lawfulness of a national practice that has subsequently ceased. Indeed, an answer to this type of question could, for example, be relevant where the aim of the question is to enable the national court to assess whether it really was necessary to change the national practice in order to bring it into line with Community law.[113] Even the fact that the disputed national legislation is subsequently amended does not in itself mean that the question referred to the Court of Justice becomes irrelevant. This is especially so where the national court informs the Court of Justice that it is the earlier legislation which applies in the main proceedings. The same applies where the question stems from a claim for compensation or a criminal case relating to a previous legal situation. But even where the referring court does not address the question of the timing of the applicability of the law, the Court of Justice will find the preliminary question admissible as it is not competent to interpret national law and thereby decide which rules should apply to the main proceedings.[114]

In *TNT Traco*, both the defendant public undertaking in the main proceedings, Poste Italiane, and the Italian government argued before the Court of Justice that

---

[112] Case C-251/00 *Ilumitrónica* [2002] ECR I-10433, paras 27–30; Case C-290/01 *Derudder* [2004] ECR I-2041, paras 37–8; and Case C-337/06 *Bayerischer Rundfunk* [2007] ECR I-11173, para 30. See also Case C-471/04 *Keller Holding* [2006] ECR I-2107, paras 25–7, where the Court of Justice chose to answer the questions both on the basis of the provisions referred to in the reference and on the basis of the previously applicable rules, since it was not clear whether the facts of the case were covered by one set of rules or the other. On this form of rephrasing of questions, see Ch 10, s 3.3.3.3.4 and Ch 11, s 2.4.

[113] Case C-324/93 *Evans Medical* [1995] ECR I-563, paras 15–17.

[114] Case C-83/92 *Pierrel* [1993] ECR I-6419, paras 31–2; and Case C-217/05 *Confederación Española de Empresarios* [2006] ECR I-11987, paras 25 and 32. For the opposite situation, where the referring court indirectly requests an examination of the national measure that has been introduced after the events in the main proceedings occurred, see Case C-302/97 *Konle* [1999] ECR I-3099, paras 32–5; and Case C-228/98 *Dounias* [2000] ECR I-577, paras 35–8.

the Court should refrain from answering a preliminary question about the relationship between the EC Treaty's competition rules and a provision in the Italian postal law which gave Poste Italiane a monopoly on the provision of certain postal services. On the one hand, the monopoly had since been terminated, and on the other hand the fine which the plaintiff competitor, TNT Traco, had paid to Poste Italiane under the earlier legislation had been repaid. The Court of Justice replied that the national court had found that, in spite of this, the case was still current, that the decision of the national court on the repayment was only an interim judgment, and that the amendment to the Italian law did not mean that the request for a preliminary ruling was devoid of purpose.[115]

In *CIA Security*, the Belgian government and one of the parties to the main proceedings argued that the referring court's question, on what legal effects were associated with the failure to notify in accordance with the so-called Draft Technical Regulations Directive (Directive 83/189), had become redundant. The main proceedings concerned a declaratory judgment and under Belgian law these kinds of proceedings were to be decided according to the law in force at the time when the court would give its ruling. Since the Belgian government had issued a new decree which had been correctly notified after the initiation of the main proceedings, and since this new decree had replaced the previous non-notified decree, only the new decree applied in the main proceedings. The Court of Justice nevertheless found the preliminary question admissible, stating that it was a matter for the national court to assess the scope of the national provisions.[116]

The Court's reasoning for accepting such questions for substantive consideration does not seem entirely consistent.

In *My*, the Court stated that it was clearly wrong when one of the parties in the main proceedings argued that the national legislation on the timing of the applicability of rules meant that the question referred had no bearing on the decision in the case. With a view to showing the relevance of the question, the Court of Justice expressed itself briefly on the correct understanding of national law.[117]

The judgment in *My* shows that when the relevance of a question depends on an interpretation of national law the Court of Justice's lack of jurisdiction to interpret national law is not always respected. Whilst the approach taken in *My* may seem appropriate in being informative for the parties, it is questionable in principle. There was nothing to prevent the Court of Justice from instead merely stating that the question depended on national law and that it should therefore be decided by the national court.

---

[115] Case C-340/99 *TNT Traco* [2001] ECR I-4109, paras 24–37.
[116] Case C-194/94 *CIA Security* [1996] ECR I-2201, paras 19–21.
[117] Case C-293/03 *My* [2004] ECR I-12013, paras 20–1.

Where a question relates to a national legal rule which is not yet adopted but is only intended to be adopted, the Court of Justice will reject the question as being hypothetical and relating to a legal situation which does not yet exist.[118]

4.11. The question concerns the legal status of the referring court

A reference for a preliminary ruling is inadmissible if it does not concern the very dispute which is pending before the referring court but rather the legal status of the national court or its judges in their personal capacities.

In *Falciola*, an Italian court asked about whether an Italian law, which restricted the immunity of Italian judges from liability for damages, prevented the judges from carrying out their duties independently and impartially. The questions were raised in a case which concerned the allocation of building and construction contracts by a local council to a particular undertaking. The Court of Justice found that it was clear from the actual wording of the order for reference that the Italian court was in doubt only as to the possible psychological reactions of certain Italian judges as a result of the enactment of the Italian law in question. Consequently, the preliminary questions did not involve an interpretation of Community law objectively required in order to settle the dispute in the main proceedings, and the Court of Justice therefore had no jurisdiction to rule on the questions submitted to it.[119]

The dispute in the main proceedings in *Nour* concerned a doctor's right to terminate various agreements on fees. During the hearing of that case, a German social security appeal tribunal referred a number of questions concerning various aspects of the tribunal's operations, in particular the calculation of the salary of the chairman of the tribunal, and the relationship between the tribunal and a subordinate body. The Court of Justice found that the questions about the payment of the chairman fell clearly outside the scope of the dispute in the main proceedings. It even appeared from the order for reference that the chairman was a party in another case concerning his salary arrangements, and that he, as a party to this other dispute, had proposed that questions should be referred to the Court of Justice corresponding to the questions which he had referred in the current case. As for the composition and operation of the subordinate body, the Court of Justice found that the question was based on an assumption that this body was not in fact able to decide disputes, so that the appeal tribunal was in practice the only instance. This issue had not been discussed between the parties in the main proceedings, it could not affect the outcome of the case, and it appeared only to have been put

---

[118] Case C-165/03 *Längst* [2005] ECR I-5637, paras 29–34.
[119] Case C-286/88 *Falciola* [1990] ECR I-191.

before the Court of Justice because it was potentially relevant to the chairman's claims for payment. The Court therefore declined jurisdiction.[120]

In contrast, a national court can refer questions concerning the extent of its duty to make references for preliminary rulings. This is so even if, at the same time as asking this procedural question, it also refers a question about a Community rule regulating the legal relations between the parties.[121] It thus does not matter that, since the referring court has already fulfilled any possible duty to refer, an answer to the question of that court's duty to refer preliminary questions by definition will have no practical consequences for the actual case. Similarly, a national court can refer a question concerning the right, under Community law, of a legal representative to represent a party in the main proceedings, regardless of whether this question has a bearing on the decision in the main proceedings.[122]

4.12. Questions concerning legislation of other Member States

Sometimes a national court has to apply the laws of another national legal system in order to solve the dispute before it. In those cases, the issue might arise whether the rules of this other legal system are compatible with Community law. Considering that general private international law does not prevent a national court from refusing to apply a legal rule from another Member State, and that it may even do so without having previously consulted the authorities of that other Member State, there are strong reasons for why the preliminary ruling procedure should also apply to such situations. Indeed, the need for a national court to obtain the advice of the Court of Justice in such cases is just as great as when a question of compatibility with Community law arises in connection with the national court's own legal system. Even so, a reference for a preliminary ruling on the compatibility with Community law of the rules of another Member State raises a number of problems. First, it will often give rise to particular difficulties for the Member State whose legislation is cast into doubt before a court in another Member State to defend its legislation merely by intervening in a preliminary ruling procedure before the Court of Justice and not also in the main proceedings before the referring court. Second, a reference concerning the validity of another Member State's rules can sometimes obscure the fact that the case is contrived.[123] Third, in such cases the risk that the preliminary ruling will be based on a misunderstanding of the relevant national legal provisions will naturally be greater.

---

[120] Case C-361/97 *Nour* [1998] ECR I-3101.

[121] Case C-344/04 *IATA* [2006] ECR I-403, paras 23–5, and Case C-210/06 *Cartesio* (ECJ 16 December 2008), paras 65–74.

[122] Case 33/74 *Van Binsbergen* [1974] ECR 1299.

[123] See, on this point, below at s 5.

According to long-established practice of the Court of Justice, the fact that a dispute raises a question about the validity of the rules of a Member State other than that of the referring national court does not in itself exclude the making of a preliminary reference.[124] In other words, the Court of Justice has powers to provide a national court with the criteria for interpretation which are necessary for deciding whether another Member State's laws are in conflict with Community law. However, at the same time the Court of Justice has also stated that in such situations particular care must be taken to ensure that the preliminary ruling procedure is not used for purposes other than those intended in the EC Treaty.[125]

For a number of years, these considerations did not lead the Court of Justice to adopt a markedly different yardstick than in ordinary cases, where the national court applied the law of its own Member State.[126] In recent years the Court of Justice has, however, taken a more restrictive approach to the admissibility of such references.

In *der Weduwe*, a Belgian judicial investigation had examined a number of offences of forgery and money-laundering in connection with taxation. In this connection a Netherlands citizen, Paul der Weduwe, was questioned as a defendant. Weduwe was resident in Luxembourg and as part of his work for two Luxembourg banks he had been employed in canvassing for clients in Belgium with a view to persuading them to place money in the Luxembourg banks in question. As part of this business, Weduwe collected money from Belgian customers and brought it to Luxembourg. Despite the obligation to give evidence to the judicial investigation, Weduwe refused to answer questions, arguing that as an employee in the financial sector he was subject to a duty of confidentiality under Luxembourg law. The investigating judge found that the Luxembourg rules on bank secrecy constituted a serious obstacle to obtaining evidence in the investigation of transactions carried out in Belgium as part of the freedom to provide services. This was so as the rules meant that employees of Luxembourg banks had to choose between infringing either the requirements of the host Member State, Belgium, on giving evidence, or the rules of the Member State of establishment, Luxembourg, on bank secrecy. On this basis the investigating judge referred some questions to the Court of Justice on the compatibility with Article 49 of the EC Treaty of both the Belgian rules on the obligation to give evidence and the Luxembourg rules on confidentiality. The Court of Justice refused to answer the questions. It started by noting

---

[124] Case C-47/90 *Delhaize* [1992] ECR I-3699; and Case 20/64 *Albatros* [1965] ECR 29. For a criticism of this see K Lipstein, 'Foglia v. Novello—Some unexplored Aspects' in F Capotorti et al (eds), *Du droit international au droit de l'intégration, Liber Amicorum Pierre Pescatore* (1987) 373.

[125] Case 244/80 *Foglia II* [1981] ECR 3045, paras 28–31.

[126] Case 261/81 *Rau* [1982] ECR 3961, paras 8–9; Case C-105/94 *Celestini* [1997] ECR I-2971, paras 19–26; and Case C-150/88 *Parfümerie Fabrik 4711* [1989] ECR 3891, paras 11–12.

that the problem only arose if the Luxembourg rules had extraterritorial effect. And even if this were the case, the conflict between the two legal systems would not arise if Luxembourg allowed the duty of confidentiality to be subordinate to conflicting national rules on the duty to give evidence. Thus, the problem only arose because the Belgian court had adopted an asymmetric interpretation of the Luxembourg rules, giving the confidentiality requirement extraterritorial effect, while this would not be the case for closely related rules on exemption from criminal liability in connection with witness testimony. However, this was not the only possible interpretation. On the contrary, both the Belgian and the Luxembourg governments had argued that the view of the Belgian court was implausible. Furthermore, the referring court had not explained why it assumed that the interpretation adopted was 'the only possible interpretation of those provisions'. The fact that the relevance of the question raised by the referring court rested on a particular interpretation of national law other than its own made it especially necessary for the referring court to state the grounds for the order for reference on this point. In these circumstances, since the referring court had not provided the Court with all the necessary information to determine whether an interpretation of the rules on free movement of services in Article 49 of the EC Treaty would serve a useful purpose in the main proceedings, the questions were held to be inadmissible.[127]

The *der Weduwe* case illustrates that the Court of Justice will no longer use its traditional approach when a reference for a preliminary ruling concerns the validity of the legislation of a legal system which is foreign to the referring court. First, the Court of Justice departed from its classic standpoint that its lack of jurisdiction to interpret national law implies that it cannot refuse to answer a preliminary question the relevance of which is based on an erroneous interpretation of national law. This departure is presumably connected with the fact that the practice referred to is not only based on formal considerations of jurisdiction, but also the fact that in classic cases the referring court must be assumed to have a far better knowledge of its own national law than does the Court of Justice. In contrast to this, the referring court seldom has direct knowledge of foreign law. Second, the yardstick was not, as it normally is, whether the question referred was clearly without relevance for the decision in the main proceedings. In fact, what was decisive was not whether the referring court's interpretation was unquestionably wrong, but rather that the interpretation was not the only one possible. In other words, it was not sufficient that the analysis of the problem *could* be relevant.

In *Bacardi-Martini*, the Court of Justice also refused to give a preliminary ruling that was aimed at enabling the referring court to assess whether another Member

---

[127] Case C-153/00 *der Weduwe* [2002] ECR I-11319.

State's legislation was compatible with Community law. The case was unusual in that, in deciding whether a company, which under English law was liable for having caused another company to be in breach of some contracts which the second company had entered into with a third company, the referring English court found it decisive to determine whether a French law was compatible with Community law. Furthermore, all the parties to the case had an interest in the French law being found incompatible with Community law. The Court of Justice repeated its remarks from *Foglia* and *der Weduwe* that it must display special vigilance when, in the course of proceedings between individuals, a question is referred to it with a view to permitting the national court to decide whether the legislation of another Member State is in accordance with Community law. For this reason, where the questions referred are intended to enable the national court to assess the compatibility with Community law of the legislation of another Member State, the Court must be informed in some detail of the referring court's reasons for considering that an answer to the questions is necessary to enable it to give judgment. In the actual case the English court had restricted itself to giving the arguments which had been made by the parties in the main proceedings. Even after being asked by the Court of Justice, the referring court had not stated whether it itself found that the answer to the question was in fact necessary in order for it to decide the case before it. The referring court had also failed to explain why the French law should be interpreted so as to give extraterritorial effect, which the French government had disputed before the Court of Justice. This lack of an independent view on a number of conditions for the relevance of the question meant that the Court of Justice did not have the requisite information to determine whether it was necessary to answer the question put. The question referred to the Court for a preliminary ruling was therefore declared inadmissible.[128]

5. Contrived Cases

As demonstrated in the preceding sections of this chapter, the duty of the Court of Justice under Article 234 is to supply all courts in the Community with the information on the interpretation of Community law that is necessary to enable them to settle genuine disputes which are brought before them. In contrast, it is

---

[128] Case C-318/00 *Bacardi-Martini* [2003] ECR I-905. R Lane, 'Article 234: A few Rough Edges Still' in M Hoskins and W Robinson (eds), *A True European, Essays for Judge David Edward* (2003) 327, 338, criticises this judgment. He emphasises that there was no doubt about the essential nature of the dispute. Moreover, a resolution of the Community law question would presumably have been decisive for the decision in the main proceedings, so he disagrees with the Court's refusal to help the referring court in the application of Community rules. In the opinion of C Naômé, *Le renvoi préjudiciel en droit européen* (2007) 98, the Court of Justice was influenced by a wish to counter forum shopping with regard to the possibility of having questions referred to the Court.

not the task of the Court to give answers to abstract or hypothetical questions. On this basis the Court has laid down that it does not have jurisdiction to decide on contrived disputes that do not concern genuine disagreements between the parties to the main proceedings.

In *Foglia*, the Court of Justice considered the consequences of an apparently contrived national case which led to a reference being made for a preliminary ruling. The parties to the case, which came before the Italian courts, were an Italian wine merchant and an Italian customer. The two parties had entered into an agreement whereby some cases of fortified wine bought by the customer should be sent to France. It was explicitly agreed that any costs imposed by the Italian or French authorities contrary to the provisions of the EC Treaty should not be borne by the buyer. A corresponding provision was included in the agreement between the wine merchant and the company responsible for shipping the wine. Upon import into France the authorities imposed a French tax on the wine, which the transport company paid and then reclaimed from the wine merchant. The wine merchant then brought a case against the buyer for the payment of the amount in question. In *Foglia I* the Court of Justice noted that the attitude of one of the parties in the national case had been neutral, that during the oral proceedings before the Court of Justice this party had stated that he was participating in the case because of the interest which a specific group of undertakings had in the outcome of the case, and that both parties had argued that the French law in question, which they had essentially described in identical terms, was contrary to Community law. It must even be assumed that the contractual clause referred to had been included with a view to provoking a court case. The Court of Justice found that if it gave a ruling in such a case, this would jeopardise the whole system of legal remedies which Community law makes available to private individuals to protect them against national legal provisions which are contrary to Community law. Furthermore, such a decision would fall outside the Court of Justice's jurisdiction, which is limited to giving national courts the elements for interpreting Community law that are necessary for deciding genuine disputes.[129]

In *Foglia II*, the Court of Justice expanded on the reasoning behind its judgment in *Foglia I*, and stated that to the greatest possible extent it leaves it to the national court to determine the necessity of making a reference for a preliminary ruling, Nevertheless, the Court of Justice has jurisdiction to examine its own jurisdiction. This means that it cannot remain passive in the assessment of such exceptional cases where such an examination may be relevant to the proper functioning of the preliminary ruling procedure. In particular the Court of Justice lacks jurisdiction to deliver advisory opinions on general or hypothetical questions. Rather its duty

---

[129] Case 104/79 *Foglia I* [1980] ECR 745.

is to assist in the administration of justice in the Member States. It should not be left to the parties to create a procedural situation in which a third party, whose situation may be affected by the judgment, does not have the possibility of presenting an appropriate defence of their interests. The Court accordingly does not have jurisdiction to reply to questions of interpretation which are submitted to it within the framework of procedural devices arranged by the parties in order to induce the Court to give its views on certain problems of Community law which do not correspond to an objective requirement inherent in the resolution of a dispute. According to the Court of Justice, a declaration that it has no jurisdiction in such circumstances does not in any way trespass upon the prerogatives of the national court but makes it possible to prevent the application of the procedure under Article 234 for purposes other than those appropriate for it. Without being expressly stated in the judgment, it was probably also a factor that the refusal to answer the questions would not have any consequences, since any court which was concerned with a genuine dispute involving the French legislation would still be able to refer the same questions for preliminary rulings. For example, the transport company in the main proceedings could have challenged the French authority's tax assessment before the French courts, and these courts could then have asked the Court of Justice for a preliminary ruling.[130]

It might be argued that in the two *Foglia* judgments the Court of Justice merely examined its own jurisdiction and that, like any other court, the Court of Justice must be entitled to do so.[131] Nevertheless, the refusal of the Court of Justice to answer preliminary questions in contrived cases has been met with considerable criticism in European legal literature.

In this connection it has been pointed out that the dispute in the main proceedings can only be shown to be contrived after having conducted a thorough examination of the facts in the main proceedings and of the behaviour and attitude of the parties to those proceedings.[132] However, according to the Court of Justice's own practice, such an examination of the facts is solely a matter for the referring court and not the Court of Justice. Moreover, an assessment of whether there is a genuine dispute between the parties is difficult to distinguish from the question of legal interest—and that question too—according to the established practice—falls first and foremost under the jurisdiction of the national courts.[133]

---

[130] Case 244/80 *Foglia II* [1981] ECR 3045.

[131] On this, see C Barnard and E Sharpston, 'The Changing Face of Article 177 References' (1997) 34 CML Rev 1113, 1123; and D Wyatt, 'Foglia No 2: the Court denies it has jurisdiction to give advisory opinions' (1982) 7 EL Rev 186, 190.

[132] A Barav, *Imbroglio préjudiciel* (1982) Revue trimestrielle de droit européen Vol 18, ss 431–83.

[133] C Gray, 'Advisory Opinions and the Court of Justice' (1983) 8 EL Rev 24, 28.

It has also been argued that the existence of a 'question' within the meaning of Article 234 of the EC Treaty is not conditional on whether the dispute before the national court is genuine, but only on whether the national court is in doubt about how a Community law question in a case before it should be solved. Since the preliminary ruling procedure is a legal remedy for the national courts, and not for the parties, it seems unreasonable to refuse to give assistance to a national court merely because the parties have a common purpose in the proceedings in question in having a national legal act overturned.[134]

Another problem is that a refusal to give a preliminary ruling means that the national court receives no guidance on whether it should refrain from applying Community law or whether it should attempt to interpret it on its own.[135] Finally, the two judgments in *Foglia* have both caused legal uncertainty and there is a risk that a national court will take offence at a rejection based on the *Foglia* principle. It has been argued that, in the long run, this might contribute to undermining the spirit of cooperation which is the basis of the preliminary ruling procedure, where the starting point is that the national courts are not obliged to refer questions to the Court of Justice.[136]

That being said, the importance of the principle on contrived cases should not be exaggerated. While the Court of Justice has been consistent in maintaining the principle, it has been very reticent about applying it in practice.

First, it is not sufficient that one of the parties in the main proceedings has manufactured the dispute. Procedural ploys by one party are not the same as procedural contrivances by both parties, as was the situation in the *Foglia* cases.[137] A dispute does not necessarily become any less genuine because it is provoked by one of the parties. Moreover, test cases can be brought before the Court of Justice under the preliminary ruling procedure even if the actual subject of the case is so small that questions of principle are the only motivation for the litigation.[138]

---

[134] A Tizzano, 'Litiges fictifs et competence préjudicielle de la Cour de Justice Européenne' (1981) Revue générale de droit international public Vol 85, pp 514–28.

[135] D Wyatt, 'Foglia No 2: the Court denies it has jurisdiction to give advisory opinions' (1982) 7 EL Rev 186, 192, proposes that in this case the national court must assume that the national law is in conformity with Community law.

[136] On this argument see K Lenaerts, 'Form and Substance of the Preliminary ruling Procedure' in D Curtin and T Heukels (eds), *Institutional Dynamics of European Integration* (1994) 355, 357.

[137] Case C-408/95 *Eurotunnel* [1997] ECR I-6315, paras 18–22; and Case C-415/93 *Bosman* [1995] ECR I-4921, paras 56 and 63–5. See also Case C-341/05 *Laval un Partneri* [2007] ECR I-11767, paras 42–50 (where, however, one might question whether any of the parties had made an improper attempt to take advantage of the possibilities offered by Community law).

[138] Joined Cases C-332/92, C-333/92, and C-335/92 *Eurico Italia* [1994] ECR I-711, paras 16–17; and Case 112/80 *Dürbeck* [1981] ECR 1095, particularly para 1 of Advocate General Reischl's Opinion.

For example, this was the situation in *FNL* where, without comment, the Court of Justice accepted for substantive consideration an action brought by a trade union against the Netherlands, where the trade union claimed that a provision in national law was contrary to Directive 79/7 on the equal treatment of men and women.[139]

Nor does it matter if one of the parties tries to achieve a result that it has not been able to achieve by lobbying for legislative changes.[140] The application of the *Foglia* principle requires that both parties are party to the contrivance of the dispute in the main proceedings.

In *Badeck*, the Court of Justice had no objection to dealing with a reference for a preliminary ruling where the main proceedings were brought by 46 members of the *Landtag* (regional assembly) of Hesse in Germany in proceedings for an abstract review of legality (so-called *Normenkontrollverfahren*).[141]

In *Meilicke*, the action in the main proceedings was brought before a German court by a shareholder against the management of the company for the provision of certain information. On the face of it the information concerned the company's increase of capital and the use made of the funds thereby raised. However, the real question was whether a specific practice of the German courts concerning disguised contributions in kind was compatible with Community law. The questions put to the Court of Justice concerned these Community rules, and the referring court stated that the plaintiff's claims could not be accepted if the German court's practice were to be found incompatible with Community law. Advocate General Tesauro found that the case had been contrived by the plaintiff. Both in legal periodicals and during the proceedings before the national court, the plaintiff had expressed the view that the German practice was contrary to Community law. The plaintiff had even adopted a standpoint that would lead to his losing the case. However, the Court of Justice refrained from applying the *Foglia* principle. Instead it stated that it was not clear, on the basis of the information from the referring court, whether the practice referred to was at all relevant to deciding the case. This led the Court of Justice to the somewhat questionable conclusion that the question was of a hypothetical nature. In this connection the Court of Justice referred to the fact that the national court had not presented all the information that would have been necessary to answer the questions presented.[142]

---

[139] Case 71/85 *FNL* [1986] ECR 3855.

[140] Case C-36/99 *Idéal Turisme* [2000] I-6049, paras 19–22. See also Case C-195/98 *Österreichischer Gewerkschaftsbund* [2000] ECR I-10497, paras 21–31; and Case C-459/99 *MRAX* [2002] ECR I-6591.

[141] Case C-158/97 *Badeck* [2000] ECR I-1987.

[142] Case C-83/91 *Meilicke* [1992] ECR I-4871. For a criticism of the judgment see para 105 in the Opinion of Advocate General Lenz in Case C-415/93 *Bosman* [1995] ECR I-4921; D Anderson, 'The Admissibility of Preliminary References' in A Barav and D Wyatt (eds), *Yearbook of European Law 1994* (1994) 179, 186ff; and A Arnull, 'Case note' (1993) 30 CML Rev 613.

Nor will the fact that a case is between a parent company and a subsidiary in itself mean that a dispute is contrived in the sense of the *Foglia* case law.[143] Similarly, a question cannot be rejected on the grounds that the plaintiff in the main proceedings lacks a legal interest in challenging the national provision or practice in question, as such a matter falls within the jurisdiction of the national court.[144]

Second, the Court of Justice will not refuse to answer a question as long as it is not manifestly apparent from the facts set out in the order for reference that the dispute is in fact fictitious.[145]

In *Cura Anlagen*, the Court of Justice stated that some of the information on the file might give rise to a suspicion that the situation underlying the main proceedings was contrived with a view to obtaining a decision from the Court of Justice on a question of Community law of general interest. However, the Court of Justice also noted that there was a genuine contract the performance or annulment of which undeniably depended on a question of Community law. The question referred was thus admissible.[146]

In *Delhaize*, both the parties in the main proceedings argued that the national legislation was incompatible with Community law. Furthermore, the plaintiff had only claimed less than one Euro in compensation although the dispute related to 3,000 hectolitres of wine. The Court of Justice did not touch on the question of whether the dispute was contrived but simply answered the questions referred.[147]

Dona concerned a provision on the prohibition of participation by foreigners in Italian professional football. The chairman of an Italian football club had asked Mr Dona to investigate whether there were foreign players who were prepared to play for the club. Dona thereupon placed an advertisement in a Belgian sports periodical. However, the club chairman refused to refund the costs for this, as he claimed that Dona had acted too hastily. Dona then brought an action before the Italian courts, claiming payment of the advertising costs. In this connection Dona claimed that some rules drawn up by a sporting federation limiting the right to take part in football matches to Italian nationals was incompatible with Community law. The Court of Justice accepted the reference for a preliminary ruling, even though there seemed to be good reasons for suspecting that the main

---

[143] Case 244/78 *Union Laitière Normande* [1979] ECR 2663; and the Opinion of Advocate General Jacobs in Case C-379/98 *PreussenElektra* [2001] ECR I-2099, para 80.

[144] Joined Cases C-320/94, C-328/94, and C-337/94–339/94 *RTI* [1996] ECR I-6471, para 40.

[145] Case 46/80 *Vinal* [1981] ECR 1563 (see in particular Advocate General Reischl's Opinion); Case 267/86 *Van Eycke* [1988] ECR 4769, paras 11–12; Case C-341/01 *Plato Plastik Robert Frank* [2004] ECR I-4883, para 30; and Case C-231/89 *Gmurzynska-Bscher* [1990] ECR I-4003, para 23.

[146] Case C-451/99 *Cura Anlagen* [2002] ECR I-3193, paras 25–7.

[147] Case C-47/90 *Delhaize* [1992] ECR I-3669.

proceedings were a contrived dispute which was merely intended to make the Court decide on the rules of the sporting federations in relation to the free movement of workers.[148]

National courts are thus not prevented from making references for preliminary rulings merely because the parties in the main proceedings agree on the need for a reference and on what the ruling should be. A case is not necessarily contrived simply because the only aim of the parties in bringing proceedings is to obtain a preliminary ruling that some specific national legal provisions are contrary to Community law.[149]

In *Jägerskiöld*, the Court of Justice found that there was insufficient basis for assuming that proceedings concerning the right to fish in another person's waters is without the agreement of the latter were an expression of a contrived dispute. In the main proceedings the defendant had not said whether he agreed with the plaintiff that the relevant national legislation was contrary to Community law. The defendant was himself the owner of waters and declared that he had his own interest in having clarification of whether he could in future offer fishing rights to others. For this reason he had supported the plaintiff's request for a reference for a preliminary ruling. Furthermore, in his oral testimony before the Court of Justice, the defendant had, while formally disputing the plaintiff's claim, in fact been critical of the national legislation. As stated by Advocate General Fennelly, it was indeed possible to entertain doubts about the genuineness of the dispute in the case, but still find that there was insufficient evidence to support a conclusion that the proceedings were obviously artificial or collusive.[150]

In *PreussenElektra*, the parties in the main proceedings agreed that the relevant German rules were contrary to Community law. Moreover, both parties had brought other proceedings with a view to having the law in question set aside. The German government therefore argued that the dispute was contrived and referred to the fact that the parties' uniform view of the law meant that they could have settled their relations without the involvement of the national courts. This was especially obvious since one of the parties owned a majority of the shares in the other party. The Court of Justice denied that the dispute must be regarded as being hypothetical. It was true that both parties had an interest in having the German law overturned. However, the legal situation between the parties was not based on an agreement, but was a direct consequence of the challenged law. Thus, the dispute in the main proceedings could not be regarded as a procedural device

---

[148] Case 13/76 *Dona* [1976] ECR 1333.

[149] Case C-412/93 *Leclerc-Siplec* [1995] ECR I-179, paras 8–16; Case C-341/01 *Plato Plastik Robert Frank* [2004] ECR I-4883, para 30; Case C-144/04 *Mangold* [2005] ECR I-9981, paras 32–9; and Case C-458/06 *Gourmet Classic* [2008] ECR I-420.

[150] Case C-97/98 *Jägerskiöld* [1999] ECR I-7319, paras 19 and 22–5.

arranged by the parties to the main action in order to induce the Court of Justice to take a position on certain problems of Community law that did not serve any objective requirement inherent in the resolution of the dispute. This conclusion was supported by the fact that the German court had permitted a third party to intervene in the case with a claim that the German law was compatible with Community law.[151]

Third, and finally, it is possible that the *Foglia* principle will only be applied in cases brought before courts in a Member State other than that whose legislation is in question.[152] Where this is the case, the Court of Justice intensifies its examination of whether the requirements for jurisdiction have been fulfilled.[153] However, even in such cases there must be almost cast iron evidence that the dispute is contrived before a reference for a preliminary ruling will be declared inadmissible under the *Foglia* jurisprudence.

In *Celestini*, the buyer of a consignment of wine had brought an action against the vendor for failure to deliver. The case had been brought in Italy in spite of the fact that (i) the wine should have been delivered in Germany, (ii) the reason for the failure to deliver was because the German authorities had controlled the wine and returned it to Italy on the grounds that it was unsuitable for human consumption, (iii) neither of the parties to the case had brought a case against the German authorities even though they agreed that the decision of the German authorities was unlawful, and (iv) the German courts had sole jurisdiction to decide on the validity of that decision. Nor did the additional circumstances that the parties had a common interest in the sale of the Italian wine in Germany, that the defendant did not dispute the jurisdiction of the Italian court, that the parties' claims and legal arguments were essentially the same, and that the parties had nevertheless with one voice requested a preliminary ruling, make it sufficiently clear that the parties jointly fabricated a dispute as a device for obtaining a preliminary ruling from the Court of Justice. As argued by Advocate General Fennelly, there was no evidence that the parties had agreed beforehand to enter into a contract with the idea at the back of their minds that, at some later stage, the content of the contract would be used to get a court in one Member State to request a preliminary ruling on the compatibility of the legislation in another Member State with Community law. The Court of Justice therefore found that it had jurisdiction to answer the questions referred to it.[154]

---

[151] Case C-379/98 *PreussenElektra* [2001] ECR I-2099, paras 31–46.
[152] This is presumably a supplementary reason why the above-mentioned Case C-83/91 *Meilicke* [1992] ECR I-4871, was not decided on the basis of the *Foglia* principle.
[153] See above at s 4.12.
[154] Case C-105/94 *Celestini* [1997] ECR I-2971, paras 19–26.

In *Van Eycke*, Mr Van Eycke had brought a case against the credit institution ASPA, claiming that ASPA had been unjustified in refusing, by reference to a Belgian decree, to open a savings account on specially advantageous terms for him, and that the decree was incompatible with Community law. When a preliminary question was referred to the Court of Justice, the Belgian government argued that the reference was not admissible since it was apparent from a number of factors that the main dispute was purely fictitious. In support of this, the government referred to the fact that Van Eycke's lawyer was an assistant lawyer in the office of ASPA's lawyer, that the parties had made a joint request that the main proceedings be adjourned with a view to making a reference for a preliminary ruling, that the disputed decree only regulated taxes and did not preclude a more advantageous savings scheme, that the parties agreed on a different forum from the defendant's, and that the case had been brought before a local court where the Belgian government had not been able to present its arguments. The Court of Justice did not, however, find it manifestly apparent from the facts set out in the order for reference that the dispute was fictitious and thus decided to consider the questions raised by the national court.[155]

In conclusion, the *Foglia* principle does not have such wide application as the original judgments in the *Foglia I* and *Foglia II* cases might have suggested. Even though the judgments are often used to support arguments that a request for a preliminary ruling should be declared inadmissible, such an argument has only been successful in the *Foglia* cases themselves. The real significance of the *Foglia* judgments is rather that they have helped create the basis for the practice described above, whereby the Court of Justice has taken upon itself the jurisdiction to examine the real relevance of a reference for a preliminary ruling.

6. The Relationship between the Preliminary Procedure and the Infringement Procedure in Articles 226 and 227 of the EC Treaty

Article 226 of the EC Treaty allows the Commission to bring proceedings against a Member State for failure to comply with Community law. Likewise, Article 227 of the EC Treaty provides that a Member State may take action against another Member State. The fact that the EC Treaty contains these specific provisions for bringing proceedings for breaches of Community law does not prevent private

---

[155] Case 267/86 *van Eycke* [1988] ECR 4769, paras 11–14. In his Opinion, Advocate General Mancini emphasised that the case had not been brought in a Member State other than the State whose legislation was in question and that the problem for the Belgian government was thus due to procedural rules in its own legal system.

individuals from bringing an action before a national court against a Member State for the same breach. Nor does this prevent a national court from making a reference to the Court of Justice for a preliminary ruling under Article 234 of the EC Treaty. Indeed, the opposite conclusion would, to a considerable extent, have deprived citizens and undertakings of their right to take action to protect their Treaty-based rights.

In *van Gend en Loos* the question arose about the relationship between Articles 226 and 227 in relation to Article 234. Three of the six Member States (at the time) made submissions in the case all arguing that a reference for a preliminary ruling could not be made where it would have been possible to use the procedure under Article 226 or Article 227. However, the Court of Justice held that the fact that the EC Treaty gave the Commission and the Member States the possibility of bringing an action before the Court of Justice against a Member State that has not fulfilled its obligations did not mean that individuals could not plead these obligations before national courts. The same applied to the fact that the EC Treaty gives the Commission ways of ensuring that obligations imposed upon those who are subject to the EC Treaty are observed. If the guarantees against the Member States' breaches of Community law were limited to the procedures in Articles 226 and 227, this would exclude any direct protection by citizens of their individual rights, and there would be the risk that recourse to the procedure would be ineffective if it were to occur after the implementation of a national decision taken contrary to the provisions of the EC Treaty. The Court of Justice also observed that the vigilance of individuals concerned to protect their rights was an effective supervision which supplemented the supervision entrusted to the Commission and the Member States by Articles 226 and 227.[156]

The fact that infringement proceedings have already been initiated in connection with a given set of circumstances will not exclude the possibility of making a reference for a preliminary ruling in connection with the same set of circumstances.[157] This applies whether or not the infringement proceedings and the reference for a preliminary ruling concern the same or different Member States. However, for practical reasons and reasons of procedural economy the Court of Justice will often combine the oral procedures in a joint hearing, and the Advocate General

---

[156] Case 26/62 *van Gend en Loos* [1963] ECR 1 (original reference: Rec 1963, p 3). Nonetheless, referring to *R v MAFF, ex p Dairy Trade Federation* [1995] COD 3; and *R (association of Pharmaceutical Importers) v Secretary of State for Health* [2001] EWCA Civ 1896 (ECR), R Gordon, *EC Law in Judicial Review* (2007) 123, notes that there have been instances where English courts have, in their discretion, declined jurisdiction to hear applications for judicial review on the basis that the cases were unsuitable for judicial review and that the complaints should have been brought by way of proceedings under Art 226 of the EC Treaty.

[157] Case 140/79 *Chemial Farmaceutici* [1981] ECR 1; and Case 142/80 *Essevi and Salengo* [1981] ECR 1413, paras 13–18.

will often prepare one opinion for both proceedings. Furthermore, the Court of Justice will often decide to give judgment at the same time in the parallel cases.[158]

Even where the Court of Justice has given judgment in an infringement case, it will be possible to make a reference for a preliminary ruling concerning the same set of circumstances.[159]

7. The Relationship between the Preliminary Procedure and the Procedure in Article 230 concerning Actions for Annulment before the Court of Justice

7.1. The *TWD* doctrine

Article 230 of the EC Treaty provides for annulment proceedings which empower the Court of Justice to review the legality of a number of Community acts. In the first instance, those having the right to institute such proceedings are the Member States and certain Community institutions. Article 230(4) also allows natural or legal persons to institute proceedings before the Court of Justice (Court of First Instance). However, this right is limited to decisions addressed to the plaintiff or decisions which, although in the form of a regulation or a decision addressed to another person, are of direct and individual concern to the plaintiff. The Court of Justice has adopted a narrow interpretation of the requirement that the plaintiff should be directly and individually concerned.[160]

Annulment proceedings must be brought within two months of the date of the publication of the measure, of its notification to the plaintiff, or, where it is neither published nor notified, from the date on which it came to the knowledge of the plaintiff.[161]

Thus, while the conditions under which a person can bring an action for annulment under Article 230 are strict, the same conditions do not apply to references

---

[158] The Court of Justice did this eg in Case C-52/00 *Commission v France* [2002] ECR I-3827; Case C-154/00 *Commission v Greece* [2002] ECR I-3879; and Case C-183/00 *González Sánchez* [2002] ECR I-3901. Judgment was given on the same day in all three cases, which concerned the interpretation of the Product Liability Directive. The first two cases were actions brought by the Commission for breach of the EC Treaty, and the third concerned a preliminary ruling. For further details on this issue, see H Schermers and J S Watson, 'Report of the Conference' in H Schermers et al, *Article 177 EEC: Experiences and Problems* (1987) 3, 40ff; and D Anderson, 'The Admissibility of Preliminary References' in A Barav and D Wyatt (eds), *Yearbook of European Law 1994* (1994) 179, 196ff.

[159] See s 4.7 above and Ch 6, s 3.3. See also Ch 6, s 4.2.3.

[160] Case C-50/00 P *Union de Pequenos Agricultores (UPA)* [2002] ECR I-6677.

[161] Art 230(5) of the EC Treaty.

for preliminary rulings. The question of *locus standi* is determined according to national law, and the conditions are often less strict than those required for initiating annulment proceedings. In addition, Community law does not impose any deadline for making a reference under Article 234. For this reason it will often be an advantage to claim the invalidity of a Community measure before a national court, rather than using the annulment procedure under Article 230. In other words, the use of the preliminary ruling procedure under Article 234 makes it possible to get round the requirements of Article 230.

A review of the validity of a legal act in connection with a preliminary ruling under Article 234 and a review in connection with an action for annulment under Article 230 constitute two different and in principle independent legal remedies, each with its own conditions for bringing an action. It follows from this that even if it may have been possible to bring a direct action to review a Community legal act under Article 230 this does not in itself prevent a national court from making a reference for a ruling on the legality of an act of a Member State which has been enacted with a view to implementing the Community act, and where it is argued that the Community act in question is unlawful.[162]

In *Rau*, a German court referred a number of questions on the interpretation and validity of some Community legal acts. Among other things it asked whether the right to challenge a Community measure under Article 230 meant that it was not possible to bring proceedings before a national court against a national measure which implemented the Community measure in question. The Court of Justice ruled that there is nothing in Community law to prevent an action from being brought before a national court against a measure implementing a decision of a Community institution where the conditions laid down by national law are satisfied. If the outcome of the dispute in such a case depends on the validity of the Community decision, the national court may refer questions to the Court of Justice for a preliminary ruling, without there being a need to ascertain whether or not the applicant in the main proceedings has the possibility of challenging the decision directly before the Court of Justice. The Court of Justice therefore found that the possibility of bringing a direct action in accordance with Article 230(4) against a decision adopted by a Community institution does not preclude the possibility of bringing an action in a national court against a measure adopted by

---

[162] Case C-197/91 *Frutticoltori Associati Cuneesi* [1993] ECR I-2639, paras 9–12. Compare this with Case 156/77 *Commission v Belgium* [1978] ECR 1881, where in an *obiter dictum* the Court of Justice stated that Arts 234 and 230 fulfil different needs and have different purposes 'and cannot justify a derogation from the principle of the time-barring of applications as a result of the expiry of the periods within which proceedings must be brought, without thereby depriving Article [230] of its legal significance'; see para 25 in the English version of the judgment (para 24 in the French version).

a national authority to implement the Community decision, including a claim that the Community decision is unlawful.[163]

As explained below in Chapter 6, Section 4.2, the Court of Justice has established that it has exclusive jurisdiction to declare a Community act unlawful. Therefore, if a party claims, before a national court, that a Community legal act is unlawful, and if the judge in the national court is inclined to agree, the national court is obliged to refer the matter for a preliminary ruling, irrespective of whether it is a court of last instance. Against this background it would have been natural to assume that a party who wishes to challenge a Community act and who has a right to bring an action under Article 230 could choose to test the validity of a Community act before a national court and thereby provoke a reference for a preliminary ruling under Article 234, instead of using the annulment procedure under Article 230. However, in *TWD Textilwerke Deggendorf*, the Court of Justice restricted the possibility of choosing freely between the two proceedings.

TWD Textilwerke Deggendorf originated in the early 1980s when the German yarn manufacturer TWD received financial aid from the German authorities. The European Commission initiated an investigation which resulted in a decision that the aid was unlawful. The decision was addressed to the German authorities. The German authorities forwarded a copy of the decision to TWD, and drew their attention to the fact that the decision could be challenged before the Court of Justice under Article 230 of the Treaty. However, neither the German authorities nor TWD brought proceedings to annul the decision. In accordance with the Commission's decision the German authorities decided to withdraw the aid. TWD brought proceedings before a German court to annul this decision. In support of its claim TWD argued that the Commission's decision was unlawful, at least in part. The German court thereupon asked the Court of Justice whether TWD was debarred from pleading the unlawfulness of the Commission's decision in a case such as that before it. The Court of Justice held first, that both a Member State and a recipient of State aid are prevented from challenging the Commission's decision on the unlawfulness of State aid under Article 230 once the period for bringing an action has expired. As regards the Member State, a failure to comply with a Commission decision so that the Commission brings proceedings for breach of the EC Treaty means that, on the grounds of legal certainty, a Member State is prevented from pleading that the Commission decision is unlawful. The Court also found that the same requirement for legal certainty prevents a recipient of aid which is subject to a Commission decision in accordance with Article 88 of the EC Treaty from calling into question the lawfulness of that decision before the national courts in an action brought against the measures taken by the national

---

[163] Joined Cases 133/85–136/85 *Rau* [1987] ECR 2289, paras 11–12.

authorities to implement that decision, if the recipient of the aid could have challenged the decision but has allowed the mandatory time limit laid down in Article 230(5) of the EC Treaty to expire. In circumstances like these, to accept that such a party could oppose the implementation of the decision in the national courts by claiming that it was unlawful would enable that party to evade the definitive nature which the decision assumes as against that party once the time limit for bringing an action has expired.[164]

As was made clear in *TWD Textilwerke Deggendorf*, the Court of Justice wanted to prevent a party being able to challenge the validity of a Community act so as to get round the time limit laid down in Article 230(5). The core of the *TWD* doctrine is thus to prevent the preliminary ruling procedure being used to circumvent the limitations in the annulment procedure.[165] In its more recent rulings the Court of Justice has maintained this core approach. However, in relation to so-called non-privileged parties (ie in particular private parties) it has restricted the application of the estoppel principle laid down in *TWD* to cases where the party entitled to bring an action has clearly and unquestionably fulfilled the strict conditions for bringing an action under the fourth paragraph of Article 230.

In *Accrington Beef*, in a dispute between some private undertakings and the UK State, the question arose of the validity of some provisions in a Community regulation. The English court referred the question to the Court of Justice for a preliminary ruling. Before the Court of Justice the UK government argued that the plaintiff undertakings were prevented from objecting to the validity of the measure before the national court as they had not brought annulment proceedings to review the disputed provisions prior to the expiry of the deadline in Article 230. In response to this the Court of Justice observed that the case concerned a regulation whose disputed provisions were addressed in general terms to categories of persons defined in the abstract and to situations determined objectively, and it was not obvious that an action by the plaintiffs would have been admissible. There was therefore nothing to prevent the validity of the regulation being reviewed in connection with a reference for a preliminary ruling.[166]

---

[164] Case C-188/92 *TWD Textilwerke Deggendorf* [1994] ECR I-833. In his Opinion in the case, Advocate General Jacobs also argued that a direct action under Art 230 provides a more appropriate procedure for challenging an individual decision than does the preliminary ruling procedure under Art 234. See also Case C-232/05 *Commission v France* [2006] ECR I-10071, paras 58–61.

[165] Para 34 in the Opinion of Advocate General Kokott in Case C-333/07 *Regie Network* (ECJ 22 December 2008); and Case C-390/98 *Banks & Co* [2001] ECR I-6117, paras 109–13, which, however, concerned a preliminary ruling in accordance with Art 41 of the ECSC Treaty. See also Case C-119/05 *Lucchini* [2007] ECR I-6199, paras 53–5. This core of the *TWD* doctrine was also reflected in a case where the illegality of a regulation was invoked on the basis of Art 241 of the EC Treaty, cf Case C-11/00 *Commission v European Central Bank* [2003] ECR I-7147, paras 74–8, and Advocate General Jacobs' Opinion in that case at para 192.

[166] Case C-241/95 *Accrington Beef* [1996] ECR I-6699, paras 14–16. See similarly Joined Cases C-346/03 and C-529/03 *Atzeni and others* [2006] ECR I-1875, para 34; and Case C-119/05

The Court has also taken into account whether the party in question in fact has been informed about his right to bring an action for annulment directly before the Court of Justice (Court of First Instance).

In *Eurotunnel* the undertaking behind the tunnel under the English Channel brought a case before a French court against an undertaking that operated a ferry service between France and England. Eurotunnel argued that the ferry operator was guilty of unfair competition by selling goods free of tax and excise duty on board its vessels. The ferry operator had been given permission to make such tax-free sales by the French authorities, and the French permission had been given under the authority of a French law which proceeded from the authorization in some directive provisions. In this connection, Eurotunnel argued before the French court that the directive provisions were invalid. The French court therefore asked the Court of Justice whether Eurotunnel could require the directive to be annulled under Article 234 when the company had not brought annulment proceedings for the review of the Community measure under Article 230. The Court of Justice ruled that, in contrast to the *TWD Textilwerke Deggendorf* case, in *Eurotunnel* there was not a situation in which an undertaking was unquestionably entitled to be informed about—and had been informed about—the possibility of bringing an action for annulment to review the Community measure which the undertaking claimed was invalid in its action before the national court. The Court of Justice also stated that it is in general doubtful whether a private party can in fact challenge a directive under Article 230. Furthermore, in the actual case it was clear that Eurotunnel would not have been entitled to bring an action under Article 230. Thus, Eurotunnel had no means of challenging the validity of the Community measure other than by bringing an action before the national court. On this basis the Court of Justice ruled that a natural or legal person may challenge before a national court the validity of provisions in directives, even though that person has not brought an action for annulment.[167]

In *Lucchini*, it seems that the party concerned had not been expressly informed of the possibility of bringing an action for annulment. It nevertheless appears from

---

Lucchini [2007] ECR 6199, paras 54–5, as well as the Advocate General's Opinion in the latter case, paras 68 and 81–3. See also Case C-441/05 *Roquette Frères* [2007] ECR I-1993, paras 39–47; and Case C-239/99 *Nachi Europe* [2001] ECR I-1197, paras 5 and 37, concerning regulations which directly and individually concern a private party. See further D Wyatt, 'The Relationship between Actions for Annulment and References on Validity after TWD Deggendorf' in J Lonbay and A Biondi (eds), *Remedies for Breach of EC Law* (1997) 55, 66.

[167] Case C-408/95 *Eurotunnel* [1997] ECR I-6315, paras 28–32. See also Joined Cases C-346/03 and C-529/03 *Atzeni and others* [2006] ECR I-1875, paras 32–3; and Case 185/83 *Rijksuniversiteit Groningen* [1984] ECR 3623, as well as the commentary on the latter case in M Broberg, 'The relationship between referrals for preliminary rulings under Article 234 and proceedings to annul Community decisions under Article 230 of the EC Treaty' in N Fenger, K Hagel-Sørensen, and B Vesterdorf (eds), *Claus Gulmann Liber Amicorum* (2006) 83, 90ff.

the Advocate General's Opinion that the party was aware of this possibility and had chosen not to exercise the right to challenge the disputed Commission decision.[168]

That the desire to prevent circumvention plays an important role in the Court's case law can also be seen by the fact that the *TWD* doctrine does not cover cases where a party that could have brought an action for annulment has in fact not claimed that the relevant Community act is invalid, but where the national court raises this question of its own motion.

In *Cassa di Risparmio di Firenze*, an Italian court made a reference concerning, among other things, the validity of a Commission decision on unlawful State aid. It was argued before the Court of Justice that the question could not be admitted, since the Commission's decision had not been challenged under Article 230. The Court of Justice rejected this objection. It held that, since the question had been referred by the national court of its own motion, the question could not be declared inadmissible by virtue of the case law resulting from *TWD Textilwerke Deggendorf*.[169]

Thus the fact that a party could have brought proceedings under Article 230(4), does not automatically mean that that party is covered by the *TWD* doctrine. A reference for a preliminary ruling on the validity of a Community measure will only be declared inadmissible if: (1) the party concerned undoubtedly could have had the validity reviewed by bringing an action under Article 230; (2) it appears indisputable that this party knew that it was entitled to bring such an action;[170] and (3) the question is not raised by the national court of its own motion, but because the party entitled to bring such an action has claimed before the national court that the Community measure is invalid.[171] Furthermore, (4) the challenge to the validity of a Community measure in a reference for a preliminary ruling cannot be dismissed if the party concerned has in fact brought an action under Article 230 within the period allowed.[172]

These four conditions apply to private parties as well as to Member States and Community institutions that have *locus standi*. However, in practice the first two

---

[168] Case C-119/05 *Lucchini* [2007] ECR I-6199.

[169] Case C-222/04 *Cassa di Risparmio di Firenze* [2006] ECR I-289, paras 72–4, and the Opinion of the Advocate General, paras 60–3. However, this is only an *obiter dictum* as the Court of Justice dismissed the question on other grounds, see paras 75–92 of the judgment.

[170] See Case C-188/92 *TWD Textilwerke Deggendorf* [1994] ECR I-833, para 24.

[171] In line with this, see Case C-178/95 *Wiljo* [1997] ECR I-585; and Case C-239/99 *Nachi Europe* [2001] ECR I-1197.

[172] See J Usher, 'The Assertion of Jurisdiction by the European Court of Justice' in P Capps, M Evans, and S Konstandinidis (eds), *Asserting Jurisdiction—International and European Legal Perspectives* (2003) 283, 291.

conditions will always be fulfilled with regard to Member States and Community institutions.[173]

It must follow from the Court of Justice's ruling in *TWD* that if a Member State has not in due time initiated annulment proceedings under Article 230 of the EC Treaty, and if subsequently it becomes a party to proceedings before a national court, it will be barred both from invoking the invalidity of the Community act and from concurring with such a claim put forward by the other party in the national proceedings. In contrast, it seems unlikely that a Member State will be prevented from invoking the invalidity of the Community act in observations that it submits as part of a preliminary ruling procedure before the Court of Justice.[174] Indeed, the Court has accepted that a Member State may intervene in a direct action under Article 230 concerning the annulment of a Community act directed to that State even though it did not itself challenge the act within the time limit.[175]

To sum up, where a party could have challenged a Community act in a direct action, it will be barred from invoking the invalidity of the Community act before a national court. The consequence of this is that in such a situation the Court of Justice will decline to answer a preliminary question on validity. Instead, the Court will merely hold that where the party concerned has not challenged the Community act under Article 230 of the EC Treaty within the time limit prescribed, the national court must consider the Community act to be binding.[176]

7.2. Discussion of the *TWD* doctrine

The Court of Justice's exclusion of certain references for preliminary rulings through the adoption of the *TWD* doctrine into the EC Treaty's system of judicial remedies has been criticised in the legal literature.[177] In this respect, the following objections to the rule in *TWD* have been raised.

---

[173] Case C-241/01 *National Farmers' Union* [2002] ECR I-9079, paras 34–9.

[174] D Anderson, 'The Admissibility of Preliminary References' in A Barav and D Wyatt (eds), *Yearbook of European Law 1994* (1994) 179, 200ff. See also D Anderson and M Demetriou, *References to the European Court* (2002) 128ff.

[175] Case T-37/97 *Foget de Clabecq* [1999] ECR II-859.

[176] The Court of Justice has taken a very similar approach vis-à-vis Art 241 of the EC Treaty, cf O Odudu, 'Case-note on Case C-11/00, *Commission of the European Communities* v. *European Central Bank*, Judgment of 10 July 2003, Full Court' (2004) 41 CML Rev 1073, 1087.

[177] See G Vandersanden, 'La procédure préjudicielle: à la recherche d'une identité perdue' in M Dony (ed), *Mélanges en hommage à Michel Waelbroeck, vol 1* (1999) 619, 632–4; and M Broberg, 'The relationship between referrals for preliminary rulings under Article 234 and proceedings to annul Community decisions under Article 230 of the EC Treaty' in N Fenger, K Hagel-Sørensen, and B Vesterdorf (eds), *Claus Gulmann Liber Amicorum* (2006) 83, 91–7, with further references. See also the Opinion of Advocate General Colomer in Joined Cases C-346/03 and C-529/03 *Atzeni and others* [2006] ECR I-1875, para 88. M Ross, 'Limits on Using Article 177 EC' (1994) 19 EL Rev 640, 643ff; V Hatzopolous, 'De l'arrêt 'Foglia-Novello' à l'arrêt "TWD Textilwerke"—La jurisprudence

First, it has been argued that Article 230(4) and Article 234 are fundamentally different. Thus, Article 230(4) entitles certain (natural or legal) persons to institute legal proceedings before the Court of Justice in order that they may in this way safeguard their rights under Community law. In contrast, Article 234 gives national courts a right to ask the Court of Justice about the interpretation or validity with respect to Community law thereby ensuring the correct and uniform application of Community law.[178] Furthermore, the annulment of a legal act under Article 230 is not the same as a declaration of invalidity under Article 234. If a legal act is annulled, in principle it ceases to exist. If a legal act is declared invalid, it continues to exist, but it cannot be applied in certain specific circumstances.[179]

Second, one might wonder whether the *TWD* case law substantially furthers one of the main arguments supporting it, namely the need to ensure the aim of legal certainty that lies behind the time limit in Article 230(5). Indeed, the *TWD* case law excludes only those who would clearly have been able to institute proceedings under Article 230(4) from having the validity of a given Community legal act tested by a reference for a preliminary ruling after the time limit in Article 230(5) has expired. In contrast, others are not prevented from challenging the validity of a legal act after the expiry of the period for bringing annulment proceedings. In other words, the Court's practice protects the substantive legal rights for these others. Hence, there will be no certainty that the validity of a Community measure is not challenged after the expiry of the time limit for bringing proceedings under Article 230(5). Moreover, the *TWD* case law is not likely to have any significance for cases concerning the validity of general Community acts such as directives and regulations. The consequences of a general act being declared invalid are, however likely to be more significant and more widespread. For this reason too, one may question to what extent the *TWD* case law actually contributes to ensuring legal certainty.

---

de la Cour de justice relative à la recevabilité des renvois préjudiciels' (1994) 3 Revue du Marché Unique Européen 195, 210ff; G Tesauro, 'The Effectiveness of Judicial Protection and Co-operation between the Court of Justice and the National Courts' in J Rosenløv and K Thorup (eds), *Ole Due Liber Amicorum* (1994) 352, 372.

[178] However, Art 234 also has an important purpose in ensuring respect for rights based on Community law—including those rights a private party may derive therefrom. In other words, this purpose is not exclusive to Art 230.

[179] In this respect see V Hatzopoulos, 'De l'arrêt 'Foglia-Novello' à l'arrêt "TWD Textilwerke"—La jurisprudence de la Cour de justice relative à la recevabilité des renvois préjudiciels' (1994) 3 Revue du Marché Unique Européen 195, 210ff. See also Case C-239/99 *Nachi Europe GmbH v Hauptzollamt Krefeld* [2001] ECR I-1197, where some plaintiffs had challenged the disputed legal act under Art 230, but where the annulment was not given effect vis-à-vis the undertaking, Nachi, which was also the addressee of the disputed legal act, but had chosen not to bring an action for annulment.

Third, it seems somewhat strange that, out of consideration for legal certainty, the natural or legal person or persons that are most directly and individually affected by a disputed Community measure should be denied the possibility of having the validity of that legal act reviewed by means of a reference for a preliminary ruling, while those who are not concerned directly and individually are not prevented from having such a review carried out. The untenable nature of this distinction is underlined when one considers the possibility of a national court referring a question about the validity of a legal act for a preliminary ruling, in a case in which the parties include both those who would have had a right to institute proceedings for annulment under Article 230(4), and those who would not have been entitled to institute such proceedings directly. This situation could arise in many different forms. In several of these different forms the ruling in *TWD Textilwerke Deggendorf* would hardly offer a persuasive solution, regardless of whether the request for a preliminary ruling is accepted or denied.[180] An example may illustrate this.

The Commission issues a decision to a Member State ordering the repayment of State aid to a shipyard. Neither the Member State concerned nor the shipyard institutes annulment proceedings before the Court of Justice (Court of First Instance). Complying with the Commission decision, the Member State requires the shipyard to repay the aid. The shipyard, however, refuses to do so, and the dispute is brought before a national court.

If the shipyard argues that no repayment should be made because the Commission decision is invalid, it follows from *TWD* that, in these circumstances, the Court of Justice will decline to rule on the validity when asked to do so in a preliminary reference. Instead the Court will merely declare that the national court must consider the Commission decision to be binding when deciding the main proceedings. However, if for instance a trade union at the shipyard is given leave to intervene before the national court in support of the shipyard and if this trade union claims that the Commission decision is invalid, the Court of Justice will probably not refuse to rule on the validity question in a preliminary reference.[181]

---

[180] For an outline of the many different forms that the situation may take, see M Broberg, 'The relationship between referrals for preliminary rulings under Article 234 and proceedings to annul Community decisions under Article 230 of the EC Treaty' in N Fenger, K Hagel-Sørensen, and B Vesterdorf (eds), *Claus Gulmann Liber Amicorum* (2006) 83. Broberg suggests that the rule in *TWD Textilwerke Deggendorf* should only be applied (1) where there is a clear attempt to evade the provisions of the EC Treaty, (2) where there are no mitigating circumstances (such as where, due to a lack of resources, a private party has not been able to initiate proceedings in accordance with Art 230), and (3) where natural or legal third parties would suffer appreciable damage if the validity of a Community legal act were put in question. See also D Wyatt, 'The Relationship between Actions for Annulment and References on Validity after *TWD Textilwerke Deggendorf*' in J Lonbay and A Biondi (eds), *Remedies for Breach of EC Law* (1997) 55, 66.

[181] Moreover, in that case, the shipyard would probably not be precluded from presenting observations before the Court of Justice arguing that the Commission decision is invalid.

This conclusion appears fairly certain where the trade union's claim is not supported by the shipyard. The question remains whether it would make a difference if, before the national court, the shipyard were to support the trade union in the latter's claim of invalidity? Also, it remains to be seen whether the answer will depend upon whether the invalidity argument was first put forward by the trade union or by the shipyard.

In other words, it remains to be settled whether the *TWD* doctrine precludes the Court from making a judicial assessment of the validity of a Community act where this validity is challenged before the national court by someone who undoubtedly did not have standing under Article 230—even if in the same main proceedings the same challenge is also made by someone who undoubtedly had such standing.

As is apparent from the above examination, the Court of Justice is faced with a dilemma between, on the one hand, countering obvious circumvention of the time limit laid down in Article 230(5) of the EC Treaty and, on the other hand, not refusing to answer preliminary questions on the validity of Community acts where such invalidity is invoked before a national court by someone who would not have had standing under Article 230.

Essentially the problem is that the same legal proceedings before a national court may include both participants that could have challenged a given Community act under Article 230 and participants that would have been barred from doing so. It is not obvious how this Gordian knot may be cut. Perhaps the better solution would be to consider other ways of preventing circumvention of the time limit laid down in Article 230(5) than that provided by the *TWD* doctrine.

6

WHEN ARE NATIONAL COURTS OBLIGED TO REFER QUESTIONS?

1. The Right to Refer and the Obligation to Refer

According to the wording of Article 234(2), a national court is free to decide whether or not to make a reference regarding the matters listed in Article 234(1). As an exception to that rule, Article 234(3), however, provides that:

> Where any such question is raised in a case pending before a court or tribunal of a Member State against whose decisions there is no judicial remedy under national law, that court or tribunal shall bring the matter before the Court of Justice.

In other words, a national court whose decision cannot be appealed against (a court of last instance) is obligated to make a reference for a preliminary ruling if the main proceedings give rise to a question about the interpretation or validity of Community law. This simple classification must be qualified on several points, however. Thus, a national court whose decisions are not subject to appeal is certainly not always required to make a reference for a preliminary ruling on Community law questions. Conversely, there are situations where national courts are required to make a reference, even if their decisions can be appealed against.

In this chapter we shall clarify when a national court has a duty to make a reference for a preliminary ruling. Section 2 analyses when a national court is regarded as being a court of last instance, as laid down in Article 234(3). Section 3 sets out when a court of last instance is exempt from the obligation to make a reference. Section 4 examines when national courts, other than those of last instance, have a duty to make a reference. Finally, Section 5 considers the legal consequences of a national court failing to comply with its obligation to make a reference.

2. National Courts Covered by Article 234(3)

The wording 'a court or tribunal of a Member State against whose decisions there is no judicial remedy' in Article 234(3) expresses a Community law concept. In the early years following the entry into force of the EC Treaty, several writers supported an institutional approach to this concept normally referred to as the theory of 'abstract appealability'. According to this theory, only the highest courts in the national legal systems were under an obligation to make a reference under Article 234(3). In support of this it was argued that the purpose of that provision was only to ensure that there were not diverging interpretations of Community law within the individual Member State, and that it was principally the highest national courts which laid down—and ensured—a uniform interpretation of the law.[1] In opposition to the theory of abstract appealability other legal writers argued for a functional approach known as the theory of 'concrete appealability'. According to this theory, what mattered was whether there was a right of appeal in the actual case in question. The proponents of the theory of concrete appealability were of the view that Article 234(3) should not only ensure, in a general manner, the uniform interpretation of Community law in the individual Member States, but also the legal protection of the rights of individuals under Community law.

---

[1] H Schermers and D Waelbroeck, *Judicial Protection in the European Union* (2001) 167, with further references.

This protection required there to be an obligation to make a reference for a preliminary ruling in all cases where there was no right of appeal.[2]

The Court of Justice has chosen to follow the theory of concrete appealability.[3] Indeed, this approach better ensures both the legal protection of individual citizens and the uniform application of Community law than would the theory of abstract appealability, had the Court adopted this approach instead.[4] Hence, it is not difficult to imagine a situation where in different lower national courts, in cases without a right of appeal, ambiguity would arise in respect of a Community law question and where the national courts would answer this question differently if there were no obligation to make a reference for a preliminary ruling.

In *Costa v E.N.E.L.*, the Italian lawyer, Costa, had refused to pay the Italian electricity supply company E.N.E.L. for supplies of electricity for an amount of less than 2,000 Italian lire. Costa had brought the case before the *Giudice Conciliatore* in Milan. The small amount of the money at issue meant that it would not be possible to appeal to a higher national court against the decision of the lower national court. The *Giudice Conciliatore* referred a number of preliminary questions to the Court of Justice. The Court of Justice held that under Article 234, national courts whose decisions could not be appealed against must refer questions concerning compliance with the EC Treaty to the Court of Justice.[5]

In *Parfums Christian Dior*, the *Hoge Raad* of the Netherlands (the Dutch Supreme Court) referred a question concerning the interpretation of the Trade Marks Directive to the Court of Justice for a preliminary ruling. In its first question the *Hoge Raad* requested clarification about which national court should be regarded as the court of last instance for the purposes of Article 234(3), where in connection with the interpretation of the Uniform Benelux Law on Trade Marks a question arose concerning the interpretation of the Trade Marks Directive. The Benelux countries had adopted common trade mark legislation which was authoritatively interpreted by references to the Benelux Court of Justice. In the case in question, according to the Uniform Benelux Law on Trade Marks, the *Hoge Raad*

---

[2] P Lasok, *The European Court of Justice—Practice and Procedure* (1994) 62; R Grass, 'L'article 177 du Traité de C.E.E.' in J Chauvin and E Trubert (eds), *Le Droit Communautaire & International devant le juge du commerce* (1989) 81, 87; and E Traversa, 'Les voies de recours ouvertes aux opérateurs économiques: le renvoi préjudiciel au titre de l'article 177 du traité CEE' (1992) Revue du Marché Unique Européen Vol 2, 51, 60.

[3] Case C-495/03 *Intermodal Transports BV* [2005] ECR I-8151, para 30, according to which the obligation to make a reference applies to supreme courts *and* to 'any other national court or tribunal against whose decisions there is no judicial remedy'. See also Advocate General Colomer at para 33 in Case 14/08 *Roda Golf & Beach Resort* (ECJ 25 June 2009).

[4] For a similar view, see judgment of 26 May 1998 by the Finnish Court of Appeal at Turku, Turun hovioikeu, 26 May 1998, No 1275/98, reported in the Sixteenth annual report on monitoring the application of Community law [1999] OJ C354/185.

[5] Case 6/64 *Costa* [1964] ECR 585.

was required to refer a question for a preliminary ruling to the Benelux Court of Justice, which would be the court of last instance in relation to the question referred to it. However, it was the *Hoge Raad* which would make the decision as the court of last instance in the main proceedings. Thus, the question was whether the *Hoge Raad* itself or the Benelux Court was the court of last instance for the purposes of Article 234(3). In answering the question, the Court of Justice stated that the aim of Article 234(3) is to prevent a Member State developing a judicial practice which is not in accordance with Community law. Since the Benelux Court decided on the interpretation of the Uniform Benelux Law on Trade Marks without there being a right of appeal, and since the decision of the *Hoge Raad* could not be appealed against according to national law, both the *Hoge Raad* and the Benelux Court were covered by the obligation to refer the question to the Court of Justice for a preliminary ruling according to Article 234(3).[6]

Due to the autonomous Community law concept of what constitutes a court for the purposes of Article 234, there might be instances where a body which, under national law, does not qualify as a court nevertheless constitutes a court of last instance under Article 234(3).

In Austria, decisions by the national regulatory telecoms authority may be appealed to the *Telekom-Control-Kommission* (Telecoms Control Commission). Whilst this body does not constitute a court within the Austrian legal system, but only a board with judicial functions, it does qualify as a court within Article 234. Moreover, there is no right of appeal to a higher review body meaning that the Telecoms Control Commission acts as a court of last instance.[7]

What is decisive for the classification as a court of last instance is whether it is possible to refer any Community law questions to the Court of Justice for a preliminary ruling after the national court in question has issued its decision. Moreover, the national court that is to hear the appealed decision must have the power to overturn those parts of the decision which a preliminary ruling may show to be incompatible with Community law. On the other hand, there is no requirement that the appeal shall have suspensory effect,[8] neither does it seem to be a requirement that there can be a new material examination of the main proceedings before the national court.

In *Lyckeskog*, Kenny Lyckeskog had been found guilty of attempted smuggling by the Strömstad District Court. The case was appealed to the Court of Appeal for Western Sweden. From the Court of Appeal the case could be appealed to the

---

6 Case C-337/95 *Parfums Christian Dior* [1997] ECR I-6013, paras 18–31.
7 See Seventeenth annual report on monitoring the application of Community law [2001] OJ C30/199.
8 Case C-210/06 *Cartesio* (ECJ 16 December 2008), paras 75–8.

Swedish Supreme Court. If such an appeal was brought by the prosecution, it would always be heard, whereas in other cases the Supreme Court had to give leave to appeal before the case could be heard. The case involved a question of Community law, and the Swedish Court of Appeal therefore asked the Court of Justice whether it was covered by Article 234(3). The Court of Justice found that the Court of Appeal was not the court of last instance. This finding was based upon the observation that it was possible to bring an appeal to the Supreme Court, and if in this connection a question was raised about the interpretation or validity of a Community rule, the Supreme Court would be required to refer the question for a preliminary ruling in accordance with Article 234(3). Thus, since the Supreme Court would be obliged to refer a question of Community law for a preliminary ruling when considering whether to grant leave to appeal, the Court of Appeal did not qualify as a court of last instance. However, under Community law the Supreme Court would presumably only be entitled to make a reference if this were made in connection with the resolution of a dispute. The Court of Justice therefore must have regarded the processing of a request to the Supreme Court for leave to appeal as a first integrated step in the dispute settlement which the appeal would comprise.[9]

As a general rule, a national court has an obligation to make a reference where the party who does not receive full support for his claims does not have a right to legal review of the decision of the case in question. In contrast, if a party receives the support of the national court in relation to his claims, it does not matter whether or not the national court agrees with that party's legal argument(s) based upon Community law. It is thus irrelevant whether a successful party agrees or disagrees with the grounds for the decision of the national court.[10]

Whether any subsequent examination of a decision of a national court is by means of an appeal to a higher national court or otherwise is immaterial. The crucial test is whether the losing party has a right to a legal review of the decision, thereby ensuring the possibility of a reference for a preliminary ruling.

In *Hoffmann-La Roche*, an undertaking had brought a case before a German court with a request that an interim order be given in interlocutory proceedings against another undertaking's use of a trade mark. The case was dealt with by summary

---

[9] Case C-99/00 *Lyckeskog* [2002] ECR I-4839, paras 17–19. The case is commented on by J Raitio in 'What is the Court of Final Instance in the Framework of Article 234(3) in Sweden?' (2003) Europarättslig Tidskrift Vol 1, ss 160–6. See also T Tridimas, 'Knocking on Heaven's Door: Fragmentation, Efficiency and Defiance in the Preliminary Reference Procedure' (2003) 40 CML Rev 9, 41 who observes that one consequence of the ruling in *Lyckeskog* is that the English Court of Appeal is not covered by Art 234(3).

[10] Case 107/76 *Hoffmann-La Roche* [1977] ECR 957, para 5, where it is stated that the requirement which arises out of the purpose of Art 234(3) will be satisfied if there is a right to an appeal 'either in all circumstances, or when the unsuccessful party so requires'.

proceedings. The referring national court's decision could not in itself be appealed. However, the losing party could require the matter to be determined in subsequent full proceedings in accordance with the usual rules of civil procedure. The Court of Justice held that a summary decision on interim measures was not covered by Article 234(3), where the legal question thus decided could subsequently be tried in an ordinary main action.[11]

A national appeal court which deals with the refusal of a lower national court to make a reference for a preliminary ruling does not necessarily constitute a court of last instance, even if the decision of the appeal court on whether to make a reference cannot be appealed to an even higher national court. Thus, the appeal court will not be the last instance if there is a subsequent possibility to appeal against the judgment of the lower national court in the main proceedings, and if in connection with the examination of this appeal there can be a reference for a preliminary ruling.[12]

There may also be situations where a court of last instance refuses to make a preliminary reference, and where this refusal can be appealed to a superior court that may overturn the refusal. Even if the refusal to make a preliminary reference may be appealed to a superior court, the lower court will still be the court of last instance within the meaning of Article 234 if the main action continues to rest with the latter court and if the ultimate ruling of this court cannot be the subject of an appeal.

A national court does not constitute a court of last instance if an appeal can only be made after leave to appeal has been granted but where the body which must grant leave to appeal is obliged to do this. In this situation the application for leave to appeal is merely a formality. Nor will a national court be regarded as a court of last instance if there is a right to seek leave to appeal, and the body granting this leave fulfils the criteria for being a national court with a right to make a reference under Article 234. Here it is necessary to make a closer examination of the role of each such body.

Presumably, two situations are likely to be particularly relevant. First, there are cases where an application for leave to appeal is brought directly before the national appeal court, and where the first step in the appeal process consists of an evaluation of whether the case should be accepted for a full hearing. In this case the appeal court will be entitled to make a reference for a preliminary ruling, and hence the lower court will not constitute a court of last instance for the purposes

---

[11] Case 107/76 *Hoffmann-La Roche* [1977] ECR 957, para 5.

[12] On a national appeal court's powers to overturn a lower national court's decision to make a preliminary reference, see Ch 9, s 2 below.

of Article 234(3).[13] Second, there may also be cases where the body considering an application for leave to appeal does not decide on the dispute in question, but merely assesses, on the basis of a discretionary evaluation, whether the case gives rise to such issues of principle that leave to appeal to a higher court should be granted. In this situation the body deciding whether to grant leave to appeal will not itself be entitled to make a reference, and hence the lower court will constitute a court of last instance for the purposes of Article 234(3). Moreover, if leave to appeal is granted in the latter situation, the court hearing the appeal will (also) be a court of last instance with a duty to refer. In other words, both the court rendering the ruling that is subject to appeal and the court hearing the appeal will be courts of last instance within the meaning of Article 234(3).

This may be compared with the ruling by the Polish Supreme Court in *Sąd Najwyższy*. Here the Supreme Court held that a Polish Court of Appeal would not be a court of last instance within the meaning of Article 234(3) when it is possible to make an extraordinary appeal in cassation from the Polish Court of Appeal to the Polish Supreme Court. Provided the losing party (or parties) has a right to make such appeal and provided the Polish Supreme Court cannot on a discretionary basis refuse to hear the case, this interpretation is in line with the one submitted here.[14]

The condition that there must be access to appeal can be fulfilled even though the appeal procedure differs according to which party loses the case.[15] What matters is whether the losing party can appeal. Conversely it must be assumed that it will not be sufficient if the right of appeal is only granted to a third party, or if one of the parties does not have a right of appeal in cases where this party does not receive full support for its claims.

In *Lyckeskog*, referred to above, the prosecution authorities had an unconditional right of appeal, whereas the accused did not have the same right. Since the accused had been found guilty in the lower national court, the Court of Justice found it necessary to look closely at his right of appeal in order to determine whether the situation was covered by Article 234(3). In other words, the Court of Justice did not find it sufficient that the prosecution authorities had an unconditional right of appeal in cases where the lower national court had not supported their claim.[16]

---

[13] Case C-210/06 *Cartesio* (ECJ 16 December 2008) paras 76–8; and (implicitly) Case C-99/00 *Lyckeskog* [2002] ECR I-4839, paras 17–18.

[14] Ruling by the Polish Supreme Court, Sąd Najwyższy–Izba Pracy, Ubezpieczeń Społecznych i Spraw Publicznych, decision of 20 February 2008, III SK 23/07, reported in the Court of Justice's newsletter REFLETS, Informations rapides sur les développements juridiques présentant un intérêt communautaire No 3, 2008, at pp 29–30.

[15] Case C-51/03 *Georgescu* [2004] ECR I-3203, para 31.

[16] Case C-99/00 *Lyckeskog* [2002] ECR I-4839, paras 14–19.

The fact that there is a possibility of an extraordinary reopening of the case—for example by a review board—does not mean that a national court of last instance is no longer a court of last instance for the purposes of Article 234.[17] The losing party has no guarantee that the case will be reopened. On the other hand, the fact that an appeal can only be made on a point of law[18] does not in itself mean that the court handing down the decision that is subject to such limited appeal is a court of last instance.[19]

Finally, in some circumstances it is not clear from the outset whether it will be possible to appeal the judgment that will be given; this is the position, for example, where access to appeal depends on the decision which the national court will take. One such situation where this will be the case is where a decision has been appealed to a national superior court and that court must choose between either finally deciding the case, meaning that a reference will not be possible following its decision, or referring the case back for a re-trial by the lower national court, meaning that it will be possible to make a preliminary ruling after the superior court's decision to refer for a re-trial.[20] In the latter situation the superior national court will not be a court of last instance. In contrast, if, in dealing with the appeal, the superior national court makes a final decision on the Community law question in dispute, it will be considered the court of last instance. In other words, in this situation the superior national court will be covered by Article 234(3) if following its decision it will not be possible to try the Community law question, either in connection with the lower national court's re-trial of the case or in any subsequent appeal of the lower national court's judgment.

3. Exceptions to the Obligation to Refer

According to its wording, Article 234(3) requires all national courts of last instance to refer questions for preliminary rulings in all situations where a case gives rise to a question of the interpretation or validity of Community law. However, the obligation to make such a reference must be understood in the light of the purpose behind Article 234, which is to ensure the uniform and correct application of

---

[17] See also C Naômé, *Le renvoi préjudiciel en droit européen* (2007), who at 39 gives as examples third party proceedings (la tierce opposition), appeal in revision (la revision), and appeal of last instance judgment (la requête civile). In contrast, the same does not apply to the appeal in cassation (le pourvoi en cassation).

[18] In French, 'un pourvoi en cassation'.

[19] Case C-210/06 *Cartesio* (ECJ 16 December 2008), paras 75–9.

[20] For other examples than the one given here, see M Dauses, 'Practical Considerations Regarding the Preliminary Ruling Procedure under Article 177 of the EEC Treaty' (1986–87) Fordham Int L J Vol 50, 538, 566.

Community law by the national courts.[21] This has considerable importance, not least today where Community law covers so many areas that there would inevitably be an excessively large number of cases referred if every court of last instance were to make a reference every time it was faced with a case that contained elements of Community law.

Section 3.1 below examines the situations in which Community law questions are not relevant to the decision on the main proceedings. Next, Section 3.2 considers the situation where the same case is dealt with by more than one 'court of last instance'. Section 3.3 reviews *acte éclairé* situations, meaning situations where in other cases the Court of Justice has already made a decision on the question. Section 3.4 analyses *acte clair* situations, ie situations where the question for interpretation has not previously been put before the Court of Justice, but where there is no real doubt about the proper interpretation of Community law. In Section 3.5 the various possibilities for making preliminary references which are not based on Article 234 are considered. Section 3.6 examines the obligation to refer where the national court makes a decision on interim measures. Finally, Section 3.7 analyses the question of the obligation of the court of last instance to refer when Community law is applied outside its formal scope of application.

3.1. The question is not relevant

A national court of last instance within the meaning of Article 234(3) does not have a duty to refer a question on the interpretation of Community law to the Court of Justice if the ruling of the Court would have no bearing on the final decision in the main proceedings.[22] As explained above in Chapter 5, Sections 2 and 4, all national courts are precluded from making a reference if the question is not relevant.

Moreover, a national court of last instance will not be required to make a reference for a preliminary ruling if it decides the main proceedings without drawing on Community law. This situation may arise where national procedural rules mean that the matter that gives rise to a problem in Community law cannot be judged, for example, because a claim under Community law is brought after the expiry of the period of limitation laid down in national law. Likewise, a national court of last instance can refrain from making a reference if, on the basis of national law, it arrives at a result that makes an otherwise relevant Community law provision obsolete for the resolution of the dispute.[23]

---

[21] Case C-2/06 *Kempter* [2008] ECR I-411, para 41.
[22] Case 283/81 *CILFIT* [1982] ECR 3415, para 10.
[23] D Vaughan, 'The Advocate's View' in M Andenas (ed), *Article 177 references to the European Court* (1994) 55, 61.

Under Community law, where the solution to a dispute before a national court raises issues of Community law, the national court must, as far as possible, take account of the relevant Community rules even if the parties do not invoke these rules in support of their claims.[24] In comparison, as a main rule, Community law does not oblige a party to introduce a claim based on Community law that he could possibly have won, with the effect that an otherwise important Community issue does not arise before the national court. Likewise, in cases other than criminal procedures, as a rule, Community law does not prevent a party from concurring with his opponent's claim even if he could have raised a counter argument based on Community law but chooses not to do so.[25] Normally there is therefore nothing to prevent one or both parties from presenting a case which might otherwise be thought to prompt questions of Community law in such a way that the national court does not have to decide on such questions.[26] In these situations the lack of relevant Community law to interpret implies that the obligation to refer laid down in Article 234(3) is not triggered even if the national court would otherwise have been obliged to make a reference to the Court of Justice.

3.2. More courts handling the case qualify as 'court of last instance'

In Section 2 above it was pointed out that in rare situations a case can be handled by two (or more) courts that both qualify as 'a court of last instance'. In these situations both courts remain under an obligation to make a preliminary reference even if they can both show that another 'court of last instance' is also involved in the same main proceedings.

Thus, if in a trademark case a court from a Benelux country qualifying as a court of last instance makes a reference to the Benelux Court, neither of these two courts of last instance can invoke the other court's involvement to show that it is not a court of last instance under Article 234(3).[27]

---

[24] See also below s 3.4.3.

[25] Joined Cases C-430/93 and C-431/03 *van Schijndel* [1995] ECR I-4705, paras 20–2; Joined Cases C-222/05–225/05 *van der Weerd* [2007] ECR I-4233, paras 28–42; and Case C-455/06 *Heemskerk* (ECJ 25 November 2008), paras 44–8.

[26] R Crowe, 'Colloquium Report—The Preliminary Reference Procedure: Reflections based on Practical Experiences of the Highest National Courts in Administrative Matters' (2004) 5 ERA Forum 435, 446 refers to an example of a Swedish case where the national tax office as party to a case decided to withdraw its case before the national court; apparently to avoid a preliminary reference to the Court of Justice. For examples from Irish practice of parties withdrawing on appeal those parts of a dispute that involve Community law, see E Fahey, *Practice and Procedure in Preliminary References to Europe: 30 Years of Article 234 EC Case Law from the Irish Courts* (2007) 60–1.

[27] *Hoge Raad's* order of 19 June 1998 whereby this court referred a question to the Benelux Court and left it to the latter to decide whether a preliminary reference should be made to the Court of Justice, cf Nederlandse Jurisprudentie 1999, No 68, reported in the eighteenth annual report on monitoring the application of community law (2000), COM(2001) 309 final, Annex VI, pp 36–7.

3.3. *Acte éclairé*—a materially identical question has already been the subject of a preliminary ruling

Article 234 is intended to ensure the uniform application of Community law in all Member States. Even if, formally, a preliminary ruling is only addressed to the referring national court, such a ruling authoritatively establishes the correct interpretation of Community law.[28] If another national court is faced with a similar question, then that other court may therefore base its decision on the answer which the Court of Justice has already given to the corresponding question. In such a situation, a national court of last instance is thus allowed, but not obliged, to make a reference.[29]

In *Da Costa*, a Dutch court of last instance referred a question which was materially identical to a question which had already been the subject of a preliminary ruling in a similar case. The Court of Justice held that albeit the reference was from a court of last instance, in this situation the national court was not obliged to make a reference of the question asked. On the other hand the national court could make the reference under Article 234 even though, on the face of it, the previous judgment seemed to have made a final settlement of the question. The Court of Justice therefore gave a preliminary ruling.[30]

Even where a previously referred question and a question which a national court of last instance is considering referring are not identical, the answer to the earlier question can mean that the law has been so unambiguously explained that there is no obligation to make a reference under Article 234(3). What is decisive is whether Article 234's underlying aim of ensuring uniform application of Community law would be put at risk if a reference were not made.[31]

The German *Bundesfinanzhof*'s judgment of 11 June 1997 provides an example of an inexpedient application of the *acte éclairé* doctrine. One of the questions that arose in the case was whether private schools are engaged in the provision of services within the meaning of the EC Treaty. In this connection the *Bundesfinanzhof* relied upon the ruling by the Court of Justice in *Humbel*.[32] This ruling, however, concerned school fees regarding education provided by the State and thus did not

---

In the actual case the Benelux Court made a preliminary reference, cf Case C-265/00 *Campina Melkunie* [2004] ECR I-1699.

[28] See Ch 12, s 3.1 below.

[29] Case 66/80 *ICC* [1981] ECR 1191, para 13; Case C-337/95 *Parfums Christian Dior* [1997] ECR I-6013, para 29; Case C-340/99 *TNT Traco* [2001] ECR I-4109, para 35; and Case C-421/06 *Fratelli Martini* [2007] ECR I-152, para 54. In this situation, under Art 104(3)(1) of the Rules of Procedure of the Court of Justice, the Court may limit itself to answering the question by a reasoned order. See Ch 11, s 1 below.

[30] Joined Cases 28–30/62 *Da Costa* [1963] ECR 31.

[31] Case 283/81 *CILFIT* [1982] ECR 3415, para 14.

[32] Case 263/86 *Humbel* [1988] ECR 5365.

provide an answer for the actual case before the *Bundesfinanzhof.*[33] Indeed, subsequently the Court of Justice ruled on the same question and reached a conclusion which conflicted with the earlier one by the *Bundesfinanzhof.*[34]

In Sweden the *Regeringsrätten* (Supreme Administrative Court) in a ruling of 26 October 2004 assessed whether an administrative decision of the Swedish authorities to prohibit a company from engaging in offering gambling services was compatible with Community law. *Regeringsrätten* found that on the face of it the prohibition was difficult to reconcile with the applicable EC Treaty provisions on free movement. Nevertheless, taking into account the practice of the Court of Justice in the field, the *Regeringsrätten* concluded that the prohibition did not conflict with Community law. This approach to the *acte éclairé* doctrine appears somewhat liberal, not least taking into consideration that in later cases in the same field the Court of Justice not only received a host of observations from a large number of Member States, but also heard the cases in the Grand Chamber.[35]

A precedent from the Court of First Instance of the European Community can also be included in the assessment as to whether an *acte éclairé* situation exists, though generally judgments from this court do not carry the same weight as a decision of the Court of Justice.

Atlanta concerned a national court's decision on interim measures in a situation where it had doubts about the validity of a Community legal act. The Court of Justice held that such interim measures must be rejected, not only in cases where in its previous practice the Court of Justice had denied that there was doubt about such validity, but also in cases where the Court of First Instance, in a judgment which had become final and binding, had dismissed on the merits a plea of illegality.[36]

A decision of the Court of First Instance can also show that a reference is relevant. This might, for example, be the case where a decision of the Court of First Instance casts doubt upon the correctness of an earlier interpretation given by the Court of Justice.

---

[33] *Bundesfinanzhof* (ECJ 11 June 1997) X R 74/95, Sammlung der Entscheidungen des Bundesfinanzhofs Bd 183, p 436, reported in sixteenth annual report on monitoring the application of Community law [1999] OJ C354/184.

[34] Case C-76/05 *Schwarz* [2007] ECR I-6849; and Case C-318/05 *Commission v Germany* [2007] ECR I-6957.

[35] *Regeringsrätten's* (ECJ 26 October 2004), *Wermdö Krog AB (tidigare Värmdö Kinesiska Restaurang AB)/Lotteriinspektionen,* reported in 22ᵉ Rapport sur le contrôle de l'application du droit communautaire, COM(2005) 570, Annex VI, pp 14–15.

[36] Case C-465/93 *Atlanta* [1995] ECR 3761, para 46.

3.4. *Acte clair*—the correct application leaves no scope for any reasonable doubt

3.4.1. Acte clair *and the* CILFIT *judgment*

It is hardly surprising that the Court of Justice has established that a court of last instance is relieved from the obligation to make a reference for a preliminary ruling where the answer would not be relevant to the decision in the main proceedings. It is correspondingly easy to acknowledge that the Court of Justice has accepted that there is no obligation to make a reference where the law has been unambiguously established in previous decisions. Arguably these two situations do not involve any substantial risk that national courts will apply Community law inconsistently. It is, however, more problematic to allow courts of last instance to refrain from making a reference for a preliminary ruling where a decision on the main proceedings requires an interpretation of Community law, and where the Court of Justice has not ruled on the issue. This entails a risk of different national courts coming to mutually conflicting conclusions. Furthermore, there will be a risk that the right to refrain from making a reference will be abused by national courts that wish to exclude the Court of Justice from deciding certain cases.[37]

Nevertheless, it regularly happens that a provision of Community law is so unambiguous that there can be no real doubt about its correct interpretation. In such a situation it would be inappropriate to require a reference to be made for a preliminary ruling. As explained above, the aim of Article 234(3) is to ensure the uniform and correct application of Community law by the national courts and to prevent a body of national case law that is not in accordance with the rules of Community law from coming into existence in any Member State.[38] This aim does not require a national court of last instance to make a reference in cases where there is no real risk of an incorrect interpretation of Community law. Furthermore, an unconditional obligation could induce one of the parties to a case to raise a Community law argument solely with the aim of delaying the proceedings.

In *CILFIT*, the question of the applicability of the theory of *acte clair* was put before the Court of Justice by the Italian Court of Cassation. In the case before the Court of Cassation the Community law aspects appeared to be so obvious that it was difficult to see any reason to make a preliminary ruling. It therefore decided to ask the Court of Justice under what conditions national courts of last instance

---

[37] A Arnull, 'The Use and Abuse of Article 177' (1989) 52 Modern Law Review Vol 52, 1987, ss 622–39; and K Alter, 'Explaining National Court Acceptance of European Court Jurisprudence: A Critical Evaluation of Theories of Legal Integration' in J Weiler, A Slaughter, and A Stone Sweet (eds), *The European Courts & National Courts* (1998) 227, 241.

[38] Case C-458/06 *Gourmet Classic* [2008] ECR I-4207 para 23; and Case C-393/98 *Gomes Valente* [2001] ECR 1327, para 17.

were obliged to refer questions of interpretation. The Court of Justice observed that the correct application of Community law could be so obvious as to leave no scope for any reasonable doubt as to the manner in which the question raised is to be resolved. In such situations a national court of last instance would not be required to make a reference for a preliminary ruling. The Court of Justice, in other words, embraced the theory of *acte clair*. However, the Court of Justice went on to lay down conditions for when a national court is justified in refraining from making a preliminary reference and instead taking upon itself the responsibility for resolving the question. In particular, the national court must not only itself be convinced as to the correct interpretation of Community law, it must also 'be convinced that the matter is equally obvious to the courts of the other Member States and to the Court of Justice'. Observing that Community law presents some characteristic features and that its interpretation gives rise to particular difficulties, the Court added that Community legislation is drafted in several languages and that the different language versions are all equally authentic. An interpretation of a provision of Community law thus involves a comparison of the different language versions. Moreover, even where the different language versions are entirely in accord with one another, Community law uses terminology which is peculiar to it and legal concepts do not necessarily have the same meaning in Community law and in the law of the various Member States. The Court rounded off its words of caution by observing that every provision of Community law must be placed in its context and interpreted in the light of the provisions of Community law as a whole, regard being had to the objectives thereof and to its state of evolution at the date on which the provision in question is to be applied. In other words, even though at first the interpretation of some Community legal act may appear obvious, it may nevertheless be much less so on closer scrutiny.[39]

The ruling in *CILFIT* is a reflection of the different roles played by the national courts and the Court of Justice. Whilst laying down a definite interpretation of the applicable national law is among the most important functions of national courts of last instance, this does not apply to Community law where the final authority for interpretation is the Court of Justice. Even though a national court of last instance may be better placed at interpreting Community law than are lower national courts, the definitive interpretation—and the consequent stability and legal certainty in the application of the law—can only be established by reference to the Court of Justice.[40] The strict conditions which the Court of Justice has attached to the application of the *acte clair* doctrine, if complied with, both maintain the Court of Justice's monopoly on questions of interpretation and minimise

---

[39] Case 283/81 *CILFIT* [1982] ECR 3415, paras 16–20.
[40] F Jacobs, 'The role of the European Court of Justice in the Development of Uniform Law' in N Jareborg (ed), *De lege, Towards Universal Law* (1995) 205, 208.

the risk of a national court of last instance adopting a wrong interpretation.[41] It should be added that even where a national court of last instance is faced with a case of *acte clair* that court is not prevented from making a preliminary reference.[42]

In the following sections we examine the application of *acte clair* in practice as well as what factors the national courts must (and may not) take into account when establishing whether a situation is one of *acte clair*.

3.4.2. *National courts' margin of discretion under the* acte clair *doctrine*

As is clear from the above, fulfilling the requirements laid down in *CILFIT* is a difficult task. Nevertheless, in practice the *acte clair* doctrine has attained considerable importance. Thus, national courts of last instance regularly refrain from making references for preliminary rulings, on the basis that with the requisite confidence they can resolve the relevant Community law issue themselves.

It seems to be a widespread opinion that, in applying the *acte clair* doctrine, national courts of last instance regularly fail to follow meticulously the conditions laid down in the *CILFIT* judgment.[43] Indeed, the case law of the Court of Justice itself provides a telling example of the failure of a national court of last instance to apply the *acte clair* doctrine correctly.

In *Kühne & Heitz*, a Dutch court of last instance refused to make a reference for a preliminary ruling on the correct interpretation of the European Community's common customs tariff in a case which concerned the tariffs applicable to poultry meat parts. Subsequently, in a different case, the Court of Justice reached the opposite conclusion to that of the Dutch court of last instance.[44]

It is difficult to state in abstract terms the degree of certainty which a national court of last instance must have in order to be able to refrain from making a reference.

---

[41] K Joutsamo, 'Community law—National law relationship—judicial cooperation under the system of preliminary rulings (Art. 177)' (1991) JFT Tidskrift utgiven av Juridiska Föreningen i Finland Årgang 126, 337, 339.

[42] Joined Cases C-428/06–434/06 *UGT-Rioja* [2008] ECR I-6747, para 43.

[43] M Andenas, 'Initiating a Reference' in M Andenas (ed), *Article 177 References to the European Court—Policy and Practice* (1994) 18; A Arnull, 'The Past and Future of the Preliminary Rulings Procedure' (2002) 13 European Business Law Review 183, 187; D Anderson and M Demetriou, *References to the European Court* (2002) 177–80; and, with special reference to Irish law, E Fahey, *Practice and Procedure in Preliminary References to Europe: 30 Years of Article 234 EC Case Law from the Irish Courts* (2007) 31–2, 46 and 48–9. See also, with regard to Swedish courts, U Bernitz, 'Kommissionen ingriper mot svenska sistainstansers obenägenhet att begära förhandsavgöranden' (2005) Europarättslig Tidskrift Nummer 1 Årg 8 ss 109–16; and, with regard to French courts, D Simon, 'La contribution de la Cour de cassation à la contruction juridique européenne: Europe du droit, Europe des juges' [2006] *Cour de cassation*, Rapport annuel 79, 82.

[44] Case C-453/00 *Kühne & Heitz* [2004] ECR I-837, paras 20–8. The judgment is further discussed in s 5.3 below.

Some have interpreted *CILFIT* so narrowly that they assume that the vast majority of the cases before national courts of last instance in which Community law is relevant must be referred to the Court of Justice.[45] Others support the view that the national courts of last instance have been given some room for discretion so that they may refrain from making a reference if they find that a question raised about Community law is based on an unreasonable interpretation of one of the parties or that the motive for proposing to make a reference is to drag out the proceedings.[46] The rather limited number of preliminary references received by the Court of Justice indicates that, as already mentioned, most of the Member States' courts of last instance have followed the latter view and so have adopted a liberal approach to the application of the *CILFIT* conditions.[47] Indeed, representatives of the national supreme courts of the European Community in a report on their use of the preliminary rulings procedure have found that 'the margin of appreciation permitted under the CILFIT criteria has clearly enabled a certain "functional flexibility" in the application of paragraph 3 of Article 234 of the EC Treaty'.[48]

Whilst the Court of Justice has never endorsed such a liberal approach, in *Intermodal Transports* it nonetheless showed itself willing to adopt a more pragmatic interpretation.

In *Intermodal Transports*, the Court of Justice had to consider whether the application of the *acte clair* doctrine was excluded where the national court of last instance intended to come to a conclusion that differed from the interpretation which an administrative authority in another Member State had reached based on the same

---

[45] H Rasmussen, 'The European Court's Acte Clair Strategy in C.I.L.F.I.T.' (1984) 9 EL Rev 242, 259; and G Vandersanden, 'La procédure préjudicielle: À la recherche d'une identité perdue' in M Dony (ed), *Melanges en hommage à Michel Waelbroeck, vol I* (1999) 619, 630. See also D Vaughan, 'The Advocate's View' in M Andenas (ed), *Article 177 References* (1994) 55, 61.

[46] D Chalmers et al, *European Union Law* (2006) 300–1, R Wainwright, 'A view from the Commission' in M Andenas (ed), *Article 177 References to the European Court—Policy and Practice* (1994) 105, 107; T Tridimas, 'Knocking on Heaven's Door: Fragmentation, Efficiency and Defiance in the Preliminary Reference Procedure' (2003) 40 CML Rev 9, 42; and J Masclet, 'Vers la fin d'une controverse? La cour de justice tempère l'obligation de renvoi préjudiciel en interprétation faite aux juridictions suprêmes (art. 177, alinéa 3, C.E.E.)' (1983) Revue du Marché Commun Vol 26, ss 363–72.

[47] M Jarvis, *The Application of EC Law by National Courts—The Free Movement of Goods* (1998) 422–4 (with further references to both literature and cases); and M Andenas, 'Initiating a Reference' in M Andenas (ed), *Article 177 References to the European Court—Policy and Practice* (1994) 18–19. According to its decision of 26 October 1990 in *Fédération nationale du commerce extérieur des produits alimentaires et Syndicat national des négociants et transformateurs de saumon*, the French *Conseil d'État* will only make a preliminary reference when it finds that the case raises 'une difficulté sérieuse d'interprétation'. Contrast this with the approach of the English House of Lords which seems to follow a stricter reading of the *acte clair* doctrine, cf C Lewis, *Judicial Remedies in Public Law* (2008) 548.

[48] H Kanninen, Association of the Councils of State and Supreme Administrative Jurisdiction of the European Union, 18th Colloquium 2002, General Report on the Colloquium subject 'The Preliminary Reference to the Court of Justice of the European Communities', 29.

Community law provision. The Court found that this was not the case. Of course this fact should cause the national court of last instance to take particular care in its assessment of whether there was no reasonable doubt as to the correct application of the Community rule, but the different interpretation could not in itself mean that the national court of last instance should make a reference. First, any divergent application of the rules in another Member State cannot influence the correct interpretation in the objective circumstances. Second, Article 234 gives the national court of last instance sole responsibility for determining whether the correct application of Community law is so obvious as to leave no scope for any reasonable doubt. Third, a national court of last instance cannot be required to ensure that the matter is equally obvious to bodies of a non-judicial nature such as administrative authorities. Finally, a national court of last instance cannot be obliged to make a reference solely because its interpretation could cast doubt upon the validity of an administrative decision in another Member State.[49]

Nevertheless, the Court of Justice has also shown that there are limits to how liberal an interpretation it is prepared to accept.

In *Gomes Valente*, the Court ruled that the fact that the Commission had refrained from bringing infringement proceedings in connection with a claimed infringement of Community law could not, in itself, dispense with the obligation to make a reference. In this connection the Court of Justice noted that the Commission is neither empowered to determine conclusively the rights and duties of a Member State nor to give Member States guarantees concerning the compatibility with the Treaty of a given line of conduct.[50] It can be added that the Commission is not obliged to initiate infringement proceedings, even where it is convinced that a Member State is in breach of Community law.[51]

3.4.3. Acte clair *and the wishes of the parties*

Preliminary references are a Community law mechanism created to ensure the homogeneous application of Community law throughout the Community. Hence, a preliminary reference does not constitute a means of redress available to the parties to a case pending before a national court. An important consequence of this is that the making of a reference for a preliminary ruling depends entirely on the national court's own assessment as to whether such a reference is appropriate and necessary. It is not contingent upon the nature of the pleas relied on by the parties. Therefore, the obligation under Article 234(3) for a court of last instance to make a reference for a preliminary ruling is not limited to situations where one

---

[49] Case C-495/03 *Intermodal Transports BV* [2005] ECR I-8151, paras 33–45. See also s 3.4.8 below.

[50] Case C-393/98 *Gomes Valente* [2001] ECR 1327, paras 15–19.

[51] See Ch 2, s 2.4.

or more parties to the main proceedings have invoked Community law before that national court.

Nor does that obligation depend on whether a party to the case requests that the national court makes use of the procedure in Article 234. This means that the fact that the parties do not disagree on the application of Community law to the actual dispute does not in itself exempt a national court of last instance from the duty to make a preliminary reference.[52] For the same reason a national court of last instance cannot decline to make a preliminary reference on the grounds that a party to the main proceedings has raised the question of making a reference too late.

Where before a national court of last instance both the plaintiff and the defendant object to the making of a preliminary reference, it would be understandable if the court were to hesitate in making a preliminary reference. Nevertheless, if the main proceedings give rise to questions on Community law that require a preliminary reference the national court cannot avoid such a reference simply because both parties are against it.[53]

Similarly, when deciding whether to make a preliminary reference a national court of last instance may not take account of a number of circumstances that are normally regarded as proper. On a strict reading of *CILFIT*, in its present format the *acte clair* doctrine does not allow the national court of last instance to take account of the importance of the case to the parties, the prolongation of the proceedings that a reference may entail, or the costs associated with the making of a preliminary reference.[54] The reason is that these factors are immaterial for whether the

---

[52] Case C-2/06 *Kempter* [2008] ECR I-411; and judgment of the Polish Supreme Court in *Re Polish Law on Employers' Insolvency* (Case II PK 17/06) [2008] 1 CMLR 41 at 1116–17. E Fahey, *Practice and Procedure in Preliminary References to Europe: 30 Years of Article 234 EC Case Law from the Irish Courts* (2007) 48–9, criticises the Irish Supreme Court for apparently putting forward a suggestion supporting the opposite view. See also M Bobek, 'Learning to Talk: Preliminary Rulings, the Courts of the New Member States and the Court of Justice' (2008) 45 CML Rev 1611, 1631. Bobek refers to a ruling by the Slovak Supreme Court where this court refused to make a preliminary reference, inter alia because the claimant was not concerned with the interpretation of the relevant Community provision.

[53] E Fahey, *Practice and Procedure in Preliminary References to Europe: 30 Years of Article 234 EC Case Law from the Irish Courts* (2007) 58, finds that *Scally v Minister for the Environment*, [1996] 1 IR 367, is an example of an Irish case where arguably a preliminary reference should have been made, but where with the assent of the parties this was not done.

[54] Advocate General's Opinion in Case C-338/95 *Wiener* [1997] ECR I-6495, in particular paras 8–10; and H Kanninen, 'La marge de manoeuvre de la juridiction suprême nationale pour procéder à un renvoi préjudiciel à la Cour de justice des Communautés européennes' in N Colneric, D Edward, J Puissochet, and D Colomer (eds), *Une communauté de droit, Festschrift für Gil Carlos Rodriquez Iglesias* (2003) 611, 620. But contrast the guidelines of the English Court of Appeal, cf 18th Colloquium of the Association of the Councils of State and Supreme Administrative Jurisdictions of the European Union, 2002, Answers to Questionnaire on Preliminary References, England and Wales, point 2.3 (available at <http://www.juradmin.eu/colloquia/2002/england_wales.pdf>).

dispute gives rise to difficult Community law questions. The Court of Justice has consistently interpreted Article 234(3) to require a preliminary reference to be made if there is doubt about the interpretation of a Community legal act so that the national courts of last instance may not apply a *de minimis* approach. Indeed, some of the most spectacular judgments of the Court of Justice have been given as preliminary rulings in which the main action has been of minor importance.[55]

Apparently, some national courts of last instance apply *de minimis* considerations when deciding whether to make a preliminary reference.[56] Moreover, a former judge of the Court of Justice has argued that in order to avoid the prolongation of a case which a preliminary reference may cause, a national court of last instance may be induced to 'see light when looking for an *acte clair*'.[57]

In *OB (by his mother and litigation friend) (FC) v Aventis Pasteur*, as part of the same legal proceedings, a preliminary reference had earlier been made. However, the question arose whether the Court of Justice's answer to the first reference was so obvious as to leave no scope for any reasonable doubt with regard to its application in the proceedings at issue. A majority of the five law lords hearing the case in the English House of Lords found that there was not *acte clair* and so decided to make a new reference to the Court of Justice. However, they added that in view of the time which had already elapsed, it was to be hoped that the Court of Justice would deal with the matter by summary order so as to shorten the preliminary procedure.[58]

In contrast to the above ruling, in *Communauté de communes du Piémont de Barr et autres*, before the French *Conseil d'État* the *commissaire du gouvernement* (Government Advocate) recommended that the case should be decided without seeking a preliminary ruling from the Court of Justice. Whilst acknowledging that the interpretation of the Community provision that was to be applied was unclear, the *commissaire du gouvernement* recommended that the French courts

---

[55] An example is Case 6/64 *Costa v E.N.E.L.* [1964] ECR 585 (of which a summary is provided in s 2 above), which established the principle of supremacy of Community law.

[56] T Tridimas, 'Knocking on Heaven's Door: Fragmentation, Efficiency and Defiance in the Preliminary Reference Procedure' (2003) 40 CML Rev 9, 42, who mentions a case before the House of Lords, where a reference for a preliminary ruling was not made, on the basis of a cost–benefit evaluation; and H van Harten, 'The Application of Community Precedent and *acte clair* by the Hoge Raad, A Case Study in the Field of Establishment and Services' (<http://ssrn.com/abstract=1113729>) who at p 19 argues that the Dutch *Hoge Raad* has applied a *de minimis* approach in conflict with the *acte clair* doctrine.

[57] L Sevón, 'What do National Judges Require of the Court of Justice of the European Communities?' in G Regner, M Eliason, and H Vogel (eds), *Festskrift til Hans Ragnemalm* (2005) 287, 288–9.

[58] *OB (by his mother and litigation friend) (FC) v Aventis Pasteur* [2008] 3 CMLR 10.

decide the issue themselves since the preliminary ruling procedure was time-consuming. The *Conseil d'État* made no reference to the Court of Justice.[59]

3.4.4. Acte clair *and the question of different language versions*

In *CILFIT* the Court of Justice observed that Community legislation is drafted in several languages and that the different language versions are all equally authentic. Therefore, the interpretation of a provision in Community law may involve a comparison of the different language versions.

A large number of cases involving interpretation of Community law do not require a comparison between different language versions. This is particularly so in fields where the Court of Justice has already rendered a considerable number of judgments which jointly provide such a clear pattern that the answer to a preliminary question, which the Court has never been faced with before, may be obvious (if the Court had earlier been faced with the question it would be a situation of *acte éclairé* rather than one of *acte clair*). In these situations the issue of interpretation that may lead the national court of last instance to a finding of *acte clair* is one of construing the Court's case law, not of comparing different language versions of a legal text. Typical examples are the concept of 'worker' as laid down in the EC Treaty's provisions on free movement or the notion of 'dominant position' as laid down in the competition rules. In these situations the question of *acte clair* first of all relates to whether the Court of Justice's case law has removed any doubts as to the correct interpretation of the relevant provision and not to the legal provision as such.

Nevertheless, in many cases involving interpretation of Community law a comparison between different language versions is relevant. When the Court rendered its judgment in *CILFIT* the Community consisted of 10 Member States and had seven official languages. Today the Community consists of 27 Member States and has 23 official languages making it unrealistic to expect a national court of last instance to be able to undertake a qualified review of the meaning of any given Community act in all 23 language versions.[60]

---

[59] *Conseil d'État, Section, 20.5.1998, Communauté de communes du Piémont de Barr et autres,* Revue française de droit administratif 1998, p 609, conc. Henri Savoie; Actualité Juridique Droit Administratif 1998, 632, Europe 1998 Act. No 238, reported in sixteenth annual report on monitoring the application of Community law, [1999] OJ C354/185.

[60] Para 99 of the Opinion of Advocate General Stix Hackl in Case C-495/03 *Intermodal Transports BV* [2005] ECR I-8151; F Jacobs, 'Approaches to Interpretation in a Plurilingual Legal System' in M Hoskins and W Robinson (eds), *A True European—Essays for Judge David Edward* (2004) 297, 303; and L Sevón, 'What do National Judges Require of the Court of Justice of the European Communities?' in G Regner, M Eliason, and H Vogel (eds), *Festskrift til Hans Ragnemalm* (2005) 287, 289–90. See also the Opinion of Advocate General Colomer in Case C-461/03 *Gaston Schul* [2005] ECR I-10513, paras 52–3.

If the *acte clair* doctrine is to be given practical importance, the national courts cannot be required to closely examine each of the official language versions of the applicable Community provisions. Advocates General Jacobs and Stix-Hackl have argued that *CILFIT* should not be regarded as requiring the national courts to examine a Community act in every one of the official Community languages, but rather as an essential caution against taking too literal an approach to the interpretation of Community provisions.[61] Similarly, a working group established by the Association of the Councils of State and Supreme Administrative Jurisdictions of the European Union have submitted that today a literal interpretation of *CILFIT*, especially as concerns the comparison of 23 language versions, is obsolete and that the *CILFIT* criteria should be interpreted 'with common sense'.[62]

On the other hand, the importance of the Community's language regime should not be ignored either. Indeed, the Court of Justice frequently refers to the importance of differences (as well as concordances) between the different language versions.[63] In order to be able to hold a situation to be covered by the *acte clair* doctrine, a national court should therefore not simply limit itself to considering its own language version of the Community act in question. Instead, it should make every endeavour to consider as many different language versions as possible; if the national court finds that for the purpose of deciding the actual case those language versions examined do not all point in the same direction, it should be very cautious in considering the case to be one of *acte clair*.[64]

---

[61] Opinion of Advocate General Jacobs in Case C-338/95 *Wiener* [1997] ECR I-6495, point 84, and Opinion of Advocate General Stix-Hackl in points 97–100 of Case C-495/03 *Intermodal Transports* [2005] ECR I-8151. The Court of Justice did not address this aspect in the two judgments. For a similar view, see also the statement by F Timmermans at p 9 in 'Summary report of the meeting of 3 December 2007 of the working group of the Association of the Councils of State and the Supreme Administrative Jurisdictions of the EU and the Network of the Presidents of the Supreme Judicial Courts of the EU on preliminary references' (available at <http://www.network-presidents.eu/IMG/pdf/Summary_report_of_december_3rd_2007.pdf>).

[62] Report of the Working Group of the Association of the Councils of State and the Supreme Administrative Jurisdictions of the EU and the Network of the Presidents of the Supreme Judicial Courts of the EU on preliminary references, published in Newsletter of the Association of the Councils of State and Supreme Administrative Jurisdictions of the European Union, No 20, p 19, available at <http://www.juradmin.eu/en/newsletter/pdf/Hr_20-En.pdf>.

[63] Case C-311/06 *Consiglio Nazionale degli Ingegneri* (ECJ 29 January 2009), paras 7, 9, and 11; Case C-517/07 *Afton Chemical Ltd* (ECJ 18 December 2008), para 35; and Case C-306/07 *Ruben Andersen* (ECJ 18 December 2008), para 33.

[64] Report of the Working Group of the Association of the Councils of State and the Supreme Administrative Jurisdictions of the EU and the Network of the Presidents of the Supreme Judicial Courts of the EU on preliminary references, published in Newsletter of the Association of the Councils of State and Supreme Administrative Jurisdictions of the European Union, No 20, p 19, available at <http://www.juradmin.eu/en/newsletter/pdf/Hr_20-En.pdf>.

3.4.5. Acte clair *and dissenting judgments*

As already stated, according to the *CILFIT* conditions the national court must not only be certain that its interpretation of Community law is correct, it must also be convinced that the matter is equally obvious to the courts of the other Member States and to the Court of Justice.[65] Hence, the question arises to what extent this requirement excludes the possibility of *acte clair* where a judgment is rendered with a dissenting opinion. Arguably, the question may also arise where there is disagreement between, on the one hand, the national court of last instance and, on the other hand, a national advocate general.[66] Four different categories of situations may be distinguished.

The first group of situations is where the difference relates to the abstract interpretation of the applicable Community law provisions that govern the relations between the parties of the case. Where the judges, who are to jointly decide a case, disagree on such abstract interpretation it is difficult to hold that all other national courts in the Community will arrive at the same interpretation as the one held by the majority. Not all national courts seem to subscribe to this view, however.

Likewise, it will normally be difficult to argue that there is *acte clair* if an appeal court applies an abstract interpretation of Community law that differs from the interpretation applied by the lower court.[67] Even where the judges of the appeal court unanimously intend to follow the same abstract interpretation of the applicable Community law provisions as did the lower court when ruling on the actual dispute, it will be rather difficult to be sure that the appeal court's interpretation will be equally obvious to all other Member State courts if a minority of the judges in the lower court supported a diverging abstract interpretation of these provisions. In either case the situation will, of course, be different if, in the period between the judgment of the lower court and the time when the appeal court is to rule on the same dispute, the Court of Justice renders one or more judgments providing legal clarification, as in these circumstances the appeal court will be faced with a situation of *acte éclairé*.

In the second group of situations the divergence between the judges has no bearing on the application of the Community law provision that governs the relation

---

[65] This may be an impossible task, as pointed out by P Wattel, '*Köbler, Cilfit* and *Welthgrove*: We Can't Go on Meeting Like This' (2004) 41 CML Rev 177, 179.

[66] For an example of the latter situation, see *Hoge Raad*, 21 March 2003, *Stichting Waterpakt and others/Ministerie van Landbouw, Natuurbeheer en Visserij and others*, Nederlands Juristenblad 2003, no 795, reported in 21ᵉ Rapport sur le contrôle de l'application du droit communautaire, COM(2004)839, Annex VI, pp I-24–I-25.

[67] Compare this with the judgment by the English House of Lords 24 July 1991 in *Regina v London Boroughs Transport Committee, ex parte Freight Transport Association Ltd* [1992] 1 CMLR 5, where the House of Lords found *acte clair* although a unanimous Court of Appeal had taken a different view on the Community Directive governing the dispute.

between the parties of the case. In this situation, a dissenting opinion does not exclude the possibility of there being *acte clair*. An example of this is where the judges merely disagree about whether the interpretation that they all favour is so obvious as to constitute *acte clair*.[68] Another example is where the judges deciding the case disagree as to whether they qualify as a court of last instance, but at the same time they do agree that the case is one of *acte clair*. Such disagreement does not exclude the possibility of there being *acte clair*.[69]

In the third group of situations, the diverging interpretations do not relate to Community law, but to the facts of the case or to national law. As the duty to make a preliminary reference does not apply to matters that the Court of Justice is not competent to answer in a preliminary ruling, it follows that dissenting opinions on such matters have no bearing on the question of whether there is *acte clair* or not.

In 2005 the Estonian Supreme Court's Constitutional Chamber was to rule on whether a provision of an Estonian law should be annulled because it was incompatible with Community law. The majority of the judges held that the Estonian law chancellor (*õiguskantsler*) did not have the competence to make a claim for annulment of an Estonian provision for non-conformity with Community law. The Supreme Court therefore could not annul the provision. A minority of six of the total of 18 judges deciding the case dissented. They argued that the Supreme Court did have the competence to annul the provision. The dissenting opinion thus concerned the interpretation of Estonian law and was not relevant to the question of whether the case was one of *acte clair*.[70]

In principle the same is true with respect to disagreement about the actual application of a Community rule (the abstract interpretation of which does not give rise to disagreement) between the judges. This follows from the fact that, formally speaking, in procedures under Article 234 the Court of Justice only gives an abstract interpretation but does not decide the actual dispute.[71] In practice, however, the Court of Justice is often ready to render judgment where in reality the abstract Community rule is applied to the facts of the case, albeit formally speaking the ruling is kept in general terms.[72] In practice it is therefore difficult to draw

---

[68] See in this respect paras 87–8 of the Opinion of Advocate General Stix Hackl in Case C-495/03 *Intermodal Transports BV* [2005] ECR I-8151.

[69] This also appears to be the approach taken by German courts of last instance, cf R Crowe, 'Colloquium Report—The Preliminary Reference Procedure: Reflections based on Practical Experiences of the Highest National Courts in Administrative Matters' (2004) 5 ERA Forum 435, 441.

[70] Riigikohtu põhiseaduslikkuse järelevalve kolleegium, 19 April 2005, case no 3-4-1-1-05, Riigi Teataja III 2005, 13, 128, reported in 23ᵉ Rapport sur le contrôle de l'application du droit communautaire, COM(2006)416, Annex VI, pp I-15–I-16.

[71] See Ch 4, s 5.6 above.

[72] See Ch 11, s 3 below.

the precise line for when disagreement on the legal qualification of the facts amongst the judges of a court of last instance necessitates a preliminary reference. Moreover, applications that are not in conformity with Community law may give rise to infringement proceedings against the Member State under Article 226, at least if those divergences of application persist.[73]

In the fourth group of situations, the judges are in agreement as to the ultimate outcome of the actual dispute, but they reach their conclusion on the basis of diverging interpretations of the applicable Community law provision. For example, in a case on free movement of goods one judge may take the view that a disputed national rule does not constitute a quantitative restriction or a measure having equivalent effect under Article 28 of the EC Treaty. The other judges find that the national rule does constitute a restriction on trade, but that this restriction is justified under Article 30 of the EC Treaty. Both the majority and the minority therefore agree that the contested national rule is lawful under Community law. In this situation it is unclear whether the decisive factor should be that the judges disagree as to the correct interpretation of the applicable Community law provision so that there is not *acte clair* or whether the decisive factor should be that all judges agree on the actual outcome of the dispute that Community law imposes on the national court so that this is a case of *acte clair*.

In 1997 the Finnish Supreme Administrative Court ruled on a case regarding access to documents transmitted to the European Commission in a competition procedure. According to a majority of the judges deciding the case, the documents were covered by Article 10 of the Finnish Constitution and therefore, as a main rule, public. Applying an exception to this main rule they nevertheless found that access should be withheld. A minority of the judges were of the view that the documents were covered by Article 20 of Council Regulation 17 which entailed that the relevant information could only be divulged if by its nature it was not covered by the obligation of professional secrecy. It thus appears that both the majority and the minority found that the documents could not be divulged, but they disagreed as to whether Council Regulation 17 applied in the actual case. Irrespective of this disagreement regarding the correct interpretation of Article 20 of Regulation 17, no preliminary reference was made.[74]

---

[73] Case C-495/03 *Intermodal Transports BV* [2005] ECR I-8151, para 44; and C Naômé, *Le renvoi préjudiciel en droit européen* (2007) 43.

[74] Judgment of 7 November 1997 by the Finnish Korkein hallinto-oikeus (Supreme Administrative Court) in case 2942/1/96, reported in fifteenth annual report on monitoring the application of Community law [1998] OJ C250/197.

3.4.6. Acte clair *and rulings by other national courts*

When a national court of last instance considers whether an interpretation of a Community act is *acte clair* it must have due regard to how other national courts (in its own as well as in other Member States) have ruled on the same interpretation of the Community act. If a national court submits to the same interpretation as the one arrived at by all other national courts, this supports a finding of *acte clair*. In contrast, it will be more difficult to argue that there is *acte clair* if other national courts have made an abstract interpretation of the relevant Community rule that conflicts with the one our national court intends to take. Indeed, it is recalled that in *CILFIT* the Court of Justice established that the test is not merely whether the national court itself is convinced about the correct interpretation of Community law; it must also be convinced that this interpretation is equally obvious to the courts of the other Member States. Therefore, if there is conflicting national case law a court of last instance should hesitate before declaring the case before it one of *acte clair*.[75]

For example, it might be questioned whether the *acte clair* doctrine was correctly applied in *Carlos Luis A.F. y Unión de Consumidores de España (UCE) v Banco Central Hispanoamericano.* Here the Spanish *Tribunal Supremo* was to consider the effect of the Council Directive on unfair terms in consumer contracts. Although a series of prior decisions by other national courts had recognised the direct effect of the Directive, the *Tribunal Supremo* denied such effect without making a preliminary reference.[76]

That being said, as explained above in Section 3.4.5, such disagreement will not exclude *acte clair* if it does not relate to the abstract interpretation of the applicable Community law provision governing the relationship between the parties in the case, but rather, for example, to the facts of the case or to national law.

With the above proviso, it will normally be difficult to argue that an interpretation of Community law qualifies as *acte clair* if a court of last instance has followed one abstract interpretation in earlier rulings, but at some later point adopts a different interpretation thereof without this being due to a ruling on the matter by the Court of Justice in the meantime.[77]

---

[75] See in this respect para 113 of the Opinion of Advocate General Stix-Hackl in Case C-495/03 *Intermodal Transports BV* [2005] ECR I-8151.

[76] *Tribunal Supremo, Sala Primera, de lo Civil,* 31.1.1998, *Carlos Luis A.F. y Unión de Consumidores de España (UCE) v Banco Central Hispanoamericano,* Repertorio Aranzadi de Jurisprudencia 1998, No 121, reported in sixteenth annual report on monitoring the application of Community law [1999] OJ C354/188. See also *Tribunal Constitucional, Sala Segunda,* 19 avril 2004, *Generalidad de Cataluña y Administración General del Estado/Herederos de Manuel Martínez Calderón,* La ley 2004, nº 1260, p 505.

[77] For an example of a national court of last instance overturning its own previous practice regarding the application of Community law, see *Raad van State* afdeling bestuursrechtspraak,

3.4.7. Acte clair *and cases pending before the Court of Justice*

The fact that another national court has put a preliminary question to the Court of Justice regarding the interpretation of the same provision in a Community act as the one at issue before a court of last instance does not, in itself, exclude the existence of *acte clair*. This approach has been taken by supreme courts of several Member States.[78] On the other hand, if such a preliminary reference is pending before the Court of Justice, this may be taken as an indication that not all national courts consider the interpretation of this provision to be *acte clair*.[79]

In 2004 the German *Bundesverfassungsgericht* (Federal Constitutional Court) overturned a ruling by the Superior Administrative Court of North Rhine-Westphalia because the latter had wrongly invoked the *acte clair* doctrine. The *Bundesverfassungsgericht* made its decision, inter alia, based on the observation that the English High Court of Justice, the Italian *Consiglio di Stato*, and the Dutch *Rechtbank s'Gravenhage* had all found that there was doubt as to whether the relevant Community act was valid or not and therefore had made preliminary references in this respect.[80]

Likewise, if the Commission has initiated infringement proceedings against a Member State under Article 226 of the EC Treaty regarding a national law's conformity with Community law, a national court of last instance should normally not invoke the *acte clair* doctrine with regard to the question of this national law's conformity with Community law on those points that are being disputed.

In 2005 the German *Bundesfinanzhof* (Federal Finance Court) ruled on the question of whether Community law precluded German tax rules under which payments of school fees to certain schools in Germany, but not payments to schools

---

7 December 2005, X./College van Burgemeesters en Wethouders van Boxtel, AB Rechtspraak Bestuursrecht 2005, 67; and *Raad van State,* afdeling bestuursrechtspraak, X./College van Burgemeesters en Wethouders van Apeldoorn, 1 February 2006, both reported in 24ᵉ rapport annuel sur le contrôle de l'application du droit communautaire, COM(2007) 398, Annex VI, pp 13–14.

[78] H Kanninen, Association of the Councils of State and Supreme Administrative Jurisdiction of the European Union, 18th Colloquium 2002, General Report on the Colloquium subject 'The Preliminary Reference to the Court of Justice of the European Communities', 30.

[79] See from Irish practice E Fahey, *Practice and Procedure in Preliminary References to Europe: 30 Years of Article 234 EC Case Law from the Irish Courts* (2007) 56, referring to *Governor and Company of the Bank of Ireland v Kavanagh*, unreported, High Court, Costello J, 19 June 1987. See also the ruling of 27 March 1995 by the Spanish *Tribunal Supremo* reported in thirteenth annual report on monitoring the application of Community law [1996] OJ C303/179; and the ruling of 27 July 2004 by the *Bundesverfassungsgericht*, 1 BvR 1270/04, NVwZ 2004, p 1346, reported in 22ᵉ Rapport sur le contrôle de l'application du droit communautaire, COM(2005) 570, Annex VI, pp 5–6.

[80] *Bundesverfassungsgericht*, 27 July 2004, 1 BvR 1270/04, NVwZ 2004, p 1346, reported in 22ᵉ Rapport sur le contrôle de l'application du droit communautaire, COM(2005) 570, Annex VI, pp 5–6.

in the rest of the Community territory, were to be treated as special expenditure leading to a reduction of income tax. The *Bundesfinanzhof* held that the German legislation denying such tax reduction was compatible with Community law. However, at the time when the *Bundesfinanzhof* issued this ruling, the Commission had commenced infringement proceedings against the very same law.[81] Hence, the ruling of the *Bundesfinanzhof* was hardly one of *acte clair*. Indeed, subsequently the Court of Justice ruled that precisely on the point in question before the *Bundesfinanzhof* Germany had been in breach of its obligations under the EC Treaty.[82]

In a situation like the one above where the Commission has initiated infringement proceedings, a court of last instance may find that suspending the procedure while awaiting the outcome of the infringement proceedings will often be an appropriate alternative to making a preliminary reference. In particular, this applies where the Commission's infringement proceedings have reached the stage where the Member State has been summoned before the Court of Justice. On the other hand, if the procedure before the national court gives rise to Community law aspects that are not likely to be answered by the Court of Justice in the infringement procedure, the national court should consider putting preliminary questions in a timely fashion, such that the Court of Justice may join the preliminary reference to the infringement procedure case (Footnote 82 bis).

A national court of last instance is not relieved of the obligation to make a reference for a preliminary ruling if the Commission does not proceed with infringement proceedings.[83] The Commission may halt the proceedings because it concludes that there is no infringement. However, as already indicated above in Section 3.4.2, quite often the Commission simply decides to use its discretion not to bring infringement proceedings even if it finds that the national measure in question raises problems in relation to Community law. Moreover, it is only the Court of Justice, and not the Commission, which can give an authoritative statement of the interpretation of Community law.

3.4.8. Acte clair *and administrative practice and legal literature*

Frequently the parties to the main proceedings will disagree about the correct interpretation of the relevant Community act. Application of the *acte clair* doctrine

---

[81] Case C-318/05, *Commission v Germany* [2007] ECR I-6957. Moreover, by a decision of 27 January 2005 the *Finanzgericht Köln* (Finance Court Cologne) had introduced a preliminary reference before the Court of Justice also raising the issue on the Community compatibility of the German legislation, cf Case C-76/05 *Schwarz v Finanzamt Bergisch-Gladbach* [2007] ECR I-6849.

[82] *Bundesfinanzhof*, 14 December 2005, XI R 66/03, Finanz-Rundschau-Ertragssteuerrecht 2005, p 751, reported in 23ᵉ Rapport sur le contrôle de l'application du droit communautaire, COM(2006) 416, Annex VI, p I-10. See also Ch 7, s 2.5.

[83] Case C-393/98 *Gomes Valente* [2001] ECR I-1327, paras 18–19, of which a summary is provided in s 3.4.2 above.

is not excluded whenever someone questions the correct interpretation. In order to apply the *acte clair* doctrine the national court need only be convinced that the matter is equally clear to other national judges and to the Court of Justice. In contrast, *acte clair* is not excluded where a national court intends to arrive at an interpretation that conflicts with that laid down by administrative authorities and legal theory.[84] Indeed, one may imagine a situation where an administrative decision on the interpretation of a Community act is brought before a national court of last instance which reverses the administrative decision whilst considering it a case of *acte clair*.

Nevertheless, if a conflicting view has been taken in administrative practice or in the legal literature this in itself may be a reason for the national court to carefully consider whether the situation truly is one of *acte clair*.

3.4.9. Acte clair—*meeting the demands of the times*

It follows from the above that there is a certain variance between, on the one hand, the strict *acte clair* conditions established in *CILFIT* and, on the other hand, the more relaxed interpretation that appears to be widely applied among national courts of last instance. As observed in Section 3.4.3 above, according to the *CILFIT* conditions, the fact that the main action itself is of limited importance cannot be given weight in deciding whether a reference must be made. However, in such a case in particular, a reference can make disproportionate demands on the time and resources of the parties to the main action, and be disproportionate to the dispute's importance to them. It appears likely that especially in these situations the national courts of last instance may be justifiably tempted to apply a less strict interpretation of the *CILFIT* conditions.[85] Thus, it has been argued that the *CILFIT* criteria

> must be assessed and applied in a rational and reasonable way, in other words 'with common sense', bearing in mind that it is in the interest of the parties, the national courts as well as the Court of Justice to avoid burdening the preliminary rulings procedure with questions that are of minor importance with a view to the unity, the coherence and development of EU law.[86]

---

[84] Case C-495/03 *Intermodal Transports BV* [2005] ECR I-8151, paras 33–45, of which a summary is provided in s 3.4.2 above.

[85] BH ter Kuile, 'To Refer or not to Refer' in D Curtin and T Heukels (eds), *Institutional Dynamics of European Integration* (1994) 381, 382.

[86] Report of the Working Group of the Association of the Councils of State and the Supreme Administrative Jurisdictions of the EU and the Network of the Presidents of the Supreme Judicial Courts of the EU on preliminary references, published in Newsletter of the Association of the Councils of State and Supreme Administrative Jurisdictions of the European Union, No 20, p 19, available at <http://www.juradmin.eu/en/newsletter/pdf/Hr_20-En.pdf>. See also p 3 in letter of 20 October 2006 sent to the Dutch minister of foreign affairs by the president of the Administrative Jurisdiction Division of the Dutch Council of State on behalf of the Council of State and the

It can also be asked whether it is appropriate for a reference for a preliminary ruling to be obligatory in cases where the Community law provision does not give rise to appreciable doubt about the interpretation that is relevant to the decision in the main proceedings, but where the national court cannot completely exclude that some other court in one of the Member States would reach a conflicting interpretation. Indeed, if all last instance courts of the Member States were rigidly to apply the *CILFIT* conditions, it is arguable that this would cause insurmountable practical problems for the Court of Justice due to the very considerable number of cases that would be referred.[87] Until now the Court of Justice has successfully evaded pronouncing itself on the situation where the interpretation of Community law does not give rise to appreciable doubt, but where the restrictive *CILFIT* conditions are nevertheless not fulfilled.

In *Lyckeskog*, the referring Swedish court asked whether a court of last instance within the meaning of Article 234(3) is obliged to request the Court of Justice for a preliminary ruling in a situation where the interpretation of the Community rule which applies to the dispute in the main proceedings does not give rise to difficulties, but where the conditions of the *CILFIT* case for applying the *acte clair* doctrine are nevertheless not fulfilled. The Court of Justice did not find it necessary to answer this question. In contrast, in his Opinion in the case Advocate General Tizzano considered the question. He argued against what the referring Swedish court seemed to propose, namely a subjective test based simply on the national court's conviction that it was in a position to resolve a question of Community law on its own in so far as the question—in the opinion of the national court—presented no problems of interpretation. The Advocate General added that the requirement laid down in *CILFIT* that it should be 'obvious' that there was no 'reasonable doubt' did not constitute a further condition. On the contrary, the 'obvious' requirement was a qualification of 'reasonable doubt' intended to emphasise that the doubt must really exist and must not be merely subjective. In the Opinion of Tizzano, the *CILFIT* conditions gave courts of last instance 'a substantial measure of discretion' and so he was anxious not to see the *acte clair* test exposed to an even higher degree of subjectivity and discretion.[88]

In *Wiener*, Advocate General Jacobs took up the question of whether it is necessary and appropriate, in view of the developments of the Community, for the

---

Presidents of the Supreme Court, the Central Appeals Tribunal and the Trade and Industry Appeals Tribunal, available at <http://www.network-presidents.eu/IMG/pdf/section_contentieux.pdf>.

[87] L Sevón, 'What do National Judges Require of the Court of Justice of the European Communities?' in G Regner, M Eliason, and H Vogel (eds), *Festskrift til Hans Ragnemalm* (2005) 287, 289–90.

[88] Case C-99/00 *Lyckeskog* [2002] ECR I-4839, paras 9 and 20 and Advocate General's Opinion. The case is summarised in s 2 above.

Court of Justice to rule in every case where a question of interpretation of Community law may arise. With respect to courts of last instance Jacobs proposed that in general they should only be obliged to make a preliminary reference where the question was of general interest.[89] Jacobs pointed out a number of developments that supported this, if an evolutionary approach were to be adopted regarding the interpretation of Article 234. Hence, he observed that Community law has been extended to many new fields, that the volume of legislation has greatly increased, and that the Court of Justice has developed a body of case law to which the national courts can resort in resolving new questions of Community law. Advocate General Jacobs also argued that in some areas of Community law, where there is already an established body of case law, increasing refinement of the case law through additional preliminary references is likely to lead to less legal certainty rather than more.[90]

More recently, in June 2005, Advocate General Colomer, in his Opinion in *Gaston Schul*, argued that the Court of Justice should moderate the terms of the *CILFIT* case law and adapt them to, as he said, 'the demands of the times'. According to Colomer the conditions laid down in *CILFIT* were justified at the time they were adopted, among other things because it had been necessary to restrict the very liberal application of the *acte clair* doctrine by certain national courts. However, the national courts' knowledge of Community law had considerably increased since 1983 when the *CILFIT* judgment had been given. Colomer equally argued that consideration for not being overwhelmed with references for preliminary rulings also favoured giving national courts greater independence. This would allow the Court of Justice to concentrate on cases which have general interest for the Community. Finally, the Advocate General observed that in those situations where the Court of Justice has relied on *CILFIT* it has made no reference at all to the requirement that the national court be convinced that its counterparts in the other Member States and the Court of Justice would interpret the contested provision in exactly the same way.[91]

Hence, all three Advocates General seem to support allowing the national courts real discretion in deciding whether a situation qualifies as *acte clair*.[92] The three

---

[89] At the Intergovernmental Conference (ICG) leading up the adoption of the Nice Treaty a proposal to this effect was tabled, but was later withdrawn, cf *Cour de cassation* (France), Rapport Annuel 2006—La Cour de cassation et la construction juridique européenne, p 99. For criticism of the proposal see C Timmermans, 'The European Union's Judicial System' (2004) 41 CML Rev 393, 401–2.

[90] Advocate General's Opinion in Case C-338/95 *Wiener* [1997] ECR I-6495. See also Advocate General Stix-Hackl's Opinion in Case 495/03 *Intermodal* [2005] ECR I-8151, paras 103–6.

[91] Advocate General's Opinion in Case C-461/03 *Gaston Schul* [2005] ECR I-10513, at paras 58–9.

[92] See also Lord Slynn of Hadley, former judge and Advocate General at the Court of Justice, in his foreword to D Anderson and M Demetriou, *References to the European Court* (2002) vi–vii.

Advocates General differ, however, as to whether the *CILFIT* conditions allow the national courts of last instance such discretion already. Tizzano was of the view that the national courts of last instance already do have this discretion, whereas Jacobs and Colomer took the opposite view.

In our opinion, the national courts should be offered some discretion in deciding whether a situation qualifies as *acte clair*. When the Court of Justice laid down the *CILFIT* conditions the Community differed significantly from the Community of today, not only with regard to the number of Member States and official languages and to the Court's case load and the time that it takes to answer a preliminary question, but also with regard to the Community law system as such which today has reached a stage where it is considerably less vulnerable than it was a quarter of a century ago. To our mind, there is still a need to strictly limit the possibility for a national court to avoid a preliminary reference in cases concerning general questions of interpretation that go beyond the confines of a single case. Indeed, in such cases there is a genuine need for uniform interpretation that should be established by the Court of Justice. In contrast, taking into consideration both the interests of the parties and the need to keep the Court's case load at a workable level, it seems less obvious that the same strict conditions should apply in cases where the issue of interpretation is unlikely to arise again, but instead is confined to the particular factual situation before the national court. In this latter situation it is submitted that it should be sufficient for *acte clair* to apply that the national court finds that the result does not give rise to appreciable doubt, but without requiring that the national court is equally convinced that all other courts will arrive at the same conclusion or that it has examined all the language versions of the relevant text.[93]

3.5. Other forms of preliminary references

In Chapter 1, Section 3, above it was shown that preliminary references to the Court of Justice may be made on legal bases other than Article 234. We now examine the duty to refer under the Euratom Treaty (Section 3.5.1). This is followed by an examination of the duty to refer within the field of justice and home affairs, ie Articles 68 of the EC Treaty and 35 of the Treaty on European Union (Section 3.5.2). Finally, we consider when there is a duty to refer under those

---

[93] A more elaborate account of how the *CILFIT* conditions may be adjusted is provided in M Broberg, 'Acte Clair Revisited: Adapting the Acte Clair Criteria to the Demands of the Times' (2008) 45 CML Rev 1383. For a sceptical view on the possibility of adjusting the *CILFIT* conditions in this way, see C Herrmann, 'Die Reichweite der gemeinschaftsrechtlichen Vorlagepflict in der neueren Rectsprechung des EuGH' (2006) Europäische Zeitschrift für Wirtschaftsrecht Vol 17, No 8, 2006, pp 231–5.

conventions that provide for the possibility of making preliminary references (Section 3.5.3).

3.5.1. Euratom Treaty

Article 150 of the Euratom Treaty on preliminary references to the Court of Justice in section 3 provides: 'Where any such question is raised in a case pending before a court or tribunal of a Member State, against whose decisions there is no judicial remedy under national law, that court or tribunal shall bring the matter before the Court of Justice.' This wording is identical to Article 234(3) and must be interpreted in the same way.

3.5.2. Justice and Home Affairs

3.5.2.1. Article 68 of the EC Treaty. Preliminary references regarding Title IV of the EC Treaty concerning 'Visas, Asylum, Immigration and Other Policies Related to Free Movement of Persons' have been laid down in Article 68. Article 68(1) provides:

> Article 234 shall apply to this Title under the following circumstances and conditions: where a question on the interpretation of this Title or on the validity or interpretation of acts of the institutions of the Community based on this Title is raised in a case pending before a court or a tribunal of a Member State against whose decisions there is no judicial remedy under national law, that court or tribunal shall, if it considers that a decision on the question is necessary to enable it to give judgment, request the Court of Justice to give a ruling thereon.

Article 68 establishes that Article 234, including the obligation in Article 234(3) for courts of last instance to refer, shall apply unless Article 68 prescribes otherwise.

Perhaps, it would be tempting to conclude that this is indeed the case. As shown above in Sections 3.1–3.4, under Article 234(3) the starting point is that a reference must be made whenever a relevant question of Community law is raised before a court of last instance. Admittedly, the *acte clair* principle means that a national court of last instance may refrain from making a reference if the correct interpretation of Community law is obvious to the court and if that court is also convinced that the matter is equally obvious to other Member State courts. Article 234(3) does not, however, confer significant discretion on national courts in this respect and it does not allow a national court of last instance to only refer if the court finds that it cannot with sufficient confidence solve the matter itself.

In comparison, Article 68(1) states that a national court has an obligation to make a preliminary reference only 'if it considers that a decision on the question is necessary to enable it to give judgment'. It would seem natural to construe this as laying down a more subjective test that vests in the national court a larger scope of discretion than does Article 234(3). Indeed, a difference in wording like the present one would make it natural to assume that different objectives were intended.[94]

Nevertheless, according to the prevailing view the obligation to refer laid down in Article 68(1) must be construed in a manner similar to Article 234(3).[95] In this respect, it is pointed out that the relevant part of the formulation of Article 68(1) stems from Article 3(1) of the Protocol on the interpretation of the Brussels Convention which provides:

> Where a question of interpretation of the Convention . . . is raised in a case pending before one of the courts listed in point 1 of Article 2, that court shall, if it considers that a decision on the question is necessary to enable it to give judgment, request the Court of Justice to give a ruling thereon.

That provision has generally been understood as implying that national courts of last instance which come within this provision are obligated to make preliminary references to the Court of Justice in the same manner as they are with regard to references under Article 234(3). It would therefore seem natural to interpret Article 68 of the EC Treaty in the same way.

It is also pointed out that, in contrast to Article 234(2), Article 68(1) prescribes that the national 'court or tribunal *shall* . . . request the Court of Justice to give a ruling'[96] whenever that is deemed necessary and that it is a general requirement for all types of preliminary references that an answer to the preliminary question is relevant for the resolution of the dispute before the referring court.[97] On that basis, the prevailing view is that the use of the word 'necessary' in Article 68(1) should not be understood as referring to a subjective assessment of the referring

---

[94] See A Staudinger and S Leible, 'Article 65 of the EC Treaty in the EC System of Competencies' (2000–2001) The European Legal Forum Vol 1, Jahr Heft 4, 225, 227.

[95] See P J G Kapteyn, 'Administration of Justice' in P J G Kapteyn et al (eds), *The Law of the European Union and the European Communities* (2008) 421, 499, G Gaja, 'The Growing Variety of Procedures Concerning Preliminary Rulings' in D O'Keeffe and A Bavasso (eds), *Judicial Review in European Union Law. Liber Amicorum in Honour of Lord Slynn of Hadley, Vol I* (2000) 143, 146, P Eeckhout, 'The European Court of Justice and the "Area of Freedom, Security and Justice": Challenges and Problems' in D O'Keeffe and A Bavasso (eds), *Judicial Review in European Union Law. Liber Amicorum in Honour of Lord Slynn of Hadley, Vol I* (2000) 153, 155, A Albors-Llorens, 'Changes in the Jurisdiction of the European Court of Justice under the Treaty of Amsterdam' (1998) 35 CML Rev 1273, 1287, T Tridimas, 'Knocking on Heaven's Door: Fragmentation, Efficiency and Defiance in the Preliminary Reference Procedure' (2003) 40 CML Rev 9, 13, and U Magnus, 'Introduction' in U Magnus and P Mankowski (eds), 'Brussels I Regulation' (2007) 41. In the opinion of P Martinet 'Article 68 CE' in P Léger (ed), *Commentaire article par article des traités UE et CE* (2000) 593, 597, the obligation to refer is in reality rather weak. This may be contrasted with C Cheneviere, 'L'Article 68 CE—Rapide survol d'un renvoi prejudicial mal compris' (2004) 5–6 Cahiers de droit européen Vols 5–6, 2004, pp 567–89 who finds that the formulation of Art 68(1) does not give a basis for finding that there is a broader margin of discretion under that provision than under Art 234.

[96] Emphasis added.

[97] See above Ch 5, s. 4.1 and s 3.1 of the present chapter.

court as to whether it is confident in resolving the matter on its own. Rather, it must be understood as simply restating the Court's practice that a national court has neither an obligation nor a right to pose a preliminary question if the answer will not be relevant for the decision in the main proceedings.

3.5.2.2. Article 35 of the EU Treaty.   Preliminary references relating to Title VI of the Treaty on European Union concerning 'Provisions on Police and Judicial Cooperation in Criminal Matters' are regulated by Article 35 of the EU Treaty. This provision does not impose an obligation to refer, but such obligation may be imposed by the individual Member State under its national law.[98]

3.5.3. Conventions

As explained above in Chapter 1, Section 3.5, a number of conventions entered into within the framework of the European Community provide for preliminary references to the Court of Justice. Some, but not all, of these conventions list those courts of last instance that are obliged to make references if they consider 'that a decision on the question is necessary to enable [them] to give judgment'.

3.6. Cases on interim measures

As already stated, a key purpose of Article 234 is to prevent one or more Member States developing a national practice which conflicts with Community law. This objective does not dictate that a national court of last instance is obliged to make a reference when making a decision in a case on interim measures, where the parties to the case subsequently have a right to have the Community law question tried.

When deciding a case involving interim measures and assessing whether a national court has a duty to make a reference for a preliminary ruling, what matters is whether both parties—in the event they have not received full support for their pleas—have a subsequent right to have the interim measures tried in such a way that there is access to make a reference for a preliminary ruling on any Community law questions which are relevant when granting the interim measures. Hence, if the decision of the national court on interim measures can be followed by a full hearing of the case, there will not be an obligation to make a reference under Article 234(3).[99]

---

[98] Treaty of Amsterdam amending the Treaty on European Union, the Treaties establishing the European Communities and certain related acts—Declarations adopted by the Conference—Declaration on Article K.7 of the Treaty on European Union [1997] OJ C340/133. For a list of the Member States which have adopted rules obliging courts of last instance to make preliminary references, see <http://curia.europa.eu/jcms/upload/docs/application/pdf/2008-09/art35_2008-09-25_17-37-4_434.pdf>.

[99] P Lasok, *The European Court of Justice—Practice and Procedure* (1994) 563.

This reasoning applies even if the decision on the granting of interim measures cannot be appealed to a higher national court and the Community law problems are relevant, new, and complex.

In *Morson and Jhanjan*, the Dutch authorities had refused to allow two women to reside in the Netherlands. The women appealed against their expulsion to a higher administrative authority. However, the appeal did not have suspensive effect, so the women simultaneously brought a case against the authorities before a Dutch court with a claim that the execution of the expulsion order should await the final decision of the authorities. The case ended up before the *Hoge Raad* (the Dutch Supreme Court) which decided to ask the Court of Justice whether Article 234(3) should be interpreted so that there was an obligation to make a reference in a situation such as the one with which the *Hoge Raad* was faced. The Court of Justice answered that the aim of Article 234(3) would be satisfied when the reference obligation applies in the proceedings which concern the substance of the case. This was so even if the substance of the case is dealt with by another jurisdictional system than that which deals with the interim measures, provided that the courts in this other jurisdictional system have the possibility of making a reference. A national court whose decision cannot be appealed against according to national law thus does not have an obligation to refer a question of interpretation to the Court of Justice if that question is raised in a case concerning interim measures and the decision which is to be taken is not binding on the national court before which the main proceedings are subsequently heard. However, this only applies if each of the parties can claim or require that a case shall be brought on the substance of the case, even before a court of a different jurisdictional system, and that during such proceedings any question of Community law on which an interim decision is taken during the summary proceedings may be re-examined and be the subject of a reference to the Court of Justice in accordance with Article 234.[100]

3.7. Application of Community law outside the scope of Community law

As shown above in Chapter 4, Section 5.3, the Court of Justice has been willing to give preliminary rulings on the interpretation of Community law even when such an interpretation is to apply outside the scope of Community law. A typical example is where a Community rule has been implemented in national law so as also to have an effect in matters which are not governed by Community law. The question is whether in such a case a national court of last instance has an obligation to make a reference under Article 234(3).

---

[100] Joined Cases 35/82 and 36/82 *Morson and Jhanjan* [1982] ECR 3723, paras 6, 9, and 10. See also Case 107/76 *Hoffmann-La Roche* [1977] ECR 957, para 5.

Some legal theorists have answered this question in the affirmative and in this connection referred to the fact that the reasoning behind the obligation to make a reference—consideration for the correct statement of the law by national courts of last instance and the uniform application of Community law in all Member States—applies equally in this situation. They also invoke the more formal consideration that since in this situation the competence to put, and to have answered, questions by preliminary rulings directly follows from Article 234, the consequence must be that the obligations provided for in this provision must apply correspondingly.[101] The present authors do not subscribe to this view. In our opinion the obligation to make a reference under Article 234 can only apply where there is an obligation to apply Community law. Moreover, the aim of extending the right to make references to cases where national legislation imitates Community rules outside their scope of application has only been to assist the national courts. It would therefore be inappropriate from the point of view of legal policy, and it would exceed the powers of the Court of Justice to supplement this right to make a reference with an obligation to make a reference in situations where a dispute concerning a *national* rule cannot be appealed to a higher national court.[102] This being said, it is submitted that a national court of last instance can be required to make a preliminary reference in this respect where it is unclear whether a given circumstance falls inside or outside the scope of Community law.

4. The Obligation of Courts Other than Those of Last Instance to Make a Reference

4.1. Overview

In the vast majority of cases only a court of last instance has a duty to make a reference. There are, however, two important exceptions, namely where a national court considers holding a Community act invalid and where it considers deviating from the Court of Justice's interpretation of a Community act. In addition it has been argued that under the Community duty of loyal cooperation all courts may be obliged to make preliminary references. These three situations are examined below.

---

[101] G Gaja, 'The Growing Variety of Procedures concerning Preliminary Rulings' in D O'Keeffe and A Bavasso (eds), *Judicial Review in European Union Law, Vol I* (2000) 143, 148; and NB Delgado and M la Casta Munoa, 'Case note on Dzodzi and Gmursynska-Bescher' (1992) CML Rev Vol 29, No 1, 152, 158.
[102] T Tridimas, 'Knocking on Heaven's Door: Fragmentation, Efficiency and Defiance in the Preliminary Reference Procedure' (2003) 40 CML Rev 9, 36ff.

4.2. References concerning invalidity

4.2.1. The duty to refer prior to a finding of invalidity

According to Article 234(1) the Court of Justice has jurisdiction to give preliminary rulings on, among other things, the validity and interpretation of acts of the
institutions of the Community and of the European Central Bank. Article 234(2)
states that national courts which are not courts of last instance may—but are not
required to—make a reference to the Court of Justice for a preliminary ruling if a
question set out in the first paragraph is raised before it. Article 234(3) provides
that there is an obligation to make a reference for a preliminary ruling if the
question is raised before a national court of last instance.

On the basis of a literal interpretation of this provision one could have assumed
that national courts covered by Article 234(2) do not have an obligation to make
a reference to the Court of Justice for a preliminary ruling when considering the
validity of a Community legal act. However, the Court of Justice came to a different conclusion when faced with this question in *Foto-Frost*.

In *Foto-Frost*, a question arose about the validity of a Commission Decision.
A German court was in doubt as to whether it had the power itself to decide the
question, and it therefore asked the Court of Justice whether a national court
could examine the validity of a Decision of the Commission. The Court of Justice
replied that according to Article 234 it has competence to give preliminary rulings
on the interpretation of the treaties, of the acts of the institutions of the Community,
and on the validity of these acts. The fact that Article 234 gives national courts,
whose decisions can be appealed against under national law, the right to make
references to the Court of Justice for preliminary rulings on interpretation and
validity does not mean that the provision has thereby established that these
national courts are themselves empowered to establish the validity of legal acts of
the Community's institutions. The Court of Justice also stated that these national
courts can decide the validity of a Community legal act. Where the national court
finds that claims of the parties on validity lack any legal basis, it can reject such
claims and find the legal act in question fully valid. When a national court acts in
this way it does not raise any doubts about the validity of a Community act.
However, the Court of Justice also remarked that, conversely, national courts are
not empowered to declare the legal acts of Community institutions to be invalid.
The main purpose of the power given to the Court of Justice by Article 234 is to
ensure the uniform application of Community law by national courts. This
requirement for uniformity is particularly important when questions are raised
about the validity of a Community act. Differences of opinion between national
courts as to the validity of Community acts could undermine the unity of the
Community legal order and the fundamental principle of legal certainty. The
Court added that this conclusion also followed from the very system of judicial

protection established by the EC Treaty and that the Court is in the best position to decide on the validity of Community acts.[103]

Thus, whilst a national court can hold a Community legal act to be valid without making a reference, it cannot itself declare such act invalid. Hence, where it considers that an argument for invalidity is well founded, it must therefore stay proceedings and make a reference to the Court of Justice for a preliminary ruling on the act's validity.[104] Just as it would be contrary to Article 234(3) if a court of last instance decided not to refer a question to the Court of Justice, for example, because it finds that the importance of the case does not justify this or because the parties jointly object to such a reference,[105] no national court can avoid making a preliminary reference on such a basis. Indeed, a national court cannot declare a Community act invalid even if similar provisions in another comparable legal act have already been declared invalid by the Court of Justice so that it could have been argued that an *acte clair* situation exists within the meaning of the *CILFIT* judgment.[106]

4.2.2. *References on validity where access to refer is restricted*

The Court of Justice has not given judgment on the extent to which the above practice applies to cases where not all national courts have been given a right to make references; this is relevant with regard to acts under Article 68 of the EC Treaty. The problem may also arise regarding Article 35 of the Treaty on European Union where a Member State has made a declaration specifying that only courts of last instance may make preliminary references under that provision or where a Member State has made no declaration at all (so that these Member State courts cannot make preliminary references under Article 35 of the Treaty on European Union). The problem essentially is that a national court may be faced with a situation where it considers a Community or a Union legal act to be invalid whilst at the same time, apparently, it is not competent to make a preliminary reference in this respect to the Court of Justice. There appear to be three possible solutions to this dilemma, though without it being possible to point to any of these as being entirely satisfactory.[107]

---

[103] Case 314/85 *Foto-Frost* [1987] ECR 4199, paras 9–18. For an example of a national court annulling a Community act before the *Foto-Frost* judgment was rendered, see Munich Finance Court, Judgment of 11 September 1985 (III, 272/79 Z 1 and 2), reported in third annual report on monitoring the application of Community law [1986] OJ C220/27.

[104] Case C-344/04 *IATA* [2006] ECR I-403, paras 27–32; and Case C-119/05 *Lucchini* [2007] ECR I-6199, paras 53–6.

[105] See s 3.4.3 above.

[106] Case C-461/03 *Gaston Schul* [2005] ECR I-10513, paras 15–25.

[107] Likewise P Eeckhout, 'The European Court of Justice and the "Area of Freedom, Security and Justice": Challenges and Problems' in D O'Keeffe and A Bavasso (eds), *Judicial Review in European Union Law. Liber Amicorum in Honour of Lord Slynn of Hadley, Vol 1* (2000) 153, 157–9, and 160.

1. One solution would be to allow a lower national court to declare a legal act invalid. Such a solution would, however, conflict with the logic of the *Foto-Frost* case. In this respect it has been argued that *Foto Frost* cannot be applied to situations where the national court has no possibility to refer the validity question to the Court of Justice so that a national court which is convinced that a legal act of the Community or of the Union is invalid, but which is not competent to make a preliminary question to this effect, may render the legal act inapplicable.[108]

2. Another solution would be that in such cases the Court of Justice assumed the competence to give a preliminary ruling on a reference from a lower national court. However, even though the consideration which made the Court of Justice require an unconditional reference in relation to Article 234 in *Foto-Frost* also applies here, that solution seems incompatible with the wordings of both Article 68 of the EC Treaty and Article 35(3)(a) of the Treaty on European Union. Indeed, both provisions unequivocally state that only courts of last instance can make references. Moreover, the Court's practice does not seem to envisage such a solution.[109]

3. Finally, it might be argued that the national court should be unconditionally required to apply a Community act which it finds invalid, and thereby be obliged to give a judgment which it finds to be materially incorrect. Such a solution would seem to be the only one which fits with both the wording of Article 68 of the EC Treaty and Article 35(3)(a) of the Treaty on European Union and the logic behind *Foto Frost*. Nevertheless, it would hardly be a satisfactory result for the purposes of legal certainty.[110]

---

[108] This approach is supported by Advocate General Mengozzi in paras 121–31 in his Opinion in Case C-354/04 P *Gestorias Pro Amnistía* [2007] ECR I-1579, G Gaja, 'The Growing Variety of Procedures concerning Preliminary Rulings' in D O'Keeffe and A Bavasso (eds), *Judicial Review in European Union Law. Liber Amicorum in Honour of Lord Slynn of Hadley, Vol I* (2000) 143, 147–8, A Arnull, 'Taming the Beast? The Treaty of Amsterdam and the Court of Justice' in D O'Keeffe and P Twomey (eds), *Legal Issues of the Amsterdam Treaty* (1999) 109, 117, and 119 and the same author in *The European Union and its Court of Justice* (1999) 70. C Naômé, *Le renvoi préjudiciel en droit européen* (2007) 45, 57–8, and 269–70 also supports this approach and she adds that the national court in particular should render the Community act inapplicable if the application of the legal act would infringe fundamental rights. Contrast, however, Advocate General Colomer in Case 14/08 *Roda Golf & Beach Resort* 25 June 2009, at para 30. Colomer observes that only the Court of Justice has jurisdiction to carry out a review of validity of Community acts.

[109] S Peers, 'Who's Judging the Watchmen? The Judicial System of the "Area of Freedom Security and Justice"' in P Eeckhout and T Tridimas (eds), *Yearbook of European Law 1998* (1999) 337, 355 points to another solution; namely that the lower national courts should make an interim measures ruling and should be obliged to make this ruling upon an appeal, in order to ensure the uniformity of EC law.

[110] This appears to be the Commission's view, cf Communication from the Commission to the European Parliament, the Council, the European Economic and Social Committee, the Committee of the Regions and the Court of Justice of the European Communities—Adaptation of the provisions of Title IV of the Treaty establishing the European Community relating to the jurisdiction of

These problems of legal certainty are particularly acute in cases where a Member State has not made any declaration in accordance with Article 35(3) of the Treaty on European Union that the courts in that Member State can make references for preliminary rulings. In this situation the Court of Justice has been given no jurisdiction in relation to the national courts in the Member State in question.[111]

4.2.3. *Findings of invalidity without (prior) preliminary reference*

The condition that a national court can only consider a Community legal act to be invalid after the Court of Justice has established this will be satisfied where the Court of Justice has held the disputed legal act to be invalid in another case. Therefore, in this situation it is not necessary to make a reference for a preliminary ruling in order to have this restated.

In *ICC*, an Italian court was faced with a number of questions concerning Community law, including the validity of a Community regulation. In a previous case the Court of Justice had already declared that the regulation in question was invalid, and the Italian court therefore asked whether a declaration on the invalidity of a Community regulation under Article 234 of the EC Treaty had general effect, or whether it only applied to the particular case. The Court of Justice stated that the scope of its judgments rendered on the basis of Article 234 should be viewed in the light of the aims of this provision and the place it occupies in the overall system of judicial protection established by the Treaties. When the Court of Justice declares a legal act of a Community institution to be invalid in accordance with Article 234, in addition to the requirement for the uniform application of Community law, there are also imperative requirements for legal certainty. It is characteristic of such a decision by the Court of Justice that a national court cannot apply a legal act that has been declared invalid without creating uncertainty about the applicable Community law. Even though a prior judgment, in which a legal act of an institution has been declared invalid, is only addressed to the national court which has referred the case to the Court of Justice, the judgment constitutes a sufficient basis for any other national court to regard the legal act as invalid. Where the Court of Justice has declared a given legal act to be invalid, all national courts can directly consider that legal act to be invalid, without there being a need for a further reference for a preliminary ruling. However, the Court of Justice also noted that national courts are not precluded from making

---

the Court of Justice with a view to ensuring more effective judicial protection of 28 June 2006 (COM(2006) 346 (final)), p 5. V Skouris, 'l'urgence dans la procédure applicable aux renvois préjudiciels' in C Baudenbacher et al (eds), *Liber Amicorum en l'honneur de Bo Vesterdorf* (2007) 59, 72 holds that this third solution reflects the present state of the law, but equally finds it to be unsatisfactory from a legal policy point of view.

[111] See further above Ch 1, s. 3.3 and in Ch 3, ss 5.3.2 and 5.3.3. The Court of Justice apparently did not consider this situation in Case C-354/04 P *Gestoras Pro Amnistía et al* [2007] ECR I-1579.

references as to whether a Community act is invalid, even where the Court has previously declared the legal act in question to be invalid.[112]

Moreover, under conditions defined by Community law, a national court can apply interim measures against the application of a Community legal act that is argued to be invalid, provided that at the same time the national court makes a reference to the Court of Justice for a preliminary ruling on the issue.[113]

4.2.4. *Evaluating the* Foto-Frost *doctrine*

There are significant substantive reasons which support the argument that only the Court of Justice may declare a Community legal act invalid. However, the Court's arguments in *Foto-Frost* give cause for thought. Thus, a natural understanding of Article 234's wording does not give solid support for the result which the Court of Justice reached in *Foto-Frost*,[114] and there is nothing indicating that the authors of the EC Treaty made a mistake when formulating the provision. As pointed out by the Advocate General in his Opinion on the case, 'the authors of the EEC Treaty had before them as a model Article 41 of the ECSC Treaty which gives the Court exclusive jurisdiction. They could have followed that example, yet did not do so.'[115] In support of the interpretation it adopted, the Court of Justice first of all argued that a national court's mistaken view that a Community legal act is invalid has different and more far-reaching consequences than a wrong interpretation. This appears quite plausible, but is not necessarily always correct. Indeed, the *Foto-Frost* case itself concerned the question of the validity of a Commission decision which was only concerned with the collection of a rather limited amount of tax from the Foto-Frost company. The validity of the actual legal act in the *Foto-Frost* case therefore, in reality, only had consequences for this company. In contrast, depending on the circumstances, a mistaken interpretation of a Community legal act can have wide-ranging consequences. The fact that the Court of Justice has not insisted on national lower courts being unconditionally required to refer such cases for a preliminary ruling can hardly be ascribed solely to the wording of Article 234. Neither can the Court of Justice's refraining from insisting on references from the lower national courts be ascribed solely to the fact that the decisions of these courts will always, according to the system of Article 234, ultimately be appealable to a national court which is obliged to make a reference for a preliminary ruling under Article 234(3). Exactly the same applies to the question of invalidity. Nevertheless, it must be acknowledged that a decision on

---

[112] Case 66/80 *ICC* [1981] ECR 1191, paras 10–14.

[113] See Ch 9, s 3 below.

[114] Prior to the *Foto-Frost* case several national courts had considered themselves entitled to declare a Community legal act invalid. The Advocate General gives a number of examples of these in para 4 of his Opinion in the *Foto-Frost* case.

[115] Para 4 of the Advocate General's Opinion in the *Foto-Frost* case.

the validity of a Community legal act will have wide-ranging consequences more frequently than will the interpretation of a Community legal act. Furthermore, a question on the validity of a Community legal act arises only relatively seldom, so that an unconditional requirement for a reference to be made will probably not lead to the Court of Justice being overburdened. In contrast, questions on the correct interpretation of Community acts arise frequently, so that an unconditional requirement for references to be made would, in practice, lead to an undesirable overburdening of the Court of Justice.

4.3. Deviating from the Court of Justice's interpretation of a Community legal act

It is for the Court of Justice to establish authoritatively the correct interpretation of Community law. Once the Court has given a decision on the validity or correct interpretation of a Community legal act, the national courts are obliged to follow the interpretation. This also applies when an interpretation has been given in a preliminary ruling.[116] As a consequence, a national court may not depart from a clearly established practice of the Court of Justice without the latter's prior acceptance.

In 1997 the German *Bundesverfassungsgericht* overturned the *Landesarbeitgericht's* ruling whereby the latter had refused to apply an interpretation established earlier by the Court of Justice. The *Bundesverfassungsgericht* held that the *Landesarbeitsgericht* could not depart from the Court of Justice's ruling without first making a preliminary reference.[117]

If a national court wishes to apply a differing interpretation it must thus make a reference for a preliminary ruling and ask a question about the correct interpretation of the Community act in question.[118] While in many cases the Court of Justice has defined an established practice, it has only very seldom expressly varied such a practice.[119]

---

[116] See below Ch 12, s 3.1.

[117] Ruling of 13 June 1997, 1 BvR 2102/95 (1997) Europäische Zeitschrift für Wirtschaftsrecht Vol 8, 575, reported in fifteenth annual report on monitoring the application of Community law [1998] OJ C250/197.

[118] See Ch 4, s 3.2.5 and F Jacobs, 'The Role of the European Court of Justice in the Development of Uniform Law' in N Jareborg (ed), *De Lege, Juridiska Fakulteten i Uppsala, Yearbook 1995* (1995) 205, 207, and the same author, 'The Effect of Preliminary Rulings in the National Legal Order' in M Andenas (ed), *Article 177 References to the European Court* (1994) 29, 30. But contrast with G Gaja, 'The Growing Variety of Procedures concerning Preliminary Rulings' in D O'Keeffe and A Bavasso (eds), *Judicial Review in European Union Law, Vol I* (2000) 143, 151.

[119] Case C-10/89 *HAG II* [1990] ECR I-3711, para 10; and Joined Cases C-267/91–268/91 *Keck and Mithouard* [1993] ECR I-6097, para 16.

4.4. The duty of loyal cooperation and preliminary references

It has been argued that by reading Article 234 together with Article 10 on the Member States' duty of loyal cooperation in the field of Community law it may be possible to derive a duty for any national court to make a reference if it contemplates interpreting a Community rule in a way which differs from that adopted by national courts in other Member States.[120] In the opinion of the present authors, the existence of such a duty is difficult to reconcile with the wording of Article 234. And indeed, as shown above in Section 3.4.8, the Court of Justice has held that even in cases covered by Article 234(3) a national court has no duty to refer merely because an administrative body has reached a conclusion other than that which the national court finds most correct. That being said, the existence of contrary interpretations by other courts and administrative bodies should be a factor weighing in favour of making a reference.[121]

5. Consequences of a National Court Disregarding its Obligation to Make a Reference

5.1. Overview

The Community is based on mutually loyal cooperation. This also applies to the cooperation between the national courts of the Member States and the Court of Justice on the basis of Article 234. The EC Treaty does not specify any sanction for a national court's failure to comply with the obligation to make a reference for a preliminary ruling. Nevertheless, four types of possible consequences may be identified in such a situation, namely infringement proceedings (Section 5.2), invalidity of the national ruling or duty to reopen a case (Section 5.3), claims for damages (Section 5.4), and breach of Article 6 of the European Convention of Human Rights (Section 5.5).

5.2. Infringement proceedings for failure to refer

It is incumbent on the Member States to ensure that their national courts fulfil the obligation to make references under Article 234. If necessary, the Commission can initiate infringement proceedings under Article 226 of the Treaty.

In 2003 the Dutch *Hoge Raad* ruled in a case where a worker was posted from the Netherlands to a German firm. The *Hoge Raad,* somewhat questionably, held that the worker did not have such attachment to the Netherlands that he could be

---

[120] J Temple Lang, 'The Duties of National Courts under Community Constitutional Law' (1997) 22 EL Rev 3, 15.
[121] See in this respect Ch 7, s 2.

considered covered by the Dutch social security scheme. The national court did not express any doubt about the interpretation of the relevant Community provisions and it did not make any preliminary reference to the Court of Justice. With this background the Commission opened proceedings against the Netherlands, arguing that the Dutch ruling constituted an infringement of the Community rules on free movement of workers.[122]

In 2004 the Commission issued a letter of formal notice to Sweden for breach of Article 234. According to the Commission the Swedish authorities should have adopted rules to ensure that the Swedish courts of last instance made references for preliminary rulings in connection with decisions on whether a right of appeal should be granted. Next, the Commission argued that reasons should be given for the refusal of the court of last instance to grant leave to appeal, so as to make it possible to assess whether the requirements of Article 234(3) were fulfilled. On this basis the Swedish Parliament adopted a 'Law on certain provisions on preliminary rulings from the Court of Justice'.[123] As a consequence of this law, if one party argues that in order to decide a case it is necessary to clarify circumstances in which the Court of Justice has powers to make a preliminary ruling, in its judgment a Swedish court must now give reasons why it has not made a reference for a preliminary ruling, if its judgment cannot be appealed against.[124]

In Germany a somewhat similar duty to give reasons for refusal to refer has been established by the *Bundesverfassungsgericht* (Federal Constitutional Court) on the basis that it can only review a lower court's refusal to make a preliminary reference if it can adequately acquaint itself with the lower court's reasons for declining to make such a reference.[125]

5.3. Failure to refer, validity of national judgments, and obligation to reopen the case-file

It may follow from national law that the setting aside of the obligation to make a reference under Article 234(3) can in itself lead to the judgment or order in question being invalid under Community law.

---

[122] *Hoge Raad,* 11 July 2003, *X te Z (Duitsland) tegen Staatssecretaris van Financiën,* AB Rechtspraak Bestuursrecht 2003, no 457, reported in 21ᵉ Rapport sur le contrôle de l'application du droit communautaire, COM(2004) 839, Annex VI, pp I-24–I-25. As for the Commission's infringement action see the Commission's press release of 9 February 2004, IP/04/178.

[123] Lag med vissa bestämmelser om förhandsavgörande från EG-domstolen, SFS 2006:502.

[124] M Schmauch, 'Lack of preliminary rulings as an infringement of Article 234 EC?' (2005) European Law Reporter Vol 11, pp 445–54; U Bernitz and A Kjellgren, *Europarättens grunder* (2002) 216; and U Bernitz, 'The Duty of Supreme Courts to Refer Cases to the ECJ: The Commission's Action Against Sweden' in N Wahl and P Cramér (eds), *Swedish Studies in European Law, Vol 1* (2006) 37, 45–6.

[125] *Bundesverfassungsgericht,* order of 9 January 2001, 1 BvR 1036/99, reported in nineteenth annual report on monitoring the application of Community law COM(2002) 324, Annex VI, pp 39–41.

In Germany the *Bundesverfassungsgericht* (the Federal Constitutional Court) has, on several occasions, annulled rulings of lower courts where these lower courts refused to make a preliminary reference. According to the *Bundesverfassungsgericht* such refusal may amount to an infringement of the German constitutional principle laid down in the *Grundgesetz* (the Basic Law) that no one may be deprived of the protection of the courts established by law.[126] The examination by the *Bundesverfassungsgericht* is limited to whether the application of Article 234 of the lower German court was manifestly unjustifiable, and in particular whether that court had totally violated its obligation to refer.[127] Moreover, in order for there to be such infringement it must be clear that the case before the German court gives rise to a question of interpretation of Community law as opposed to a question of application of Community law to the particular factual situation facing the court.[128]

In contrast, Community law itself does not contain a principle according to which a breach of the obligation to refer laid down in Article 234(3) entails the decision of the national court becoming invalid. This is so regardless of the fact that Article 234 has direct effect in the national legal systems. Indeed, the Court of Justice has recognised the importance of the principle of *res judicata* in the legal systems of both the Community and the Member States. It has thus held that, in order to ensure both stability of the law and legal relations and the sound administration of justice it is important that judicial decisions are definitive and can no longer be called into question after all rights of appeal have been exhausted or after the expiry of the time limits.[129] Therefore, Community law does not require a national court to disapply domestic rules of procedure conferring finality on a decision, even if to do so would enable the national court to remedy an infringement

---

[126] *Bundesverfassungsgericht*, order of 9 January 2001, 1 BvR 1036/99, reported in nineteenth annual report on monitoring the application of Community law COM(2002) 324, Annex VI, pp 39–41; and *Bundesverfassungsgericht*, ruling of 29 July 2004, 2 BvR 2248/03 (2004) Deutsches Verwaltungsblatt JG 119 1411, reported in 23ᵉ Rapport sur le contrôle de l'application du droit communautaire, COM(2006) 416, Annex VI, p I-5. Also in Austria the *Verfassungsgerichtshof* (Constitutional Court) has annulled a ruling by a lower court for breach of Art 234(3), cf *Verfassungsgerichtshof*, 30 September 2003, B 614/01, (2004) Europäische Zeitung für Wirtschaftsrecht JG 15 222, reported in 21ᵉ Rapport sur le contrôle de l'application du droit communautaire, COM(2004) 839, Annex VI, pp I-7–I-8.

[127] Order of the *Bundesverfassungsgericht* of 30 January 2002, 1 BvR 1542/00 (2002) Neue Juristische Wochenschrift Heft 20 1486, reported in twentieth annual report on monitoring the application of Community law COM(2003) 669, Annex VI, pp 6–7. Compare the decision of the Dutch *Raad van State, afdeling bestuursrechtspraak*, 16 November 2005, X, (2006) AB Rechtspraak Bestuursrecht AFL 14 124, and of the Dutch *Centrale Raad van Beroep*, 17 November 2006, *X/Raad van Bestuur van de Sociale Verzekeringsbank* (2007) AB Rechtspraak Bestuursrecht AFL 8 57, according to which breach of a Dutch court of the obligation to refer a preliminary question under Art 234 does not, according to Dutch law, constitute a reason to revise a decision that has become final.

[128] F Mayer, 'The European Constitution and the Courts', in A von Bogdandy and J Bast (eds), *Principles of European Constitutional Law* (2006) 281, 290 with further references.

[129] Case C-224/01 *Köbler* [2003] ECR I-10239, para 38.

of Community law.[130] This principle applies both to situations where the infringement consists of a national ruling that is contrary to Community law with regard to substance and to infringements of a procedural nature such as, for example, an omission to respect Article 234(3).

In two respects the Court of Justice has, however, qualified that finding.

First, the principle of *res judicata* plays a less prominent role when a national judgment is at odds with a decision of a Community institution that has become final and where those who clearly had standing to challenge the decision have not done so. In this situation not only the finality of the national court's decision must be protected but also that of the Community decision. Moreover, it is one thing for a national court to make an incorrect decision, but quite another to render a decision that encroaches on the sole competence of a Community institution.[131]

Second, in certain situations Community law imposes on an *administrative* body an obligation to review a final administrative decision even though that decision has been upheld by a national court of last instance. There is not a general obligation for the administrative body to make such a review. However, where the administrative decision in question has become final as a result of a judgment of a national court ruling at final instance and where, in the light of a subsequent decision given by the Court of Justice, it becomes clear that this judgment is based on a misinterpretation of Community law which was adopted without a preliminary reference to the Court of Justice under Article 234(3), the national administrative body responsible for the case will have to exercise all possible discretion under national law in order to review the administrative decision notwithstanding that the decision has received judicial confirmation. The Court of Justice thus accepts that the matter is regulated by national law, and that the situation just mentioned is to be considered as compatible with Community law if national law does not allow the administration to reopen the case. Nevertheless, at the same time the Court requires the competent administrative body to exercise any discretion it may have under national law in a manner that makes it possible to review the administrative act.

In *Kühne & Heitz*, a Dutch court of last instance refused to make a reference for a preliminary ruling on the correct interpretation of the European Community's common customs tariff in a case which concerned the tariffs applicable to poultry meat parts. Subsequently, in a different case, the Court of Justice reached the opposite conclusion to that of the Dutch court of last instance. The importer

---

[130] Case C-126/97 *Eco Swiss* [1999] ECR I-3055, paras 46–8; and Case C-234/04 *Kapferer* [2006] ECR I-2585, paras 19–24. See also BH ter Kuile, 'To Refer or not to Refer' in D Curtin and T Heukels (eds), *Institutional Dynamics of European Integration* (1994) 381, 384.

[131] Case C-119/05 *Lucchini* [2007] ECR I-6199. See further A Biondi, 'Case note' (2008) 45 CML Rev 1459, and above in Ch 5, s 7.

concerned in the Dutch case thereafter applied to the Dutch court to have its case reopened whereupon the Dutch court made a reference to the Court of Justice for a preliminary ruling. The Court of Justice held that the Dutch court had been wrong in not originally making a reference for a preliminary ruling. This did not automatically mean that the Dutch authorities had a duty to reopen the case. However, under Dutch law the national courts had power to reopen a case, and since the importer had requested that the case be reopened as soon as it became aware of the Court of Justice's decision, it followed from the general Community principle of loyal cooperation that the case should be reopened.[132]

As is apparent from the above summary, in *Kühne & Heitz* the Court placed emphasis on the fact that the person concerned complained to the administrative body immediately after becoming aware of the decision of the Court of Justice. Subsequently, however, the Court stated that Community law does not impose any time limit on how late a party can ask for a reopening of the national proceedings. Consequently, the matter must be settled in accordance with the principle of procedural autonomy which means that Member States remain free to set reasonable time limits for seeking remedies, in a manner consistent with the Community principles of effectiveness and equivalence.[133]

The obligation for the relevant administrative body to reopen the case is not dependent on whether the parties to the main proceedings relied on Community law before the national court. This is because Article 234 institutes a direct cooperation between the Court of Justice and the national courts by means of a procedure which is independent of any initiative by the parties. Indeed, the obligation to reopen the case arises even if the national court did not consider the Community law issue at all, as long as under the relevant national procedural rules the national court may raise of its own motion a plea alleging infringement of Community provisions.[134] To make the obligation to reopen the wrongful administrative decision conditional upon the legal pleas of the parties concerned would not sit well with the obligations of courts of last instance laid down in Article 234(3). Considering that the aim of the preliminary ruling procedure goes beyond merely ensuring judicial protection for the parties to the specific case, the fact that a national court of last instance has overlooked the significance of a question of interpretation of Community law, and thereby has violated Article 234(3), should not be held against the individual concerned.

---

132 Case C-453/00 *Kühne & Heitz* [2004] ECR I-837, paras 20–8.
133 Case C-2/06 *Kempter* [2008] ECR I-411 and the comment on the case by N Fenger, 'Review of final administrative decisions contrary to EU Law' (2008) European Law Reporter Vol 5, 150 155–6.
134 Case C-2/06 *Kempter* [2008] ECR I-411, paras 34–46.

5.4. Damages for failure to refer

Refraining from making references cannot in itself lead to a duty to pay damages under Community law. However, where it later turns out that a decision of a national court of last instance was taken in violation of Article 234(3) this may be relevant in assessing whether the Member State in question must pay damages for any loss that has been suffered due to the judgment.

In *Köbler*, an Austrian professor claimed a length-of-service increment which his public employer refused. Köbler therefore brought a case against his employer. The case required an interpretation of Community law, and the Austrian court of last instance therefore made a reference for a preliminary ruling. However, the reference was subsequently withdrawn before the Court of Justice had given its ruling, and the national court decided the case, finding against Professor Köbler. Köbler thereafter brought a case claiming compensation for the loss he had suffered as a result of the failure of the Austrian court to obtain a preliminary ruling and of its subsequent incorrect application of Community law. Essentially, the question was whether the Member States can be liable to pay compensation for the incorrect decisions of their national courts, and if so on what conditions. The Court of Justice established that the principle that a Member State is obliged to compensate for the loss caused to citizens from infringements of Community law for which the Member State in question is responsible also applies when the infringement is due to a decision of a national court of last instance. The conditions for the existence of liability to pay compensation are the same as otherwise apply to the Member States' infringements of Community law. This means that the Community provision which is set aside must be intended to give rights to citizens, the infringement must be sufficiently serious, and there must be a direct causal connection between the infringement of the obligation of the Member State and the loss suffered. The Court of Justice made it clear that the principle of liability for breach of Community law concerns the Member States' duty to pay compensation, and does not entail the personal liability of the judges.[135]

In *Traghetti del Mediterraneo*, the Court of Justice stated that Community law precludes national legislation which excludes all State liability for damage caused to individuals by an infringement of Community law attributable to a national court adjudicating at last instance, on the grounds of an interpretation of the provisions of law or of an assessment of the facts and evidence carried out by the national court. Community law also precludes national legislation which limits State liability solely to cases of intentional fault or serious misconduct on the part

---

[135] See C-224/01 *Köbler* [2003] ECR I-10239.

of the national judges, to the extent that such limitation goes further than the conditions laid down in the judgment in *Köbler* summarised above.[136]

To assess whether a superior court has incurred liability due to a sufficiently serious infringement of Community law can be quite a delicate task for a lower national court. Moreover, a problem of incapacity (bias) can arise if the matter is to be brought before the court of last instance that is held to have committed the infringement.

In a case before the Swedish Supreme Court a party argued that this court had committed a significant procedural error, as it had not made a reference for a preliminary ruling before deciding a case. The Supreme Court however denied that it had been under an obligation to make such a reference in the actual case.[137]

In practice it will probably be a rare occurrence that a judgment of a national court will justify an award of compensation under Community law.[138] Thus, according to Advocate General Jacobs (as he then was) a Member State will really only be held liable under the *Köbler* ruling in a case of bad faith.[139]

5.5. Failure to refer and Article 6 of the European Convention of Human Rights

The question of whether a national court's failure to make a preliminary reference constitutes a breach of Article 6 of the European Convention of Human Rights has arisen on several occasions; in particular where the preliminary reference has been from a national court to another body (court) within the same national system.

In *Coëme*, the European Court of Human Rights was asked to consider whether the Belgian Court of Cassation had committed an infringement of Article 6 of the European Convention on Human Rights when it refused to make a preliminary reference to the Belgian 'Administrative Jurisdiction and Procedure Court' on certain issues relating to the main proceedings. The European Court of Human Rights first observed that the European Convention on Human Rights does not,

---

[136] See Case C-173/03 *Traghetti del Mediterraneo* [2006] ECR I-5177, paras 24–46. See also the ruling by the French *Conseil d'État* of 18 June 2008 in case no 295831, *Gestas*, and the ruling by the Austrian *Verfassungsgerichtshof* (Constitutional Court) of 13 October 2004 in case A5/04, reported in 22ᵉ Rapport sur le contrôle de l'application du droit communautaire, COM(2005) 570, Annex VI, p 16.

[137] K J Dhunér, 'Sweden' (2005) IBA Legal Practice Division Antitrust Newsletter Vol 18, 27.

[138] *Re Accountants Aptitude Tests* (Case III ZR 294/03) [2006] 2 CMLR 55, where a claim for compensation for failure to make a preliminary reference was rejected by the German *Bundesgerichtshof* (Federal Supreme Court).

[139] R Crowe, 'Colloquium Report—The Preliminary Reference Procedure: Reflections based on Practical Experiences of the Highest National Courts in Administrative Matters' (2004) ERA Forum 435, 444.

as such, guarantee any right to have a case referred by a domestic court to another national or international authority for a preliminary ruling. Moreover, it observed that there was no absolute right to have a preliminary question referred to a court. This was so even where a particular field of law may be interpreted only by a court designated by statute and where the legislation concerned requires other courts to refer to that court, without reservation, all questions relating to that field. The European Court of Human Rights added, however, that 'it is not completely impossible that, in certain circumstances, refusal by a domestic court trying a case at final instance might infringe the principle of fair trial, as set forth in Article 6 § 1 of the Convention, in particular where such refusal appears arbitrary'.[140]

Arguably, the reasoning in the European Court of Human Rights' ruling in *Coëme* may be applied to a national court's failure to make preliminary references to the European Court of Justice. It thus follows that it cannot be completely ruled out that a failure to make a preliminary reference may constitute a breach of Article 6 of the European Convention of Human Rights. If ever such a situation were to arise, it seems most likely that it would do so where the failure is committed by a court of last instance that arbitrarily refuses to make a preliminary reference.

In *Canela Santiago v Spain*, the European Court of Human Rights held that the Spanish Supreme Court's failure to make a preliminary reference to the Court of Justice did not constitute an infringement of Article 6 of the European Convention of Human Rights because the Supreme Court had set out its reasons for not making a preliminary reference. Accordingly, the refusal to make a preliminary reference could not be regarded as arbitrary.[141]

---

[140] *Coëme and others v Belgium* ECHR 2000-VII, para 114. See also the two unreported decisions to which the European Court of Human Rights refers in para 114 in *Coëme* as well as *Wynen and Centre Hospitalie Interrégional Edith-Cavell v Belgium* ECHR 2002-VIII, paras 41–3.

[141] *Canela Santiago v Spain* (Application No 60350/00) Decision of 4 October 2001. See also M Breuer, 'State Liability for Judicial Wrongs' (2004) 29 EL Rev 243, 251; and H Schermers and D Waelbroeck, *Judicial Protection in the European Union* (2001) 272.

7

WHEN OUGHT A REFERENCE FOR A PRELIMINARY RULING BE MADE?

1. Overview

In Chapters 4–5 we assessed what kinds of questions a national court may refer to the Court of Justice and in what situations such references may take place. Chapter 6 then identified the situations where this competence to pose preliminary questions is not only an option for the national court, but an obligation under Community law, for example, because the national court contemplates setting aside a legal act taken by a Community institution or because there is no right of appeal against its decision and the conditions for *acte clair* are not fulfilled. In this chapter, it is assumed that the national court, on the one hand, is faced with a question of Community law that it may refer for a preliminary ruling according to the criteria described in Chapters 4–5, but, on the other hand, is not bound to do so according to the criteria identified in Chapter 6. In other words, Chapter 7 concerns the situation where the national court has discretion in its decision as to whether or not it should refer a preliminary question to the Court of Justice, and the purpose of the chapter is to analyse (1) the different criteria that form the basis for the national court's discretionary decision, and (2) to what extent Community law interferes with that discretion.

The chapter begins by identifying, in Sections 2.1–2.4, the different criteria that in general form the basis for the national court's decision as to whether or not it should make use of the preliminary reference procedure. Section 2.5 then deals with the particular situation where a similar question is already pending before the Court of Justice or where the national court has a cluster of parallel cases before it and must decide whether to make a preliminary reference in all cases or only in one or a few test cases. In Section 3, we discuss to what extent a national court not sitting as a court of last instance should refrain from posing a preliminary question because such a question could also be posed during a possible appeal procedure. Finally, Section 4 examines at what stage of the proceedings it is most appropriate to refer a preliminary question and, inter alia, discusses to what extent points of fact and national law ought to be clarified before it is decided whether to make use of the preliminary procedure.

2. Determining the Relevant Criteria

2.1. The need for judicial assistance

The Court of Justice has refrained from laying down rules for when a preliminary question should be referred by courts not covered by Article 234(3) and has held that it is up to the national court itself to decide whether or not it wants to make a preliminary reference.[1] Therefore, national courts whose decisions can be appealed against have a wide measure of discretion in deciding whether a question should be referred to the Court of Justice, which is reflected in the significant differences between the numbers of preliminary references made by the courts of the different Member States.[2] Nevertheless, it is possible to identify a range of criteria which most national courts use in their assessment of whether or not to involve the Court of Justice in the resolution of the case before them.

Of these criteria the most important is probably the degree of doubt that the national court entertains in how to interpret the relevant Community rule. The more the national court is in doubt, the more reason it has, all things being equal, to refer. It is, however, not a straightforward exercise to set a general standard as to how much doubt a national court should have about the correct interpretation of Community law before it is appropriate for it to bring the matter before the Court of Justice.

From a Community law perspective, it is for each national court itself to decide this issue.[3] On this basis, some national courts have found that the procedure laid down in Article 234(2) should only be applied if the case raises really difficult and

---

[1] Case 166/73 *Rheinmühlen* [1974] ECR 33, paras 2–4.
[2] See Ch 2 above.
[3] The Court of Justice will for example not declare a preliminary question inadmissible simply because the case may also be decided solely on the basis of national law, see Ch 5, s 4.6 above.

important points of Community law and the answer of the Court of Justice, moreover, can be expected to have a conclusive effect on the outcome of the national proceedings.[4] Other national courts have chosen to refer merely because they were not completely sure about the correct interpretation of a Community rule and found it likely that the ruling would be of help for the resolution of the main proceedings.[5] In favour of the latter view it has been pointed out that only the Court of Justice has a panoramic view of the Member States and an intimate familiarity with the functioning of the Community, that the preliminary procedure furthermore has the advantage of making it possible to receive observations from the Community institutions and all Member States, and that the Court of Justice's choice between alternative submissions might not only depend on purely legal considerations, but also on policy reasons.[6]

Legal literature has also provided widely differing recommendations. While some authors argue that national courts should show restraint and in general have the requisite confidence to decide points of Community law themselves,[7] others favour a stronger involvement of the Court of Justice. In the opinion of the present authors, it would not be appropriate for national courts not sitting as courts of last instance, in general, to make use of the preliminary procedure in cases where they only have little doubt about the correct interpretation of Community law. Not only would such a liberal approach eliminate the distinction in Article 234 between appealable and non-appealable decisions, it would also ignore the fact

---

[4] Lord Denning in *HP Bulmer v J Bollinger SA* [1974] Ch 401.

[5] According to Sir Thomas Bingham MR in *R v International Stock Echange, ex p Else Ltd* [1993] QB 534; [1993] 1 All ER 420, 426, an English court should be willing to refer unless it can resolve the issue itself with complete confidence. If the court has any real doubt, it should ordinarily refer. See the broadly similar cases of *Customs and Excise Commissioners v Littlewoods Organisation plc* [2001] EWCA Civ 1542; [2001] STC 1568, paras 116–18; and *Professional Contractors' Group v Commissioners of Inland Revenue* [2001] EWCA Civ 1945, paras 90–1. See further DPJ Walsh, 'The Appeal of an Article 177 EEC Referral' (1993) Modern Law Review Vol 56, No 6, pp 881–6; C Lewis, *Judicial Remedies in Public Law* (2008) 553-4; M Hoskins, 'Discretionary References: To Refer or not to Refer' in M Hoskins et al (eds), *A True European, Essays for Judge David Edward* (2004), 345, 346; and D Anderson and M Demetriou, *References to the European Court* (2002) 130ff.

[6] J Bingham in *Customs and Excise Commissioners v Samex ApS* [1983] 3 CMLR 194, para 31.

[7] D Andersson, 'The Application of the General Principles of Community Law by the Courts of England', *Cour de cassation*, Paris Colloquium, 4–5 December 2000, cited in D Vaughan and M Gray, 'Litigating in Luxembourg' (2007) Jersey and Guernsey Law Review Vol 11, point 42. cf the so-called '2000 Due Report' from a Reflection Group set up by the Commission. With a view to reducing the length of preliminary proceedings, the Reflection Group suggested different measures to encourage national courts to apply Community law themselves. Compare the reaction from Council of Bars & Law Societies of Europe (CCBE) in this organisation's observations to the IGC. According to the CCBE, in the majority of the Member States it was practising lawyers' experience before national courts that it was already extremely difficult to obtain a preliminary reference, cf further, A Arnull, 'The Past and Future of the Preliminary Rulings Procedure' in M Andenas and J Usher (eds), *The Treaty of Nice and Beyond: Enlargement and Constitutional Reform* 345, 349.

that Community law is an integral part of national law and that it is a normal task of the national courts to decide on difficult legal questions. Indeed, the natural forum for Community law is just as much the national courts (and administrative authorities) as it is the Court of Justice. Moreover, as will be shown below in Section 2.2, the disadvantages relating to, amongst other things, time and costs connected to the preliminary ruling procedure should not be underestimated.

That being said, it would be equally unfortunate if national courts whose decisions are subject to appeal were to take the position that they should be highly reticent in making preliminary references and only do so exceptionally when they were very much in doubt about the correct interpretation of a given Community provision.[8] Rather, the proper course is an approach where the criteria concerning the relative difficulty in interpreting Community law is not applied as a stand-alone condition; instead the question of whether to refer should be made on the basis of a combined assessment of a number of factors as will be shown below. Indeed, such is also the practice of most national courts.

First, the advantages of a preliminary ruling can be limited if the case can be decided independently of Community law. For this reason it is understandable that national courts sometimes seek to decide a case solely on the basis of national law where this may properly be done in order to avoid making a preliminary reference.[9]

It might also be appropriate to take account of whether the question concerns a legal issue which can be expressed in abstract terms or whether it rather concerns a dispute about how an already well-established and fine-tuned Community law principle should be applied to a particular factual situation, the assessment of which depends heavily on a concrete evaluation of the special circumstances of the individual case. In the latter case a preliminary ruling might sometimes not cast significantly more light on the problem that the national court is facing, but merely result in the Court of Justice reiterating already well-known abstract criteria, leaving the actual application of these criteria to the referring court.[10] One such

---

[8] In practice it may be delicate for a party to the main proceedings to persuade a national court that the court is not sufficiently competent to decide the Community law aspect of a case without assistance from the Court of Justice, see likewise H Schermers and D Waelbroeck, *Judicial Protection in the European Union* (2001) 274.

[9] See in this respect Ch 6, s 3.1 above, and with regard to German courts Crowe, 'Colloquium Report, The Preliminary Reference Procedure: Reflections based on Practical Experience of the Highest National Courts in Administrative Matters' (2004) 5 ERA Forum 435, 438. What perhaps amounts to too strong an emphasis on this consideration can be found in the decision of the Irish Supreme Court in *Doyle v An Taoiseach* [1986] Irish Law Reports Monthly 693.

[10] With regard to the precision with which the Court of Justice formulates a preliminary ruling see Ch 11, s 3 below. As argued by J Pertek, *La pratique du renvoi préjudiciel de droit communautaire* (2001) 9, the distinction between interpretation and application can be quite unclear in practice and give rise to much confusion as to whether a given issue falls within the competence of the national court or may be referred for a preliminary ruling.

example would be cases regarding whether a given consumer contract must be considered 'unfair' in the sense of Directive 93/13 on unfair terms in consumer contracts. In this type of case the issue in dispute is often not the correct abstract interpretation of the Community law provision in question, but rather how the law should be applied to the facts, ie a task that first and foremost falls on the national court.[11]

In legal theory it has been argued that there can be more reason to make a reference if a case raises questions about the significance of different language versions and/or the need for a special purpose-made interpretation, as the Court of Justice is generally better placed than a national court to carry out such an examination.[12] Moreover, a national court of one Member State should be more ready to make a preliminary reference where it is faced with a question as to whether the national law of another Member State contravenes Community law. In this situation a preliminary reference will offer that other Member State the opportunity of presenting before the Court of Justice its point of view on whether its law infringes Community law.[13] Similarly, where the practice of other Member States is relevant for the correct interpretation of the applicable Community measure, a preliminary reference may often be appropriate in view of the fact that the Court of Justice may receive observations from those other States and, if necessary, itself invite those States to provide the relevant information.

Finally, in some situations it can be relevant that only the Court of Justice has the power to restrict the temporal effect of a given interpretation of a Community legal measure so that the interpretation laid down by the Court will only apply from a specific point in time. This factor might for example be conducive to making a preliminary reference in cases concerning the validity of a general tax law where the consequence of a judgment holding the tax law to be contrary to Community law can be far-reaching, unless the Court chooses to make a temporal restriction of its interpretation thereby precluding a flood of law suits for repayment of taxes already paid.[14]

---

[11] Paras 25–30 in the Opinion of Advocate General Geelhoed in Case C-237/02 *Freiburger Kommmunalbauten* [2004] ECR I-3403. See similarly with regard to the question of whether, in connection with its transfer, an undertaking has maintained its original personality and is therefore covered by the Directive on the rights of employees in connection with the transfer of undertakings D Wyatt, 'Procedures and Principles' in M Andenas (ed), *Article 177 References to the European Court—Policy and Practice* (1994) 77, 81.

[12] M Hoskins, 'Discretionary References: To Refer or not to Refer' in M Hoskins et al (eds), *A True European, Essays for Judge David Edward* (2004) 345, 347ff. This point has also been expressed in English legal practice; cf Sir Thomas Bingham, 'The National Judge's view' in M Andenas (ed), *Article 177 References to the European Court—Policy and Practice* (1994) 43, 47.

[13] D Anderson and M Demetriou, *References to the European Court* (2002) 143. For the special requirements for the formulation of the preliminary reference in such cases; see Ch 5, s 4.12 above.

[14] See Ch 12, s 5 below.

2.2. Delay and cost

The time taken to obtain a preliminary ruling must also be taken into account. Admittedly, in *Pafitis* the European Court of Human Rights ruled that this period of the overall procedure should not be included when calculating whether the parties have had access to a court within a reasonable time in accordance with Article 6 of the European Convention on Human Rights.[15] Nevertheless, the wish to provide a speedy resolution to the dispute obviously must be attributed considerable weight in many cases.

The Rules of Procedure of the Court of Justice allow for an accelerated procedure or for giving special priority to certain references. However, both avenues are only open in special cases, and in its assessment of whether to apply these special procedures the Court of Justice does not normally attach much weight to the individual interests that a party to the main proceedings may have in a speedy resolution of the case.[16] The Court also increasingly uses the possibility of deciding obvious cases either by reasoned order or by a judgment without an Advocate General giving an Opinion.[17] This means that the procedure is speeded up somewhat, but it still often takes more than a year from the reference being received by the Court of Justice until the Court rules on the preliminary question. Moreover, it is solely for the Court of Justice to decide whether to apply the above procedures and so the national court will not know in advance whether any of them will be applied in the case at hand. It is therefore very rare that preliminary questions are referred in cases concerning interim relief; to some extent this may also be due to the fact that the point of Community law may later arise when the substance of the claim is considered.[18]

Considerations of the total cost of a case due to the making of a preliminary reference can also be relevant. Indeed, although the parties to the main proceedings are not obliged to participate in the preliminary proceedings before the Court of Justice most prefer to do so.[19] However, the parties' costs of participating in a preliminary reference procedure are generally not likely to be higher than those incurred in possible appeal proceedings.

Therefore, an argument that a preliminary reference should not be made because of the costs that this may inflict on the parties may not be persuasive if a preliminary

---

[15] *Pafitis v Greece*, judgment of 26 February 1998, (Application No 20323/92), para 95; see similarly Case E-2/03 *Asgeirsson* [2003] EFTA Court Report 185, para 24.

[16] See Ch 10, s 5 below.

[17] See Ch 11, s 1 below.

[18] See, however, Case C-65/98 *Eyüp* [2000] ECRI-4747, where the Austrian *Verwaltungsgerichtshof* submitted a preliminary reference in a precautionary measure procedure; and Case C-213/89 *Factortame* [1990] ECR I-2433, where the English House of Lords made a reference concerning the interim suspension of the application of a national law.

[19] See Ch 10, s 4.4.1 below.

ruling can be expected to make an appeal superfluous.[20] The same line of argument applies if it appears likely that the dispute will in any case give rise to a preliminary ruling, so that the question is in reality only whether the reference should be made by the present court or in connection with a probable later appeal. Finally, in criminal cases considerations pertaining to costs can hardly have the same weight as in civil cases.

2.3. The wishes of the parties

The above considerations pertaining to costs and the length of proceedings make it natural to also consider the wishes of the parties to the main proceedings. Formally speaking, the preliminary procedure does not as such constitute a dispute resolution procedure; rather it is a non-contentious stage in the procedure before the national court.[21] It follows that Article 234 does not provide a judicial remedy for the parties to the main proceedings. Therefore the mere fact that one party—or even all the parties—contends that the dispute gives rise to a question concerning the interpretation of Community law which should be referred to the Court of Justice does not mean that the national court or tribunal concerned is compelled to make a preliminary reference.[22] Nor can the parties force a national court to make a preliminary reference by entering into an agreement to this effect before the dispute arises.[23] From a Community law point of view, the question of making a reference is not subject to negotiation and agreement of the parties. The right and the duty to make a reference have been vested in the national courts not only to enable them to make sure that the citizen's Community law rights are respected, but also more generally to ensure the uniform and correct application of Community law in all Member States. For the same reason, a national court may make a reference even if neither of the parties to the main proceedings has argued that the case raises questions of Community law, and even if all involved parties object to the making of such a reference.

In *Salonia*, the defendant in the main proceedings argued that the Court of Justice did not have jurisdiction to rule on the referred preliminary questions, among other things because neither the plaintiff nor the defendant had relied on

---

[20] See also C Lewis, *Judicial Remedies in Public Law* (2008) 555, with reference to the English cases *R v Dairy Produce Quotas Tribunal Ex p Hall and Sons (Dairy Farmers) Ltd* [1988] 1 CMLR 592; and *R v Pharmaceutical Society of Great Britain Ex p Association of Pharmaceutical Importers* [1987] 3 CMLR 951.

[21] Case 62/72 *Bollmann* [1973] ECR 269, para 4; and Case 5/72 *Grassi* [1972] ECR 107, para 4.

[22] Case 283/81 *CILFIT* [1982] ECR 3415, para 9. Cf also Joined Cases 31/62 and 33/62, *Milchwerke Heinz Worhmann* ECR English special edition 501; Case 101/63 *Wagner* ECR English special edition 195; Case C-344/04 *IATA* [2006] ECR I-403, para 28; and the decision of the English Court of Appeal in *R v Secretary of State for Social Services, ex p Bomore Medical Supplies Ltd* [1986] 1 CMLR 228.

[23] Case 93/78 *Mattheus* [1978] ECR 2203, para 5.

Community law in their claims. The Court of Justice rejected that argument stating that Article 234 did not imply that it was only competent to answer a preliminary question if one or more of the parties to the main proceedings had raised a question about the interpretation or validity of Community law; the Court was equally competent when such a question was raised *ex officio* by a national court that found that a decision on the question was necessary before giving judgment.[24]

In practice, however, the parties to the main proceedings play an important role in the national court's decision of whether or not to refer.[25] Often, the initiative of suggesting that a reference should be made comes from one of the parties, although national practice varies considerably in this respect. Especially in those legal systems where the role of counsel in clarifying the case is considerable, such as Great Britain, Ireland, and Denmark, references for preliminary rulings are generally made at the initiative of the parties.[26] This has even led some to argue that, in the UK at least, the reality behind the preliminary procedure is closer to a litigant–Court of Justice relationship (with the national court acting as a relay between the two) than a national court–Court of Justice dialogue as frequently proclaimed by the Court of Justice.[27]

Moreover, it is probably not very often that a national court not sitting as a court of last instance makes a reference against the wishes of both parties, unless the court suspects that the parties have a common improper interest in avoiding a clarification of the application of Community law to the case; the latter may, for example, be the case in connection with the interpretation of a contract that may be contrary to Article 81 of the EC Treaty on agreements which distort competition.

In *Ex parte Schering Chemicals Ltd*, the fact that neither party wanted a preliminary reference was a factor which the English High Court took into account in its decision not to refer.[28]

---

[24] Case 126/80 *Salonia* [1981] ECR 1563, paras 5–7; and similarly Case C-290/05 *Nádasdi* [2006] ECR I-10115, para 32. Similarly, Case C-446/98 *Fazenda Pública* [2000] ECR I-11435, paras 47–8; Joined Cases C-87/90–89/90 *Verholen* [1991] ECR I-3757, paras 11–16; and Case C-261/95 *Palmasani* [1997] ECR I-4025, para 20.

[25] For the role of the parties in the actual drafting of a preliminary reference see below Ch 8, s 1.

[26] H Kanninen, Association of the Councils of State and Supreme Administrative Jurisdiction of the European Union, 18th Colloquium 2002, General Report on the Colloquium subject 'The Preliminary Reference to the Court of Justice of the European Union', point 4.1, but see also J H H Weiler and R Dehousse, *Primus inter Pares, the European Court and National Courts: Thirty Years of Cooperation* (1992), according to which approx. 40 per cent of the preliminary cases referred to the Court of Justice were not initiated by the parties, but were referred by the national court of their own motion.

[27] D Chalmers, 'The Much Ado about Judicial Politics in the United Kingdom: A Statistical Analysis of Reported Decisions of United Kingdom Courts invoking EU Law 1973–1988', Harvard Jean Monnet Working Paper 1/00, points I and VII.

[28] *R v Secretary of State for Social Services, ex p Schering Chemicals Ltd* [1987] 1 CMLR 277, para 99.

In *Portman Agrochemicals*, Mr Justice Brooke of the English High Court noted that both parties to the case had pointed out that the delays connected to obtaining a preliminary ruling were such that the case would be moot by the time a ruling was given. Although lacking confidence in his ability to adequately resolve the issue, the High Court judge decided, in the interests of the parties and in consideration of the time and cost involved in obtaining a preliminary ruling, that he would interpret the relevant directive himself.[29]

In contrast, if both parties encourage the national court to make a preliminary reference, this may weigh as one amongst a number of factors in the national court's assessment of whether to make a reference. That being said, it would be unfortunate if a 'references by consent practice' was established;[30] even where all the parties to a dispute favour a preliminary reference, the national court should only make such a reference if it finds that it needs assistance from the Court of Justice to correctly decide the case. The national court should also be alert to cases where a party's request for a reference is a delaying tactic.[31] It has been suggested that a request for a preliminary ruling should be more readily accepted where the party seeking the reference will be the one to suffer the adverse effects of delay.[32] Conversely, reticence in referring might sometimes be more proper in cases where the party which, in the preliminary view of the national court, will be most likely to bear the costs of litigation, is opposed to making a reference to the Court of Justice.

Not all national courts fully subscribe to the above characterisation of the preliminary procedure as a non-contentious cooperation between courts not entailing rights for the parties to the main dispute.

It is also arguable that the pronouncements of the European Court of Human Rights, that in special cases a decision not to refer may raise problems in relation to Article 6 of the European Convention on Human Rights, build on an understanding of the preliminary procedure which differs from the one formulated by the Court of Justice.[33]

---

[29] *R v Ministry of Agriculture, Fisheries and Food, ex p Portman Agrochemicals Ltd* [1994] 3 CMLR 18, paras 20–1. According to a Report of 4 June 2008 of the European Parliament's Committee on Legal Affairs (A6-0224/2008, p 25), many judges refrain from using the preliminary procedure because of the delay involved.

[30] *Portsmouth City Council v Richards & Quietlynn* [1989] 1 CMLR 673 para 111.

[31] The decision by the Chancery Division of the English High Court in *Wychavon District Council v Midland Enterprises (Special Event) Ltd* [1988] 1 CMLR 397, where the High Court refused to make a preliminary reference, inter alia, because it was believed that the defendants' real concern was to obtain a two-year delay before it was finally concluded that they had acted criminally.

[32] R Gordon, *EC Law in Judicial Review* (2007) 127, with reference to *Generics UK Ltd v Smithkline and French Laboratories Ltd* [1990] 1 CMLR 416, 435.

[33] See Ch 6, s 5.5 above.

Arguments that a party to the main proceedings has a right to have the Court of Justice involved in the resolution of the dispute through a preliminary reference have for good reasons tended to be put forward where arguably the national court has been under a duty to make a reference because it has been sitting as a court of last instance within the meaning of Article 234(3). A Spanish ruling, however, seems to build on the view—which in our opinion is not so convincing—that the right to a fair hearing in itself may require that national courts obtain a preliminary ruling from the Court of Justice before they take a decision that adversely affects the parties arguing in favour of such a reference.

In *Real Club Náutico de Gran Canaria*, a Spanish court decided that a tax provision concerning the Canary Islands was inapplicable since, according to that court, the provision in question was identical to another Spanish provision that the Court of Justice had already declared contrary to Community law. The Spanish court reached its decision without first making a preliminary reference. The government of the Canary Islands appealed the decision to the Spanish Constitutional Court (Tribunal Constitucional) arguing that it had been deprived of the right to effective judicial protection as ensured by the Spanish Constitution. The Constitutional Court agreed with that claim noting that it could not concur with the lower Spanish court that the precedent from the Court of Justice was relevant for the case at hand.[34]

According to some political scientists, preliminary references are more likely to occur if a court doubts whether the parties will comply with its decision.[35] In our opinion, such speculations are far from realistic. Of course it sometimes happens that national courts in cases concerning a politically or economically important piece of national legislation choose to make a preliminary reference even if they feel fairly confident that the national law is contrary to Community law. It might indeed be convenient for a national court to obtain the backing of the Court of Justice before striking down this kind of national legislation. Nevertheless, in this situation a preliminary reference is not so much made out of the national court's fear of non-compliance with its own judgment; rather it seems more likely that the reference is made because the national court only wishes to take such a draconian step after having obtained the confirmation of the Court of Justice that it is indeed an appropriate one to take.

---

[34] Judgment of 19 June 2006 from the *Tribunal Constitucional, Sala Segunda*, nº 194/2006, *Gobierno de Canarias v Real Club Náutico de Gran Canaria*, BOE, nº 172, suplemento de 20/07/2006. See further in s 2.5 below concerning situations where a similar issue is already pending before the Court of Justice.

[35] S Nyikos, *The European Court of Justice and National Courts: Strategic Interaction within the EU Judicial Process* (2001) 8.

2.4. The wish not to overload the Court of Justice

It is sometimes argued that when deciding whether or not to make a preliminary reference the national court should also take account of more abstract and general considerations pertaining to the functioning and development of Community law.[36] Indeed, if all national courts made preliminary references without showing any kind of self-restraint, this would not only mean that the processing time for each case would become unacceptably long, it would also overwhelm the Court of Justice with cases to such an extent that it would be unable to fulfil its functions effectively. In particular, the English courts have referred to this consideration in support of showing restraint with regard to preliminary references.[37]

Following the same line of reasoning it has also been suggested that a national court should be more ready to refer if it finds the issue in question to be one of principle and/or of wide-ranging practical importance. Conversely, a national court should be less inclined to make a preliminary reference if the question relates to a problem which is unlikely to arise outside the specific circumstances of the case and has no real bearing on the unity, coherence, and development of Community law.[38]

Obviously, a well functioning system for preliminary rulings is of considerable importance. Moreover, it can hardly be denied that the number of references has an influence on the speed and quality of the Court's work. However, it is not obvious that national courts should have particular regard to the issue of how 'interesting' the case is from a Community perspective when deciding whether to make a preliminary reference. Rather, the main focus of the national courts must be upon the cases that are before them. Viewed from this perspective the likelihood that a clarification of a given question is unlikely to contribute to the general development of Community law may carry only limited weight.[39] In addition, it might not

---

[36] See most notably Advocate General Jacobs in his Opinion in Case C-338/95 *Wiener* [1997] ECR I-6495, paras 20–1.

[37] This approach was set forth by Lord Denning as early as in the case of *HP Bulmer v J Bollinger SA* [1974] Ch 401. See further *Customs and Excise Commissioners v BAA plc* [2002] EWCA Civ 1814; [2003] STC, paras 47–8; *Centralan Property Ltd v Customs and Excise Commissioners* [2003] EWHC 44 (Ch), paras 17–22; and *R v IRC Professional Contractors' Group* [2002] 1 CMLR 46.

[38] L Sevón, 'How should I make a Reference? The National Judge and Preliminary Rulings' in M Levin et al (eds), *Festskrift till Ulf Bernitz* (2001) 209, 214; and M Hoskins, 'Discretionary References: To Refer or not to Refer' in M Hoskins et al (eds), *A True European, Essays for Judge David Edward* (2004) 345, 347. In *R v Pharmaceutical Society of Great Britain, ex p Association of Pharmaceutical Importers* [1987] 3 CMLR 951, the referring English court put emphasis on the question having significant practical importance for the Community in general. Similarly, in *R v Secretary of State for Trade and Industry, ex p Trade Union Congress* [2001] 1 CMLR 5, the English Divisional Court decided to refer, inter alia, because the point in question also affected other Member States.

[39] See similarly G Vandersanden, 'La procédure préjudicielle: À la recherche d'une identité perdue' in M Dony (ed), *Mélanges en hommage à Michel Waelbroeck, vol I* (1999) 619, 636. See also the

always be easy for a national court to assess the Community-wide significance of the problem that it is facing.

2.5. Similar cases are pending

If an identical or corresponding question is already pending before the Court of Justice, the need for a reference will normally be less obvious. Indeed, in cases where a national court has already submitted a question on the same matter, it is quite common for other national courts not to submit a new question, but merely to postpone consideration of the case while waiting for the Court of Justice to render its preliminary ruling.[40] The same consideration applies when the Commission has brought infringement proceedings under Article 226 of the EC Treaty before the Court of Justice regarding the same matter as the one before the national court (Footnote 40 bis) or where the national court itself has already referred a preliminary question in another case and now faces a similar issue in the new proceedings.

There will, however, be grounds for making an additional reference if there is doubt as to whether the Court of Justice's ruling in the already pending case will also be useful as an answer in the case where a reference is being contemplated. Otherwise there is a risk that a reference may be necessary at a later stage, leading to further delays. It is therefore, for example, not advisable to refrain from making a preliminary reference in cases where it is unclear whether any difference in the factual context of the cases in question will be relevant for the interpretation of Community law. The same applies where it is doubtful whether the preliminary question already referred will be answered, for example because the referring court has only posed the question for the eventuality that the Court of Justice will answer another question in a particular way.

In *Greenpeace*, the Dutch *Raad van State* had to decide whether to refer a preliminary question in a case concerning a permit for small-scale field trials using genetically modified strains of maize in three municipalities. In hearing the dispute the *Raad van State* took cognisance of a pending order for reference made by the French *Conseil d'État* asking the Court of Justice for an interpretation of the Directive which also found application in the Dutch case.[41] The *Raad van State*, however, decided to refer its own questions, inter alia, because the preliminary questions in the French case related to the French administrative organisation of

---

discussion in H Schermers et al, *Article 177: Experiences and Problems* (1987) 14 and 67; and R Gordon, *EC Law in Judicial Review* (2007) 127.

[40] Compare C Lewis, *Judicial Remedies in Public Law* (2008) 557, according to which English courts have not been dissuaded from making a reference because similar issues are already before the Court of Justice. See also Ch 5, s 6.

[41] Case C-552/07 *Azelvandre* (ECJ 15 February 2009).

départements and *cantons*. In the opinion of the *Raad van State* an answer from the Court of Justice based on these territory descriptions would not necessarily be directly relevant to the Dutch situation. Subsequently, after having received the judgment in the French case, the *Raad van State* withdrew its reference.[42]

In November 1978, a Danish High Court decided to suspend the procedure in a case between a private plaintiff and the Danish tax authorities because the Commission had brought infringement proceedings before the Court of Justice against Denmark on the same legal matter. The private plaintiff appealed the decision to the Danish Supreme Court which ruled that if the High Court were to put preliminary questions to the Court of Justice it should do this at a sufficiently early stage for the Court of Justice to take these questions into account vis-à-vis the infringement proceedings. The Supreme Court therefore rescinded the decision to suspend the procedure.[43]

In *Friends of the Irish Environment Limited,* the issue was whether a provision in the Irish Planning and Development Act was compatible with Directive 85/337 on environmental impact assessment. The Irish High Court decided to stay the proceedings, but without making a preliminary reference. The High Court justified this decision by referring to the fact that the Commission had issued a reasoned opinion in which it claimed that the Irish provision in question did not respect the directive. In the opinion of the High Court this made it more appropriate to stay the proceedings than to make a reference, as the time it would take for the Court of Justice to issue a preliminary ruling would not be less than the time it would take to rule on a possible infringement action. Moreover, in the opinion of the High Court, the Irish State should be given the opportunity of complying with its obligations before the issue was brought before the Court of Justice.[44]

In our opinion, the reasoning in *Friends of the Irish Environment Limited* is open to criticism for the mere fact that it is by no means certain that a reasoned opinion will lead to infringement proceedings before the Court of Justice. Moreover, even if the Irish High Court had made a preliminary reference this would not in itself preclude the Irish State from amending the provision in dispute before the Court of Justice would be able to render a ruling.

---

[42] Joined Cases C-359/08–361/08 *Stichting Greenpeace Nederland,* removed from the Court's register by order of 2 April 2009. For another example of simultaneous references of more or less identical questions see Case C-203/08 *Betfair* (pending) and Case C-258/08 *Ladbrokes Betting and Gaming* (pending) where the Dutch *Raad van State* and *Hoge Raad* respectively decided to refer questions concerning the legality of the Dutch legislation on exclusive gambling rights.

[43] *Hans Just v Ministeriet for Skatter og Afgifter,* UfR 1979 p 117.

[44] High Court, 15 April 2005, *Friends of the Irish Environment Limited, Tony Lowes v Minister for the Environment, Heritage and Local Government, Ireland, Attorney General, Galway County Council* [2005] IEHC 123.

When choosing between making one or more simultaneous references where a cluster of broadly identical cases are pending before the same national court, it will often be natural from the point of view of efficiency for both the national court and the Court of Justice that the questions be pooled as much as possible. However, the national court should take account of the fact that although the Court of Justice accepts test cases, it will only answer a preliminary question if a ruling on the referred question is relevant for deciding the particular national proceeding in which the question was referred. It is thus not enough that an answer to the question will be important for other cases pending before the same court, and this is so even if an answer to the preliminary question would make further references unnecessary.[45]

In the Netherlands the conservation measures under the Community's common fisheries policy were enforced under criminal law. A lower Dutch court made a preliminary reference in *Romkes* regarding the validity of certain Community regulations on fishing quotas. At the same time several other similar Dutch cases relating to the same fishing quotas were also pending, but it was considered unnecessary to make requests for a preliminary ruling in these other cases as the *Romkes* case embodied the interests of all Dutch fishermen.[46]

In *Oliehandel Koeweit*, the Dutch *Raad van State* posed broadly similar questions in five different, but simultaneous, cases in order to present the Court of Justice with a clear picture of the different situations in which the relevant Community law question arose.[47]

In *Metock*, the parties to a number of different proceedings before the Irish High Court were third-country nationals married to non-Irish Union citizens. For the purpose of making a preliminary reference to the Court of Justice, the Irish court pooled all cases and stated the origins of each couple and how long they had been married. Thereupon the High Court distilled three questions from the totality of the immigration cases and incorporated them into the single order for reference.[48]

Finally, the national court might take into account the wish of the parties to be put in a position whereby they can present observations directly before the Court of Justice. Indeed, they will only be able to do so if a reference is made in the very dispute that they are participating in, but not if the national court stays the

---

[45] See Ch 5, s 4.1 above.
[46] Case 46/86 *Romkes* [1987] ECR 2671.
[47] Joined Cases C-307/00–311/00 *Oliehandel Koeweit* [2003] ECR I-1821.
[48] Case C-127/08 *Metock* [2008] ECR I-6241. For another example, see Case C-459/9 *Mrax* [2002] ECR I-6591.

proceedings in order to await the ruling in another case, be that a case before the same national court or a case before another court. [49]

In *ABNA*, the French *Conseil d'État* had found it unnecessary to refer a preliminary question to the Court of Justice because the same issue had been raised in a pending reference from a UK court. One of the parties to the French case thereupon asked the Court of Justice for permission to submit observations in the English case arguing that otherwise it would be deprived of its rights of defence as the outcome of the English reference was expected to also determine the outcome of the case before the French court. The Court of Justice refused to allow the observations to be submitted. The argument pertaining to rights of defence should have been made before the *Conseil d'État* as it was for the national courts to consider whether such considerations should lead them to pose preliminary questions even if the Court of Justice was expected to rule on the matter because of an already pending case raising the same issue. [50]

In *Tum and Dari*, the English House of Lords referred questions for a preliminary ruling to the Court of Justice concerning the Additional Protocol to the Association Agreement between Turkey and the EC. [51] Subsequently, a similar question arose in a dispute that came before the Dutch *Raad van State* in *Günes*. The Dutch *Raad van State* was aware of the reference in *Tum and Dari,* but nevertheless chose to make a preliminary reference thereby also giving the parties in the Dutch case the opportunity to submit written observations to the Court of Justice. In its preliminary reference the *Raad van State* referred to the UK case and stated that it was possible that the outcome of the UK case would be relevant to the questions put in the Dutch case. Having received the judgment in the UK case, the *Raad van State* requested the parties in *Günes* to present observations on whether there was reason to pursue the preliminary reference. Having obtained these observations it concluded that there were no such reasons and withdrew the reference. [52]

In *Nationaal Overlegorgaan Sociale Werkvoorziening and others*, several cases relating to the same substantive matter came before the Dutch *Raad van State*. Once the *Raad van State*, in a meeting attended by the various trial chambers, had decided that a reference for a preliminary ruling ought to be made, the question arose as to whether the reference should relate to one or more of the cases. Whilst the three cases were partly identical each case also had its own specific elements, and the parties differed for each case. The *Raad van State* decided to make simultaneous requests for a preliminary ruling in all three cases, primarily in order to

---

[49] See Ch 10, s 3.1 below.
[50] Case C-453/03 *ABNA* (ECJ 30 March 2004).
[51] Case C-16/05 *Tum and Dari* [2007] ECR I-7415.
[52] Case C-296/05 *Günes*, removed from the Court's register on 21 November 2007.

ensure that all parties could submit written observations to the Court of Justice. At the Court of Justice, the three cases were joined for the purposes of the oral and written part of the procedure.[53]

Indeed, not all national legal orders allow for a stay of proceedings in order to await a preliminary ruling from the Court of Justice.

In *Caribo*, the outcome of the case pending before the Tribunale di Bologna turned on the interpretation of provisions of Community law on which the Court of Justice had already been asked to give a preliminary ruling. The Italian court therefore ordered a stay of proceedings. That order was appealed to the Corte di cassazione which annulled it. According to the Corte di cassazione, where an Italian court not being a court of last instance considers that the outcome of a case before it depends on a question of interpretation of Community law, that court must either refer a preliminary question to the Court of Justice or itself answer the question. In contrast, such a court is not entitled to stay proceedings while waiting for the Court of Justice to deliver judgment on a preliminary question made by another court as such a step would deprive the parties to the case of the opportunity of participating in the procedure before the Court of Justice and thereby of their constitutional right to a contradictory process.[54]

3. From which Court should a Reference be Made?

In the following section we will discuss whether a national court which has discretion as to whether to make a reference ought to take account of whether a preliminary reference may be made in the course of a possible appeal.

It is sometimes suggested that in general courts not sitting as courts of last instance ought to show reticence with regard to making references. The argument is that the damaging effects of inconsistent interpretation of Community rules in their rulings are less significant than rulings by courts of last instance. Therefore, considerations which normally disfavour a reference should be given greater weight.

---

[53] Joined Cases C-383/06–385/06 *Nationaal Overlegorgaan Sociale Werkvoorziening and others* [2008] ECR I-1561.

[54] Ruling of 14 September 1999 by the Corte di cassazione, Sezione II civile, No 9813, *Caribo v Ministero delle Finanze*, Il massimario del Foro italiano. 1999, col 1030. The case is summarised in the European Commission's 2000 survey of the application of Community law by national courts, [2001] OJ C30/192 at pp 195–6. Compare the more recent ruling of 21 June 2006 in *INIS v Maragon*, No 14411, where the Italian court came to the opposite conclusion in a case concerning repayment of illegal State aid. See also, broadly similar to the first decision of the Italian Corte di cassazione, the ruling by the Austrian *Oberster Gerichtshof* of 14 January 1997, 4 Ob 2386/96b and 4 Ob 2391/96p. Compare M Jarvis, *The Application of EC Law by National Courts* (1998) 429, who argues that such repeat references are an unnecessary waste of resources that can be avoided by better coordination within the national judicial system.

While it is correct that the risk that a decision of a lower court will create an unwarranted precedent is less than if the decision is rendered by a court of last instance, it may be questioned whether the argument takes sufficient account of the parties' legitimate interests in obtaining a correct decision.[55] Rather, the correct approach must be to identify the concrete circumstances in the specific case speaking for and against a lower court making a reference.

In *Glaxo Group Ltd*, the English High Court had considered it necessary to refer a series of questions to the Court of Justice for a preliminary ruling.[56] The decision to refer was then brought before the Court of Appeal. The Court of Appeal rejected the appeal, stating that the High Court was right to consider that the questions arising in the case before it were not clear and that the matter should be referred to the Court of Justice. It added that the High Court enjoyed discretion as to whether preliminary questions should be referred to the Court of Justice or whether the matter of a reference should be deferred to an appeal court. The Court of Appeal declared that it would not interfere with the High Court's exercise of its discretion unless the High Court had either failed to take into account a matter which it should have done, or had wrongly taken into account matters which it should not have done or was clearly wrong.[57]

Especially where the relevance and formulation of the question depends to a large degree on disputed facts which may only be finally settled on appeal it might be appropriate not to refer and instead leave it to the appeal court to determine whether a reference is desirable.[58] Otherwise, one runs the risk that a new reference will have to be made during the appeal procedure if the appeal court takes a different view on the facts.

In contrast, where it is clear that the answer to an easily definable question of Community law is decisive for the resolution of the dispute in the main proceedings, considerations of procedural efficiency will generally favour a reference being made by the first instance court. This may be the case, for example, where the dispute concerns the correct implementation of Community law in national law. The same applies when it appears likely that the clarification of the Community law aspects of a case might obviate the need for comprehensive and unnecessary presentation of evidence.

---

[55] D Anderson and M Demetriou, *References to the European Court* (2002) 154.

[56] High Court of Justice (England and Wales), Chancery Division, Patents Court, 28 February 2000, *Glaxo Group Ltd and Others v Dowelhurst Ltd and Swingwad Ltd* [2000] 2 CMLR 571–652. The case referred was Case C-143/00 *Boehringer Ingelheim and others* [2002] ECR I-3759.

[57] Court of Appeal (England and Wales) Civil Division, 29 March 2000, *Glaxo Group Ltd and Others v Dowelhurst Ltd and Swingward Ltd* [2000] Eu LR 660. See with regard to appeals of references Ch 9, s 2 below.

[58] H Schermers and J S Watson, 'Report of the Conference' in H Schermers et al (eds), *Article 177: Experiences and Problems* (1987) 4ff; and P Lasok et al, *Judicial Control in the EU* (2008) 172.

Finally, there can be situations where one or more of the parties to the main proceedings is so intent on obtaining a ruling from the Court of Justice that for this reason alone they will engineer a preliminary reference through an appeal to a court of last instance which will be obliged to make a reference, unless one of the exceptions to the obligation of such a court to make a reference applies.[59] In the view of the present authors, however, it is questionable whether a lower court should give weight to this consideration.

4. At what Stage in the Main Proceedings should a Reference be Made?

Under Community law it is up to the national court to decide at what stage of the proceedings it wishes to make a preliminary reference. This applies even if the timing of the preliminary reference may mean that the defendant in the main proceedings is deprived of the possibility of responding before the reference is formulated and dispatched to the Court of Justice.[60]

In *Corsica Ferries*, the preliminary question was raised in an *ex parte* summary procedure where an adversarial procedure would only take place if the decision was appealed by the party against whom judgment was given. The Court of Justice held that Article 234 does not make the reference to the Court subject to there having been an *inter partes* hearing in the proceedings in the course of which the national court refers the questions for a preliminary ruling. Nor could the reference be declared inadmissible by reason of the fact that it was impossible for the referring court to obtain any evidence other than the written evidence produced by the applicant. On the other hand, these characteristics of the national procedure could not justify a relaxation of the general requirement that the national court gives the Court a detailed account of the factual and legal context in which the question has arisen. In the case at hand the description of the factual and legal context did indeed appear inadequate in some respects. The Court was therefore prevented from replying with the desired precision to certain of the questions

---

[59] See Ch 6, s 3 above.

[60] Joined Cases 36/80–71/80 *Irish Creamery Milk Suppliers Association* [1981] ECR 735, paras 6–8; Case 72/83 *Campus Oil* [1984] ECR 2727, paras 9–11; Case 14/86 *Pretore di Salò* [1987] ECR 2545, para 11; Case C-348/89 *Mecanarte* [1991] ECR I-3277, para 48; Case C-60/02 *X* [2004] ECR I-651, paras 23–9; and Case C-470/03 *AGM-COS.MET* [2007] ECR I-2749, paras 41–7. In Case 199/82 *San Giorgio* [1983] ECR 3595, paras 7–9, the Italian government argued in vain that the question should be rejected, since the reference had been made at the introductory stage of the proceedings solely by the president of the referring court in spite of the fact that under Italian law the final judgment was to be given by the full court.

raised and had no other choice but to hand down a ruling where it left open certain aspects of the questions raised.[61]

In *Høj Pedersen*, it was argued before the Court of Justice that for the purposes of one of the preliminary questions the referring national court had not clarified whether the facts of the case were such as it had assumed before making the reference. In response, the Court of Justice held that the need to provide an interpretation of Community law which is helpful to the national court makes it essential to define the legal context in which the interpretation requested should be placed. Therefore, depending on the circumstances, it could be an advantage if the facts of the case were established and if questions of purely national law were settled before the preliminary reference was made. However, the Court also held that these observations did not limit the discretion of the national court as it is this court that is best placed to judge at what stage of the proceedings it needs a preliminary ruling.[62]

As emphasised in both *Corsica Ferries* and *Høj Pedersen*, the Court of Justice will often only be able to give an interpretation of Community law which can be useful to the national court if the preliminary reference presents in sufficient detail the factual and legal context which forms the background to the referred question. Depending on the circumstances, it can, however, be difficult for the national court to identify the exact question of law that gives rise to doubt before the facts have been established. Similarly, so long as the facts have not been duly established, the national law context in which the Community law issue arises may remain unclear. Hence, the national court may find itself in a position where it can neither assess whether a preliminary ruling is really necessary nor be able to formulate the preliminary reference with the requisite clarity. Thus, it is generally recommended that a national court refrains from formulating and referring questions before it has established with sufficient clarity the factual and national law elements of the case.[63]

---

[61] Case C-266/96 *Corsica Ferries France* [1998] ECR I-3949, paras 21–8. See also Case 52/76 *Benedetti* [1977] ECR 163, para 10.

[62] Case C-66/96 *Høj Pedersen* [1998] ECR I-7327, paras 43–6.

[63] Joined Cases 36/80–71/80 *Irish Creamery Milk Suppliers Association* [1981] ECR 735, para 6; Case C-343/90 *Lourenco Dias* [1992] ECR I-4673, para 19; and O Due, 'Danish Preliminary References' in D O'Keeffe and A Bavasso (eds), *Judicial Review in European Union Law* (2001) 363, 374. See also, with special regard to criminal cases, the statement of the English House of Lords in *Henn and Darby* [1980] 2 CMLR 229, 232–3 according to which in a criminal trial upon indictment it will seldom be a proper exercise of judgment to seek a preliminary ruling before the facts of the alleged offence have been ascertained. With reference to *South Pembrokeshire District Council v Wendy Fair Makerts Ltd* [1994] 1 CMLR 213, 223–4, R Gordon, *EC Law in Judicial Review* (2007) 110, similarly argues that in English judicial review challenges it will rarely be appropriate for a reference to be made at, or prior to, the permission stage of an application for judicial review. Compare the ruling of 9 November 2006 *Attridge Law and another v Coleman* [2007] 2 CMLR 24. For further

In *JämO*, the national court referred a number of preliminary questions with a view to clarifying whether differences in the payment of two groups of employees could constitute unlawful sex discrimination on the basis of different pay for work of equal value. The questions were referred before the national court had considered whether the work of the two groups in fact had the same value, as this would require extensive research associated with major costs. The Court of Justice found that it was in possession of the information necessary to enable it to give a ruling on the questions referred. It added, however, that the referring court's description of the factual and legal context appeared to be incomplete. In various respects it was therefore unable to reply to the questions raised with the precision that it would have wished to.[64]

In the *Bundesverwaltungsgericht's* judgment of 28 January 1997, the question arose as to the stage in national proceedings at which a preliminary question should be referred. On an appeal from a judgment of the Hamburg *Oberverwaltungsgericht* ordering the expulsion of a Turkish national, the *Bundesverwaltungsgericht* held that German law warranted expulsion as a general preventive measure in the case at hand. However, the *Bundesverwaltungsgericht* went on to consider whether Decision No 1/80 of the EEC–Turkey Association Council militated against expulsion as a general preventive measure. It found that it could not answer that question without an interpretation of the decision from the Court of Justice. Since, however, a reference should only be made if the preliminary ruling would be relevant to the national court's decision, and since it had not been shown that the applicant was active on the normal labour market as required for Decision 1/80 to apply to him, the Court annulled the judgment of the *Oberverwaltungsgericht* and referred the case back to it for retrial and further examination of the facts, possibly involving a reference to the Court if Justice.[65]

Even though it is generally recommended only to make a preliminary reference after the facts of the case have been established, there are nevertheless a few situations in which it may be appropriate to make a reference before all aspects of the facts have been established. Occasionally, the answer given by the Court of Justice to questions of interpretation raised in a reference is decisive in establishing which facts are relevant for the adjudication of the case in the main proceedings. In such situations, grounds of procedural efficiency speak in favour of deferring taking evidence until its significance for the decision of the case has become clear.

---

references to English case law on the matter, see H Schermers and D Waelbroeck, *Judicial Protection in the European Union* (2000) 276.

[64] Case C-236/98 *JämO* [2000] ECR I-2189, paras 30–4.

[65] Judgment of the *Bundesverwaltungsgericht* of 28 January 1997, 1 C17/94 [1997] Neue Zeitschrift für Verwaltungsrecht, 10. Jahrgang, 1119 and [1998] OJ C257/170.

And indeed, the Court of Justice accepts that a national court refers questions that are based on a non-verified assumption that Community law is applicable.[66]

In *Enderby*, the English Court of Appeal referred a question as to how far an employer had a duty to give objective reasons for why a particular occupation which was primarily carried on by men was better paid than another occupation which was primarily carried on by women. Before the Court of Justice the German government argued that the question could not be answered before it had been decided whether the two occupations should be regarded as comparable as was required for the Equal Pay Directive to apply. In the view of the government this was not the case and it was therefore irrelevant whether or not the differences in pay could be objectively justified. The Court of Justice rejected this argument, noting that the Court of Appeal had decided to deal with the question of whether the differences in pay were objectively justified before deciding whether the occupations in question were of equal value, since this could necessitate a more detailed examination of the evidence. The preliminary questions had thus been referred on the assumption that the occupations in question were of equivalent value. The questions were clearly not unconnected with the dispute in the main proceedings, and the Court of Justice could therefore answer them without itself deciding on the validity of an assumption which was a matter for the national court to decide subsequently, if this were shown to be necessary.[67]

Moreover, in special situations it might not only be that an early reference makes it possible to avoid unnecessary disputes about the facts; it might even be that the Community law aspects are so unclear that the national court has difficulty in determining what facts are relevant before the Court of Justice's preliminary ruling has established the legal context in which the facts are to be considered.[68]

In *Schmidberger*, an Austrian court had referred several preliminary questions to the Court of Justice about whether a Member State was liable to pay compensation for failure to take measures against a manifestation that blocked a public road. The question presumed that damage had been suffered although this had not been proved before the referring court. The Austrian government therefore argued that the questions were hypothetical and that, in any case, they had been referred at too early a stage in the proceedings, since it had not yet been shown

---

[66] Case C-350/03 *Schulte* [2005] ECR I-9215, paras 41–5; and the Opinion of Advocate General Lenz in Case C-324/93 *Evans Medical* [1995] ECR I-563, paras 22–3. See also paras 34–8 in the Opinion of Advocate General Jacobs in Case C-39/94 *SFEI* [1996] ECR I-3547; and Ch 5, s 4.3 above, and Ch 8, s 3.2.3 below.

[67] Case C-127/92 *Enderby* [1993] ECR I-5535, paras 11–12. See also Case C-303/06 *Coleman* [2008] ECR I-5603, paras 28–32, and *Thetford Corporation v Fiamma Spa* [1987] 3 CMLR 266.

[68] F Jacobs, 'When to Refer to the European Court' (1974) 90 The Law Quarterly Review 486, 490ff.

with sufficient certainty what facts were relevant to the decision on the dispute. The Court of Justice declared the reference admissible. Not only did it follow from the Court's established case law that it is up to the national court to decide at which stage in the proceedings it is appropriate to make a preliminary reference. In the actual case the referring court had, moreover, convincingly explained why the dispute could only be decided if the Court of Justice answered the questions. Among other things this concerned the circumstances which should be taken into account in connection with presenting evidence of the damage that the plaintiff claimed to have suffered. Hence, it was not unreasonable for the referring court to seek an answer on what type of damage could be taken into account in the event of a breach of Community law before pronouncing itself on the evidence required in the actual case.[69]

Finally, it might be appropriate to make the reference at an early stage of the national proceedings in order not to delay the case unnecessarily in situations where the facts are agreed and a decision on a point of Community law is unavoidable.

In *R (ABNA Ltd)*, it was found appropriate to pose preliminary questions at an early stage of the procedure as the issue in dispute was the validity of secondary Community law and the specific facts of the case were believed to be of less importance for the resolution of that issue.[70]

It would be unfortunate if a national court were required to reopen a case which has already been set for judgment with a view to making a preliminary reference to the Court of Justice. It is therefore advisable for the parties to raise the question of a reference before the national court as early as possible. Similarly, if the national court during its own preparation of the case becomes uncertain about the application of possibly relevant Community rules, it will often be appropriate for it to invite the parties to make submissions about the Community law aspects of the case and the need for a preliminary reference.

---

[69] Case C-112/00 *Schmidberger* [2003] ECR I-5659, paras 29 and 39–40.
[70] *R (ABNA Ltd) v Secretary of State for Health and Foods Standards Agency* [2004] 2 CMLR 39.

8

THE FORM AND CONTENT
OF A REFERENCE

1. Introduction

An order for reference to the Court of Justice must obviously be formulated in such a way as to be in accordance with Article 234 of the EC Treaty. The questions asked must, in other words, fall within the jurisdiction of the Court of Justice. Therefore, they may not (directly) concern the actual application of Community law to the case in question, nor may they invite the Court of Justice to perform an evaluation of the facts in the main proceedings, nor may they relate to the interpretation or validity of national law.

Apart from this, the procedure for preliminary references is relatively unregulated. In order for the preliminary reference process to work effectively, the Court of Justice has, however, gradually laid down a number of requirements for how a reference should be formulated. This chapter identifies these requirements and makes recommendations as to how a reference should be framed. However, a few remarks may first be beneficial regarding the respective roles of the referring court and the parties to the main proceedings.

Under Community law a national court that contemplates making a preliminary reference is not required to consult the parties to the proceedings on the questions that it considers referring. On the other hand, Community law does not deny the parties any influence over the design of a reference; on the contrary, while emphasising the discretion of the national court, the Court of Justice has itself emphasised the usefulness of hearing the parties.[1]

National practice varies with regard to the role played by the parties in preparing a preliminary question. Whilst eg the Austrian Administrative Court, the Supreme Court of Belgium, the German Federal Administrative Courts, the French Council of State, and the Supreme Court of Spain all draft a preliminary reference without much involvement of the parties, the parties play an important role in this respect in for example Ireland, the United Kingdom, and Denmark. Indeed, this may go so far that the role of the national court primarily is to confirm an agreement by the parties. Thus, in these Member States it is often left to the parties to draw up a draft for the order for reference, including a description of the facts, and not just for the actual questions to be referred.[2]

Whilst the latter approach has practical advantages, experience has shown that it may also lead to an exaggeration of the complexity of the legal problems and to an inflation of the number of questions, including questions which may prove to be neither particularly important for the resolution of the case nor especially difficult to answer for the referring court. Moreover, the parties are not—and cannot be expected to be—objective vis-à-vis the case and this is likely to affect both the formulation of the questions and the presentation of the facts. Therefore, where a national court leaves it to the parties to make a draft for the reference it is important that the court retains firm control over the reference so that the parties' influence does not become excessive; otherwise there will be a risk that the reference will reflect too much the claims of the parties and be less concise and suitable for obtaining a preliminary ruling.[3]

In any event, it is recommended that the national court consults the parties on the proposed questions before submitting the reference to the Court of Justice. Such involvement may not only forestall complications after the Court of Justice has handed down its judgment; it may also help the national court improve the preliminary reference, for instance by correcting or supplementing the facts given therein or by enabling the court to make the questions more to the point. Indeed, it may

---

[1] See above Ch 7, s 4.

[2] H Kanninen, Association of the Councils of State and Supreme Administrative Jurisdiction of the European Union, 18th Colloquium 2002, General Report on the Colloquium subject 'The Preliminary Reference to the Court of Justice of the European Communities', 29.

[3] Criticism of the lenient practice of some national courts in allowing the parties too much influence on the drafting of the reference has been aired, inter alia, by former President of the Court of Justice, Ole Due, cf O Due, 'Danish Preliminary References' in D O'Keeffe and A Bavasso (eds), *Judicial Review in European Union Law* (2001) 363, 374. See also D Anderson and M Demetriou, *References to the European Court* (2002) 199ff, with further references. The problem is also discussed by H Schermers and JS Watson, 'Report of the Conference' in H Schermers et al (eds), *Article 177: Experiences and Problems* (1987) 12.

even be that following such consultation with the parties the national court finds that a reference is not necessary and instead decides the questions itself.

2. The Form of the Reference

It is not a formal requirement that a preliminary question is explicitly formulated as such, as long as it is clear from the reasons given in the order for reference what issues are raised.[4] Nevertheless it is unquestionably an advantage if the reference is built up around one or more questions. The formulation of an actual question makes it easier for the Court of Justice to identify the issues in doubt which the national court seeks help in resolving. In addition, upon receipt of the reference, a brief statement is published for information purposes in the Official Journal of the European Union, series C. This information normally takes the form of stating the questions asked.

Community law does not contain any special rules on the procedure by which national courts must decide on making a reference for a preliminary ruling; this is a matter for national law.[5] Thus, for instance, where a reference is made by a collegial court, Community law does not regulate whether the questions must be formulated and approved by all the judges, or whether, for example, the presiding judge or a delegated judge can be authorised to draw up and refer the questions.[6] Nor does Community law bind national courts with regard to whether the reference is made by a decision, an order, or a judgment.[7] In this respect national practice varies although the most common form in which a submission for a preliminary reference is made is as a regular decision or an interim decision of a normally constituted session of the referring court.[8] Indeed, Community law does not preclude a preliminary reference being made as part of a final judgment with respect to matters not covered by the reference for a preliminary ruling; however, the desirability of having a reference that is to the point and does not require unnecessary translation work militates in favour of not combining these two decisions into one single order.[9]

---

[4] Case 1/71 *Cadillon* [1971] ECR 75, para 4; Case C-107/98 *Teckal* [1999] ECR I-8121, paras 25, 28, and 35; and Case C-296/00 *Expo Casa Manta* [2002] ECR I-4657, para 25.

[5] Case 13/61 *Bosch* ECR (English special edition) 45.

[6] Case 75/63 *Unger* ECR (English special edition) 177.

[7] Case C-373/90 *X* [1992] ECR I-131, para 1, where the reference was made in the form of a letter; and Case C-116/00 *Laguillaumie* [2000] ECR I-4979, para 10.

[8] H Kanninen, Association of the Councils of State and Supreme Administrative Jurisdiction of the European Union, 18th Colloquium 2002, General Report on the Colloquium subject 'The Preliminary Reference to the Court of Justice of the European Communities', 36.

[9] Ibid.

The reference should not be sent via diplomatic channels but directly to the Court of Justice, addressed to the Registry of the Court of Justice, Boulevard Konrad Adenauer, L-2925 Luxembourg. Community law does not contain deadlines in relation to the time which may elapse between the decision to make a reference and the receipt of the questions by the Court of Justice. However, with a view to limiting the length of the proceedings, the questions should be sent as soon as possible.[10]

The order for reference should be drawn up in the language of the proceedings of the referring court (provided that this is one of the official languages of the European Union). In order to minimise the risk of misunderstanding, the reference should be made in one document rather than several with cross-references between them.[11]

With a view to providing the Court of Justice with the best possible basis for giving a ruling that can be applied, the referring court should not merely forward the order for reference itself, but also a copy of all the relevant documents in the case.[12] The reference should also state the names and addresses of the parties and their legal representatives so that the Court of Justice can easily inform them of the receipt of the reference and of the deadline for presenting observations in the case. If a party changes his legal representative, he should notify the Court of Justice of this change as soon as possible.

3. The Content of a Reference

3.1. The need for a thorough order for reference

The Court of Justice tries to avoid making abstract and thereby unforeseeably wide-ranging decisions. Its rulings must be applied in order to ensure a correct and uniform application of Community law, and the Court of Justice, therefore, seeks to give the referring court an answer which provides that court with the best possible help for deciding the dispute in the main proceedings. If the Court of Justice has not been adequately apprised of the factual and legal background to the

---

[10] R Barents et al, *European Courts Practice* (2004) para 31.095. In Case 208/80 *Lord Bruce of Donington* [1981] ECR 2205, the Court of Justice first received the questions nearly a year after the national court had decided to make a reference.

[11] Where the referring court requests the Court of Justice to apply the special urgent procedure relating to cases concerning the area of freedom, security, and justice, that request should be submitted in a document separate from the order for reference itself, or in a covering letter expressly setting out the request so that the Court's Registry is able to establish immediately that the file must be dealt with in a particular way, see s 3.2.6 below.

[12] The entire case file is not automatically sent to the Advocate General and the participating judges. Thus, it is not always part of the documentation used in the consideration of the reference. However, the members of the Court of Justice will have the opportunity to consult the documentation at the Court's Registry, and this sometimes happens.

questions submitted, there is a risk that its reply may be beside the point resulting in an incorrect application of Community law in the main proceedings.

On the basis of the information in the preliminary reference, the observations presented directly to the Court, and any enclosed case file of the main proceedings, the Court of Justice will often be able to establish the necessary information about the factual and legal background to the case. However, this task can make unreasonable demands on the resources and time of the Court of Justice which is entitled to expect that the national courts ensure that there is sufficient information on a case referred for a preliminary ruling. Even where the Court of Justice does its utmost to gain an overview of the case, the risk of misunderstanding cannot be entirely ruled out. Moreover, the Court of Justice can only avoid answering hypothetical questions if the national court states the reasons why it finds that a ruling on the questions referred is necessary for deciding the dispute in the main proceedings.[13] There is thus a close connection between on the one hand the Court of Justice's control over the exercise of its jurisdiction and the requirement that a preliminary ruling should actually be of use to the referring court, and on the other hand the consequent requirement that there should be an adequate description of the questions at issue and their background.

In *EVN*, the object of the review proceedings brought in the main proceedings was, inter alia, the annulment of an invitation to tender in its entirety and the annulment of a series of individual conditions in the contract documents and of a number of decisions of the contracting authority relating to the requirements established by the award and selection criteria used in the tender in question. It transpired from the referring Austrian court's order for a preliminary reference that all the decisions and conditions whose annulment was sought in the main proceedings had a decisive effect on the outcome of the tender procedure. In contrast, the referring court had not provided any explanation as to the precise reasons why it considered that an answer to the question of the compatibility of a provision in the Austrian legislation with the Community rules on public procurement was relevant to the case pending before it. Since there was no information before the Court of Justice to show that an answer to that issue was needed in order to resolve the dispute, the Court of Justice regarded the questions as hypothetical and, accordingly, inadmissible.[14]

In *Plato Plastik*, the referring court sought, among other things, guidance on whether the Austrian system for recovering and recycling waste was compatible

---

[13] Case C-343/90 *Lourenco Dias* [1992] ECR I-4673, para 15; Case C-378/93 *La Pyramide* [1994] ECR I-3999, para 13; and Case C-75/04 *Hanssens* (ECJ 21 January 2005), paras 9 and 13–14. On the requirement that the answer to a question given in a preliminary ruling must be relevant to the decision in the main proceedings, see Ch 5, s 3 above.

[14] Case C-448/01 *EVN* [2003] ECR I-14527, paras 73–83.

with the competition rules, the fundamental freedoms, and the proportionality principle. After deciding on the admissibility of several other questions in the same case, the Court of Justice stated that it was not clear that an answer to the remaining questions would have any effect on the outcome of the main proceedings. Consideration of the existence of any such effect and, if necessary, the examination of those questions were further complicated by the fact that the order for reference contained little information on the factual situation. Moreover, the referring court had not explained the connection between each of the provisions of Community law of which it sought interpretation, and the factual situation. Without this information, it was not possible to ascertain the specific problem of interpretation which could arise in relation to each provision. Therefore, as the particulars in the order for reference were too imprecise with regard to the legal and factual situations to which the questions related, the Court was unable to ascertain the specific problem of interpretation of Community law and to give a useful interpretation in that respect. It thus declined to answer those questions.[15]

In *Austroplant-Arzneimittel*, the Court of Justice had asked the referring court to explain the basis for the claim of the plaintiff in the main proceedings, as well as clarification of how an answer to the questions asked could be relevant to the decision of the case. In its reply, the national court had essentially restricted itself to setting out the arguments made by the plaintiff and saying that the case raised a question about Austria's implementation of Directive 89/105 on the transparency of measures regulating the pricing of medicinal products. However, the national court did not indicate in more detail which provisions in the directive were questioned, nor did it describe how the national law might have implemented them incorrectly. The Court of Justice found that the national court's reply did not contain a necessary explanation of how an answer to the national court's preliminary questions could be relevant to the main proceedings. It therefore declined to answer these questions.[16]

The requirement for the order for reference to throw light on the relevance of the questions applies in particular when the questions cast doubt on the validity of the legislation of a Member State other than that in which the referring court is situated.[17]

In *Bacardi-Martini*, the Court of Justice stated that it displays special vigilance when, in the course of proceedings between individuals, a question is referred to it with a view to permitting the national court to decide whether the legislation of another Member State is in accordance with Community law. For this reason,

---

[15] Case C-341/01 *Plato Plastik Robert Frank* [2004] ECR I-4883, paras 37–40.
[16] Case C-54/03 *Austroplant-Arzneimittel* (ECJ 12 March 2004).
[17] See also Ch 5, s 4.12.

where the questions referred are intended to enable the national court to assess the compatibility with Community law of the legislation of another Member State, the Court must be informed in some detail of why the referring court considers that an answer to the questions is necessary to enable it to give judgment. In the case in question the national court had limited itself to stating the arguments which one of the parties in the main proceedings had put forward. In the opinion of the Court of Justice the referring court had not lived up to this requirement. Not even after being asked to explain the relevance of the question referred, had the national court stated whether it found that an answer to the question was in fact necessary to enable it to make a decision. Nor had the national court explained why the foreign law should be interpreted in such a way as to make the question relevant. The question would only be relevant if the legislation in question were given extraterritorial effect. However, before the Court of Justice the government of the Member State whose legislation was the subject of the question had disputed that the legislation had such extraterritorial effect. On this basis the Court of Justice found that it did not have the material before it to show that it was necessary to rule on the compatibility with the EC Treaty of legislation of a Member State other than that of the referring court. The question was thus declared inadmissible.[18]

Finally, the information provided in an order for reference must not only be such as to enable the Court of Justice to reply usefully but must also enable the governments of the Member States and other interested parties to submit observations pursuant to Article 23 of the Statute of the Court of Justice. If the preliminary reference does not make it possible to clearly identify the relevant legal topic, there is a risk that those States and other bodies will refrain from presenting their observations to the preliminary case and thus deprive the Court of Justice of relevant information and arguments. There is also a risk that a State may feel ambushed by a preliminary ruling on legal questions of major importance about which it had a significant interest in expressing a view before the Court of Justice makes its ruling, but could not detect because of the low quality of the reference. This situation is underlined by the fact that not only can a preliminary ruling indirectly overrule the national law, which is relevant to the case before the court, but it can also overrule equivalent legislation in other Member States. On this basis, the Court of Justice has stated that, by means of its examination of the admissibility of questions, it will ensure that the possibility to submit observations is safeguarded, bearing in mind that, by virtue of the above-mentioned provision, only the orders for reference are notified to the interested parties.

---

[18] Case C-318/00 *Bacardi-Martini* [2003] ECR I-905.

The practice was laid down in *Holdijk* where the Danish government argued that the incompleteness of the preliminary references did not enable it to submit observations on the substance of the case. The Court of Justice acknowledged that, as a matter of principle, Article 23 of the Court's Statute means that an order for reference must give an account of the relevant facts and national law in such a way as to make it clear to the Member States and Community institutions what the case is about.[19]

The first reference for a preliminary ruling in 1961 already demonstrated that an incomplete and superficial order for reference might, in practice, make it impossible, on the one hand, for those entitled to present observations to make meaningful submissions, and on the other hand, for the Court of Justice to give a ruling that is sufficiently precise to be usable by the referring court.[20] Until the mid 1990s, the Court of Justice nevertheless adopted a mild approach and only in very rare cases refused to give rulings on unsatisfactorily formulated references. Instead, it reacted to them by giving vague and abstract rulings of limited value for the referring court. However, a change of practice was introduced in 1993 with *Telemarsicabruzzo*,[21] since when dismissal of defective references has become the norm.

This change in practice was not unconnected with the different challenges with which the Court of Justice had then begun to be faced. Previously the Court had reason to encourage the national courts to make references and thereby to strengthen both knowledge about Community law and the recognition thereof while at the same time establishing the basic principles in the interplay between national law and Community law. Today, among other things because of the preliminary rulings procedure, these aims have largely been realised, even though there may still be significant challenges in respect of the newer Member States. Presently, the challenges tend to be related to resource limitations. In order for the Court of Justice to have time for a thorough examination of each case it is necessary to keep down the number of references.[22] The Court's practice in dismissing inadequate references has, however, not been used to eliminate 'uninteresting' cases, as is known from the *certiorari* principle applied by the US Supreme Court. Even though the Court's tightening up of the practice seems to reflect a policy decision, it is only used to dismiss cases where it would be difficult to render a judgment

---

[19] Joined Cases 141/81–143/81 *Holdijk* [1982] ECR 1299, paras 5–8. See similarly Case C-207/01 *Altair Chimica* [2003] ECR I-8875, para 25.

[20] Case 13/61 *Bosch* [1962] ECR (English special edition) 45. See also Case 52/76 *Benedetti* [1977] ECR 163, para 20.

[21] Joined Cases C-320/90–322/90 *Telemarsicabruzzo* [1993] ECR I-393.

[22] A Arnull, 'Case note on the *Telemarsicabruzzo* case' (1994) CML Rev Vol 31, No 2, 377, 384. On the motives for the Court of Justice's change in practice, see also A Arnull, 'Case note on the *Telemarsicabruzzo* case' (1994) 31 CML Rev Vol 31, No 2, 377, 528ff.

which gives a useful answer to the referring court. Hence, the tighter practice is not used as a strategic mechanism to actively reduce the volume of cases handled.[23]

It has been argued that the stricter practice of the Court of Justice risks leading to a lack of uniformity in the application of the law. Unless it chooses to make a renewed reference after its first reference has been dismissed, a national court is left to its own devices. This involves a risk that it will take a decision based on a mistaken application of Community law.[24] This criticism is not convincing. The alternative to the Court dismissing a reference is not that it gives a detailed answer, where the facts and the national law are integrated in a preliminary ruling in such a way as to really be decisive for the dispute in the main proceedings. On the contrary, the alternative is that the Court renders a vague and meaningless response which will in any event not give the national court genuine guidance in deciding the main proceedings.[25]

It has also been argued that the Court's practice risks deterring national courts from making references, for fear of being met with an inadmissibility order. In this connection it has been emphasised that very few judges, in the course of their career, have more than one, or at most a very few occasions to formulate an order for reference. It can thus be difficult for a national court, where neither the judge nor the parties to the case are used to working with Community law, to formulate a precise and detailed order for reference.[26] However, this risk is considerably reduced by the fact that the Court of Justice has published an information note on how a reference should be framed.[27] Moreover, the incentive to make a reference is hardly likely to be increased if, instead of rejecting the reference as inadmissible, the national court receives a preliminary ruling which is formulated in such general terms that it will be of little use.

3.2. Guidelines for the drafting of a reference for a preliminary ruling

3.2.1. Introduction

As stated above in Section 2, there are no formal requirements as to the form of a preliminary reference. However, the referring court should have due regard for the special requirements flowing from the aim and process of the preliminary ruling

---

[23] T Tridimas, 'Knocking on Heaven's Door: Fragmentation, Efficiency and Defiance in the Preliminary Reference Procedure' (2003) 40 CML Rev Vol 40, 9, 22ff. See also Ch 1, s 6.4.

[24] A Arnull, 'The Past and Future of the Preliminary Rulings Procedure' (2002) 13 European Business Law Review 183, 186.

[25] Case 14/86 *Pretore di Salò* [1987] ECR 2545, para 16.

[26] A Arnull, 'The Past and Future of the Preliminary Rulings Procedure' (2002) 13 European Business Law Review Vol 13, 183, 186.

[27] Information note on references from national courts for a preliminary ruling ([2005] OJ C143/1). This information note is also available on the Court of Justice's website at <http://www.curia.europa.eu>.

procedure. It is thus important that the reference contains a precise identification of the question referred and a thorough description of the facts of the main proceedings as well as of the relevant national law. Moreover, the reference should be easily understandable without it being necessary to seek additional information from other documents. These requirements will be analysed in more detail in the following section.

3.2.2. Identification of the question referred

First of all, a reference for a preliminary ruling must state the precise grounds on which the referring court raises the question about the interpretation of Community law and finds it necessary to refer a question to the Court of Justice for a preliminary ruling.[28] In other words, the legal issues at stake must be identified clearly in the order for reference.

In *Illumitrónica*, the referring court wanted guidance on whether a Commission decision on the post-clearance recovery of customs duties was valid. The Court of Justice noted that nothing in the order for reference served to actually identify the relevant Commission decision. Consequently, the Court was unable to adjudicate on this point.[29]

There are substantial differences as to how closely national courts link the formulation of a question to the actual facts of the case. There is nothing to stop a national court from choosing to formulate the question for a preliminary ruling relatively openly and abstractly, while giving the necessary information to enable the Court of Justice to understand the facts of the case and the national law background in the reasons given for the question. That notwithstanding, in general it is preferable for the question not to be unnecessarily wide. Conversely, it is not desirable to ask a great number of questions and sub-questions with a view to covering every conceivable factual or legal hypothesis which the ingenuity of counsel can devise.[30] Where such questions may remain open, it is better to emphasise this in the accompanying reasons for the question raised.

A preliminary question ought, moreover, to be formulated so as to take account of the limits to the Court of Justice's jurisdiction under Article 234. This means that the question should not concern the facts or national law, nor should it directly

---

[28] Case C-101/96 *Italia Testa* [1996] ECR I-3081, para 6; Case C-480/04 *D'Antonio* (ECJ 22 February 2005), para 5; Case C-167/94 *Grau Gomis* [1995] ECR I-1023, para 9; and Joined Cases C-72/07 and C-111/07 *Blanco Perez* [2007] ECR 81, para 18.

[29] Case C-251/00 *Ilumitrónica* [2002] ECR I-10433, para 71.

[30] D Edward, and C Bellamy, 'Views from European Courts' in G Barling and M Brealey (eds), *Practitioners' Handbook of EC Law* (1988) 36, as well as D Anderson and M Demetriou, *References to the European Court* (2002) 200.

ask whether national law is compatible with Community law.[31] Instead, a question may ask whether the relevant Community law rule precludes a national provision with certain specific characteristics. Indeed, it is possible to ask whether Community law precludes 'a national provision *such as* the one laid down in Article X of Law no Y of Member State Z'.[32]

It is often just as much on the basis of the referring court's reasoning as on the basis of the question itself that the Court of Justice can identify the Community law elements about which there are doubts. Moreover, it is highly recommended for the referring court to identify the provisions of Community law of which it seeks an interpretation, as this makes the work of the Court of Justice significantly easier. Admittedly, in the early cases it was stated that an express reference to individual provisions of Community law was not a precondition for admissibility of a reference.[33] Likewise, in its guidelines to national courts on making references for preliminary rulings, the Court of Justice has not explicitly established such a requirement. However, in its more recent case law the Court of Justice has indicated the importance of the national court giving, at the very least, some explanation of the reasons for the choice of the Community provisions of which it requests an interpretation.

Similarly, the referring court must give an account of the link that it has established between those provisions and the national legislation applicable to the dispute.[34] The Court of Justice has even refused to admit a question purely on the grounds that the referring court had '*provided no information at all on the reasons for its choice of the Community provisions referred to*' in the question submitted for preliminary ruling.[35]

---

[31] Case C-320/88 *Shipping and Forwarding Enterprise Safe* [1990] ECR I-283; Case C-130/93 *Lamaire* [1994] ECR I-3215; Case C-342/97 *Lloyd Schuhfabrik Meyer & Co* [1999] ECR I-3819, para 11; Case C-40/01 *Ansul* [2003] ECR I-2439, para 44; and Case C-198/01 *CIF* [2003] ECR I-8055, para 62.

[32] See also Ch 4, s 5.6 and Ch 11, s 3.

[33] Case C-235/90 *Morvan* [1991] ECR I-5419; Case 20/87 *Gauchard* [1987] ECR 4897, paras 6–9; and Case 35/85 *Tissier* [1986] ECR 1207, paras 5–11.

[34] Case C-386/07 *Hospital Consulting* [2008] ECR I-67, paras 33–4; Case C-305/07 *RAI* (ECJ 9 April 2008); Case C-467/06 *Consel Gi. Emme* (ECJ March 2008), paras 15–16, Case C-116/05 *Dhumeaux* (ECJ 1 December 2005), para 21; Case C-116/00 *Laguillaumi,* [2000] ECR I-4979, para 16; Case C-399/98 *Ordine degli Architetti* [2001] ECR I-5409, para 105; and Case C-167/94 *Grau Gomis* [1995] ECR I-1023, para 9. As stated by R Lane, 'Article 234: A Few Rough Edges Still' in M Hoskins and W Robinson (eds), *A True European, Essays for Judge David Edward* (2003) 327, 334, 'The question may well betray a Community law context and the point to be determined, but it is for the national court to make it reasonably clear what it is and why it is so; with the Court of Justice no longer scrabbling for work, it has no duty to divine a question which may be, but is not clearly, there.'

[35] Case C-237/04 *Enirisorse* [2006] ECR I-2843, paras 21–2, and similarly Case C-380/05 *Centro Europa 7* [2008] ECR I-349, paras 53–6. It might have influenced the result in these two cases that it was difficult to see how the provisions in question could be relevant for the resolution of

In *Simoncello*, an Italian court had referred a question on the application of, among other things, the Treaty rules on the free movement of workers and the right of establishment. However, the court had not stated any reasons why it regarded these provisions as being relevant, and neither the order for reference nor the subsequent observations to the Court of Justice made it possible to make a link between these provisions and the facts in the main proceedings, which concerned the failure of an Italian company to report to the Italian authorities on the employment status of some Italian workers. Furthermore, no information had been given indicating that the company in question intended to make use of the right of establishment. On this basis, the Court of Justice stated that it was not in a position to give a useful answer to the question referred for a preliminary ruling. It therefore declared the question manifestly inadmissible.[36]

In *Laserdisken*, a Danish city court had asked the Court of Justice for guidance on whether Articles 28, 30, 81, and 82 of the EC Treaty and/or Directive 92/100 prevented the owner of an exclusive right to hire out video films from prohibiting the hiring out of copies of a film in Denmark, even though permission had been given for hiring out copies of the film in another Member State. The Court of Justice noted that the order for reference gave no explanation of the reasons for which it raised the question of the effect of the competition provisions in Articles 81 and 82 of the EC Treaty in connection with the matters of fact and law in the main proceedings. In the absence of such information the referring court had failed to put the Court of Justice in a position to give an interpretation of those articles which could be of use to the former. Hence, the preliminary questions were regarded as inadmissible in so far as they concerned the interpretation of these two Treaty provisions.[37]

It will often be useful to summarise the claims and arguments of the parties to the dispute concerning the question referred. This will better bring out the critical issues of the case just as it might occasionally make it unnecessary for the parties themselves to present observations to the Court of Justice. That being said, it will normally not be sufficient that the referring court merely passes on the arguments of the parties without at the same time setting out its own understanding of the relevant factual and legal issues. This is particularly so if the parties' presentations of the facts and the legal situation under national law vary widely since, in such a situation, the Court of Justice would not be able to obtain, from the observations

---

disputes before the referring courts. It is not unlikely that this somewhat formal and inflexible approach would have been different if the identified provisions of Community law had seemed obvious or at least relevant. Contrast Case C-350/07 *Kattner Stahlbau* (ECJ 5 March 2009), paras 26–7.

[36] Case C-445/01 *Simoncello* [2003] ECR I-1807, para 23.
[37] Case C-61/97 *Laserdisken* [1998] ECR I-5171, paras 9–10.

of the parties, a more precise impression of the problems on which the referring court seeks a ruling.[38]

There is no requirement that the referring court states how it believes that the questions of Community law raised should be interpreted. Practice is thus determined by the different Member States; thus whilst German and Dutch courts often put forward their own view as to the answer to be given to the referred questions most other Member States have been rather cautious in this respect.[39] Such reticence is understandable as the national court might find that its credibility could be damaged if its suggestion was not followed, and it might even be feared that an obligation to suggest an answer could work as an unintended disincentive for some national courts to refer. In addition, it has been argued that requiring a proposal on how to answer the question referred would make the Court of Justice superior to the national supreme courts which in turn could adversely affect the relationship of cooperation between the latter courts and the Court of Justice.[40]

Nevertheless, such suggestions for how the questions could be answered can sometimes make it easier for the Court of Justice to identify the background to the question asked and thus the critical issues at stake. Indeed, in its information note concerning the special urgent preliminary procedure provided in Article 104b of the Court's Rules of Procedure, the Court explicitly suggests that, in so far as it is able to do so, the referring court shall state its view on the answer to be given to the question(s) referred. Such a statement makes it easier for those participating in the procedure to define their positions just as it facilitates the Court's decision, thereby contributing to the rapidity of the procedure.[41] Formulating its own view of the Community law point at stake may also help the referring court in securing that the relevant information is indeed presented in the order for reference, and

---

[38] Case C-447/01 *DLD Trading Company I* (ECJ 21 March 2002). This order was followed by Case C-216/03 *DLD Trading Company II* (ECJ 1 April 2004), in which the Court of Justice again refused to answer the question.

[39] According to S Nyikos, *The European Court and National Courts* (2001) 116, in a selection of 574 preliminary references made between 1961 and 1995, the referring court provided its own suggestion to the referred question in 41.3 per cent of the references. This figure is, however, hardly representative as half of the selected data material related to references from German courts, ie from courts that have shown a particular willingness to put forward their own view on the referred question. The German practice might be linked to the fact that where German courts make references to the German *Bundesverfassungsgericht* the reference is accompanied by the referring court's own proposed answer to the question raised.

[40] See the summary of the statements made by Judge Schäder of the Swedish Supreme Administrative Court in R Crowe, 'Colloquium Report, The Preliminary Reference Procedure: Reflections based on Practical Experience of the Highest National Courts in Administrative Matters' (2004) 5 ERA Forum 435, 440. Compare A Dashwood and A C Johnston, *The Future of the Judicial System of the European Union* (2001) 68.

[41] With regard to the urgent procedure, see Ch 10, s 5.3 below, and Case C-446/02 *Gouralnik* (ECJ 30 April 2004).

that the question asked does in fact give rise to real doubt. In addition, by presenting its own view on the Community law point the referring court may be able to influence the ruling of the Court of Justice. Where the national court procedure provides for an advisory opinion on the legal aspects of the main action—such as the opinion of a national advocate general—the referring court may consider submitting the relevant parts of this opinion together with the preliminary questions.

3.2.3. *Information about the facts*

The order for reference should also describe those parts of the facts pertaining to the main proceedings which can be relevant to the Court of Justice's interpretation of the relevant Community provisions.[42]

If the question is referred before the relevant facts have been finally established in the main proceedings, the national court should explain the facts and the hypotheses which lie behind the reference in a manner that enables the Court of Justice to focus on those aspects of Community law that could be necessary for the national court to make a decision in the main proceedings. In other words, in such a situation the referring court should give an account of the various scenarios with regard to the possible understandings of the facts which form the basis of the referred questions.

There are three ways in which a national court can ensure this. First, the referring court can ask the Court of Justice to base its reply on a specific hypothesis.[43] This method reduces the volume of questions in the individual reference and normally reduces the workload of the Court of Justice. It does, however, entail a risk that the reference will later turn out to have been futile if it appears that the hypothesis was not borne out.[44] Indeed, it may even be necessary to make a supplementary reference. This means that this method is most suitable where the alternative interpretation of the facts will not involve Community law. It might also be appropriate if the correct interpretation of Community law will not give rise to doubt should it be shown that the alternative situation is the correct one.

Second, the national court can choose to refer several alternative questions, just as in its reasons it can give possible scenarios for the final finding of facts.

---

[42] Case C-454/08 *Seaport Investments Limited* (ECJ 20 May 2009); Case C-358/04 *Valdagnese* (ECJ 14 June 2005), paras 8–10; Case C-458/93 *Saddik* [1995] ECR I-511, para 12; and Case 52/76 *Benedetti* [1977] ECR 163, paras 19–22. According to J Korte, *Primus inter Pares: The European Court and National Courts. The Follow-up by National Courts of Preliminary References ex. Art 177 of the Treaty of Rome: A Report on the Situation in the Netherlands* (1991) 90ff, in a study of 152 Dutch references approximately 30 per cent of those suffered from some form of insufficient information on the facts without those insufficiencies being grave enough to lead to the case being inadmissible.

[43] Case C-127/92 *Enderby* [1993] ECR I-5535.

[44] See further above Ch 5, s 4.3, and Ch 7, s 4, and below Ch 12, s 2.1.

Finally, by means of supplementary questions the national court can request the Court of Justice to give a ruling on how a given point on which the parties do not agree will affect the answer to the main question. Thereby, depending on the answer given in the preliminary ruling, the national court might avoid having to decide difficult questions of law and conduct cumbersome investigations on the facts.

In the two latter situations efforts should be made to keep the extent of the questions at a reasonable level and formulated sufficiently broadly so that the Court of Justice can itself assess how best to answer the questions.[45]

It might sometimes be difficult for a national court to determine in advance which factual elements the Court of Justice will attach importance to when deciding on the question referred. For this reason it is, on the one hand, advisable that a relatively detailed review of the facts of the case should be given, and that the reference should also mention facts the relevance of which might seem limited. On the other hand, one should not overlook that the order for reference must be translated. In order to ensure as quick and as accurate a translation as possible, the reference should not be unnecessarily long. Moreover, where a reference is voluminous, the Court of Justice might decide to translate only a summary.[46] According to the Court of Justice's information note on references from national courts for a preliminary ruling, a maximum of about 10 pages is often sufficient to set out in a proper manner the context of a reference for a preliminary ruling.[47] The reference should be written in simple, clear language, with short sentences.

In *Bellamy*, the referring court wanted to know whether Articles 28 and 30 of the EC Treaty prevented the application of a national provision which imposes an obligation to use in all advertising material such a description of a foodstuff as may be provided by law or regulation, where the omission of that description might mislead the consumer. The Court of Justice noted that the referring court had confined itself to stating that the national rule at issue in the main proceedings applied in criminal proceedings in which Mrs Bellamy was being prosecuted for 'having failed in the advertising for the product to use in a clearly visible manner a description of the foodstuff, thereby misleading consumers as to the nature of

---

[45] See similarly O Due, 'Danish Preliminary References' in D O'Keeffe and A Bavasso (eds), *Judicial Review in European Union Law* (2000) 363, 374. For less felicitously formulated questions see Joined Cases 36/80 and 71/80 *Irish Creamery* [1981] ECR I-735; Case 83/78 *Pigs Marketing Board* [1978] ECR 2347; and Joined Cases 115/81 and 116/81 *Adoui and Cornuaille* [1982] ECR 1665.

[46] Cf Art 104 of the Court's Rules of Procedure. According to V Skouris, 'L'urgence dans la procédure applicable aux renvois préjudiciels' in C Baudenbacher et al (eds), *Liber Amicorum en l'honneur de Bo Vesterdorf* (2007) 59, 62ff, of the 251 references that the Court received in the period between 1 October 2005 and 31 December 2006, summaries of the references were made in 22.

[47] Point 22 of the note.

the foodstuff, in this case by describing the product as pasteurised whole fresh milk'. However, this description of the offence which Mrs Bellamy was alleged to have committed was far from sufficient information to enable the Court of Justice to give a ruling that could be used by the referring court. The national court had not made clear whether or not the advertising in question was found on the product's packaging, nor was it explained what was the specific omission alleged against Mrs Bellamy. Furthermore the parties who had presented observations to the Court of Justice disagreed about what Mrs Bellamy was accused of. Thus, Mrs Bellamy had herself explained that she was being prosecuted for having used the term 'pasteurised whole fresh milk', thus giving the impression that the milk was fresh although it had been pasteurised. In contrast, the Commission had stated that Mrs Bellamy had been prosecuted for having used the term 'Breakfast Milk', and for not having used the statutory description 'pasteurised whole fresh milk'. In these circumstances the Court of Justice found itself unable to give a useful answer to a number of the questions referred.[48]

Anssens concerned the relationship between certain French taxes on motor vehicles and the prohibition on discriminatory taxes in Article 90 of the EC Treaty. It was not clear from the reference whether the vehicle which had been subject to tax in the main proceedings had been manufactured in France or in some other Member State. This information was necessary for determining whether the Treaty provision referred to was applicable at all. If the vehicle was manufactured in France, the situation would be purely internal and would not fall within the scope of Community law. Nor had the referring court stated whether the vehicle had been imported into France directly from a third country, which would also have meant that Article 90 was not applicable. Furthermore, the referring court had not given a detailed description of the French law. On this basis the Court of Justice refused to give a ruling. However, it added a number of comments on when a national taxation system will be in accordance with Article 90. The judgment illustrates that, even though questions may be declared inadmissible, a national court may nevertheless obtain helpful guidance from the Court of Justice's explanation of why an order for reference does not contain the necessary information to enable the Court of Justice to give a preliminary ruling on the substance of the case.[49]

In assessing whether a preliminary reference has presented the facts of the case in an adequate manner the Court of Justice takes as its basis the allocation of jurisdiction in Article 234 on the establishment of the facts. There is thus no need to give

---

[48] Case C-123/00 *Bellamy* [2001] ECR I-2795, paras 23–7.
[49] Case C-325/98 *Anssens* [1999] ECR I-2969, paras 10–14. See also Case C-234/05 *de Becker* (ECJ 27 October 2005).

an account of the evidence that has led the referring court to the description of the facts set out in the order for reference.

In *van der Kooy*, the referring court stated that a ship had links with the Netherlands Antilles. The French government said that the question should be refused a substantive hearing, arguing that it was not possible to see, on the basis of the order for reference, why the referring court believed that there was such a link. To this the Court of Justice remarked that, while the documentation for the reference was indeed very succinct, the Court of Justice both could and should base its consideration on the premises which the referring court regarded as having been established. In the actual case, this meant that the Court of Justice had to give a ruling on the basis that the ship had a connection with the Netherlands Antilles. The lack of detailed evidence to support this finding could not justify the dismissal of the reference.[50]

In order to ascertain whether the information supplied by the referring court satisfies the requirements pertaining to a reference, the nature and scope of the questions raised will also be taken into consideration.[51] Where the referring court finds that certain conditions of Community law are fulfilled, and therefore limits its reference to the remaining questions, it will normally be sufficient if the description of the case allows a view to be taken solely of the problems actually referred, but not of the problems which the referring court finds that it has itself resolved.[52]

The need for a detailed account of the facts is particularly important in the area of competition law, where the facts and the legal situation are often complex. On many occasions an order for reference has given the Court of Justice sufficient information to answer questions about the Treaty provisions on freedom of movement, but not to answer questions on the application of the competition rules.[53]

---

[50] Case C-181/97 *Van der Kooy* [1999] ECR I-483, paras 26–30. See similarly Case C-13/05 *Navas* [2006] ECR I-6467, paras 26–30.

[51] Case C-94/07 *Raccanelli* [2008] ECR I-5939, para 26.

[52] Case C-368/98 *Vanbraekel* [2001] ECR I-5363, paras 20–5.

[53] Case C-250/06 *United Pan-Europe Communications Belgium* [2007] ECR I-11135, paras 13–23; Case C-295/05 *Asemfo* [2007] ECR I-2999, paras 25–45; Case C-134/95 *USSL* [1997] ECR I-195, para 15; Case C-341/95 *Betatti* [1998] ECR I-4355, paras 66–72; Case C-284/95 *Safety Hi-Tech* [1998] ECR I-4301, paras 68–74; Case C-108/98 *RI.SAN* [1999] ECR I-5219; Joined Cases C-51/96 and C-191/97 *Christelle Deliège* [2000] ECR I-2549, paras 26–40; Case C-176/96 *Lehtonen* [2000] ECR I-2681, paras 27–30; Case C-341/01 *Plato Plastik Robert Frank* [2004] ECR I-4883, paras 32–40; and Case C-72/03 *Carbonati Apuani* [2004] ECR I-8027, paras 9–14. See also Case C-134/03 *Viacom Outdoor II* [2005] ECR I-1167, paras 20–33, where the Court of Justice stated, after it had dismissed a previous reference relating to the same main proceedings in Case C-190/02 *Viacom Outdoor I* [2002] ECR I-8297, that even a renewed reference did not contain sufficient information to enable it to give a proper and usable ruling on the problems under competition law. See similarly Case C-157/90 *Banchero I* [1993] ECR I-1085; Case C-387/93 *Banchero II* [1995] ECR I-4663, paras 18–19 and 23; Case C-326/95 *Banco de Fomento e Exterior I*

In *Cannito*, an Italian court had referred a number of questions to the Court of Justice concerning compensation and the limitation period following a breach of Articles 81 and 82 of the EC Treaty. The Court of Justice stated that the orders for reference did not contain sufficient explanation of the legislation applicable to the dispute. Nor had the referring court given an account of the factual circumstances on which its questions were based. For example it had not stated what the alleged infringements consisted of. In these circumstances it was to no avail that the order for reference referred to the facts found in other judgments or in a decision of the competent competition authority. The reference was therefore held to be inadmissible.[54]

Conversely, there will often be less need for a detailed account of the facts and legal circumstances of the main proceedings where the question is of a technical nature, enabling the Court of Justice to give a relevant answer even without knowledge of the background to the dispute.[55] In this connection it is also relevant how generally the questions are framed and whether they can be answered on an abstract basis, or whether they in reality invite the Court of Justice to assist in a concrete application of a discretionary rule.[56]

3.2.4. Information about national law

The order for reference should also give an account of the relevant provisions of national law. If the preliminary reference merely contains a reference to the provisions or to an Internet site where the legal text is reproduced, without either quoting or restating them, the Court of Justice as well as the Member States and EU institutions might face great difficulty in understanding the case in its proper context and in their own language. For the same reason, abbreviations or short names for legal text should be either avoided or explained.

Moreover, use of terminology that is particular to the legal system of the referring court should be avoided or explained as neither the Court of Justice nor the EU institutions or Member States which might want to present observations before the Court can be expected to be familiar with the national legal system in which the question has arisen. In other words, the reference should be drafted so that it can be understood by lawyers who do not have prior knowledge of the legal

---

[1996] ECR I-1385; Case C-66/97 *Banco de Fomento e Exterior II* [1997] ECR I-3757; Case C-101/96 *Italia Testa* [1996] ECR I-3081; and Joined Cases C-128/97 and C-137/97 *Testa and Modesti* [1998] ECR I-2181. In all three sets of cases, not only the first but also the renewed reference was dismissed in whole or in part since even the renewed references did not contain a description of the case that enabled the Court of Justice to give a clear and relevant response.

[54] Joined Cases C-438/03, C-439/03, and C-2/04 *Cannitto* [2004] ECR I-1605, paras 7–13. See also Case C-386/92 *Monin I* [1993] ECR I-2049, para 7.

[55] Case C-316/93 *Vaneetweld* [1994] ECR I-763, para 13.

[56] Joined Cases C-58/95, C-75/95, C-112/95, C-119/95, C-123/95, C-135/95, C-140/95, C-141/95, C-154/95, and C-157/95 *Gallotti* [1996] ECR I-4345, para 9.

principles and concepts that apply in the legal system of the referring court. Depending on the subject matter of the case and the relevant national law there might be a need to address such principles or concepts which may be peculiar to a national legal system and which are not necessarily familiar to the judges of the Court of Justice taking part in the case, even if the relevant principles and concepts would be obvious to a lawyer of the State of the referring court.[57]

In *Odine degli Architetti*, the Court of Justice stated that, among other things, the referring court had not given details of the aspects of Italian law which could potentially be in conflict with Community law. In the absence of such informa-tion, it was not possible to identify the specific problem arising in the main pro-ceedings concerning the interpretation of Community law. The question was therefore declared inadmissible.[58]

In *Tarantik*, Advocate General Jacobs stated that a detailed account of national law was often required in cases concerning fiscal issues, where the national legisla-tion may well be highly complex and where it is likely to be impossible to assess the full implications of one aspect of the system in the absence of complete infor-mation concerning the functioning of the system as a whole.[59]

In *Colapietro*, the Court of Justice was requested to assess whether a rule in national law, which imposed penalties for the infringement of various provisions of Community law, was disproportionate in relation to the nature of the infringe-ments. The Court held that the principle of loyalty under Article 10 of the EC Treaty obliged the Member States to impose effective but proportionate sanctions for the breach of Community rules. However, the referring court had not described the national law imposing penalties, nor had the Court of Justice received infor-mation on the character and extent of the disputed activities or of the penalties to which the accused could be subject under national law. The Court of Justice therefore refused to answer the question.[60]

3.2.5. *The order for reference must be understandable without the need to refer to other documents*

The order for reference must be self-explanatory as it is only the order for reference itself, and no other documentation relating to the case, that is forwarded to the

---

[57] C Naômé, *Le renvoi préjudiciel en droit européen* (2007) 229, and likewise below in Ch 10, s 4.3.3, concerning observations presented in the case before the Court of Justice.

[58] Case C-399/98 *Odine degli Architetti* [2001] ECR I-5409, paras 104–7. See similarly Case C-258/98 *Carra* [2000] ECR I-4217, para 20; Case C-257/95 *Brestle* [1996] ECR I-233, para 17; Case C-252/00 *Vendeweerd* (ECJ 9 December 2000), paras 11–12 and 15–17, and Case C-500/06 *Corporación Dermoestética* (ECJ 17 July 2008), paras 26–8. Indications of this were already given in earlier cases; see for example Case 244/78 *Union Laitière Normande* [1979] ECR 2663, paras 5–6.

[59] Opinion of Advocate General Jacobs in Case C-421/97 *Tarantik* [1999] ECR I-3633, para 22.

[60] Case C-391/00 *Colapietro* (ECJ 19 January 2001).

Member States and EU institutions etc entitled to present observations in the proceedings for a preliminary ruling. Indeed, as a rule documents annexed to the preliminary reference are not translated and will not be presented to the judges who are going to rule on the preliminary reference; although it does happen that (typically) the Judge-Rapporteur or the Advocate General requests access to the annexes.

In *Colonia Versicherung*, the order for reference did not contain a description of the facts in the case, of national law, or of the reasons for the national court's doubts about the correct interpretation of Community law. Instead, the order for reference referred to the submissions of the parties to the main proceedings. In the view of the Court of Justice, these references were, however, insufficient to ensure that those who had a right to present observations to the Court of Justice could effectively exercise this right. The questions were therefore inadmissible.[61]

In *Viacom Outdoor*, the referring court had attached to a very brief order for reference various documents relating to the main proceedings, and in particular appended various procedural documents, including several acts and regulations relating to bill-posting. The Court of Justice recalled that it is for the referring court to explain, in the order for reference, the factual and legislative context of the dispute in the main proceedings, the reasons which have led the court to raise the question of the interpretation of certain provisions of Community law in particular, and the connection which it establishes between those provisions and the national law applicable to the case. As this had not happened, the reference was declared manifestly inadmissible.[62]

In *Pigs Marketing Board*, a Member State had such difficulties in identifying the legal problems that lay behind the long list of questions in the order for reference that it requested the Court of Justice to indicate beforehand the questions which it regarded as relevant, in order to permit that State to work out its position for the oral hearing. The Court of Justice refused this request, since a categorisation of the questions as being more or less relevant would risk locking the Court of Justice into a fixed position in its final judgment, and it would also make it more difficult for others entitled to make observations to present their views.[63]

---

[61] Case C-422/98 *Colonia Versicherung* [1999] ECR I-1279, para 8.

[62] Case C-190/02 *Viacom Outdoor I* [2002] ECR I-8287, paras 13–25. This differs from the situation where, when the Court of Justice has admitted a question for a preliminary ruling, it often uses information from the documentation relating to the main proceedings where these are put before it; see Case 251/83 *Haug-Adrion* [1984] ECR 4277, para 9; Case C-168/95 *Arcaro* [1996] ECR I-4705, para 21; Case C-262/97 *Engelbrecht* [2000] ECR I-7321j, para 33; Case C-107/98 *Teckal* [1999] ECR I-8121j, para 34; and Case C-220/98 *Estée Lauder* [2000] ECR I-117, para 21.

[63] Case 83/78 *Pigs Marketing Board* [1978] ECR 2347, paras 22–3 and 31.

The fact that it is only the order for reference itself and no other documentation relating to the case that is being translated and forwarded to those who are entitled to present observations in the proceedings for a preliminary ruling also means that an appeal court making a reference should not content itself with merely referring to a lower court's description of the facts, however thorough and articulate that description might be; instead the referring court should either provide its own summary of the facts in the reference or quote the facts as established by the lower court.[64]

In *Laguillaumie*, the national court had referred a number of questions concerning, among other things, the competition rules of the EC Treaty and Directive 83/189/EEC laying down a procedure for the provision of information in the field of technical standards and regulations. The order for reference had not explained what the connection was between the Community provisions which the referring court sought an interpretation of, the facts of the case, and the national law which were to be applied in the main proceedings. Thus, the referring court had not explained what the alleged abuse of a dominant position consisted of, or what national provision made an interpretation of the above-mentioned Directive necessary. It made no difference that the national court had annexed to the order for reference the documentation relating to the national proceedings. Only the order for reference constitutes the basis for proceedings before the Court of Justice, and it was only this order which was notified to the interested parties. The Court of Justice therefore declined jurisdiction.[65]

The practice of the Court of Justice is, however, not completely unambiguous in balancing, on the one hand, the consideration of giving the Member States the possibility of making meaningful written observations on the basis of a clearly identified problem, and, on the other hand, the desire not to reject a reference for a preliminary ruling where the totality of the information provided to the Court of Justice enables it to provide the referring court with a useful reply. Naturally, the Court of Justice has been dismissive of allowing a Member State to invoke Article 23 of the Statute of the Court, laying down a right for the parties, the Member States, and the EU institutions to present observations in the preliminary case, in order to prevent the Court from answering questions on which that Member State does not seek a judicial ruling. This applies in particular to inadmissibility arguments made by the Member State from which the reference has been made.

---

[64] C Naômé, *Le renvoi préjudiciel en droit européen* (2007) 227.

[65] Case C-116/00 *Laguillaumie* [2000] ECR I-4979. See also Case C-307/95 *Max Mara* [1995] ECR I-5083, paras 7–8; Case C-9/98 *Agostini* [1998] ECR I-4261, paras 6–9; Case C-196/96 *Lahlou* [1996] ECR I-3945, para 5; Case C-2/96 *Sunino* [1996] ECR I-1543, para 5; Joined Cases C-28/98–29/98 *Charreire and Hirtsmann* [1999] ECR I-1963, para 11; Case C-422/98 *Colonia Versicherung* [1999] ECR I-1279, paras 7–10; Case C-166/06 *Eurodomus* [2006] ECR I-90, para 12; and Case C-438/06 *Omar Greser* [2007] ECR I-69, para 10.

Indeed, that State will normally be particularly well-positioned to understand the facts and legal circumstances of the preliminary questions, and may even be a party to the main proceedings.

Frequently the written observations of the parties give the Court of Justice sufficient information to enable it to give a meaningful interpretation of the relevant Community provisions in relation to the circumstances that are the subject of the main proceedings. Where that is the case, the Court tends to answer the question referred, even if the order for reference does not in itself give the Member States a satisfactory basis for exercising their right to present detailed and yet case-specific observations in the case.[66]

The Court of Justice often uses the observations of the Member States and EU institutions in order to assess whether the reference has been sufficiently comprehensive. Thus, the Court has often rejected inadmissibility arguments because of insufficient information in the reference on the grounds that in its written observations the Member State or EU institution concerned actually managed to correctly identify the problem which the reference for a preliminary ruling seeks to have clarified.[67] The Court, moreover, often considers it sufficient that, with a view to the oral hearing, the Member States are made aware of any supplementary information through other observations presented to the Court or through subsequent information provided by the referring court, for example as a result of it answering a question from the Court of Justice. It thus suffices that, by the date of the oral hearing at the latest, the Member States and EU institutions have a reasonable oversight and understanding of the preliminary question and its possible resolution so that they are able to decide whether they want to develop their observations during the hearing.[68]

An incomplete reference can sometimes be understood on the basis of previous references, whether in the same case or in other cases.[69] That does not mean,

---

[66] Case C-506/04 *Wilson* [2006] ECR I-8613j, paras 40–1; and Joined Cases C-480/00 and others *Azienda Agricola Ettore Ribaldi* [2004] ECR I-2943, paras 71–5, but compare paras 89–92.

[67] Case C-345/06 *Heinrich* (ECJ 10 March 2009), para 35.

[68] Case C-6/05 *Medipac* [2007] ECR I-4557, paras 30–6; Case C-506/04 *Wilson* [2006] ECR I-8613, paras 40–4; Case C-293/03 *My* [2004] ECR I-12013, paras 16–19; Case C-46/02 *Fixtures Marketing* [2004] ECR I-10365j, paras 22–5; Case C-444/02 *Fixtures Marketing* [2004] ECR I-10549j, paras 13–14; Case C-207/01 *Altair Chimica* [2003] ECR I-8875, paras 23–8; Case C-109/99 *ABBOI* [2000] ECR I-7247, paras 41–7; Case C-56/99 *Gascogne Limousin Viandes* [2000] ECR I-3079, paras 29–31; Case C-35/99 *Arduino* [2002] ECR I-1529, paras 28–31; Joined Cases C-180/98–184/98 *Pavlov* [2000] ECR I-6451, paras 53–4; Joined Cases C-115/97–117/97 *Breentjens* [1999] ECR I-6025, paras 40–4; Case C-176/96 *Lehtonen* [2000] ECR I-2681, paras 25–7; and Case C-373/95 *Maso* [1997] ECR I-4051, paras 30–1.

[69] Joined Cases C-133/93, C-300/93, and C-362/93 *Crispoltini II* [1994] ECR I-4865, paras 18–19; Case C-399/96 *Europièces* [1998] ECR I-6965, para 24; Joined Cases C-51/96 and C-191/97 *Christelle Deliège* [2000] ECR I-2549, para 38; Joined Cases C-115/97–117/97 *Breentjens* [1999] ECR I-6025, para 41; Joined Cases C-421/00, C-426/00, and C-16/01 *Sterbenz* [2003] ECR

however, that it is sufficient for a referring court simply to refer to another reference concerning other parties. First, those questions might not be known to the parties to the dispute before the referring court. Second, this approach poses problems in relation to the rights of the Member States and EU institutions to present observations in the preliminary case before the Court of Justice under Article 23 of the Statute of the Court.[70]

Under Article 104(5) of the Court's Rules of Procedure, it may, after hearing the Advocate General, request clarification from the referring court.[71] In practice the Registrar of the Court of Justice occasionally seeks to give the referring court the opportunity to supplement inadequate references.[72] After having obtained such clarifications, the Court provides the parties to the main proceedings and all others entitled to present observations in the preliminary case with the possibility of commenting, in writing or during an oral procedure, on the referring court's clarification.

Moreover, Article 54a of the Rules of Procedure allows the Court of Justice to request the parties to the main proceedings, the Member States, and the EU institutions to submit further information on the background to the case, just as the Court can invite these bodies to give an assessment of the possible consequences of a given decision.[73]

In *Wijsenbeek*, the Irish government argued that some questions concerning Article 14 of the EC Treaty were inadmissible because the reference did not contain information as to whether the party in the main proceedings had started his journey to the Netherlands in another Member State or in a third country. The Court of Justice noted that the party in question had explained that his flight came from Strasbourg and that this had not been contested in any of the other observations made to the Court. Consequently, the judgment making the reference

---

I-1065, para 21; and Joined Cases C-453/03, C-11/04, C-12/04, and C-194/04 *ABNA* [2005] ECR I-10423, para 49.

[70] Case C-12/07 *Autostrada dei Fiori and Aiscat* [2007] ECR I-162, para 24.

[71] Case C-265/05 *Naranjo* [2007] ECR I-349, para 23, where the Court of Justice asked the referring court for information about the relevant national law. See also Case C-20/05 *Schwilbert* [2007] ECR I-9447, para 22; Case C-231/03 *Coname* [2005] ECR I-7287, para 9; and C Naômé, *Le renvoi préjudiciel en droit européen* (2007) 140–4 and 232. In a resolution of 9 July 2008 on the role of the national judge in the European judicial system (A6-0224/2008), point 30, the European Parliament has called upon the Court of Justice to consider involving the referring judge more closely in its proceedings, including enhancing the possibilities of clarifying the reference.

[72] Case C-3/04 *Poseidon Chartering* [2006] ECR I-2505, para 11, and D Edward, 'Reform of Article 234 Procedure: The Limit of the Possible' in D O'Keeffe and A Bavasso (eds), *Judicial Review in European Union Law, vol I* (2000) 119, 121ff. Edward also states that a number of courts have shown themselves unable or unwilling to react to such opportunities, for example because the questions have been drafted by the parties to the main proceedings so that the referring court is unable to oversee such a reformulation without reconvening the hearing.

[73] Case C-20/03 *Burmanjer* [2005] ECR I-4133, para 8.

together with the written and oral observations gave the Court sufficient informa-tion to enable it to interpret the rules of Community law in relation to the situa-tion which was the subject of the main proceedings. The reference was therefore admissible.[74]

Where the Court of Justice is not in possession of information about the facts or national law necessary for giving a correct answer to the preliminary question, it must *ex officio* refuse to answer it. This is so not because of a self-standing require-ment for a thorough presentation of the case, but merely because the preliminary ruling process can only work in practice if the Court has the information neces-sary to understand the legal and factual circumstances of the case and, thereby, to provide the referring court with a useful reply. In other words, the boundary drawn is functional, and a reference will not be dismissed if an otherwise brief or incomplete presentation does not prevent the Court of Justice from understan-ding the legal questions referred to it.[75]

In *Van Straaten*, the Court of Justice stated that 'although the grounds of the order for reference are succinct and lack structure, the information which they contain is sufficient' to enable the Court to give correct and useful answers to the questions.[76]

In *Raccanelli*, the Court of Justice similarly held that

> while there may be gaps in the reference for a preliminary ruling, both in relation to the presentation of the facts of the main proceedings and the grounds for the refer-ence, the Court none the less has sufficient information to enable it to determine the scope of the questions raised and to interpret the Community provisions at issue so as to reply usefully to those questions.[77]

The above-mentioned considerations also entail that an incomplete order for reference will not be viewed more positively merely because it is a follow-up to a previous reference on the same case which has earlier been declared inadmissible on the ground of an insufficient description of the dispute in the main proceedings.[78]

---

[74] Case C-378/97 *Wijsenbeek* [1999] ECR I-6207, paras 18–23. See also Case C-476/01 *Kapper* [2004] ECR I-5205, paras 23–30; Case C-472/93 *Spano* [1995] ECR I-4321, para 26; Case C-17/94 *Gervais* [1995] ECR I-4353, para 21; Case C-56/98 *Modelo* [1999] ECR I-6427, para 18; and Case C-18/01 *Korhonen* [2003] ECR I-5331, para 25.

[75] Case C-322/98 *Kachelmann* [2000] ECR I-7505, para 20; Case C-295/97 *Piaggio* [1999] ECR I-3735, paras 22–3; and Case C-39/94 *SFEI* [1996] ECR I-3547, para 27.

[76] Case C-150/05 *Van Straaten* [2005] ECR I-9327, para 35.

[77] Case C-94/07 *Raccanelli* [2008] ECR I-5939, para 30. See similarly Case C-48/07 *Les Vergers du Vieux Tauves* (ECJ 22 December 2008), para 19.

[78] See the judgments referred to in s 3.2.3 above, n 53, and Case C-229/03 *Herbstrith* (ECJ 1 April 2004), compared with Case C-430/01 *Herbstrith* (ECJ 21 March 2002).

Depending on the deficiencies in the order for reference, the Court of Justice will sometimes be able to set out one or more expressly stated assumptions for the relevance of its preliminary ruling and leave it to the referring court to decide the extent to which the ruling is indeed relevant to the main proceedings.[79] Sometimes such deficiencies will not entirely prevent the Court of Justice from giving an interpretation of the Community rule in question, but 'merely' force the Court to give a general and abstract interpretation which does not take account of the particular circumstances of the actual case.[80] Although formally receiving an answer to its questions, the referring court may only derive limited value from such an abstract ruling.

In *Karlsson*, the Court of Justice stated that, as a matter of principle, in pursuing aims of agricultural policy, Member States may be justified in exempting certain producers from an otherwise general obligation even if the situation of these producers is analogous to that of competing producers. However, neither the grounds in the order containing the reference nor the observations made by the interveners in the case were sufficiently detailed to enable the Court to expand on when such treatment was justified.[81]

Several scholars have criticised the practice of the Court of Justice in dismissing references on the grounds of deficient presentation of the dispute in the main proceedings. The criticism has been directed not so much at the principle behind the Court's case law, but rather, it has been argued that the case law is inconsistent and therefore does not give national courts the necessary guidance.[82]

It is true that the case law does not always appear to be entirely consistent. However, any inconsistency should be of little importance for the national courts. A national court ought not to be satisfied with drawing up an order for reference on the basis of the vague minimum requirements which the Court of Justice has laid down for accepting a preliminary question as admissible. Rather, the benchmark should be much higher, as the referring court should seek to frame its questions in such a way

---

[79] Case C-371/97 *Gozza* [2000] ECR I-7881, paras 27–8; and Case C-400/96 *Harpegnies* [1998] ECR I-5121, para 21. See also Ch 11, s 2.4 below.

[80] See Case 222/78 *Beneventi* [1979] ECR 1163, paras 13 and 19–20; and Case C-266/96 *Corsica Ferries France* [1998] ECR I-3949, paras 15–18 and 24–5; as well as Ch 7, s 4, and Ch 11, s 3.3.

[81] Case C-292/97 *Karlsson* [2000] ECR I-2737, para 51.

[82] P Oliver, 'Recevabilité des questions préjudicielles: La jurisprudence des années 1990' (2001) Cahiers de droit européen Vols 1–2, 2001, 15, 29; R Lane, 'Article 234: A Few Rough Edges Still' in M Hoskins and W Robinson (eds), *A True European, Essays for Judge David Edward* (2003) 327, 336ff; D O'Keeffe, 'Is the Spirit of Article 177 under Attack? Preliminary References and Admissibility' (1998) 23 EL Rev Vol 23, 509, 514; as well as C Barnard and E Sharpston, 'The Changing Face of Article 177 References' (1997) 34 CML Rev Vol 34, 1113, 1150. The last named authors find that the level of completeness required for an order for reference depends on how interesting either the Advocate General or the Judge-Rapporteur finds the case.

as to give the Court of Justice the best possible basis for giving a ruling that is both relevant and provides the referring court with thorough and exhaustive guidance on all the Community law aspects of the case.

Moreover, it would be inappropriate for the Court of Justice to develop a practice with uniform but inflexible formal requirements for making a reference. As already stated, the quality requirements regarding the preliminary reference have two objectives: first, to avoid the Court of Justice delivering judgments that do not correspond to the reality behind the main dispute, thereby risking leading to an incorrect application of Community law; and second, to ensure that the Member States and the EU institutions entitled to present observations in the case have a reasonable basis on which to present those observations. This necessarily means that a case-by-case assessment is unavoidable. There is no reason to refuse to give a preliminary ruling if, in spite of a superficial reference, the Court of Justice manages to identify the problem which lies behind the question. A consistent application of precise requirements laid down as to the content of a reference would risk resulting in references being dismissed when there was no real need to do so. From the point of view of national judges, one of the advantages of the preliminary rulings procedure is that it gives the judge the possibility of obtaining help without conveying the impression of the judge being unqualified or helpless. A strict application of formalised requirements for elucidating preliminary references would risk undermining this aspect of Article 234.

That being said, one might sometimes wish that the Court of Justice could be more consistent with regard to how far the requirement for clarity of a reference should be based solely on the order for reference or whether it is sufficient that the issues at stake have been identified at the latest at the oral hearing. In principle there is nothing that prevents the Court from making more systematic use of its right to request clarification from the national court under Article 104(5) of the Rules of Procedure, referred to above.[83]

3.2.6. *Requesting the application of the urgent preliminary ruling procedure in the area of freedom, security, and justice*

As described in more detail below in Chapter 10, Section 5.3, a special urgent preliminary ruling procedure exists for areas covered by Title VI (Articles 29 to 42) of the Treaty on European Union concerning police and judicial cooperation in criminal matters, and Title IV (Articles 61 to 69) of Part Three of the EC Treaty

---

[83] For a similar argument see W Alexander, 'La Recevabilité des renvois préjudiciels dans la perspective de la réforme institutionelle de 1996' (1996) Cahiers de droit européen Vol 32, 561, 572; and D O'Keeffe, 'Is the Spirit of Article 177 under Attack? Preliminary References and Admissibility' (1998) 23 EL Rev Vol 23, 509, 512. According to D Anderson and M Demetriou, *References to the European Court* (2002) 290, Art 104(5) is not used for this purpose. However, Case C-265/05 *Naranjo* [2007] ECR I-349, para 23, does not seem to support this statement.

concerning visas, asylum, immigration, and other policies related to free movement of persons, including judicial cooperation in civil matters. The urgent procedure, which is laid down in Article 23a of the Court's Statute and Article 104b of its Rules of Procedure, entails special requirements for the formulation of the preliminary reference supplementing the general requirements described above in this chapter.[84]

First, the request for the urgent preliminary ruling procedure must be submitted in a form that enables the Registry of the Court to establish immediately that the file must be dealt with in a particular way. Accordingly, the request should be submitted in a document separate from the order for reference itself, or in a covering letter expressly setting out the request.

Second, according to Article 104b(1) of the Rules of Procedure, in order to enable the Court of Justice to decide quickly whether the urgent preliminary ruling procedure should be applied, the request should state the reasons which, in the view of the referring court, justify the application of that exceptional procedure. To that end, it should set out clearly and precisely the legal and factual background to the case, and should also describe the particular legal and/or factual matters which establish the need for an urgent ruling, such as, for example, the existence in national or Community law of mandatory time limits for giving a ruling or the serious consequences which could result, for the person concerned, from any delay in ruling on the questions referred.

In so far as it is able to do so, the referring court should briefly state its view on the answer to be given to the question(s) referred. Hopefully such a statement will encourage the submission of written or oral observations that are as relevant as possible. At the same time, the urgency mandates that the order for reference be succinct, as this helps to ensure the rapidity of the procedure.

Third, again with a view to ensuring speedy case-handling, the referring court should state the email address or any fax number which may be used by the Court of Justice, together with the email addresses or any fax numbers of the representatives of the parties to the proceedings. A copy of the signed order for reference together with a request for the urgent preliminary ruling procedure should be sent to the Court by email[85] or by fax[86] so that processing of the reference and of the request can begin upon receipt of the emailed or faxed copy. Also the originals of those documents must be sent to the Registry of the Court as soon as possible.

---

[84] See also the Court of Justice's information note on the urgent preliminary ruling procedure applicable to references concerning the area of freedom, security, and justice.

[85] <ECJ-Registry@curia.europa.eu>.

[86] (00 352) 433 766.

9

PROCEEDINGS BEFORE THE REFERRING COURT AFTER A REFERENCE HAS BEEN MADE

1. The Case Remains Pending before the National Court

Article 23 of the Statute of the Court of Justice presupposes that the national court stays the proceedings when it refers a preliminary question to the Court of Justice and this is indeed a normal consequence of making a preliminary reference. However, to make a preliminary reference does not imply that the case as such is transferred to the Court of Justice. On the contrary, the main proceedings remain pending before the referring court and that court thus retains jurisdiction to take any procedural measures which it is empowered to take under national law. For example, it may order protective measures to safeguard the interests of the parties pending the judgment of the Court of Justice.[1] Furthermore, Community law does not prevent the referring court from withdrawing a preliminary question, and there is no duty to give reasons for such a withdrawal.[2]

---

[1] See on this issue s 3 below.
[2] Case C-317/95 *Canadane Cheese Trading* [1997] ECR I-4681; Case C-534/08 *KLG Europe Eersel* (ECJ 18 February 2009); and Case C-233/99 *Hansen* (ECJ 21 March 2002).

Frequently a preliminary reference is withdrawn because the main proceedings before the referring court are terminated—for instance due to a settlement or withdrawal of appeal.[3]

In *Zabala Erasun*, following a reference to the Court of Justice for a preliminary ruling, the defendant Spanish government acquiesced to the claims of the plaintiff and paid the unemployment benefits claimed by the latter. Furthermore, the government declared that the payment, with retrospective effect, should be regarded as being covered by the scope of the applicable Community law rule, as the plaintiff had argued in the main proceedings. Finally, the government submitted that the preliminary reference should be withdrawn, as the dispute no longer existed. However, the referring court maintained its request for a preliminary ruling. Indeed, it informed the Court of Justice that, since the case was no longer pending before it but had been referred to the Court of Justice, it was not in a position to terminate the case and withdraw the preliminary questions. The Court of Justice replied that it follows from Article 234 that where a national court makes a reference for a preliminary ruling only the request for interpretation or a decision on validity is addressed to the Court; the case as such is not transferred. The national court therefore remains seized of the case, which is still pending before it. Accordingly, Community law does not preclude a national court which has made a preliminary reference from finding that in national law the claims of the appellants have been acceded to and, where appropriate, that the main proceedings are thereby terminated. On this basis, the Court of Justice declared that it did not have jurisdiction as long as the Spanish court had not confirmed that, under Spanish law, the proceedings had been terminated.[4]

Another common reason for withdrawing a preliminary reference is that following the reference a judgment of the Court of Justice, on an issue similar to that raised in the preliminary reference, has rendered the matter *acte éclairé* so that the referring court can now confidently decide the matter itself without first obtaining a preliminary ruling.[5] Depending on the stage of the preliminary proceedings, the referring court might, however, find it more appropriate to maintain the reference.

In *Royscott Leasing Ltd and others v Commissioners of Customs and Excise*, in connection with Directive 77/388, the English Court of Appeal refused to withdraw

---

[3] Case C-396/06 *Kramme* (removed from the Court's register on ECJ 11 April 2008); Case C-408/07 *Ruf* (removed from the Court's register on ECJ 2 February 2009); and Case C-175/06 *Tedeso* (removed from the Court's register on ECJ 27 September 2007).

[4] Joined Cases C-422/93–424/93 *Zabala Erasun* [1995] ECR I-1567.

[5] See Ch 5, s 4.7 above, and eg Case C-514/08 *Atenor Group* (removed from the Court's register on ECJ 29 March 2009); Case C-584/08 *Real Madrid Football Club* (removed from the Court's register on ECJ 29 March 2009); Case C-389/07 *Azlan Group plc* (removed from the Court's register on ECJ 18 August 2008); and Case C-203/05 *Vodaphone 2* (removed from the Court's register on ECJ 20 August 2008).

a request for a preliminary ruling which it had made to the Court of Justice despite an intervening ruling by the latter in another case relating to the same directive. In the opinion of the Court of Appeal there was only reason to withdraw a preliminary reference if it was clear that a ruling on the question posed had become entirely without interest. That condition was not met in the instant case. Indeed, as the Court of Justice had not suggested that the preliminary reference should be withdrawn, it apparently did not itself find that the issue had already been decided in the other case. Moreover, the proceedings before the Court of Justice were at an advanced stage as the hearing was imminent and the Advocate General was to deliver his Opinion in about two months' time. Hence, to withdraw the reference would not entail a substantial reduction of the length of the national proceedings. Rather to the contrary, at this advanced stage of the proceedings withdrawing the reference for a preliminary ruling could unduly prolong the case as a whole.[6]

It may also happen that a judgment from the Court of Justice handed down after the preliminary reference has been made induces the referring court to either withdraw or add questions to those already posed.[7]

Only the referring national court can ask the Court of Justice to remove a request for a preliminary ruling from its case register.[8] In contrast, as the procedure in Article 234 is wholly independent of the will of the parties to the main proceedings, even a joint request to strike a preliminary reference from the register will be in vain. The parties may nevertheless draw the Court's attention to developments in the national proceedings and thereby induce it to ask the referring national court whether it maintains its preliminary reference. Unfortunately, national courts do not always respond to the Court's questions, and in such situations it has happened that the Court of Justice has removed a preliminary case from its register where it seemed apparent from other information available to the Court of Justice that the national proceedings had been terminated.[9]

---

[6] Court of Appeal (England and Wales), 5 November 1998, *Royscot Leasing Ltd and others v Commissioners of Customs and Excise* [1999] 1 CMLR 903, paras 5–6.

[7] Case C-311/94 *Ijssel-Vliet Combinatie* [1996] ECR I-5023; Case C-385/99 *Müller-Fauré* [2003] ECR I-4509; and Case C-156/01 *Van der Duin* [2003] ECR I-7045.

[8] On the possibility of appealing a preliminary reference within the national judicial system, see s 2 below.

[9] Case C-132/07 *Beecham Group* (ECJ 12 March 2009). See further R Barents et al, *European Courts Procedure* (2004) para 17.023; and C Naômé, *Le renvoi préjudiciel en droit européen* (2007) 134. For a similar situation before the EFTA Court see Case E-5/97 *European Navigation* [1998] EFTA Court Report 59.

2. Appeal against a Decision to Make a Preliminary Reference

Whilst a rule of national law whereby a court is bound on points of law by the rulings of a superior court cannot on this ground alone deprive a lower court of its power, provided for under Article 234, to refer questions to the court for a preliminary ruling, this provision does not preclude a decision to refer a preliminary question being subject to those remedies that are normally available under national law.[10]

Traditionally, this has been interpreted to imply that Community law allows a decision to make a preliminary reference to be overturned by an appellate court according to national rules on the administration of justice.[11] Depending on national law, such an appeal can for example be based on an argument that the referring court does not have jurisdiction under national law, that there has been a procedural mistake, or that the assumed relevance of the preliminary question is based on an incorrect interpretation of national law.

Unless informed that an appeal has suspensory effect under national law, the Court of Justice does not defer its dealing with a preliminary reference solely because the decision to make the preliminary reference has been appealed.[12] In principle, proceedings for the preliminary ruling before the Court of Justice can thus be completed while the question of the reference or its content is still pending before the national appellate court. In such cases the Court of Justice will render its ruling without regard to the objections which have caused the reference to be appealed.[13] However, once the Court of Justice has been informed that the decision to make a preliminary reference has been annulled on appeal, it has traditionally abided by that decision and removed the preliminary case from its

---

[10] Case 146/73 *Rheinmühlen-Düsseldorf* [1974] ECR 139, para 3; and see further Ch 3, s 6.2, above.

[11] K Lenaerts et al, *Procedural law of the European Union* (2006) 59ff; H Schermers and D Waelbroeck, *Judicial Protection in the European Union* (2001) 249ff; C Soulard, 'Techniques de formulation de la question préjudicielle: les rôles respectifs de la jurisdiction nationale et de l'avocat' in V Christianos (ed), *Evolution récente du droit judiciare communautaire vol I* (1994) 73, 78; M Jarvis, *The Application of EC Law by National Courts* (1998) 429; R Barents et al, *European Courts Procedure* (2004), paras 31.081–31.086 and 31.143; and D Anderson and M Demetriou, *References to the European Court* (2002) 195, 215–17 and 305. See for an English example Court of Appeal, Civil Division, 16 July 2002, *R (on the application of A) v Secretary of State for the Home Department* [2002] European Law Reports 580; for a German example judgment of the *Bundesverwaltungsgericht* of 28 January 1997, 1 C 17/94 [1997] Neue Zeitschrift für Verwaltungsrecht 1119; and, with regard to the Netherlands, R Crowe, Colloquium Report, The Preliminary Reference Procedure: Reflections based on Practical Experience of the Highest National Courts in Administrative Matters (2004) 5 ERA Forum 435, 437.

[12] Case 127/73 *BRT* [1974] ECR 51, para 9; Case 106/77 *Simmenthal* [1978] ECR 629, para 10; and Case C-132/87 *Nationaal Instituut vor Landbouwkrediet* (ECJ 20 January 1988).

[13] Joined Cases 2/82–4/82 *Delhaize Frères* [1983] ECR 2973, paras 8–9.

case register.[14] Conversely, in the past the Court of Justice has accepted that a national appellate court modified a preliminary question or added new questions to those already posed by the lower court.[15]

The judgment in *Cartesio* has, however, qualified that approach and underlined the autonomy of the referring court.

In *Cartesio*, a Hungarian court asked whether it was in accordance with Article 234 that Hungarian law conferred a right to bring an appeal against an order making a preliminary reference thereby limiting the power of the lower courts to refer questions for a preliminary ruling. The Court of Justice first restated its established case law according to which Article 234 does not preclude a decision of a national court to make a preliminary reference being subject to the remedies that are normally available under national law. It added, however, that the outcome of such an appeal could not limit the referring court's jurisdiction to make a preliminary reference if it considered that a case pending before it raised questions on the interpretation of provisions of Community law necessitating a ruling by the Court of Justice. In this respect, the Court stated that Article 234 confers an autonomous jurisdiction on the referring court to make a preliminary reference. This autonomous jurisdiction would be called into question, if—by varying the order for reference, by setting it aside, and by ordering the referring court to resume the proceedings—the appellate court could prevent the referring court from exercising the right to make a preliminary reference. Therefore, it was solely for the referring court to draw the proper inferences from a judgment delivered on an appeal against its decision to refer and, in particular, to come to a conclusion as to whether it would be appropriate to maintain the preliminary reference, or to amend it or to withdraw it.[16]

The Court's statement that Article 234 does not preclude a decision to make a preliminary reference subject to appeal under national law is difficult to reconcile with its conclusion that the lower court's competence to make a preliminary reference cannot be restricted by national rules permitting the appellate court to quash or amend the order for a preliminary reference.

At the very least, the judgment implies that it is only the referring court that has the power to instruct the Court of Justice of the consequences under national law of an appeal against its decision to make a preliminary reference. Consequently, the Court of Justice will not strike a preliminary reference from its register merely

---

[14] Case 65/77 *Razanatsimba* [1977] ECR 2229, paras 5–6; Case C-34/90 *Plapied and Gallez* (ECJ 24 April 1991); Case C-269/92 *Bosman* (ECJ 8 December 1993); Case C-310/94 *Ardon* (ECJ 16 January 1996); and paras 48–9 in Advocate General Colomer's Opinion in Case C-132/07 *Beecham Group* (ECJ 12 March 2009).

[15] Joined Cases C-297/88 and C-197/89 *Dzodzi* [1990] ECR I-3763, paras 8–9.

[16] Case C-210/06 *Cartesio* (ECJ 16 December 2008), paras 88–98.

because the appellate court informs it that the decision to make a preliminary reference has been quashed on appeal. On such a narrow reading of the judgment it is unlikely to have any significant practical consequences, since Community law will fully respect national law both on the possibility to appeal decisions to make a preliminary reference and on the legal effects of such appeal decisions, including the binding effect that they have on the lower referring court. This reading of the judgment would square nicely with the Court's practice up to *Cartesio*.

Nonetheless, there seem to be convincing arguments to support the view that the ruling in *Cartesio* goes further. Thus, whilst accepting that an appeal may be made against a decision to make a preliminary reference, the Court of Justice at the same time appears to hold that Community law vests in the referring lower court the power to ignore a decision of an appellate court overturning or amending the decision to refer. In other words, Community law seems to entail that the appellate court's decision does not have its usual binding force on the lower court and that the appellate court's ruling instead becomes a mere advice to the referring court.[17] This reading finds support in the Court's statement that

> the *outcome* of such an appeal cannot limit the jurisdiction conferred by Article 234 EC on that court to make a reference to the Court if *it* considers that a case pending before it raises questions on the interpretation of provisions of Community law necessitating a ruling by the Court.[18]

Moreover, if the referring court were bound by the appellate court's decision that the reference should be withdrawn or altered, why then would the Court of Justice be at pains to stress that

> a court at first instance remains free to refer questions to the Court pursuant to Article 234 EC, *regardless* of the existence of a rule of national law whereby a court is bound on points of law by the rulings of a superior court? (Footnote 18 bis)

And why would the Court continue by observing that:

> the autonomous jurisdiction which Article 234 EC confers on the *referring* court to make a reference to the Court would be called into question, *if*—by varying the order for reference, by setting it aside and by ordering the referring court to resume the proceedings—the appellate court could prevent the referring court from exercising the right, conferred on it by the EC Treaty, to make a reference to the Court?[19]

Finally, the Court underlined:

> [it is for the] referring court to draw the proper inferences from a judgment delivered on an appeal against its decision to refer and, in particular, to come to a conclusion as to whether it is *appropriate* to maintain the reference for a preliminary ruling, or

---

[17] See similarly J Engström, 'Case Law of the European Union Courts, Leading Judgments 16 December 2008 to 28 February 2009' (2009) ERA Forum 308.
[18] Para 93 of the judgment, emphasis added. 18 bis: para 94 of the judgment, emphasis added.
[19] Paras 94–5 of the judgment, emphasis added.

to amend it or to withdraw it . . . such revocation or amendment being matters on which that court *alone* is able to take a decision.[20]

This statement does not sit well with an interpretation that under national law the lower court is bound by an appeal decision to recall a preliminary reference.

Under this latter and more far-reaching reading of *Cartesio*, the consequences of the judgment are likely to vary between the different Member States. On the one hand, the ruling will not have much impact in those Member States where it already follows from national law that a preliminary reference cannot be made subject to appeal. This appears to be the case in Austria,[21] Belgium,[22] Ireland,[23] and Italy.[24] On the other hand, in those Member States where a decision to make a preliminary ruling may be subject to appeal, the judgment will, in principle, imply a substantial change of national procedural law. Nevertheless, it appears somewhat doubtful whether in practice the ruling in *Cartesio* will have substantive consequences. After all, the judgment accepts that an appellate court may pronounce itself on a lower court's decision to make a preliminary reference, and it does not seem likely that many lower courts will ignore an appellate court ruling that a preliminary reference be withdrawn or amended even if Article 234 vests in the lower court the power to disregard such a ruling.

Finally, the principle laid down in *Cartesio* only applies where the dispute in the main proceedings also continues before the referring court after the appellate court has rendered its decision. In contrast, if either the appeal itself or the decision of the appellate court means that the case is no longer pending before the referring court, then the referring court loses its competence to maintain a preliminary reference in spite of an appellate court's decision to the contrary.

In *De Nationale Loterij,* the Belgian *rechtbank van koophandel te Hasselt* referred two preliminary questions concerning the relationship between the EC Treaty rules on free provision of services and a Belgian law granting monopoly rights to Nationale Loterij, Belgium's public gaming company. This decision to make a preliminary reference was appealed to the *hof van beroep te Antwerpen* which found that the case law of the Court of Justice provided sufficient clarity for the resolution of the case. It therefore annulled the decision to make a preliminary reference and at the same time ruled on the substance of the case. Hence, the question arose whether the Court of Justice could strike the case from its register merely on the basis of the appellate court's decision or whether the ruling in *Cartesio* entailed

---

[20] Paras 96–7 of the judgment, emphasis added.
[21] Decision of the *Oberster Gerichtshof* of 9 December 1997 Case 16 Ok 9/96.
[22] Decision of the *Cour d'appel de Bruxelles*, 5 March 1999, No 322/96, summarised in the European Commission's 2000 Survey concerning the application of Community law by National Courts [2001] OJ C30/192, p 194.
[23] *Campus Oil v Minister for Industry and Energy* [1983] The Irish Reports 82.
[24] Case No 7636, order of 24 May 2002 *Foro italiano* 2002, I, Col 3090.

that only the referring court could withdraw the question. In this regard the Court of Justice recalled that in *Cartesio* the main proceedings remained pending before the referring court in their entirety since it was only the referring court's decision to make a preliminary reference to the Court of Justice that had been appealed. In such a situation, the referring court's power to make a preliminary reference could not be called into question by the application of national rules permitting the appellate court to set aside the reference and order the referring court to resume the domestic law proceedings. However, this result could not be transposed to the altogether different situation in the main proceedings in *Loterij* where the appellate court itself decided the dispute in the main proceedings and thereby had taken upon itself to ensure the application of Community law. In this latter situation, the dispute was no longer pending before the referring court, and it was therefore not decisive that the referring court had not itself withdrawn the preliminary question. Hence, the Court of Justice found it unnecessary to answer the preliminary question.[25]

3. Interim Relief

3.1. Overview

As described above in Section 1, a preliminary reference does not entail that the main proceedings are transferred from the referring court to the Court of Justice. Rather, the case remains pending before the national court. Hence, the Court of Justice has no jurisdiction to entertain an application for interim relief in a preliminary reference case, and it is therefore exclusively for the referring court to grant interim relief in order to ensure the legal protection which persons derive from Community law.[26]

However, as will be shown in the following section, this does not mean that Community law remains indifferent to the issue of interim protection. The analysis starts out in Section 3.2 by identifying the situations where a national court has competence to order interim protection under Community law. Section 3.3 then provides an account of the different criteria that form part of a decision to provide interim relief under Community law.

3.2. The competence of national courts to order interim relief

3.2.1. *Possible conflicts between national law and Community law*

A national court seised of a dispute governed by Community law must be in a position to grant interim relief against a national law or administrative order that

---

[25] Case C-525/06 *De Nationale Loterij* (ECJ 24 March 2009).
[26] Case C-186/01 R *Alexander Dory* [2001] ECR I-7823, paras 6–10.

is claimed to be incompatible with Community law in order to ensure the full effectiveness of the judgment to be given on the existence of rights claimed under Community law.[27]

Similarly, the principle of effectiveness requires that a national court which refers a preliminary question to the Court of Justice in order to resolve a problem of compatibility between Community law and a national law or administrative measure must be able to suspend the application of the relevant national measure while awaiting the preliminary ruling.[28]

In the situations just described, the dispute solely concerns the issue of whether a national legislative provision or administrative act infringes Community law and so the legality of a Community act is not called into question. Where no Community act is called into question, Community law leaves it to the domestic legal system of each Member State to determine the conditions under which interim relief is to be granted. The only proviso is that these conditions may not be less favourable than those applying to similar domestic actions (principle of equivalence) and must not render it excessively difficult to obtain interim judicial protection of rights conferred by Community law (principle of effectiveness).[29] Provided these conditions are met, Community law does not restrict the possibility under national law of granting interim relief. Indeed, such relief does not suspend the immediate enforcement of the relevant Community rule; rather to the contrary, by temporarily disapplying the contested national provision, any potential Community law problem will disappear provisionally.

3.2.2. *Possible conflicts between different Community rules*

National courts may also suspend the enforcement of a national measure based on a Community act where the legality of the latter is contested. However, in such cases both the procedural and the substantive rules for the granting of interim relief are different to those applicable in the situations described above where the application for interim protection is not based on a claim of illegality of a Community act.

First, the decision as to whether to suspend the operation of a national measure issued in accordance with a contested Community act is not first and foremost regulated by national law. Rather, the national court must apply both national and Community law. Thus, while the issue remains governed by national procedural law as regards the making and examination of the application for interim

---

[27] Case C-432/05 *Unibet* [2007] ECR I-2271, paras 66–77; and Case C-226/99 *Siples* [2001] ECR I-277, para 19.
[28] Case C-213/89 *Factortame* [1990] ECR I-2433.
[29] Case C-432/05 *Unibet* [2007] ECR I-2271, paras 78–83.

relief, the substantive conditions for ordering the suspension are regulated by Community law and are thus the same for all Member States. Moreover, these uniform conditions are largely identical to those regulating the same matter in cases brought before the Court of Justice (and the Court of First Instance) in accordance with Article 242 of the EC Treaty.[30] According to that provision, the bringing of actions before the Court of Justice does not have suspensory effect. However, the Court of Justice may, if it considers that circumstances so require, order that the application of the contested act be suspended.

Second, it is a condition that at the same time as ordering the suspension, the national court makes a preliminary reference to the Court of Justice for a ruling on the validity of the disputed Community act, should the validity question not already have been brought before the Court in another case.[31] Indeed, this requirement follows logically from the Court's case law according to which it has exclusive competence to declare a Community act invalid.[32]

In *Zuckerfabrik*, the Court of Justice stated that a national court can suspend the application of a national administrative act issued in accordance with a disputed Community regulation until the Court of Justice, via a preliminary reference from the national court, has decided whether the regulation is invalid. In this connection the Court of Justice emphasised the importance of ensuring effective legal protection. It also acknowledged that the result could hardly be otherwise, as in earlier case law it had established that interim relief should be possible in relation to national legislation that was potentially contrary to Community law.[33] Finally, the result also followed from the need to have a coherent Community system for interim relief. Indeed, when, by an order under Article 242 of the EC Treaty, the Court of Justice can, in a direct action, suspend the application of a contested Community regulation, it would be unreasonable if a national court could not postpone the application of a national measure issued under that very regulation. Turning to the actual conditions for granting interim relief, the Court held that the uniform application of Community law is a fundamental requirement of the

---

[30] Joined Cases C-143/88 and C-92/89 *Zuckerfabrik Süderditmarschen* [1991] ECR I-415, paras 22–27; Joined Cases C-453/03, C-11/04, C-12/04, and C-194/04 *ABNA* [2005] ECR I-10423, para 104; and Case C-334/95 *Krüger* [1997] ECR I-4517, paras 43–4. As to the rare situation where a national court hearing an application for interim measures considers adopting protective measures vis-à-vis a non-Community authority because a likely infringement of Community law would otherwise be imminent see Case C-17/98 *Emesa Sugar* [2000] ECR I-675, paras 66–73.

[31] In an order of 29 October 2003 in *Société Techna*, Droit Administratif, January 2004, p 32, the French *Conseil d'État, Section du contentieux*, decided to order interim relief against the French implementing provision of a Community directive without making a preliminary reference to the Court of Justice on the validity of the directive in question as an English court had already referred that question to the Court.

[32] See Ch 6, s 4.2 above.

[33] See s 3.2.1 above.

Community legal order. Consequently, the power to suspend the enforcement of administrative measures based on a contested Community regulation had to be subject to uniform conditions in all Member States. Moreover, precisely because of the above-mentioned need for coherence between interim relief before the Court of Justice and interim relief before the national courts, the conditions should correspond to those that would apply to the Court itself under Article 242 in direct actions.[34]

Under Article 242 of the EC Treaty, an application may not be made to postpone the application of a negative administrative act (eg an administrative act that rejects an application for a grant or a permit).[35] Indeed, in such a situation a postponement of the contested act would not change the legal position of the applicant, who would still not have received even a temporary grant or permit. Such a party might nevertheless have the same need for interim protection. Article 243 of the EC Treaty therefore provides that the Court of Justice may prescribe any necessary interim measures. For example, the Court can require the Commission to issue a temporary marketing permit, despite the existence of a disputed Community rule that restricts rights thereto.

The case law described above on the competence of national courts to order interim protection against national measures which implement Community rules the legality of which is called into question reflects a desire for a cohesive approach to the grant of interim remedies. This aim applies both where an applicant seeks suspension of enforcement of a national administrative measure adopted on the basis of the contested Community act and where that applicant applies for interim measures of the kind covered by Article 243 of the EC Treaty. The Court of Justice has therefore ruled that the interim legal protection which national courts must afford to individuals under Community law should be the same in the two situations. Thus, national courts have the competence to issue positive orders provisionally disapplying a contested Community act pending a preliminary ruling by the Court on the validity of that act. It has also been held that due to the need for coherence in the system of interim remedies, the national courts' jurisdiction with regard to the issuing of such orders must be exercised by analogy with Article 243 of the EC Treaty.

In 1993 the Community adopted a regulation on the import of bananas which meant that a number of German undertakings, including the fruit importer *Atlanta,* were put in a difficult position. The regulation was administered via the

---

[34] Joined Cases C-143/88 and C-92/89 *Zuckerfabrik Süderditmarschen* [1991] ECR I-415, paras 14–33.
[35] Case C-89/97P R *Moccia Irme* [1997] ECR I-2327, para 45; and Case C-206/89 R *S* [1989] ECR 2841, para 14.

issuing of import licences by the national authorities. Atlanta applied for an import licence, but was refused, and it therefore brought an action against this decision. The German court questioned whether the import rules laid down in the regulation were valid and made a preliminary reference to that effect.[36] At the same time, the German court made a separate preliminary reference to the Court of Justice asking whether it could make a positive order provisionally disapplying the regulation in question pending a preliminary ruling by the Court on its validity. The Court of Justice recognised that a national court could grant such positive interim relief. This was so, as the interim legal protection which the national courts must afford to individuals under Community law must be the same, whether they seek suspension of enforcement of a national administrative measure adopted on the basis of a Community regulation or the grant of other forms of interim measure. However, a national court may only order such a positive measure, rendering the regulation whose validity is challenged provisionally inapplicable as regards the applicant, on the same conditions as those which apply when the Court of Justice is dealing with an application for interim measures under Article 243 of the EC Treaty.[37]

The judgments in *Zuckerfabrik* and *Atlanta* show that the alignment with Articles 242 and 243 of the EC Treaty also applies where the otherwise applicable national law on interim protection would have resulted in a wider interim protection than that provided under Community law. In other words, Community law not only imposes minimum conditions for when interim protection should be granted, it also restricts the national courts' competence to grant such relief since granting this relief will mean the temporary disapplication of the contested Community rule before its invalidity has been established.

The competence of national courts to provide for positive interim relief does not go so far as to allow for such measures in cases where the existence and extent of the applicant's Community rights are yet to be established in a future legal act that has still to be adopted by the Community legislator.

In *Port*, a German court asked whether it could order provisional measures in proceedings for the grant of interim relief until such time as the Commission had adopted a decision allowing certain forms of import of bananas from third countries under an import licence. The Court of Justice noted that this situation was different from the situation at issue in *Zuckerfabrik* and *Atlanta*, described above. Indeed, the issue was not the possible granting of interim relief in the context of the implementation of a Community regulation whose validity was being contested, but rather related to granting traders interim judicial protection in a

---

[36] Case C-466/93 *Atlanta* [1995] ECR I-3799.
[37] Case C-465/93 *Atlanta* [1995] ECR I-3761.

situation where, by virtue of a Community regulation, the existence and scope of traders' rights had to be established by a Commission decision which the Commission had not yet adopted. With regard to this latter situation, the EC Treaty makes no provision for a reference for a preliminary ruling by which a national court can ask the Court of Justice to rule that an institution has failed to act. Consequently, national courts have no jurisdiction to order interim measures pending action on the part of the institution. Rather, judicial review of the alleged failure to act must be exercised exclusively by the Court of Justice and the Court of First Instance. In other words, an application for interim protection could only be made before the Community courts under Article 243 of the EC Treaty in connection with proceedings brought for failure to act.[38]

3.3. The conditions for granting interim relief

3.3.1. Overview

The following section examines the basic conditions for the national court to be able to order interim remedies, namely:

1. that there is reasonable doubt about the legality of the contested act;
2. that there is urgency; and
3. that no countervailing public or private interest in the continuous and unin-terrupted application of the contested act weighs more heavily than the applicant's interest in obtaining interim relief.

In addition to these three conditions the rules on interim relief before the Court of Justice and the Court of First Instance contain two supplementary conditions: first, the main action must not be manifestly inadmissible, eg because it has been brought too late or because the plaintiff lacks standing.[39] And, second, the interim protection sought may not prejudice the outcome of the main action.

The Court of Justice has not yet ruled whether these two additional conditions also apply in situations where the question on interim relief arises before a national court.

However, it must be presumed that this is not so with regard to the situation described above in Section 3.2.1, ie where the interim relief is sought against national law. It would nevertheless be natural to assume that, as a matter of national law, most national courts would also refuse to order interim relief if these conditions were not fulfilled. That being said, where it is uncertain under national law whether an action to safeguard respect for an individual's rights under Community law is admissible, Community law requires that the national court must be able to

---

[38] Case C-68/95 *Port* [1996] ECR I-6067, paras 46–62.
[39] Case C-380/04P R *Bactria* (ECJ 13 December 2004).

grant the interim relief necessary in order to ensure that those rights are respected.[40]

Also with regard to the situation described above in Section 3.2.2 a national court should display considerable caution before refusing interim protection on the ground that the main action is not likely to be admissible since, in principle, the question of the admissibility of the main action should not be examined in relation to an application for interim relief as this will prejudice the merits of the case.[41]

3.3.2. Doubt as to validity

It is a classical condition for interim relief that, following an initial assessment, it is not evident that the applicant's claim in the main proceedings is without any merit (often referred to as the case having *fumus boni iuris*).

With regard to the situation described above in Section 3.2.2, the Court of Justice has, out of regard for the effectiveness of the Community legal system, held that interim relief suspending the enforcement of a contested Community act or of a national measure implementing that act may be adopted only if the factual and legal circumstances relied on by the applicant are such as to persuade the national court that 'serious doubts' exist as to the validity of the contested Community act. In this respect, when making the interim order, the national court cannot restrict itself to referring the question of the validity of the Community act to the Court of Justice for a preliminary ruling, but must, in addition, set out the reasons for why it considers that the Court of Justice should find the act to be invalid.[42]

On the face of it, it may seem surprising that the Court of Justice insists on such a high threshold for the requisite doubt. Indeed, the Court of Justice has held that, in cases before it, it is sufficient that 'it cannot be ruled out from the outset that the main action is well founded'.[43] However, there are important differences between, on the one hand, the situation where a national court has to decide whether a party should be allowed temporarily not to comply with a Community rule, and, on the other hand, the interests which the Court of Justice (and the Court of First Instance) must take account of in proceedings where it is up to those two courts to decide whether to order interim relief against a Community act under Articles 242 and 243 of the EC Treaty.

First, the question of the validity of the disputed Community act is not decided by the national court, but by the Court of Justice, the latter being the sole competent

---

[40] Case C-432/05 *Unibet* [2007] ECR I-2271, para 72.
[41] Case T-85/05 R *Dimos Ano Liosion* [2005] ECR II-1721, paras 37–47; Case C-313/90 R *CIRFS* [1991] ECR I-2557; Case T-107/96 R *Pantochim* [1996] ECR II-1361; Case C-12/95 P *Tramasa* [1995] ECR I-467; and Case T-610/97 R *Carlsen* [1998] ECR II-48.
[42] Case C-465/93 *Atlanta* [1995] ECR I-3761, para 36.
[43] Case C-76/08 R *Commission v Malta* [2008] ECR I-64, para 30.

authority to declare a Community act invalid. Hence, the national court itself should not merely have doubts about the validity of the contested Community act; it must also entertain a justified assumption that the Court of Justice will find that the claim of invalidity is 'not without substance'. Second, it may be presumed that the national court has greater difficulty than the Court of Justice in evaluating whether the Community act is invalid so that its doubt about this may arise more easily than before the Court of Justice. Third, an interim decision of the Court of Justice must not prejudge the decision in the main proceedings and the Court of Justice is therefore barred from making a more substantive preliminary assessment of the validity of the disputed Community act when deciding whether to grant an interim remedy.[44] In contrast, a national court is not so barred since it cannot itself declare a Community provision to be invalid and thus its assessment of the Community act's validity has no prejudicial effects.

When assessing the conditions for the grant of interim relief, the national courts are, moreover, obliged to respect the Community courts' rulings on the matter in question. Thus, if in an action for annulment the Court of Justice or the Court of First Instance has dismissed on the merits a claim of invalidity of a Community act the national court is barred from ordering interim protection in reaction to a claim of illegality on the same grounds. The same applies if in the context of a reference for a preliminary ruling on validity the Court of Justice has held that the reference has disclosed nothing to affect the validity of that act.[45]

As stated above in Section 3.2.1, where a dispute is solely about whether a national measure is compatible with Community law without contesting the validity of a Community act, Community law leaves it to national law to regulate the precise conditions for interim relief. It only interferes if under national law it is excessively difficult to obtain interim remedies for the protection of Community rights. Until now the Court of Justice has not pronounced itself on how much doubt the national courts may require concerning the legality of the contested national measure.

In *R v Secretary of State for Transport, ex p Factortame (No 2)*, Lord Goff of the UK House of Lords held that an English court should not restrain a public authority by interim injunction from enforcing apparently authentic law unless it is satisfied, having regard to all the circumstances, that the challenge to the validity of the law is prima facie so firmly based as to justify such an exceptional course being taken.[46]

---

[44] Cf Art 36 of the Court's Statute and Art 86 of its Rules of Procedure as well as Case C-393/96 R *Antonissen* [1997] ECR I-441.

[45] Case C-465/93 *Atlanta* [1995] ECR I-3761, para 46.

[46] [1991] 1 AC 603, 673C.

3.3.3. Urgency

Under Community law, in addition to the requirement for reasonable doubt, measures suspending the application of a contested legal act may be granted only in the event of urgency. A national court dealing with the application for interim relief must therefore examine the circumstances particular to the case before it and consider whether it is likely that immediate enforcement of the measure that is the subject of the application for interim relief would result in serious and irreversible damage to the applicant that could not be made good if the Community act were to be declared invalid.[47] Indeed, there is no need to suspend the application of the contested act if a later annulment of the act would give the affected party the necessary remedy, either in itself or in combination with an economic compensation.[48] Similarly, a national court may not suspend the application of measures taken in accordance with a contested Community act if the main proceedings can be decided before a loss becomes irreparable.[49] The same applies if the requested interim relief is unable to prevent the threatened loss.

It is for the party claiming serious and irreparable damage to establish its existence. While it is not necessary to show that the damage will occur with absolute certainty, a sufficient degree of probability being enough, the applicant is none the less required to prove the facts which are considered to found the prospect of such damage and demonstrate why interim relief is likely to prevent the damage from occurring.[50]

In principle, purely pecuniary damage cannot be regarded as irreparable as it can be the subject of future pecuniary compensation.[51] That being said, there may be situations where such damage cannot subsequently be compensated, for instance because it will not be possible to prove the extent of the damage or because the party that will be required to compensate the loss will not be able to do so.

Similarly, interim relief may be justified where it appears that, if the protection is not granted, the applicant will find itself in a situation which could jeopardise its

---

[47] Joined Cases C-143/88 and C-92/89 *Zuckerfabrik Süderditmarschen* [1991] ECR I-415, paras 28–9; and Case C-465/93 *Atlanta* [1995] ECR I-3761, paras 40–1.

[48] Case 176/88 R *Hanning* [1988] ECR 3915, para 13; and Case T-108/94 R *Candiotte* [1994] ECR II-249, paras 24–9.

[49] Case T-229/97 R *CEFS* [1997] ECR II-1649.

[50] Case C-130/95 *Giloy* [1997] ECR I-4291, paras 37–40; Case C-329/99 PR *Pfizer Animal Health* [1999] ECR I-8343, para 75; Case C-149/95P R *Atlantic Container Line* [1995] ECR I-2165, paras 38–47; and Joined Cases C-51/90 R and C-59/90 R *Cosmos-Tank* [1990] ECR I-2167, paras 18–32; Case T-291/04 R *Enviro Tech Europe* [2005] ECR II-475, paras 72–3; Case C-39/03 R *Artegodan* [2003] ECR I-4485; Case T-151/01 R *Duales System Deutschland* [2001] ECR II-3295, para 197; Case T-41/97 R *Antillean Rice Mills* [1997] ECR II-447, paras 47–59.

[51] Case C-257/90 *Italsolar* [1990] ECR I-3841, para 15; Case T-6/97 R *Comafrica and Dole* [1997] ECR II-291, para 46; and Case T-43/98 R *Emesa Sugar* [1998] ECR II-3055, paras 62–71.

very existence or irremediably alter its position in the market.[52] However, in the latter situation it is a condition that the applicant shows not only that the disputed legal act damages its market position, but also that obstacles of a structural or legal nature would prevent it from regaining a significant proportion of the lost market share even if the contested legal act were to be annulled in the main action.[53]

3.3.4. Balancing the interests

Finally, it is a condition for instituting interim relief against the application of a contested Community act that the applicant's interests in the relief outweigh opposing public or private interests in the immediate and continuous application of that act.

In *UK v Commission*, interim relief was sought against a Commission decision on certain emergency measures—including an export prohibition—to fight BSE (mad cow disease). The Court of Justice held that the maintenance of the disputed export prohibition would probably result in damage to commercial and social interests, and that part of such damage would not easily be reparable if the UK's claim in the main action were to be upheld. However, the likely damage could not outweigh the serious harm to public health which could be caused by a suspension of the contested decision. Hence, the application for interim relief was refused.[54]

When performing this balancing test, the national court must examine whether the Community measure in question would be deprived of all effectiveness if not immediately implemented. Depending on the nature of the case, the court must also try to foresee the cumulative effects that would arise if a large number of courts were to adopt interim measures for similar reasons.[55] This applies in particular when an objection is made to the validity of a general rule such as a Community regulation. Indeed, to the extent that other undertakings find themselves in the same situation as the applicant, it must be expected that an order granting interim relief in such a situation may lead to a cascade of similar orders thus resulting in a virtual suspension of the contested act. Similarly, regard must be had for the interest of any third party in not having the implementation of an administrative act delayed.[56]

---

[52] Case T-169/00 R *Esedra* [2000] ECR II-2951, para 45; Case T-378/02 R *Technische Glaswerke Ilmenau* [2003] ECR II-2921; Case T-148/04 R *Travel Solutions Belgium* [2004] ECR II-3027, para 46; Case T-411/07 R *Aer Lingus Group* [2008] ECR II-411, para 131; Case T-475/07 R *Dow AgroSciences* [2008] ECR II-92, para 71; and Case T-246/08 R *Melli Bank* [2008] ECR I-146, para 34.

[53] Case T-369/03 R *Arizona Chemical* [2004] ECR II-205; Case T-303/94 R *European Dynamics* [2004] ECR II-4621; and Case T-95/09 R *United Phosphorus* (ECJ 28 April 2009), para 35.

[54] Case C-180/96 R *UK v Commission* [1996] ECR I-3903.

[55] Case C-465/93 *Atlanta* [1995] ECR I-3761, paras 46–8.

[56] Case T-96/92 R *CCE Grandes Sources* [1992] ECR II-2579, para 39. In comparison, consideration for the interests of third parties cannot be taken into account when assessing urgency; see Case T-417/05 R *Endesa* [2006] ECR II-18.

Also the financial risk for the Community must be taken into consideration. Hence, where there is a possibility that the interim protection sought may involve such financial risk, granting the interim protection might be made conditional upon the applicant providing adequate guarantees, such as the depositing of money or other security.[57] By analogy with the case law under Article 242, it must, however, be assumed that the national court can decide not to require such guarantee if the party seeking exemption from providing the guarantee adduces evidence that it is impossible for it to provide such guarantee, at least without imperilling its existence.[58] Otherwise, in many situations the requirement to provide such guarantee would in practice render a claim for interim relief impossible, as the applicant would not be able to discharge such an undertaking if it turns out that his substantive claim is unsuccessful.

A national court may also take account of national financial or other public interests, be that in situations where the interim protection sought is directed solely at a national measure or where the applicant indirectly seeks protection against a Community act. At least under the same conditions as those outlined above, Community law cannot be assumed to preclude that the national court makes the ordering of interim relief conditional upon the applicant providing adequate guarantees.[59]

---

[57] Joined Cases C-143/88 and C-92/89 *Zuckerfabrik Süderditmarschen* [1991] ECR I-415, para 32; and Case C-465/93 *Atlanta* [1995] ECR I-3761, para 45.

[58] Case T-11/06 R *Romana Tabacchi* [2006] ECR II-2491; Case T-79/03R *IRO* [2003] ECR II-3027; and Case T-252/03 R *FNICGV* [2004] ECR II-315.

[59] eg decisions of English courts in *R v Inspectorate of Pollution, ex p Greenpeace* [1994] 1 WLR 570; and *R v Secretary of State for the Environment, ex p Royal Society for the Protection of Birds* (1995) 7 Admin LR 434. See further R Gordon, *EC Law in Judicial Review* (2007) 101–3.

10

THE PROCEDURE BEFORE
THE COURT OF JUSTICE

1. Overview

The procedure for references for preliminary rulings given in the form of a judgment consists of the following stages:

- Translation of the reference into all the official languages, and the subsequent publication of a summary of the reference in the Official Journal of the European Union.[1]

- Submission of written observations.

---

[1] Art 104 of the Court's Rules of Procedure. As explained in Ch 5, s 4.7, already at this stage the Court's Registrar will examine whether the case raises questions which have been decided in previous judgments, and if so send copies of these judgments to the referring court so that the latter can decide whether the reference should be upheld or wholly or partially withdrawn. According to C Naômé, *Le renvoi préjudiciel en droit européen* (2007) 120, where it is very likely that the preliminary reference will be dismissed as inadmissible by way of an order, the reference will, until its

- Translation of the written observations into French, the working language of the Court of Justice. At the same time the President of the Court assigns the case to a Judge-Rapporteur just as the First Advocate General assigns it to one of the Advocates General.

- Drawing up by the Judge-Rapporteur of a Preliminary Report (*rapport préalable*). This report is made for internal use and treated as confidential. It identifies the relevant legal issues and their likely ramifications. It is used, inter alia, to decide whether the reference should be dismissed as inadmissible by way of a reasoned order and, if not, how many judges should take part in deciding the case, whether there is a need for an oral hearing, and whether it should be decided with or without an Advocate General giving an Opinion. The Preliminary Report is discussed at a so-called General Meeting (*réunion générale*).

- Drawing up by the Judge-Rapporteur of a Report for the Hearing, giving a factual presentation of the case and of the written observations that have been received. Prior to the oral procedure the Report for the Hearing is translated and transmitted to those entitled to present observations to the Court.

- The oral procedure, which is normally concluded with the Advocate General's Opinion.[2]

- Deliberation and voting by the judges and preparation of the judgment.

- Translation of the judgment.

- Signing and delivery of the judgment.

Of the 16.8 months that it took on average to give a preliminary ruling in 2008,[3] about one third was spent on translation of the decision to make a reference, of the written observations received, and of the judgment itself.

2. Notification of the Decision to Make a Reference

According to Article 23 of the Statute of the Court of Justice, it is for the referring court itself to notify the Court of Justice of its preliminary question. Following the Court's receipt of the preliminary reference, the question is published in the Official Journal and notified to the parties in the main proceedings, the Commission, and the governments of the Member States.[4] Notification is also

---

admissibility has been decided, only be translated into French and not notified to the States and Community institutions.

[2] As will be explained below at s 4.4, the Court dispenses still more frequently with the oral procedure. Similarly, as explained below at Ch 11, s 1, it is increasingly common that the Court proceeds without an Opinion of the Advocate General.

[3] Point 12 in the statistics chapter of the 2008 Annual Report of the Court of Justice.

[4] On the right of other public bodies to present observations in cases that concern them see K Mortelmans, 'Observations in the Cases governed by Article 177 of the EEC Treaty: Procedure and Practice' (1979) 16 CML Rev 557, 560.

given to the Council or to the European Central Bank if the act the validity or interpretation of which is in dispute originates from one of them, and to the European Parliament and the Council if the act the validity or interpretation of which is in dispute was adopted jointly by those two institutions.[5] Moreover, the Registrar also gives notice of the reference for a preliminary ruling to the EFTA Surveillance Authority and to the three EFTA States that are party to the EEA Agreement (Iceland, Liechtenstein, and Norway).

Where an agreement relating to a specific subject concluded by the Council and one or more non-Member States provides that those States are entitled to submit observations where a court of a Member State refers a question falling within the scope of the agreement to the Court of Justice for a preliminary ruling, the decision of the national court containing that question shall also be notified to the non-Member State(s) concerned. For example, the non-Member States Iceland and Norway, which are parties to an association agreement to the Schengen Agreement, will be notified of preliminary questions concerning the Schengen Agreement in order to allow them to present observations in cases on that agreement. In this situation Article 104 of the Court's Rules of Procedure provides that the decision of the referring court shall be communicated to the non-Member State in the original language version together with a translation of the decision or, where appropriate, of a summary into one of the official EU languages, to be chosen by the third State concerned.

According to Article 104 of the Court's Rules of Procedure, where appropriate, on account of the length of the referring court's reference, a full translation thereof may be replaced by the translation of a summary of the reference into the other official languages. The summary shall include the full text of the preliminary question(s). It shall also, in so far as that information appears in the national court's decision, summarise the subject matter of the main proceedings and the essential arguments of the parties in the main proceedings, and provide a succinct presentation of the reasoning in the reference for a preliminary ruling and the case law and the provisions of Community and domestic law relied on.[6]

Until now the notification has been made in the form of a registered letter. However, the Court is examining the possibility of using electronic means, a method that has already been introduced regarding the special procedure for urgent cases in the area of freedom, security, and justice.[7]

---

[5] In practice, the Court notifies the institutions to a greater extent so that the institutions themselves assess whether to submit observations, subject to control by the Court.

[6] See also above Ch 8, s 3.2, where it is advised that the national court keeps this provision in mind when drafting the reference.

[7] See s 5.3.1 below. The Court of Justice does not grant access to the preliminary reference to persons and bodies not covered by Art 23 of its Statute. The same applies to the case file of the national proceedings that the referring court has sent to the Court's Registrar.

3. Observations on the Preliminary Reference

3.1. Those entitled to submit observations

The parties to the main proceedings and the Commission are always entitled to submit observations.

Presumably, the same is the case for the Member States, although so far the Court of Justice has not finally settled whether a Member State may present observations in cases on Community rules that do not apply in the Member State in question, for example because that State either has invoked an opt-out clause or has not exercised an opt-in clause in the area concerned.

In *Tessili*, the Court allowed the UK and Ireland to submit observations in a preliminary reference from a German court concerning the Brussels Convention notwithstanding the fact that neither of these States was a party to the Convention. To a large extent the Court based its reasoning on the fact that the two States were required to become parties to the Convention at a later stage. Hence, the ruling does not directly lay down the law for situations where a Member State is not required to accede to the relevant Community rule in the future.[8]

The prevailing view, however, seems to be that such Member State observations must be allowed considering that any case may raise issues of general legal or political importance affecting even Member States that are not bound by the particular provision in question.[9] Indeed, in relation to observations in preliminary references made under the European Union's third pillar, Article 35(4) of the EU Treaty prescribes that any Member State may present observations in cases where the Court is seised according to Article 35(1), regardless of whether that State has accepted the competence of the Court of Justice in accordance with Article 35(2).

It is for each Member State to lay down in its legal order which body or bodies may submit observations on its behalf. Where the internal constitutional competence pertaining to the preliminary questions is divided between different bodies of a Member State this has sometimes led to different bodies of that State submitting observations on different questions in a given case. Moreover, where a public body is party to the main proceedings, it is for the State in question to decide whether the observations should also be made by State bodies other than the one taking

---

[8] Case 12/76 *Tessili* [1976] ECR 1473.

[9] C Naômé, *Le renvoi préjudiciel en droit européen* (2007) 110 ; R Barents et al, *European Courts Procedure* (2004) para 31.118; and D Anderson and M Demetriou, *References to the European Court* (2002) 242. Where a State accedes to the European Community after a preliminary reference has been made, that State may participate in the preliminary procedure as from the date of accession, see C Naômé, *Le renvoi préjudiciel en droit européen* (2007) 110.

part in the national proceedings. Occasionally, this has led to the same State presenting different views on the same question.[10]

As regards the Council and the European Central Bank the right to present observations is limited to cases where an act whose validity or interpretation is in dispute originates from one of them. With regard to the European Parliament, Article 23 of the Court's Statute affords this institution the right to submit observations on preliminary references concerning acts adopted 'jointly' by it and the Council. In contrast, Article 23 does not explicitly afford the Parliament the right to submit observations in cases that concern its Protocol and Rules of Procedure which have been adopted by the Parliament alone. Nevertheless, since Article 23 of the Court's Statute affords the Parliament the right to submit observations in preliminary references concerning the validity or interpretation of an act for which it is a co-legislator, *a fortiori,* it must also have this right when a preliminary reference concerns the interpretation of an act that has the Parliament as its sole author.[11]

As concerns the EFTA Surveillance Authority and the EFTA States that are party to the EEA Agreement, the right to present observations before the Court of Justice is limited to situations where the preliminary question concerns one of the fields covered by the EEA Agreement. This condition is fulfilled not only when the preliminary question refers to provisions in the EEA Agreement, but also when the answer to the question hinges upon the interpretation or validity of a provision in Community law that has a counterpart in the EEA Agreement.[12]

With regard to third countries, Article 23 prescribes that observations can be presented to the extent that these countries are entitled to be notified of the reference according to the rules described above in Section 2 of this chapter.

Natural or legal persons may only submit observations to the Court of Justice if they are either parties to the main proceedings or have been granted the right to intervene in those proceedings before the referring court in accordance with national rules on the administration of justice.[13]

In *Biogen*, a company that was not party to the main proceedings sought leave to intervene in the preliminary procedure before the Court of Justice in order to submit observations on the preliminary reference. In support of its request, the

---

[10] Case C-195/98 *Österreichischer Gewerschaftsbund* [2000] ECR I-10497; and Case C-49/98 *Finalarte Sociedade de Construção Civil* [2001] ECR I-7831.

[11] Joined Cases C-200/07 and C-201/07 *Marra* (ECJ 21 October 2008), paras 21–3.

[12] As for the EFTA Court, Art 97 of the Rules of Procedure of the EFTA Court provides that also the Commission and the Community (including all the EU Member States) may present observations in preliminary cases before the EFTA Court.

[13] Case 35/80 *Denkavit Nederland* [1981] ECR 45; and Case 2/74 *Reyners* [1974] ECR 631. See also R Barents et al, *European Courts Procedure* (2004) paras 23.020–23.022.

company argued that Article 40 of the Statute of the Court of Justice gives natural and legal persons the right to intervene in cases before the Court. The Court of Justice rejected the request, stating that the preliminary procedure did not envisage contentious proceedings designed to settle a dispute but prescribed a special procedure whose aim is to ensure a uniform interpretation of Community law by cooperation between the Court of Justice and the national courts and enabling the latter to seek the interpretation of Community provisions which they have to apply in disputes brought before them. The right to present observations before the Court of Justice in connection with a reference for a preliminary ruling therefore has to be assessed exclusively on the basis of Article 23 of the Statute. The Court of Justice went on to state that the reference in this provision to 'the parties' referred solely to the parties to the action pending before the national court.[14]

In *Satakunnan Markkinapörssi and Satamedia*, the European Data Protection Supervisor applied for leave to submit observations on a preliminary question concerning Directive 95/46 on the protection of individuals with regard to the processing of personal data and on the free movement of such data. In support of his application, the Supervisor pointed to the fact that the Court had, in previous orders, recognised his right to intervene in direct actions before it. Moreover, he argued that the subject matter of the reference for a preliminary ruling was clearly within the limits of the task conferred on him. The Court declared the application inadmissible noting that Article 23 refers only to the parties to the action before the national court and that the Supervisor was not involved in this action.[15]

In *ABNA*, the French *Conseil d'État* had found it unnecessary to make a preliminary reference to the Court of Justice because the issue facing the *Conseil d'État* had already given rise to a pending reference from a UK court. One of the parties in the case before the *Conseil d'État* thereupon asked the Court of Justice for permission to present observations in the UK preliminary reference case arguing that otherwise it would be deprived of its rights of defence. The Court turned down that request. The argument pertaining to rights of defence should have been made before the *Conseil d'État* as it was for the national courts to consider whether such considerations should lead them to refer preliminary questions themselves even if the Court of Justice was expected to rule on the matter because of pending cases raising the same issue.[16]

---

[14] Case C-181/95 *Biogen* [1996] ECR I-717.

[15] Case C-73/07 *Satakunnan Markkinapörssi and Satamedia* [2007] ECR I-7075. See also the order in Case 6/64 *Costa* 1964 ECR (English special edition) 614; Case 62/72 *Bollmann* [1973] ECR 269, para 4; Case 19/68 *De Cicco* 1968 ECR (English special edition) 473; Case C-305/05 Ordre des Barreaux francophones et germanophones (order of 9 June 2005); Case C-368/06 *Cedilac* [2008] ECR I-12327; and K Mortelmans, 'Observations in the cases governed by Article 177 of the EEC Treaty: Procedure and Practice' (1979) 16 CML Rev 557, 559.

[16] Case C-453/03 *ABNA* (ECJ 30 March 2004), and see further above ch 7, s 2.5, and C Naômé, *Le renvoi préjudiciel en droit européen* (2007) 136-137.

The legal orders of the Member States name and classify the various participants in procedures before the national courts in different ways. However, the right to submit observations to the Court cannot depend on those terminological and formal differences. The objective of Article 23 of the Court's Statute is to give persons potentially affected by the Court's preliminary ruling the opportunity to present their views on the questions to be decided. Therefore, all persons who take part in national proceedings will be considered to be parties within the meaning of Article 23 of the Statute, and it is therefore submitted that this provision includes not only interveners, but also *amici curiae* in the main proceedings where this concept is recognised in the relevant national legal system.[17]

If someone is given leave to intervene in the main proceedings after a reference has been made to the Court of Justice, he will also be entitled to submit observations to the Court of Justice from the date when leave is granted, for example in connection with the oral procedure before the Court of Justice.

In *Transporoute,* the plaintiff in the main proceedings was declared insolvent after the national court had made a reference for a preliminary ruling. However, the national court allowed the administrator in insolvency to continue the main proceedings, and the Court of Justice therefore allowed the administrator to submit observations in the preliminary proceedings.[18]

A failure to present written observations does not affect the possibility of later presenting oral observations in the preliminary proceedings. Moreover, the fact that a party neither submits written nor oral observations does not imply that the Court of Justice will infer that that party implicitly consents to what is being stated and argued by others before the Court.[19]

The person or body submitting observations to the Court of Justice is entitled to make these observations public.[20] Moreover, unless the referring court itself hides the names of private parties, the Court of Justice publishes these names in the list of both pending and closed cases, even where the preliminary reference originates in a Member States where the names of private parties are not made public. Acting ex officio or upon a duly reasoned request the Court may, however, choose not to

---

[17] See further Advocate General Jacobs in his Opinion in Case C-379/98 *PreussenElektra* [2001] ECR I-2099, paras 69–71; Case C-27/89 *SCAPE* [1990] ECR I-1701; and Case C-230/96 *Cabour and Nord Distribution Automobile* [1998] ECR I-2055. An *amicus curiae* (Latin for 'friend of the court') is not a party, but contributes information on the case with a view to assisting the relevant court to reach the right decision.

[18] Case 76/81 *Transporoute* [1982] ECR 417. See also Case C-192/99 *Kaur* [2001] ECR I-1237; and Case C-432/92 *Anastaciou* [1994] ECR I-3087. In the latter case a company was given leave to intervene by the national court less than a week before the oral hearing in Luxembourg and thus could present oral observations in the case.

[19] See s 4.4 below.

[20] Case C-376/98 *Germany v Parliament and Council* [2000] ECR I-2247.

divulge the names of a party in the main proceedings where the subject matter of the case justifies this.[21]

3.2. Observations by Community institutions and Member States

The Commission always submits observations in preliminary reference proceedings. If a question directly concerns the validity of one of the Council's legal acts it often—although certainly not always—submits observations. The Council has also submitted observations where an attack on another measure indirectly puts one of its own acts in issue. Moreover, it has submitted observations where the question concerned the interpretation of international agreements concluded between the Community and third States.

Rule 121 of the Parliament's Rules of Procedure establishes that if a case before the Court of Justice involves the questioning of the validity of an act of Parliament, only exceptionally shall the Parliament abstain from submitting observations. Rule 121(4) of the European Parliament's Rules of Procedure regulates, inter alia, the provision of observations in preliminary proceedings. Before their adoption the Rules of Procedure did not explicitly provide for the provision of observations. However, in a letter of 10 December 1997 to the President of the European Parliament the Chairman of the Committee on Legal Affairs and Citizens' Rights had expressed the view that the Parliament had an obligation to defend the validity of its legal acts. With only few exceptions the Parliament therefore submitted observations in all preliminary proceedings that gave rise to questions of validity of its legal acts. In contrast, the Parliament has only exceptionally submitted observations in other types of case.

One such example is *Heinrich*, where the Parliament presented observations in a case where the subject matter in dispute was connected to the actions of the Parliament's Civil Liberties Committee against disproportionate and ineffective counter-terrorism measures.[22]

Generally speaking the observations of the Community institutions are of great value to the Court of Justice. In addition to assisting it in identifying the relevant case law, the institutions' observations may contain recommendations for expanding or limiting a given line in the Court's case law. Moreover, the Community institutions often provide a useful account of the legislative history of secondary Community legislation just as they sometimes give an account of the financial and

---

[21] Case C-13/94 *P v S and Cornwall County Council* [1996] I-2413; Case C-384/98 *D* [2000] ECR I-6795; and see further C Naômé, *Le renvoi préjudiciel en droit européen* (2007) 178–9.
[22] Case C-345/06 *Heinrich* (ECJ 10 March 2009).

policy considerations which lie behind the relevant Community act and the context in which this act operates.[23]

That being said, the Court of Justice is, of course, aware that the Community institutions are not completely neutral parties.[24] This is especially true where the case concerns the legality of an act issued by the institutions. Moreover, sometimes the different members of the Council interpret the relevant Community act in divergent ways. Thus, depending on the circumstances, the Court may receive information which a Community institution puts forward in connection with a reference for a preliminary ruling with a certain healthy scepticism.

As for the EFTA Surveillance Authority, the possibility of presenting observations before the Court of Justice is seen as a most useful way of furthering homogeneity between the legal orders of the Community and the EEA. When the case before the Court of Justice raises questions that are specific to the EEA legal order, as a rule the Authority will present observations. It will normally also appear before the Court when a preliminary question raises issues of Community law that are similar to those that have arisen in a case pending before the Authority. Especially where the relevant EFTA State also presents observations in the case the net effect may be that a case that would otherwise have been pleaded before the EFTA Court in reality finds its solution via a judgment by the Court of Justice.

In *Lindmann*, concerning taxation of lottery gains, the Court of Justice was asked to assess the compatibility of Finnish legislation with Article 49 of the EC Treaty. As that provision corresponds to Article 36 of the EEA Agreement and since, for all practical purposes, the Finnish legislation was similar to Norwegian provisions against which the EFTA Surveillance Authority had issued a reasoned opinion, both the Authority and Norway submitted observations to the Court of Justice. When the Court of Justice found the Finnish legislation incompatible with Community law, Norway changed its own legislation before the Authority had occasion to bring the matter before the EFTA Court.[25]

Moreover, the EFTA Surveillance Authority occasionally submits observations in preliminary cases before the Court of Justice where problems similar to those raised in the case before the Court may arise under the EEA Agreement. Sometimes, the mere fact that a preliminary reference raises a particularly interesting question

---

[23] R Wainwright, 'A view from the Commission' in M Andenas (ed), *Article 177 References to the European Court—Policy and Practice* (1994) 105, 106. In addition, since the Commission intervenes in all preliminary cases, it is able to generate knowledge of value for its supervision of the Member States' follow-up on the preliminary rulings.

[24] See J Pertek, *La pratique du renvoi préjudiciel de droit communautaire* (2001) 115, who opposes the use of the words 'amicus curiae' to describe the Commission's observations in preliminary cases.

[25] Case C-42/02 *Lindmann* [2003] ECR I-13519.

of EC and EEA law has, in itself, prompted the Authority to submit observations.[26]

As for the Member States, both the total number of observations and the number of observations relative to the number of preliminary references have increased over the last decade.[27] This upward trend is presumably a reflection of the fact that governments have become more aware of the wide-reaching consequences that a preliminary ruling might have for the Member States' room for manoeuvre. It probably also reflects an increased belief that such observations may influence the decisions of the Court of Justice. In this respect, a Member State can sometimes have an interest in arguing a view before the Court of Justice which it has been unable to persuade the other Member States to accept when the Community provision in question was negotiated in the Council.

The Member States' observations can be of considerable assistance to the Court of Justice by pointing out the likely practical, financial, or political consequences of a given decision. In particular, where a preliminary reference concerns a Member State's own legislation, it will often be useful for the Court to receive a detailed account of the relevant national provisions, the considerations that lie behind these provisions, and the practice of the national courts in applying them. Such information not only gives the Court a better basis for solving the specific dispute but may, depending on the circumstances, also improve the possibility of giving a more precise judgment that avoids examining hypothetical issues.[28] Similarly, a Member State might help to cast light on the rules pertaining to the referring body where there are doubts as to whether this body constitutes a court within the meaning of Article 234. That being said, as was also the case with respect to observations made by the Community institutions, information provided by a Member State must, of course, be assessed with due regard to the interests which that Member State may have in presenting the facts and national law in a way that best furthers the interests of that State.

The practices of the different Member States as to when to present observations differ significantly both with regard to the number and the type of cases. While some

---

[26] N Fenger et al, 'European Free Trade Agreement (EFTA) and European Economic Area (EEA)', in R Blanpain (ed), *International Encyclopedia of Law, International Organisations, vol 1, supplement 24* (2005) 134–5.

[27] In a study of 572 cases covering the period from 1961 to 1995 S Nyikos, *The European Court and National Courts: Strategic Interaction within the EU Judicial Process* (2001) 114, found that Member States had presented written observations in 50.5 per cent of the cases referred from their own legal system. According to the same study the Court of Justice followed the result proposed by the Member State government of the referring court in 44.1 per cent of the cases in which that government submitted observations.

[28] As to the Court's readiness to depart from the understanding of national law presented in the reference due to arguments made in observations before the Court, see below at s 3.3.3.4.

Member States readily present observations in a case, 'merely' because it raises an issue of principle, other Member States are more reticent about submitting observations in cases that do not raise questions about the compatibility with Community law of their own national laws or administrative practice. Indeed, even if a preliminary reference concerns the compatibility of a Member State's national laws or practice, some Member States may leave it to the national administrative authority that is a party to the main proceedings to present the Member State's views to the Court of Justice.[29] Irrespective of these appreciable differences between the various Member States, it is possible to discern a tendency where still more States move away from submitting the bulk of their observations in their own national cases, and instead increasingly pick out the cases according to the subject matter and legal issues raised by the individual case. Perhaps this shift is a reflection of the fact that a preliminary ruling de facto may overrule not only the national legislation which is the subject of the national procedure giving rise to the preliminary reference, but also similar legislation of other Member States. It is therefore only natural that Member States other than the one from which the reference originates also submit observations in such preliminary proceedings. In this respect it appears that some Member States have thematic priorities in their participation strategy. Thus, while virtually all Member States occasionally make observations in cases concerning direct taxation, the Scandinavian Member States tend to be particularly active in environmental matters and in cases concerning the right of access to documents held by the EU institutions. In comparison, several Mediterranean Member States appear to focus on agricultural issues. Moreover, France appears to be especially active regarding services of general interest and the development of general principles of Community law.[30]

In *Placania*, eight governments submitted observations arguing that national monopolies on gaming did not infringe the rules in the EC Treaty on establishment and free movement of services. All of those eight States themselves had some

---

[29] According to M Granger, 'States as successful Litigants before The European Court of Justice: Lessons from the "Repeat Players" of European Litigation' in *Croatian Yearbook of European Law and Policy 2006* (2006) 27, 37, the Netherlands was at that time the Member State that, in the last years preceding the article, had submitted the largest number of observations followed by Germany, the United Kingdom, France, Austria, Greece, Italy, and Belgium. On the practice of the different States, see further M Granger, 'When Governments go to Luxembourg' (2004) EL Rev 3, 9ff. As for the corresponding issue of observations before the EFTA Court by the Commission, the EFTA Surveillance Authority, the EFTA States, and the EU Member States, see C Baudenbacher, 'The EFTA Court Ten Years on' in T Orlygsson, P Tresselt, and C Baudenbacher (eds), *The EFTA Court Ten Years on* (2005) 1, 31–4. On the practice of the Danish government see N Fenger and M Broberg, *Præjudicielle forelæggelser for EF-domstolen* (2008) 253–4.

[30] See M Granger, 'States as successful Litigants before The European Court of Justice: Lessons from the "Repeat Players" of European litigation' in *Croatian Yearbook of European Law and Policy 2006* (2006) 27, 38–9.

form of gaming monopolies.[31] When shortly thereafter the same issue came before the EFTA Court in *Ladbrokes*, that Court received observations from a total of 11 States, in addition to observations from the two parties as well as from the Commission and the EFTA Surveillance Authority.[32]

In *Laval*, in addition to observations submitted by the Commission, the EFTA Surveillance Authority and the parties to the main proceedings, 14 Member States, as well as the two EFTA States, Iceland and Norway, presented observations. This was due to the considerable importance in economic, political, and legal terms that the preliminary questions gave rise to with respect to the rights of trade unions to take measures against foreign service providers not willing to enter into collective agreements in the host State.[33]

Presumably each government first weighs the advantages of presenting observations in such situations—ie to improve the likelihood of receiving a ruling that caters for the government's views—against the risk of openly exposing a potential problem in its national legal order vis-à-vis Community law.

Where several Member States are going to present similar arguments, the Court encourages the States to coordinate their respective observations, especially with respect to the oral hearing. Indeed, such cooperation may not only save the Court from unnecessary repetition, but perhaps also lead to a fuller presentation of the socio-economic context of the issue at stake.

3.3. Influencing the scope of the preliminary ruling through the presentation of observations

3.3.1. *The preliminary ruling procedure does not have any parties* stricto sensu

Article 234 of the EC Treaty introduces a means of direct cooperation between the Court of Justice and the national courts. Formally speaking, this cooperation takes place within the framework of a non-contentious procedure. Thus, although, in reality, there is a distinct adversarial feel to a preliminary proceeding, neither the parties to the main proceedings nor anybody else entitled to present observations in the preliminary procedure have the status of parties before the Court of Justice; they are merely invited to state their view and may thus be likened to *amici curiae*. For the same reason, they are not entitled to take procedural initiatives of their own as part of the preliminary procedure.[34] Similarly, the rights and obligations pertaining to 'parties' laid down in the Court's Statute and its Rules of

---

31 Joined Cases C-338/04, C-359/04, and C-360/04 *Placanica* [2007] ECR I-1891.
32 Case E-3/06 *Ladbrokes* [2007] EFTA Court Report 85.
33 Case C-341/05 *Laval* [2007] ECR I-11767.
34 Case 62/72 *Bollmann* [1973] ECR 269, para 4; Case 44/65 *Hessische Knappschaft* [1965–68] ECR 965 (English special edition).

Procedure are not generally applicable to persons and bodies presenting observations in a preliminary procedure.

3.3.2. The subject matter of the preliminary question

It is solely for the national court to determine the content of the question it puts before the Court of Justice. In connection with the proceedings before the Court of Justice, the parties in the main proceedings can only submit suggestions with regard to the interpretation of the content of the reference and with regard to the answers to the questions referred.[35] Hence, those entitled to submit observations during the preliminary procedure before the Court of Justice cannot challenge the relevance of a preliminary question on the grounds that the referring court has decided to initiate the proceedings under Article 234 on the basis of a misunderstanding of the factual or legal problems in the main proceedings.[36] Nor can they amend or expand, or for that matter narrow, the content of the question.[37]

This is in particular the case when the party concerned has argued unsuccessfully before the national court for an expansion of the scope of the questions referred.[38] It is strictly applied in relation to the question of which national legal provisions the preliminary ruling should relate to. If the national court has restricted its reference to a legal problem that is derived from a specific rule under national law, not even the most compelling set of observations would persuade the Court of Justice to frame its preliminary ruling so as to have regard for other legal problems that are derived from different national rules. Similarly, the Court of Justice is wary about accepting requests from those entitled to submit observations to change the theme of the question in order to cover problems of Community law which are not contained in the reference.[39]

---

[35] Case C-261/95 *Palmisani* [1997] ECR I-4025, paras 30–1.

[36] See above Ch 5, s 4.5, as well as Case C-364/92 *Eurocontrol* [1994] ECR I-43, paras 12–13; Case C-456/98 *Centrosteel* [2000] ECR I-6007, paras 11–12; and Case C-442/05 *Zweckverband zur Trinkwasserversorgung* [2008] ECR I-1817, paras 20–7.

[37] Case 174/84 *Bulk Oil* [1986] ECR 559, paras 53–4; Case 311/84 *CBEM* [1985] ECR 3261, paras 9–10; Case C-30/93 *AC-ATEL* [1994] ECR I-2305, paras 14–20; Case C-189/95 *Franzén* [1997] ECR I-5909, paras 78–9; Case C-435/97 *WWF* [1999] ECR I-5613, paras 28–9; Case C-366/99 *Griesmar* [2001] ECR I-9383, paras 21–4; Case C-466/00 *Kaba* [2003] ECR I-2219, paras 40–1; Case C-438/01 *Design Concept* [2003] ECR I-5617, paras 12–15; Case C-236/02 *SLOB* [2004] ECR I-1961, paras 29–30; and Case C-390/06 *Nuova Agricast* [2008] ECR I-2577, paras 42–4. See equally with regard to cases under Art 35 of the EU Treaty Case C-404/07 *Katz* (ECJ 9 December 2008), paras 37–8; and Case C-296/08 *Santesteban Goicoechea* [2008] ECR I-6307, paras 43–7.

[38] Opinion of Advocate General Fennelly in Joined Cases C-64/96 and C-65/96 *Uecker and Jaquet* [1997] ECR I-3171, para 26. See also Case C-262/97 *Engelbrecht* [2000] ECR I-7321, paras 21–2; Case C-305/05 Ordre des Barreaux francophones et germanophones *[2007] ECR I-5305, paras 17–20*; and Case C-196/89 *Nespoli and Crippa* [1990] ECR I-3647, paras 9–10, where the national court had emphasised which questions it wanted answered.

[39] Joined Cases C-376/05 and C-377/05 *Brünsteiner* [2006] ECR I-11383, paras 25–9; Case 299/84 *Neumann* [1985] ECR 3663, paras 11–12; Case C-337/88 *SAFA* [1990] ECR I-1, para 20;

In *Syndesmos*, the referring court essentially wanted guidance on whether the provisions of the Second Company Law Directive precluded increases in the capital of a company where such increases had not been authorised by the annual general meeting of shareholders and no pre-emptive subscription rights had been made available to the existing shareholders. Before the Court of Justice the parties in the main proceedings put forward various arguments about problems that were not covered by the referring court's preliminary questions. It was for instance being debated whether individuals who, before a national court, seek to rely on rights based on a general principle of law must have a legitimate interest in invoking that principle. It was also argued that the Community legislator did not have competence to legislate on matters of insolvency law and other collective procedures for the satisfaction of creditors' claims. The Court of Justice declined to consider these arguments. According to the allocation of jurisdiction in proceedings for preliminary rulings, it was solely for the national court to determine the subject matter of the question referred. If necessary, the national court could make a fresh reference to the Court of Justice if it considered it necessary to obtain a further ruling on the interpretation of Community law for the purpose of taking a decision in the main proceedings.[40]

In *Felicitas*, a German court had asked the Court of Justice to interpret Article 5 of Directive 69/335 concerning indirect taxes on the raising of capital. The plaintiff in the main proceedings argued that it was necessary first to reply to the question underlying the referring court's preliminary question, namely whether a transaction such as that concerned in the main proceedings constituted a transaction subject to capital duty within the meaning of the directive. The Court of Justice noted that this underlying question would necessitate an interpretation of provisions of the directive other than that referred in the order for reference. Since the underlying question was not covered by the preliminary reference and since the national court had expressed no doubt that a transaction such as that concerned in the case was subject to capital duty, the Court of Justice declined to rule on the underlying question.[41]

Case C-196/89 *Nespol and Crippa* [1990] ECR I-3647, para 23; Case C-297/94 *Bruyère and others* [1996] ECR I-1551, paras 13 and 19–20; Case C-408/95 *Eurotunnel* [1997] ECR I-6315, paras 33–4; Case C-124/97 *Läärä* [1999] ECR I-6097, paras 23 and 26; Case C-67/98 *Zenatti* [1999] ECR I-7289, paras 22–3; Case C-465/98 *Darbo* [2000] ECR I-2297, paras 18–19; Case C-402/98 *ATB* [2000] ECR I-5501, paras 28–31; and Case C-28/04 *Tod's and Tod's France* [2005] ECR I-5781, para 16. See also Ch 11, s 2.5.

[40] Case C-381/89 *Syndesmos Melon tis Eleftheras Evangelikis Ekklisias* [1992] ECR I-2111, paras 18–19.

[41] Case 270/81 *Felicitas* [1982] ECR 2771, paras 8–9. See similarly with regard to the EFTA Court Case E-10/04 *Piazza* [2005] EFTA Court Report 76, para 30.

In the same way, neither the parties to the main proceedings nor others entitled to submit observations before the Court of Justice can require the Court to make a more fundamental reformulation of the subject of the preliminary reference.

In *Sehrer*, a German court had requested the Court of Justice to rule on a question of the compatibility with Community law of a German provision which required that Mr Sehrer pay a health insurance contribution on a supplementary retirement pension paid to him from France. Before the Court of Justice, both the Commission and the German government argued that the real problem was not the lawful German contribution. Rather the problem was that France also required payment of a health insurance contribution. In their view, account should only be taken of the basis for the calculation of the German contribution if the prior collection of the contribution in France was compatible with Community law. Advocate General Colomer agreed in principle that the contribution required under French law was probably contrary to Community law and, moreover, the real source of Mr Sehrer's problem. However, the referring court had chosen to limit its question to the validity of the German contribution, and it was not for the Court of Justice to refuse to give a ruling on the question, nor could it extend the scope of the question to include a ruling on the French law. The Court of Justice agreed with its Advocate General. It added moreover that the referring court in its order for reference had expressed doubts as to whether the duty under French law to pay sickness insurance contributions conferring no benefit entitlement was compatible with Community law. However, the German court had chosen not to include this issue in its preliminary reference since it could only be tried by the French courts, and because Mr Sehrer himself had preferred to put the validity of the German sickness insurance contributions in issue on the grounds that they were at a higher rate than the French contributions. The Court of Justice therefore found it appropriate only to reply to the question submitted by the national court.[42]

This reticence to change the subject matter of the questions referred is based on a number of interlinked considerations. First, the Court of Justice cannot give rulings on hypothetical questions.[43] Second, the Court of Justice must respect the allocation of jurisdiction made in Article 234 between itself and the national courts, according to which it is for the national courts to decide which issues of Community law they need help to solve. Indeed, the Court of Justice does not take over the case before the national court as a result of the reference; the case remains pending before the national court and the Court of Justice only becomes involved to the extent that the national court finds this desirable. Third, often the

---

Court of Justice will not have the necessary information about the facts or the national law to enable it to foresee the consequences of expanding a question referred.[44] Finally, changing the preliminary questions would hardly be compatible with the rights of those persons and bodies covered by Article 23 of the Court's Statute, to be able to submit observations before the Court, given that, in accordance with that provision, it is only the decision to make a reference that is notified to them.[45]

3.3.3. Supplementing or departing from the facts of the reference

3.3.3.1. The main rule. Under Article 234, the Court of Justice does not have the authority to decide the facts in the main proceedings with binding effect for the national court.[46] For this reason, the Court of Justice will, as a point of departure, base itself upon the referring court's presentation of the facts in the main proceedings when answering the latter's preliminary questions.[47] Even when a party to the main proceedings convincingly argues before the Court that the facts are other than those described in the order for reference, the Court normally sticks to the account of the facts given in the reference.

In *Phytheron International*, the referring court had given a very short description of the facts in the main proceedings about a dispute on the exhaustion of trademark rights relating to certain goods. During the proceedings before the Court of Justice it was stated that the goods were not manufactured in Turkey, as was otherwise stated in the order for reference, but instead in Germany. Notwithstanding this, the Court of Justice chose to answer the preliminary questions only on the basis of the facts as they appeared from the order for reference. Indeed, to base its ruling on the facts mentioned in the course of proceedings before it would have entailed that the very substance of the problem raised by the questions referred would be changed. It would also mean that the Court would have had to address a question of principle on which it had not yet had occasion to decide, on the basis of facts which required clarification to enable a proper answer to be given. Also the fact that the owner of the trademark was not a party to the main proceedings, and therefore could not present his arguments before the Court of Justice, meant that the Court could not disregard the presentation of the facts contained in the order for reference. Finally, to alter the substance of questions referred for a preliminary

---

[44] Case C-108/98 *RI.SAN* [1999] ECR I-5219, paras 12–17; and Case C-124/97 *Läärä* [1999] ECR I-6097, paras 23 and 26.

[45] Case C-235/95 *AGS* [1998] ECR I-4531, para 26; Case C-412/96 *Kainuun Liikenne Oy* [1998] ECR I-5141, paras 21–4; and Case C-420/97 *Leathertex* [1999] ECR I-6747, para 22. See also above Ch 8, s 3.2.5.

[46] See above Ch 4, ss 5.1 and 5.5, and below Ch 12, s 2.1.

[47] See Ch 5, s 4.5. See also P Lasok, *The European Court of Justice—Practice and Procedure* (1994) 349 and 353.

ruling would be incompatible with the Court's function under Article 234 and with its duty to ensure that those entitled to submit observations under Article 23 of the Statute can exercise that right effectively.[48]

In *Dumon and Fromont*, a French court asked the Court of Justice to rule on the legal effect of the fact that France had disregarded an obligation to inform the Commission in connection with the implementation of a directive. Both the Commission and the French government disputed the relevance of the question, arguing that France had in fact informed the Commission. They therefore suggested that rather than answering the question as it was put, the Court of Justice should hold that the obligation to provide information imposed by the directive had in fact been complied with. The Court replied that changing the reference for a preliminary ruling would not be compatible with its tasks under Article 234. Rather, it was up to the referring court to assess whether this new information, presented in the course of the proceedings before the Court of Justice, was useful, or indeed necessary, in resolving the dispute in the main proceedings. The Court of Justice thereafter gave its ruling and held that the directive did not prevent the application of a provision such as that introduced into French law, even if the Commission had not been notified.[49]

The following sections analyse the types of case where the Court of Justice nevertheless departs from this main principle and thus takes account of supplementary information presented to it during the preliminary procedure or even bases itself on an understanding of the facts or of national law that differs from that stated in the order for reference.

3.3.3.2. Supplementing the referring court's description of the facts.
Originally, the axiom behind Article 234 was that Community law could be interpreted *in abstracto*, and that it was therefore possible to establish a clear division of jurisdiction, where the Court of Justice first gives an abstract ruling on the law, upon which the national court applies this interpretation to the facts of the main proceedings.[50] The Court of Justice was thus regarded as a kind of legal data bank that operated in a fact-free environment. However, it soon became clear that it was seldom possible to maintain such a division of competences in practice.[51]

---

48 Case C-352/95 *Phytheron International* [1997] ECR I-1729, paras 9–14. See also Joined Cases 103/77 and 145/77 *Royal Scholten-Honig* [1978] ECR 791, paras 2–4, and Case C-330/07 *Jobra* (ECJ 4 December 2008), paras 12–18. In situations like the one in *Phytheron International* it would perhaps be appropriate for the Court of Justice to inform the referring court of the observations submitted to the Court of Justice with a view to the referring court evaluating whether to maintain the question as originally asked or to reformulate it.

49 Case C-235/95 *Dumon and Fromont* [1998] ECR I-4531.

50 See Ch 4, s 5.6.

51 See below Ch 11, s 3.1.

The Court's Rules of Procedure allow it to admit evidence during a preliminary procedure. Hence, both a party to the main proceedings and any other body entitled to submit observations to the Court of Justice may introduce facts not mentioned in the reference. This applies regardless of whether or not the information has been put before the referring court. Indeed, in its 'Notes for the Guidance of Counsel' the Court explicitly invites those presenting observations in preliminary proceedings to bring to its attention the factual circumstances of the case before the referring court and the relevant provisions of the national legislation at issue.[52]

Moreover, so as to enable the Court to better understand the questions referred to it, the Court not only values, but sometimes even calls for, evidence to complete or explain the background of the facts as stated in the preliminary reference. Especially where the referring court has framed its questions in general terms, the Court of Justice will be inclined to examine them in the light of the observations of the parties to the main proceedings.[53] Thereby, the Court will be able to design its answer to the facts in the main proceedings and the relevant national law. In the same way, where the referring court has asked a question on the validity of a Community rule, but has not given any details on the possible grounds for the alleged invalidity in the order for reference, the Court of Justice will take as its point of departure the arguments for invalidity which have been made by the parties to the main proceedings.[54]

The above practice deviates from the Court's previous case law as laid down in *Bosch* in which the Court stated that it could not take account of different, apparently uncontested, pieces of factual information which had been put forward in the course of the proceedings. The Court thereby referred to the then categorically enforced principle that in a preliminary ruling the establishment of the facts of the case fell within the exclusive jurisdiction of the national courts, and that the Court of Justice could only interpret Community law *in abstracto*, and not even indirectly apply the law to the facts.[55]

---

[52] Notes for the Guidance of Counsel in written and oral proceedings before the Court of Justice of the European Communities of January 2007, point 9. The notes are available at the Court's web-page <http://www.curia.europa.eu>. With regard to the right to object to such supplementary evidence being entered into the Court's case file, eg because it has been obtained illegally or concerns internal legal advice, see the Court's order in Case C-221/06 *Stadtgemeinde Frohnleiten* [2007] ECR I-2613, and C Naômé, *Le renvoi préjudiciel en droit européen* (2007) 181.

[53] Case 109/79 *Maïseries de Beauce* [1980] ECR 2883, paras 14–15; Case 245/81 *Edeka* [1982] ECR 2745, paras 7–10; Case 251/83 *Haug-Adrion* [1984] ECR 4277, paras 8–10; Case C-213/90 *ASTI* [1991] ECR I-3507, para 9; Case C-107/97 *Rombi and Arko-Pharma* [2000] ECR I-3367, paras 48 and 61; and Case C-535/03 *Unitymark* [2006] ECR I-2689, paras 28 and 49–51.

[54] Case C-323/88 *Sermes* [1990] ECR I-3027, para 13. See correspondingly Case C-359/89 *SAFA* [1991] ECR I-1677, paras 13–14; Joined Cases 103/77 and 145/77 *Royal Scholten-Honig* [1978] ECR 791, paras 16–17; and Case 41/72 *Getreide-Import* [1973] ECR 1, para 2.

[55] Case 13/61 *Bosch* [1962] ECR (English special edition) 45.

Normally, the Court of Justice is particularly open to including contextual information that can clarify the general background to a problem before it, as long as this new information does not cast doubt on the facts that are given in the order for reference in relation to the actual dispute. This applies in particular to information which can have greater relevance for the abstract interpretation of the legal rule in question rather than the specific application of the rule in the actual case.[56]

3.3.3.3. The facts presented in the reference are being disputed.

3.3.3.3.1. The degree of fact-finding performed by the referring court. As stated in the preceding sections, the Court of Justice is relatively open to supplementing the facts of the case, as laid out in the reference from the national court, as long as the supplementary facts complement rather than change the presentation given in the reference. In contrast, the Court is more reticent about accepting information that casts doubt on the referring court's understanding of the facts in the main proceedings, or even contradicts the order for reference. This is particularly the case where the issues in question have been subject to a presentation of evidence in the proceedings before the national court.

In comparison, in relation to factual information about which the referring court has not taken special measures to obtain evidence, the Court of Justice has occasionally, although not often, chosen to frame its ruling on the basis of a different understanding of the facts than the one expressed in the preliminary reference if the conflicting evidence presented to the Court seems to be indisputable.

In *Mesbah*, the preliminary question was based on an understanding of the facts according to which the respondent in the main proceedings had acquired Belgian citizenship 'apparently in the mid 1970s'. During the proceedings before the Court of Justice, the respondent and the Belgian government both argued that the respondent had only become a Belgian citizen in 1985. They both also claimed that in 1998 the respondent had also had Moroccan citizenship. In support of their statements, the respondent and the Belgian government presented a certified extract from the national Belgian register and a certificate issued by the Consulate General of Morocco in Brussels. This information could not merely be regarded as a supplementary fact, since it essentially contradicted the information given in the order for reference. However, the Court of Justice reformulated the question so as to accord with the facts of the case as they had been corrected by the observations.[57]

---

[56] P Lasok, *The European Court of Justice—Practice and Procedure* (1994) 351. As an illustration of this see Case 327/82 *Ekvo* [1984] ECR 107, paras 8–16.

[57] Case C-179/98 *Mesbah* [1999] ECR I-7955, paras 24–6. See similarly Case C-511/03 *Ten Kate Holding Musselkanaal* [2005] ECR I-8979, paras 39–40.

3.3.3.3.2. Undisputed facts that arise after the reference is made. Where the parties to the main proceedings agree about factual circumstances that have arisen after the reference for a preliminary ruling has been made, the Court of Justice has generally been willing to reformulate the preliminary question so as to take into account the agreed view of the parties about the actual problem in the case as it stands at that time. In these situations, the Court of Justice will normally not consult the referring court before reformulating the issue to be answered.[58]

In *Nijhuis*, a Dutch court referred two questions concerning a right to an invalidity pension under Regulation 1408/71. During the proceedings before the Court of Justice, both parties to the main proceedings and the Commission were in agreement that, after the reference for a preliminary ruling had been made, another Community regulation had entered into force clearly giving the plaintiff a right to the disputed payment. On this basis the Court of Justice limited its preliminary ruling to dealing with the period before the second regulation entered into force.[59]

After receiving the response to the preliminary question, it is up to the referring court to verify the Court of Justice's assessment of the evidence and thereby also the relevance of the preliminary ruling for the resolution of the dispute in the main proceedings. Indeed, as already mentioned, the Court of Justice cannot determine the facts of the case in the main proceedings with binding effect for the national court.[60] Where the Court of Justice departs from the understanding as presented in the reference, the preliminary ruling will only be binding for the referring court in so far as it concurs with the understanding of the facts of the case on which the preliminary ruling is based.[61] For that reason too, the Court of Justice tends only to base its preliminary ruling on facts deviating from those presented in the reference when it believes that in its final judgment the referring court will confirm the correctness of the understanding of the facts on which the preliminary ruling is based.

3.3.3.3.3. A party corrects information on the facts against his own interest. Occasionally, the Court of Justice has also deviated from the referring court's presentation of the facts where, in a way that weakens his own case, a party to the main proceedings himself corrects a fact mentioned in the preliminary reference. In proceedings for preliminary rulings, the Court of Justice is not bound by the admissions of the parties since one of the main purposes of the procedure is to

---

[58] Again, from the point of view of legal policy, it would be worth considering whether it would not be helpful if there were a more comprehensive ongoing dialogue between the Court of Justice and the national court while a case is pending before the Court of Justice.

[59] Case C-360/97 *Nijhuis* [1999] ECR I-1919, para 24.

[60] See above at Ch 4, s 5.6.

[61] See below at Ch 12, s 2.1.

clarify a question of general interest applicable to all.[62] However, if on the basis of the information presented to the Court of Justice, it is both undisputed and apparent that the referring court, without having looked into the matter in any great detail, has overlooked some important factual information, the Court of Justice has at times been willing to reformulate the preliminary question so that it is cohesive with its own understanding of the facts, and thereby to provide the referring court with an answer that is useful for the resolution of the dispute in the main proceedings.

In *Tabouillot*, various questions were referred to the Court of Justice about the relationship between Article 90 of the EC Treaty prohibiting discriminatory taxes and some French provisions on the taxation of vehicles. The plaintiff in the main proceedings himself informed the Court of Justice that he had imported the vehicle in question directly from the USA. Article 90 is not applicable in such situations, but the plaintiff in the main proceedings argued that the Court should nevertheless answer the questions referred, since he would be able to claim such a ruling at national level in support of the principle that all taxpayers in France should be treated equally under the tax rules. The Court of Justice found that nothing in the order for reference gave reason to believe that a preliminary ruling was sought with a view to clarifying this aspect. On the contrary, it seemed clear that the national court had only referred the questions because it had mistakenly believed that the disputed vehicle had been imported from another Member State. The Court of Justice therefore reformulated the questions so that they related to the rules pertaining to a vehicle imported into a Member State from a third country, and held that, with regard to such cases, Community law did not preclude the French rules in question. In contrast, the Court of Justice did not rule on whether the French rules were compatible with Community law in cases where a vehicle was imported from another Member State.[63]

3.3.3.3.4. Those entitled to present observations disagree on the correction of a fact. As a clear rule, the Court of Justice will only base its ruling on the additional factual information brought forward in the preliminary procedure if the new information is undisputed by all who submit observations in the preliminary case. Where that is not the case, the Court has no other choice than to refer to the facts of the case as described by the national court in its reference. This is especially so in cases where the new information seems difficult to reconcile with the understanding of the facts set out in the preliminary reference.[64]

---

62 P Lasok, *The European Court of Justice—Practice and Procedure* (1994) 352ff.
63 Case C-284/96 *Tabouillot* [1997] ECR I-7471. See also Ch 4, s 5.3.5.
64 Case 240/87 *Deville* [1988] ECR 3513, paras 13–17. See also K Lenaerts, 'Form and Substance of the Preliminary Ruling Procedure' in D Curtin and T Heikels (eds), *Institutional Dynamics of*

Even where an observation in the preliminary ruling procedure before the Court of Justice contains new factual information that is not disputed in other observations presented as part of this procedure, the Court will be hesitant to base its ruling firmly on this new information if one or more of the parties to the main proceedings, who would have an interest in disputing the new information, have not presented observations to the Court and thus not been available for questions from the Court as to the accuracy of the new information. Indeed, not appearing before the Court in a preliminary procedure does not mean that the party concerned consents to what is being said and claimed by others during the preliminary reference procedure. Therefore, it would not be without pitfalls if the Court were to attach importance to such new information. If, during the proceedings for the preliminary ruling, the observations give the Court of Justice the impression that the referring court probably has an incorrect understanding of the facts, the Court will usually make this discernable from its preliminary ruling by encouraging the referring court to make a new examination of the facts.[65] In such situations the Court may also give alternative answers or merely emphasise that its ruling is based on a given assumption about the facts.

The case law of the Court of Justice contains at least one example of the Court entirely setting aside the national court's evaluation of the facts even though the parties to the main proceedings disagreed about whether the national court was wrong about the facts.

In *Casa Uno*, an Italian court had asked the Court of Justice to rule on whether some Italian rules on business opening hours were contrary to the provision in Article 28 of the EC Treaty on the free movement of goods. Before deciding on the case, the Court of Justice sent one of its earlier rulings to the referring court, making it clear that national rules on sales were only covered by Article 28 if the rules affected the sales of foreign goods differently and more restrictively than the sale of corresponding domestic goods. The Italian court nevertheless asked the Court of Justice to proceed to a ruling, stating essentially that particular features of the Italian commercial market meant that the legislation in question discriminated indirectly against imported goods. This finding was disputed by the defendant authority, by the Greek government, and by the Commission. On the other hand, the plaintiff supported the argument which had persuaded the referring court. The Court of Justice held that it had been presented with no evidence that the aim of the rules at issue was to regulate trade in goods between Member States. Nor was there any evidence that, viewed as a whole, the Italian rules could lead to

---

European Integration (1994) 355, 366, and 368; and P Lasok, *The European Court of Justice—Practice and Procedure* (1994) 349.

[65] Case 99/83 *Fioravanti* [1984] ECR 3939, para 10.

unequal treatment between national products and imported products as regards access to the market. In this connection, the Court emphasised that national rules whose effect was to generally limit the marketing of a product, and therefore also its importation, could not on that ground alone be regarded as limiting access to the market for those imported products to a greater extent than for similar national products. It thereafter ruled that Article 28 did not apply to national rules on shop opening hours which applied to all retailers in the country and which, both in law and in fact, affected the marketing of national products and products from other Member States in the same way.[66]

The judgment in *Casa Uno* has been criticised for exceeding the Court's jurisdiction under Article 234.[67] And indeed, even if it is difficult not to agree with the Court of Justice that the referring court's argument in *Casa Uno* was somewhat far fetched, it is still remarkable that, without taking evidence, the Court of Justice set aside the referring court's evaluation of the facts while at the same time maintaining that the legal test was whether foreign goods were in law or in fact put in a worse position than domestically produced goods. Nevertheless, the Court's approach seems justified, as the disputed information did not relate to facts *stricto sensu*, but rather to an *assessment* of the likely factual general effects of a given piece of legislation. Whereas the national courts are clearly better placed to assess evidence directly concerning the individual characteristics of the parties to the dispute (such as whether one of the parties is more or less than 18 years old or has impaired vision), it might be considerably more difficult for a national court to make findings about the general characteristics of a given market situation. It is therefore not unreasonable that in the latter situation the Court of Justice has shown itself more inclined to supplement or even to differ from the referring court's description of the facts.[68]

3.3.3.3.5. Cases concerning the validity of Community rules. The willingness of the Court of Justice to itself establish the facts of a case is particularly apparent where questions are raised about the validity of a Community act since only the Court of Justice can declare a Community act invalid. Thus, the Court is forced to give an unconditional answer and cannot, as in cases of interpretation, confine itself to establishing legal criteria on the basis of which the national court must find the relevant facts and make the final assessment. Moreover, only exceptionally can the assessment of questions of validity be made in the abstract, but it will

---

[66] Joined Cases C-418/93, C-419/93, C-420/93, C-421/93, C-460/93, C-461/93, C-462/93, C-464/93, C-9/94, C-10/94, C-11/94, C-14/94, C-15/94, C-23/94, C-24/94, and C-332/94 *Casa Uno* [1996] ECR I-2975, paras 20–8.

[67] R Lane, 'Article 234: A Few Rough Edges Still' in M Hoskins and W Robinson (eds), *A True European, Essays for Judge David Edward* (2003) 327, 340–1.

[68] D Anderson and M Demetriou, *References to the European Court* (2002) 84ff, and below at s 3.3.3.3.5 concerning question on the validity of Community acts.

often depend on the factual effects of the disputed act. In this respect, it will often be necessary to take account of evidence from other Member States to which the parties to the main proceedings and the referring court often only have limited access.[69] If, in such cases, the Court of Justice were to base itself entirely on the national court's presentation of the facts, it would mean that to a considerable degree the evaluation of the validity of a Community act would rely on the quality and extent of evidence given by the parties to the main proceedings. Such a result would be unacceptable, and thus the general allocation of competences between the Court of Justice and the referring court in Article 234 cases does not meet the needs in these cases. Indeed, especially in cases concerning the validity of a Community act, it would be wrong to view the preliminary procedure as purely non-contentious proceedings where it is solely for the referring court to establish the facts. In reality, such preliminary cases have significant adversarial elements in which the Community institution that has issued the contested act behaves more like a defendant than a neutral observer.

Hence, in cases concerning the validity of Community acts, the Court of Justice does not consider itself bound by the national court's presentation of the facts.[70] This is particularly so in the typical situations where the Community institution that has issued the contested act is not party to the proceedings before the national court and thus has not been able to present evidence supporting the legality of the act before that court. Moreover, in these cases, the Court of Justice is willing to take account of information not mentioned in the reference even where the parties do not agree about whether or not the facts of the case are correctly described in the order for reference. The Court's willingness to engage in fact-finding independently of the referring court is particularly apparent with regard to facts that are not specifically related to the actual behaviour of the parties to the procedures before the national court, but more generally relate to the market situation or to other factual elements that are likely to be relevant for the assessment of the validity of the disputed Community act.[71]

3.3.3.3.6. Rules of evidence.   Since, formally, preliminary ruling proceedings are not in the nature of a dispute, the ordinary rules on the burden of proof and the

---

[69] T Koopmans, 'The Technique of the Preliminary Question—a view from the Court of Justice' in H Schermers et al (eds), *Article 177: Experiences and Problems* (1987) 327, 330.

[70] Gathering of evidence has taken place in eg Joined Cases 117/76 and 16/77 *Ruckdeschel* [1997] ECR 1753, paras 8–9; Case 131/77 *Malic* [1978] ECR 1050, paras 3–6; and Case C-212/97 *Angelopharm* [1994] ECR I-171, paras 22–3.

[71] Case C-337/88 *SAFA* [1990] ECR I-1. See also the Opinion of Advocate General Reischl in Case 36/79 *Denkavit* [1979] ECR 3439, 3461ff; the Opinion of Advocate General Warner in Case 51/76 *EMI Records* [1976] ECR 811, 854; G Bebr, 'General Report' in H Schermers et al (eds), *Article 177: Experiences and Problems* (1987) 345, 352–4; and P Lasok, *The European Court of Justice—Practice and Procedure* (1994) 352.

requirements for evidence in direct proceedings before the Court of Justice do not fully apply. That being said, the rules on the burden of proof relating to the preliminary procedure are quite similar to those used in direct proceedings. Thus, also in preliminary procedures, the one who makes potentially disputed assertions on the facts in his observations before the Court must discharge the burden of underpinning these assertions with factual evidence.[72] Similarly, the Court of Justice can sometimes conclude that a submission may be presumed to be correct since the one having an interest in disputing the submission was present at the preliminary procedure and did not dispute the submission even though he had ample opportunity to do so. In such cases, the Court may choose to render its preliminary ruling on this basis, even though the fact in question is not discussed in the order for reference.[73] In contrast, as already indicated, this approach is not normally possible where the one who would have an interest in disputing the assertions has not presented observations in the preliminary procedure.

The special procedure with a single round of written observations and a short oral procedure (if any[74]) gives only limited possibilities for persons and bodies entitled to present observations to the Court to challenge the evidential value or relevance of information submitted. As a matter of principle, it might be argued that the preliminary procedure for that reason alone contains serious flaws with regard to judicial protection. In practice, these flaws are, however, normally not of major importance. Indeed, as demonstrated above in Sections 3.3.1–3.3.3, the Court usually refrains from integrating disputed facts in its preliminary ruling in a manner that deviates from the referring court's understanding of the facts where there is even the slightest doubt about the correctness of the conflicting factual information that has been provided in observations before the Court. Instead, the Court will frame its ruling in general terms or give alternative solutions which seek to take account of the different possible factual situations with which the national court may be confronted.[75]

However, this approach cannot be used in cases concerning the validity of Community acts, as the question of validity must be decided by the Court of Justice itself. In these cases the lack of procedural rules to protect the parties in the main proceedings means that in reality they have limited scope for challenging factual information which may be put forward in the course of the preliminary ruling proceedings, for example, by one of the Community's institutions.[76] This is

---

[72] P Lasok, *The European Court of Justice—Practice and Procedure* (1994) 421.

[73] Case 311/85 *VVM* [1987] ECR 3801; Case 148/85 *Forest* [1986] ECR 3449, para 11; and Case 433/85 *Feldain* [1987] ECR 3521, para 16; as well as D Anderson and M Demetriou, *References to the European Court* (2002) 82.

[74] See below at s 4.4.

[75] See ss 3.3.3.1 and 3.3.3.3.4, as well as Ch 11, s 2.4.

[76] See s 4.3 below.

particularly the case where the question of the validity of a Community act is raised for the first time in a written observation to the Court, meaning that a Community institution's counterarguments in support of the validity of the act are only presented in the oral proceedings.

3.3.3.4. Departing from the referring court's interpretation of national law.

As demonstrated above, to some extent the Court of Justice allows the parties to supplement the facts of a case as contained in the order for reference. In comparison, there is a greater need to be prudent in allowing the parties to the main proceedings and others entitled to submit observations to correct a national court's interpretation of national law. Indeed, the Court of Justice nearly always rejects such claims on the principle that it must base its ruling on the interpretation of national law which the referring court has adopted. This is the case even where the referring court's interpretation is being disputed by the very government that has issued the national rules in question.

In *Orfanopoulos*, the German government disputed the way in which the referring German court had explained the German rules. Referring to the allocation of jurisdiction between the Court of Justice and the national courts, the Court of Justice dismissed this objection and based its preliminary ruling on the legal situations as defined and described by the German court.[77]

However, there is nothing to prevent the Court of Justice from drawing express attention, in its ruling, to the fact that doubts have been raised about the correctness of the statement relating to national law.

In *Pusa*, a Finnish court made a reference for a preliminary ruling on the compatibility with Community law of the Finnish Law on enforcement. In its observations to the Court of Justice, the Finnish government gave an interpretation of this law. The Court held that it was not for it to rule on the interpretation of provisions of national law and that it therefore had to base itself on the legislative context, as described in the preliminary reference. For the same reason, it was for the referring court alone to ascertain whether the interpretation put forward by the Finnish government before the Court of Justice was well founded. However, since the order for reference did not contain any information that contradicted the Finnish government's interpretation, the Court of Justice found it most appropriate to rule on whether the Finnish Law on enforcement was contrary to Community law, in the event that the Finnish law was interpreted as suggested by the government.[78]

---

[77] Joined Cases C-482/01 and C-493/01 *Orfanopoulos* [2004] ECR I-5257, para 43. See also Case C-136/03 *Dörr* [2005] ECR I-4759, paras 45–6; and Case C-246/04 *Turn- und Sportunion Waldburg* [2006] ECR I-589, paras 17–22.

[78] Case C-224/02 *Pusa* [2004] ECR I-5763, para 29.

In a few exceptional cases the Court of Justice has departed from the principle that it does not have competence to interpret national law and has used arguments from observations in the preliminary procedure to effectively set aside the referring court's interpretation of national law. Such deviations seems less surprising in the few situations where the referring court is not interpreting its own national laws, but that of another State as the presumption of the national court being more appropriate to interpret national law cannot apply in these situations.[79] The Court has also, however, in two judgments de facto set aside the interpretation that a national court has given of rules from its own legal system.

In *Roquette Frères*, the Court of Justice noted that the referring French district court had based itself on the premise that the national provision at issue in the main proceedings drew a distinction between actions arising from a finding by a national court, that a provision of domestic law was unlawful in the light of a superior rule of national law, and those arising from a finding by the Community judicature, that a provision of domestic law was unlawful in the light of Community law. However, with reference to the observations of the Commission and those of the French and Italian governments, the Court of Justice found that the French law drew no such distinction. On the contrary, it referred in general to all judicial decisions indicating that the rule of law applied in levying a charge was incompatible with a superior rule of law, without being directed specifically at decisions emanating from the Community judicature or cases of incompatibility with Community law. In this connection the Court of Justice referred to information submitted by the French government that the French *Cour de cassation* had consistently refuted the interpretation of the relevant French law put forward by the referring court. The Court of Justice then referred to its case law according to which, in instances where a national court has based a preliminary question on a misunderstanding of *Community law*, the Court may reformulate the question so that the answer will be of genuine value to the referring court. In this connection the Court of Justice did not distinguish between reformulations that were due to a misunderstanding of Community rules and reformulations that were based on a disagreement about the understanding of national law. The Court thereupon reformulated the question so as to base its ruling on an understanding of *national law* which differed from the one provided by the referring court.[80]

Lenz concerned a question from an Austrian court about whether some Austrian tax rules were contrary to the EC Treaty rules on the free movement of capital. In the preliminary procedure, the plaintiff in the main proceedings, the Austrian government, and the Commission all argued that the question did not concern

---

[79] See above Ch 5, s 4.12, and Ch 8, s 3.1.
[80] Case C-88/99 *Roquette Frères* [2000] ECR I-10465, paras 16–19.

the tax system which was applicable in Austria at the material time. The Court of Justice then invited the Austrian government to provide more information on the Austrian tax system. Having received this additional information, the Court accepted the arguments brought forward in the observations and stated that the national provisions referred to in the order for reference did not provide for a tax deduction 'such as that indicated by the referring court, even on a broad interpretation of the law'. In those circumstances, the Court saw no need to reply to the question.[81]

In *Ordini degli Achitetti*, the Court of Justice refused an invitation made in an observation to the Court to apply an interpretation of Italian law that differed from the one set forth by the referring court. The Court of Justice, however, reached this conclusion on the basis of a number of concrete factors which indicated that the national court's interpretation was correct. The Court's decision was thus not based on a general rule that by definition it must apply the referring court's interpretation.[82]

These examples of the departure from the axiom that it is solely for the referring court and not for the Court of Justice to rule on the interpretation of national law are rare and difficult to reconcile with the Court's frequent assertion of the limits to its jurisdiction under Article 234. Presumably, the above-mentioned judgments do not indicate a general trend towards a redefinition of the Court's competence in preliminary cases. Rather, the better view is to consider these departures from the main rule to be a manifestation of pragmatism in situations where, on the basis of both the observations presented to the Court and the Court's own enquiries, it seems clear that the relevance of the question referred is based on an obviously wrong interpretation of the national law and where the national court has presented no reasons for why it has arrived at the contested interpretation.[83]

3.3.3.5. The Court of Justice's access to information on the facts and on national law. It is crucial for the Court's ability to give an answer that will be of use to the referring court that it has reasonable certainty that its ruling is based on a correct understanding of the facts and the national law in the main proceedings.[84] Where neither the order for reference nor the observations in the preliminary ruling proceedings give the Court such certainty, the question arises as to whether it

---

[81] Case C-315/02 *Lenz* [2004] ECR I-7063, paras 51–5. One might wonder if it would not have been beneficial if the Court had invited the referring court to comment on the arguments raised in the preliminary procedure before dismissing the question as hypothetical. For an overview of the Court's practice of when to ask the referring court for clarification see C Naômé, *Le renvoi préjudiciel en droit européen* (2007) 140–4 and 232.

[82] Case C-399/98 *Ordini degli Achitetti* [2001] ECR I-5409, paras 76–86.

[83] See also above Ch 5, s 4.5.

[84] D Edward, 'The Problem of Fact-finding in Preliminary Proceedings under Article 177' in H Schermers et al (eds), *Article 177: Experiences and Problems* (1987) 216ff.

can, on its own initiative, take steps to obtain the information as part of the proceedings.

In principle, the general rules in the Court of Justice's Statute and Rules of Procedure relating to measures of enquiry also apply to cases for preliminary rulings.[85] According to Article 24 of the Statute, the Court of Justice may require 'the parties' to produce all documents and to supply all information which it considers desirable. For preliminary rulings this means that the Court may make such requests to the parties to the main proceedings and all other bodies entitled to present observations to the Court during the preliminary procedure. The Court may for example invite a Member State not party to the main proceedings to supply all information which the Court considers necessary.[86] Sometimes the Court asks those who have submitted written observations on a case to provide further information about some specific problems.[87] Also, the Member State whose national law is affected by the dispute in the main proceedings is regularly asked to give a report on the facts and the national law. The Court will then be able to use this report in its preliminary ruling, unless the report is contested by others who are entitled to submit observations.[88] Similarly, the Court sometimes asks a Community institution to give specific information, regardless of whether the institution has submitted written observations on the case in question.[89]

Normally the information is obtained through a written request from the Court's Registrar. Thus, an actual order is hardly ever issued. A request by the Court of Justice for documentation or provision of information is not enforceable by the national courts. Where there is a refusal to provide the documents or information required, the Court of Justice takes 'formal note' of this, and may draw its conclusions with respect to the evidence, inter alia, by using the evidential rule that refusal to provide evidence must be due to the fact that such evidence would not be beneficial to the person refusing to provide it, cf Article 24 of the Court's Statute.

Furthermore, according to Article 25 of the Court's Statute and Article 47 of its Rules of Procedure, the Court may at any time entrust any individual, body,

---

85 P Lasok, *The European Court of Justice—Practice and Procedure* (1994) 365.
86 In Case 168/84 *Berkholz* [1985] ECR 251, the Court of Justice requested the Member State concerned to send an expert to the oral proceedings.
87 Case C-250/92 *Gøttrup-Klim* [1994] ECR I-5641, para 19; and Case C-379/87 *Groener* [1989] ECR 3967.
88 Case C-343/90 *Lourenco Dias* [1992] ECR I-4673, para 52. As shown in ss 3.3.3.3.4 and 3.3.3.3.6 above, if others entitled to present observations dispute the information provided the Court of Justice may not evaluate the evidence itself, but must leave this to the national court, and it must therefore either formulate its preliminary ruling in vague terms or give alternative rulings for the national court's alternative findings.
89 Case 208/80 *Lord Bruce of Dennington* [1981] ECR 2205.

authority, committee, or other organisation it chooses with the task of giving an expert opinion. Formally, Article 47 also enables the Court of Justice to summon a witness. However, in practice these measures are not used in preliminary ruling procedures. The aim of such measures is normally to obtain clarification of disputed facts and, as has been shown above, such clarification normally falls outside the jurisdiction of the Court of Justice under Article 234.[90]

Finally, under Article 104(5) of the Rules of Procedure, the Court of Justice may request clarification from the national court. The Court regularly uses this provision to resolve doubt about the relevance of the reference or to obtain more knowledge of the facts or the national law in the main proceedings.[91] Normally such information is obtained prior to the oral proceedings. Those entitled to present observations to the Court will thereby have the opportunity to comment on the information in their oral observations, should the Court decide to hold an oral hearing.

4. The Procedure before the Court of Justice

According to Article 103 of the Court's Rules of Procedure, the procedure for preliminary rulings is governed by the general provisions of the Rules of Procedure, subject to adaptations necessitated by the nature of references for a preliminary ruling. When the Court of Justice has received a preliminary reference, a Judge-Rapporteur and (normally) an Advocate General are appointed in the same way as for direct actions. Moreover, at the Court's administrative meeting following the conclusion of the written procedure, the members of the Court decide which chamber the case will be referred to.

In the following section we first consider representation in Section 4.1, and then we examine the language regime in preliminary references in Section 4.2. Next, in Section 4.3 we turn to the written procedure followed by an examination of the oral procedure in Section 4.4.

4.1. Representation

According to Article 19 of the Statute of the Court of Justice, the Member States and the Community institutions are represented before the Court by an agent appointed for each case; the agent may be assisted by an adviser or by an attorney. The same applies to the EFTA Surveillance Authority and the three EFTA States that are party to the EEA Agreement. There is thus no requirement that the agent

---

[90] P Lasok, *The European Court of Justice—Practice and Procedure* (1994) 104.
[91] R Barents et al, *European Courts Procedure* (2004) para 11.017.

concerned is a lawyer or merely has a legal education, just as it is not a prerequisite that the agent is an employee of the State or institution in question.

As for the representation of the parties in the main proceedings and their personal attendance, according to Article 104(2) of the Rules of Procedure, the Court of Justice must take account of the referring court's rules of procedure. Hence, persons who have a right of audience before the referring court can also appear before the Court of Justice. This applies whether or not they are licensed to act as an attorney. If the national procedural rules do not require a party to have legal representation, then the party can also appear in person before the Court of Justice.[92] Similarly, in that situation a party to the main proceedings can be represented by a family member such as his spouse or father[93] just as, for example, a member of the party's staff may appear before the Court of Justice.[94]

The provision in Article 104(2) is not strictly enforced, and the Court has, for example, accepted observations from lawyers who did not have the right to plead before the referring court.[95]

4.2. Language

According to Article 29(2) of the Rules of Procedure, the language of a preliminary case is the referring national court's language of procedure. This applies to both written and oral proceedings. Thus, each case has its 'own' language, and only one of the 23 official languages will be the language of the case.[96] An exception is made where cases are joined and the language of the case is different for each: in such circumstances the language of each of the cases joined becomes the language of the joined case so that there will be more languages of the case.

Whilst the use of the language of a third country will not be authorised, exceptionally the Court of Justice may authorise the use of another of the official EU languages for the oral procedure provided one of the parties to the main proceedings

---

[92] Case C-168/91 *Konstantinidis* [1993] ECR I-1191; Case C-19/92 *Kraus* [1993] ECR I-1663; Case C-282/91 *de Wit* [1993] ECR I-1221; and Case C-285/01 *Burbaud* [2003] I-8219.

[93] Case C-77/95 *Zûchner* [1996] I-5689 and Case C-337/97 *Meeusen* [1999] ECR I-3289.

[94] Case C-249/97 *Gruber* [1999] ECR I-5295.

[95] R Barents et al, *European Courts Procedure* (2004) paras 13.068 and 31.133ff; and J Pertek, *La practique du renvoi préjudiciel de droit communautaire* (2001) 119ff, according to whom the Court accepts legal representation by a solicitor in the context of a preliminary reference from a national court even though only a barrister may appear before the referring national court. See also D Anderson and M Demetriou, *References to the European Court* (2002) 249ff, concerning legal representatives who do not have a right of audience in the State of the referring court, but who are licensed attorneys in another Member State. Anderson and Demetriou argue that in such cases there ought to be a right of audience before the Court of Justice in proceedings for preliminary rulings.

[96] Catalonian courts normally render their judgments in Catalan. Notwithstanding this, they make preliminary references only in Castillian (Spanish), see C Naômé, *Le renvoi préjudiciel en droit européen* (2007) 126.

makes a duly substantiated request, and after the opposing party in the main proceedings and the Advocate General have been heard. Such an authorisation can be
an advantage to a party who does not speak the language of the referring court.

Whereas the Court in direct proceedings has only accepted that a party or an
intervener pleads in a language other than the language of the case where special
circumstances exceptionally justify this,[97] is has applied a more lenient practice in
procedures for preliminary rulings, where the choice of language is not normally
a matter for the parties, just as the parties have no control over whether the case is
referred to the Court of Justice. The Court seems inclined to accept oral observations in preliminary cases in languages other than the language of the case, as long
as this is requested in writing well before the hearing and provided those persons
and bodies entitled to present observations do not object.[98]

Permission to use a language other than the language of the case applies only to the
person so authorised by the Court. This means that in these cases more languages
will be used in the procedure.

The Member States submit their observations in their own language whereupon
the Court of Justice's translation service will be responsible for the translation into
the language of the case. The written and oral observations made by the Community
institutions are given in the language of the case. Third countries which participate in proceedings for a preliminary ruling in accordance with Article 23(4) of
the Court's Statute and Article 29(3) of its Rules of Procedure may be permitted
to use another of the official languages of the EU than the language of the case.
The Court can also authorise the three EFTA States which are parties to the EEA
Agreement, as well as the EFTA Surveillance Authority to use one of the official
languages of the EU other than the language of the case. In practice the three
EFTA States as well as the EFTA Surveillance Authority always request, and are
allowed, to present both their written and oral observations in English.

Any supporting documents expressed in a language other than the language of the
case must be accompanied by a translation into the language of the case. This
requirement can be derogated from under special circumstances.[99] In the case of
lengthy documents, translations may be confined to extracts. However, at any
time the Court may, of its own motion or at the request of a party, call for a fuller
or even complete translation. The translation need not be made by an authorised

---

[97] Case T-121/95 *EFMA* [1997] ECR II-87.
[98] D Vaughan et al, *Butterworths European Court Practice* (1993) 76. According to C Naômé, *Le
renvoi préjudiciel en droit européen* (2007) 128, the Court receives around five such applications each
year of which two to three are normally granted.
[99] Case T-11/95 *BP Chemicals* [1996] ECR II-599; and Case T-121/95 *EFMA* [1997] ECR
II-87.

translator, as long as it is made clear that it is not an official translation. If more than one language is used in a case, any person or body entitled to present observations can receive a translated version from the Registrar. However, due to the workload weighing on the Court's translators, such a translation can take time. Moreover, the Court may require such parties to pay for the costs of translation themselves.[100] For these reasons it will often be more appropriate for the person or body in question to arrange for the translation of the document themselves.

While it is extremely rare that a preliminary procedure will involve witnesses or experts, the rule in Article 29 of the Rules of Procedure, according to which a witness or expert witness can use any of the 23 official languages, and moreover may be authorised to speak in a language that is not one of the official languages if he is unable to express himself in one of these, still applies to preliminary proceedings.

According to Article 29(5) of the Rules of Procedure, the President of the Court and the Presidents of Chambers may use one of the official EU languages other than the language of the case when conducting oral proceedings. The same applies to the Judge-Rapporteur in preparing the Preliminary Report and the Report for the Hearing, and for judges and Advocates General in putting questions, and Advocates General in delivering their Opinions. The Registrar arranges for translation into the language of the case.

It often happens that at the oral hearing a member of the Court poses a question to the lawyer pleading the case in a language that differs from the one used by the lawyer when making his observations. In such situations the lawyer is advised not to reply in the language in which the question is put even if he is capable of doing so. First, because the lawyer has not been allowed to use that other language, and, second, because it may confuse the interpreters who will expect him to answer in the language in which he has presented his observations.[101]

4.3. The written proceedings

4.3.1. Introduction

According to Article 20 of the Court's Statute, the procedure before the Court consists of two parts: written and oral. Whereas the former is described in this section, the oral procedure is analysed below in Section 4.4.

In order to assist those taking part in the proceedings before the Court of Justice it has issued 'Notes for the Guidance of Counsel'.[102] These notes contain a number of useful recommendations as to how both written and oral observations can best

---

[100] D Vaughan et al, *Butterworths European Court Practice* (1993) 77.
[101] See also C Naômé, *Le renvoi préjudiciel en droit européen* (2007) 243.
[102] The notes are available at the Courts webpage <http://www.curia.europa.eu>.

be framed, including in preliminary ruling proceedings. The following analysis provides a review of the relevant provisions in the Statute and the Rules of Procedure as well as recommendations that are supplementary to the 'Notes for the Guidance of Counsel'.

4.3.2. *Deadlines and requirements regarding submission of observations*

There is a two-month deadline for the submission of written observations. This period begins to run from the date on which the party or person in question acknowledges receipt of the registered letter giving notice. The period is calculated on the basis of the rules in Chapter 9 of the Rules of Procedure, which means that the prescribed time limits are extended on account of distance by a period of 10 days regardless of the actual distance.[103] The Court has no competence to extend the deadline, even upon application. However, exceeding the deadline may be accepted in the event of *force majeure*, a concept that is given a narrow interpretation.[104]

The written observations and any correspondence concerning the case should be addressed to: 'Court of Justice of the European Communities, Registry, L-2925 Luxembourg'. It is also possible to deliver the relevant documents directly to the Registry offices at the Court (Boulevard Konrad Adenauer, Luxembourg-Kirchberg), or, outside office hours, to the Court's reception desk which is open 24 hours a day. There is thus no requirement that the observations arrive during working hours.

The observations can also be lodged by fax on (352) 43 37 66 or by email: <ECJ. Registry@curia.europa.eu>. The observations are considered to have arrived when they have been received in the Registry by either of these electronic means, provided that the signed original document is lodged at the Registry within the following 10 days. The observations do not need to be served on the (other) parties to the main proceedings or those (others) entitled to present observations before the Court of Justice under Article 23 of the Court's Statute.

The Rules of Procedure do not regulate whether the original observations should be accompanied by copies and if so the number thereof. In the Court's 'Notes for the Guidance of Counsel' it is only stated that in direct actions, the

---

[103] Art 81(2) of the Rules of Procedure. See further in R Barents et al, *European Courts Procedure* (2004) para 19.063ff; and P Lasok, *The European Court of Justice—Practice and Procedure* (1994) 208ff. The Rules of Procedure of the EFTA Court do not contain a corresponding rule. Thus, observations in cases before that court must be presented within the two-month deadline. Shorter deadlines apply in cases concerning the accelerated procedure, see s 5.2 below.

[104] K Lenaerts et al, *Procedural law of the European Union* (2006) 611; R Barents et al, *European Courts Procedure* (2004) paras 19.125 and 31.126; C Naôme, *Le renvoi préjudiciel en droit européen* (2007) 131; and D Anderson and M Demetriou, *References to the European Court* (2002) 259ff.

original pleading and all the annexes to it must be lodged together with five copies for the Court and, for the purposes of notification, a copy for every other party to the proceedings. Nevertheless, the Registrar of the Court is appreciative if in preliminary cases the original is accompanied by seven copies thereby saving the Court Registry the time taken in making copies.[105]

The original of the written observations must be signed by counsel for the party concerned and accompanied by all annexes referred to in it.[106] There are no rules about what kind of annexes etc may be attached. Hence, it is possible, for example, to submit expert observations obtained at the initiative of one of the parties to the main proceedings, just as the parties in cases concerning the customs tariff often provide the Court with samples of the object whose classification is in dispute. In evaluating the evidential weight of the annexes, the Court of Justice has regard for the special circumstances that characterise the preliminary rulings procedure.[107] The Court of Justice does not allow notes for use in subsequent oral proceedings to be submitted as one of the documents of the case.[108]

There is no obligation to give an address for service in Luxembourg. All service of documents from the Court of Justice is by registered post, with acknowledgement of receipt. However, parties entitled to make observations can agree that service of documents to them can be made by fax or some other form of electronic communication.

4.3.3. Content and structure of written observations

There are no formal requirements as to the structure of the written observations. As for the content, one should be aware that oral proceedings in the preliminary rulings procedure have a different and less important role than oral proceedings in many of the courts of the Member States.[109] The written observations should therefore exhaustively set out the arguments in support of the party's view of the case. As the case file of the referring court is neither translated nor forwarded to those others entitled to present observations, the observations should be self-explanatory and not merely consist of references to pleadings or other procedural documents from the main proceedings.

---

[105] C Naômé, *Le renvoi préjudiciel en droit européen* (2007) 240.

[106] Art 37(1) of the Rules of Procedure. See also P Lasok, *The European Court of Justice—Practice and Procedure* (1994) 301ff. In order to avoid duplication, it is advisable that the parties to the main proceedings agree, if possible, to submit a common bundle of annexes.

[107] See s 3.3.3.3.6 above.

[108] In contrast, the EFTA Court accepts such notes to be submitted in connection with oral proceedings.

[109] See s 4.4 below.

If a party entitled to present observations is in full agreement with the description of the facts of the case set out in the order for reference, it is sufficient to state this without repeating the facts.[110] This will save the Court of Justice from unnecessary translation, and thus has the advantage that the case can be dealt with more quickly. In contrast, where the party concerned disagrees with the referring court on the description of facts or national law, the written observations should describe the relevant facts or national provision and point to where there is disagreement. Moreover, often the judge coming from the referring court's Member State does not sit on the case. Thus, to some extent it might fall to the lawyers for the parties to the main proceedings to provide details on points of substantive law or procedure pertaining to the relevant national legal system which are necessary for a full understanding of the case. Similarly, if there is a need to address principles which may be peculiar to a national legal system and which are not necessarily familiar to the judges of the Court of Justice taking part in the case, particular care should be taken when explaining legal provisions or principles, even if these would be obvious to a lawyer of the State of the referring court. That being said, in view of the translation workload and the time involved in making the translations, repetition must be avoided.

In a single reading of the observations, the Court should be able to apprehend the essential matters of fact and law. Moreover, it is advisable that the observations are written in such a way that they are easy to translate with the least possible risk of mistakes and inaccuracies. Since, in most cases, the judges and the Advocate General will read pleadings in a language other than that in which they are drafted, counsel should bear in mind that if the meaning of a text is obscure in the original language there is a risk that the translation will exacerbate this obscurity. Indeed, this risk is aggravated not only by the occasional impossibility of translating directly from one language to another without passing through a 'language pivot'; the risk for added obscurity also follows from the fact that it is not always possible, in the transition from one language to another, to find an accurate translation of the 'legal jargon' which may be used before national courts. Therefore, meticulously drafted sentences over which the draftsman has laboured for hours in order to pin down that elusive phrase or the perfect *bon mot* may not survive the translation process, and treasured nuances—especially of legal language—may be lost or obscured.[111]

The above-mentioned two-month deadline (plus 10 days) for submitting written observations runs simultaneously for all those entitled to present observations. The person drafting the written observations must therefore do this without

---

[110] D Edward and C Bellamy, 'Views from European Courts' in G Barling and M Brealey (eds), *Practitioner's Handbook of EC Law* (1988) 27, point 37.

[111] Ibid, 27, point 27.

necessarily having knowledge of the arguments which may be put forward in other observations. Moreover, there is only one round of observations so that those entitled to present observations do not have the opportunity to comment on the other observations in writing. Such comments can only be given during the oral proceedings.[112] Thus, the written observation should address, as far as possible, all the arguments which can be expected to be put forward by others entitled to present observations.

The absence of a second round of written observations is based on the wish not to further increase the length of time for dealing with the preliminary case. This aim is certainly laudable. However, the absence of a right to make written comments on the observations of others has been criticised for not ensuring a proper adversarial procedure. This applies in particular when the question referred for a preliminary ruling casts doubt on the validity of a legal act where the party or body issuing this legal act is not involved in the main proceedings. For example, a party who claims before the national court that a regulation is invalid will only be able to respond to the relevant Community institution's defence of the validity of the regulation in connection with the oral proceedings.[113] The same applies in cases where a reference for a preliminary ruling concerns the compatibility with Community law of a national legal act, and the Member State in question is not a party to the case before the referring court.

Sometimes the Court of Justice seeks to make up for these disadvantages by asking questions of those who take part in proceedings before it, so that they can focus on those topics that the Court finds important, and if necessary supplement their written observations. The questions will often be put at the same time as the Court forwards the Judge-Rapporteur's Report for the Hearing to those entitled to present observations in the preliminary proceedings. In addition, the problem relating to a lack of an adversarial procedure is diminished by the Court's practice of normally giving an abstract response where there is doubt about the facts and the national legal context, leaving it to the national court to clarify unclear or disputed circumstances and thereafter to bring the case within the scope of the abstract response.[114]

Only the observations themselves are translated into the language of the case. In principle, any supplementary annexes are not translated, nor are they always sent

---

[112] K Mortelmans, 'Observations in the cases governed by Article 177 of the EEC Treaty: Procedure and Practice' (1979) 16 CML Rev 557, 565, has argued that, strictly speaking, there is nothing to stop a legal or natural person entitled to present observations making more than one written submission during the two-month period. At the same time, he notes that in practice it would not normally be possible to comment on the observations of other parties, since nearly all observations are sent to the Court of Justice close to the deadline.

[113] See s 3.3.3.3.5 above.

[114] See ss 3.3.3.3.4 and 3.3.3.3.6 above, and Ch 11, ss 2.4 and 3.3. See also Ch 8, s 3.2.5.

to those others entitled to present observations in the preliminary case.[115] For this reason, important arguments should be included in the main statement rather than relegated to an annex. If a legal or natural person entitled to present observations wishes to rely on a particular passage in an annex, this passage should either be quoted in the main statement or clearly identified with a precise reference.

It is recommended that the observations include references to the relevant case law of the Court of Justice. When a judgment of the Court is cited in the observations, full details should be given, including the names of the parties or, at least, the name of the applicant. In addition, when citing a passage from a judgment of the Court or from an Opinion of an Advocate General, the number of the paragraph or the page number on which the passage in question is to be found should be indicated.

There is no need to give long accounts of the Court's own judgments as these must be assumed to be known by the Court. On the other hand, depending on the circumstances, it may be appropriate to give accounts of decisions of national courts or arbitration decisions, and the same applies to judgments of international courts and other decisions of international bodies.

4.3.4. *Length of the written observations*

There are no formal restrictions on the length of written observations. However, 10 pages in a normal case and 30 pages in a complex case should normally be enough. The judges usually do not begin to work on a case before the observations have been translated, and the longer the observations are, the more time it will take to make the translations—thus affecting the total time it takes for the Court to render judgment. It has also been suggested that when the observations are too long only the Judge-Rapporteur will read them whereas the remaining judges hearing the case will merely consult the Report for the Hearing.[116] Regardless of whether this is so, it is recommended that the observations should be drafted so that it is easy to make a summary thereof in the Report for the Hearing. One possible way to do this is to include brief summaries of the arguments advanced.

4.3.5. *The Report for the Hearing*

The Court of Justice forwards observations received to all those entitled to submit observations and not merely to those who have in fact submitted observations on

---

115 As to the ensuing issues pertaining to rights of defence see Case C-491/06 *Danske Svineproducenter* [2008] ECR I-3339, paras 20 and 24.

116 D Anderson and M Demetriou, *References to the European Court* (2002) 263ff. Compare D Richards and M Beloff, 'View from the Bar' in G Barling and M Brealey (eds), *Practitioners' Handbook of EC Law* (1988) at 2.16.

the case.[117] Moreover, on the basis of the written observations, the Judge-Rapporteur prepares a Report for the Hearing which includes a distillation of the written observations. As is the case for the observations themselves, the Report for the Hearing is sent to all those entitled to present observations. The Court of Justice tries to ensure that this happens at least three weeks before the oral procedure. After receiving the Report for the Hearing, the recipients are invited to verify that there are no errors in the information contained in the Report. If they consider that errors are present, they are requested to inform the Registrar and to suggest such amendments as they consider appropriate.[118] As far as possible, such suggestions for corrections should not be postponed until the oral proceedings.

4.4. The oral procedure

4.4.1. Not all cases are heard orally

Originally, nearly all preliminary cases were heard orally. However, with a view to reducing the Court's workload as well as the length of the proceedings, it has become increasingly normal for the Court to dispense with the oral procedure.

First, the procedure for a preliminary ruling does not contain an oral stage if the Court of Justice decides to give its decision by means of a reasoned order in accordance with Article 104(3) of the Rules of Procedure.[119]

Second, for other cases, the provision in Article 104(4) of the Rules of Procedure prescribes that the procedure includes an oral part, but at the same time allows the oral procedure to be dispensed with. In practice, the Court only holds a hearing in proceedings for a preliminary ruling if one of the parties to the main proceedings or others entitled to present observations to the Court so request. Such request must be submitted within three weeks of receipt of the written observations. That period may be extended by the President of the Court. Relevant grounds for requesting oral proceedings could for example be that new arguments have been put forward in other written observations, or could be disagreement as to the description of the facts given in another statement or in an answer to a question from the Court. An indication should be given as to which points one wishes to deal with in the oral proceedings.[120]

---

[117] Until January 1994, the Report for the Hearing was published in the European Court Reports in all the official languages. This practice was dispensed with in order to reduce costs connected to translation and to speed up the publication of the Court Reports. Today, the Report for the Hearing, which is drawn up in French, is only translated into the language of the case.

[118] The Court's 'Notes for the Guidance of Counsel', point C.1.b. As noted by C Naôme, *Le renvoi préjudiciel en droit européen* (2007) 241, it is worth the effort of suggesting the requisite corrections as the Report is often used as basis for the draft judgment.

[119] On the choice between a judgment and a reasoned order, see Ch 11, s 1.

[120] D Anderson and M Demetriou, *References to the European Court* (2002) 268.

It is for each person or body entitled to present observations at the oral hearing to decide whether there is reason to do so. On the one hand, the fact that a person has not requested an oral hearing does not preclude that person from presenting oral observations should the case be heard orally. Thus, the Commission only rarely requests an oral hearing whereas, as a rule, it attends any oral hearing should one be held. On the other hand, in its 'Notes for the Guidance of Counsel', the Court stresses that refraining from presenting oral arguments will never be construed as constituting acquiescence in the arguments put forward by others. On that basis, the Court invites counsel to consider 'whether oral argument is really necessary or whether a simple reference to the written observations or pleadings would suffice'.[121]

Anyone who is entitled to present written observations is also entitled to attend the oral hearing, whether or not they have used their right to present written observations. In fact, making oral observations can be particularly important for a Member State or other body entitled to present observations if they only become aware of the nature and importance of the case by reading the written observations.

4.4.2. Setting the date for the oral hearing

The Court of Justice does not usually consult (counsel for) those entitled to attend the oral hearing before setting the date for the hearing. The summons will often be served with only a few weeks' notice. The proceedings are held in public unless the Court, of its own motion or on application by those entitled to submit observations, decides otherwise. Such a decision is only made where serious reasons so dictate.[122] Lawyers are required to be robed. The Court has robes available for those who have not brought their own.

4.4.3. Time allowed for addressing the Court

It is the established practice of the Court to ask for a prior indication of the length of the oral observations of each of those who will make use of the right to speak. This should not normally exceed 20 minutes. For cases dealt with by Chambers consisting of three judges, observations should not exceed 15 minutes. Requests for permission for more time must be justified and must reach the Court of Justice at least 15 days before the date of the hearing. The Court's decision on the request will be notified to the applicant at least one week before the hearing. Dispensations from the normal time limits are not readily given. In fact, the Court occasionally invites counsel to confine the length of their speeches to less than that indicated. Similarly, in its 'Notes for the Guidance of Counsel' the Court states that experience

---

[121] See the Court's 'Notes for the Guidance of Counsel', point C.6.
[122] Art 31 of the Court's Statute.

has shown that the time allowed for oral observations is generally not fully used by counsel accustomed to appearing before the Court.[123] The Court is quite willing to cut short a lawyer who exceeds the allotted time. The time allotted for the oral submission does not include time used to reply to questions asked by the members of the Court. The same applies to the time used for the short reply that can be made at the end of the session.

For reasons connected with the efficient conduct of the hearing, each person or body entitled to present oral arguments should only have one person to actually make the oral submission before the Court of Justice. Notwithstanding this, replies to questions asked by the Court do not have to be delivered by the same person who addressed the Court in the oral submission. Moreover, following a duly reasoned written application made at least two weeks before the date of the hearing, the Court might grant permission for a second person to present part of the oral observations. In that case, the total duration of the oral arguments must still keep within the usual time limits for such presentations as set out above. According to the 'Directions relating to Hearings' that accompany the Court's convocation for the oral hearings, only in exceptional circumstances will such a second person be allowed. It is, however, quite common practice for the Commission to present its observations using several lawyers when a case raises issues that are covered by different teams in its Legal Service. Only the person who made the oral submission is allowed to present the reply, and where two lawyers have been allowed to present the main observations, only one of them will be allowed to give the reply.

4.4.4. *Content and conduct of the oral hearing*

In the light of the knowledge which the Court of Justice already possesses of all the documents lodged in the course of the written procedure, the oral procedure should normally be used to:

1. provide a more detailed analysis of the dispute, by clarifying and expounding the more complex points and those which are more difficult to grasp;
2. submit any new arguments prompted by recent events occurring after the close of the written procedure;
3. reply to the arguments put forward by others in their written pleadings;
4. reply to the arguments put forward in the oral pleadings in the short reply at the end of the hearing itself;
5. answer the questions put by the Court.[124]

---

[123] The Court's 'Notes for the Guidance of Counsel', point C.5.
[124] Ibid, point C.2.

Before the hearing commences, the Court of Justice invites those who are going to plead to a brief private meeting in order to settle the arrangements for the hearing. In some cases, the judges and the Advocate General that are to hear the case indicate particular matters which they would like to be developed in the oral observations. Where the Court has requested the participants in the hearing to concentrate their oral submissions on certain points, the submissions should only deal with other aspects of the case if this is particularly important for the Court's decision; at the very least the Court's indications should serve as a guide as to what points should be dwelt upon in the speech. At the preparatory private meeting there is no interpretation available, nor will the judges require that the communication takes place in French if another language known to at least some of the participating judges is preferred by the participants.

The order in which the oral observations are given is that the plaintiff (or appellant) in the main proceedings makes the first observation, followed by the defendant (or respondent), others participating in the procedure before the referring court, the Member States and any third countries in alphabetical order, the Council, the European Parliament and the EFTA Surveillance Authority, and finally the Commission.

The Court of Justice recommends that each oral presentation is introduced by an overview of the observations about to be made. Similarly, it might be useful to indicate when one point in the observations is concluded and the next begins.

Reference to previous decisions of the Court of Justice should use the full reference, including the case number. Where passages from a judgment are intended to be read out, an indication should be given of the paragraph quoted from.

Where several of those entitled to present observations wish to make the same arguments, it is recommended that the observations be coordinated with a view to limiting the duration of the oral procedure and avoiding repetition.[125] Where such coordination has not been made those pleading should be ready to adapt their presentations so as to avoid repeating at length points already made by previous speakers.

As stated above in Section 4.3.3, the written procedure does not provide for the possibility of making written comments on the written observations of others. Furthermore, by the time of the oral proceedings, the participating judges may be expected to have studied the written observations or, at least, the summaries given in the Report for the Hearing. For this reason, it is generally advisable that the oral observations focus on countering the arguments that others may have made in

---

[125] Indeed, before the hearing in Case C-475/03 *Banca popolare di Cremona* [2006] ECR I-9373 the Court invited representatives of the Member States to coordinate their oral observations.

their written observations rather than merely repeating the points which have already been expressed in one's own prior written observations. Similarly, especially for those who do not speak first, it is normally not necessary to recall the factual and legal background to the case. That being said, it can be a good idea to take account of the fact that all judges may not have studied equally thoroughly those parts of the written observations that are not summarised in the Report for the Hearing.

There is no bar to introducing information and arguments that have not been presented in the written observations.[126] Parties entitled to present observations must therefore be prepared for matters that have not been touched on in the written observations to be the subject of discussion and questioning by the Court of Justice. In contrast, as a clear rule further documents may only be submitted during the oral proceedings in response to a question from the judges.[127] However, exceptionally the Court of Justice has accepted such presentation of documents where the others entitled to present observations have received the document without objecting to its being put before the Court.[128]

The Court allows for a succinct reply once all observations have been presented. Such a reply should focus exclusively on the arguments put forward by others during the hearing. In other words, the right to make a reply should not be used to summarise or repeat one's own arguments. Moreover, abstaining from making a reply will not be taken to imply that the arguments made in other submissions are not contested. When making a reply it is recommended to start by indicating what circumstances will be commented on and to keep the response as brief as possible.[129]

According to Article 57 of the Court's Rules of Procedure, in the course of the hearing the judges and the Advocate General may put questions to those making the submissions. This is frequently done to clarify the facts of the case or national law. Often the judges or the Advocate General will ask more argumentative questions in order to test the strength of a legal argument. Where questions of a more technical nature are put, these may be answered by any accompanying experts. These experts are not normally required to present evidence of their qualifications, nor are they sworn in as witnesses. The questions may be put both during and after the presentation of the oral submission; hence, it is important to be

---

[126] R Barents et al, *European Courts Procedure* (2004) para 31.113; and P Lasok, *The European Court of Justice—Practice and Procedure* (1994) 343.

[127] Case C-491/06 *Danske Svineproducenter* [2008] ECR I-3339, paras 20 and 23.

[128] D Anderson and M Demetriou, *References to the European Court* (2002) 279.

[129] O Due, 'Presenting the Case Orally—The Judge's view' in D Vaughan et al, *Butterworth's European Court Practice* (1993) iv.

ready to deal with interruptions during the presentation and, furthermore, to appreciate that the answering of questions is an important part of the hearing.[130]

4.4.5. Considerations pertaining to interpretation

The members of the Court of Justice do not necessarily follow the oral observations in the language in which they are made, but often listen to the simultaneous interpretation. This imposes certain constraints and it is important to be attentive to these in order to ensure that what is said is fully understood by the members of the Court. Therefore, as stated by the Court, those making the oral pleadings must regard the interpreter as an essential partner in the presentation of their argument.[131]

The Court advises against making oral submissions by reading out from a manuscript. Indeed, an address prepared in writing is generally made up of longer and more complicated sentences and the speaker will often be inclined to read too quickly to allow for satisfactory interpretation. Therefore, it might be preferable to base the oral submission on well-structured notes, using simple terms and short sentences.[132] Similarly, technical jargon should be avoided, and care should be taken in the use of witty remarks and the like that might not be easily translatable.[133]

It is important to speak sufficiently slowly to enable the interpreters to interpret. Indeed, in ensuring that the length of the speech will not surpass the time allotted, due account must be taken of the need to speak at a tempo appropriate for simultaneous interpretation. This is especially so with regard to interpretation between the smaller languages as this is often done via one of the major languages, thereby increasing both the risk of misunderstandings and the total time of interpretation. Moreover, even if the interpreters might sometimes be able to follow a fast rhythm, it should not be overlooked that it is more difficult for the listener to follow attentively a speech where the verbal and non-verbal communication are dissociated from one another. For the same reason, one should not assume that judges not seeking eye contact with the speaker are not listening. Indeed, some concentration might be lost if they seek visual contact with the person pleading, as they are not actually listening to the voice of the speaker, but to the—delayed—voice of the interpretation. This also means that a speech which is being complemented

---

[130] R Barents et al, *European Courts Procedure* (2004) para 12.048.

[131] The Court's 'Notes for the Guidance of Counsel', point C.4.

[132] See, in addition to the Court's 'Notes for the Guidance of Counsel', Sir Gordon Slynn (former member of the Court), *Litigating in Luxembourg* (1988) 12.

[133] See in the same vein D Richards and M Beloff, *Practitioners' Handbook of EC Law* (1998) at 2.22, according to whom: 'Unless the interpreter can interpret, one's choicest phrases are so much chaff—gone with the wind.'

with gestures or facial expressions becomes separated from what the bench is hearing. This factor should be duly taken into account when addressing the Court.

The Court's interpreters normally prefer the use of a steady and continuous rhythm, not too fast and without abrupt pauses, even if the pauses were intended to help the interpreters keep up. The interpreters can only hear what is spoken into the microphone, so it is important to make sure that the microphone is switched on and to talk into it. It is also a good idea to pause between switching on the microphone and beginning to speak, so that the interpreters have a chance to prepare themselves. Indeed, some lawyers have made it a habit to begin their presentation with some more general matters that are not essential to the submission.

Whether the oral observation is made by reading out from a manuscript or given on the basis of notes, it is recommended that copies of the text or notes be given to the interpreters to make it easier for them to undertake the simultaneous interpretation. It is possible to deliver the material directly to the interpreters' booths before the hearing. However, it is generally advisable that all relevant information concerning the probable content of the oral observations is forwarded in advance to the Court's Directorate for Interpretation by fax ((352) 4303 3697) or email (<interpret@curia.europa.eu>). This is particularly important where there are passages to be quoted or where the case concerns topics with which the interpreters cannot be expected to be familiar (for example technical areas with special terminology). If the interpreters are provided with the relevant material in good time, they will be better able to prepare themselves, give a better rendering of the oral observations, and ensure that they are not disconcerted by technical terms or citations of texts or figures. The relevant text will only be communicated to the interpreters.

The different court rooms all have headphones so that those participating in the hearing can listen to the observations of others via the interpretation provided. Where a person or body is represented by more than one lawyer in the oral procedure, it is recommended that the lawyer not making the submission listen to the interpretation of his colleague's speech in order to verify that the interpreters can follow and that no misinterpretation takes place.

The oral proceedings are generally viewed as less important than the written. While the written observations are thoroughly translated, and often discussed in detail in the judgment itself, the oral observations are, as mentioned, subject to simultaneous interpretation, with the consequent risk of mistakes and failure to understand immediately the points which a party is trying to get across. Moreover, the judges do not deliberate over the outcome of the case immediately following the hearing, but normally wait for the Opinion of the Advocate General and the circulation of a draft judgment by the Judge-Rapporteur. Hence, there will often be several months between the hearing and the time when the judges will need to once again devote attention to the case, and therefore arguments made in the hearing might not always be remembered in detail by the participating judges. To some extent this inconvenience is alleviated by the Court's practice of recording the oral proceedings and transcribing them afterwards. The transcription is only available to the judges and their staff.[134] The recording is only made using the French language channel. This means that at those points where, for one reason or another, the French interpreter has been unable to make the interpretation, the transcript will simply provide a note that no translation was available; this may for example occur where the comments were made so rapidly that it was impossible for the interpreter to keep up.

4.4.6. *Closure of the oral procedure*

After the oral observations have been made, but before the formal closure of the oral proceedings, the Advocate General delivers his Opinion.[135] Only the conclusion itself is read out. On average the Opinion is ready two months after the hearing in which the oral observations are made. However, there are considerable variations in the time taken by Advocates General to write their Opinions. Unless the proceedings are reopened for exceptional reasons, the Court will not allow any observation after the Opinion has been delivered.[136]

Following a change of the Court's Statute in connection with the Nice Treaty, the Court may now decide that an Advocate General shall not give an Opinion. Such a decision can be taken where the Court considers that the case raises no new points of law.[137] Moreover, there will be no Opinion of the Advocate General where the case is decided by way of a reasoned order in accordance with Article 104(3) of the Court's Rules of Procedure (Footnote 177 bis).

5. Expedited Procedures

5.1. Overview

In principle, the Court of Justice deals with the cases in the order in which they are received.[138] However, whilst all cases should of course be decided as rapidly as possible, some cases present particular characteristics that entail a special need for a speedy resolution. The Court disposes of several ways of allowing it to accelerate a preliminary procedure.

---

[134] Joined Cases C-74/00 P and C-75/00 P *Falck* [2002] ECR I-7869, para 69.
[135] Art 59 of the Rules of Procedure.
[136] See s 6 below.
[137] Art 20, fifth paragraph, of the Court's Statute; 137 bis: See further below at Ch 11, s 1.
[138] Art 55 of the Court's Rules of Procedure.

First, the Court may decide the case by a reasoned order, under Article 104(3) of the Rules of Procedure. In this way it dispenses both with the oral arguments of those entitled to submit observations and with the written Opinion of the Advocate General.

Second, if the Court believes that there should be an oral hearing whilst at the same time the proceedings should be expedited, Article 20 of the Statute allows the Court to decide the case by a judgment whilst dispensing with the Advocate General's written Opinion.

These two procedures constitute the Court's most important instruments for speeding up the resolution of preliminary cases on a larger scale. Indeed, in a number of cases the Court has been able to answer the preliminary question in less than a year.[139]

Third, according to Article 55(2) of its Rules of Procedure, on proposal by the referring court or by one or more of the persons or bodies entitled to submit observations, the President may, in special circumstances, order that a case be given priority over others. Such prioritisation does not affect the time limits for providing observations in the case or other time limits applying to the 'external' participants in the case. It merely means that the Court will give priority to the resolution of the case in its internal planning, translation, and case distribution. This can sometimes result in the case being decided approximately six months ahead of what is normal for a preliminary case.[140]

Fourth, the Court may apply a so-called accelerated procedure to all types of preliminary cases. This procedure is described below in Section 5.2.

Finally, a special urgent procedure has been introduced for cases referred for a preliminary ruling in the areas covered by Title VI of the Union Treaty or Title IV of Part Three of the EC Treaty. This procedure is analysed below in Section 5.3.

5.2. The accelerated procedure laid down in Article 104a of the Court's Rules of Procedure

5.2.1. *Procedure*

According to Article 104a of the Rules of Procedure, the President may exceptionally decide to apply an accelerated procedure thereby derogating from the normal procedural scheme governing a reference for a preliminary ruling. Application of Article 104a is only possible where a ruling on the question put to the Court is a matter of 'exceptional urgency' due to the circumstances of the case. The Court

---

[139] E Barbier de La Serre, 'Accelerated and Expedited Procedures Before the EC Courts, A Review of the Practice' (2006) 43 CML Rev 783, 811ff with further references. See further below at Ch 11, s 1.
[140] Case C-213/89 *Factortame* [1990] ECR I-2433.

takes the decision to apply Article 104a in the form of a reasoned order on a proposal from the Judge-Rapporteur and after hearing the Advocate General. Application of the accelerated procedure to a case cannot be decided *ex officio* by the Court. Neither can the parties to the main proceedings, nor any other of those entitled to present observations in the preliminary procedure, invite the Court to apply this accelerated procedure. The accelerated procedure can only be requested by the referring court, either on its own initiative or at the suggestion of the parties in the main proceedings.

If the request for an accelerated procedure is granted, the President of the Court (or the President of the Chamber dealing with the case) may immediately fix the date for the hearing. The date can thereby be notified to the parties in the main proceedings and to those other persons referred to in Article 23 of the Court's Statute at the same time as they are being notified of the preliminary reference. Written observations may thereafter be lodged within a period prescribed by the President. This period may not be less than 15 days (plus the usual extension by a period of 10 days on account of distance according to Article 81(2) of the Rules of Procedure), but it can still be appreciably shorter than the normal time limit in preliminary cases of two months (and 10 days).

The President may request that the matters addressed in the observations be restricted to the essential points of law raised by the question referred. The work of the Court's translation service is thereby alleviated and, consequently, the time spent on translating the observations is shortened. Prior to the hearing the written observations are notified to those entitled to submit observations.

Under the accelerated procedure, the Advocate General does not present an Opinion, but he will be present at the hearing, and the Court will only rule after hearing the Advocate General's View, be that by a written or an oral statement.[141]

Hence, it can be seen that the accelerated procedure essentially consists of shortening the different steps of the normal preliminary procedure without dispensing with any of them. The procedure thereby puts extra strain on both those entitled to present observations to the Court of Justice and on the Court itself. In 2008 the average time for deciding a case under the accelerated procedure was 4.5 months whereas the average time for all preliminary references was 16.8 months.[142]

5.2.2. *The notion of 'exceptional urgency'*

The provision in Article 104a sets a high threshold for its application. Not only is it a requirement that there is 'exceptional urgency', but even where that threshold

---

[141] As a rule these Views are published in the same way as the Opinions. Exceptionally, however, the Court may decide that the Advocate General's View shall not be made public.

[142] Point 12 in the statistics chapter of the Court's 2008 Annual Report.

is met, it is still within discretion of the President of the Court to decide whether to use the accelerated procedure. Moreover, so far the Court has interpreted the provision restrictively, having in mind that the application of the accelerated procedure necessarily entails delay of the processing of other cases whereas Article 104a was not intended to introduce a system where different kinds of cases are dealt with at different speeds.[143] Indeed, in the period 2004–08, only in two of the 34 cases where use of the accelerated procedure had been requested did the Court grant the request.[144]

The economic interests of the parties to the main proceedings are not of such a nature as to establish the exceptional urgency within the meaning of Article 104a, however significant and legitimate they may be.[145] Indeed, even if the risk of economic loss invoked by the referring court is real, this does not in itself demonstrate exceptional urgency.[146] Moreover, application of the accelerated procedure presupposes that, presumably, it may prevent a risk that would otherwise materialise if the case were dealt with by way of an ordinary procedure.[147] In the same vein, the urgency must relate to the actual facts of the main proceedings and not to extraneous elements and hypothetical facts that are unlikely to materialise.[148]

The Court has held that the duration of a criminal case before the referring court is not a consideration which in itself can establish exceptional urgency within the meaning of Article 104a.[149] Nor is it sufficient that a reference for a preliminary ruling has been made in connection with the application of interim measures or in interlocutory proceedings. The accelerated procedure can thus not be used as an alternative to the referring court itself ordering interim relief in the main proceedings.[150]

Neither is it sufficient that there are a large number of similar cases pending before the national courts and that the preliminary ruling may affect the outcome of these other cases.[151] Likewise, the fact that a large number of persons are involved

---

[143] V Skouris, 'L'urgence dans la procédure applicable aux renvois préjudiciels' in C Baudenbacher et al (eds), *Liber Amicorum en l'honneur de Bo Vesterdorf* (2007) 59, 66ff.

[144] Point 15 in the statistics chapter in the Court's 2008 Annual Report.

[145] Case C-81/04 *Richert* (ECJ 1 April 2004); Case C-341/04 *Bondi* (ECJ 15 September 2004); Case C-11/05 *Frisland Coberco* (ECJ 18 March 2005); Case C-467/06 *Consel Gi Emme* (ECJ 23 January 2007); Case C-351/07 *CEPAV DUE* (ECJ 19 October 2007); Case C-201/08 *Plantanol* (ECJ 3 July 2008); and Case C-384/08 *Attanasio Group* (ECJ 4 December 2008).

[146] Case C-115/06 *Racke* (ECJ 3 May 2006); and Case C-174/05 *Stichting Zuid-Hollandse Milieufederatie* (ECJ 2 June 2005).

[147] Case C-385/05 *CGT* (ECJ 21 November 2005).

[148] Case C-300/04 *Eman* (ECJ 23 September 2004 and 18 March 2005).

[149] Case C-375/08 *Pontini* (ECJ 29 September 2008).

[150] Joined Cases C-363/04–365/04 *Michaniki* (ECJ 17 November 2004); Case C-12/07 *Austrada dei Fiori* (ECJ 23 March 2007); and Case C-33/07 *Jipa* (ECJ 3 April 2007). See also Ch 9, s 3.

[151] Case C-330/05 *Granberg* (ECJ 24 October 2005); Case C-385/05 *CGT* (ECJ 21 November 2005); and Case C-439/08 *VEBIC* (ECJ 3 December 2008).

in main proceedings does not, as such, constitute such exceptional circumstances as to justify the application of an accelerated procedure.[152] Indeed, the Court of Justice has held that in general not even the interest attached to a speedy resolution of a controversy as to the legality of a directive or a regulation fulfils the conditions for an application of the accelerated procedure.

In *International Air Transport Association*, the Court refused to use the accelerated procedure in connection with a reference for a preliminary ruling on the validity of Regulation 261/2004 on common rules on compensation and assistance to passengers in the event of denied boarding and of cancellation or long delay of flights. In support of the application of the accelerated procedure, the national court argued that the regulation could lead to serious financial harm to the airlines concerned. However, the Court of Justice ruled that this was normally the case with the entry into force of new Community rules, so the case could not be regarded as exceptional within the meaning of Article 104a of the Rules of Procedure.[153]

In contrast, the accelerated procedure has been used both in a case concerning public health and in a case concerning married couples who had been deprived of their right to family life.

Article 104a was applied for the first time in *Jippes*; a dispute on the validity of a Community prohibition on vaccinations against foot and mouth disease. In this case the Court of Justice took account of the number of outbreaks, the speed with which the disease spread, and the fact that the slaughter of a number of animals would be avoided if the disputed prohibition of vaccination were to be found invalid.[154]

In *Metock*, the preliminary questions concerned residence permits for third country nationals who had married EU nationals having exercised their right to free movement. The referring court requested that the accelerated procedure be applied, inter alia, because as long as the case was pending, some of the third country nationals were being held under arrest and all were deprived of the opportunity of leading a family life with their spouse and children. The Court held that the right to respect for private and family life, as laid down in Article 8 of the European

---

[152] Case C-283/06 *Kögaz* (ECJ 21 November 2005); Case C-368/06 *Cedilac* (ECJ 25 September 2006); Case C-201/08 *Plantanol* (ECJ 3 July 2008); and Joined Cases C-403/08 and C-429/08 *Football Association Premier League* (ECJ 3 December 2008). See also with regard to proceedings that might have consequences for the national employment market, Case C-341/05 *Laval* (ECJ 15 November 2005).

[153] Case C-344/04 *IATA* (ECJ 29 September 2004). See similarly on the question of the validity of a Directive, Joined Cases C-154/04 and C-155/04 *Alliance for Natural Health* (ECJ 7 May 2004).

[154] Case C-189/01 *Jippes* [2001] ECR I-5689, para 45.

Convention for the Protection of Human Rights, is among the fundamental rights protected in Community law. In addition, the ruling of the Court could remove the uncertainty affecting the situations of the applicants in the main proceedings and, therefore, their family lives. Consequently, a reply from the Court within a very short period could bring a swifter end to this uncertainty and the Court therefore decided to apply the accelerated procedure.[155]

5.3. The urgent procedure in the area of freedom, security, and justice

5.3.1. Overview of the urgent procedure

As is apparent from the above analysis, the accelerated procedure laid down in Article 104a is only intended to be applied infrequently in certain narrowly defined circumstances. The Article 104a procedure therefore does not provide an adequate system for treating entire categories of cases that require particular speed. This is so, first, because the accelerated procedure comprises the same procedural stages as does the normal preliminary ruling procedure and, second, because the increased speed is achieved primarily by giving absolute priority to the case in question at all stages. In this way the accelerated procedure necessarily has a detrimental impact on the speed with which all other pending cases are treated.[156]

In cases concerning disputes about visas and asylum, expulsion decisions issued under immigration law, parental responsibility, and custody of children, an urgent resolution of a preliminary question is often needed, however. The same is true with regard to cases relating to the enforcement of European arrest warrants and criminal cases involving the detention of a suspect. The new paragraph 4 that will be added to Article 234, when or if the Lisbon Treaty enters into force, must be read in this light.[157] According to this new provision the Court of Justice shall act with the minimum delay when a preliminary question is raised in a case pending before a court of a Member State with regard to a person in custody.

Article 23a of the Court's Statute and Article 104b of its Rules of Procedure therefore contain a special urgent preliminary ruling procedure that may be applied to cases currently covered by Title IV of the EC Treaty and Title VI of the Treaty on European Union.[158] The objective is to enable the Court of Justice to decide such cases within a particularly short time whilst not delaying the handling of other

---

[155] Case C-127/08 *Metock* (ECJ 17 April 2008).

[156] K Lenaerts, 'The rule of Law and the coherence of the judicial system of the European Union' (2007) 44 CML Rev 1625, 1654.

[157] Art 234 will be numbered Art 267 following the entering into force of the Lisbon Treaty.

[158] As explained in more detail above at Ch 3, s 5.3, today references regarding Title IV of the EC Treaty are limited to national courts against whose decisions there is no judicial remedy. If the Lisbon Treaty is ratified this limitation will be abandoned which in turn is likely to lead to a substantial increase in the number of references where the urgent procedure may apply.

pending cases, and indeed in 2008 the average time for handling such cases was a mere 2.1 months. This special procedure differs from both the ordinary and the accelerated preliminary ruling procedures notably on the following points:

- First, as soon as they arrive at the Court of Justice, cases subject to the urgent preliminary ruling procedure will be assigned to a chamber of five judges specifically designated for this procedure.

- Second, the written procedure is limited to the parties to the main proceedings, the Member State from which the reference is made, and the European Commission, as well as those other Community institutions whose measure may be at issue in the reference. All bodies referred to in Article 23 of the Statute will be able to participate in the oral procedure, where they can express their view, inter alia, on the written observations that have been lodged.[159]

- Third, for the most part the communication in these cases will be conducted electronically, ie by fax or email.[160]

5.3.2. Conditions for the application of the urgent preliminary ruling procedure

The urgent preliminary ruling procedure only applies in the areas covered by Title VI (Articles 29 to 42) of the EU Treaty and Title IV (Articles 61 to 69) of Part Three of the EC Treaty. It is for the Court of Justice to decide whether the urgent procedure is to be applied. Such a decision is generally only taken on a reasoned request from the referring court. Exceptionally, the Court may decide of its own motion to deal with a reference under the urgent preliminary ruling procedure, where that procedure appears, prima facie, to be required. For this reason the Court has systematically examined all such cases in order to evaluate whether there is reason to apply the urgent procedure.

As the urgent procedure puts considerable strain on the Court as well as those participating in the procedure, it should only be used where it is of paramount importance that the Court makes its decision as speedily as possible. In 2008, the Court received six requests for an application of the urgent procedure of which three were granted.[161]

The urgent procedure was applied for the first time in *Rinau*. This case concerned the interpretation of Regulation 2201/2003 concerning jurisdiction and the recognition and enforcement of judgments in matrimonial matters and matters of parental responsibility (the Brussels II bis Regulation). The referring Lithuanian

---

[159] See in this respect s 3.1 above.

[160] For the special considerations as to how the national court should formulate and transmit a preliminary reference that it wishes to be dealt with under the urgent procedure see above at Ch 8, ss 3.2.2 and 3.2.6.

[161] Point 16 in the statistics chapter of the Court's 2008 Annual Report.

court asked whether it had to recognise a decision of a German court whereby the mother of a child living in Lithuania had to send her daughter to the father living in Germany or whether the Lithuanian court itself could make its own determination of the case without being bound by the decision of the German court. The preliminary reference as such was submitted to the Court on 14 May 2008 followed by an application for the use of the urgent procedure under Article 104b received by the Court on 22 May 2008. In support of the request the referring court argued that it was necessary to act urgently on the ground that any delay could damage the relationship between the child and the parent with whom she did not live and that this damage could be irreparable. The referring court also relied on the need to protect the child against any possible harm and the need to ensure a fair balance between the interests of the child and those of its parents. Already the day after having received the request to apply the urgent preliminary procedure the Court acceded thereto. Four days after having received the request, the Court fixed a two-week time limit for lodging written observations. At the same time the Court invited comments on two issues that it found particularly relevant for the resolution of the preliminary question. Oral hearings took place just over a month after the Court received the request for the application of the urgent procedure and observations were presented by six governments in addition to the parties to the main proceedings and the Commission. The judgment was handed down on 11 July 2008, ie less than two months after the Court had received the preliminary reference.[162]

In *Santesteban Goicoechea*, the Court received a preliminary reference from a French court on the European arrest warrant and surrender procedures in extradition proceedings concerning Mr Santesteban Goicoechea and a request that the reference be dealt with under the urgent procedure. As grounds for that request the referring court stated that, after serving a sentence of imprisonment, Mr Santesteban Goicoechea was being detained solely for the purpose of extradition ordered in the extradition proceedings in which the reference was made. Four days after receipt of the request the Court decided to apply the urgent procedure. A hearing was held less than a month later and judgment was given less than a week thereafter.[163]

5.3.3. *The decision whether or not to apply the urgent procedure*

As soon as the preliminary reference is received and a request for an urgent procedure is made by the national court, the Court will notify the reference in its original language to the parties to the main proceedings, the Member State from which

---

[162] Case C-195/08 PPU *Rinau* [2008] ECR I-5271.
[163] Case C-296/08 *Santesteban Goicoechea* (ECJ 12 August 2008). See also Case C-388/08 *Leymann and Pustovarov* [2008] ECR I-6307.

the reference is made, the Commission and, where the validity or interpretation of one of their measures is at issue, to the European Parliament and the Council. Thereby, the first steps can be taken immediately in the language of the case. At the same time, the parties, the Member State, and the institution(s) in question are directly informed that dealing with the reference under the urgent preliminary ruling procedure is being considered.

Within the Court of Justice, the translation of the preliminary reference is given immediate emergency priority and is translated into the Court's working language without delay. This translation allows the designated chamber to determine quickly whether to apply the urgent preliminary ruling procedure. In other words, the Court does not await the translation of the reference into all the other official languages and the ensuing notification to the other Member States.

On the expiry of the period laid down for the submission of written observations, the Court will send the preliminary reference to the other persons and bodies referred to in Article 23 of the Statute. The letter is accompanied by a translation of the reference into the relevant Community language, where appropriate in summary form. Moreover, as is the case for all references for a preliminary ruling, the letter is accompanied by the written observations submitted to the Court together with a translation thereof into French, the Court's working language. Thereby, the residual group comprising Member States other than the one from which the reference originates will also obtain a basis for deciding whether or not to present oral observations at the hearing.

If the Court decides that the reference is not to be dealt with under the urgent procedure, the case will instead be dealt with under the ordinary procedure for preliminary rulings. This decision is communicated to the national court. Even though the decision is not reasoned, the national court may deduce that the Court of Justice has found that there was not sufficient urgency to justify the application of the urgent procedure.

Where the Court declines to apply the urgent procedure, the parties to the main proceedings, the State from which the reference originates, and the institutions in question will have an advantage over the other persons referred to in Article 23 of the Statute, as the latter group will receive the text of the reference for a preliminary ruling, in their language, only at a later date. In contrast, where the Court decides to deal with the reference under the urgent procedure, the advance notice of the reference given to the parties to the main proceedings, the State from which the reference is made, and the institutions referred to in the first paragraph of Article 23 of the Statute has the advantage of allowing those concerned to familiarise themselves with the reference and to hold any discussions necessary in order to rapidly draft any written observations they may wish to make.

5.3.4. *The written procedure*

The urgent preliminary ruling procedure seeks to take account of the need for the Member States to have a real opportunity to participate in these types of cases while at the same time guaranteeing that the proceedings are handled very swiftly so that the national court can decide the case before it as soon as possible. Save in exceptional cases, discussed below, the urgent procedure contains a written part. However, for reasons of assuring maximum speed, the written part is confined to the parties to the main proceedings, the Member State to which the referring court belongs, the Commission and, where relevant, the Community institution(s) whose measure is at issue.

According to Article 104b(2), the time limit for presenting written observations under the urgent procedure is set by the chamber hearing the case. Presumably, the Court will fix this limit having due regard to the degree of urgency and the complexity of the case. In contrast to the normal preliminary procedure the Rules of Procedure do not lay down a fixed period.[164] The urgent procedure does not prescribe any minimum length. However, in a non-binding statement the Council has called upon the Court not to set a period of less than 10 working days in order to give the Member States enough time to draft written observations or prepare oral arguments.

In the interests of efficiency and speed, the Court may specify a maximum length for written observations and invite those who may present such observations to concentrate on certain specific points.

Exceptionally, the particular circumstances of the case or its legal background may require the Court to give a ruling within a shorter time frame than that achievable under the urgent procedure. For that reason in cases of such extreme urgency Article 104b(4) of the Rules of Procedure, allows the Court to omit the written stage of the procedure and only hold a hearing. This eliminates all the time consuming elements associated with the submission and translation of written observations.

According to Article 104(6) of the Rules of Procedure, procedural documents in an urgent preliminary procedure can be lodged or served by email, fax, or other technical means of communication available to the Court. The same applies to any other communication to and from the Court in such a procedure. This provision—which deviates from the general regime in the Rules of Procedure—is seen as essential to ensure the rapid treatment of cases dealt with under the urgent procedure.

---

[164] This is in parallel to the accelerated procedure, cf s 5.2.1 above.

5.3.5. *The oral observations in the urgent procedure*

The possibility of presenting oral observations ensures that the Court hears the parties to the main proceedings, the Member State concerned, the relevant Community institutions, and other bodies entitled to present observations in preliminary proceedings. Moreover, the Court may counterbalance the fact that these bodies have not had the opportunity to submit written observations by conducting an extended hearing. Indeed, the oral hearing in an urgent procedure can be quite different from the oral hearing in a normal preliminary reference case; for instance it may last much longer than what is usual in preliminary reference cases.

As in the accelerated procedure, the designated chamber will decide the case shortly after the hearing and after having heard the Advocate General, who will seek to present his view within a day or two of the hearing. The judgment will then be translated into all languages in the usual way, but as a matter of priority into the language of the case, in order for the Court of Justice to deliver judgment as quickly as possible.

6. Gathering of Further Evidence and Reopening the Oral Proceedings

According to Article 60 of the Court's Rules of Procedure, after hearing the Advocate General, the Court may at any time order any measure of inquiry to be taken or expand or reopen a previous inquiry.[165] A request for the acceptance of evidence made after the oral proceedings will be admitted only if it relates to facts which may be decisive and which the party making the request could not have put forward before the close of the oral procedure.

Bosman concerned the compatibility of the football player transfer systems with the rules on the free movement of workers in Article 39 of the EC Treaty. After the conclusion of the oral proceedings in the preliminary reference, one of the parties to the main proceedings asked the Court of Justice to allow a measure of enquiry with a view to obtaining fuller information on, among other things, the role played by transfer fees in the financing of small or medium-sized football clubs. The Court dismissed this request, as the party in question could have made the submission before the close of the oral procedure. This was especially so as the opposing party to the main proceedings, in his written observations to the Court, had dealt with some of the questions about which there was now a request for

---

[165] The decision on the gathering of further evidence thereafter takes place in accordance with Art 45(1) of the Rules of Procedure.

further evidence without this having prompted the presentation of evidence at the oral proceedings.[166]

According to Article 61 of the Rules of Procedure, the Court may also order the reopening of the oral procedure. A case can be reopened where, for example, the Court finds that there is insufficient information about it, or that it ought to be decided on the basis of an argument which had not been discussed between the parties.[167] Cases may also be reopened where the oral proceedings have been restricted to certain questions, or if new circumstances have come to light which may be relevant for deciding the case.[168] Whereas the purpose of reopening in such situations is to guarantee a contradictory procedure, reopening can also be ordered for the more practical reason that the term of one or more of the participating members of the Court expires before the case has been decided.[169] The same applies if the case is referred to a chamber composed of a greater number of judges after the oral proceedings.[170] The provision in Article 61 allows for some discretion as to when to reopen the oral procedure. Hence, it allows for a case not to be reopened, even where a party has not had the possibility of presenting arguments about certain circumstances before the closing of the oral proceedings, unless these circumstances are significant for the decision in the case.[171]

Hitherto the Court has not been willing to accommodate requests for reopening oral proceedings on the basis of a disagreement with the Opinion of the Advocate General.[172] Indeed, neither the Statute nor the Rules of Procedure contain

---

[166] Case C-415/93 *Bosman* [1995] ECR I-4921, paras 52–4. See also Case C-73/97 P *Comafrica and Dole* [1999] ECR I-185.

[167] Case C-163/90 *Legros* [1992] ECR I-4625; Case C-299/99 *Philips* [2002] ECR I-5475, paras 17-22; Joined Cases C-270/97 and C-271/97 *Deutsche Post* [2000] ECR I-929, para 30; Case C-184/01 P *Hirshfeldt* [2002] ECR I-10173; Case C-336/03 *easyCar* [2005] ECR I-1947; Case C-347/03 *ERSA* [2005] ECR I-3785; Case C-329/03 *Trapesa* [2005] ECR I-9341; and Case C-496/04 *Slob* [2006] ECR I-8257, para 32. See also Case C-215/03 *Schnitzer* (ECJ 10 January 2003), where, by mistake, one of the parties to the main proceedings had not received the observations presented by others to the Court.

[168] Case C-380/01 *Schneider* [2004] ECR I-1389, para 19; and Joined Cases C-216/99 and C-222/99 *Ricardo Prisco* [2002] ECR I-6761.

[169] Case C-246/95 *Coen* [1997] ECR I-403.

[170] Case C-292/04 *Meillicke* (ECJ 7 April 2006); Case C-285/01 *Burbuad* [2003] ECR I-8219; Joined Cases C-267/91 and C-268/91 *Keck and Mithouard* [1993] ECR I-6097; and Case 155/79 *AM & S* [1982] ECR 1575.

[171] Joined Cases T-236/01, T-239/01, T-244/01–T-246/01, T-251/01, and T-252/01 *Tokai Carbon* [2004] ECR II-1181.

[172] Case C-8/96 *Locamion* [1997] ECR I-7055; Case C-284/96 *Didier Tabouillot* [1997] ECR I-7471; Case C-73/97 P *Comafrica and Dole* [1999] ECR I-185; Case C-147/02 *Alabaster* [2004] ECR I-3101, paras 33–5; Case C-181/02 P *Kvaerner* [2004] ECR I-5703; Case C-127/02 *Waddenvereniging* [2004] ECR I-7405; Case C-210/03 *Swedish Match* [2004] ECR I-11893; Case C-30/02 *Recheio—Cash & Carry* [2004] ECR I-6051, paras 11–13; Joined Cases C-544/03 and C-545/03 *Mobistar* [2005] ECR I-7723, paras 22–5; Case C-331/04 *ATI EAC* [2005] ECR I-10109, paras 14–17; Joined Cases C-346/03 and C-529/03 *Atzeni and others* [2006] ECR I-1875,

provisions whereby the parties can present observations with a view to commenting on the Opinion of the Advocate General.

In *Makedoniko Metro*, one of the parties to the main proceedings requested that the oral procedure be reopened so that further information about the subject matter of the main proceedings could be given to the Court. In its request, the party argued that the Advocate General had been wrong in reformulating the preliminary question and in the understanding of facts on which this reformulation was based. The Court observed, first, that, in accordance with settled case law, it may, where appropriate, reformulate a question referred for a preliminary ruling in order to avoid exceeding its jurisdiction and to provide the referring court with an answer that will be of assistance to it. Second, it noted that it is for the national court to decide what constitutes the subject matter of the main proceedings. Hence, the submissions which would be put forward in the course of a reopened oral procedure would relate solely to questions falling within the jurisdiction of the referring court. On that basis, the Court concluded that there was nothing in the request to indicate that it was necessary to reopen the oral procedure or that it would serve any useful purpose to do so.[173]

In *Radlberger Getränkegesellschaft*, the Court was invited to reopen the oral hearing following an Opinion of the Advocate General that was claimed to discuss a series of issues which were not covered in the written or oral procedure and which allegedly revealed a misappraisal of the arguments relied on in observations before the Court. The Court, however, rejected the request as it considered that it was in possession of all the facts necessary for it to answer the preliminary questions and that the relevant facts had been the subject of argument presented before it.[174]

This practice is understandable. Indeed, to systematically confer a right to submit observations in response to the Opinion of the Advocate General would have to be followed by a corresponding right, for the others entitled to present observations before the Court, to reply to those observations so as not to infringe the principle of an adversarial process. That in turn would not only cause practical

---

paras 25–7; Case C-259/04 *Emanuel* [2006] ECR I-3089, paras 14–17; and Case C-484/06 *Ahold* (ECJ 10 July 2008), paras 19–23; but compare Case C-35/98 *Verkooijen* (ECJ 17 September 1999), where the case was reopened after the parties to the main proceedings jointly informed the Court that the Opinion of the Advocate General was based on a misunderstanding of the relevant national law. See in respect of the national court, Case C-380/01 *Schneider* [2004] ECR I-1389, para 19. The Advocate General may also request the reopening of the oral proceedings, but the Court of Justice is not bound by such a request.

[173] Case C-57/01 *Makedoniko Metro* [2003] ECR I-1091, paras 32–8. See also Joined Cases C-453/03, C-11/04, C-12/04, and C-194/04 *ABNA* [2005] ECR I-10423, paras 41–3.

[174] Case C-309/02 *Radlberger Getränkegesellschaft* [2004] ECR I-11763, paras 20–4. See also Case C-434/02 *Arnold André* [2004] ECR I-11825, paras 24–7; and Case C-138/05 *Stichting Zuid-Hollandse Milieufederatie* [2006] ECR I-8339, paras 21–5.

difficulties but would also considerably prolong the procedure.[175] However, the Court's practice has been met with some criticism from those entitled to submit observations as well as from the referring courts.

In *Emesa Sugar*, one of the parties to the main proceedings sought leave to submit written observations after the Advocate General had delivered his Opinion. In this respect, the party relied on the case law of the European Court of Human Rights concerning the scope of Article 6(1) of the European Convention of Human Rights and in particular on the judgment of 20 February 1996 in *Vermeulen v Belgium*.[176] In that judgment the European Court of Human Rights had held that it constituted a breach of Article 6(1) that Belgian law did not allow for a right of an accused to reply to the Opinion of the *Procureur Général's* department at the Belgian Court of Cassation before judgment was given in the case against him. The *Procureur Général* had as its main duty, at the hearing and at the deliberations, to assist the Court of Cassation and to help ensure that its case law is consistent. To this end the *Procureur* gave an Opinion which derived its authority from the *Procureur Général's* department itself. The Court of Justice held that this judgment by the European Court of Human Rights could not be transposed to the Opinions of the Court of Justice's Advocates General. First, in accordance with Articles 221 and 222 of the EC Treaty, the Court of Justice consists of judges and is assisted by Advocates General. Article 223 lays down identical conditions and the same procedure for appointing both judges and Advocates General. Moreover, it follows from the Court's Statute that the Advocates General have the same status as the judges, including with regard to their impartiality and independence. Second, the Advocates General, none of whom is subordinate to any other, are not public prosecutors nor are they subject to any authority, nor are they entrusted with the defence of any particular interest in the exercise of their duties. It was in this context that the role of the Advocate General must be viewed. In accordance with Article 222 of the EC Treaty, his duty is to make reasoned submissions on cases brought before the Court of Justice, in order to assist the Court in the performance of the task assigned to it. These submissions are made in open court and on the basis of complete impartiality and independence. The Opinion of the Advocate General does not form part of the proceedings between the parties, but rather opens the stage of deliberation by the Court. It is not therefore an opinion addressed to the judges or to the parties which stems from an authority outside the Court. Rather, it constitutes the individual reasoned opinion, expressed in open court, of a member of the Court of Justice itself. The Advocate General

---

[175] For a discussion of how the parties could be given the opportunity to comment on the Opinion of the Advocate General see C Naômé, *Le renvoi préjudiciel en droit européen* (2007) 154–5.

[176] Reports of Judgments and Decisions, 1996 I, p 224.

thus takes part, publicly and individually, in the process by which the Court reaches its judgment, and therefore in carrying out the judicial function entrusted to it. Accordingly, the application for leave to submit written observations in response to the Opinion delivered by the Advocate General was dismissed.[177]

In *Kaba I*, after the Advocate General had presented his Opinion, one of the parties to the main proceedings informed the Court of his doubts as to the accuracy of certain factual issues on which the Opinion appeared to be based. Arguing that these inaccuracies amounted to exceptional grounds justifying the reopening of the oral procedure, the party shortly thereafter lodged further observations. The Registrar of the Court, however, returned these additional observations and did not accept them as forming part of the Court file. Moreover, the Court gave judgment not basing itself on the understanding of the facts that had been advanced by the party. Following the Court's judgment, the party argued before the national court that the preliminary ruling had been based on a misunderstanding of the facts found in the first order for reference and of the relevant national law. In those circumstances, the national court was unsure whether the proceedings before the Court had been conducted in accordance with Article 6(1) of the European Convention of Human Rights. It therefore decided to stay the proceedings for a second time and ask two more preliminary questions, the first inviting the Court to answer whether Article 6 of the European Convention of Human Rights had indeed been respected in the preliminary procedure in the first reference, and the second asking the Court whether it would have arrived at the same result in the first judgment had it based itself on the facts as set out in the submissions that the Court refused to include in its file. In *Kaba II*, the Court first replied to the second question answering that its judgment would not have been different had it taken into consideration the facts presented in the refused submission. Having thus addressed the doubts which led the national court to refer fresh questions for a preliminary ruling the Court found it unnecessary to reply to the first question concerning compliance with the European Convention of Human Rights.[178]

---

[177] Case C-17/98 *Emesa Sugar* [2000] ECR I-665 (order) and [2000] ECR I-675, para 18 (judgment).
[178] Case C-356/98 *Kaba* [2000] ECR I-2623, and Case C-466/00 *Kaba II* [2003] ECR I-2219.

11

THE PRELIMINARY RULING

1. Judgment or Order?

Traditionally, decisions on questions referred for a preliminary ruling have been given in the form of a judgment. However, where a question referred to the Court of Justice is identical to a question on which the Court has already ruled, it may, according to Article 104(3) of the Court's Rules of Procedure, after hearing the Advocate General, give its decision by reasoned order.[1] The same applies where the answer to such a question may be clearly deduced from existing case law, or where the answer to the question referred for a preliminary ruling admits of no reasonable doubt.

The aim of allowing decisions to be made by means of an order is to ease the burden of the Court of Justice and to reduce the time taken to deal with a case.

---

[1] Joined Cases C-9/01–12/01 *Monnier* (ECJ 18 June 2001), and Joined Cases C-405/96–408/96 *Société Beton Express* [1998] ECR I-4253. This procedure is also applied when the Court of Justice has suspended the processing of a preliminary case while awaiting the resolution of another case before the Court raising identical questions, cf Case C-256/99 *Hung* (ECJ 12 July 2001).

Indeed, the use of Article 104(3) means that the case can be decided solely on the basis of the written submissions and without the Advocate General being required to give an Opinion.

The procedure for deciding whether or not to apply Article 104(3) of the Rules of Procedure differs according to the reasons for which it is invoked. Where the Court of Justice considers using the simplified procedure because the result admits of no reasonable doubt, it must inform the referring court of its intention to make a decision by means of an order and give the parties in the main proceedings and other interested parties the opportunity to express a view thereon. In contrast, in the two other situations covered by the provision, ie where a question is identical to a question on which the Court has already ruled, or where the answer can be clearly deduced from existing case law, the Court is no longer obliged to inform the national court and to hear the parties before it can give its decision by order. Moreover, even where the Court of Justice must hear the referring court and those entitled to make submissions, practice shows that it can be difficult to convince the Court that a decision should be made in the form of a judgment. In order to make best use of the possibilities offered by the simplified procedure, the Court seeks to decide whether to apply the procedure laid down in Article 104(3) even before the commencement of the written procedure. Thus, if at the time when the case is attributed to a referring judge, it appears evident that it could be disposed of under the simplified procedure, the Court may at that early stage inform the referring court and the parties that it favours this procedure.

Whereas it is easy to see when this procedure is being applied because the Court has already ruled on the question or because the answer can easily be deduced from existing case law, the Court has hitherto been more reticent in explaining why a case does not give rise to any reasonable doubt and for this reason is covered by Article 104(3). Nevertheless, it seems clear that the most important requirement is that the Court finds the answer to be straightforward. In most of the rulings, this is reflected by a clear (and often short) line of argument. Another important factor appears to be that prior case law may be advanced in support of the answer albeit without this amounting to *acte éclairé*.[2] The provision is also used in cases where the Court of Justice concludes for the first time that a given national legislation is contrary to the fundamental provisions of the EC Treaty.[3] Moreover, whilst the

---

[2] Case C-424/01 *CS Communications & Systems Austria* [2003] ECR I-3249; Case C-395/02 *Transport Service* [2004] ECR I-1991; Joined Cases C-162/03, C-185/03, C-44/04, C-45/04, C-223/04, C-224/04, C-271/04, and C-272/04 *Azienda Agricola Balconi Andrea* (ECJ 21 June 2005). On *acte éclairé*, see Ch 6, s 3.3.

[3] Case C-268/03 *De Baeck* [2004] ECR I-5961; Case C-206/03 *SmithKline Beecham* [2005] ECR I-415; and Case C-307/99 *OGT Fruchthandelsgesellschaft* [2001] ECR I-3159, where the provision was applied in relation to a question about the (lack of) direct effect of the WTO Agreement and the TRIPS Agreement.

most straightforward cases are normally allocated to chambers of three judges (ie the smallest chambers), several Article 104(3) cases have been decided by five-judge chambers.[4] Finally, in a large proportion of the cases it would seem as if the interpretation will likely be of only limited general relevance to national court cases other than the one in the main proceedings.[5]

Pursuant to the fifth sub-paragraph of Article 20 of the Court's Statute, the Court may also, after hearing the Advocate General, proceed to a judgment without an Opinion. After the Court has been given this opportunity, it is in fact faster for the Court to hand down such a judgment than it is to give a reasoned order in cases where no oral hearing is requested by one or more of those entitled to present observations pursuant to Article 23 of the Statute.[6] Moreover, Article 104(3) only grants the Court a right to proceed by way of a reasoned order when the conditions set out in this provision are fulfilled, but the Court is never obligated to use this possibility; it may always choose to decide the case in the form of a judgment.[7] Consequently, the simplified procedure laid down in Article 104(3) has become less important as a practical tool for reducing the time it takes to process a preliminary reference case.[8] And indeed, rendering judgment without obtaining an Opinion from the Advocate General is now more common than the use of an order under Article 104(3); according to the Court's 2008 Annual Report, about 41 per cent of the judgments delivered in 2008 were delivered without an Opinion. In comparison, in 2007 the simplified procedure laid down in Article 104(3) was used in approximately 10 per cent of all decisions terminating the Court's procedure in preliminary reference cases.[9]

---

[4] Case C-518/99 *Richard Gaillard* [2001] ECR I-2771; Case C-175/00 *Verwayen-Boelen* [2002] ECR I-2141; and Joined Cases C-307/00–311/00 *Oliehandel Koeweit BV* [2003] ECR I-1821. In Case C-242/99 *Johann Vogle* [2000] ECR I-9083, the order was rendered by the full court.

[5] Case C-446/02 *Hauptzollamt Hamburg Jonas v Gouralnik & Partners* [2004] ECR I-5841; Case C-115/03 *Eco Eridania* (ECJ 28 September 2004); and Case C-447/04 *Autohaus Ostermann* [2005] ECR I-10407. Indeed, in some cases the Court of Justice appears to deliberately limit the applicability of the ruling to the specific case. On the application of the provision in practice, see M Broberg, 'Acte Clair revisited: Adopting the *acte clair* criteria to the demand of the times' (2008) 45 CML Rev 1383, 1393; and T Tridimas, 'Knocking on Heaven's Door: Fragmentation, Efficiency and Defiance in the Preliminary Reference Procedure' (2003) 40 CML Rev 9, 18ff. Tridimas finds that the provision has considerable potential for acting as a filter for references for preliminary rulings as it gives the Court of Justice the possibility of deciding which of its previous decisions it will re-evaluate.

[6] C Naômé, *Le renvoi préjudiciel en droit européen* (2007) 192.

[7] Case C-411/00 *Swoboda* [2002] ECR I-19567, para 32.

[8] C Naômé, *Le renvoi préjudiciel en droit européen* (2007) 33.

[9] The 2007 Annual Report of the Court of Justice, Section C 7, p 86. On the background to the rule see N Burrows and R Greaves, *The Advocate General and EC Law* (2007) 20ff. The rule will not necessarily diminish the Advocate General's influence on the Court's practice; indeed, it has been argued that it may strengthen this influence—see Advocate General Mischo referred to in K Mortelmans, 'The Court Under the Influence of its Advocates General: An Analysis of the Case Law on the Functioning of the Internal Market' in P Eeckhout and T Tridimas (eds), *Yearbook of European Law 2005* (2006) 127, 172.

Regardless of whether the decision is made by a judgment or an order, the Court's decision will be without dissenting opinions as its Rules of Procedure do not provide for this possibility.[10] The decision is sent to the referring court and to all those who were originally informed about the preliminary reference.

2. Reformulating the Question Referred

2.1. Overview

While the Court of Justice has jurisdiction to interpret Community law, it is for the national court to apply the Court of Justice's interpretation in the main action. Or, to put it differently, within the framework of the procedures for preliminary rulings, it is for the national court to decide whether Community law applies in the case before it, and whether a given national law provision is in accordance with Community law. This means that the question for preliminary ruling should be formulated, in principle, as an abstract enquiry about the interpretation of Community law, and not as a question about how the dispute in the case before the national court should be decided.[11]

Where a national court nevertheless refers such a direct question, the Court of Justice will seldom dismiss it. Instead, it will seek to reformulate the question so as to respect the allocation of jurisdiction between the Court of Justice and the national court.

In *Placanica*, which concerned a criminal prosecution in connection with a game of chance, an Italian court referred to the Court of Justice a question as to whether an Italian legal provision was compatible with the Treaty rules on freedom of establishment and the freedom to provide services. In its question the Italian court requested the Court of Justice to consider whether the criminal provisions which were referred to in the indictment in the main action could apply in the Member State. Several of the Member States that submitted observations in the case argued that the Court of Justice should refuse to rule on the question as it concerned the interpretation of national law. In its decision, the Court of Justice emphasised that it was for the national courts and not for the Court of Justice to interpret national provisions. The Court of Justice also stated that, on a literal reading of the question referred for a preliminary ruling, it had been asked to rule on the compatibility with Community law of a provision of national law. Although the Court could

---

[10] On the advantages and disadvantages of this, see D Edward, 'Reform of Article 234 Procedure: The Limit of the Possible' in D O'Keeffe and A Bavasso (eds), *Judicial Review in European Union Law, vol I* (2000) 119, 132–4.

[11] See further above in Ch 4, s 5.6 and Ch 8, s 3.2.2.

not answer that question in the terms in which it was framed, there was nothing to prevent it from giving the national court guidance as to the interpretation of Community law to enable the latter to rule on the compatibility of national law with Community law.[12]

Similarly, the Court of Justice will not refuse to answer an inappropriately framed reference, as long as the reference contains the information which is necessary for the Court to make a usable ruling.[13]

According to some political scientists the Court of Justice's decision as to whether it should redefine the issues presented to it by the referring court is to a considerable extent determined by what they have labelled the Court's 'own policy agenda' of further integration.[14] Thus, it has been argued that the Court exploits an 'institutional loophole' in the preliminary procedure in order to increase its autonomy as a court and that it primarily does so when the ruling in question is not likely to come under extensive scrutiny by a wider audience. We are not going to engage in a discussion of these conspiracy theories. However, we would like to make clear from the outset that we do not subscribe to these theories. Of course judges do not operate in a political void, but to claim that they engage in 'strategic manoeuvring' in order to pursue hidden 'agendas'—without really underpinning these claims on serious documentation—appear to us to be exaggerated.[15]

The remainder of this chapter is devoted to an examination of the way in which the Court of Justice either limits or reformulates the questions referred in order, on the one hand, to uphold the division of tasks between itself and the national courts and, on the other hand, to be able to tailor its decision to the specific case, so that the referring court is given the best conditions for applying the preliminary ruling in its own decision.[16]

---

[12] Case C-338/04 *Placanica* [2007] ECR I-1819, paras 36–8. See also Case C-342/97 *Lloyd Schuhfabrik Meyer & Co* [1999] ECR I-3819, paras 11–12; Case C-295/05 *Asemfo* [2007] ECR I-2999, paras 26 and 34; and Case C-443/06 *Hollmann* [2007] ECR I-8491, paras 17–22. If it is not possible to reformulate the question so as to respect the allocation of jurisdiction, the Court of Justice will refuse to answer the question; see eg Joined Cases C-175/98 and C-177/98 *Lirussi and Bizzaro* [1999] ECR I-6881, paras 36–9; and Case C-318/98 *Fornasar* [2000] ECR I-4785, paras 30–3.

[13] See Ch 4, s 5.6, and Ch 8, s 3.2.5.

[14] S Nyikos, *The European Court of Justice and National Courts: Strategic Interaction within the EU Judicial Process* (2001) 8, 35, and 124–6.

[15] We are likewise sceptical of Nyikos' suggestion that in cases where the Court of Justice renders very general rulings leaving a wide margin of discretion to the national court when deciding the main action, such general rulings are motivated out of fear that the national court would refuse to comply with a preliminary ruling if it were more specific so as to leave a narrower margin of discretion to the national court, cf Nyikos (n 14 above) 37, with further references.

[16] According to C Naômé, *Le renvoi préjudiciel en droit européen* (2007) 195 and 219, once the preliminary question has arrived at the Court of Justice, it acquires a life of its own. The dogma that

2.2. The preliminary question is narrowed down

Sometimes a preliminary question relates to Community law in its entirety, without specifying which particular provisions the national court considers to be relevant.[17] In such cases, if the Court of Justice is able to identify potentially relevant provisions of Community law, it will limit its examination to these provisions. The Court may also limit the extent of the question as such. For example, where the question concerns the validity of a Community rule, the Court of Justice has sometimes adopted an interpretation that removes the basis for the objection to validity and thus makes the preliminary question hypothetical.[18] Similarly, the Court consistently refrains from answering questions whose relevance lapses on the basis of the answer the Court has given to other questions in the same case.[19]

The Court of Justice most frequently reformulates preliminary questions where the questions exceed the Court's powers under Article 234. Typical examples are questions concerning the correct interpretation of national law,[20] questions concerning the assessment of facts and evidential issues,[21] and questions asking the Court to rule directly on the compliance of national law with Community law.[22] In such cases, the Court of Justice declines to answer the question in the form it has been put and instead provides the national court with a ruling on the interpretation of Community law so as to enable that court to determine whether such compatibility exists in order to decide the case before it.[23]

Outside these situations too, the Court of Justice has a marked tendency to reformulate a question so that it can be answered in such a way as to give the greatest help to the referring court to make the correct decision in the main proceedings.

In *Mau*, the Court of Justice observed that the questions referred partly concerned the interpretation of national law and the assessment of its conformity with Community law. Since the Court did not have jurisdiction to reply to such questions, it found it necessary, as a preliminary step, to define the subject matter of the reference for a preliminary ruling. The Court further noted that the documents

---

it is solely for the referring court to decide the tenor of a question is therefore not always reflected in practice.

[17] See Ch 8, s 3.2.2.
[18] Case C-334/95 *Kruger* [1997] ECR I-4517, paras 20–3.
[19] Joined Cases C-52/97–54/97 *Viscido* [1998] ECR I-2629, para 17.
[20] See Ch 4, s 5.2 above.
[21] See Ch 4, s 5.5 above.
[22] See Ch 4, s 5.6 above.
[23] Case 83/78 *Pigs Marketing Board* [1978] ECR 2347, paras 25–6; Case 35/85 *Tissier* [1986] ECR 1207, paras 5–11; Case C-134/95 *USSL No 47 di Biella* [1997] ECR I-195, para 17; Case C-175/99 *Mayeur* [2000] ECR I-7755, para 22; and Case C-228/98 *Dounias* [2000] ECR I-577, para 36.

before it showed that the national court was faced with essentially two problems concerning the calculation of salary claims and the effect of national law being in conflict with Community law. The Court then went on to examine those two problems before replying specifically to the questions referred, in the form that these questions had to be reformulated by the Court in order to respect the division of the competence between the Court of Justice and the referring court.[24]

Whilst seeking to assist the referring court in the resolution of the actual dispute, the Court sometimes also chooses to reformulate a question in such a way as to make it unnecessary for it to decide on controversial or doubtful questions of law. Thus, for that reason alone, reformulation should not be seen as an indication that the referring court did not manage to make a proper reference.

In *Caterino*, an Italian court referred a question to the Court of Justice on whether a provision in a directive on the transport of waste only applied to professional waste collection or whether it also applied to any commercial undertaking which transported its own waste. The question arose from a criminal case against a person whose business could not be characterised as being that of a professional waste collector. According to the referring court, the prohibition in Italian law implementing the directive only applied to cases where waste was transported by those who carried on business as waste removers. However, in connection with the handling of the criminal prosecution, the question arose as to whether criminal liability could be inferred directly from the directive. The Court of Justice refrained from answering this question. Instead, it referred to the established case law that a directive cannot of itself impose obligations on an individual and cannot therefore be relied upon as such against an individual.[25]

From time to time, national courts refer preliminary questions that are based on an incorrect interpretation of Community law. In such cases, instead of merely answering the question in the form they are asked, the Court of Justice will normally inform the referring court of the correct interpretation of the Community rules in question. Normally, the answer will thereby show that the question is irrelevant for the resolution of the dispute in the main proceedings. This approach gives the referring court a usable answer which can either form the basis of a renewed reference for a preliminary ruling, or which can help it decide the dispute in the main proceedings.

---

[24] Case C-160/01 *Mau* [2003] ECR I-4791, paras 18–20.

[25] Case C-311/99 *Caterino* (ECJ 29 May 2001); and similarly Case C-80/06 *Carp* [2007] ECR I-4473. To some extent these decisions contradict the judgment in Case C-318/98 *Fornasar* [2000] ECR I-4785, paras 25–8, where in similar circumstances the Court of Justice answered the question referred, despite the fact that the defendant in the main proceedings had argued that a directive could not create criminal liability in relation to national law.

In *Celestri,* the Court of Justice was requested to decide on the validity of a Commission communication from 1981 amending the basic prices of certain iron and steel products. The Court noted that this communication did not apply to the facts in the main proceedings since these were dealt with in a Commission recommendation from 1978. Furthermore, the national court's question was to be understood as calling in question the validity of the 1981 communication only on the assumption that the communication was applicable at the time of the events in question. The Court of Justice thereafter found that it was not necessary to give a ruling on the validity of the Commission communication.[26]

In *Bulthuis-Griffioen,* a question was referred to the Court of Justice about the interpretation of the term 'systematically aim to make a profit' in Article 13 of the Sixth VAT Directive. The Court stated that, in order to provide the national court with a reply which would assist in resolving the main proceedings, it was first necessary to ascertain whether the provision was in fact applicable in the main proceedings. In the view of the Court of Justice this was not the case, as the national court had overlooked that the relevant part of the provision only applied to legal persons and not to the natural person who was a party in the main proceedings. In those circumstances, the Court of Justice found that it was not necessary to answer the preliminary question as such. Instead, the reply given to the national court was that the directive was to be interpreted as meaning that a trader who is a natural person was not covered by the provision in question.[27]

Sherson Lehmann Hutton concerned various questions on the rules in the Brussels Convention on jurisdiction in proceedings concerning contracts concluded by consumers. The Court of Justice noted that it was apparent from the order for reference that the main proceedings were brought not by a private individual, but by a company. Therefore, instead of merely answering the question referred, the Court first considered whether a plaintiff, such as the plaintiff in the main proceedings, could be regarded as a consumer that benefitted from the special rules governing jurisdiction laid down by the Convention with respect to consumer contracts. The Court found that this was not the case and concluded on that basis that it was not necessary to give a ruling on the specific questions that had been put to it.[28]

---

[26] Case 172/84 *Celestri* [1985] ECR 963. Similarly Case C-451/93 *Delevant* [1995] ECR I-1545, paras 12–19; Case C-315/93 *Flip CV* [1995] ECR I-913, paras 16–19; and Case C-336/95 *Trevejo* [1997] ECR I-2115, paras 9–16.

[27] Case C-453/93 *Bulthuis-Griffioen* [1995] ECR I-2341.

[28] Case C-89/91 *Sherson Lehmann Hutton* [1993] ECR I-139. Similarly Case C-98/06 *Freeport* [2007] WCR I-8319, paras 31–3; Case C-104/01 *Libertel* [2003] ECR I-3973, paras 22–43; and Case C-321/03 *Dyson* [2003] ECR I-687.

Where the relevance of the Community rules referred to in the preliminary question gives rise to doubt, the Court of Justice will normally interpret these rules. Depending on the level of doubt, it will then either stick to the doctrine that it is the referring court that is best positioned to evaluate the relevance of the question,[29] or it will, while answering the question referred, draw the attention of the referring court to the fact that the Court entertains doubt about the relevance of the question, thereby indirectly encouraging the referring court to examine the question more closely.

In *William Hilton & Sons*, the Court of Justice stated that it was possible that the facts of the case were such that the question should be decided solely on the basis of national law. The Court then answered the preliminary question on the premise that the Regulation which the question concerned was in fact applicable to the facts of the case.[30]

In *Douwe Egberts*, several of those entitled to present observations in the preliminary procedure raised doubts as to whether the product concerned in the main proceedings was covered by the directive which the national court wanted interpreted. The Court of Justice remarked that it found it appropriate to reply to the questions referred on the basis of the premise of the order for reference, namely that the product did have the characteristics in question so as to come within the scope of the directive.[31]

2.3. Inclusion of other Community law provisions

The Court of Justice shows no reticence in taking into account other Community law provisions than those referred to in the order for reference. In order to be able to give a useful answer to the questions asked, the Court can provide the referring court with all the elements of interpretation of Community law that are relevant for deciding the dispute in the main proceedings. This frequently means that the Court refers to Community rules which the national court appears not to have taken into account.[32]

---

[29] See Ch 5 and Ch 10, s 3.3.3.1.
[30] Case C-30/00 *William Hilton & Sons* [2001] ECR I-7511, paras 35–9.
[31] Case C-239/02 *Douwe Egberts NV* [2004] ECR I-7007.
[32] Case C-315/88 *Pennacchiotti* [1990] ECR I-1323, para 10; Case C-280/91 *Viessmann* [1993] ECR I-971, para 17; Case C-130/92 *OTO* [1994] ECR I-3281, paras 14–15; Case C-42/96 *SIF* [1997] ECR I-7089, paras 27–9; Case C-410/96 *Ambry* [1998] ECR I-7875, paras 18–21; Case C-87/99 *Consorzio per la tutela del formaggio Gorgonzola* [1999] ECR I-1301, para 16; Case C-121/00 *Hahn* [2002] ECR I-9193, para 21; Case C-304/00 *Strawson* [2002] ECR I-10737, paras 57-58; Case C-469/00 *Ravil* [2003] ECR I-5053, para 27; Case C-271/01 *Coppi* [2004] ECR I-1029, paras 21–9; Case C-387/01 *Weigel* [2004] ECR I-4981, para 44; Case C-60/03 *Wolff & Müller GmbH* [2004] ECR I-9553, paras 24–7; Case C-275/06 *Promusicae* [2008] ECR I-271, paras 42–6; and Case C-205/07 *Gysbrechts* (ECJ 16 December 2008), paras 29–34.

This is the case not only when the provisions are additional to those which are referred to in the order for reference, but also when only those provisions not referred to are relevant to the decision in the main proceedings.

As explained above in Section 2.2, where a preliminary question concerns a different Community law rule than that which the Court of Justice finds relevant to the main proceedings, the Court will not normally give a ruling by interpreting the Community provision referred to in the preliminary reference since such an answer would be both irrelevant and hypothetical. Instead, the Court will simply answer the question by interpreting the relevant Community provision.[33] Such reformulation of a preliminary question arises, for example, where a national court refers to the Treaty rules on freedom of movement and the Court of Justice concludes that the issue in question has been harmonised by a directive or a regulation.[34] The same it true where the preliminary question refers to provisions which have either not entered into force or are no longer in force at the relevant date for the main proceedings. In such situations, the Court of Justice has chosen to deal with the question by interpreting the Community provisions which were in force at the material time rather than by interpreting the provisions mentioned in the preliminary reference.[35]

In *Gerritse*, the Court of Justice was asked to assess whether some German tax rules infringed the right of establishment in Article 43 of the EC Treaty. The Court noted that the citizen concerned was resident in the Netherlands and that the taxation measure in dispute related to a business carried on for a limited period in Germany. It therefore found that the question was more concerned with the freedom to provide services laid down in Article 49 of the EC Treaty than with the right of establishment, and it thus answered the question, as reformulated, by reference to Article 49.[36]

---

[33] Case 54/84 *Paul* [1985] ECR 915, paras 6–12; Case C-246/95 *Coen* [1997] ECR I-403, paras 14–17; Case C-352/95 *Phytheron International* [1997] ECR I-1729, paras 9–14; Case C-107/98 *Teckal* [1999] ECR I-8121, paras 39–40; Joined Cases C-393/99 and C-394/99 *Hervein* [2002] ECR I-2829, para 24; Case C-230/98 *Schiavon Silvano* [2000] ECR I-3547, paras 33–8; Joined Cases C-228/01 and C-289/01 *Bourrasse and Perchicot* [2002] ECR I-10213, paras 29–33; and Case C-321/03 *Dyson* [2007] ECR I-693, paras 19–26. For a comparison with the previous practice, see Case 10/65 *Deutschmann* [1965] ECR 469.

[34] Case C-241/89 *SARP* [1990] ECR I-4695, paras 6–10; and Case C-346/06 *Rüffert* [2008] ECR I-1989, paras 18–19. It might of course also occasionally be the other way around, see Case C-6/05 *Medipac* [2007] ECR I-4557, paras 31–2.

[35] Case C-251/00 *Ilumitrónica* [2002] ECR I-10433, paras 27–30; Case C-271/01 *COPPI* [2004] ECR I-1029, paras 21–9; and Case C-337/06 *Bayerische Rundfunk* [2007] ECR I-11173, para 30. Compare Case C-273/98 *Schlebusch* [2000] ECR I-3889, paras 19–24. See also Ch 5, s 4.9 above.

[36] Case C-234/01 *Gerritse* [2003] ECR I-5933, paras 23–4.

The Court's readiness to reformulate the preliminary question is sometimes criticised for intruding on the competence of the national court to decide for itself which problems it needs assistance with. In the great majority of cases, this criticism is unwarranted. Admittedly, there have been occasions when the referring court has found the Court of Justice's reformulation of the problem to be less than beneficial for the solution to the problem and where the Court of Justice thus did not succeed in giving the guidance sought.[37] However, the reformulation of the question is normally merely a natural consequence of the fact that, when the national court has laid out the factual basis of the dispute, the Court of Justice is best qualified to decide on the content of Community law and thus is the most capable of deciding which Community rules are relevant for the decision in the main proceedings. Only in this way can the Court of Justice attain the purpose of the preliminary ruling procedure. Indeed, it would not be in the spirit of cooperation underpinning Article 234 if the Court of Justice were to provide the referring court with an answer that would not assist the latter in reaching a correct decision. By guiding the referring court towards the relevant elements of Community law the Court of Justice is much more faithful to that spirit of cooperation.[38] If the Court had not taken that approach, the dialogue between courts introduced by Article 234 would have depended too much on the particular national court which refers the question, so that, depending on the way that court worded the question referred for a preliminary ruling, it could determine the answer. Indeed, it has happened that the Court has given divergent answers to the very same factual situation because of different formulations of the preliminary questions in the different cases.[39]

Where the Court of Justice finds that a Community rule not referred to by the referring court is irrelevant to the resolution of the dispute in the main proceedings, it will normally dismiss a request from a party entitled to present observations before the Court that this other Community rule should be included in the preliminary ruling.[40] However, in special circumstances, the Court of Justice has agreed to assess a Community rule which the Commission has found relevant in its observations only to dismiss the Commission's interpretation of the rule in question. This departure from normal practice has hitherto occurred when the Commission's view of the law concerned a problem that was important both in

---

[37] C Barnard and E Sharpston, 'The Changing Face of Article 177 Proceedings' (1997) 34 CML Rev 1113, 1120.

[38] M Dauses, 'Practical Considerations Regarding the Preliminary Ruling Procedure under Article 177 of the EEA Treaty' (1986–87) 10 Fordham Law Review Int LJ 538, 564.

[39] Paras 33–6 of the Opinion of Advocate General Colomer in Case C-55/00 *Gottardo* [2002] ECR I-143.

[40] See Ch 10, ss 3.3.2 and 3.3.3 above.

principle and practice, and where the Court has thus found it appropriate to clarify the law so that future cases on the same problem could be avoided.

In *Lindfors*, the Court of Justice was asked to decide whether Directive 83/183 on tax exemptions applicable to permanent imports from a Member State of the personal property of individuals gave Union citizens the right to import a used car free of tax when moving to another Member State. The Commission argued that this was so. At the same time the Commission argued that the provision in Article 18 of the EC Treaty, on the fundamental right to freedom of movement for Union citizens, was relevant to the case. In the opinion of the Commission, the combined effect of the directive and this Treaty provision was that the receiving Member State could not impose a registration tax when the registration was due to the fact that a Union citizen, in connection with moving his place of residence, wanted to import his car which had previously been registered in the Member State he was leaving. The Court of Justice held first that the directive did not prevent the imposition of a registration tax, as argued by the Commission. It then assessed the relevance of Article 18 of the EC Treaty, even though this provision had not been mentioned in the preliminary question. The Court thereafter dismissed the Commission's interpretation of this provision and held that Article 18 should not be interpreted as meaning that a Union citizen could not be worse off from a tax point of view than the situation he was in before moving.[41]

2.4. Alternative answers

If there is reasonable doubt about whether the Community rule referred to in the preliminary question is the only provision which is relevant to the case, the Court of Justice sometimes gives supplementary interpretations of other potentially relevant provisions. It is then for the national court to decide which rules are applicable to the resolution of the dispute in the main proceedings.[42] It might, however, also choose merely to state that there are other Community provisions which could be relevant for the decision in the main proceedings, without itself interpreting them in its preliminary ruling.[43]

In *Cipra and Kvasnicka*, two questions were referred on the interpretation of Regulation 3820/85 on the harmonisation of certain social legislation relating to road transport (including rules on rest periods for drivers). From the facts as described by the referring court, however, it appeared likely that the journey in question had taken place outside the borders of the European Union. In that case,

---

[41] Case C-365/02 *Lindfors* [2004] ECR I-7183, paras 31–4. See also Case C-183/95 *Affish* [2003] ECR I-4315.
[42] Case C-359/89 *SAFA* [1991] ECR I-1677, para 6; and Case C-67/89 *Berkenheide* [1990] ECR I-2615, paras 16–20.
[43] Joined Cases C-228/90–234/90 and C-353/90 *Simba* [1992] ECR I-3713, paras 19–22.

the situation would not be regulated by the regulation but by the AETR Agreement. On this basis the Court of Justice decided to give an interpretation both of the regulation and of the AETR Agreement, stating that it was then up to the referring court to decide, on the basis of the facts in the main proceedings, whether the case should be decided according to the rules in the regulation or the rules in the agreement.[44]

In *Pennacchiotti*, the national court referred a question for a preliminary ruling on the Community rules on quality wines. The Court of Justice noted that under the Community rules the Frascati wine concerned in the main proceedings could be both a sparkling wine and a 'quality wine produced in a specified region'. Since the documentation in the case did not make it possible to establish whether the case concerned one or both kinds of wine, the Court of Justice interpreted the Community rules in respect of both kinds of wine. This meant that the Court of Justice took account of Community rules other than those referred to in the order for reference.[45]

If a referring court has not given sufficient information about the relevant national legal provision, the Court will sometimes provide the referring court with alternative answers to the question put. More often it will, however, merely state the factual and the national law aspects about which the national court should obtain information in order to decide on the points which the preliminary ruling does not solve.[46]

In *Sapod Audic*, the Court of Justice was asked whether the national legal act that applied in the main proceedings was a technical regulation as defined in Directive 83/189 laying down a procedure for the provision of information in the field of technical standards and regulations. In the view of the Court of Justice the answer to this depended on whether there was an actual obligation under national law to comply with the legal act in question. Information was not given about this in the order for reference. On the basis of the information available to the Court, it was most natural to assume that the national provision did not impose such an obligation. The Court therefore chose to give a primary response to the question asked according to which it assumed that the national rules did not impose such an obligation. However, at the same time it gave a subsidiary answer according to which it assumed that there was indeed such an obligation under the national rules.[47]

---

[44] Case C-439/01 *Cipra and Kvasnicka* [2003] ECR I-745, paras 14–26.
[45] Case C-315/88 *Pennacchiotti* [1990] ECR I-1323, paras 7–10. Cf also Case C-400/96 *Harpegnies* [1998] ECR I-5121, paras 13–22.
[46] Case C-127/92 *Enderby* [1993] ECR I-5535, paras 26–9.
[47] Case C-159/00 *Sapod Audic* [2002] ECR I-5031. See similarly Case C-216/01 *Budvar* [2003] ECR I-13617, paras 143–73.

2.5. Potentially relevant issues that do not form part of the preliminary reference

As can be seen from the above, the Court of Justice often gives a ruling on the basis of Community rules other than those referred to in the reference in instances where it may do so without changing the core of the problem which lies behind the question referred. In contrast, the Court is more reticent in cases where an assessment of other Community rules will raise problems other than those which the national court has chosen to lay before the Court of Justice.

Hence, in cases concerning the interpretation of Community law, the Court of Justice only seldom extends the scope of a preliminary ruling beyond the question asked. As stated above in Chapter 10, Section 3.3, the parties in the main proceedings and others entitled to present observations to the Court of Justice can only rarely persuade the Court to enter into issues other than those identified in the preliminary reference. It is similarly unusual that the Court, on its own initiative, rules on issues that differ from those to which the reference seeks an answer. If the Court of Justice finds that a case can give rise to further considerations and questions, it will normally merely mention those issues while stating that it will not give a ruling on them as questions have not been referred in this respect.[48] To simplify somewhat, one could say that, on the one hand, the Court ensures that any question from the referring court is answered correctly even if it is based on an incorrect understanding of Community law, but, on the other hand, the Court does not ensure that the question actually referred is the only relevant one and that no other issues of Community law are left unresolved.

The reticence of the Court is particularly apparent with regard to the question of which national provisions a preliminary ruling should indirectly relate to. If the referring court has limited its question to a legal problem that arises from specific national rules, the Court of Justice will not frame its preliminary ruling so as to relate to different problems that arise from other national rules.

The reluctance to widen the subject of a reference does not only apply in relation to which national rules the preliminary ruling should relate to. The Court of Justice is also careful about changing the subject of a question in relation to Community law problems which have not been referred to in the order for reference.[49] For example, it will not normally discuss competition law problems when the national court has only referred a question about the right of freedom of movement. This reticence is especially marked if the national court expressly states

---

[48] Case C-338/89 *Danske Slagterier* [1991] ECR I-2315, para 14; Case C-131/97 *Carbonari* [1999] ECR I-1103, paras 51–3; Case C-438/01 *Design Concept* [2003] ECR I-5617, paras 12–15; and Case C-12/02 *Grilli* [2003] ECR I-11585, para 36.

[49] Case C-67/98 *Zenatti* [1999] ECR I-7289, paras 22–3.

that it is not requesting an interpretation of certain specified problems.[50] Even outside such situations, the practice of the Court shows a tendency not to extend the scope of a reference.

In *Becu*, two questions were referred to the Court of Justice about the relationship between, on the one hand, the rules in the EC Treaty on competition and the prohibition of discrimination on the grounds of nationality and, on the other hand, certain Belgian rules under which the loading and unloading of ships had to be carried out by recognised dockers. The Court of Justice held that the competition rules did not apply since the Belgian rules had not been adopted by an undertaking within the meaning of Article 81 of the EC Treaty. As for the question of discrimination on the grounds of nationality, the general prohibition in Article 12 of the Treaty was applicable neither to workers nor to the provision of services, as these should be assessed under Articles 39 and 49 of the EC Treaty. However, there was nothing in the case that suggested that foreign citizens were treated less advantageously than Belgian citizens. The Court of Justice added that the order for reference did not ask whether the national rules could constitute a non-discriminatory restriction under Articles 39 or 49. It could thus not give a ruling on this. Referring to its practice on related problems, the Court nevertheless commented that the national court could look more closely into this problem and in this connection give consideration to different elements that the Court listed in the judgment, with a view to deciding the question itself.[51]

The Court's approach is to a large extent due the fact that it cannot give rulings on hypothetical questions and that it is for the national courts themselves to decide which issues of Community law they require help to solve. Moreover, if the Court were to change the content of a preliminary question, it would effectively undermine the rights of Member States, as well as those of EU institutions and others that are entitled to submit observations before the Court under Article 23 of the Statute of the Court.[52] Finally, the Court's approach is justified by the fact that often it will not have the necessary information about the facts or the national law to be able to foresee the consequences of expanding a question referred.[53]

---

[50] Case 247/86 *Alcatel* [1988] ECR 5987, paras 7–8; and Case C-262/97 *Engelbrecht* [2000] ECR I-7321, paras 21–2.

[51] Case C-22/98 *Becu* [1999] ECR I-5665, paras 34–6.

[52] On its own, this consideration is generally considered to be of less weight than the objective of helping the referring court in resolving the dispute in the main proceedings, see Ch 8, s 3.2.5 above and similarly G Bebr, 'The preliminary proceedings of Article 177 EEC–Problems and suggestions for improvement' in H Schermers et al (eds), *Article 177: Experiences and Problems* (1987) 345, 348; and J Bengoetxea et al, 'Integration and Integrity in the Legal Reasoning of the European Court of Justice' in G de Búrca and J Weiler (eds), *The European Court of Justice* (2001) 43, 54.

[53] See Ch 10, s 3.3.2 above and also Ch 5, s 4, and Ch 8, s 3.2.5 above.

That being said, there are no clear boundaries between, on the one hand, situations where the Court includes Community provisions other than those referred to in the reference without redefining the issue at stake, and, on the other hand, situations where such an inclusion of other provisions raises problems other than those which the national court has chosen to lay before the Court of Justice. The Court's practice seems to be flexible giving it substantial leeway to take the approach it finds most suited to the individual case. Presumably, it plays a significant role in whether the Court finds that a review of other provisions may reveal a problem relating to Community law which could affect the outcome of the decision in the main proceedings.[54] However, the Court of Justice can only involve Community rules other than those which the referring court wants interpreted if the order for reference contains a description of the factual and legal circumstances of the case enabling the Court to give a relevant and appropriate answer to the questions for interpretation to which these other Community rules may give rise. For this reason it is hardly surprising that the Court's propensity to keep strictly to the question referred is most pronounced where the order for reference does not provide it with the necessary basis to foresee the consequences of extending the scope of the question.[55]

In *RI.SAN*, in a number of observations submitted to the Court of Justice it was argued that the preliminary ruling should take account of Directive 92/50 on the award of public service contracts, even though the referring court had expressly excluded that the directive could be relevant. The Court of Justice indicated that the referring court's statement was possibly due to a misunderstanding of its scope. However, even if the directive were relevant for the resolution of the dispute in the main proceedings, the referring court had not provided the factual information that was required to enable the Court to rule on the interpretation of the directive. In those circumstances, the Court had no other choice than to confine its answer to the Community provisions expressly mentioned in the preliminary questions.[56]

In *Merckx*, the referring court sought information on whether a provision in a directive on safeguarding of employees' rights in the event of transfers of undertakings applied in a situation where the rights of a car distributorship were transferred from one company to another. While answering this question, the Court of Justice stated that regard for the circumstances in the main proceedings also made it necessary to rule on the interpretation of another provision in the same directive regulating the rights of employees affected by the transfer. Presumably, this extension of the question was based on the fact that the dispute before the national

---

[54] Case C-295/97 *Piaggio* [1999] ECR I-3735, paras 22–5 and 44–50.
[55] Case C-124/97 *Läärä* [1999] ECR I-6097, paras 23 and 26.
[56] Case C-108/98 *RI.SAN* [1999] ECR I-5219, paras 12–17.

court concerned whether the employees were obliged to accept the transfer. If the Court of Justice had only ruled on the question actually referred, the ruling would presumably have given the impression that those employees who were affected by the transfer could not object to the continuation of the contract of employment with the new employer. By reformulating the question, and in this connection establishing that an employee could oppose the continuation of the contract of employment with the new employer, the Court of Justice made it clear that its interpretation of the provision mentioned in the question did not in itself decide the dispute in the main proceedings.[57]

If the national court has limited the scope of its preliminary questions due to a misunderstanding of Community law, the Court of Justice sometimes chooses to indirectly widen the scope of the questions where this can be done without introducing problems which, by their nature, are different from the question put.[58]

The tendency to include Community rules other than those referred to in the order for reference is not only dependent on the information given in the reference. It also relates to which Community provisions the case concerns. Thus, certain Treaty provisions are characterised by the fact that they are subject to a more or less uniform interpretation or by the fact that they form an integrated whole. Where this is the case, the Court of Justice has shown itself to be more ready to include other Community provisions which are connected to those referred to in the reference.

In *Claeys*, the national court had only referred to the prohibition of customs duties and charges having equivalent effect, as laid down in Article 25 of the EC Treaty. In its ruling, the Court of Justice also included the closely related provision in Article 90 on the prohibition of discriminatory taxes.[59]

The willingness of the Court of Justice to consider Community provisions that are not referred to in the order for reference also seems to depend on whether it prefers to avoid dealing with a controversial question which the inclusion of such provisions would entail, or whether, on the contrary, it wants to use the opportunity to

---

[57] Joined Cases C-171/94 and C-172/94 *Merckx* [1996] ECR I-1253.

[58] Case C-62/00 *Marks & Spencer* [2002] ECR I-6325, paras 22–33. Cf also Joined Cases C-482/01 and C-493/01 *Orfanopoulos* [2004] ECR I-5257, paras 90–5.

[59] Case C-114/91 *Claeys* [1992] ECR I-6559, paras 8–12. Similarly, it is not unusual for the Court of Justice to express a view on Treaty provisions on freedom of movement other than those referred to in the order for reference; see eg, as mentioned in s 2.3 above, Case C-234/01 *Gerritse* [2003] ECR I-5933, paras 23–4; and Case C-55/94 *Gebhard* [1995] ECR I-4165. See also Case C-107/98 *Teckal* [1999] ECR I-8121, paras 39–40, where the national court had correctly identified the Community law problem as concerning public procurement, but had referred to a different directive than that which in fact applied.

give a wider clarification of the law than is necessary for the purpose of deciding the main proceedings.[60]

In *Keck*, a French court had asked whether a French provision which prohibited the retailing of goods at a loss was compatible with the 'the principles of the free movement of goods, services and capital, free competition in the Common Market and non-discrimination on grounds of nationality' laid down in the EC Treaty. The Court of Justice began its response by noting that the provisions on the free movement of persons, services, and capital were not relevant for the resolution of the dispute, which concerned the marketing of goods. Furthermore, the prohibition of discrimination on the grounds of nationality could not be relevant for the decision in the main proceedings, since the French law applied to any sales activity carried out within the national territory, regardless of the nationality of those engaged in it. Finally, the national court had not referred to specific competition rules, but merely to the Community's overall purpose of free competition. In these circumstances, having regard to the written and oral arguments presented to the Court, and with a view to giving a useful reply to the referring court, the appropriate course was to look at the prohibition of resale at a loss from the perspective of the free movement of goods. The Court of Justice then gave one of Community law's most striking and leading decisions, in which it expressly overruled its own previous case law.[61]

In *Trojani*, a Belgian court referred a number of questions about various Treaty provisions on Union citizenship and freedom of movement for persons and services. The questions all related to the rights of a French citizen to reside in Belgium. The Court of Justice answered these questions in the negative. It then stated that the questions had been referred in connection with a dispute the purpose of which was to decide whether Mr Trojani had a right to special social assistance, and from the facts of the case it appeared that Mr Trojani was lawfully resident in Belgium. Indeed, the municipal authorities of Brussels had in the meantime issued him with a residence permit. On its own initiative, the Court of Justice then examined the significance of the general prohibition of discrimination on the grounds of nationality in Article 12 of the Treaty. It concluded that, even if Community law allowed the residence permit to be conditional on Mr Trojani being self-sufficient, this did not mean that Belgium could discriminate against Mr Trojani in respect of social assistance when the Belgian authorities had themselves granted him a right of residence.[62]

---

[60] See s 3.6 below.
[61] Joined Cases C-267/91 and C-268/92 *Keck and Mithouard* [1993] ECR I-6097, paras 4–10 and 16. See also Case C-203/90 *Gutshof-Ei* [1992] ECR I-1003, para 12.
[62] Case C-456/02 *Trojani* [2004] ECR I-7573.

2.6. Questions on the validity of a Community provision

The tendency of the Court of Justice to consider *ex officio* issues not raised in the preliminary reference is more pronounced when the case concerns the validity of a Community provision. In connection with a reference for a preliminary ruling, the Court of Justice can, on its own initiative, examine whether a disputed Community act is invalid on grounds other than those stated in the order for reference.[63] Indeed, when dealing with a question of the interpretation of a Community act, the Court of Justice does have the competence to reformulate the question so as to make it a question about validity and thereafter determine that the legal act in question is invalid.[64]

This practice has been criticised as being contrary to the allocation of jurisdiction provided for in Article 234. However, such criticism overlooks the purpose behind Article 234, which is to ensure that Community law is given uniform interpretation, and the fact that one of the most important tasks of the Court of Justice is to ensure that the Community institutions exercise their powers within the framework laid down in Community law. Where doubt arises about the validity of a Community act, the Court of Justice can thus not be bound only to consider the arguments that have been made by the parties to the main proceedings. On the contrary, it is desirable that the Court of Justice should, as far as possible, ensure that the national authorities do not apply a Community act which is in fact invalid. The real concerns about the practice referred to relate rather to the right of the Community institution that has issued a potentially invalid legal act, to comment on the possible grounds for its invalidity where these grounds have not been set out in the order for reference. In practice the Court of Justice seeks to solve this problem by putting questions to the Community institution concerned either before or during the oral hearing.

That being said, where the preliminary question only concerns the correct interpretation of the act, the Court will rarely, of its own motion, examine the validity of that act.[65] Similarly, where the preliminary question concerns the validity of a Community act, the Court rarely considers whether the act in question is invalid

---

63 Case 158/80 *Rewe* [1981] ECR 1805, paras 19 and 27.

64 Case 16/65 *Schwarze* [1965] ECR 131; Case 62/76 *Strehl* [1977] ECR 211; Case C-37/89 *Weiser* [1990] ECR I-2395; and Case C-395/00 *Cipriani* [2002] ECR I-11877. See also Joined Cases C-95/99, C-98/99, and C-180/99 *Khalil* [2001] ECR I-7413; and the Opinion of Advocate General Mancini in Case 316/86 *Krücken* [1988] ECR 2213, 2226ff.

65 In contrast, the Court sometimes reformulates a question about the validity of a Community provision in order to make it a question about the interpretation of the provision. Thus, the Court of Justice regularly finds that a question about the validity of a Community act is based on a wrong interpretation thereof, and that a correct interpretation means that the question of invalidity becomes hypothetical, see s 2.2 above.

for other reasons than those touched upon in the order for reference.[66] Indeed, even where one of the parties to the main proceedings before the referring court has put forward grounds of invalidity other than those mentioned in the preliminary reference, the Court sometimes finds it inappropriate to extend its examination on the validity issue to those other grounds.[67]

Former Advocate General Slynn has suggested that in cases of doubt, or where the Court thinks it needs further argument, it should restrict itself to indicating the possibility of invalidity without ruling on it. In comparison, in a clear case the Court should reformulate a question of interpretation to an issue of invalidity if the validity question is fundamental to the issue in the main proceedings.[68]

3. Tailoring the Preliminary Ruling to the Facts of the Case

3.1. The extent to which the Court of Justice itself makes the legal classification of the facts

As explained in Chapter 4, Section 5.6, in respect of Article 234 it is, in principle, the task of the Court of Justice only to interpret Community law, but not to apply it in the actual case. On this basis preliminary rulings were originally given in abstract and general terms. What lay behind this practice was presumably a view that the distinction between abstract interpretation and its application to the facts required the Court of Justice to leave a certain scope for the national court concerning the application of the ruling.[69] The distinction between interpretation and application is far from unambiguous, however. Furthermore, an abstract and general answer will often be of limited value to the referring court, just as there sometimes will be a risk that different national courts will apply the

---

[66] As stated in Ch 4, s 3.4 above, the fact that the Court of Justice has interpreted secondary Community legislation in a previous judgment, without finding it invalid, does not mean that the Court of Justice is thereby prevented from finding this piece of Community legislation invalid in a later decision.

[67] Case C-390/06 *Nuova Agricast* [2008] ECR I-2577, paras 42–4; and Case C-305/05 *Ordre des barreaux francophones et germanophones* [2007] ECR I-5305, paras 17–19. Compare, however, Case C-183/95 *Affish* [2003] ECR I-4315, paras 27–8; and Case C-322/88 *Sermes* [1990] ECR I-33027, para 13.

[68] Opinion of Advocate General Slynn in Case 313/86 *Lenoir* [1988] ECR 5391, 5410. Such an example is provided by Case C-61/98 *De Haan Beheer* [1999] ECR I-5003, where the Court of Justice noted that the act in question had been debated in both the written and oral observations. See also C Naômé, *Le renvoi préjudiciel en droit européen* (2007) 203–4, who argues for a balance of the relevant interests, including that of a right to a fair hearing for the Community institution concerned.

[69] See Ch 10, s 3.3.3.2 above, and further K Lenaerts, 'Form and Substance of the Preliminary ruling Procedure' in D Curtin and T Heukels (eds), *Institutional Dynamics of European Integration* (1994) 355, 364.

interpreted Community provision in divergent ways, contrary to the purpose behind Article 234.

On this basis, the Court of Justice has long been moving towards a more concrete style of interpretation, where the preliminary ruling is formulated in a manner that takes into account relevant aspects of the facts in the main proceedings and of the national law. Thereby, depending on the circumstances, an interpretation will be given which is still formulated in abstract terms but which in reality is tantamount to application.[70] This is regularly expressed in the rulings themselves in the formulation whereby a given factual and legal situation, such as the one before the referring court, is or is not in accordance with Community law. Indeed, sometimes the Court of Justice states that even if the actual application is a matter for the jurisdiction of the national court, the Court of Justice has enough information to decide the application of the law itself.[71]

In *Morgan*, the operative part of the judgment reads as follows:

> Articles 17 EC and 18 EC preclude, *in circumstances such as those in the cases before the referring court*, a condition in accordance with which, in order to obtain an education or training grant for studies in a Member State other than that of which the students applying for such assistance are nationals, those studies must be a continuation of education or training pursued for at least one year in the Member State of origin of those students.[72]

In *Förster*, part of the operative part of the judgment holds that

> [a] student *in the situation of the applicant in the main proceedings* cannot rely on Article 7 of Regulation (EEC) No 1251/70 of the Commission of 29 June 1970 on the right of workers to remain in the territory of a Member State after having been employed in that State in order to obtain a maintenance grant.[73]

In *Oto*, the Court of Justice answered a preliminary question as follows:

> A tax such as the national consumption tax introduced into Italian law by Article 13 of Decree-Law No 953 of 30 December 1982, subsequently Article 4 of Law No 53 of 28 February 1983, does not constitute a charge having an effect equivalent to a customs duty on imports within the meaning of Article 12 of the EEC Treaty. . . . A tax of that kind does not come within the scope of Article 95 of the Treaty in so far as it is applicable to goods imported directly from non-member countries.[74]

---

[70] C-284/95 *Safety Hi-Tech* [1998] ECR I-4301, paras 18–19; Case C-167/97 *Seymour Smith* [1999] ECR I-623, para 68; and Case C-77/02 *Steinicke* [2003] ECR I-9027, paras 58–9. See also L Weitzel, 'La reformulation de la question préjudicielle' in V Christianos (ed), *Evolution récente du droit judiciare communautaire vol I* (1994) 83, 94.

[71] Case C-251/00 *Ilumitrónica* [2002] ECR I-10433, paras 46–53.

[72] Joined Cases C-11/06 and C-12/06 *Morgan* [2007] ECR I-9161 (emphasis added).

[73] Case C-158/07 *Förster* (ECJ 18 November 2008) (emphasis added).

[74] Case C-130/92 *Oto* [1994] ECR I-3281.

In *Krawczynski*, one of the preliminary questions was answered as follows:

Article 33(1) of Sixth Council Directive 77/388/EEC . . . is to be interpreted as not precluding an excise duty such as that provided for in Poland by the Law on Excise Duty . . . of 23 January 2004, which is charged on all sales of motor vehicles before their first registration on national territory.[75]

According to a former member of the Court of Justice, this practice implies that 'the national judge is thus led in hand as far as the door; crossing the threshold is his job, but now a job no harder than a child's play'.[76] Similarly, another former member of the Court has stated that the Court of Justice's rulings have in reality decided the main proceedings in 'an extremely high proportion of cases'.[77] These statements are corroborated by a study indicating that in almost 60 per cent of the cases where the position of national authorities was at issue, the Court of Justice left no discretion whatsoever to the referring court.[78]

In the following section, an account will be given of the different factors that influence the degree to which the Court of Justice decides to integrate the facts and national legal provisions into its interpretation of Community law so as to hand down a judgment that in reality determines the outcome of the main proceedings.

3.2. The nature of the question

The nature of the question referred naturally plays a significant role in the type of the answer given. As a rule, the more technical and less abstract a question, the more precise and concrete the answer will be. Conversely, the Court of Justice will not normally itself decide whether, for instance, a criminal law sanction is disproportionate in the actual case, since such an assessment will depend on a number of concrete circumstances which would be best examined directly before the

---

[75] Case C-426/07 *Krawczynski* [2008] ECR I-6021. See also Case C-118/96 *Safir* [1998] ECR I-1897; Case C-294/97 *Eurowings* [1999] ECR I-7447; Case C-322/98 *Kachelmann* [2000] ECR I-7505; Case C-60/00 *Carpenter* [2002] ECR I-6279; Case C-351/00 *Niemi* [2002] ECR I-7007; Case C-353/00 *Keeping Newcastle Warm* [2002] ECR I-5419; Case C-126/01 *GEMO* [2003] ECR I-13769; Case C-261/01 *van Calster* [2003] ECR I-12249; Case C-294/01 *Granarolo* [2003] ECR I-13429; Case C-138/02 *Collins* [2004] ECR I-2703; and Case C-94/07 *Raccanelli* (ECJ 17 July 2008).

[76] F Mancini, 'A Constitution for Europe' (1989) CML Rev Vol 16, 595.

[77] F Jacobs, 'The Effect of Preliminary Rulings in the National Legal Order' in M Andenas (ed), *Article 177 References to the European Court–Policy and Practice* (1994) 29.

[78] J Weiler, *Primus Inter Pares: The European Court and National Courts: Thirty Years of Cooperation*, unpublished study of 1992. See also Ch 12, s 1 below, concerning the number of disputes where the parties settle out of court after the preliminary ruling has been rendered. In a Report of 4 June 2008 from the European Parliament's Committee on Legal Affairs (A6-0224/2008), p 23, 89 per cent of 123 national courts having made preliminary references found that the Court's preliminary ruling was readily applicable to the facts of the case.

national court where the evidence is given.[79] Similarly, where a question concerns the lawfulness of the activities of a natural or legal person represented neither before the referring court nor before the Court of Justice, the Court will presumably be inclined to give a rather vague ruling thereby evading directly expressing a view thereon.[80]

In deciding on the precision and degree to which the answer shall be tailored to the particular factual situation before the referring court, the Court of Justice also takes into consideration how much need there is to ensure uniform solutions in all Member States with regard to the point of law in question. Thus, in relation to cases concerning customs tariffs classifications, it is natural for the Court of Justice to give a ruling in such concrete terms that it effectively decides whether the goods in question fall under one or other of the customs categories, as otherwise forum shopping might arise. Similarly, where the question referred concerns the interpretation of Community rules with a view to deciding the compatibility of a national law with Community law, the Court of Justice often finds it appropriate to give an answer that effectively decides the case in the main proceedings. The only restriction in these cases is that the preliminary ruling must be formulated in a manner so as to be applicable by any other court that is confronted with the same problem. The ruling therefore must at the same time be sufficiently concrete to give the referring court the guidance necessary to decide the dispute in the main proceedings correctly, and sufficiently abstract to be of general application.[81] Especially where the Court is aware of variations in national decisions applying the relevant Community law provision, it may be more inclined to hand down a ruling that effectively determines the compatibility of national law with Community law.[82]

In comparison, it can be argued that the Court of Justice should accord more discretion to the national courts by using vague and abstract terms when interpreting a vague legal standard the main principles and overall content of which have already been established, but where the correct application of the law in the actual case depends largely on the particular factual situation in the main proceedings. Indeed, the national courts are in a better position than the Court of Justice to obtain reliable information about the facts of the case and have a more detailed knowledge of the relevant provisions of national law. Moreover, it would be understandable if the Court chooses to focus on laying down the guiding principles for

---

[79] T Tridimas, 'Proportionality in Community Law, Searching for the Appropriate Standard of Scrutiny' in E Ellis (ed), *The Principle of Proportionality in the Laws of Europe* (1999) 65, 78.

[80] H Schermers and D Waelbroeck, *Judicial Protection in the European Union* (2001) 306.

[81] D Edward and C Bellamy, 'Views from European Courts' in G Barling and M Brealey (eds), *Practitioner's Handbook of EC Law* (1988) 27, 30.

[82] C Lewis, *Judicial Remedies in Public Law* (2008) 540.

the interpretation of the Community provision in question rather than engaging in the actual application of well-established criteria. Indeed, national courts should be acknowledged as being active and responsible participants in the day-to-day implementation of Community law.

3.3. The content and formulation of the preliminary reference

Sometimes the Court of Justice gives a ruling which is so abstract that it can be difficult to apply to the facts of the main proceedings. The reason for this is often that the Court of Justice has received insufficient information about the facts of the case, its socio-economic background, or the relevant national legislation.[83] This means that it is important for the referring court to give a thorough description of the facts of the case.[84]

In *Gourmet*, a Swedish court asked the Court of Justice whether a general prohibition on advertising for alcoholic drinks constituted a restriction on the free movement of goods and services. If the Court of Justice answered this question in the affirmative, the referring court wanted the Court of Justice's assessment of whether such a prohibition could be assumed to be justified on the grounds of the protection of the life and health of humans, and whether it was proportionate. The Court of Justice answered the first question in the affirmative. Thereafter it stated that in principle an advertising prohibition could be regarded as justified as a means of combating alcoholism. As for deciding whether the Swedish advertising prohibition was in accordance with the principle of proportionality, the Court of Justice stated that the decision 'calls for an analysis of the circumstances of law and of fact which characterise the situation in the Member State concerned, which the national court is in a better position than the Court of Justice to carry out'. In reality the Court of Justice therefore left the decision in the hands of the referring Swedish court, which subsequently found that the prohibition was not proportionate.[85]

In *Geffroy*, the Court of Justice was asked to consider whether various provisions in Community law constituted an obstacle to the application of a national law on the labelling of foods which prevented buyers or consumers from being misled. The Court of Justice stated that in principle it was not a matter for it to decide

---

[83] Case 77/72 *Capolongo* [1973] ECR 611, paras 7–8; and Case C-292/97 *Karlsson* [2000] ECR I-2737, para 51.

[84] See Ch 8, s 3.2.3 above.

[85] Case C-405/98 *Gourmet* [2001] ECR I-1795, para 33. The drawback of leaving the assessment to the referring court is illustrated by the fact that a Norwegian Supreme Court, when faced with almost identical Norwegian legislation in a judgment of 24 June 2009, found this legislation to be compatible with the corresponding provisions in Arts 11 and 13 of the EEA Agreement. See also Case C-222/95 *Parodi* [1997] ECR I-3899, paras 27–8; where the Court of Justice's open-ended ruling gave rise to conflicting rulings in French courts, cf *Cour de cassation* Rapport Annuel 2006, p 114.

whether the labelling of certain products was such as to mislead buyers or consumers. It would only be so if the information presented in the case appeared to the Court of Justice to be sufficient, and it found that the answer was obvious. However, in the case before it the Court of Justice did not have the necessary information to rule on this point. It therefore restricted itself to giving more general directions with a view to helping the national court in its decision.[86]

As explained above in Chapter 10, Section 3.3, the Court of Justice will often supplement the information in a preliminary reference with the information that the parties to the main dispute, the Member States, and the EU institutions have presented to the Court in their observations. However, only when the supplementary information is undisputed will it be integrated into the ruling so as to tailor it to the specific situation before the referring court.[87] Where this condition is not fulfilled, the Court's lack of competence to rule on the facts in the main proceedings means that it has no other choice but to give an abstract reply indicating those issues of fact the referring court must establish in order to fill in the 'blanks' left in the preliminary ruling.[88]

3.4. Policy considerations

It is difficult to draw a precise line between, on the one hand, a permissible concrete interpretation of the facts in a ruling which tends towards being directly applicable and, on the other hand, an impermissible interpretation of disputed facts and national law. For this reason it should be no surprise that the Court of Justice has been subject to criticism by national courts and by jurists for being both too concrete and too abstract.[89] In our opinion, it would be unfortunate if the Court of Justice were to avoid dealing with difficult questions concerning the compatibility of national law with Community law by hiding behind the argument that it lacks jurisdiction to decide on the actual facts of the case. Indeed, in a great number of cases the Court of Justice has established that its jurisdiction does go as far as to integrate undisputed facts and national legal provisions in its preliminary rulings with a view to making them sufficiently precise to give the national court effective guidance, and at the same time ensuring the uniform application of Community law.

---

[86] Case C-366/98 *Geffroy* [2000] ECR I-6579, paras 18–23. See also Case C-510/99 *Tridon* [2001] ECR I-7777, para 58. In this case the Court of Justice stated that the application of the proportionality principle to the national legislation in question required a scientific examination and an individual examination of the actual circumstances of the case, and that it was a matter for the national court to undertake this.

[87] See Ch 10, s 3.3.3.3.4 above.

[88] K Lenaerts, 'Form and Substance of the Preliminary ruling Procedure' in D Curtin and T Heukels (eds), *Institutional Dynamics of European Integration* (1994) 355, 367.

[89] See Ch 12, s 2.1 below.

A ruling which integrates the facts of the case and the national rules in this way also has the advantage that the Court avoids having to give a ruling on legal circumstances and factual situations that are not the subject of the dispute in the main proceedings. This means that the Court of Justice does not have to decide on issues where other cases could provide a better basis for clarification and development of the law.[90] Similarly, a preliminary ruling may be concretely and precisely framed due to differences of opinion between the judges involved. This applies both in cases where the judges agree on the outcome of the case, but not on the interpretation of the rules behind the decision, and where a majority of the judges seek to engage the minority in the reasoning by making it highly specific, thus narrowing the *ratio decidendi* of the ruling so that it does not prejudge the outcome of future cases. Another advantage of a preliminary ruling being precise and specific is that the parties to the main proceedings will have less need to continue proceedings before the referring court and that such a precise ruling may thereby save time for the resolution of the dispute between the parties.[91]

Finally, a reference for a preliminary ruling is sometimes made, not so much because the national court is seriously in doubt about the correct interpretation of Community law, but because it nevertheless wants the authority and support of the Court of Justice before overruling a national law or a previous judicial ruling of a higher court. In such cases, it is important that the Court provides the referring court with an answer that fits that underlying consideration.[92]

There are, however, also policy considerations which speak in favour of the Court of Justice rendering more general preliminary rulings. One pertains to the Court's workload and is addressed below in Section 3.5. A closely related one is avoiding the risk that the Court's focus might drift from the interpretation and development of Community law to the actual application in the main proceedings. If the Court engages in what is in reality application, this may attract a virtually infinite number of preliminary questions. A prominent role of the Court of Justice is to safeguard the unity and consistency of Community law. However, while this certainly necessitates that the Court outlines the overall interpretation of the many Community rules, a quest for full uniformity in application is not only impossible to achieve, but is also likely to put an undesirable strain on the Court's limited resources.

Moreover, if the Court were to narrowly focus its interpretation on the main proceedings giving rise to the preliminary question this would likely mean that

---

[90] K Lenaerts, 'Form and Substance of the Preliminary ruling Procedure' in D Curtin and T Heukels (eds), *Institutional Dynamics of European Integration* (1994) 355, 369.

[91] B Rodger, *Article 234 and Competition Law* (2008) 84 with further references.

[92] P Dyrberg, 'What should the Court of Justice be doing' (2001) EL Rev Vol 26, 291, 296.

the preliminary answers would be given a less general application and so would be of less use in other cases before national courts, thereby giving rise to further questions from these other courts. In contrast, if the preliminary ruling is not closely attached to the facts of the main proceedings giving rise to the preliminary question, it will be clearer that it has general application.[93] With this background it is arguable that the Court should formulate preliminary rulings at a higher level of generalisation than it frequently does at present. On the other hand, if the Court of Justice were to refuse to assist the referring judge whenever this assistance could be qualified as *quasi* application of Community law to the main proceedings, the latter may well perceive this refusal as a rebuke and arguably it would be difficult to reconcile with the spirit of cooperation which the Court itself holds so high.[94]

As indicated above, the Court is faced with a dilemma between the three conflicting aims, namely (1) to leave it to the referring court to rule on the actual application of Community law in the main proceedings, (2) to ensure that the referring court is given genuine guidance, and (3) to ensure that reasonable uniformity is achieved regarding the application of Community law. The dilemma in how to weigh these conflicting aims against one another is illustrated in a number of cases on the relationship between national rules restricting the opening hours of retailers and the Treaty provisions on the free movement of goods.[95] In *Torfaen Borough Council*, the Court of Justice was asked to consider how the proportionality test in Articles 28 and 30 of the Treaty should be applied to English rules on Sunday trading. However, the Court of Justice left the decision on this question to the national court, as it ruled that what was decisive was whether the prohibition laid down in Article 28 covered national measures governing the marketing of products where the restrictive effect of such measures on the free movement of goods exceeded the effects intrinsic to trade rules. The question of whether the effects of specific national rules did in fact remain within that limit was, according to the Court, a question of fact to be determined by the national court.[96] Less than two years later the Court of Justice was faced with nearly identical questions in references from Belgian and French courts. Here the Court of Justice ruled that the disputed national rules did not go too far in relation to the proportionality principle.[97] When the Court of Justice in *B&Q* again received a question on the compatibility with Community law of the English rules on opening hours, it stated that it was

---

[93] Advocate General Jacobs in para 21 of his Opinion in Case C-338/95 *Wiener* [1997] ECR I-6495.

[94] C Timmermans, 'The European Union's Judicial System' (2004) 41 CML Rev 393, 402.

[95] The Court of Justice later changed its practice in this area so that, in principle, the rules on the opening hours of retailers are no longer covered by the Treaty provisions on the free movement of goods in Art 28 of the Treaty.

[96] Case 145/88 *Torfaen Borough Council* [1989] ECR 3851, paras 15–16.

[97] Case C-312/89 *Conforama* [1991] ECR I-997; and Case C-332/89 *Marchandise* [1991] ECR I-1027.

in possession of all the information necessary to decide the question, and it thereafter itself chose to apply Community law to the facts of the case. In this connection the Court did not indicate what information had not been given in *Torfaen*, but had now come to its knowledge.[98]

3.5. The work load of the Court of Justice

In addition to the factors mentioned above, it might be assumed that the practice of the Court of Justice is influenced by a desire not to be swamped with references for preliminary rulings. The value of the preliminary ruling procedure necessarily requires the system to function reasonably. As already argued above in Section 3.4 of this chapter, the Court of Justice must therefore ensure that important cases are not drowned in a flood of cases which do not involve any points of principle. The more the Court insists on giving a general answer that does not go into the actual circumstances of the individual case, the less incentive national courts will have to refer questions of Community law that are closely linked to the factual circumstances of the main proceedings without having any wider and more general application. Notwithstanding this, the Court seems to consider it important that its preliminary rulings should not be expressed so as to deter national courts from making references.[99]

In *Clinique*, a question was referred to the Court of Justice on whether the Treaty rules on the free movement of goods precluded the application of a national provision under which the import and sale of cosmetics could be prohibited because, according to the national authorities, the use of the name 'Clinique' for the goods could mislead consumers into thinking that the goods concerned were medical goods. Advocate General Gulmann found that such a use of the national provisions entailed a restriction on trade. He, however, also concluded that under Community law it was proper to protect consumers from being misled. The question was therefore whether the application of the national provision in the actual case went further than necessary in order to achieve that objective. The Advocate General recommended that instead of making this assessment itself, the Court of Justice should only point to some general criteria and leave it to the referring court to apply the rules in the actual case. In this connection he emphasised that the case did not raise any question of the compatibility of national law with the Treaty rules on freedom of movement, but only the application of these rules in the specific case—an application which would require a concrete assessment of whether, in the circumstances, consumers would in fact be misled. If the Court of Justice itself made that decision, it risked interpreting Community law in relation to

---

[98] Case C-169/91 *B & Q* [1992] I-6635, para 14.
[99] P Dyrberg, 'What should the Court of Justice be doing?' (2001) EL Rev Vol 26, 291, 296; and T de la Mare, 'Article 177 in Social and Political Context' in P Craig and G de Burca (eds), *The Evolution of EU Law* (1998) 215, 222.

circumstances about which it did not have enough information. Moreover, the Court's workload argued against taking on the task of ensuring the uniform application of general provisions such as those in this case. The Court of Justice did not follow the advice of its Advocate General. On the contrary, it gave an interpretation which was specific to the case, in which it concluded that Community law did indeed preclude a national measure which prohibits the importation and marketing of a product classified and presented as a cosmetic on the ground that the product bears the name 'Clinique'.[100]

In *Wiener*, the referring court invited the Court of Justice to rule on whether the term 'nightdresses' within the meaning of the Common Customs Tariff was to be interpreted as covering exclusively 'other' undergarments which, in view of their characteristics, are clearly intended only to be worn as nightwear, or whether the term also covered products which, on the basis of their appearance, were intended mainly, but not exclusively, to be worn in bed. Advocate General Jacobs recommended that the Court of Justice should not give a specific answer to the question which would effectively determine the outcome of the case. In his view, the work of the Court of Justice would grind to a halt under the burden that would be imposed if it continued to resolve such issues instead of merely laying down general criteria for the application of the Customs Tariff. Even if it were possible for the Court of Justice to answer the question in the specific case, this would not be desirable. The Advocate General argued further that the role of the Court of Justice was to lay down interpretative principles so the national courts could themselves resolve the disputes before them. Thus, the Court of Justice ought not to give specific answers, but merely repeat the principles of interpretation that had been developed in previous cases and leave it to the national court to decide the particular issue with which it is confronted. In the view of the Advocate General, such a practice was especially appropriate in cases concerning the tariff classification for a specific product, and it could be used with advantage, for example, in relation to the classification of goods under the Waste Directive. The Court of Justice did not follow the advice of the Advocate General, but gave a rather precise answer which presumably decided the dispute in the main proceedings.[101]

In *Freiburger Kommunalbauten*, a German court asked the Court of Justice to assist the referring court with the application of Article 3 of Directive 93/13 on unfair terms in consumer contracts in relation to a specific contract. The relevant provision in the directive provided that: '[a] contractual term which has not been individually negotiated shall be regarded as unfair if, contrary to the requirement of good faith, it causes a significant imbalance in the parties' rights and obligations

---

[100] Case C-315/92 *Clinique* [1994] ECR I-317.
[101] Case C-338/95 *Wiener* [1997] ECR I-6495.

arising under the contract, to the detriment of the consumer.' The Court of Justice ruled that, both in its reference to the term 'good faith' and to significant imbalances in the parties' rights and obligations, the provision only contained an abstract definition of which contractual terms will be regarded as unreasonable. However, it added that under Article 234 of the Treaty 'it should not rule on the application of these general criteria to a particular term, which must be considered in the light of the particular circumstances of the case in question'. This meant that it was for the referring court itself to assess whether the contractual terms fulfilled the criteria for being regarded as unreasonable within the meaning of the directive. The Court of Justice added that it would have had jurisdiction to give a more specific interpretation of the provision if it had found that the term was unfair without having to consider all the circumstances in which the contract was concluded and without having to assess the advantages and disadvantages that this term would have under the national law applicable to the contract. It thus accepted the Opinion of Advocate General Geelhoed who had argued that national courts must play a central role in ensuring compliance with the directive, without the need to constantly make preliminary references to the Court of Justice as to whether a contractual term is unfair:

> This is not merely a question of the clear demarcation of powers as between the Community and the Member States, but also one of the economical use of legal remedies. Given the general nature of the term 'unfair', the multiplicity of terms, both as regards form and content, which currently appear in consumer agreements could give rise to continual references for preliminary rulings.[102]

3.6. New legal principles

Where the Court of Justice develops a new legal principle, it may use subsequent preliminary rulings as a means to develop the principle further and establish more precise criteria for its application. In such situations, the Court will therefore often in the first subsequent decisions be inclined to give a quite precise and fact-specific answer. Later, when guidelines for how the new principle should be applied have been established through those rulings, the Court will sometimes be more reticent about making concrete applications of the principle in order to accustom the national courts to solving such problems themselves.

An example of this is the Court's development of the Member States' liability for breaches of Community rules. In the first judgments in this field, the Court went quite far in giving an interpretation *'in concreto'* that effectively determined whether there was liability in the specific cases before the referring court.[103] Once the general guidelines had been established, and the Member States had been

---

[102] Case C-237/02 *Freiburger Kommmunalbauten* [2004] ECR I-3403, paras 19–25, as well as paras 25–30 in the Opinion of the Advocate General.
[103] eg Case C-392/93 *British Telecom* [1996] ECR I-1631, para 41.

reassured that the assessment of liability was relatively mild, the Court began increasingly to leave the actual application of the principle to the referring courts.[104]

There have also been cases where the Court of Justice consciously defines the relevant legal problem raised in the preliminary question more broadly than is necessary for the decision in the main proceedings. This approach is, *inter alia*, used to give a principle, which is laid down in the preliminary ruling, an effect that goes beyond the scope of the actual case.[105]

In some cases, this practice has led the Court of Justice to lay down principles that later turned out to be too far-reaching, so that it has been necessary to limit or significantly modify this in subsequent cases.[106]

One such example is the Court's practice regarding whether a Member State's failure to implement a Directive means that national time limits for initiating proceedings and periods of limitation must be suspended in relation to claims that are based on the Directive in question. In *Emmott*, the Court answered this question in the affirmative and based this on the general need for proper and prompt implementation of Directives.[107] However, in all subsequent cases the Court has effectively refused to follow the consequences of the principle expressed in *Emmott*. In the first of these cases the Court sought to limit the scope of *Emmott* through an analysis of the special purposes of different kinds of deadlines.[108] Subsequently, the Court has refrained from emphasising the purpose behind the rule imposing a deadline and has merely assessed whether the national rule respects the fundamental principles of equal treatment and effectiveness. Ultimately, the Court has ruled that 'the solution adopted in *Emmott* was justified by the particular circumstances of that case, in which the time-bar had the result of depriving the applicant of any opportunity whatever to rely on her right to equal treatment under a Community directive'.[109] In assessing whether this is the case, today the Court only attaches importance to whether the national authority has, by disloyal conduct, contributed to a citizen not seeking to challenge the decision of the authority in due time.[110]

---

[104] It still happens though that the Court of Justice itself takes an unequivocal stand on whether the infringement concerned constitutes a sufficiently serious breach capable of rendering the Member State concerned liable in damages, see eg Case C-452/06 *Synthon* [2008] ECR I-7681, paras 36 and 46. See also, with regard to the EFTA Court, Case E-8/07 *Nguyen* [2008] EFTA Court Report 224.

[105] See s 2.5 above.

[106] J Bengoetxea et al, 'Integration and Integrity in the Legal Reasoning of the European Court of Justice' in G de Búrca and J Weiler (eds), *The European Court of Justice* (2001) 43, 59.

[107] Case C-208/90 *Emmott* [1991] ECR I-4269.

[108] Case C-338/91 *Steenhorst-Neerings* [1993] ECR I-5475.

[109] Case C-188/95 *Fantask* [1997] ECR I-6783. See also Case C-410/92 *Johnson* [1994] ECR I-5483; and Case C-90/94 *Haahr* [1997] ECR I-4085.

[110] Case C-260/96 *Spac* [1998] ECR I-4997; Joined Cases C-279/96–281/96 *Ansaldo Energia* [1998] ECR I-5025; and Case C-228/96 *Aprile* [1998] ECR I-7141.

12

THE EFFECTS OF THE
PRELIMINARY RULING

1. Introduction

When the Court of Justice gives a preliminary ruling, in principle it does not decide on the resolution of the actual case before the national court, but only gives a ruling on the validity or interpretation of one of the legal acts referred to in Article 234(1).[1] Hence, the preliminary ruling constitutes merely an interim stage in the national proceedings which continue after the Court's ruling having regard to the clarification of Community law that has now been established.[2]

There are no provisions of Community law governing the subsequent continuation of these proceedings. Depending on the preliminary ruling, the case may be withdrawn or settled out of court so that no judgment on substance is issued in

---

[1] See Ch 4, s 5.6, Ch 8, s 1, and Ch 11, s 3.
[2] See Ch 5, s 1, and Ch 9, s 1.

431

the main proceedings. Indeed, this often happens due to the sometimes very conclusive and case-specific preliminary rulings.[3]

Where the case is not withdrawn, it is up to the national court, acting under national law, to decide whether the parties should be given an opportunity to address the referring court on the implications of the preliminary ruling for the main proceedings. Sometimes the Court's preliminary ruling will in reality settle the main proceedings so that the subsequent proceedings may be quite brief. Often, however, the ruling will leave some questions open so that there will be a need for presenting more evidence.

In this chapter, Section 2 deals with the effects of a preliminary ruling on the main proceedings. Section 3 then examines the effect of the ruling on cases other than the one that has given rise to the preliminary reference. Following this, Section 4 discusses the legal significance of the Advocate General's Opinion. Section 5 analyses the temporal effect of a preliminary ruling. Finally, the question of the interpretation and revision of a preliminary ruling is dealt with in Section 6.

2. The Effects of a Preliminary Ruling for the Main Proceedings

2.1. National courts dealing with the case

The response that the Court of Justice gives to a preliminary question binds the referring court in its application of Community law.[4] Hence, if the referring court fails to comply with a preliminary ruling it not only risks its decision being reversed on appeal; it also constitutes a breach of Community law so that the Commission may commence an infringement action under Article 226 of the EC Treaty against the State concerned. Moreover, failure to comply with a preliminary ruling can constitute such a serious infringement of Community law that it will trigger State liability. Indeed, the Court of Justice has ruled that there can be an infringement of Community law incurring liability if a national court does not make a reference for a preliminary ruling in a situation where it has a duty to do so, and on this basis renders a judgment which is not in accordance with Community law.[5] A Member

---

[3] In a study of 313 cases from the period 1961–95 it was found that the preliminary ruling led the parties to desist in 40.9 per cent of the examined cases, cf S Nyikos, *The European Court and National Courts: Strategic Interaction within the EU Judicial Process* (2001) 164. A broadly similar result was arrived at in a study of the referring courts' reactions with respect to all preliminary rulings that had been rendered in the field of competition law up until May 2004, cf B Rodger, *Article 234 and Competition Law* (2008) 85.

[4] Case C-446/98 *Fazenda Pública* [2000] ECR I-11435, para 49; Case 52/76 *Benedetti* [1977] ECR 163, para 26; and Case 69/85 *Wünsche* [1986] ECR 947, para 13.

[5] See Ch 6, s 5.4.

State may even more readily incur liability if a national court obtains a preliminary ruling from the Court of Justice and thereafter decides on the case in the main proceedings in a way which is obviously contrary to the preliminary ruling.

Not only the referring court, but also any appeal court which decides on the case in the main proceedings is bound by a preliminary ruling on the case in question.[6] The same applies to any other national court dealing with the case at a later stage of the proceedings.

The binding effect of a preliminary ruling applies not only to its operative part of the preliminary ruling, but must also be understood on the basis of the grounds for the preliminary ruling.

In *Bosch*, a German court referred a question to the Court of Justice about the correct interpretation of a Council regulation, and in particular on the interpretation of an earlier preliminary ruling in which the Court of Justice had interpreted the regulation. In its answer the Court of Justice repeated the central premise of the original ruling and added that the judgment's operative part should be understood in the light of the grounds of the judgment.[7]

The binding effect of a preliminary ruling does not mean that the referring court is prevented from making a new preliminary reference.[8] Indeed, national courts have sometimes found that the main proceedings gave rise to further questions concerning Community law and that a second preliminary ruling would be desirable or even necessary in order to answer these further questions. It has also happened that a renewed reference is made because the national court is in doubt about the correct meaning of a preliminary ruling that has been given previously. In comparison, a national court is barred from making a renewed reference in order to challenge the validity of an earlier preliminary ruling.[9]

Studies show that national courts only very rarely take issue with the result arrived at in the preliminary ruling. Examples of non-compliance are rare and so to the extent that there is a genuine enforcement problem related to the preliminary ruling procedure this does not lie in failure to comply with the Court's preliminary ruling in those cases where a question has been referred; rather it stems from those cases where Community law is being ignored without the national court making

---

[6] K Lenaerts et al, *Procedural Law of the European Union* (2006) 193; and R Grass, 'L'article 177 du Traité de C.E.E.' in J Chauvin and E Trubert (eds), *Le droit communautaire & international devant le juge du commerce* (1989) 81, 101. For references to English and German appellate courts acknowledging this binding effect see D Anderson and M Demetriou, *References to the European Court* (2002) 326ff.

[7] Case 135/77 *Bosch* [1978] ECR 855.

[8] Case C-466/00 *Kaba II* [2003] ECR I-2219, para 39. See also Ch 5, s 4.7.

[9] See Ch 4, s 3.2.5; and Case 69/85 *Wünsche* [1986] ECR 947, paras 10–16. The case is summarised in s 6 below.

a preliminary reference.[10] This is hardly surprising as the willingness to make a preliminary reference normally also implies a readiness to give effect to the preliminary ruling. Indeed, under the parallel rules of the EEA Agreement the EFTA Court's answer to a preliminary reference under Article 34 of the so-called Surveillance and Court Agreement does not bind the referring court, but merely has the effect of an advisory opinion.[11] However, there have been no instances up to now where the referring court has chosen not to follow the EFTA Court's interpretation.

Questions concerning the binding effect of a preliminary ruling have, however, arisen in cases where in its ruling the Court of Justice has gone beyond the issue referred to it and has answered a question that, strictly speaking, had not been put to it by the referring court.

In France, the *Conseil d'État* had previously taken the stand that a preliminary ruling from the Court of Justice only binds a referring French court to the extent that the preliminary ruling stays within the preliminary question as formulated by the referring court. In contrast, it was legitimate not to follow the Court's ruling to the extent that it answered questions not raised in the reference. Thus, for example, if in a preliminary ruling the Court of Justice limited the temporal effect of that ruling, without the referring court having asked any question thereon, only the interpretation of the relevant Community rule would be binding on the

---

[10] In an examination covering the period 1961–95, Nyikos found only overt non-compliance in two cases of the total of 313 reviewed cases (approximately 0.6 per cent of all cases examined). Of those two cases, at least one of them cannot, in our opinion, be seen as non-compliance. Nyikos also found that in six cases (approximately 2 per cent of all cases examined) after having obtained the preliminary ruling the national court used what she labels 'evasion through reinterpretation', cf S Nyikos, *The European Court and National Courts: Strategic Interaction within the EU Judicial Process* (2001) 164. As an example of such 'evasion' Nyikos gave Case 131/79 *Santillo* [1980] ECR 1585 (summarised below) where the referring UK court concurred with the Court of Justice that Community law had not been respected, but nevertheless found the breaches immaterial for the validity of the contested decisions. In a study of 388 preliminary references by German courts J Schwarze, *Die Befolgung von Vorabentscheidungen des Europäischen Gerichtshof durch deutsche Gerichte* (1988) 39, found that the referring courts displayed an overwhelming readiness to follow the ruling of the Court of Justice. Thus, in this regard it was not possible to identify any shortcomings in the ensuing decisions of the national court in more than 92 per cent of the cases. Indeed, even where exceptionally the national court considered the Court of Justice's ruling not to be correct, the former would consider itself bound by the preliminary ruling. In an analysis of 152 decisions by Dutch courts no examples of deliberate defiance of preliminary rulings was found. However, the study found one clear and one less clear example of wrongful application of the preliminary ruling, probably due to a misreading of the Court's judgment, cf J Korte, *Primus inter Pares: The European Court and National Courts. The follow-up by National Courts of Preliminary References ex. Art 177 of the Treaty of Rome: A Report on the Situation in the Netherlands* (1991) 65, 69–71, and 87ff. Also J Usher, 'Compliance with Judgments of the Court of Justice of the European Communities' in M Bulterman and M Kuijer (eds), *Compliance with Judgments of International Courts* (1996) 87, 106ff, and 109 finds that examples of non-compliance are few and far between.

[11] See above Ch 1, s 4.

referring court, whereas the temporal limitation of that interpretation would not.[12] This approach by the French *Conseil d'État* was hardly compatible with the principle that the judgments of the Court of Justice are also binding on national courts which have not made a preliminary reference. And it was particularly unhelpful with regard to cases concerning the validity of Community acts.

Fortunately, in its ruling in *Société De Groot* concerning annulment proceedings against a ministerial provision regulating the marketing of shallots, the *Conseil d'État* has now reversed its position. On the view that the assessment of the lawfulness of the French provision depended on the interpretation of two Community directives, the *Conseil d'État* referred a preliminary question to the Court of Justice on the relationship between the provision and those directives. In its judgment in *De Groot,* the Court of Justice did not only rule on the aforementioned directives: noting that the plaintiffs in the main proceedings had also invoked Article 28 of the EC Treaty, it also examined the relationship between the French rule and that provision regardless of the fact that the *Conseil d'État* had decided not to pose a preliminary question concerning the rules on free movement of goods. The Court of Justice concluded that the French rule in question did in fact violate Article 28.[13] Following this preliminary ruling, the *Conseil d'État* held that, although this interpretation of Article 28 had not been the object of the preliminary reference, it was indeed binding on the *Conseil d'État.*[14]

Similarly, questions concerning the binding effect of a preliminary ruling have sometimes arisen before the referring court when it has been argued that the Court of Justice has exceeded its competence under Article 234 because it has based its preliminary ruling on an understanding of the facts in the main proceedings not shared by the referring court.

In *Arsenal*, the English High Court had referred a preliminary question concerning the right of a trademark owner to prohibit the use of his mark by a third party. In its preliminary ruling the Court of Justice referred to the special circumstances in the main proceedings and stated that the character of the third party's use of the trademark in the actual case was such that the trademark owner could object to it.

---

[12] *Conseil d'État, Section du contentieux*, 26 juillet 1985, affaire n° 42.204, *Office national interprofessionnel des céréales (ONIC)* Rec p 233. In contrast, in a judgment of 10 December 1985 the French *Cour de cassation* found that the French courts were bound to follow the ruling of the Court of Justice also in situations like the one outlined here, see *Bulletin des arrêts de la Cour de cassation— Chambres civiles*, 1985, IV, pp 247–8. See further Sèners, 'La portée d'un arrêt de la Cour de justice des Communautés européennes rendu sur question préjudicielle' (2007) Revue française de droit administrative Vol 6, November–December 2003, 373; and C Naômé, *Le renvoi préjudiciel en droit européen* (2007) 214. On temporal limitation of preliminary rulings, see s 5 below.

[13] Case C-147/04 *De Groot* [2006] ECR I-245.

[14] *Conseil d'Etat, Section du contentieux, 3ème et 8ème Sous-sections réunies*, 11 December 2006, n° 234560, *Société De Groot en Slot Allium BV et Bejo Zaden BV*, A.J.D.A., 22 janvier 2007, p 136.

Holding that it was only bound with regard to the Court of Justice's findings as to the law applicable to the facts as established by the national court, and holding that the Court of Justice had made a finding of fact, namely that use of the trademark was liable to affect the origin of the goods, the High Court concluded that the Court of Justice had acted *ultra vires*. The High Court therefore held that it was not bound by the preliminary ruling. The High Court thereupon reached the opposite result to that which the Court of Justice had reached. This decision was appealed to the English Court of Appeal. The Court of Appeal agreed that the ruling of the Court of Justice seemed to include conclusions on the facts of the case and that these conclusions were not binding on the national court. However, in contrast to the High Court the Court of Appeal found that the Court of Justice's finding of the facts was compatible with the assessment of the facts made by the national court, and it therefore came to the same conclusion as that reached by the Court of Justice.[15]

The Court of Justice accepts that a preliminary reference is sought before the facts are finally established, be that by the referring court or in a later appeal procedure.[16] Therefore, where the answers given by the Court of Justice relate to a factual or legal situation that turns out not to be relevant for deciding the main proceedings before the national court, the question of a preliminary ruling's binding effect does not arise vis-à-vis the main proceedings giving rise to the preliminary reference. Indeed, as stated by the Court itself, the preliminary ruling is binding on the national courts 'as to the interpretation of the Community provision and acts in question'.[17] It follows that both the facts and the national law applicable to the case do not come within the Court's jurisdiction even if they have been integrated into the preliminary ruling in order to enable the Court to provide the referring court with an answer that is useful for the resolution of the main proceedings.

The national court may therefore, for example, end up deciding the main proceedings on the basis of a point of national procedural law without ever applying the interpretation of Community law provided for in the preliminary ruling.[18] Similarly, there may well be situations where, for reasons which have not been

---

[15] Case C-206/01 *Arsenal* [2002] ECR I-10273; and *Arsenal Football Club v Reed* [2003] 2 CMLR 25. The case is discussed in P Kerr, 'Trade Mark Tangles' (2004) EL Rev Vol 29, No 3, 345, 356ff; and R Lane, 'Article 234: A Few Rough Edges Still' in M and W Robinson (eds), *A True European, Essays for Judge David Edward* (2003) 327, 341.

[16] See above in Ch 5, s 4.3, and Ch 7, s 4.

[17] Case 52/76 *Benedetti* [1977] ECR 163, para 26.

[18] Advocate General Maduro in para 13 of his Opinion in Case C-210/06 *Cartesio* (ECJ 16 December 2008), P Lasok, *The European Court of Justice–Practice and Procedure* (1994) 353; and above Ch 5, s 4.3, and Ch 10, s 3.3.3.3.2.

subject to the preliminary ruling, the Court's judgment proves not to be relevant for the resolution of the main proceedings.

In *Data Delecta*, the Swedish *Högsta Domstolen* (Supreme Court) had referred a preliminary question concerning whether Community law precluded a Member State from requiring plaintiffs from another Member State to lodge security for the costs of legal proceedings when no similar requirement applied to nationals of that State. The Court of Justice held that such a procedural rule constituted direct discrimination on grounds of nationality and was incompatible with Community law. The Swedish Supreme Court thereupon concluded that even if it were bound by the preliminary ruling, it was nevertheless for the Supreme Court itself to decide whether the circumstances of the particular case before it fell within the scope of the relevant Community provision. In the actual case the action in question was for payment for goods which had been delivered before Sweden's accession to the European Union. Consequently, Community law, including the Court of Justice's ruling, did not apply to the facts in the main proceedings, and the Supreme Court therefore concluded that the UK plaintiff should indeed lodge security for the costs of the legal proceedings.[19]

Where the Court of Justice builds its preliminary ruling on a set of facts that differs from the one described by the referring court, a procedural problem may arise if the referring court is not itself competent to establish the facts, eg because it is bound by the facts as established by a lower court. In this situation, the different assessment of the facts by the Court of Justice might even make it difficult for the national court to comply with the preliminary ruling without violating its own national rules of procedure.[20]

In *Familiapress*, the *Handelsgericht Wien* had made a preliminary reference concerning an Austrian law the effect of which was to prohibit the distribution of periodicals containing prize puzzles or competitions. The Court of Justice held that Article 28 of the EC Treaty did not preclude the application of such legislation provided that the prohibition was proportionate to the objective pursued, especially as regards the maintenance of press diversity. The preliminary ruling assumed that the newspapers offering the chance of winning a prize in games, puzzles, or competitions were in competition with small newspaper publishers

---

[19] Decision of 30 November 1996, Case Ö 1195/94; and Case C-43/95 *Data Delecta* [1996] ECR I-4661. One might wonder first why the Swedish Supreme Court did not rule on this intertemporal question before deciding on whether to make a preliminary question and, second, why the Court of Justice found the reference admissible; indeed, in its subsequent case law the Court has refused to answer preliminary references where, at the material time in the case before the referring court, the State in question was not a Member of the EU and thus not bound by Community Law. See in this respect above at Ch 4, s 5.4.

[20] C Naômé, *Le Renvoi préjudiciel en droit européen* (2007) 221.

who were deemed to be unable to offer comparable prizes and that the prospect of winning was liable to bring about a shift in demand. The Court of Justice, however, left it to the national court to determine whether those conditions were satisfied on the basis of a study of the national press market concerned. After an interim appeal of the main proceedings was brought before the Austrian *Oberster Gerichtshof*, this court considered it impossible under Austrian law for it to call on experts to study the market conditions and consumer habits in question as part of such interim proceedings. On that basis, the *Oberster Gerichtshof* considered it sufficient if the plaintiff established the likelihood that these conditions had been met and otherwise left it to the lower court trying the substantive issue to determine whether in reality the conditions had been met.[21]

In *Ten Kate*, the Dutch *Hoge Raad* heard an appeal in cassation from the Dutch Court of Appeal. Since the case raised issues of Community law, the *Hoge Raad* made a preliminary reference. The Court of Justice noted that it appeared from the observations of the Netherlands government and the Commission that the factual situation differed from that assumed by the *Hoge Raad* in its reference and that it was therefore necessary to recast the preliminary question.[22] In the opinion of the *Hoge Raad*, this new information and different reading of the facts could not be taken into consideration for the purpose of an appeal in cassation. On the other hand, in a re-examination of the case the Dutch Court of Appeal could not ignore the new facts on which the preliminary was based. The *Hoge Raad* recalled that in exceptional cases Dutch law allows new facts to be taken into consideration during an appeal procedure and it found that in the situation at hand such exceptional circumstances were present. The *Hoge Raad* added that when a case is referred back to an appeal court following a preliminary ruling of the Court of Justice, and when that ruling is based on facts that cannot be found in the preliminary reference, the parties to the main proceedings must be allowed a right to comment on and dispute the Court's understanding of the facts.[23]

It is the national court that applies the preliminary ruling to the facts in the main proceedings.[24] In some cases it appears debatable whether in this regard the national court has been faithful to the preliminary ruling.

---

[21] Case C-368/95 *Familiapress* [1997] ECR 1-3689; and *Oberster Gerichtshof*, order of 23 March 1999, 4 ob 249/98s. *Vereinigte Familiapress zeitungsverlags-und vertriebs GmbH v Heinrich Bauer Verlag*, Wirtschaftsrechtliche Blätter 1999, p 378. The latter order is summarised in the Commission's Seventeenth Annual Report on monitoring the application of Community law [2001] OJ C30/198.

[22] Case C-511/03 *Ten Kate* [2005] ECR I-8979, paras 35–6 and 39–40.

[23] *Hoge Raad*, 22 December 2006, nj 2007, 161.

[24] See Ch 4, s 5.6, and Ch 11, s 3.1.

One of the more spectacular and, it is submitted, less fortunate, applications of a preliminary ruling is found in *Brasserie du Pêcheur*. The background to this case was that a French brewery had been excluded from the German beer market because French beer did not fulfil the German *Reinheitsgebot* ('purity requirement'). Later the German *Reinheitsgebot* was found to be contrary to Community law, and the French brewery therefore claimed compensation from the German State for the loss it had suffered from its exclusion from the market. The referring German court (*Bundesgerichthof*) thereupon asked what conditions apply for imposing liability on a State in such a situation. The Court of Justice replied in a manner that made it natural to assume that the German State had committed a sufficiently serious and manifest breach so as to incur liability, at least with regard to the losses incurred in the period following the date when the Court of Justice had delivered judgment in the infringement proceedings that had earlier been issued against Germany. However, in its judgment the *Bundesgerichthof* concluded that to the extent that there was a direct causal connection between the infringement and the loss, this infringement could not be regarded as being sufficiently serious. In other words, the German State was not liable to pay compensation.[25]

In *Santillo*, the Court of Justice held that social danger resulting from the presence of a foreigner must be assessed by the competent national authority at the time when the decision ordering expulsion is made against him. This was so, since 'a lapse of time amounting to several years between the recommendation for deportation and the decision of the administration is liable to deprive the recommendation of its function as an opinion' within the meaning of the relevant Community Directive. Nevertheless, upon receipt of the interpretation the referring English court found that a lapse of four and a half years between the recommendation for deportation and the issue of a deportation order did not deprive the recommendation of its force, as there was no evidence that the position had in any way changed or that the considerations which had caused the recommendation to be made had been altered in a sense favourable to the foreigner involved.[26]

---

[25] Judgment of 24 October 1996, Entscheidungen des Bundesgerichtshofes in Zivilsachen Bd. 134, p 30. A summary of the *Bundesgerichthof*'s judgment is provided in [1997] OJ C332/206. For criticism of the ruling of the *Bundesgerichthof*, see P Oliver, 'Casenote to Cases C-46/93 and C-48/93, Brasserie du Pêcheur v Germany, and The Queen v Secretary of State for Transport ex parte Factortame [1996] ECR I-1029' (1997) 34 CML Rev 635, 657. For an example of a less convincing application of preliminary rulings within the field of competition law, see B Rodger, *Article 234 and Competition Law* (2008) 112–15 and 244–9 concerning the referring Italian court's application of the judgment in Case C-179/90 *Porto di Genova* [1991] ECR I-5889.

[26] Case 131/79 *Santillo* [1980] ECR 2917; *R v Secretary of State for the Home Department, ex parte Santillo* [1981] QB 778. See critical to the national ruling J Usher, 'Compliance with Judgments of the Court of Justice of the European Communities' in M Bulterman and M Kuijer (eds), *Compliance with Judgments of International Courts* (1996) 87, 107; and S Nyikos, *The European Court and National Courts: Strategic Interaction within the EU Judicial Process* (2001) 154ff and 174ff.

Following the Court of Justice's ruling in *Ypourgos Ergasias*, according to which the Greek legislation on tourist guides was incompatible with Article 49 of the EC Treaty concerning the free provision of services, the Greek Council of State found that, in the main proceedings which had given rise to the preliminary question, there was no sufficient cross-border element for that provision to apply. Hence, the applicant could not rely on Community law.[27]

A preliminary ruling rejecting arguments that a Community act is invalid does not have the effect of concluding *res judicata* that the act in question is valid. Indeed, the Court never holds in positive terms that the examined Community act is valid, but merely concludes that its examination has disclosed nothing to affect the validity of the act.[28] In this way the Court keeps the door open for a finding of invalidity in subsequent cases, including in a new preliminary proceeding originating from the same national court based on new arguments for the alleged illegality.

2.2. The parties to the main proceedings

While both the referring court and any subsequent appeal court are bound directly by the preliminary ruling, the situation is different with regard to the parties to the main proceedings. These parties do not have the status of parties in the preliminary ruling procedure.[29] They are thus no more bound by a preliminary ruling stemming from main proceedings to which they are parties than by any other decision of the Court of Justice. Whilst they can rely on the Court of Justice's ruling in the proceedings before the national court in order to demonstrate the content of Community law, it is only the national court's decisions which they can require to be enforced, for example through sheriff court proceedings. Moreover, if they act in a manner incompatible with the preliminary ruling they will, formally speaking, not be in violation of the preliminary ruling as such, but only of the relevant Community provision that was subject to the ruling.[30]

This does not, however, entail that the parties to the main proceedings giving rise to the preliminary ruling may legitimately ignore that ruling so long as the referring court has not rendered judgment on the matter. For instance, a preliminary ruling finding that a given national tax measure is incompatible with Community law may be so straightforward and unconditional that the relevant tax authorities

---

[27] Case No 5302/1995 of the Greek Council of State; and Case C-398/95 *Ypourgos Ergasias* [1997] ECR I-3091.

[28] Case C-127/07 *Société Arcelor Atlantique et Lorraine* (ECJ 16 December 2008); Joined Cases C-362/07 and C-363/07 *Kip Europe* (ECJ 11 December 2008); and Case C-375/07 *Heuschen* (ECJ 20 November 2008).

[29] See above Ch 10, s 3.3.1.

[30] See the Opinion of Advocate General Mancini in Case 14/86 *Pretore di Salò* [1987] ECR 2545, para 7; and P Lasok, *The European Court of Justice—Practice and Procedure* (1994) 494.

on the basis of Community law will have an obligation to stop enforcing the national tax measure even before the national court has ruled on the matter. Indeed, the authorities of the Member State concerned have an independent obligation to take all measures necessary to ensure that Community law is complied with within that State. While they retain the choice of the measures to be taken, those authorities must in particular ensure that national law is changed so as to comply with Community law as soon as possible and that the rights which individuals derive from Community law are given full effect.[31] If the Member State does not do this, the Commission may bring an infringement action and there may even be a basis for a claim for compensation under Community law.

3. The Effect of a Preliminary Ruling in Other Cases

3.1. Other national courts

In the early years of Community law it was debated among legal theorists what effect a preliminary ruling of the Court of Justice has other than in relation to the main proceedings. While some legal writers then took the view that preliminary rulings are not generally applicable and that legally speaking they do not bind courts other than those involved in solving the dispute giving rise to the preliminary ruling, today the prevailing view is the opposite.[32]

Indeed, the general significance of a preliminary ruling to matters other than the main proceedings which have given rise to it may be likened to the effect of a judgment of a national supreme court, in a continental legal system that generally extends beyond the dispute with which this judgment is immediately concerned.

First, as a matter of principle, preliminary rulings are declaratory; ie they lay down how existing Community law must be understood as from the day of its entry into force. The interpretation given by the Court of Justice thus constitutes an integral

---

[31] Joined Cases C-231/06–233/06 *Jonkman* [2007] ECR I-5149, paras 38–41.

[32] J Combrexelle, 'L'impact de l'arrêt de la Cour: étendue et limites des pouvoirs du juge national' in V Christianos (ed), *Evolution récente du droit judiciaire communautaire, vol I* (1994) 113, 115; F Jacobs, 'The Role of the European Court of Justice in the Development of Uniform Law' in N Jareborg (ed), *De Lege, Juridiska Fakulteten i Uppsala, Årsbok 1995* (1995) 205, 207; F Jacobs, 'The Effect of Preliminary Rulings in the National Legal Order' in M Andenas (ed), *Article 177 References to the European Court* (1994) 29, 30; E Traversa, 'Les voies de recours ouvertes aux opérateurs économiques: le renvoi préjudiciel au titre de l'article 177 du traité CEE' (1992) 2 Revue du Marché Unique Européen 51, 66; and D Anderson and M Demetriou, *References to the European Court* (2002) 334ff. For an example where a Member State court has acknowledged the *erga omnes* effect of preliminary rulings, see the ruling by Voivod Administrative Court in Warsaw, *Brzezinski v Dyrektor Izby Celnej* (Case III SA/Wa 254/07) [2008] 3 CMLR 28, para 11.

part of the Community law rule in question.[33] If, for example, the Court of Justice rules that a provision in a directive is intended to create exhaustive (or full) harmonisation, then this finding has general application and is not limited to the main proceedings which gave rise to the reference for a preliminary ruling, unless the Court itself should decide otherwise.

Second, the preliminary ruling procedure is aimed at ensuring a uniform interpretation of Community law. To achieve this objective the interpretation of a Community rule given in a preliminary ruling must have general validity and also bind all other courts having to interpret that Community rule.[34]

Third, in several respects the Court of Justice has shown that it attaches general validity to its own preliminary rulings. Thus, it acknowledges the precedential value of preliminary rulings in the very same way as it does in relation to direct actions.[35] Furthermore, the Court has held that national courts can rely on a preliminary ruling in another case declaring a Community act invalid, despite the fact that the national courts are themselves prevented from declaring Community acts invalid.[36] A preliminary ruling whereby a Community act is declared invalid thus has effects beyond the main proceedings in respect of which the reference for the preliminary ruling was made.[37]

Correspondingly, the *acte éclairé* doctrine means that a national court which otherwise has a duty to make a preliminary reference can refrain from doing so, if the Court of Justice has already clarified the question in an earlier decision.[38] Here too the Court of Justice gives its earlier preliminary decisions wider effect. Similarly, when considering the temporal effect of preliminary rulings, the Court of Justice not only takes into account effects going beyond the proceedings which gave rise to the original reference, but also decides on that question with general effect for all other national courts. Thus, when the Court has held that its interpretation in a preliminary ruling should be given a temporal limitation, this part of the judgment is binding on all national courts that are later faced with the same question as the one giving rise to the preliminary ruling. This general effect is also apparent from the fact that the Court of Justice only allows a temporal limitation to be laid

---

[33] See s 5.1 below.

[34] K Lenaerts et al, *Procedural Law of the European Union* (2006) 195ff; and A Trabucchi, 'L'effet "erga omnes" des décisions préjudicielles rendues par la Cour de justice des Communautés européennes' (1974) Revue trimestrielle du droit européen Vol 10, 56, 78.

[35] Compare Case C-445/05 *Werner Haderer* [2007] ECR I-4841, para 18; and Case C-465/93 *Atlanta* [1995] ECR I-3761, para 46, with Case C-422/05 *Commission v Belgium* [2007] ECR I-4749, para 62.

[36] Case 66/80 *ICC* [1981] ECR 1191, paras 9–18.

[37] D Anderson and M Demetriou, *References to the European Court* (2002) 149 and 334ff.

[38] See Ch 6, s 3.3.

down in the first ruling that it renders on the question.[39] Also in this respect, the preliminary ruling is thus accorded normative effects for other cases than the one giving rise to the preliminary ruling.

Fourth, it is precisely the general effect of preliminary rulings which is the reason why Article 23 of the Court's Statute vests in the Member States and several Community institutions a right to make submissions in connection with the preliminary ruling procedure.[40] There is thus a logical connection between the procedure before the Court and the scope of the decision which it can give.

The general effect of preliminary rulings means that all national courts are obliged to apply not only the operative part of a preliminary ruling, but also its *ratio* when interpreting Community law. This obligation exists whether or not the national court in question sits as a court of last instance.[41]

Arguably, an exception to this exists in those situations where the Court of Justice has made a preliminary ruling in a case where the preliminary question concerns the interpretation of legal measures that have been modelled upon Community law measures. On the one hand, the Court's preliminary ruling will be binding on all national courts which are faced with the same question of interpretation under Community law regardless of the fact that the Court's ruling was given on the basis of a preliminary reference in a case where Community law as such did not actually apply. On the other hand, Community law cannot be binding on national courts outside Community law's scope of application. Therefore, under Community law the Court's ruling cannot be binding on other national courts that are 'merely' to apply a national rule that is modelled upon Community law. However, the national courts may of course be bound by the Court's ruling by virtue of national law. Indeed, we may recall from Chapter 4, Section 5.3, that where a national court makes a preliminary reference with regard to the interpretation of legal measures that have been modelled upon Community law measures, the Court will only consider the reference to be admissible if under national law the referring court will be bound by the preliminary ruling. Hence, at least with regard to other courts from the same national legal system as the referring court it

---

[39] See s 5.2.1 below.

[40] K Lenaerts et al, *Procedural Law of the European Union* (2006) 195; and F Jacobs, 'The Role of the European Court of Justice in the Development of Uniform Law' in *De Lege, Juridiska Fakulteten i Uppsala, Årsbok 1995* (1995) 205, 207.

[41] A Trabucchi, 'L'effet "erga omnes" des décisions préjudicielles rendues par la Cour de justice des Communautés européennes' (1974) Revue trimestrielle du droit européen Vol 10, 56, 71ff; but compare A Toth, 'The Authority of Judgments of the European Court of Justice: Binding Force and Legal Effects' in F Jacobs (ed), *Yearbook of European Law 1984* (1986) 1, 61, and 66.

must be assumed that they will also be bound by the preliminary ruling by virtue of national law.[42]

3.2. Parties in other national proceedings, Community institutions, and Member States

Parties in national proceedings other than that giving rise to the preliminary ruling are not directly bound by previous preliminary rulings. However, since these parties are bound by Community law, and since this law must be understood as interpreted by the Court of Justice, the net effect is that they indirectly, and in a broader sense of the word, become bound by a preliminary ruling regardless of the fact that they were not parties to the proceedings that gave rise to the preliminary ruling. In the same broad sense of the word preliminary rulings bind Community institutions and Member States indirectly.

3.3. The Court of Justice

The Court of Justice does not consider itself bound by its own previous preliminary rulings.[43] However, as far as possible it seeks to ensure a uniform interpretation of Community law. In drafting its preliminary rulings it will therefore try to establish concordance with previous decisions, be that in preliminary proceedings or in direct actions. This has significant parallels with the Scandinavian doctrine of precedent in relation to a court's own previous decisions, but differs from the Anglo-Saxon doctrine of *stare decisis*, under which previous decisions are regarded as binding.[44]

---

[42] See further Ch 4, ss 5.3.2–5.3.5.

[43] Opinion of Advocate General Warner in Case 112/76 *Manzoni* [1977] ECR 1647 (1661–3); the Opinion of Advocate General Lagrange in Joined Cases 28/62–30/62 *Da Costa* [1963] ECR 31 (original reference: Rec 1963, p 61); and D Anderson and M Demetriou, *References to the European Court* (2002) 324ff. As for newer examples of de facto overrulings of previous case law see Case C-299/05 *Commission v Council and European Parliament* [2007] ECR I-8695; Case C-2/06 *Kempter* [2008] ECR I-411; Case C-119/06 *CELF* [2008] ECR I-469; and Case C-127/08 *Metock* [2008] ECR I-6241, para 59. For older examples see Case C-10/89 *Hag* [1990] ECR I-3711, para 10; and Joined Cases C-267/91 and C-268/91 *Keck and Mithouard* [1993] ECR I-6097, para 16.

[44] See F Jacobs, 'The Effect of Preliminary Rulings in the National Legal Order' in M Andenas (ed), *Article 177 References to the European Court* (1994) 29, 29ff; A Toth, 'The Authority of Judgments of the European Court of Justice: Binding Force and Legal Effects' in F Jacobs (ed), *Yearbook of European Law 1984* (1986) 1, 32ff; A Arnull, 'Owning up to Fallibility: Precedent and the Court of Justice' (1993) 30 CML Rev 247; G Tridimas and T Tridimas, 'National courts and the European Court of Justice: a public choice analysis of the preliminary reference procedure' (2004). International Review of Law and Economics Vol 24, issue 2, June 2004, pp 125–45; and M Dauses, 'Practical Considerations Regarding the Preliminary Ruling Procedure under Article 177 of the EEA Treaty' (1986–87) 10 Fordham Int LJ 538, 572ff who also remarks that the special characteristics of common law makes it less easy to compare the ruling of the Court of Justice with national supreme courts from common law systems.

4. The Legal Significance of the Opinions of the Advocates General

It often happens that the Advocate General advises on matters which the Court of Justice does not itself touch upon in its ruling. This is particularly so where the Court only rules on some of the questions referred. Indeed, the Advocate General will often provide an answer to a preliminary question even if he or she considers the reference to be inadmissible or the question to be irrelevant. Moreover, even where the Court actually deals with all the issues raised in the Opinion, the Opinion may place the case in a broader context than will the judgment as the latter is often formulated in a more concise manner that does not provide much insight into the underlying legal issues.

An Advocate General's Opinion does not have binding effect. A national court cannot, therefore, consider a question of interpretation or validity as having been settled solely on the basis of such an Opinion. Notwithstanding this, the Opinion should not be wholly disregarded. It is presumably most correct to characterise the Advocate General's Opinion as being a source of law which can and should be taken account of when clarifying the state of the law, much in the same way as writings of leading legal theorists.[45]

5. The Temporal Effect of a Preliminary Ruling

5.1. The main rule

The interpretation which the Court of Justice gives to a rule of Community law clarifies and defines the meaning and scope of that rule as it must be or ought to have been understood and applied from the time of its coming into force. In other words, the interpretation has effect *ex tunc*, not *ex nunc*.[46] In the same way, in

---

[45] On the functions and importance of the Advocates General see K Mortelmans, 'The Court under the Influence of its Advocates General: An analysis of the case law on the functioning of the Internal Market' in P Eeckhout and T Tridimas, *Yearbook of European Law 2005* (2006) 127; and T Tridimas, 'The role of the Advocate General in the development of Community law' (1997) 34 CML Rev 1349. While using different methods, both Tridimas and Mortelmans conclude that, in the respective fields of law examined, the Court has followed its Advocate General in between 85 and 90 per cent of all cases, see Mortelmans, op cit, p 149, and Tridimas, op cit, p 1362. However, both authors also underline the dangers of such a quantitative criterion which risks the qualitative value of the Advocate General's contribution to the development of Community law being overlooked, as an Opinion may cast new light on an issue even if the Court does not follow the Advocate General.

[46] Joined Cases 66/79 and 127/79–128/79 *Salumi* [1980] ECR 1237, paras 9–12; Case C-62/93 *BP Soupergaz* [1995] ECR I-1883, para 39; and Joined Cases C-177/99 and C-181/99 *Ampafrance*

principle a preliminary ruling declaring a Community act invalid has retroactive effect, similar to a judgment annulling an act.[47]

The principle that a preliminary ruling lays down the correct interpretation *ex tunc* does not prevent the application of national rules regarding the legal effect of previous national court rulings. Indeed, the Court of Justice has recognised the importance of the principle of *res judicata*. It has thus held that in order to ensure both stability of the law and legal relations it is important that judicial decisions are definitive and cannot be called into question after all rights of appeal have been exhausted. Community law therefore allows a national judgment to stand even if it is based on an understanding of the law which is subsequently overturned by a preliminary ruling. And this is so even if it follows from the later preliminary ruling that the result reached in the national case is incompatible with Community law.[48]

The only conditions in such situations are that the national rules on the legal force of judicial decisions treat claims based on national law and Community law in the same manner (principle of equivalence) and that they are not framed in such a way as to render impossible in practice the exercise of rights conferred by Community law (principle of effectiveness). Under the same proviso, national rules on prescription and time limits for bringing legal action may mean that a preliminary ruling will have no consequences for legal relationships the legal effects of which may no longer be enforced.[49]

5.2. Circumstances which justify limiting the temporal effect

5.2.1. Overview

It follows from the above that the interpretation given in a preliminary ruling must be applied also to legal relationships established before the delivery of the preliminary ruling. Such a ruling may therefore call into question legal relationships established in good faith. For that reason, in application of the general principle of legal certainty inherent in the Community legal order, the Court of Justice may in exceptional circumstances limit the temporal effect of a preliminary ruling.

[2000] ECR I-7013, para 66. From Member State practice, see the ruling by the Voivod Administrative Court in Warsaw, *Brzezinski v Dyrektor Izby Celnej* (Case III SA/Wa 254/07) [2008] 3 CMLR 28, para 11.

[47] Case C-228/92 *Roquette Frères* [1994] ECR I-1445, para 17.

[48] Case C-453/00 *Kühne and Heitz* [2004] ECR I-837, para 21; Case C-224/01 *Köbler* [2003] ECR I-10239, para 38; and Case C-234/04 *Kapferer* [2006] ECR I-2585, paras 19–24. On State aid cases see Case C-119/05 *Luccini* [2007] ECR I-6199, paras 59–63. For the possibility of obtaining damages against the State concerned in such a situation, see above at Ch 6, s 5.4.

[49] Opinion of Advocate General Tesauro in Joined Cases C-485/93 and C-486/93 *Simitzi* [1995] ECR I-2655, para 16; and Case C-125/01 *Pflücke* [2003] ECR I-9375.

Such a limitation on the temporal effect of the ruling can only be made by the Court of Justice, and not by a national court, since the uniform application of Community law would otherwise be put at risk.[50] Moreover, the limitation can be laid down only in the first judgment ruling on the interpretation sought, but not in later rulings. Indeed, there must necessarily be one single occasion when a decision is made on the temporal effects of the requested interpretation of the Community provision in question. Otherwise both the need for equal treatment of the Member States and of other persons subject to Community law and the requirements arising from the principle of legal certainty would be jeopardised.[51]

As will be shown in the following section, several conditions must be fulfilled for the temporal effects of a preliminary ruling to be limited. First, the affected individuals or national authorities must have been prompted to adopt practices which did not comply with Community law by reason of objective, significant uncertainty regarding the implications of the relevant Community provisions (see below Section 5.2.2). Second, without a limitation on the temporal effect the preliminary ruling must be liable to cause serious financial consequences because a considerable number of measures have been taken on the basis of the now over-turned legal provision (see below Section 5.2.3). Third, an exemption from a possible temporal limitation must be made for those who have initiated legal proceedings prior to the handing down of the preliminary ruling (see below Section 5.2.4). In Section 5.2.5 some supplementary remarks are made concerning cases where the temporal limitation is sought against preliminary rulings that declare Community acts invalid.

5.2.2. *Lack of legal clarity and good faith*

5.2.2.1. General considerations. The first condition for imposing a limitation in time on a preliminary ruling is that the affected individuals and national authorities must have been prompted to adopt practices which did not comply with Community law by reason of objective, significant uncertainty regarding the

---

[50] Case 826/79 *Mireco* [1980] ECR 2559, para 9; and Case C-292/04 *Meillicke* [2007] ECR I-1835, paras 32–41. As for the possibility of the EFTA Court issuing advisory opinions with temporal limitations see H Haukeland Fredriksen, 'Bokanmeldelse av Niels Fenger og Morten Broberg, Præjudicielle forelæggelser for EF-Domstolen' (2008) Tidsskrift for Rettsvitenskap Årg 121, 613–21.

[51] Case 309/85 *Barra* [1988] ECR 355, paras 13–14; Case C-57/93 *Vroege* [1994] ECR I-4541, para 31; Case C-415/93 *Bosman* [1995] ECR I-4921, para 142; Case C-426/07 *Krawczynski* (ECJ 17 July 2008), paras 40–7; and Case C-158/07 *Förster* (ECJ 18 November 2008), para 66. For a criticism of the Court's case law see W Alexander, 'Temporal Effects of Preliminary Rulings' in A Barav and D Wyatt (eds), *Yearbook of European Law 1988* (1990) 11. A request to limit the temporal effect of a preliminary ruling can be made as late as during the oral proceedings; see eg Joined Cases C-485/93 and C-487/93 *Simitzi* [1995] ECR I-2655, para 29; Case C-330/95 *Goldsmiths* [1997] ECR I-3801, para 27; Case C-104/98 *Buchner* [2000] ECR I-3625, para 37; and Case C-366/99 *Griesmar* [2001] ECR I-9383, para 70.

implications of the relevant Community provisions. It is thus not enough that the relevant actors have acted in good faith concerning the validity of the provisions of Community law or national law that the preliminary ruling has found the Community provision to be flawed. Indeed, it is characteristic of most of the cases where the Court of Justice has chosen to limit the temporal effect of a preliminary ruling that the ruling could be considered to represent a development of Community law, ie that there were reasonable grounds for expecting the opposite outcome.

In *Cabanis-Issarte*, the Court of Justice changed its 20-year-old practice on Articles 2 and 3 of Regulation 1408/71, so that these provisions could be relied on to a greater extent by an employee's surviving spouse. Under these circumstances, overriding considerations of legal certainty precluded legal situations which had been definitively settled in accordance with the Court's previous case law thereafter being called into question as a consequence of the Court's departure from its own precedents. It was therefore decided that the judgment could not be relied on in support of claims concerning benefits relating to periods prior to the date of its delivery.[52]

In *Bosman*, the Court of Justice ruled that the EC Treaty's provisions on the free movement of workers precluded certain rules laid down by a sporting association under which, on the expiry of contracts entered into with their clubs, professional football players could only be employed by another club if the latter club paid the former club a transfer fee or a fee to compensate for the costs of training and development. The Court acknowledged that the special characteristics of the transfer rules of sporting associations could have created some uncertainty as to whether those rules were compatible with Community law. Overriding considerations of legal certainty therefore militated against calling into question legal situations whose effects had already been exhausted. However, the time limitation could be allowed only in respect of those fees which had already been paid, or at least were due, on the date of the judgment. In the same judgment the Court of Justice also set aside the use of nationality clauses which restricted the number of foreign members on a team. The Court refused to allow a temporal limitation on the effect of this part of its judgment, since it was not reasonable for those concerned to have considered that the discrimination resulting from those clauses was compatible with the rules on the free movement of workers.[53]

In *Sürül*, the Court of Justice was asked to rule on Decision No 3/80 of the EEC–Turkey Council of Association on the application of the social security schemes of the Member States to Turkish workers and members of their families. The Court held that this decision should be interpreted so as to prevent a Member State from

---

[52] Case C-308/93 *Cabanis-Issarte* [1996] ECR I-2097, paras 46–8.
[53] Case C-415/93 *Bosman* [1995] ECR I-4921, paras 139–46.

requiring in certain circumstances that a Turkish worker should have an unlimited right of residence in order to be granted child benefit for his child who lives together with the Turkish worker in the Member State in question, if for that purpose nationals of that State are required only to be resident there. During the preliminary proceedings a number of Member States argued that such a ruling would undermine a large number of legal relationships established on the basis of national legislation which had been in force for some time. It would thus result in serious financial repercussions for the social security systems of those States. The Court replied that it was the first time it had been called on to interpret the relevant provision and that one of its previous judgments could well have created a situation of uncertainty as to the right of Turkish citizens to rely on the decision. In those circumstances, pressing considerations of legal certainty precluded any reopening of the question of legal relationships which had been definitively determined before the delivery of the judgment where that would retroactively throw the financing of the social security systems of the Member States into confusion.[54]

Conversely, the Court of Justice has sometimes refused to limit the temporal effect of a judgment, by stating that the interpretation of the relevant provision did not cause significant uncertainty.

In *Commission v France*, the Court of Justice overturned an almost 20-year-old collective agreement, because it was contrary to the provision on equal treatment in Article 7 of Regulation 1612/68. The Court refused to limit the temporal effect of its judgment since already at the time when the collective agreement was made judgments had been given by the Court which indicated that the agreement would not be in compliance with Community law. The French government's argument that the judgment would impose on the French authorities a heavy financial burden amounting to as much as FF 192 million could not lead to any other conclusion.[55]

In *Bautiaa*, the Court of Justice rejected a request from the French government to limit the judgment's temporal effects in a case concerning a French duty on capital contributions made in the context of mergers. First, the financial consequences which might ensue for a government owing to the unlawfulness of a tax could not in themselves justify limiting the effects of a judgment of the Court.[56] Second, the government had not shown that, in the period during which the duty had been imposed, Community law could reasonably have been understood as meaning that the duty was lawful. In this connection it made no difference that a declaration

---

[54] Case C-262/96 *Sürül* [1999] ECR I-2685, paras 106–13.
[55] Case C-35/97 *Commission v France* [1998] ECR I-5325, paras 45–53. See also Case C-347/00 *Perez* [2002] ECR I-8191, paras 44–7; and Case C-17/05 *Cadman* [2006] ECR I-9583, paras 42–3.
[56] See in this respect s 5.2.3 below.

made at the Council meeting at which the relevant Community provision was adopted suggested that Community law was not an obstacle to the French duty. This was so given that it was settled case law that declarations recorded in Council minutes in the course of preparatory work leading to the adoption of a directive could not be used for the purpose of interpreting that directive where no reference was made to the content of the declaration in the wording of the provision in question. The declaration therefore had no legal significance.[57]

5.2.2.2. The behaviour of Community institutions.

The condition relating to lack of legal clarity is primarily assessed objectively, without reference to the subjective understanding of the Member State or persons concerned. That being said, the Court of Justice is more ready to limit the temporal effect of a preliminary ruling if the Community institutions or other Member States have contributed to the uncertainty.[58]

In *Blaizot*, the Court of Justice held that the EC Treaty's prohibition on discrimination on the grounds of nationality applied to the payment of a registration fee for admission to study veterinary medicine. The Court acknowledged that this ruling constituted a new development in Community law. Furthermore, the Commission had previously assumed that the EC Treaty did not preclude a national law such as the one in question and had notified this to the Member States. Thereby, the Commission might reasonably have led the national authorities to consider that the legislation which the ruling now indirectly set aside was in conformity with Community law. In those circumstances, pressing considerations of legal certainty precluded any reopening of the question of past legal relationships where that would retroactively throw the financing of university education into confusion. The temporal effect of the ruling was thus limited accordingly.[59]

In *Barber*, the Court of Justice interpreted the term 'pay' in Article 141 of the EC Treaty as including certain forms of pension rights. This interpretation was contrary to that adopted by the Council in two directives. Given this, and given that the Court of Justice's interpretation would mean that the financial balance of many pension schemes would be upset retroactively, the Court limited the effect of the ruling to pension rights acquired after the ruling was given.[60]

---

[57] Joined Cases C-197/94 and C-252/94 *Bautiaa* [1996] ECR I-505, paras 44–56.
[58] Case C-437/97 *EKW* [2000] ECR I-1157, paras 53–8; and Case C-228/05 *Stradasfalti* [2006] ECR I-8391, paras 70–7. Compare with the Court's earlier practice in Joined Cases 142/80 and 143/80 *Essevi* [1981] ECR 1411, para 34, where it was not clear what significance should be attributed to the Commission's view on the question.
[59] Case 24/86 *Blaizot* [1988] ECR 379, paras 25–34.
[60] Case 262/88 *Barber* [1990] ECR I-1889, paras 40–5.

In *Legros*, the Court of Justice set aside a French rule on dock dues related to the French overseas departments. At the same time it limited the temporal effect of the ruling on the grounds that the particular characteristics of the dock dues and the specific identity of the French overseas departments had created a situation of uncertainty regarding the lawfulness of the dues under Community law. That uncertainty was reflected by the conduct of the Community institutions. Indeed, the Commission had decided not to pursue an infringement procedure which it had originally initiated against the French rules in question. Moreover, the Commission had proposed that the Council should adopt a decision which would allow the dock dues to be maintained temporarily. The Court found that, taken together, those circumstances could have led the French Republic and the local authorities in the French overseas departments reasonably to consider that the applicable national legislation was in conformity with Community law.[61]

Under its general powers to supervise compliance with the EC Treaty, the Commission has wide discretion in assessing whether it is appropriate to initiate infringement proceedings.[62] Hence, the fact that the Commission has been aware of the existence of a national rule without objecting to it is not in itself sufficient reason to limit the temporal effect of a preliminary ruling that, indirectly, declares the national rule to be incompatible with Community law.[63]

In *Cooke*, the United Kingdom asked the Court of Justice to limit the temporal effect of a judgment concerning the common agricultural policy. According to the UK, without a temporal limitation of its effects, the preliminary ruling would involve considerable administrative and practical complications, since the UK authorities would be obliged to re-examine up to 10,000 files in the light of the interpretation given by the Court. The UK also argued that it had acted in good faith about the lawfulness of the national practice. In particular, notwithstanding the repeated requests for clarification and information which it had sent to the Commission over a five-year period, the Commission had not warned the UK of any error of interpretation which it was committing. The Court of Justice replied that, even though the Commission had not replied to several letters from the UK authorities, several years before the judgment was rendered the UK had been aware that the Commission had doubts about the validity of the interpretation

---

[61] Case C-163/90 *Legros* [1992] ECR I-4625, paras 28–36.

[62] See Ch 2, s 2.4 above.

[63] Case C-137/94 *Richardson* [1995] ECR I-3407, para 35. See also the related question of the temporal limitation of a judgment in infringement proceedings Case C-359/97 *Commission v UK* [2000] ECR I-6355, paras 88–96. In Case 43/75 *Defrenne II* [1976] ECR 455, para 73, the Court of Justice emphasised that, despite the warnings given, the Commission had not brought proceedings against the Member States in question. The Court of Justice held that this could have reinforced the wrong impression about the effects of the Treaty provisions. Given the more recent practice, it is unlikely that this older case is still indicative of the state of the law.

adopted by the UK. Indeed, in a meeting the Commission had expressed that it did not agree with that interpretation. None of these circumstances had led to a change of attitude by the UK, and the UK could therefore not validly claim that the Commission's stance had led it reasonably to consider that its interpretation was in conformity with Community law. In any case, the administrative and practical difficulties claimed did not amount to the 'serious difficulties' that are generally required for limiting the temporal effect of a judgment, especially since it would be up to the undertakings concerned to show that they fulfilled the conditions which the Court of Justice had laid down in its judgment.[64]

In *Lancry*, the French government argued that the temporal effect of the judgment declaring a Community decision invalid should be limited, inter alia, because the validity issue had been touched upon in an earlier case about a closely related rule without this leading the Court of Justice to declare the Community decision invalid. The Court of Justice refused the request. It held that whilst it was true that in the earlier judgment it had not ruled on the validity of the Community decision that it had now found invalid, at the hearing in the earlier case, the French government had itself argued that the Court was not called upon, in those proceedings, to rule on the validity of the decision. The French government could therefore not reasonably have inferred from the Court's silence on that point that the Community decision was valid. This was especially so, as in his Opinion in the earlier case the Advocate General had argued that the Community decision was incompatible with Community law.[65]

On the other hand, if the Commission has actually commenced infringement actions against the Member State concerned for upholding the national act that the preliminary ruling indirectly finds incompatible with Community law, this will be a strong argument against limiting the temporal effect of the preliminary ruling.[66]

The requirement of legal uncertainty and good faith implies that a preliminary ruling should be limited in time only for the period during which the uncertainty persists. Hence, where, for example, another judgment has cast light on the issue after the preliminary reference was introduced, but before the preliminary ruling in which the temporal limitation is sought, the Court will not limit the temporal effects until the time of the preliminary ruling, but will only be ready to limit the effects until that earlier date when the other judgment clarified the matter.

---

[64] Case C-372/98 *Cooke* [2000] ECR I-8683, paras 39–47. See similarly Joined Cases C-453/02 and C-462/02 *Linneweber* [2005] ECR I-1131, para 43.

[65] Joined Cases C-363/93, C-407/93, C-408/93, C-409/93, C-410/93, and C-411/93 *Lancry* [1994] ECR I-3957, para 44.

[66] Joined Cases C-367/93–377/93 *Roders* [1995] ECR I-2229, para 45.

In *Carbonati Apuani*, the Court of Justice found that a tax imposed on goods which crossed a territorial boundary within a Member State should be dealt with in the same way as the dock dues at issue in the *Legros* case summarised above.[67] It also found that the considerations of legal certainty that had induced the Court to impose a temporal limitation in *Legros* similarly applied to the tax at issue in *Carbonati Apuani*. In contrast, there were no grounds for limiting the effects of the judgment with regard to the time following the judgment in *Legros*, since after that date the national authorities should have been aware that the contested duty was incompatible with Community law.[68]

5.2.2.3. Legitimate expectations for Member States?   In general, it is easier to fulfil the requirement of good faith where a preliminary ruling, if not limited in time, will interfere in legal relationships between private parties. Conversely, more is required before a Member State can succeed in arguing that it was reasonable for it to expect that the legislation which the preliminary ruling indirectly sets aside was compatible with Community law, so that on this basis, the ruling should only be given effect *ex nunc*.

In *Ampafrance*, the Court of Justice set aside a Council decision whereby France had been allowed a derogation from the Sixth VAT Directive. The French government argued that the temporal effect of the judgment should be limited, since both the Commission's support for the special arrangement and the Council's decision had led the government to assume that the derogation was compatible with Community law. The Court of Justice replied that the principle of legitimate expectations was generally relied upon by individuals and traders in situations where they had legitimate expectations created by the public authorities. In contrast, that principle could not be relied on by a Member State in order to avoid the consequences of a decision of the Court of Justice declaring a Community decision invalid, since that would jeopardise the possibility for individuals to be protected against conduct of the public authorities based on unlawful rules. The Court of Justice added that the French government had largely contributed to the adoption of the Council decision. In these circumstances the government could not reasonably believe that the decision was valid.[69]

---

[67] Case C-163/90 *Legros* [1992] ECR I-4625, referred to above in the present section.

[68] Case C-72/03 *Carbonati Apuani* [2004] ECR I-8027, paras 36–42. See also Joined Cases C-485/93 and C-486/93 *Simitzi* [1995] ECR I-2655, paras 29–34; Case C-128/93 *Fisscher* [1994] ECR I-4583, paras 25–8; Case 69/80 *Worringham and Humphreys* [1981] ECR 767, paras 29–33; and Case 61/79 *Denkavit Italiana* [1980] ECR 1205, paras 16–21. On this issue see also paras 130–87 in the Opinion of Advocate General Stix-Hackl in Case C-475/03 *Banca popolare di Cremona* [2006] ECR I-9373; and paras 71–87 in the Opinion of Advocate General Jacobs in the same case.

[69] Joined Cases C-177/99 and C-181/99 *Ampafrance* [2000] ECR I-7013, paras 67–70.

The ruling in *Ampafrance* seems to suffer from an inconsistency. On the one hand the Court categorically holds that a Member State is precluded from relying on its own expectations whilst on the other hand the Court equally comments upon the French government's subjective bad faith. Unless the latter comment is merely intended as a factual reply to the French government's arguments, the two observations do not go well together as any discussion of the government's possible good faith should be legally irrelevant if the Court really adheres to its unconditional statement that, as a matter of principle, Member States are always precluded from relying on their own expectations. Moreover, the consequence of such a categorical application of the principle of legitimate expectations would be that there could never be a temporal limitation of the effects of a judgment in a case where a national tax measure is found to be incompatible with Community law, or in a case where a restriction of a public benefit is overturned. As several of the cases referred to above demonstrate, such a strict interpretation is, however, not the current law. For this reason, the judgment should probably be read narrowly so that it only entails that expectations of a Member State as to the validity of a given piece of legislation cannot in themselves justify a temporal limitation on a preliminary ruling.

5.2.3. *Serious financial consequences*

As stated above, in order to place a temporal limitation on the effects of a preliminary ruling it is also a condition that, without such limitation, the ruling risks causing serious financial consequences because a significant number of legal arrangements have been established on the basis of the legal provision that has now been found incompatible with Community law.

If the financial consequences are not serious, the Court of Justice will refuse to limit the temporal effects of the judgment without necessarily assessing whether the conditions concerning lack of legal certainty and good faith, discussed above, are fulfilled.[70]

On the other hand, even the most burdensome financial consequences which might ensue for a Member State from a preliminary ruling do not in themselves justify limiting the temporal effects of the ruling.[71] After all, if it were otherwise, the most serious infringements would receive more lenient treatment in so far as

---

[70] Case C-138/07 *Cobelfret* (ECJ 12 February 2009), paras 66–70; Case C-290/05 *Nádasdi* [2006] ECR I-10115, paras 61–8; Case C-209/03 *Bidar* [2005] ECR I-2119, para 70; and Case C-446/04 *Test Claimants in the FII Group Litigation* [2006] ECR I-11753, paras 221–5.

[71] Case C-423/04 *Richards* [2006] ECR I-3585, para 41; Joined Cases C-453/02 and C-462/02 *Linneweber* [2005] ECR I-1131, para 44; Case C-294/99 *Athinäiki Zithopia* [2001] ECR I-6797, para 39; and Case C-104/98 *Buchner* [2000] ECR I-3625, para 41. See also Joined Cases C-197/94 and C-252/94 *Bautiaa* [1996] ECR I-505, paras 44–56; and Case C-35/97 *Commission v France* [1998] ECR I-5325, paras 45–53, both of which are summarised in s 5.2.2.1 above.

it is those infringements that are likely to have the most significant financial implications for Member States. Furthermore, to limit the effects of a judgment solely on the basis of such considerations would considerably diminish the judicial protection of the rights which citizens and undertakings derive from Community law.[72]

In *Dansk Denkavit*, the Danish government asked the Court of Justice to limit the temporal effect of the judgment which indirectly set aside a Danish law on obligatory employment market contributions as contrary to the Sixth VAT Directive. In support of its request the government described the serious consequences which such a decision could have for Denmark's public finances and its judicial system. The contributions in question had contributed approximately four per cent of the Danish State's total revenue during the period in question. If only a fraction of the 150,000–200,000 undertakings that had paid employment market contributions were to bring litigation to claim repayment, this would lead to the collapse of the Danish judicial system. In response, the Court of Justice merely noted that the Danish government had not shown that Community law could reasonably be construed as permitting such a levy at the time when the contested contributions were introduced. Furthermore, some weeks after the contributions had been introduced the Commission—which the Danish government had informed prior to adopting the proposal that formed the basis of the law on employment market contributions—drew to the attention of the Danish government the problems relating to the Sixth VAT Directive to which the contributions could give rise.[73]

In *Griesmar*, the French government had argued that a judgment with effect *ex tunc* would throw the financial equilibrium of retirement pensions for civil servants into disarray, since such retroactive application would have an estimated cost of between FF 3 and 5 billion a year. The Court of Justice nevertheless refused to limit the temporal effects of its ruling as the French rule in question differed significantly from those rules which had been at issue in earlier judgments cited by the government in order to demonstrate the existence of objective and significant uncertainty as to the validity of the French rule. The Court added that, in any event, it had not been established that the number of civil servants who would be able to prove that the judgment gave them a right to a recalculated pension was such as to give rise to serious economic repercussions.[74]

---

[72] Joined Cases C-367/93–377/93 *Roders* [1995] ECR I-2229, para 48.

[73] Case C-200/90 *Dansk Denkavit* [1992] ECR I-2217, paras 20–3. With the benefit of hindsight one can hardly say that the argument about the public finances was in fact justified, since subsequently in most cases the Danish State succeeded in arguing that the employers had passed on the costs to the consumers and so there was no loss for the State to compensate.

[74] Case C-366/99 *Griesmar* [2001] ECR I-9383, paras 70–8.

In *Skov Æg*, concerning a reference from a Danish court, the Court of Justice held that claims under the Product Liability Directive should be addressed to the producer only and thus not to the supplier. The Court thereby differed from the interpretation hitherto adopted under Danish law. The Danish government applied for a temporal limitation of the effects of the judgment. In support of this it relied in particular on the serious consequences for legal certainty and the financial implications which the judgment could entail for injured persons in a large number of actions relating to product liability which had been decided on the basis of the understanding of the law which the preliminary ruling would overturn. The Court of Justice replied that Danish law entitled a supplier to be indemnified by the producer. For this reason alone the application for a limitation of the temporal effect of the judgment was rejected.[75]

Nor can the consideration that it will be very difficult to establish the facts on which any claims would be based to justify the temporal limitation of the effect of a preliminary ruling. Instead, this aspect must be considered as part of the concrete evaluation of the evidence in connection with each claim. Indeed, the burden of proof normally lies on the person relying on the facts alleged, so that any difficulties which a claimant might have in this regard would in any event be prejudicial to his case.[76]

However, in *EKW*, which concerned the legality of an Austrian tax law and where the *ex tunc* illegality of this law would affect several million transactions, each of limited value, the Court of Justice ruled that a right for all tax subjects to challenge the tax which the judgment had set aside would 'retroactively cast into confusion the system whereby Austrian municipalities are financed'. The condition that an *ex tunc* application of the judgment would cause serious financial consequences was thus fulfilled.[77] This judgment seems to be less harsh than the practice which the Court of Justice had followed hitherto in relation to State (ie non local government) taxes or charges.

An application for a temporal limitation on the effects of a judgment must, in any event, be based on well-documented and detailed prognoses and assumptions in order to be accepted. If this is not the case, it can in itself lead to the Court of Justice refusing to accept such an application.[78]

---

[75] Case C-402/03 *Skov Æg* [2006] ECR I-199, paras 49–53.

[76] Case C-137/94 *Richardson* [1995] ECR I-3407, paras 36–7; and Case C-372/98 *Cooke* [2000] ECR I-8683, para 43.

[77] Case C-437/97 *EKW* [2000] ECR I-1157, para 59.

[78] Case C-313/05 *Brzeziński* [2007] ECR I-519, paras 58–60; Case C-446/04 *Test Claimants in the FII Group Litigation* [2006] ECR I-11753; Case C-524/04 *Test Claimants in the Thin Cap Group Litigation* [2007] ECR I-2107, paras 129–33; and Case C-481/99 *Heininger* [2001] ECR I-9945, para 49.

5.2.4. *Relationship to pending proceedings*

In those cases where the Court of Justice limits the temporal effects of an interpretation, at the same time it exempts from the temporal limitation those who have initiated legal proceedings before national courts prior to the handing down of the preliminary ruling.[79] Indeed, if no such exemption were made these parties would be precluded from effective legal protection and the intended benefit of Article 234 would be forfeited.

This practice means that a citizen or undertaking who has not yet initiated proceedings but is awaiting the outcome of a case pending before the Court of Justice should consider bringing an action if the question of whether there are grounds to restrict the temporal effects of the ruling is raised before the Court. In this way the citizen or undertaking may avoid the practical effect of a limitation on the temporal effects of a preliminary ruling. Alternatively, the party concerned can seek to obtain an undertaking from the opposing party that the latter will not invoke any possible limitation of the temporal effects of the preliminary ruling.

5.2.5. *Temporal limitation in cases concerning the validity of Community measures*

In essentially the same manner as for judgments concerning interpretation, the Court of Justice can limit the temporal effect of a preliminary ruling concluding that a Community act is invalid while at the same time making an exception for those who had initiated proceedings prior to the handing down of the preliminary ruling.[80] The principle underlying Article 233 of the EC Treaty, allowing the Court to require a Community institution whose act has been annulled to take the necessary measures, can also be invoked in the context of invalidity given on a reference for a preliminary ruling.[81]

---

[79] eg Case C-415/93 *Bosman* [1995] ECR I-4921, para 144.

[80] See, in addition to Joined Cases C-363/93, C-407/93, C-408/93, C-409/93, C-410/93, and C-411/93 *Lancry* [1994] ECR I-3957, referred to in s 5.2.2.2 above, and Joined Cases C-177/99 and C-181/99 *Ampafrance* [2000] ECR I-7013, referred to in s 5.2.2.3 above, Case C-228/92 *Roquette Frères* [1994] ECR I-4445; Case C-228/99 *Silos* [2001] ECR I-8401, paras 35–9; and Joined Cases C-38/90 and C-151/90 *Lomas* [1992] ECR I-1781, para 23. On the variations in the formulation of the temporal limitation see C Naôme, *Le renvoi préjudiciel en droit européen* (2007) 215ff. On the temporal effect of a preliminary ruling holding that a Community act, before it has been published, has no binding effect in so far as it imposes obligations on individuals see Case C-345/06 *Heinrich* (ECJ 10 March 2009), paras 64–70. On the situation where the question is not whether to limit the temporal effect of a judgment, but to limit the effects of a judgment concerning the actual enforceability of a Community act in a Member State, see Case C-161/06 *Skoma-Lux* [2007] ECR I-10841, paras 63–73.

[81] Case 4/79 *Providence Agricole de la Champagne* [1980] ECR 2923.

6. Interpretation and Revision of a Preliminary Ruling

Article 43 of the Court's Statute and Article 102 of the Rules of Procedure provide that, if the meaning or scope of a judgment is in doubt, the Court must construe it on application by any party or Community institution which establishes that they have an interest therein. However, as there are, in the formal sense of the word, no parties to a preliminary procedure, neither the parties to the main proceedings nor any other entitled to present observations under Article 23 of the Court's Statute can rely on these provisions. Where there is doubt about the true meaning of a preliminary ruling, such doubt must be clarified by means of a new preliminary reference.[82]

In *Reisebüro Binde*, the Court of Justice held that it is for the referring court alone to assess whether it has obtained sufficient guidance from the preliminary ruling or whether it is necessary to refer the matter once more to the Court of Justice. Accordingly, the parties to the main proceedings cannot rely on Article 43 of the Court's Statute and Article 102 of the Rules of Procedure in order to seek revision of a preliminary ruling. Only the national court to which such a ruling is addressed may, if appropriate, submit new considerations to the Court of Justice which might lead the Court to give a different answer to a question submitted earlier.[83]

In *Wünsche I*, a German court referred a number of questions to the Court of Justice concerning the validity of a Commission regulation. On the basis of statistical information given by the Commission, among other things, the Court held that consideration of the preliminary question had disclosed no factor such as to affect the validity of the regulation.[84] The undertaking, Wünsche, which was a party to the main proceedings, considered that the preliminary ruling was contrary, inter alia, to the principle of the right to be heard. The undertaking therefore managed to persuade the German court to make a new reference to the Court of Justice concerning the validity of the Court's preliminary ruling, and the German court also repeated its question concerning the validity of the regulation. In *Wünsche II*, the Court of Justice stated that a preliminary ruling conclusively determines a question of Community law and is binding on the national court for the purpose of the decision to be given in the main proceedings. The provisions in the Court's Statute and Rules of Procedure relating to the exceptional review procedures available for challenging the authority of the Court's judgments are exhaustive and thus do not apply to judgments given by way of preliminary ruling. The authority of a preliminary ruling does not preclude the referring court

---

82 Case 40/70 *Sirena* [1979] ECR 3169. See also Ch 4, s 3.2.5, and Ch 5, s 4.7.
83 Case C-116/96 *Reisebüro Binder* [1998] ECR I-1889.
84 Case 345/82 *Wünsche I* [1984] ECR 1995.

from making a further reference to the Court of Justice before giving judgment in the main proceedings. However, this right does not extend to referring further questions to the Court of Justice as a means of contesting the validity of a previously delivered judgment, as this would call into question the allocation of jurisdiction under the preliminary ruling procedure. Hence, a preliminary ruling does not rank among the acts of Community institutions whose validity is open to review in proceedings under Article 234, and the Court therefore had no jurisdiction to give a ruling on the question concerning the validity of the preliminary ruling in *Wünsche I*.[85]

In accordance with Article 66 of the Court's Rules of Procedure, the Court of Justice may rectify clerical mistakes, errors in calculation, and obvious slips such as translation errors in a preliminary ruling. However, since formally speaking there are no parties in preliminary ruling procedures this rectification must be undertaken by the Court of its own motion, as Article 66 only allows a 'party' to apply for this to be done, and this term only refers to parties in proceedings before the Court of Justice. The term thus does not include persons etc who are parties to the main proceedings before the national court, nor does it include those who have, or could have, presented observations before the Court of Justice in the preliminary proceedings.[86] Not even the referring court can invoke the provision in Article 66 of the Rules of Procedure.

---

[85] Case 69/85 *Wünsche II* [1986] ECR 947.

[86] P Lasok, *The European Court of Justice—Practice and Procedure* (1994) 106ff and 494; R Barents et al (eds), *European Courts Procedure* (2004) para 31.141; and C Naômé, *Le renvoi préjudiciel en droit européen* (2007) 194. In the same way, the provision in Art 67 of the Rules of Procedure on supplementing a judgment on the costs of proceedings does not apply to preliminary rulings; see P Lasok, *The European Court of Justice—Practice and Procedure* (1994) 499. The same is true as concerns the provision in Art 44 of the Court's Statute regarding a review of a preliminary ruling; see Case 69/85 *Wünsche II* [1986] ECR 947; and P Lasok, op cit, 524ff.

13

LITIGATION COSTS AND LEGAL AID

1. Litigation Costs

According to Article 104(6) of the Rules of Procedure of the Court of Justice, it is for the referring court to decide on the allocation of costs in connection with a reference for a preliminary ruling.

In *Clean Car Autoservice I*, in accordance with Article 104(6) of the Rules of Procedure, the Court of Justice ruled that it was for the referring Austrian court to decide on the apportionment of the litigation costs.[1] On that basis, the Austrian court awarded Clean Car Autoservice an amount of costs which was calculated on the basis of a fixed scale that did not take account of the special costs connected with the reference for a preliminary ruling. Clean Car Autoservice argued that this scale was contrary to Community law. It therefore brought a new action before another Austrian court concerning the amount of the costs awarded. In *Clean Car Autoservice II*, that second Austrian court made a preliminary reference inviting the Court of Justice to rule on how Article 104(6) of the Rules of Procedure should be interpreted if a Member State had not prescribed any national rules enabling national courts to decide on the costs of a reference for a preliminary ruling. Before the Court of Justice, the defendant public authority and the Austrian government both contended that the preliminary reference was inadmissible arguing, inter alia, that Article 104(6) is merely a rule on jurisdiction that concerns neither the principle nor the extent of any right to recover costs incurred in proceedings for a preliminary ruling. The Court of Justice found the preliminary reference admissible, since the question referred was specifically intended to ascertain whether the right to recover

---

[1] Case C-350/96 *Clean Car Autoservice I* [1988] ECR I-2521.

those costs could be founded on Article 104(6). The Court then held that it was in principle for the internal legal order of each Member State to determine the rules applicable to payment of costs incurred by the parties to the main proceedings when a reference was made for a preliminary ruling. However, such national rules must not be less favourable than those governing similar domestic actions not involving Community law (the principle of equivalence). Nor may they render virtually impossible or excessively difficult the exercise of rights conferred by Community law (the principle of effectiveness). The latter principle would not preclude rules according to which the successful party in proceedings before a national court is entitled to recover certain of the costs incurred, but which contain no particular provisions as regards the costs occasioned in those proceedings by a procedural step, such as a reference for a preliminary ruling under Article 234.[2]

The provision in Article 104(6) covers the parties to the main proceedings and any other persons or entities who intervene before the national court. Others entitled to present observations before the Court of Justice under Article 23 of the Court's Statute are responsible for their own costs. Hence, the national court should not make a ruling with regard to these.

A Member State that is a party to the main proceedings may be awarded costs relating to the preliminary reference by the national court. In such cases, it is thus recommended that, in its observations to the Court of Justice, the State concerned indicate whether the observations are presented in its capacity as a party to the main proceedings before the referring court or merely as one entitled to present observations under Article 23 of the Court's Statute.[3]

The proceedings before the Court of Justice as such are free and there are thus no court fees.

2. Legal Aid

According to Article 104(6) of the Rules of Procedure of the Court of Justice, the Court may in special circumstances grant, by way of legal aid, assistance for the purpose of facilitating the representation or attendance of a party in connection

---

[2] Case C-472/99 *Clean Car Autoservice II* [2001] ECR I-9687, paras 12–22. See also Case 62/72 *Bollmann* [1973] ECR 269, in which the Court of Justice stated that it was up to the referring court to decide, by applying national law, to what extent the costs related to the preliminary ruling procedure should be included in the calculation of costs.

[3] K Mortelmans, 'Observations in the cases governed by Article 177 of the EEC Treaty: Procedure and Practice' (1979) 16 CML Rev 557, 568ff, with reference to earlier practice. Where a preliminary ruling results in a direct action before the Court of Justice or the Court of First Instance, the costs awarded in the direct action will not include the costs that may have accrued from the making of a submission in the previous preliminary ruling procedure; see P Lasok, *The European Court of Justice—Practice and Procedure* (1994) 440.

with preliminary ruling proceedings before the Court. The legal aid covers, fully or partly, the costs incurred both for written and oral observations and includes basic lawyers' fees as well as hotel costs.[4]

The Court does not seem to have defined what it considers to constitute 'special circumstances' within the meaning of Article 104(6). However, it must be assumed that the provision is aimed at situations where, due to lack of means, a party is unable to defend his rights without legal aid and it is not possible to obtain this under national law. It is also natural to assume that the Court will have regard for whether it is likely that the preliminary reference will be considered admissible. In contrast, it is not obvious that importance will be attached to the expected outcome of the reference since the preliminary ruling procedure, in principle, is non-contentious.[5]

In a preliminary reference case, the party concerned must first seek legal aid from the competent authorities in his own country.[6] Hence, where a national authority has already refused to give any, or to give full, legal aid it can be an advantage to attach this decision to the application for aid to the Court of Justice. The application should at least give information about the possibilities for legal aid in the proceedings under national law and the amount of costs which are expected to be incurred as a consequence of the preliminary procedure.

In order to establish his lack of means, the person concerned must provide the Court with all relevant information such as a certificate from the competent national authority to that effect. The Court has hitherto accepted declarations from public bodies such as tax authorities and social services authorities as well as from employers, if relevant. Sworn declarations from applicants themselves have also been regarded as sufficient.[7] It is advisable to seek guidance from the Court's Registry about the requirements for documentation before submitting the application.

An application for legal aid can be made before the preliminary reference is received by the Court of Justice and up to the point of the hearing. There is no obligation to be represented by legal counsel in connection with the preparation and submission of such an application.

An order granting or refusing legal aid is not subject to appeal. Where the application for legal aid is refused in whole or in part, the order will state the reasons for that refusal.

---

[4] On the discretionary criteria which are included in setting the amount of legal aid, see R Barents et al, *European Courts Procedure* (2004) para 16.032.

[5] P Lasok, *The European Court of Justice—Practice and Procedure* (1994) 150; and R Barents et al, *European Courts Procedure* (2004) para 16.034.

[6] The Court's Notes for the Guidance of Counsel. Naturally, the Court will not grant legal aid to cover costs that are already covered under such national schemes, see Case C-60/03 *AJ W* (ECJ 19 May 2004).

[7] R Barents et al, *European Courts Procedure* (2004) para 16.036; and P Lasok, *The European Court of Justice—Practice and Procedure* (1994) 150ff.

BIBLIOGRAPHY

Albors-Llorens, 'Changes in the Jurisdiction of the European Court of Justice under the Treaty of Amsterdam' (1998) 35 CML Rev 1273.

Alexander, W, 'Temporal Effects of Preliminary Rulings' in A Barav and D Wyatt (eds), *Yearbook of European Law 1988* (1990) 11.

——, 'La Recevabilité des renvois préjudicielles dans la perspective de la réforme institutionelle de 1996' (1996) Cahiers de droit européen 561.

Alter, K, 'The European Court's Political Power' (1996) 19 West European Politics 458.

——, 'Explaining National Court Acceptance of European Court Jurisprudence: A Critical Evaluation of Theories of Legal Integration' in J Weiler, A Slaughter, and A Stone Sweet (eds), *The European Courts & National Courts* (1998) 227.

——, *The European Court's Political Power* (2009).

Anagnostaras, G, 'Preliminary problems and jurisdiction uncertainties: the admissibility of questions referred by bodies performing quasi-judicial functions' (2005) 30 EL Rev 878.

Andenas, M, 'Initiating a Reference' in M Andenas (ed), *Article 177 References to the European Court – Policy and Practice* (1994) 18.

Anderson, D, 'The Admissibility of Preliminary References' in A Barav and D Wyatt (eds), *Yearbook of European Law 1994* (1996) 179.

Anderson, D and M Demetriou, *References to the European Court* (2002).

Arnull, A, 'The Use and Abuse of Article 177' (1989) Modern Law Review 622.

——, 'Case note' (1993) CML Rev 613.

——, 'Owning up to Fallibility: Precedent and the Court of Justice' [1993] CMLR 247.

——, 'The evolution of the Court's jurisdiction under Article 177 EEC' (1993) 18 EL Rev 129.

——, 'Case note on the *Telemarsicabruzzo* case' (1994) CML Rev 377.

——, 'Taming the Beast? The Treaty of Amsterdam and the Court of Justice' in D O'Keefe and P Twomey (eds), *Legal Issues of the Amsterdam Treaty* (1999) 109.

——, *The European Union and its Court of Justice* (1999) 70.

——, 'The Past and Future of the Preliminary Rulings Procedure' (2002) 13(3) European Business Law Review 183.

——, 'The Past and Future of Preliminary Rulings Procedure' in M Andenas and J Usher (eds), *The Treaty of Nice and Beyond: Enlargement and Constitutional Reform* 345.

——, 'Judicial Architecture or Judicial Folly? The Challenge Facing the EU' in A Dashwood and A C Johnston, *The Future of the Judicial System of the European Union* (2001) 41.

Association of the Councils of State and the Supreme Administrative Jurisdictions of the EU and the Network of the Presidents of the Supreme Judicial Courts of the EU on preliminary references, Report of the Working Group, published in Newsletter of the Association of the Councils of State and Supreme Administrative Jurisdictions of the European Union, No 20, p 19, available at <http://www.juradmin.eu/en/newsletter/pdf/Hr_20-En.pdf>.

Azizi, J, 'Opportunities and Limits for the Transfer of Preliminary Reference Proceedings to the Court of First Instance' in I Pernice et al (eds), *The Future of The European Judicial System in a Comparative Perspective* (2005) 241.

Barav, A, *Imbroglio préjudiciel* (1982) Revue trimestrielle de droit européen 431.

Barbier de La Serre, E, 'Accelerated and Expedited Procedures Before the EC Courts, A Review of the Practice' (2006) CML Rev 783.

Barents, R, et al, *European Courts Procedure* (2004).

Barnard, C and E Sharpston, 'The Changing Face of Article 177 Proceedings' (1997) CML Rev 1113.

Baudenbacher, C, 'The EFTA Court Ten Years on' in T Orlygsson, P Tresselt, and C Baudenbacher (eds), *The EFTA Court Ten Years on* (2005) 1.

Bebr, G, 'The Existence of a Genuine Dispute: An Indispensable Precondition for the Jurisdiction of the Court under Article 177 EEC Treaty' (1980) CML Rev 525.

——, 'Arbitration Tribunals and Article 177 of the EEC Treaty' (1985) CML Rev 489.

——, 'The preliminary proceedings of Article 177 EEC – Problems and suggestions for improvement' in H Schermers et al (eds), *Article 177: Experiences and Problems* (1987) 345.

——, 'General Report' in H Schermers et al (eds), *Article 177: Experiences and Problems* (1987) 345.

Bengoetxea, J, et al, 'Integration and Integrity in the Legal Reasoning of the European Court of Justice' in G de Búrca and J Weiler (eds), *The European Court of Justice* (2001) 43.

Bernitz, U, 'Kommissionen ingriper mot svenska sistainstansers obenägenhet att begära förhandsavgöranden' (2005) Europarättslig Tidskrift 109.

——, 'The Duty of Supreme Courts to Refer Cases to the ECJ: The Commission's Action Against Sweden' in N Wahl and P Cramér (eds), *Swedish Studies in European Law, Vol 1* (2006) 37.

Bernitz, U and A Kjellgren, *Europarättens grunder* (2002).

Berramdane, A, 'Les limites de la protection juridictionnelle dans le cadre du titre VI du traité sur l'Union européenne' (2007) 2 Revue du droit de l'Union Européenne 433.

Betlem, G, 'Case note to Case C-346/93 Kleinwort Benson Ltd v City of Glasgow District Council', [1995] ECR I-615, (1996) CML Rev 137.

Bobek, M, 'Learning to talk; Preliminary Rulings, The courts of the new Member States and the Court of Justice' (2008) CML Rev 1611.

Bontinck, G, 'The TRIPs Agreement and the Court of Justice: A New Dawn? – Some Comments About Joined Cases C-300/98 and C-392/98 *Parfums Dior* and *Assco Gerüste*', Jean Monnet Working Paper 16/01.

Breuer, M, 'State Liability for Judicial Wrongs' (2004) 29 EL Rev 243.

Broberg, M, 'The relationship between referrals for preliminary rulings under Article 234 and proceedings to annul Community decisions under Article 230 of the EC Treaty' in N Fenger, K Hagel-Sørensen, and B Vesterdorf (eds), *Claus Gulmann Liber Amicorum* (2006) 83.

——, '*Acte Clair* revisited: Adapting the *acte clair* criteria to the demands of the times' (2008) CML Rev 1383.

——, 'Preliminary References by Public Administrative Bodies: When Are Public Administrative Bodies Competent to Make Preliminary References to the European Court of Justice?' (2009) 15 European Public Law 207.

——, 'The preliminary reference procedure and questions of international and national law' in P Eeckhout and T Tridimas (eds), *Yearbook of European Law 2009* (forthcoming).

Burley, A and W Mattli, 'Europe Before the Court: A Political Theory of Legal Integration' (1993) International Organization 41.

Burrows, N and R Greaves, *The Advocate General and EC Law* (2007).

Carrubba, C and L Murrah, 'Legal Integration and Use of Preliminary Ruling Process in the European Union' (2005) International Organization 399.

Chalmers, D, 'The Much Ado about Judicial Politics in the United Kingdom: A Statistical Analysis of Reported Decisions of United Kingdom Courts invoking EU Law 1973-1988', Harvard Jean Monnet Working Paper 1/00.

Chalmers, D, et al, *European Union Law* (2006).

Cheneviere, C, 'L'Article 68 CE – Rapide survol d'un renvoi prejudiciel mal compris' (2004) 5–6 Cahiers de droit européen 567.

Colomer, R, 'La réforme de la Cour de justice opérée par la traité de Nice et sa mise en oeuvre future' (2001) 37(4) Revue trimestrielle de droit européen 705.

Combrexelle, J, 'L'impact de l'arrêt de la Cour: étendue et limites des pouvoirs du juge national' in V Christianos (ed), *Evolution récente du droit judiciaire communautaire, vol I* (1994) 113.

Craig, P and G de Búrca, *EU Law, Text, Cases and Materials* (2007).

Crowe, R, Colloquium Report, The Preliminary Reference Procedure: Reflections based on Practical Experience of the Highest National Courts in Administrative Matters (2004) 5 ERA Forum 435.

Curtin, D and R H van Ooik, 'Revamping the European Union's enforcement systems with a view to eastern enlargement', WRR Working Documents no. W110, The Hague 2000.

Dashwood, A, 'Preliminary Rulings on the Interpretation of Mixed Agreements' in D O'Keeffe and A Bavasso (eds), *Judicial Review in European Union Law. Liber Amicorum in Honour of Lord Slynn of Hadley, Vol 1* (2000) 167.

Dashwood, A and A C Johnston, 'Synthesis of the Debate' in A Dashwood and A C Johnston (eds), *The Future of the Judicial System of the European Union* (2001) 55.

Dauses, M, 'Practical Considerations Regarding the Preliminary Ruling Procedure under Article 177 of the EEA Treaty' (1986–87) 10 Fordham Int L J 538.

Davies, G, 'Abstractness and concreteness in the preliminary reference procedure: implications for the division of powers and effective market regulation' in NN Shuibhne (ed), *Regulating the Internal Market* (2006) 210.

Delgado, N B and M la Casta Munoa, 'Case note on Dzodzi and Gmursynska-Bescher' (1992) CML Rev 152.

Dhunér, K J, 'Sweden' (2005) IBA Legal Practice Division Antitrust Newsletter 27.

Dougan, M, *National Remedies Before the Court of Justice – Issues of Harmonisation and Differentiation* (2004) 3.

Due, O, 'Presenting the Case Orally – The Judge's view' in D Vaughan et al, *Butterworth's European Court Practice* (1993) iv.

——, 'Danish Preliminary References' in D O'Keeffe and A Bavasso (eds), *Judicial Review in European Union Law* (2001) 363.

Due, O, 'The Working Party Report' in A Dashwood and A C Johnston (eds), *The Future of the Judicial System of the European Union* (2001) 87.

Due Report (Report by the Working Party on the Future of the European Communities' Court System).

Dutch Council of State, letter of 20 October 2006 sent to the Dutch minister of foreign affairs by the president of the Administrative Jurisdiction Division on behalf of the Council of State and the Presidents of the Supreme Court, the Central Appeals Tribunal and the Trade and Industry Appeals Tribunal, available at <http://www.network-presidents.eu/IMG/pdf/section_contentieux.pdf>.

Dyrberg, P, 'What should the Court of Justice be doing' (2001) 26 EL Rev 291.

Eeckhout, P, 'The European Court of Justice and the "Area of Freedom, Security and Justice": Challenges and Problems' in D O'Keeffe and A Bavasso (eds), *Judicial Review in European Union Law. Liber Amicorum in Honour of Lord Slynn of Hadley, Vol. 1* (2000) 153.

——, *External Relations of the European Union – Legal and Constitutional Foundations* (2004).

Edward, D, 'The Problem of Fact-finding in Preliminary Proceedings under Article 177' in H Schermers et al (eds), *Article 177: Experiences and Problems* (1987) 216ff.

——, 'Reform of Article 234 Procedure: The Limit of the Possible' in D O'Keeffe and A Bavasso (eds), *Judicial Review in European Union Law, Vol I* (2000) 119.

Edward, D and C Bellamy, 'Views from European Courts' in G Barling and M Brealey (eds), *Practitioner's Handbook of EC Law* (1988) 27.

Engström, J, 'Case Law of the European Union Courts, Leading Judgments 16 December 2008 to 28 February 2009' (2009) ERA Forum.

Fahey, E, *Practice and Procedure in Preliminary References to Europe: 30 Years of Article 234 EC Case Law from the Irish Courts* (2007).

Fenger, N, 'Article 177' in H Smit and P Herzog (eds), *The law of the European Community: a commentary on the EEC Treaty* (1997).

——, 'Review of final administrative decisions contrary to EU Law' [2008] European Law Reporter 150.

Fenger, N, et al, European Free Trade Agreement (EFTA) and European Economic Area (EEA)' in R Blanpain (ed), *International Encyclopedia of Law, International Organisations, vol 1, supplement 24* (2005).

Fenger, N and M Broberg, *Præjudicielle forelæggelser for EF-domstolen* (2008).

Gaja, G, 'The Growing Variety of Procedures Concerning Preliminary Rulings' in D O'Keeffe and A Bavasso (eds), *Judicial Review in European Union Law. Liber Amicorum in Honour of Lord Slynn of Hadley, Vol I* (2000) 143.

Garbagnati Ketvel, M-G, 'The Jurisdiction of the European Court of Justice in Respect of the Common Foreign and Security Policy' (2006) 55 International and Comparative Law Quarterly 77.

——, 'Almost, but not quite: The Court of Justice and judicial Protection of Individuals in the Third Pillar' (2007) 6 European Law Reporter 223.

Gilliaux, P, *Le renvoi préjudiciel à la Cour de justice des Communautés européennes – Rapport belge* (2002) 4.

Golub, J, 'Modelling Judicial Dialogue in the European Community' EUI, Robert Schuman Working Paper 58/96.

——, 'The Politics of Judicial Discretion: Rethinking the Interaction between National Courts and the European Court of Justice' (1996) 19(2) West European Politics 360.

Gordon, R, *EC Law in Judicial Review* (2007).

Gori, G, 'La notion de juridiction d'un État membre au sens de l'article 234 CE' in N Fenger, K Hagel-Sørensen, and B Vesterdorf (eds), *Claus Gulmann Liber Amicorum* (2006) 155.

Granger, M, 'When Governments go to Luxembourg' (2004) 29 EL Rev 3.

——, 'States as successful Litigants before The European Court of Justice: Lessons from the 'Repeat Players' of European Litigation' in *Croatian Yearbook of European Law and Policy 2006* (2006) 27.

Grass, R, 'L'article 177 du Traité de C.E.E.' in J Chauvin and E Trubert (eds), *Le droit communautaire & international devant le juge du commerce* (1989) 81.

Graver, H P, 'The Effects of EFTA Court Jurisprudence on the Legal Orders of the EFTA States' in C Baudenbacher, P Tresselt, and T Örlygsson (eds), *The EFTA Court – ten years on* (2005) 79.

Gray, C, 'Advisory Opinions and the Court of Justice' (1983) EL Rev 24.

Groussot, X, et al, *Empowering National Courts in EU Law* (2009).

Harding, C, 'Who goes to Court in Europe?' (1992) 17 EL Rev 105.

van Harten, H, 'The Application of Community Precedent and *acte clair* by the Hoge Raad, A Case Study in the Field of Establishment and Services' (<http://ssrn.com/abstract=1113729>).

Hartley, T C, *The Foundations of European Community Law* (2007).

Hatzopolous, V, 'De l'arrêt 'Foglia-Novello' à l'arrêt "TWD Textilwerke" – La jurisprudence de la Cour de justice relative à la recevabilité des renvois préjudiciels' (1994) 3 Revue du Marché Unique Européen 195.

Haukeland Fredriksen, H, "Om mangelen på tolkningsspørsmål fra norske domstoler til EFTA-domstolen" (2006) Jussens Venner 386.

——, 'Bokanmeldelse av Niels Fenger og Morten Broberg, Præjudicielle forelæggelser for EF-Domstolen' [2008] Tidsskrift for Rettsvitenskap 613.

Heliskoski, J, 'The Jurisdiction of the European Court of Justice to Give Preliminary Rulings on the Interpretation of Mixed Agreements' (2000) Nordic Journal of International Law 395.

Herrmann, C, 'Die Reichweite der gemeinschaftsrechtlichen Vorlagepflict in der neueren Recthsprechung des EuGH' (2006) Europäische Zeitschrift für Wirtschaftsrecht 231.

Herrmann, K, 'Gebrauchtwagenhandel – Wie Richter aus neuen EU-Mitgliedstaaten den Dialog mit dem EuGH aufnehmen' (2007) 18 Europäische Zeitschrift für Wirtschaftsrecht 385.

Hertz, K, *Danish Arbitration Act 2005* (2005).

Hill, J, *International Commercial Disputes* (2005).

Holdgaard, R, 'Principles of Reception of International Law in Community Law' in P Eeckhout and T Tridimas (eds), *Yearbook of European Law 2006* (2007) 263.

——, 'Case note on Case C-431/05 *Merck Genéricos* [2007] ECR I-7001, (2008) CML Rev 1233.

Hoskins, M, 'Discretionary References: To Refer or not to Refer' in M Hoskins et al (eds), *A True European, Essays for Judge David Edward* (2004) 345.

House of Lords, European Union Committee, 10th Report of Session 2007–08, The Treaty of Lisbon: an impact assessment.

Jacobs, F, 'When to Refer to the European Court' (1974) 90 The Law Quarterly Review 486.

——, 'The Role of the European Court of Justice in the Development of Uniform Law' in N Jareborg (ed), *De Lege, Juridiska Fakulteten i Uppsala, Årsbok 1995* (1995) 205.

——, 'The Effect of Preliminary Rulings in the National Legal Order' in M Andenas (ed), *Article 177 References to the European Court* (1994) 29.

——, 'Introducing the Court's Paper' in A Dashwood and A C Johnston, *The Future of the Judicial System of the European Union* (2001) 9.

——, 'Approaches to Interpretation in a Plurilingual Legal System' in M Hoskins and W Robinson (eds), *A True European – Essays for Judge David Edward* (2004) 297.

Jacqué, J and J Weiler, 'On the Road to European Union – A new Judicial Architecture: An Agenda for the Intergovernmental Conference' (1990) CML Rev 185.

Jarvis, M, *The Application of EC Law by National Courts – The Free Movement of Goods* (1998).

Jour-Schröder, A and C Konow, 'Die Passerelle des Art. 42 EU-Vertrag' (2006) 18 Europäische Zeitschrift für Wirtschaftsrecht 550.

Joutsamo, K, 'Community law – National law relationship – judicial cooperation under the system of preliminary rulings (Art. 177)' (1991) JFT Tidskrift utgiven av Juridiska Föreningen i Finland 337.

Kanninen, H, 'General Report on the Colloquium subject "The Preliminary Reference to the Court of Justice of the European Communities"' 34–36, Association of the Councils of State and Supreme Administrative Jurisdiction of the European Union, 18th Colloquium 2002.

——, 'La marge de manoeuvre de la juridiction suprême nationale pour procéder à un renvoi préjudiciel à la Cour de justice des Communautés européennes' in N Colneric, D Edward, J Puissochet, and D Colomer (eds), *Une communauté de droit, Festschrift für Gil Carlos Rodriquez Iglesias* (2003) 611.

Kapteyn, P J G, 'Administration of Justice' in P J G Kapteyn et al (eds), 'The Law of the European Union and the European Communities' (2008) 421.

Kerr, P, 'Trade Mark Tangles' (2004) EL Rev 345.

Kilpatrick, C, 'Community or Community of Courts in European Integration? Sex Equality Dialogues between UK Courts and the ECJ' (1998) European Law Journal 121.

Komninos, A, 'Article 234 EC and National Competition Authorities in the Era of Decentralisation' (2004) 29 EL Rev 106.

Koopmans, T, 'The Technique of the Preliminary Question – a view from the Court of Justice' in H Schermers et al (eds), *Article 177: Experiences and Problems* (1987) 327.

——, 'The Future of the Court of Justice of the European Communities' in A Barov and D A Wyatt *Yearbook of European Law 1991* (1993) 1.

Korte, J, *Primus inter Pares: The European Court and National Courts. The follow-up by National Courts of Preliminary References ex. Art 177 of the Treaty of Rome: A Report on the Situation in the Netherlands* (1991).

Koutrakos, P, 'The Interpretation of Mixed Agreements under the Preliminary Reference Procedure' (2002) 7 European Foreign Affairs Review 25.

ter Kuile, B H, 'To Refer or not to Refer' in D Curtin and T Heukels (eds), *Institutional Dynamics of European Integration* (1994) 381.

Lane, R, 'Article 234: A Few Rough Edges Still' in M and W Robinson (eds), *A True European, Essays for Judge David Edward* (2003) 327.

Lasok, P, *The European Court of Justice – Practice and Procedure* (1994).

Lasok, P, et al, *Judicial Control in the EU* (2008).

Lauwaars, R H, 'Institutional Structure' in P J G Kapteyn et al (eds), *The Law of the European Union and the European Communities* (2008) 175.

Lenaerts, K, 'Form and Substance of the Preliminary ruling Procedure' in D Curtin and T Heukels (eds), *Institutional Dynamics of European Integration* (1994) 355.

——, 'The unity of European law and the overload of the ECJ – the system of preliminary rulings revisited' in I Pernice et al (eds), *The Future of The European Judicial System in a Comparative Perspective* (2005) 212.

——, 'The rule of Law and the coherence of the judicial system of the European Union' (2007) CML Rev 1625.

Lenaerts, K and P Van Nuffel, *Constitutional Law of the European Union* (2005).

Lenaerts, K, et al, *Procedural Law of the European Union* (2006).

Lewis, C, *Judicial Remedies in Public Law* (2008).

Lipstein, K, 'Foglia v. Novello – Some unexplored Aspects' in F Capotorti et al (eds), *Du droit international au droit de l'intégration, Liber Amicorum Pierre Pescatore* (1987) 373.

Maduro, M, *We, the Court – The European Court of Justice & the European Economic Constitution* (1998).

Magnus, U, 'Introduction' in U Magnus and P Mankowski (eds), *Brussels I Regulation* (2007) 41.

Mancini, F, 'A constitution for Europe' (1989) CML Rev 595.

de la Mare, T, 'Article 177 in Social and Political Context' in P Craig and G de Burca (eds), *The Evolution of EU Law* (1998) 215.

Martinet, P, 'Article 68 CE' in P Léger (ed), *Commentaire article par article des traités UE et CE* (2000) 597, 593.

Masclet, J, 'Vers la fin d'une controverse? La cour de justice tempère l'obligation de renvoi préjudiciel en interprétation faite aux juridictions suprêmes (art. 177, alinéa 3, C.E.E.)' [1983] Revue du Marché Commun 363.

Mattli, W and A Slaughter, 'Revisiting the European Court of Justice' (1998) 52 International Organization 177.

Mattli, W and A Slaughter, 'The Role of National Courts in the Process of European Integration: Accounting for Judicial Preferences and Constraints' in A Slaughter, A Stone Sweet, and J Weiler (eds), *The European Court and National Courts – Doctrine and Jurisprudence – Legal Challenge in Its Social Context* (1998) 253.

Mayer, F, 'The European Constitution and the Courts', in A von Bogdandy and J Bast (eds), *Principles of European Constitutional Law* (2006) 281.

Moitinho de Almeida, L P, 'La notion de juridiction d'un État membre (article 177 du traité CE)' in R Iglesias, O Due, R Schintgen, and C Elsen (eds), *Mélanges en hommage à Fernand Schockweiler* (1999) 463.

Mortelmans, K, 'Observations in the cases governed by Article 177 of the EEC Treaty: Procedure and Practice' (1979) CML Rev 557.

——, 'The Court under the Influence of its Advocates General: An analysis of the case law on the functioning of the Internal Market' in P Eeckhout and T Tridimas, *Yearbook of European Law 2005* (2006).

Naômé, C, *Le renvoi préjudiciel en droit européen* (2007).

——, 'EU Enlargement and the European Court of Justice' in E Best et al, *The Institutions of the Enlarged European Union* (2008) 100.

Nyikos, S, *The European Court and National Courts: Strategic Interaction within the EU Judicial Process* (2001).

Odudu, O, 'Case-note on Case C-11/00, *Commission of the European Communities v. European Central Bank*, Judgment of 10 July 2003, Full Court' (2004) 41 CML Rev 1073.

O'Keeffe, D, Case note to Case C-3/90 *Bernini* [1992] ECR I-1071, (1992) CML Rev 1215.

O'Keeffe, D, 'Is the Spirit of Article 177 under Attack? Preliminary References and Admissibility' (1998) 23 EL Rev 509.

Oliver, P, 'Casenote to Cases C-46/93 and C-48/93, Brasserie du Pêcheur v Germany, and The Queen v Secretary of State for Transport ex parte Factortame' [1996] ECR I-1029, (1997) 34 CMLR 635, 657.

——, 'Recevabilité des questions préjudicielles: La jurisprudence des années 1990' (2001) 1–2 Cahiers de droit européen 15.

Peers, S, 'Who's Judging the Watchmen? The Judicial System of the "Area of Freedom Security and Justice"' in P Eeckhout and T Tridimas (eds), *Yearbook of European Law* (1998) 337.

Pertek, J, *La pratique du renvoi prejudiciel de droit communautaire* (2001).

Petite, M, 'La Cour de justice dans la cooperation judiciaire: réalités et perspectives?' speech given at Seminar of the members of the European Union Supreme Judicial Courts Network and representatives of the European Union institutions, Tuesday 22 November 2005, Brussels, pp 8-9 (available at <http://www.rpcsjue.org/IMG/pdf/petite.pdf>).

Pitarakis, J, and G Tridimas, 'Joint Dynamics of Legal and Economic Integration in the European Union' (2003) European Journal of Law and Economics 357.

Póltorak, N, '*Ratione Temporis* Application of the Preliminary Rulings Procedure' (2008) 45 CML Rev 1357.

Prechal, S, 'Community Law in National Courts: The Lessons From Van Schijndel' (1998) CML Rev 681.

——, 'The Preliminary Procedure: a role for legal scholarship?' in *The Uncertain Future of the Preliminary Rulings Procedure*, Symposium Council of State, the Netherlands, 30 January 2004.

Prechal, S, et al, *'Europeanisation' of the Law: Consequences for the Dutch Judiciary* (2005).

Raitio, J, 'What is the Court of Final Instance in the Framework of Article 234(3) in Sweden?' (2003) Europarättslig Tidskrift 160.

Rasmussen, H, *FIDE 1980, vol 1* (1980) 313.

——, *On Law and Policy in the European Court of Justice* (1986).

——, 'The European Court's Acte Clair Strategy in C.I.L.F.I.T.' (1984) 9 EL Rev 242.

——, 'Issues of Admissibility and Justiciability in EC Judicial Adjudication of Federalism Disputes under Article 177 EEC' in H Schermers et al (eds), *Article 177 EEC: Experiences and Problems* (1987) 379.

——, 'Docket Control Mechanisms, the EC Court and the Preliminary References Procedure' in M Andenas (ed), *Article 177 References to the European Court – Policy and Practice* (1994) 83.

——, 'Remedying the Crumbling EC Judicial System' (2004) CML Rev 1071.

Richards, D and M Beloff, 'View from the Bar' in G Barling and M Brealey (eds), *Practitioners' Handbook of EC Law* (1988).

Riechenberg, K, 'Note concernant les renvois préjudiciels qui réinterrogent la Cour' in V Christianos (ed), *Evolution récente du droit judiciare communautaire, vol I* (1994) 99.

Rodger, B, *Article 234 and Competition Law* (2008).

Rosas, A, 'The European Union and Mixed Agreements' in A Dashwood and C Hillion (eds), *External Relations Law of the European Community* (2000) 200.

Ross, M, 'Limits on Using Article 177 EC' (1994) EL Rev 640.

Schepel, H and E Blankenburg, 'Mobilizing the European Court of Justice' in G de Búrca and J Weiler (eds), *The European Court of Justice* (2001) 9.

Schermers, H, 'Problems and Prospects' in A Dashwood and A C Johnston (eds), *The Future of the Judicial System of the European Union* (2001) 31.

Schermers, H and D Waelbroeck, *Judicial Protection in the European Union* (2001).

Schermers, H and J S Watson, 'Report of the Conference' in H Schermers et al (eds), *Article 177: Experiences and Problems* (1987) 12.

Schmauch, M, 'Lack of preliminary rulings as an infringement of Art 234 EC?' (2005) 11 European Law Reporter 445.

Schwarze, J, *Die Befolgung von Vorabentscheidungen des Europäischen Gerichtshof durch deutsche Gerichte* (1988) 39.

Sèners, F, 'La portée d'un arrêt de la Cour de justice des Communautés européennes rendu sur question préjudicielle' (2007) 11 Revue française de droit administratif 373.

Sevón, L, 'How should I make a Reference? The National Judge and Preliminary Rulings' in M Levin et al (eds), *Festskrift till Ulf Bernitz* (2001) 209.

——, 'What do National Judges Require of the Court of Justice of the European Communities?' in G Regner, M Eliason, and H Vogel (eds), *Festskrift til Hans Ragnemalm* (2005) 287.

Simon, D, 'Questions préjudicielles' [1991] Journal du droit international 455.

——, 'La contribution de la Cour de cassation à la construction juridique européenne: Europe du droit, Europe des juges' [2006] *Cour de cassation*, Rapport annuel 79.

Slynn, Sir Gordon, *Litigating in Luxembourg* (1988) 12.

Slynn of Hadley, Lord, foreword to D Anderson and M Demetriou, *References to the European Court* (2002).

Skouris, V, 'Self-conception, Challenges and Perspective of the EU Courts' in I Pernice et al (eds), *The Future of The European Judicial System in a Comparative Perspective* (2005) 19.

——, 'l'urgence dans la procédure applicable aux renvois préjudiciels' in C Baudenbacher et al (eds), *Liber Amicorum en l'honneur de Bo Vesterdorf* (2007) 59.

Soulard, C, 'Techniques de formulation de la question préjudicielle: les rôles respectifs de la jurisdiction nationale et de l'avocat' in V Christianos (ed), *Evolution récente du droit judiciare communautaire, vol. I* (1994) 73.

Staudinger, A and S Leible, 'Article 65 of the EC Treaty in the EC System of Competencies' (2000–2001) 4 The European Legal Forum 225.

Stone Sweet, A and T Brunell, 'The European Court and the National Courts: A statistical analysis of preliminary references 1961–1995', Jean Monnet Working Paper No 14/1997.

——, 'The European Court, National Judges and Legal Integration: A Researcher's Guide to the Data Set on Preliminary References in EC Law 1958–98' (2001) 6(2) European Law Journal 117.

Temple Lang, J, 'The Duties of National Courts under Community Constitutional Law' (1997) 22 EL Rev 3.

Tesauro, G, 'The Effectiveness of Judicial Protection and Co-operation between the Court of Justice and the National Courts' in J Rosenløv and K Thorup (eds), *Ole Due Liber Amicorum* (1994) 352.

Timmermans, C, 'The European Union's Judicial System' (2004) CML Rev 393.

——, 'General Aspects of the European Union and the European Communities' in P J G Kapteyn et al (eds), *The Law of the European Union and the European Communities* (2008) 53.

——, in 'Summary report of the meeting of 3 December 2007 of the working group of the Association of the Councils of State and the Supreme Administrative Jurisdictions of the EU and the Network of the Presidents of the Supreme Judicial Courts of the EU on preliminary references' at p 9 (available at <http://www.network-presidents.eu/IMG/pdf/Summary_report_of_december_3rd_2007.pdf>).

Tizzano, A, 'Litiges fictifs et competence préjudicielle de la Cour de Justice Européenne' [1981] Revue génerale de droit international public 514.

Toth, A, 'The Authority of Judgments of the European Court of Justice: Binding Force and Legal Effects' in F Jacobs (ed), *Yearbook of European Law 1984* (1986) 1.

Trabucchi, A, 'L'effet "erga omnes" des décisions préjudicielles rendues par la Cour de justice des Communautés européennes' (1974) 10 Revue trimestrielle du droit européen 56.

Traversa, E, 'Les voies de recours ouvertes aux opérateurs économique: le renvoi préjudiciel au titre de l'article 177 du traité CEE' (1992) 2 Revue du Marché Unique Européen 51.

Tridimas, G and T Tridimas, 'National courts and the European Court of Justice: a public choice analysis of the preliminary reference procedure' (2004) 24(2) International Review of Law and Economics 125.

Tridimas, T, 'The role of the Advocate General in the development of Community law' (1997) CMLR 1349.

——, 'Knocking on Heaven's Door: Fragmentation, Efficiency and Defiance in the Preliminary Reference Procedure' (2003) CML Rev 9.

——, 'Proportionality in Community Law, Searching for the Appropriate Standard of Scrutiny' in E Ellis (ed), *The Principle of Proportionality in the Laws of Europe* (1999) 65, 78.

Usher, J, 'Compliance with Judgments of the Court of Justice of the European Communities' in M Bulterman and M Kuijer (eds), *Compliance with judgments of International Courts* (1996) 87.

——, 'The Assertion of Jurisdiction by the European Court of Justice' in P Capps, M Evans and S Konstandinidis (eds), *Asserting Jurisdiction – International and European Legal Perspectives* (2003) 283.

Vandersanden, G, 'La procédure préjudicielle: À la recherche d'une identité perdue' in M Dony (ed), *Mélanges en hommage à Michel Waelbroeck, vol I* (1999) 619.

Vaughan, D, 'The Advocate's View' in M Andenas (ed), *Article 177 references to the European Court* (1994) 55.

Vaughan, D, et al, *Butterworths European Court Practice* (1993).

Vesterdorf, B, 'A Constitutional Court for the EU?' in I Pernice et al (eds), *The Future of the European Judicial System in a Comparative Perspective* (2005) 83.

Vink, M, M Claes, and C Arnold, 'Explaining the Use of Preliminary References by Domestic Courts in EU Member States: A Mixed-Method Comparative Analysis' Paper presented at the 11th Biennial Conference of the European Studies Association April 2009.

Wainwright, R, 'A view from the Commission' in M Andenas (ed), *Article 177 References to the European Court – Policy and Practice* (1994) 105.

Walsh, D P J, 'The Appeal of an Article 177 EEC Referral' (1993) Modern Law Review 881.

Wattel, P, '*Köbler, Cilfit* and *Welthgrove*: We Can't Go on Meeting Like This' (2004) CML Rev 177.

Weiler, J, 'The European Court, National Courts and References for Preliminary Rulings – The Paradox of Success: A Revisionist View of Article 177 EEC' in H Schermers, C Timmermans, A Kellermann and J Watson (eds), *Article 177 EEC: Experiences and Problems* (1987) 366.

——, 'Journey to an Unknown Destination: A Retrospective and Prospective of the European Court of Justice in the Arena of Political Integration' (1993) 31(4) Journal of Common Market Studies 417.

Weiler, J and R Dehousse, *Primus inter Pares, the European Court and National Courts: Thirty Years of Cooperation*, unpublished study, Florence 1992.

Weitzel, L, 'La reformulation de la question préjudicielle' in V Christianos (ed), *Evolution récente du droit judiciare communautaire, vol I* (1994) 83.

Wind, M, et al, 'The Uneven Legal Push for Europe, Questioning Variation when National Courts go to Europe' (2008) European Union Politics 487.

Wyatt, D, 'Foglia No 2: the Court denies it has jurisdiction to give advisory opinions' (1982) EL Rev 186.

——, 'Procedures and Principles' in M Andenas (ed), *Article 177 References to the European Court – Policy and Practice* (1994) 77.

——, 'The Relationship between Actions for Annulment and References on Validity after TWD Deggendorf' in J Lonbay and A Biondi (eds), *Remedies for Breach of EC Law* (1997) 55.

INDEX